core

SWING advanced programming

ISBN 0-13-083292-8

90000

9 780130 832924

PRENTICE HALL PTR
CORE SERIES

* Sun Microsystems Press/Prentice Hall title.

core
SWING advanced programming

KIM TOPLEY

Prentice Hall PTR
Upper Saddle River, NJ 07458
www.phptr.com

Library of Congress Cataloging-in-Publication Data

Topley, Kim.
　　Core Swing : advanced programming / Kim Topley.
　　　　p. cm. -- (Prentice Hall PTR core series)
　　ISBN 0-13-083292-8
　　　　1. Graphical user interfaces (Computer systems) 2. Swing (Computer file) 3. Java
　　(Computer program language) 4. Java foundation classes. I. Title. II. Series.
QA76.9.U83 T66 1999
005.13'3--dc21　　　　　　　　　　　　　　　　　99-057903

Production Editor: *Vanessa Moore*
Compositors: *Sean Donahue, Vanessa Moore*
Acquisitions Editor: *Greg Doench*
Editorial Assistant: *Mary Treacy*
Marketing Manager: *Bryan Gambrel*
Manufacturing Manager: *Alexis R. Heydt*
Cover Design: *Talar Agasyan*
Cover Design Direction: *Jerry Votta*
Art Director: *Gail Cocker-Bogusz*
Project Coordinator: *Anne Trowbridge*

© 2000 Prentice Hall PTR
Prentice-Hall, Inc.
Upper Saddle River, NJ 07458

Prentice Hall books are widely used by corporations and government agencies for training,
marketing, and resale. The publisher offers discounts on this book when ordered in bulk quantities.
For more information, contact
　　　　Corporate Sales Department
　　　　Prentice Hall PTR
　　　　One Lake Street
　　　　Upper Saddle River, NJ 07458
　　　　Phone: 800-382-3419; FAX: 201-236-7141
　　　　E-mail (Internet): corpsales@prenhall.com

Printed in the United States of America

10　9　8　7　6　5　4　3　2　1

ISBN 0-13-083292-8

Prentice-Hall International (UK) Limited, *London*
Prentice-Hall of Australia Pty. Limited, *Sydney*
Prentice-Hall Canada Inc., *Toronto*
Prentice-Hall Hispanoamericana, S.A., *Mexico*
Prentice-Hall of India Private Limited, *New Delhi*
Prentice-Hall of Japan, Inc., *Tokyo*
Pearson Education Asia Pte. Ltd.
Editora Prentice-Hall do Brasil, Ltda., *Rio de Janeiro*

For Berys, Andrew, Katie, and Max.

Contents

CHAPTER 8   Drag-and-Drop   710

Preface

There is no doubt that, in the two years or so since the first production version of Swing was released, it has gradually taken over from the Abstract Window Toolkit (AWT) as the preferred graphical component set for client-side Java applications. With this increase in reliance on Swing has come a greater demand for development staff who are familiar with its intricacies and who know how to go beyond the obvious and get the best out of the powerful components that Swing contains. The Swing application programming interface (API) is huge, but that's not the worst problem for commercial developers. The issue is not so much that there is a very broad API—the real problem is that much of what you can do is hidden away under the covers and not very clearly outlined in the documentation that Sun provides. What's more, the Swing toolkit has a relatively low-level API and, although the components make very good building blocks, in real-world applications you need to enhance them to make them fully usable. Take, for example, the text components. On the face of it, they are relatively simple to use and give you a lot features in the basic API. But what if you want an input field that only accepts numbers? What about limiting the number of characters that the user can type into the field, or forcing letters to uppercase even if the user types them in lowercase? You won't find these features documented in the API, but the text components are built around a framework that makes it possible to plug in these enhancements, provided you know what you are doing. This book aims to show you some of the techniques you can use to make best use of Swing.

Because Swing is such a large topic, authors can take one of two approaches when writing about it. One possibility is to try to cover the whole API in a single book. This leads either to something very large (and probably overwhelming for most readers) or to something that is smaller, but broad and shallow and therefore risks not giving the reader enough information on anything. The alternative is to address only the most important parts of the API, the ones that most developers will use most of the time, but to cover it in enough detail that the reader can find exactly what he/she needs. It would also have to contain enough background to allow the reader to work out extra details from the source code. The latter approach is the one that I adopted in *Core Java Foundation Classes*, one of the first Swing books published. In trying to keep the number of pages down to something manageable, I had to leave out of *Core Java Foundation Classes* some of the more esoteric parts of the Swing API, such as the Undo package, in order to be able to give full coverage to the basics of the architecture and to the more sophisticated components, `JTable` and `JTree`, which were completely new to AWT developers.

Core Swing: Advanced Programming picks up where *Core Java Foundation Classes* left off, both expanding on some of the areas already covered in some detail in the first book and also introducing areas that *Core Java Foundation Classes* could not address. For example, even though *Core Java Foundation Classes* covered the text components far more thoroughly than most of the other Swing books available at the time (and since), there still remained a lot to say about them. This book tells you everything you need to know to build the enhanced text fields that you need in order to create a professional, commercial user interface and much more. In the first chapter, for example, you'll see how to create a text field that only accepts valid numbers, where the allowed input format is specified as a property of the component and how to perform other checks or transformations on the text that the user types.

To ensure their relevance to the problems being faced by real-world developers, many of the examples and topic areas covered in this book were chosen because they are frequently discussed on the Java GUI-related Internet news groups. If, like many contributors to the `comp.lang.java.gui` newsgroup, you've looked at Swing's HTML support and wanted to make full use of it but been daunted by its complexity (and the fact that it isn't documented anywhere), you'll need to read Chapter 4, which contains 200 pages almost entirely dedicated to this single topic, while Chapter 8 shows you how to make use of the Java 2 drag-and-drop feature, together with Swing components, to enhance the usability of your application's user interface. The central example of this chapter shows you how to add drag-and-drop features to a `JTree` that gives a visual representation of a file system, thus allowing you to create a basic Windows Explorer-type application with only a few lines of code. You'll also find detailed coverage of the Undo package and two chapters that show you exactly how to make the best use of the rendering and editing facilities of `JTable`.

Who This Book Is For

This book is intended for software developers who already have a good working knowledge of Swing, GUI programming techniques, and the Java programming language and want to extend their knowledge of Swing to build better applications. This is not an introductory text on any of these three topics, although you will find that there is some basic refresher material at the start of some of the chapters, in particular those that cover the text components. You do not, however, need to be an authority on Swing to make use of this book. Almost all of the existing Swing books should give you the basic knowledge you'll need to read this one. Not surprisingly, I would recommend *Core Java Foundation Classes* as a suitable place to start with Swing if you are looking for a beginner's text, although *Core Java 2* Volumes 1 and 2 (Prentice Hall) also contain enough material to be used as a starting point.

What You'll Need

In order to compile and run the examples that accompany this book, you'll need to have a computer with both the Java Development Kit and the Swing packages installed. Since this is not an introductory text, I assume that you have already used Swing, so it is very likely that you already have access both to Swing and either JDK 1.1 or Java 2. If you don't, you can download them from Sun's Web site at `java.sun.com`.

The material in this book is applicable both to JDK 1.1 and Java 2, with the exception of Chapter 5, which discusses bi-directional text, and Chapter 8, which covers the drag-and-drop feature. Drag-and-drop is available only in Java 2, while bi-directional text can theoretically be used with JDK 1.1, but the font support needed for languages for which it is required is not present in JDK 1.1, thus limiting its usefulness. If your are going to use JDK 1.1, you can download it from the following URL:

`http://java.sun.com/products/jdk/1.1`

At the time of writing, JDK 1.1.8 is the most recent release of JDK 1.1 and is the one that was used to test the example code on the CD-ROM. Since Swing is not a core component of JDK 1.1, you will need to download and install it separately from:

```
http://java.sun.com/products/jfc/download.html
```

where you will find Swing 1.1.1, the final version of Swing that will be released for use with JDK 1.1.

On the other hand, if you intend to use the Java 2 platform, you can download it from

```
http://java.sun.com/products/jdk/1.2
```

Java 2 includes Swing, so you do not need to download it separately. The examples in this book were tested with JDK 1.2.2.

Installation instructions for both the JDK and Swing are available from Sun's Web site. When installing the software, be sure to set the PATH and CLASSPATH variables correctly. You will also need to set the CLASSPATH variable when using the example code, as described in "About the CD-ROM" later in this Preface.

How This Book Is Organized

The first five chapters of this book deal almost exclusively with the Swing text components. Although superficially simple, these components are built on a complex and flexible software architecture that makes it possible to customize or extend them to accomplish almost any task. However, since there is little documentation for these components available in the JDK, the main problem that most developers encounter is working out how to exploit the text controls to the fullest.

Chapter 1 deals with the simple JTextField and JPasswordField components. In many applications, the user will interact almost exclusively with these single-line controls. If your application has a predominantly form-based interface, you'll need to know exactly how to customize these two controls to make it easy for the user to complete forms and to minimize the possibility of incorrect information being entered. The chapter begins with an overview of the text package and shows the architecture that underlies all of the text controls, much of which will be familiar if you have read *Core Java Foundation Classes* or a similar introductory Swing book. The rest of the chapter shows you how to create specialized text controls, including a text field that only allows the user to type valid numeric values, and another one that tracks what the user types and "autocompletes" the field from a list of legal values so that the user may only need to type a small number of characters to select the input value required.

Chapter 2 looks at how the text package deals with more complex text that can mix multiple fonts, colors, and other styles. This chapter shows you how to use the Swing JTextPane control to display programmatically-created text and how to control the layout of lines and paragraphs on the screen.

Chapter 3 builds on the material covered in the first two chapters by showing you how to change the appearance of the text in a text control without changing the way in which the data is represented internally. This is possible because the Swing text components rely on classes called "views" to draw their content onto the screen. Views use the text stored in the text control plus attributes supplied along with it to determine what to draw. This chapter shows you how to create custom views that use existing or private attributes to display the same data in various different ways. A popular application of this technique, and the central example of this chapter, is the ability to create a text field that adds formatting to the text that it contains, without the formatting being held in the data itself. You might use this feature to have a series of digits displayed as a telephone number, such as

```
(123)-456-7890
```

without needing to have the parentheses and the hyphens store in the text field itself, the advantage of which is that the application does not need to have code to remove them when it reads the telephone number from the text field.

You'll also see how to use private attributes with JTextPane to add extra facilities, such as a paragraph with a colored background or wrapped with a custom border.

Chapter 4 is probably the most interesting of the text-related chapters. This chapter deals with the JEditorPane control, which can be used to render and edit files that contain plain text, HTML, or encoded Rich Text Format (RTF). You'll see how to load the text into the JEditorPane, how to write out modifications, how to use it to display Web pages held locally or on the Internet, and how to implement the correct behavior for hypertext links. Much of this material has been covered, to some degree, in other Swing books, even some of the most basic ones. Here, though, it is just the introduction to the second part of the chapter, which contains a detailed examination of the Swing HTML package. Using the material in this chapter, you'll be able to load HTML into JEditorPane much faster than you can if you use the standard JEditorPane setPage method. You'll see how to use the HTML package to load and analyze an HTML page without displaying it to the user and to extract information from it, such as a list of the links to other pages that it contains. You'll also see the internal data structures used by JEd-itorPane when it is displaying HTML and how to programmatically modify them to change the way in which the content is displayed.

Chapter 5 describes the built-in support for bi-directional text, an internationalization feature which allows text in languages such as Arabic that are predominantly read from right to left to be rendered properly when displayed on the screen. Although you can use this facility without really being aware of it (in the sense that the text components know when text should be rendered right to left without intervention by the developer), there are several subtle points that you need to understand if you are developing an application that might be used in an environment in which the reading order is not the usual left to right that you are probably most familiar with. Chapter 5 covers these points by showing you how the text components handle bi-directional text and how their internal structure is affected by it.

Chapters 6 and 7 cover JTable rendering and editing, respectively. These topics probably cause more confusion for developers than any other aspect of the Swing API, even though (and, in fact, probably because) the underlying concepts are fairly simple. Chapter 6 begins by covering the rendering mechanism, then proceeds to show how you can customize it to add special effects to an entire table, to a specific row or rows, or to a single cell. You'll also see how to make use of tooltips to present more detailed information to the user. Chapter 7 covers the related topic of in-cell editing with JTable. This feature is almost certainly one of the least understood parts of the JTable API, judging by the number of times it crops up in the newsgroups. The first part of Chapter 7 confronts the major point of confusion straight away—the fact that the editing component does not permanently reside in the table, but appears only when it is required—by describing in detail the interaction between the table, the mouse and keyboard and the editor itself. This discussion is illustrated by combining editing and rendering techniques to give the impression that a table has a button in each row. The button looks and behaves like a real button, even though it is not actually present most of the time. In this chapter, you'll also see how to take control of the mechanics of the editing process and make it easier for a user to quickly update data in a table by adding support for tabbing between editable columns using the TAB key, a feature that is not available by default. The same technique can, of course, be used to add other usability features to the table.

Chapter 8 describes the Java 2 drag-and-drop feature and is the only part of this book that is not applicable if you are going to be using JDK 1.1 for the foreseeable future. Drag-and-drop is not part of the Swing package, but it does come under the broader heading of the Java Foundation Classes. By adding drag-and-drop support to your application, you can make it much easier for the user to copy or move data (in whatever form) between different parts of your application or even to or from a different one. This chapter starts by outlining the basic architecture of the drag-and-drop subsystem and then shows you how to implement both the "drag source" and the "drop target" for different types of information, including text and graphical components. Finally, you'll see a complete implementation of what is probably the most frequently discussed drag-and-drop related facility—a tree that supports moving or copying of data by dragging nodes, which represent the data, with the mouse and dropping them on the target node. The best feature of this example is that the source and target of the operation don't have to be in the same application and, in fact, it works even if the source or target of the operation is a native (non-Java) application.

One of the more unusual features of Swing is a complete package dedicated to giving the user undo and redo operations performed from the user interface. The code in this package is leveraged by the Swing text components to allow developers to roll back changes made in simple input fields or even in the more complex JTextPane and JEditorPane where a user might modify not only content but also fonts, colors, and text alignment. Although the underlying support for these operations is present in the text controls, you still have to do some work to make it available to the user. Chapter 9 shows you not only how to do this, it also shows the architecture of the Undo package, how to use the undo mechanism in other situations which have nothing to do with text handling, and how to extend it to add some useful features that are not available straight out of the box.

Conventions Used in This Book

Courier font is used to indicate Java code, both in the listings and in the shorter code extracts that you'll find included in the text. The same font is also used to indicate key words and class names (such as JFrame). In some cases, we show a code extract and then explain how to modify it to change its behavior. In this case, the code that is added or modified is shown in a **bold courier font**.

The following icon is used to call out material that is of significance and that the reader should be alerted to:

This icon flags information that deserves special attention, such as an interesting fact about the topic at hand, or that the reader may want to keep in mind while programming. These callouts are called Core Notes. It also may flag information that, while useful, may cause unexpected results or serious frustrations. These are called Core Alerts. And, finally, this icon also flags particularly useful information that will save the reader time, highlight a valuable programming tip, or offer specific advice on increasing productivity. These are refered to as Core Tips.

About the CD-ROM

The CD-ROM that accompanies this book has the following directory structure:

```
EXAMPLES
    EXAMPLES.ZIP

COREJFC
    CH10.PDF

SOFTWARE
    NETBEANS
        NBDX2212.EXE
        NBDX2212.SH
    SWINGBUILDER
        SB2.EXE
        SWINGBUILDER-2_0-2_NOARCH.RPM
```

The Example Source Code

The source code for all of the examples in this book are provided in a ZIP file in the EXAMPLES directory of the CD-ROM. The same source code is used both for JDK 1.1 and Java 2. Before extracting and installing the examples, you should make sure you have a working JDK and that your environment is set up properly so that you can run the Java compiler and run compiled Java code.

Extracting the Example Source Code

To use the examples, you need to extract them from the ZIP file and compile them. Although you can install them anywhere you like, throughout this book we'll assume that you use a directory called

```
c:\AdvancedSwing\Examples
```

as the base location for the example source code. If you are working on a UNIX platform, you will probably install the example source code under your home directory and you will have to make the necessary adjustments to the path names that appear in this book. The simplest way to extract the example code is to use a visual tool like `WinZip` or the DOS command line program `pkunzip`. Alternatively, you can use the JDK `jar` command; assuming that your CD-ROM appears as drive D, the following commands will install the example source code:

```
cd c:\AdvancedSwing\Examples
jar xvf D:\Examples\Examples.zip
```

The example code is arranged so that the examples for each chapter have their own separate package and this is reflected in the directory structure, which makes it easy to see which source code relates to each chapter of the book. The examples for Chapter 1 reside in the package `Advanced-Swing.Chapter1`. In terms of your machine's file system, the source code for these examples will be found in the directory

```
C:\AdvancedSwing\Examples\AdvancedSwing\Chapter1
```

Much of the example code is reproduced in the book, but this is not always the case. Where there is repetition or there is a relatively large amount of code that is part of the example but that does not help to explain the points being described, only the most interesting portions of the example will be shown. You can always find the complete source code for any example in the appropriate directory, using the name of the main class of the example to find the source file concerned. In all cases in which code has been omitted you will find a note to this effect.

Updates to the examples will be posted from time to time on the author's Web site at `http://www.topley.demon.co.uk/corebooks.html`.

Compiling the Examples

The examples on the CD-ROM have been tested with both JDK 1.2.2 and Swing 1.1.1 on JDK 1.1.8. Compiled class files are included for the Java 2 platform. If you are intending to use the example code with JDK 1.1 or if you want to try out your own modifications to them, you will need to recompile them.

Before attempting compilation, make sure that your CLASSPATH is properly set. The CLASSPATH will need to include the base directory for the example code as well as the location of the JDK and the Swing packages (at least for JDK 1.1). If you already have a working JDK 1.1 environment, all you need to do is put the directory

```
C:\AdvancedSwing\Examples
```

in your CLASSPATH. Here is a typical CLASSPATH for JDK 1.1.8 and Swing 1.1.1:

```
c:\AdvancedSwing\Examples;c:\jdk1.1.8\lib\classes.zip;c:\
    swing-1.1.1\swingall.jar
```

Note that it is very important to include the base directory for the examples in the CLASSPATH, *not* the directories in which the examples themselves reside. Thus, for example, it would be **incorrect** to include in the CLASSPATH the directory

```
c:\AdvancedSwing\Examples\AdvancedSwing\Chapter1
```

If you are using Java 2, the JDK software is not accessed via the CLASSPATH variable and you only need to include a reference to the example code in your CLASSPATH. The following DOS command would be sufficient to set up the CLASSPATH for Java 2:

```
set CLASSPATH=c:\AdvancedSwing\Examples
```

Once you have the correct CLASSPATH, you should compile the examples in each directory separately. For example, to compile the examples for the first two chapters, you should do something like this:

```
cd c:\AdvancedSwing\Examples\AdvancedSwing\Chapter1
javac *.java
cd c:\ AdvancedSwing\Examples\AdvancedSwing\Chapter2
javac *.java
```

The class files will be placed in the same directory as the corresponding source. Note that, if you are using JDK 1.1, you should not attempt to compile the examples for Chapters 5 and 8, since these apply to Java 2 only.

Running the Examples

Exact instructions for running each example appear along with the description of the source code throughout the book. A typical command line for executing an example looks like this:

```
java AdvancedSwing.Chapter1.TextFieldExample
```

The important thing to note is that you must supply the full name of the class, including the package prefix. It would be incorrect to try to short circuit this by using only the terminal part of the name, even if you attempt to adjust the CLASSPATH to compensate. Thus, for example, the following does *not* work:

```
set CLASSPATH=c:\AdvancedSwing\Examples\AdvancedSwing\Chapter1
java TextFieldExample
```

The COREJFC Directory

The COREJFC directory contains a complete copy of Chapter 10 of *Core Java Foundation Classes* in PDF format. In order to make use of this file, you will need to use a program such as Adobe's Acrobat Reader, which can be downloaded from:

```
http://www.adobe.com/products/acrobat/readstep.html
```

Chapter 10 of *Core Java Foundation Classes* contains an in-depth discussion of the Swing JTree component and demonstrates, among other things, how to use JTree to display a hierarchical view of a file system similar to the one used by Windows Explorer. One of the more useful features of Windows Explorer is the ability to copy, move, and link files in the file system by dragging and dropping icons in the Explorer window. Drag-and-drop was not available in JDK 1.1, but it is a part of Java 2. In Chapter 8 of this book, we build on the *Core Java Foundation Classes* implementation and show you how to add drag-and-drop capability to a tree. If you don't have a copy of *Core Java Foundation Classes*, you will find the PDF file on the CD-ROM useful since you will need to review the original implementation before studying the extension to it shown in this book.

The SOFTWARE Directory

The SOFTWARE directory contains two substantial pieces of software that you will almost certainly find useful as a Swing developer. You may install and use either or both of these packages on your system without paying a royalty to the company that produces them, but you should read the license terms at the back of this book before doing so. By installing the software on your system, you are deemed to accept the terms of the license. Note that neither Prentice Hall nor the author provides any support for this software. If you have any problems installing this software, please refer to the developers' Web sites as indicated in the following paragraphs.

NetBeans

NetBeans is a complete integrated development environment implemented in Java and uses Swing components for its user interface. The CD-ROM contains two versions of the Developer X2 version 2.1.2 product, one for Windows and the other for UNIX. To install NetBeans, you must already have Java 2 installed on your system. Both copies of the software are located in the SOFTWARE\NETBEANS directory of the CD-ROM.

To install the Windows version, just double-click the file nbdx2212.exe. The installation is performed using a standard InstallShield installer. UNIX users should change directory to SOFTWARE/NETBEANS and use the Bourne Shell to run the installer:

```
sh nbdx2212.sh
```

NetBeans is a free IDE, so the software on the CD-ROM is a fully working version. If you have any difficulty installing or using NetBeans, you can get help at:

```
http://www.netbeans.com/support.html
```

SwingBuilder

SwingBuilder is a utility that allows you to visually create Swing-based user interfaces. Unlike NetBeans, it is not a complete development environment. Instead, it is one component of a suite of IDE tools produced by SwingSoft, a UK-based company who can be contacted via their Web site at http://www.swingsoft.com, where you can also find details of the other IDE component that they provide. SwingBuilder is written entirely in Java and is bundled with the Java Runtime Environment version 1.1.8 and Swing version 1.1, so you do not need to have either the JDK or Swing already installed to make use of it. Unlike most GUI builders, SwingBuilder does not generate code from your user interface design. Instead, it saves either a compact binary representation of your component layout, or it can create an XML file. At runtime, software provided by SwingSoft and included with SwingBuilder reads either of these formats and recreates the user interface.

The CD-ROM contains an evaluation copy of SwingBuilder that was packaged especially for this book, in the SOFTWARE\SWINGBUILDER directory.

To install this software, Windows users should double-click or run the file sb2.exe. For Linux users, an RPM package is provided. To install this, use the command

```
rpm -i SwingBuilder-2_0-2_noarch.rpm
```

Feedback

No book is perfect and this one is unlikely to be an exception to that rule. Even though it has been through a long period of revision and technical review, there are, of course, errors still to be found and improvements still to be made. If you find an error or if there is something that you think might make the book more useful, we want to know about them. Please send comments and corrections to the following e-mail address:

```
kt@topley.demon.co.uk
```

Further Information

Java is a fast-moving subject and Swing is still one of its fastest changing parts. To keep up with developments, reading books is not enough. The best place for up-to-date information is, of course, the JavaSoft Web site at http://java.sun.com.

JavaSoft provides an online Swing magazine, called *The Swing Connection*, which is regularly updated and can be found at http://java.sun.com/products/jfc/tsc/.

The Prentice Hall Web site, http://www.phptr.com, is regularly updated with pointers to discussion groups or author events at which you can directly question the authors of Prentice Hall's Java and Swing books. As well as these open forums, questions on *Core Swing: Advanced Programming* and *Core Java Foundation Classes* can always be sent to the author's e-mail address (shown above). I promise to respond as quickly as I can, but not always immediately!

Finally, there are several active newsgroups devoted to discussion of the Java platform. The following two groups in particular frequently discuss Swing and JFC-related issues:

```
comp.lang.java.gui
comp.lang.java.programmer
```

Acknowledgments

Most of the time, writing a book is a lonely occupation that involves only the author, a laptop computer, and quite a lot of software. Fortunately, at the beginning and end of the process, the author gets to work with other human beings to get the job started and completed.

The process starts with the acquisitions editor. In my case, I have been lucky enough to convince Greg Doench not just once, but twice, that he really needs to publish my work. *Core Java Foundation Classes* took a year to complete, which was long enough, but *Core Swing: Advanced Programming* was in development for eighteen months—well over twice the time that I had originally expected to spend on it. My thanks go to Greg not only for giving me a second opportunity to write about Swing, but also for being so patient as the expected completion dates came and went; and to Greg's assistant, Mary Treacy, for organizing such mundane but important things as a contract and royalty checks.

I am grateful to the technical reviewers for this book, Cameron Laird and Robert Evans, for carefully reading the manuscript in draft form and spotting some (and hopefully most) of the many mistakes that are inevitable in a book of this size covering a topic that has changed quite a lot over the period of the book's development. My thanks in advance to those readers who spot the remaining errors, and to those who have already alerted me to the minor mistakes in my first book, *Core Java Foundation Classes*, that were not caught before its publication!

When the writing and review process are finally complete, the book is in the hands of the Prentice Hall production team. Anne Trowbridge and Sean Donahue did a great job respectively managing the production process and laying out some of the chapters in readiness for printing. Thanks also to the copy editor, Bernadette Murphy Bentley, and proofreader, Stephanie English, for correcting my grammar and my non-American spelling. Most of all, though, I am extremely grateful to my production editor, Vanessa Moore, not only for making the sure the book's Word files were accurately converted to the finished product that you now hold in your hands, but also for ensuring that everyone involved, including me, delivered what they were supposed to on the dates that they had promised. And, although I really shouldn't mention it here, thanks also to Vanessa for taking the time while she was on vacation there to collect information about Barcelona so that my family would be able to make the best of our visit there this Spring.

Two companies, NetBeans and SwingSoft, were generous enough to allow me to include their software on this book's CD-ROM. I'd particularly like to express my thanks to John Bridges and Eddie Chan of SwingSoft who not only agreed to allow me to use their software, but also took the time to build an evaluation version especially for this book.

Finally, my thanks once again to my family, Berys, Andrew, and Katie, who put up one more time with my continued absence and the always untidy state of my working environment. I promise not to do this again for a while—at least not for the rest of this century!

Kim Topley
November, 1999

THE SWING TEXT COMPONENTS: CREATING CUSTOMIZED INPUT FIELDS

Topics in this Chapter

- Introduction to the Swing Text Components
- Text Component Architecture
- Custom Text Components
- Keymaps and Keyboard Bindings
- Creating a Custom Caret

Chapter 1

The Swing text components are much more powerful than their Abstract Window Toolkit (AWT) counterparts. This is partly because of the more complete application programming interface (API) that the Swing components provide, but the most useful new features come from the model-view-controller architecture around which the new components are built. There is so much functionality available from the Swing text components and so many ways to customize them that a whole book could be devoted to the subject. In this chapter, the first of five that discuss the text components, you'll first see an overview of the new text controls. After this introductory material, some of which should already be familiar to you, you'll see how to add new functionality to the simpler text components (JText-Field, JPasswordField, and JTextArea) by subclassing them, by creating new model classes, and by plugging in custom components, such as a new cursor.

The Swing Text Components

All the Swing text components are derived from JTextComponent, which is a subclass of JComponent. Swing provides five fully functional text controls, three of which provide replacement functionality for the AWT TextField and `TextArea` components and two that are entirely new. The class hierarchy of the Swing text components is shown in Figure 1-1. Although Figure 1-1 shows all the text components in the Swing package, it doesn't show the complex set of model and view classes that are used to implement them. Much of the power of these components, especially the new `JEditorPane` and `JText-Pane` controls, comes from the generalized and flexible architecture that underlies them. Later in this chapter, you'll see how to exploit this architecture to create customized text components that are suited to particular tasks. For example, you'll see several examples of text fields that validate the user's keystrokes as they are typed. Before looking at how to create custom components, let's look at what the basic controls are capable of.

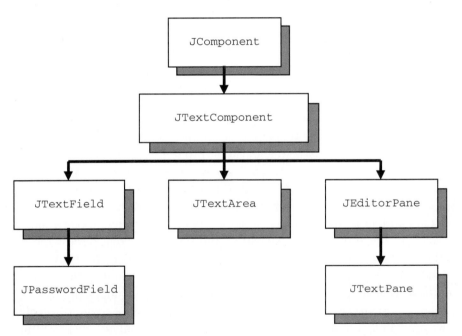

Figure 1-1   Swing text component class hierarchy.

The *JTextField* and *JPasswordField* Components

`JTextField` and `JPasswordField` are the simplest of all the text components. They both contain a single line of text, which may be supplied by the application program or typed by the user. The main difference between these two controls is that `JPasswordField` doesn't directly display its content—

instead, it uses a single character (usually an asterisk) to represent each character that it contains, so that it is possible to see how many characters have been typed, but not what they are. As its name suggests, `JPasswordField` is intended to be used as a simple way to accept a user's password. Because it is derived from `JTextField`, everything that applies to `JTextField` is also true of `JPasswordField`. For brevity, the rest of this section will refer only to `JTextField`. However, everything that follows is true also of `JPassword-Field`.

Creating a Text Field

When you create a `JTextField`, you can specify some or all of the following attributes:

- The `Document` in which it will hold its text.
- The initial content of the text field.
- The number of columns to be displayed.

As you'll see later, all the text components hold their content in an object that implements an interface called `Document`. Different text components use different `Documents` tailored to their specific needs; `JTextField` uses an instance of the `PlainDocument` class to store text. This class, and the other `Document` classes, will be covered later in "Storing Document Content" on page 34.

If you supply a text string to initialize the control, the text will be stored in the `Document` and displayed when the component appears on the screen. If you don't supply any text, the control starts out empty. The `setText` method can be used to change the text. When the user presses RETURN in a text or password field, an `ActionEvent` is generated. Application programs can register an `ActionListener` to receive this event and use the `getText` method to retrieve whatever the user typed in the control.

Text Field Size

When you create a text field, you can specify its width in columns as an argument to the `JTextField` constructor; you can also set the width using the `setColumns` method. Note, however, that setting the number of columns does not constrain the amount of text that the control can hold— restricting the number of characters that the user can type into a text field requires you to create a custom `Document` class, as you'll see in "A Text Field with Limited Input Capacity" on page 42. The only effect that setting the column count has is to control the text field's preferred width, which is determined as follows:

- If the column count has been set, the preferred width of the control is the number of columns multiplied by the width of the letter m in the font selected into the text field.
- If the column count has not been set, the preferred width is the size of the text in the text field in the currently selected font.

Sometimes, of course, the text field won't be given its preferred width. This is often the case in form layouts where input fields are allowed to stretch across their host container. In general, then, setting the column count only acts as a hint to the text field that might help it select a suitable field width; the text itself could be wider or narrower than the horizontal space occupied by the text field.

Content Alignment

Because the width of the text field is not necessarily the same as that of the text it contains, there is the matter of text alignment to consider. There are three natural ways to align the text within a text field:

- The beginning of the text aligned to the left of the text field.
- The end of the text aligned to the right of the text field.
- The center of the text aligned in the center of the text field.

You can specify the alignment of the text using the `setHorizontal-Alignment` method, which takes a single argument with one of the following values:

- `JTextField.LEFT`
- `JTextField.RIGHT`
- `JTextField.CENTER`

By default, left alignment is used. When the text is right-aligned, the text field's insertion cursor appears at the right side of the control, after the text. Any new text typed by the user is added there, moving the existing content to the left. In a text field with center alignment, the cursor again appears at the right of any existing text and new characters are added at its right end, but in this case the text is moved in such a way as to keep its center aligned with the middle of the control.

Figure 1-2 shows five text fields configured in slightly different ways. The code for this example is shown in Listing 1-1.

Figure 1-2 JTextField examples.

Listing 1-1 Configuring Text Fields

```
package AdvancedSwing.Chapter1;

import javax.swing.*;
import javax.swing.text.*;
import java.awt.*;

public class TextFieldExample {
    public static void main(String[] args) {
        JFrame f = new JFrame("Text Field Examples");
        f.getContentPane().setLayout(new FlowLayout());
        f.getContentPane().add(new JTextField
                ("Text field 1"));
        f.getContentPane().add(new JTextField
                ("Text field 2", 8));
        JTextField t = new JTextField("Text field 3", 8);
        t.setHorizontalAlignment(JTextField.RIGHT);
        f.getContentPane().add(t);
        t = new JTextField("Text field 4", 8);
        t.setHorizontalAlignment(JTextField.CENTER);
        f.getContentPane().add(t);
        f.getContentPane().add(new JTextField
                ("Text field 5", 3));

        f.pack();
        f.setVisible(true);
    }
}
```

To try this example, use the command:

```
java AdvancedSwing.Chapter1.TextFieldExample
```

Let's look at each of the text fields in turn, working from the left. The first field (with content "Text Field 1") is created using default alignment and size. As a result, it makes itself wide enough to hold its content and aligns the text on the left. Because the control is at the optimal size for its content, it is difficult to see that the text is left-aligned. The second field, however, has an explicitly specified column width of 8 and you can clearly see in this case that the text is aligned to the left. It may surprise you that the text field is actually larger than its content, given that it is supposed to be eight columns wide and that the text string it contains has 12 characters. The reason for this, of course, is that the width of the control is calculated as the width of eight letter m's in the text field's assigned font. In this case, the 12-character content happens to take up less room than eight m's in the same font.

Core Note

If you were to use a constant-width font, the number of columns would correspond to the number of characters that the text field could display.

The third and fourth text fields differ from the second only in their alignment: they are initialized with right- and center-alignment, respectively. The effect of the alignment is clearly visible in Figure 1-2. If you click in the first text field and then use the TAB key to get to the third field, you'll see that the insertion point is initially placed to the left of the text and that anything that you type moves automatically to the left as you type it. Move the focus to the fourth field using the TAB key and type a few more characters and you'll see that the text in this control always arranges to be centered in the visible area.

The fifth text area is created with a column width of 3, which turns out to be too small to display its content. Nothing is actually lost however—all the text is still in the control. Indeed, if you use the TAB key to get to this control, and then use the arrow keys on your keyboard to move the cursor to the right, you'll find that the text will scroll left as the cursor reaches the right side of the text field, bringing into view the text that was initially out of the visible area. This scrolling capability is provided automatically by JTextField. As you'll see, however, the other text controls do not scroll by default.

Scroll Offset

If you want, you can control the text field's scrolling capability from within your application using the following three methods:

- `public int getScrollOffset();`

- `public void setScrollOffset(int offset);`
- `public void scrollRectToVisible(Rectangle r);`

The `getScrollOffset` method returns the text field's current scroll off-set, which is the number of pixels of the text string that are out of view to the left of the control's visible area. This value is, therefore, zero when a text field with left alignment is initially displayed. If you were to scroll the text to the left so that the first few characters went out of view, the scroll offset would increase by the number of pixels of the rendered string lost from view. The `setScrollOffset` method allows you to explicitly set a new scroll offset, which has the effect of changing the text positioning within the view. Setting the scroll offset to zero moves the left side of the text in a left-aligned control to the left of the control. As you might expect, setting a positive value causes some of the text to move out of view to the left. However, a negative scroll offset does not result in leading space between the left side of the control and the text that it contains—instead, it is treated as zero.

The `scrollRectToVisible` method is an alternative way to move the text within the viewing area. The only member of the `Rectangle` argument that this method uses is the x value, which is taken as a signed offset from the *current* scroll position. Thus, a positive value causes the scroll offset to increase, moving the text to the left, while a negative value causes the text to move to the right. Again, you can't use this method to set a negative scroll offset—attempting to do so results in the scroll offset being set to zero. There are, therefore, two equivalent ways to ensure that the start of the text is visible in a text field:

```
JTextField t = new JTextField("Text Field", 3);
t.setScrollOffset(0); // Directly sets scroll offset to zero
t.scrollRectToVisible(new Rectangle(-t.getScrollOffset(),
                                    0, 0, 0));
```

The *JTextArea* Control

`JTextArea` is a two-dimensional control that allows you to display more than one line of text. To this end, you can create a text area by initializing it with a string in which the separate lines are delimited by newline characters, so that each line of the string appears on a different line of the control. You can also explicitly specify the number of rows and columns that the `JTextArea` should occupy. As with `JTextField`, of course, specifying these values only influences the text area's preferred size and does not necessarily determine its actual width or height.

Text Area Size, Scrolling, and Wrapping

The actual size of a text area depends on the number of rows and columns that you specify either in the constructor or with the setRows and/or set-Columns methods and on two other factors:

- Whether the text area is embedded in a JScrollPane.
- Whether the text area has line wrapping enabled.

The easiest way to see how these attributes interact is to look at an example. The code in Listing 1-2 creates six text areas containing the same four lines of text, but initialized in slightly different ways. If you run this example using the command:

```
java AdvancedSwing.Chapter1.TextAreaExample
```

you get the result shown in Figure 1-3.

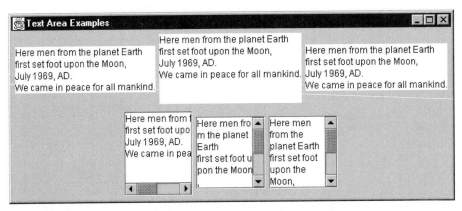

Figure 1-3 JTextAreas with various scrolling and wrap settings.

Let's first consider the text areas on the top row of Figure 1-3. All these areas contain the same text, which is four lines long because it has three embedded newline characters. The control at top left is created without specifying the number of rows and columns to be used and, as a result, the text area is as wide and as tall as it needs to be to exactly fit the text. The other two text areas on the top row are configured with six rows and ten columns and three rows and eight columns respectively. However, you can see that, despite the fact that they specify different column counts, they are the same width. Furthermore, the rightmost text area has four rows even though three were specified in the constructor. This demonstrates that a text area expands to occupy as much space as it needs, assuming that the layout manager allows it to, even if an attempt is made to constrain it by configuring specific row and column counts.

Listing 1-2 Configuring Text Areas

```
package AdvancedSwing.Chapter1;

import javax.swing.*;
import javax.swing.text.*;
import java.awt.*;

public class TextAreaExample {
    public static void main(String[] args) {
        JFrame f = new JFrame("Text Area Examples");
        JPanel upperPanel = new JPanel();
        JPanel lowerPanel = new JPanel();
        f.getContentPane().add(upperPanel, "North");
        f.getContentPane().add(lowerPanel, "South");

        upperPanel.add(new JTextArea(content));
        upperPanel.add(new JTextArea(content, 6, 10));
        upperPanel.add(new JTextArea(content, 3, 8));

        lowerPanel.add(new JScrollPane(
                        new JTextArea(content, 6, 8)));
        JTextArea ta = new JTextArea(content, 6, 8);
        ta.setLineWrap(true);
        lowerPanel.add(new JScrollPane(ta));

        ta = new JTextArea(content, 6, 8);
        ta.setLineWrap(true);
        ta.setWrapStyleWord(true);
        lowerPanel.add(new JScrollPane(ta));

        f.pack();
        f.setVisible(true);
    }

    static String content = "Here men from the
        planet Earth\n" +
                "first set foot upon the Moon,\n" +
                "July 1969, AD.\n" +
                "We came in peace for all mankind.";
}
```

The second row of Figure 1-3, however, shows that the situation is different when a text area is wrapped in a `JScrollPane`. The text areas in the bottom row are all created with six rows and eight columns and you can see that the visible area of the scroll pane is six rows high. The width of the visible area is, in fact, the same as eight letter m's in the font used by the text area, although it is difficult to see this because the font is not constant-width. When a text area is wrapped in a scroll pane, then the scroll pane's view port is sized to match the number of rows and columns specified for the text area itself, again assuming that the layout manager does not apply other constraints.

Because we know that it is not possible to fit all the text into an eight-character-wide display area, it is clear that some of the lines will either be too wide and need to be scrolled into view, or they will need to wrap onto the following line. By default, the text area does not wrap text; the text area on the left of the bottom row is set up in this way and, as you can see, three lines of text overflow the display area to the right. As a result of this, the scroll pane's horizontal scroll bar appears. However, because there are only four lines of text and the text area has six rows, there is no need for a vertical scroll bar.

There are two `JTextArea` methods that control text wrapping and a complementary pair that allow you to retrieve the current settings:

- `public void setLineWrap(boolean wrap);`
- `public boolean getLineWrap();`
- `public void setWrapStyleWord(boolean word);`
- `public boolean getWrapStyleWord();`

As noted earlier, by default, no wrapping is performed and `getLineWrap` returns `false`. If you invoke `setLineWrap` with argument `true`, the text area will fill each line of the scroll pane's visible area and wrap at its right boundary, splitting words without regard to word breaks—therefore, words can be divided over line boundaries. This effect can be seen in the lower middle text area. When line wrapping is enabled, the text always ends at the right edge of the control so there is no need for a horizontal scroll bar, but a vertical scroll bar is required because the resulting text can no longer be displayed in six lines. The scroll pane works out for itself which scroll bars it needs to display based on the text area's preferred size and the size of its viewport.

When line wrapping is enabled, you can also force breaks to occur at word boundaries by invoking the `setWrapStyleWord` method with argument `true`, as has been done with the rightmost text area. Here you can see that the text is not broken indiscriminately, giving a much better effect. Again, a vertical scroll bar is needed to allow all the text to be seen.

Line and word wrapping can also be used when the text area is not enclosed in a scroll pane, but they only have any effect when the layout manager of the container surrounding the control does not allocate it the horizontal space that it needs to display its longest line of text. When this happens, the text is broken in the same way as shown in the preceding example and the vertical space requirement will increase to account for the overflow lines. Of course, if the layout manager also constrains the height of the text area, it may not be possible to display all the text, and some number of lines will be lost at the bottom of the control.

JEditorPane and *JTextPane*

JEditorPane and JTextPane are deluxe text components that have no AWT equivalents. These two controls can be used to render simple text in the same way as JTextArea, and can also be used to display more complex text with multiple fonts and colors. JEditorPane is, in effect, a window onto a pluggable document editor. It can be configured to display text held externally in arbitrary formats by connecting it to an *editor kit* that knows how to interpret a particular document encoding format and render the corresponding content on the screen.

Swing comes with two complete editor kits that can be used to display documents encoded in HTML (Hypertext Markup Language) and RTF (Rich Text Format). Plugging an HTML editor kit into a JEditorPane, for example, turns it into a simple Web browser, with the capability of loading pages over the network and following hypertext links. You can also switch the JEditorPane into edit mode, in which case you can edit the HTML page content on the screen and then save the resulting document, which will result in the corresponding HTML being written out. In other words, you can use JEditorPane as a rough-and-ready HTML editor. This facility is also available for RTF documents.

JTextPane is a subclass of JEditorPane that allows you to create your own documents with arbitrary combinations of font, color, and any other attribute you care to associate with text or with any other active content that you might embed in the document. Using JTextPane you can, for example, mix text with images or with Swing components that bring some active element to the document. The programming interfaces that allow you to do this are relatively straightforward, although the data model that underlies both JTextPane and JEditorPane is rather complex. You'll see some of the complexity of these components in the first few chapters of this book.

Common Text Component Features

All the text components are derived, directly or indirectly, from `JText-Component` and inherit several common features from this class. This section provides an overview of the most important of these features.

Editable and Enabled States

By default, when you create a text component, the user will be able to change its content by typing or by selecting new text from the clipboard. Sometimes it is useful to create a read-only text component, or to be able to determine at runtime whether the control's content should be editable. For example, consider an application that provides an input form that allows a user to change field values and update the corresponding data source (such as a database). Usually, the form might use text controls with editing enabled. However, it might be necessary to display the same form in read-only mode, perhaps because the user does not have permission to change the underlying data, or simply as part of a separate "view" function that does not allow update. To make this possible, `JTextComponent` provides the following methods:

- `public void setEditable(boolean editable);`
- `public boolean isEditable();`

Invoking `setEditable(false)` stops the user from typing into the component or selecting data into it from the clipboard (see "Selection and Data Transfer" on page 16). It is still possible, however, to select text from a read-only control and place it onto the clipboard. Figure 1-4 shows a selection of text components, some of which are read-only. You can run this example using the command:

```
java AdvancedSwing.Chapter1.EditabilityExample
```

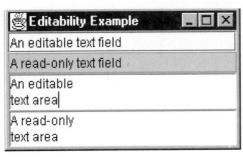

Figure 1-4   Editable and read-only text components.

The two components at the top of this figure are text fields. Of these, the first is editable, while the second has been made read-only. If you try to type into the second text field, you'll find that you can't. Notice that, in this case, the fact that this component is read-only is obvious to the user because its background color is different from that of the editable text field directly above it. This change in background color is carried out automatically by the text field's look-and-feel class. However, you can't rely on this visual cue—while it works with the Metal look-and-feel, both the Windows and Motif text fields don't change color when they become read-only. By contrast, the text areas at the bottom of the figure look identical even in the Metal look-and-feel, but the bottom one is read-only while the one above it is not.

As well as making a text component read-only by using `set-Editable(false)`, you can also enable or disable it using the following methods inherited from `Component`:

- `public void setEnabled(boolean enabled);`
- `public boolean isEnabled();`

A disabled text component acts as if it were read-only and changes its visual appearance to reflect the fact that it cannot be modified. The Metal implementation, for example, does this by shading the text, as shown in Figure 1-5.

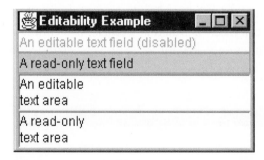

Figure 1-5 A disabled text field.

The example shown in Figure 1-5 can be run with the following command:

```
java AdvancedSwing.Chapter1.EditabilityExample disable
```

When this example is running, the text field at the top is initially enabled, as it is in Figure 1-4. After 10 seconds, it will be disabled and the text content will change to indicate that this has happened. The text field is enabled again 10 seconds later, and so on.

The distinction between a read-only text component and a disabled component is an important one. Usually, you choose to make a field read-only because the field that it represents should not be editable in the context of the form that it is part of, perhaps because the field is computed from other fields or should never be editable by the user for other reasons. By contrast, you would disable a text component to make it read-only for a short time. For example, you might choose to disable a text component after the user has filled in a form and pressed the OK button, to show that no further input is possible until the current operation is complete. When the operation finishes, you would enable the text components for further input. Whichever choice you make, any characters that the user attempts to type into the text field are ignored.

Focus Accelerator Keys

As an aid to keyboard navigation, JTextComponent allows an accelerator key to be associated with each text component. When this key is pressed at the same time as the ALT key, the text field will receive the keyboard input focus. This facility is useful when you are creating a form with many input fields that could be filled in any order or when you want the user to be able to jump immediately to any particular field without needing to use the mouse. Because a text component with a focus accelerator key has no way to indicate to the user that there is a focus accelerator or which key to use, it is common to use the accelerator key as the mnemonic key for a JLabel associated with the text component, as shown in Figure 1-6.

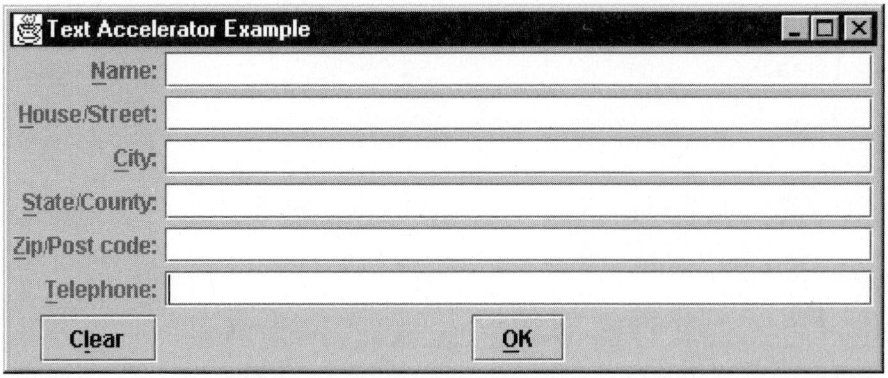

Figure 1-6 Text components and focus accelerators.

Here, each text field has an associated label, one letter of which is underlined to indicate that a focus accelerator for the corresponding text field is available. To see how this works, type the command:

```
java AdvancedSwing.Chapter1.TextAcceleratorExample
```

When the form appears on the screen, press ALT+c, being sure that the "c" is lowercase. When you do this, you'll find that the cursor moves to the input field labeled City. Similarly, pressing ALT+h moves the input focus to the House/Street field, and so on.

Core Alert

Some versions of Swing have a bug that causes the accelerator key to appear in the text field. For example, if you use ALT+c to move the focus to the field labeled City followed by pressing ALT+h to move the focus elsewhere, the "h" will appear in the City field. This bug was fixed in Swing 1.1.1.

Creating a text field with an associated label is a three-step process, an example of which might look like this:

```
JTextField t = new JTextField(35);
t.setFocusAccelerator('c');
JLabel l = new JLabel("City:", SwingConstants.RIGHT);
l.setDisplayedMnemonic('c');
```

The JTextComponent setFocusAccelerator method is used to define the accelerator key; you can also retrieve the current accelerator key using getFocusAccelerator, which returns "\0" if there is none. These methods are defined as follows:

- `public void setFocusAccelerator(char key);`
- `public char getFocusAccelerator();`

The key supplied to setFocusAccelerator may be either upper- or lowercase (assuming it is alphabetic); either way, the user must press the corresponding key together with ALT but *without* SHIFT, whether the programmer specifies "c" or "C" in the code. The following line ensures that a text component has no associated accelerator:

```
t.setFocusAccelerator('\0');   // \0 clears any registered
                               // accelerator
```

The JLabel setDisplayedMnemonic method results in the supplied character being underlined when the label displays its text. It is your responsibility to arrange for the characters used as the accelerator for the text field and as the label mnemonic match.

Selection and Data Transfer

JTextComponent supports cut-and-paste operations via the system clipboard using the underlying AWT data transfer mechanism, a full description of which you'll find in *Core Java 2, Volume 2: Advanced Features* (Sun Microsystems Press/Prentice Hall). Let's look at how this works as seen by both the user and programmer.

The User's View of Text Component Cut-and-Paste Operations

From the user's point of view, copying, deleting, and pasting text from a Swing text field is the same as it would be in a native application. The first step is to create a selection, which is done by clicking where the selection is to begin and then dragging it left or right to the other end of the selection. As the mouse is dragged, the text that will be part of the selection is highlighted.

Core Note

The Swing text components implement selection using two pluggable subcomponents—the Caret*, which is responsible for drawing the cursor and keeping track of where the mouse is as it is dragged over the content of the text component, and the* Highlighter *which, as its name suggests, is responsible for highlighting the selected text. Both of these elements can be customized to produce different effects if desired. You'll see an example of a customized* Caret *later in this chapter and of a customized* Highlighter *in Chapter 3.*

Having created the selection, the user can copy or delete it onto the clipboard using a gesture that is look-and-feel dependent. Text that has been copied to the clipboard can then be pasted into another text field using another look-and-feel dependent gesture. The key bindings for these operations in the Metal, Motif, and Microsoft Windows look-and-feels are shown in Table 1-1.

Table 1-1 Text Component Key Bindings Cut and Paste		
Operation	*Java and Windows*	*Motif*
Copy	CTRL+c	CTRL+INSERT
Cut	CTRL+x	SHIFT+DELETE
Paste	CTRL+v	SHIFT+INSERT

Note that data transfer doesn't operate simply within a single Java application, or even just between two Java applications. It is also possible to transfer data into and out of platform native applications. For example, start the text field example shown in Figure 1-5 using the command

```
java AdvancedSwing.Chapter1.EditabilityExample disable
```

and select some text from the bottom text area. With the selected text highlighted (as shown in Figure 1-7, in which the text "read-only" has been selected), copy it onto the clipboard using the correct key sequence for your active look-and-feel from Table 1-1.

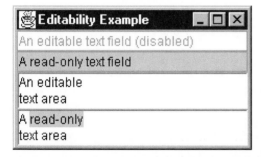

Figure 1-7 Selecting text onto the clipboard from a text component.

With the text copied onto the clipboard, click somewhere in the editable text area so that the insertion cursor appears and then press the keys that perform a paste action (for example, CTRL+v). This will cause the text "read-only" to be inserted after the mouse insertion point. Now start a native text editor (for example, Notepad on Windows or vi under UNIX), open a new document, and paste the clipboard content into it. Again, you'll find that the text "read-only" is inserted. To complete this example, type some more text into the native editor, select it and copy it onto the clipboard, and then paste it into the editable text area of the Java application. By experimenting with the Java example and the native application, you should be able to verify that you can copy text from a text field whether or not it is editable. You can't copy data from a disabled text component and, of course, you can't cut data from a text component that is either read-only or disabled and the text that you attempted to delete will not even be copied to the clipboard. Similarly, you cannot paste data into a text component unless it is both editable and enabled.

The Programmer's View

`JTextComponent` provides an API for implementing delete, copy, and paste operations should you wish to do so. The methods you can use are as follows:

- `public int getSelectionStart();`
- `public int getSelectionEnd();`
- `public void setSelectionStart(int start);`
- `public void setSelectionEnd(int end);`
- `public void select(int start, int end);`
- `public void selectAll();`
- `public void setCaretPosition(int pos);`
- `public void moveCaretPosition(int pos);`
- `public void copy();`
- `public void cut();`
- `public void paste();`

Assuming the user has made a selection, the first two methods return the start and end position of the selection as offsets from the start of the text in the text field, counting the first character as offset 0. If there is no selection, these methods return identical values that correspond to the location of the input cursor (or caret). You can create a selection programmatically by using `setSelectionStart` and `setSelectionEnd` to individually set the start and end offsets, or in a single call using `select` or `selectAll`, the latter of which selects everything in the text component. These four methods are provided for compatibility with the AWT text components. New code should instead use `setCaretPosition` to mark the start of the selection and `moveCaret-Position` to indicate the end. This pair of calls creates a selection consisting of the range of characters between offset given to `setCaretPosition` and the one passed to `moveCaretPosition`. Note that however you create a selection, the end offset must be equal to or greater than the start offset.

The job of moving data to or from the clipboard is done by the `copy`, `cut`, and `paste` methods. These convenience functions extract the selected text and move it to the clipboard or copy data in from the clipboard by using the

AWT data transfer facility, which is discussed further in Chapter 8. In the case of a paste operation, the data overwrites whatever is currently selected in the text component, or is inserted straight after the caret position if there is no selection. You can position the caret before the paste operation occurs by using the `setCaretPosition` method (which creates an empty selection at the offset specified), or select the text to be overwritten with the content of the clipboard by using `setCaretPosition` followed by `moveCaretPosition`.

Text Components, Text Wrapping, and Scrolling

As you saw earlier, unless you are dealing with a `JTextField` or a `JPass-wordField`, you usually need to place text components inside a `JScrollPane` to ensure that all their content will be accessible to the user. You also saw, in Listing 1-2, that `JTextArea` has methods that allow you to control whether text that is too long to be displayed in the space allocated to it should wrap to the next line or should continue past the end of the visible area, necessitating the use of a horizontal scroll bar. Those methods are, however, specific to `JTextArea`. In this section, you'll see how the more complex `JEditorPane` and `JTextPane` controls handle scrolling and word wrapping.

Controlling Line and Word Wrapping

As you've already seen in this chapter, `JTextArea` does not wrap text by default, but has additional methods that allow you to change this behavior if you want, whereas `JTextField`, for which line wrapping makes no sense, incorporates its own scrolling mechanism that allows text that does not fit in the component's visible area to be brought into view by moving the cursor. The other standard text components, `JEditorPane` and `JTextPane`, always wrap text. However, you can suppress word wrapping for these two components if you want.

When a component is mounted in a `JScrollPane`, it can elect to be treated in one of two ways:

- The component can have its width set to the width of the `JScrollPane`'s viewport.
- The component can retain its preferred width.

If you want to avoid line wrapping because you want to force each line of text to occupy one line on the screen, you need to make your text component retain its preferred width so that if the text is wider than the viewport, it is formatted on one line and a horizontal scroll bar is created.

The key to this is the `Scrollable` interface, which contains the following method (among others):

```
public boolean getScrollableTracksViewportWidth();
```

When the component mounted in its viewport implements the `Scrollable` interface, the `JScrollPane` calls the component's implementation of this method when determining how to set the component's horizontal size. If this method returns `true`, the component's horizontal size will be made to match that of the viewport. If it returns `false`, the component will be given its preferred horizontal size. There is a similar method that independently controls the component's height.

`JTextComponent`'s implementation of `getScrollableTracksViewport-Width` returns `true` if the preferred width of the text component is smaller than the width of the `JScrollPane`'s viewport and `false` otherwise. This means that the text component will be stretched to match the width of the visible area if it would otherwise be too narrow to fit. On the other hand, if the text component requires more horizontal space than is available, it is not reduced in size to fit the viewport. Either way, the text in the control would not wrap with this policy. `JTextArea` has a slightly different implementation that behaves in the same way as `JTextComponent` unless line wrapping is enabled, in which case it returns `true`, so that the component's width will be forced to match the width of the viewport when wrapping is required. `JEditorPane`, which is also derived from `JTextComponent`, has a slightly more complex implementation that returns `true` most of the time, except when the viewport size is smaller than the minimum width or larger than the maximum of its content, when it returns `false` to maintain the minimum or maximum size. `JTextPane`, a subclass of `JEditorPane`, always returns `true` from `getScrollableTracksViewportWidth`. In other words, both `JTextPane` and `JEditorPane` will wrap text.

To change the wrapping behavior of, say `JTextPane`, you need to subclass it and override its `getScrollableTracksViewportWidth` method to return `false` when appropriate. The simplest solution would be to always return `false` from this method and this would work, in the sense that the text would never wrap. However, this approach has a flaw. What would happen if the viewport were wider than the space required by the longest line of text? In this case, because the `JTextPane` would only be as wide as its longest line of text requires, the extra space to its right would be unoccupied—the background of the viewport would show through. In the Metal look-and-feel with default colors installed, this results in the viewport containing a `JTextPane` with a white background on the left and a gray empty space to the right, followed by the vertical scroll bar if one is necessary. A better solution is shown in Listing 1-3.

Listing 1-3 A Text Pane Without Line Wrapping

```java
package AdvancedSwing.Chapter1;

import javax.swing.*;
import javax.swing.text.*;
import javax.swing.plaf.*;
import java.awt.*;

public class NonWrappingTextPane extends JTextPane {
    public NonWrappingTextPane() {
        super();
    }

    public NonWrappingTextPane(StyledDocument doc) {
        super(doc);
    }

    // Override getScrollableTracksViewportWidth
    // to preserve the full width of the text
    public boolean getScrollableTracksViewportWidth() {
        Component parent = getParent();
        ComponentUI ui = getUI();

        return parent != null ?
            (ui.getPreferredSize(this).width
            <= parent.getSize().width) :
                true;
    }

    // Test method
    public static void main(String[] args) {
        String content =
            "The plaque on the Apollo 11 Lunar Module\n" +
            "\"Eagle\" reads:\n\n" +
            "\"Here men from the planet Earth first\n" +
            "set foot upon the Moon, July, 1969 AD\n" +
            "We came in peace for all mankind.\"\n\n" +
            "It is signed by the astronauts and the\n" +
            "President of the United States.";
        JFrame f = new JFrame("Non-wrapping Text
            Pane Example");
        JTextPane tp = new JTextPane();
        tp.setText(content);
```

Listing 1-3 A Text Pane Without Line Wrapping (continued)

```
        NonWrappingTextPane nwtp = new NonWrappingTextPane();
            nwtp.setText(content);

        f.getContentPane().setLayout
            (new GridLayout(2, 1));
        f.getContentPane().add(new JScrollPane(tp));
        f.getContentPane().add(new JScrollPane(nwtp));

        f.setSize(300, 200);
        f.setVisible(true);
    }
}
```

In this example, the `NonWrappingTextPane` is a subclass of `JTextPane` in which the `getScrollableTracksViewportWidth` method has been overridden to produce the desired effect. If you type the command

```
java AdvancedSwing.Chapter1.NonWrappingTextPane
```

you'll see a frame with two panes containing the same text mounted one above the other, as shown in Figure 1-8.

Figure 1-8   Text panes with and without line wrap.

The pane at the top is a standard `JTextPane`. If you adjust the width of the frame so that it is too narrow to show all the text, you'll find that the text in the top pane wraps as necessary. No horizontal scroll bar will appear, but the number of lines of text will grow, as evidenced by the vertical scroll bar. By contrast, the text in the lower control doesn't wrap—instead, a horizontal scroll bar appears when you make the viewport too small. If you make the frame wider than the longest line of text, you'll see that both text panes grow to fill the horizontal space available. In particular, the lower text pane does not suffer from the flaw described earlier.

To make this work, the `getScrollableTracksViewportWidth` method is implemented as follows:

- When the viewport width is smaller than the desired width of the text pane, return `false`. This makes the `JScrollPane` size the text pane at its full width, avoiding the wrapping and resulting in a horizontal scroll bar.
- When the viewport is wider than the text, return `true`. Now, the text pane will be stretched horizontally to occupy all the space in the viewport.

You can see the details in Listing 1-3. When the text pane is mounted in a `JScrollPane`, its parent is the viewport itself and the width of that component is the width of the viewport as it appears on the screen. The point to note here is how the text pane's preferred size is determined. The most obvious way to get this would be to call `getPreferredSize` and extract the width from the returned `Dimension` object. However, this would result in a stack overflow, because `getPreferredSize` for `JTextPane` is inherited from `JEditorPane`. However, the `JEditorPane` implementation of this method calls `getScrollableTracksViewportWidth`, which we are reimplementing here by calling `getPreferredSize`! Instead, our `getScrollableTracksViewportWidth` method needs the real preferred size of the text component, without taking into account whether it is mounted in a `JScrollPane`. This information is available from the `getPreferredSize` method of the text pane's user interface (UI) component, which can be obtained by calling the `getUI` method of `JComponent`.

Program-Controlled Scrolling of Text Components

Another common requirement of text components mounted in scroll panes is to programmatically scroll to a known location. For example, you might want to scroll the text component when conducting a text search to highlight an instance of the search string that is not currently visible. You can provide this behavior by using the `JComponent scrollRectToVisible` method, which works equally well for text components. The only problem is working out where the text that you want to scroll to is located within the scroll pane's viewport.

Listing 1-4 shows a subclass of JTextPane (AppendingTextPane) that has a new method called appendText. This method takes a String as its only argument and adds it to the end of the text pane's current content. Then, it arranges for the scroll pane that the text pane is mounted in to scroll so that the new text is visible. This feature is useful for implementing a debugging console, where it is useful to be able to keep track of output as it appears, without having to continually click the scroll bar to bring it into view.

Listing 1-4 A Text Pane with Automatic Scrolling

```
package AdvancedSwing.Chapter1;

import javax.swing.*;
import javax.swing.text.*;
import java.awt.*;
import java.awt.event.*;
import java.text.*;
import java.util.*;

public class AppendingTextPane extends JTextPane {
    public AppendingTextPane() {
        super();
    }

    public AppendingTextPane(StyledDocument doc) {
        super(doc);
    }

    // Appends text to the document and ensure that
    // it is visible
    public void appendText(String text) {
        try {
            Document doc = getDocument();

            // Move the insertion point to the end
            setCaretPosition(doc.getLength());

            // Insert the text
            replaceSelection(text);
```

Listing 1-4 A Text Pane with Automatic Scrolling (continued)

```
                // Convert the new end location
                // to view co-ordinates
                Rectangle r = modelToView(doc.getLength());

                // Finally, scroll so that the new text is visible
                if (r != null) {
                    scrollRectToVisible(r);
                }
            } catch (BadLocationException e) {
                System.out.println("Failed to append text: " + e);
            }
        }
    }

    // Testing method
    public static void main(String[] args) {
        JFrame f = new JFrame("Text Pane with Scrolling
            Append");
        final AppendingTextPane atp =
            new AppendingTextPane();
        f.getContentPane().add(new JScrollPane(atp));
        f.setSize(200, 200);
        f.setVisible(true);

        // Add some text every second
        Timer t = new Timer(1000, new ActionListener() {
            public void actionPerformed(ActionEvent evt) {
            String timeString = fmt.format(new Date());
                atp.appendText(timeString + "\n");
            }

            SimpleDateFormat fmt =
                new SimpleDateFormat("HH:mm:ss");
        });
        t.start();
    }
}
```

You can try out this new text component by typing the command:

```
java AdvancedSwing.Chapter1.AppendingTextPane
```

This program creates an empty text pane and starts a timer. Every second, a `String` containing the current time is appended to the text pane. If you let this example run for a few seconds, the text pane will fill up. However, the latest time will always be displayed because the text pane scrolls automatically to bring it into view, as shown in Figure 1-9.

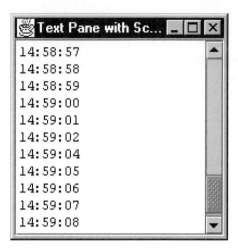

Figure 1-9 Automatic scrolling of text components.

The `appendText` method contains the code that arranges for the scrolling. The first problem is to actually append the text to the existing content. This is done by using the `replaceSelection` method, which replaces whatever is currently selected by the `String` passed as its argument. Immediately before this method is called, `setCaretPosition` is called to place the insertion point at the end of the current content. As noted earlier, calling `setCaret-Position` (without a subsequently call of `moveCaretPosition`) creates an empty selection, so the following `replaceSelection` is effectively an insertion at the end of the text pane.

To scroll the new text into view, `scrollRectToVisible` is called. This method needs a `Rectangle` that describes the section of the viewport that should be made visible. At this stage, all we have is the offset within the text pane at which the new text was inserted, which was obtained from the `getLength` method of the `Document` underlying the text pane. Fortunately, `JTextComponent` has a method called `modelToView` that takes a model offset and returns a `Rectangle` describing the location of that offset within the document view. This `Rectangle` can be passed directly to `scrollRectTo-Visible` to obtain the desired effect. Note that we first check that the `Rectangle` returned by `modelToView` is not `null`: This is necessary because this method returns `null` if the text component has not yet been painted.

Adding Functionality to the Basic Text Components

The Swing text components provide a lot of functionality. However, if you understand the way in which they are built, you can get much more out of them either by subclassing the components themselves or by reimplementing some of the pieces that make them up. This section looks first at the architecture of the text components. When you've seen the overall picture, you'll then see how to create extended text components that, for example, validate input as it is being typed by the user.

Text Component Architecture

Figure 1-10 shows the major pieces that make up a text component. This view is a logical one, rather than a class-based one. The diagram shows an imaginary document containing three paragraphs held in the Document object, represented lower left. The paragraphs are delimited by newline characters. The actual layout of this text on the screen is shown in the top left. Here, the text is split into three paragraphs aligned vertically above each other and the content of the first paragraph has been selected by dragging the mouse over it. The cursor is assumed to be positioned after the word "paragraph."

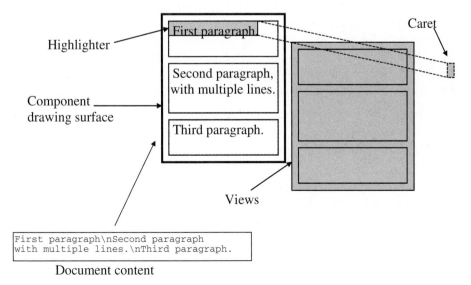

Figure 1-10 Text component architecture.

The selected text is highlighted using an object called the *highlighter*, which draws directly onto the component's drawing surface. The highlighter is represented by the shaded area over the text of the first paragraph. In front of the component surface is a logical representation of the *views* that actually render the text onto the screen. Here, there is a view for each paragraph. As you'll see in Chapter 3, there are more view objects in a real text component; the figure shows only the paragraph views for the sake of simplicity. Finally, the cursor is drawn using an object called the *caret*. Like the highlighter, the caret draws directly on the component's drawing surface.

The Document

The document stores the data that the text component displays and the attributes that are associated with it or with other objects within the *document*. While `JTextField`, `JPasswordField`, and `JTextArea` can only display text and are limited to a single font and two colors (one for the background and another for the foreground), both `JEditorPane` and `JTextPane` support multiple fonts and colors and can host more interesting content, such as icons and components in addition to text. The document holds all the information that describes the content of the component, including the fonts and colors.

The methods that maintain the document contents are defined by the `Document` interface. The Swing package includes two concrete implementations of this interface that are used by the standard text components. `Plain-Document` is used to hold text only. It has no methods for supporting the more complex formatting possible with the `JEditorPane` and `JTextPane` components, which use a document class called `DefaultStyledDocument`. In addition to these basic document classes, the HTML support provides a third one, `HTMLDocument`, which is derived from `DefaultStyledDocument`. The standard document types and the `Document` interface are discussed in "Storing Document Content" on page 34.

The Highlighter

Every text component has an associated highlighter, which is used to show the portion of the text that is currently selected. A highlighter is an implementation of the `Highlighter` interface, of which the `DefaultHigh-lighter` class in the Swing text package is an example. When the component is created, an instance of the class `DefaultHighlighter` is initialized and associated with it. `DefaultHighlighter` is a simple implementation that highlights selected text by changing its background color to the selection color of the text component that it is associated with, which is usually extracted from the `UIDefaults` object of the installed look-and-feel.

Although there is at most one selection in a text component at any given time, and hence at most one area highlighted to show the selection, a highlighter can actually be used to color an arbitrary set of ranges within a document. Each range is controlled by a class implementing the interface `Highlighter.HighlightPainter`. When a `Highlighter` needs to draw its associated highlights, it uses the corresponding `HighlightPainter` to do so. The `DefaultHighlighter` class uses the `DefaultHighligher.Default-HighlightPainter`, which fills a rectangular area with a solid color, to do its painting. Highlighters are discussed in more detail in Chapter 3.

The Caret

The caret (otherwise known as the cursor) is principally concerned with displaying the point where text will be inserted in response to keystrokes. By default, the cursor is drawn as a thin vertical line. However, when bi-directional text is in use (see Chapter 5), it is augmented by a small black blob that shows which way the current text region flows.

The caret can be provided by any class that implements the `Caret` interface. There is a default implementation called `DefaultCaret` that provides all the functionality required by the standard text components. The caret is not usually look-and-feel dependent, but its color and the rate at which it blinks when its associated component has the keyboard focus are configured in the selected look-and-feel's `UIDefaults` table.

The caret listens to property change, focus, mouse, and mouse motion events that occur within its text component and `DocumentEvents` from the component's `Document`. By responding to focus and mouse events, the caret is fulfilling part of the controller role of the MVC model. The other part of the controller, the part that handles keyboard input, is implemented by `JTextComponent`, although much of the work is delegated to the text component's installed editor kit.

Property change events are used to detect a change of `Document` within the text component so that the caret can register itself as a `Document-Listener` on whatever is the current `Document`. `DocumentEvents` are generated when the content of the text component's model changes; a change in document content can affect the visual position of the caret if text is added or removed before the location of the caret in the document.

Focus events are used to switch the caret on and off. In the default implementation, the caret is visible only when the text component has the focus.

When the component gains the focus, the caret paints itself at its current location; when the focus is lost, the caret is removed.

Finally, mouse events are used to control the caret's position and to manage the selection of text. The caret maintains two distinguished positions within the document referred to as the *mark* and the *dot*. The dot always corresponds to the caret's current position, while the mark is the position to which the caret was last moved by clicking the mouse. The range of the document between the mark and the dot is the selection. Suppose that the user clicks the mouse somewhere inside a text component. This position becomes both the mark and the dot. Because the mark and the dot now occupy the same place in the document, there will be no selection. If the user now drags the mouse, the caret follows the mouse by moving the dot to the position reported by the last mouse drag event. The mark, however, is left behind. Because dragging the mouse causes a selection to be created, the caret is responsible for making the selection visible by arranging for the component's highlighter to repaint the background of the selected text. A custom highlighter may, of course, use other means to display the selection, such as underlining the affected range of text. Methods that allow the programmer to control the selection (such as `select`, `selectAll`, etc.) also control the caret by setting the dot and mark directly.

If you want, you can change the appearance of the caret by substituting your own implementation of the `Caret` interface using the `JTextComponent` `setCaret` method. There is an example that shows how this is done later in this chapter.

The Editor Kit

Although not shown in Figure 1-10, the editor kit provides much of the functionality of the text components. There are four editor kits provided with the Swing text packages:

- `DefaultEditorKit`
- `StyledEditorKit`
- `HTMLEditorKit`
- `RTFEditorKit`

Broadly speaking, an editor kit knows how to handle a document with a particular content type. `DefaultEditorKit` is used with simple text components (`JTextField`, `JPasswordField`, and `JTextArea`) that use a single font and a single foreground color. `StyledEditorKit` is more complex and handles arbitrary attributes that can be applied to the whole document, to paragraphs, or to ranges of characters. This editor kit is used by JTextPane and is the superclass of both HTMLEditorKit and RTFEditorKit, which use the text and attribute handling inherited from StyledEditorKit to read and display HTML and RTF documents respectively. These two editor kits are typically plugged into a JEditorPane.

The editor kit is responsible for the following:

- Creating the appropriate type of Document to support the same facilities as the editor kit. DefaultEditorKit creates a PlainDocument; StyledEditorKit and RTFEditorKit both use a DefaultStyledDocument; and HTMLEditorKit uses an HTMLDocument, which is derived from DefaultStyledDocument. The editor kit creates the Document when the text component that it is hosted by is created, unless the programmer has installed a specific Document type by passing it to the component's constructor.

- Loading document content from an input stream (or reader) or writing content to an output stream (or writer). The editor kit read and write methods are usually invoked indirectly via the same methods of JTextComponent. There is a connection between the editor kit and the format of the data in the input stream. For example, the HTMLEditorKit expects to read an input stream that contains text and HTML tags and writes output in the same format. DefaultEditorKit and StyledEditorKit handle only plain text, so you can't save the formatting applied programmatically to a JTextPane in a file and recover it later, unless you override the StyledEditorKit write method to store the attributes in a private format and implement the read method so that you can restore them.

- Creating the View objects needed to draw the content of a text component on the screen. View objects are described in "Views" below, and in more detail in Chapter 3.

- Providing a set of editing actions that can be connected to keyboard actions for use by the end-user. This aspect of the editor kit is described in "Keymaps and Key Bindings" on page 86.

Views

Text components are drawn by objects derived from the abstract View class. There are several standard subclasses of View that handle various aspects of the drawing process. The views that will be used to draw a particular component depend on the component type and on its actual content. Classes called `PlainView` and `WrappedPlainView` are used by `JTextArea`, while two others called `FieldView` and `PasswordView` are used by `JTextField` and `JPasswordField`, respectively. For the simple text components, only one `View` type is required to manage the whole document and the component itself knows how to create its own specific kind of `View`.

Core Note

This is not strictly true, because there is an inner class of `WrappedPlainView` *that manages line wrapping. For now, we'll sacrifice strict accuracy in the interests of making it easier to understand exactly how* `View`s *are used. You'll see the complete truth in Chapter 3.*

Other components have a hierarchy of `View`s, each of which knows how to display part of the control's content. The most important `View` objects are listed in Table 1-2.

Table I-2 Swing View Classes	
`FieldView` and `PasswordView`	These views are used by `JTextField` and `JPassword-Field` respectively. They draw text in a single-line display area. `FieldView` is derived from `PlainView`. `PasswordView` is a subclass of `FieldView` that differs only in that it renders each character in the model using the configured echo character instead of the corresponding characters from the text component's selected font.
`PlainView` and `WrappedPlainView`	`PlainView` and `WrappedPlainView` are used by `JTextArea` and draw two-dimensional text. The `PlainView` does not wrap lines that are too long to fit within the visible area allocated to them—it simply truncates them. `WrappedPlainView` is a subclass of `PlainView` that wraps by breaking the text at white-space boundaries when word wrapping style is in use, or when the line is full if it is not.
`BoxView`	`BoxView` is a "container" view that acts a little like the Swing `Box` component. Its function is to manage child views by arranging them horizontally or vertically. In practice, this view is used as the main view of a `JTextPane` or a `JEditorPane` and manages the entire document, laying out `ParagraphViews` vertically, one above the other.

Table 1-2 Swing View Classes (continued)	
`ParagraphView`	As its name implies, this is used to manage the layout of the contents of a paragraph from a `JEditorPane` or `JText-Pane`. A `ParagraphView` creates paragraphs by building rows consisting of `LabelViews`, `IconViews`, and `ComponentViews` as appropriate.
`LabelView`	`LabelView` is the basic view that actually renders text from the underlying document. A `LabelView` may or may not map onto a single line of the view area of a text component. However, a `LabelView` is never more than one row long.
`IconView`	An `IconView` takes care of displaying inline images stored as instances of the Swing `Icon` interface.
`ComponentView`	Similarly, `ComponentView` hosts a `Component` and places it inline in the document flow. Although you can place an AWT `Component` in a document, you are more likely to use a lightweight component derived from `JComponent` to avoid the usual problems inherent in mixing AWT and Swing components.

In the case of `JTextPane` and `JEditorPane`, different elements of the document are managed by different `View` objects. To avoid hard-coding this relationship into the components themselves, the editor kit is used as a factory that creates the appropriate `View` objects based on the nature of the piece of the document being rendered. For example, in the case of `JText-Pane`, for each paragraph in the document, `StyledEditorKit` would create a `ParagraphView` to represent it and this `ParagraphView` would be added to another `View` called `BoxView` that manages the vertical layout of the document. Each piece of the paragraph would, in turn, be managed by a `Label-View` if it consists of plain text. `JTextPane` and `JEditorPane` can also include `Icons` and arbitrary `Components` inline with the text. When a `Styled-EditorKit` is installed in one of these components, these objects are drawn by `Views` of type `IconView` or a `ComponentView`. A custom editor kit might have private `View` objects that render text, `Icons`, or `Components` differently and would return instances of its own customized objects from its `factory` method. You'll see an example of a text component that uses a custom `View` component, along with a more detailed discussion of the way in which `Views` work, in Chapter 3.

Storing Document Content

Now that you've seen the overall architecture of the text components, it's time to write some real code. The simplest aspect of all the text components is the underlying document model. Even though there are three different document models in the Swing text package, they are all derived from a common base class (called `AbstractDocument`) and they all fundamentally do the same thing. Basically, the job of the data model is to store the text that will ultimately be displayed on the screen and information that describes (logically, not physically) how it should be formatted. These two aspects are actually neatly separated from each other. In this section, you'll see how the text is stored and how it can be manipulated without regard to the formatting information. Knowing how this works, you'll be able to create, among other things, useful subclasses of `JTextField` that perform various kinds of input validation, or help users by trying to guess what they want to type by comparing the input keystrokes to a predefined list of possible values. Later, you'll see how the text can be enhanced with attributes such as color and font changes and how paragraph structure can be imposed on top of what would otherwise be linear text.

The Document Interface

The `Document` interface controls how data that is stored within the text component's model is accessed and updated. In short, it is the interface to the data model. As noted in the previous paragraph, the data model stores both text and attributes and `Document` provides the hooks needed to retrieve and store both types of information. It does not, however, dictate how that information should be stored—that's left to concrete implementations to determine. The methods defined by the `Document` interface are listed in Table 1-3.

Insertion and Removal of Text

The first five methods in this interface are by far the most important as far as this section is concerned. The `insertString` and `remove` methods respectively allow content to be added to or removed from the data model. At this level, the document is considered to be composed of a sequence of Unicode characters; for convenience, `insertString` allows you to add a group of characters together by taking its data in the form of a `String` rather than as individual characters.

Table 1-3 The Document Interface

```
public int getLength();

public void insertString(int offset, String str,
    AttributeSet a) throws BadLocationException;

public void remove(int offs, int len) throws
    BadLocationException;

public String getText(int offset, int length) throws
    BadLocationException;

public void getText(int offset, int length, Segment txt)
    throws BadLocationException;

public Position getStartPosition();

public Position getEndPosition();

public Position createPosition(int offs) throws
    BadLocationException;

public Object getProperty(Object key);

public void putProperty(Object key, Object value);

public void addDocumentListener(DocumentListener listener);

public void removeDocumentListener(DocumentListener
    listener);

public void addUndoableEditListener(UndoableEditListener
    listener);

public void removeUndoableEditListener(UndoableEditListener
    listener);

public Element[] getRootElements();

public Element getDefaultRootElement();

public void render(Runnable r);
```

Positioning within the data model is specified by using an offset from the beginning of the document. These offsets refer not to the characters themselves, but to the "gaps" between successive characters. Offset 0, for example, refers to the location just before the first character of the document and, if the document contains n characters in all, the position before the last character has offset (n - 1), while the position after the last character is at offset n.

The insertString method takes an offset as its first parameter. When this method is called, the implementation is expected to place the data in the String passed as the second argument into the data model at the location directly following the given offset. Any data originally at that offset is moved down to offset (offs + length), where length is the number of characters in the supplied String. When inserting content, you can also specify an AttributeSet. As its name suggests, an AttributeSet stores attributes, such as color or font information, that will be associated with the data in the model. Attributes are generally only meaningful for text components derived from JEditorPane; they will be described in the next chapter. When there are no attributes to store, as is the case for JTextField, JPasswordField, and JTextArea, this argument has the value null.

The remove method deletes content from the model, moving whatever follows the removed text up to occupy its original location. Because of this, the model always appears to be compact—there are never any unoccupied offsets anywhere in the data.

Both insertString and remove throw a BadLocationException if you try to address a range of offsets that is not entirely within the model. This means that the starting offset may not be negative and must be less than the number of characters in the model. The length argument must similarly be zero or positive and, in the case of the remove method, it must be such that the value of (offset + length) is less than the length of the model. If you supply a range of offsets that is invalid, the resulting BadLocationException contains the value of the first illegal offset in the range, which can be obtained using the offsetRequested method.

Core Note

As you'll see in later chapters, inserting and removing text has a direct effect on other parts of the document model and on the View components used to render the model onto the screen. At the moment, however, you can forget about those secondary effects, because they are dealt with separately. Views, for example, are updated as a result of events sent from the model when its content changes.

Retrieving Model Content

The two getText methods allow you to inspect the content of the model. The first variant copies the data from the specified range into a newly created String object. While this may be convenient for some purposes, it is not the most efficient way to access the model. The second `getText` method accepts a `Segment` object, defined as follows:

```
public class Segment {
    public char[] array;
    public int offset;
    public int count;
    public Segment();
    public Segment(char[] array, int offset, int count);
    public String toString();
}
```

The second variant of `getText` is usually a more efficient way to inspect the model, because it often avoids the need to copy the data. To use it, you create a `Segment` object using the first constructor shown above and simply pass it to `getText` along with the offset and length of the part of the document that you want access to. The `getText` method then sets the `array`, `offset`, and `count` members to point to a character array that contains the data in the specified range. The character at the first offset in the specified range can be obtained as follows:

```
try {
    Segment seg = new Segment();
    model.getText(offset, length, seg);
    char firstChar = seg.array[seg.offset];
} catch (BadLocationException e) {
    // Handle illegal access
}
```

In some cases, the `array` member will actually point to the real document content, thus avoiding the need to copy the data out of the model. For this reason, the data returned by this method must *not* be modified. In other cases, however, a copy of the model content will be returned. Callers of `get-Text` should not make any assumptions about whether the data returned is a copy or the real data, because this depends on the implementation of the underlying data storage mechanism.

Positions

Although the `insertString`, `remove`, and `getText` methods use absolute offsets to specify locations within the model, this is often not a convenient way to manipulate text, mainly because offsets can become invalid when text is added to or removed from the model. If you have a pointer to the start of a paragraph in the form of an offset, you can continue to access the start of the paragraph using that offset provided nothing inserts or removes data in the area that precedes the paragraph. If this does happen, there is no easy way to find the start of the paragraph again.

To make it possible to track logical locations within a document, the model provides `Position` objects. A `Position` object is tied to a particular offset in the model that is specified when the `createPosition` method is called. Once you've got a `Position` object for a given location, it remains attached to that location even if its offset changes later. To obtain the offset that corresponds to a `Position` at any given time, you can use the `getOffset` method. For example, suppose the model contains 100 characters and you want to keep track of the character that is initially located at offset 50. Consider the following code sequence:

```
Position paraPos = model.createPosition(50);
System.out.println("Initial offset = " + paraPos.getOffset());
model.remove(10, 20);
System.out.println("Final offset = " + paraPos.getOffset());
```

The first call to `println` would show that the `Position` created by the first line has associated offset 50. After the `remove` method completes, 20 characters from offsets 10 through 29 will have been removed, so everything that was at offset 30 and higher will have moved down to fill up the gap. In particular, the character initially at offset 50 will have moved to offset 30 and the second call to `println` would show that the offset in the `Position` object is now 30. The `Position` object continues to track the point it was initially associated with regardless of what changes are made to the model.

The `getStartPosition` and `getEndPosition` methods create `Position` objects that always correspond to the start and end of the document respectively. In this respect, they don't actually track a given offset in the document, but rather always stay attached to its start and end, even if text is added at the front of the document or at the end.

Properties

The `getProperty` and `putProperty` methods allow arbitrary values addressed by arbitrary keys to be stored in the document model. The various `Document` implementations use this feature to store information that could be used during rendering or for some other type-specific purpose. For example, `PlainDocument` holds the default tab spacing that will be used to decide where to move the caret when the TAB key is pressed under the property name `tabSize`; the associated value being an `Integer`. More interestingly, the `HTMLDocument` type uses a common property defined by `Document` called `title` to store the value associated with the HTML TITLE tag.

When building custom text components or custom document models, you can create and store your own properties using this mechanism.

Event Handling

The four methods `addDocumentListener`, `removeDocumentListener`, `addUndoableEditListener`, and `removeUndoableEditListener` are used to allow events within the text model to be monitored. The latter two are part of the undo/redo mechanism that will be covered in Chapter 9. The other two methods allow listeners to receive notification of content changes within the document model, which cause `DocumentEvent`s to be generated.

> **Core Note**
>
> If you're familiar with the AWT text components, a `DocumentEvent` is the Swing equivalent of the AWT `TextEvent`. Unlike `TextEvent`, which is a class, `DocumentEvent` is actually an interface. Real `DocumentEvent`s in Swing are instances of the class `DefaultDocumentEvent`, which implements the `DocumentEvent` interface. `DefaultDocumentEvent` is an inner class of `AbstractDocument`. You'll find more on this in Chapter 9.

A `DocumentEvent` is created when any of the following occurs:

- Something is inserted into the model.
- Something is deleted from the model.
- The attributes associated with some part of the model are changed.

`DocumentEvent` has methods that allow you to extract the offset of the first affected character, the length of the region affected, the `Document` in which the change was made, and the event type, which will be one of `Document-Event.INSERT`, `DocumentEvent.REMOVE`, and `DocumentEvent.CHANGE`. These events are used internally by the text component's `View` objects to update its on-screen representation. The offset and length values can be used to work out exactly which `View`s are affected by whatever change has been made, which makes it possible to optimize the screen update process.

A typical application might use a `DocumentEvent` to be notified that some change has occurred in a text component that may require state elsewhere in the application to be updated. For example, suppose the application presents a dialog box consisting of a `JTextField` and an associated `OK` button that would dismiss the dialog and cause the content of the text field to be processed, perhaps as a person's name or e-mail address. When the text field is empty, it would not be useful for the button to be active, so a well-written application would create the dialog with the button disabled. As soon as a single character has been typed, however, the content of the text field might be valid, so the button should be enabled. If the user types some characters and then deletes them, leaving the text field empty, the button should be disabled again. The application can implement these semantics by receiving DocumentEvents from the JTextField. Here is how a suitable listener might be registered:

```
JTextField textField = new JTextField(20);
DocumentListener l = new DocumentListener() {
    // Implementation not shown
};
textField.getDocument().addDocumentListener(l);
```

The important thing to note about this code is that the listener has to be registered with the Document, not the text field, because JTextComponent does not have convenience methods to delegate registration to the Document.

The DocumentListener interface is defined as follows:

```
public interface DocumentListener extends EventListener {
    public void insertUpdate(DocumentEvent e);
    public void removeUpdate(DocumentEvent e);
    public void changedUpdate(DocumentEvent e);
}
```

In this example, the insertUpdate method would be called when content has been added to the JTextField and it would respond by enabling the OK button. Similarly, removeUpdate is entered when something is deleted from the text field. It would probably get the length of the document content and disable the OK button if the text field were now empty.

Because a DocumentEvent is generated when any change of any kind is made to the content of a text component, you might think that you could listen to DocumentEvents as a way of monitoring characters typed into the text field with a view to checking if they are valid. For example, you might try to implement a text field that only allows uppercase characters to be typed by attaching a listener to the text field and either removing lowercase characters or forcing them to uppercase within the listener code. However, this technique does not work, because the Swing Document implementations do not allow you to change their content from with a DocumentListener. The reason for this is clear—if it were allowed, changing the document content from within the DocumentListener would cause another DocumentEvent, which could result in your `DocumentListener` methods being invoked recursively. As you'll see in the next section, there are better and more direct ways to create text fields that verify or act immediately upon input passed to them, without using `DocumentEvents`. It is, however, perfectly practical to use these events when the action you take in response does not affect the text field, as is the case with the example of the `OK` button that you have just seen.

Elements and Rendering

The `getRootElements` and `getDefaultRootElement` methods of the `Document` interface are concerned with maintaining the superstructure that sits over the raw text that allows the more complex text components to display formatted text and mix them with images and components. This aspect of the data model will be covered in Chapter 3.

The `render` method is a convenience that makes it possible for the text component to be safely drawn onto the screen without the potentially disruptive effects of document updates during the drawing process. This is achieved by locking the document to prevent other threads attempting to change its content or the associated attributes, and then invoking the `run` method of the `Runnable` passed to the `render` method. The `Document` methods that update the document content are expected to synchronize with the rendering process by obtaining a write lock before making any changes. The locking is implemented within the standard `Document` implementations, so there is no need to be concerned with the details unless you plan to override the `insertString` or `replace` methods as implemented in `AbstractDocument`.

Implementing Text Fields with Input Validation

`JTextField` is a perfectly usable general purpose input field, but it doesn't have any means of validating that the user is typing characters that are acceptable when taking into account the way in which the content of the field will actually be used by an application. This is not surprising, of course, because there are countless ways to use a text field, all of which require different validity checks to be made. Nevertheless, it is possible to adopt a general strategy for the implementation of a text field that provides some kind of input validation, and in this section, you'll see two examples that illustrate how to use the architecture of the Swing text components to get control at the appropriate points to make whatever checks are required.

A Text Field with Limited Input Capacity

For our first example, let's create a text field that imposes an upper limit on the number of characters that can be typed into it. This is a very common requirement in applications that interface with databases with fixed-length fields, because it would not be acceptable to allow the user to try to enter a value whose size exceeds that of the corresponding field in the database. Although the code to check the length could be added to the application, having an off-the-shelf component that can do the job is better from the point of view of code reuse and also creates a better user interface, because it is possible to stop accepting keystrokes when the maximum size of the input field has been reached, rather than allowing the user to type something unacceptable and providing feedback later.

How would you implement such a text field? There are several possible ways to do this. Let's look at three of them.

Limiting Input using a DocumentListener

You've already seen one possible solution earlier in this chapter in connection with `DocumentEvents`. Perhaps the most obvious thing to do is to create a subclass of `JTextField` that can be given the maximum field size as an argument to its constructor, which then registers a `DocumentListener` on its own document. With this approach, each time the user added a character to the text field or removed characters, the `DocumentListener` would be informed and its `insertUpdate` method would check how many characters had been typed so far. If the number of characters exceeded the configured limit, the content would be truncated to the maximum size and written back to the model. Unfortunately, we know that this cannot be done because you cannot change the content of the document from within the `DocumentListener` implementation. Perhaps you could get around this restriction by using the `SwingUtilities invokeLater` method to defer the modification so that it would be made outside the critical phase of the document update. One problem with this technique is that, as viewed from outside the component, some number of characters would be added to the text component and then taken away again. This is a confusing state of affairs—only real document updates should be seen by the user and reflected to any other `DocumentListeners` that might be registered on the component.

Furthermore, making changes and immediately removing them also needlessly complicates any possible support for undo/redo that you might want to provide for your enhanced text field, because the internal changes will appear as distinct actions from the point of view of the undo mechanism. At worst, this might mean that users will see these phantom changes if they want to make use of the redo mechanism to reverse actual edits on the text field. For example, suppose you implement a bounded-length text field in this way and then add the ability for the user to use CTRL-z to undo the last edit and CTRL-Y to redo the last undone change. Suppose also that there is a maximum of 10 characters allowed in the input field and that the user inadvertently typed an 11-character string. At this point, the text component intervenes and removes the 11th character, leaving 10 characters in the data model. Now suppose the user types CTRL-z. What should this do? Arguably, it should remove the 10th character typed, because the insertion of the 11th character never really happened. However, the sequence of events in the model has actually been:

1. Type the 10th character.
2. Type the 11th character.
3. Delete the 11th character.

Now, unless the undo mechanism is aware of what is happening under the covers in the enhanced text field, it will respond to CTRL-z by undoing the deletion of the 11th character, creating an 11-character text field again. At this point, the text component's internal DocumentListener will notice that this is illegal and arrange to remove it, leaving the original 10 characters. In other words, CTRL-z has actually done something within the component, but left its content and appearance unchanged. This is not correct behavior. While it might be possible to devise some way to work around this, it would almost certainly create a complex implementation that is difficult to maintain. Not surprisingly, there is a better way.

Listening to Keyboard Input

If trying to change the content of the model after it has been updated is not an acceptable solution, how about stopping the excess characters getting into the model in the first place? This has got to be a better solution, because it immediately avoids creating document events and undoable edit events for state changes that shouldn't really have happened. One possible way to do this would be to capture the keyboard events that are generated as the user types into the text component. Each time a new character is typed, the keyboard event would be intercepted and the number of characters in the model would be checked. If the model is already full, the newly typed key would be rejected by consuming the event, so that the logic within the text component that would insert the new key into the model would never see it. It is certainly possible to catch and suppress key events in this way, but this approach is also not without problems.

Consider, for example, what your key event handler would actually need to do. In principle, when each key is typed, it would get the length of the model and compare it to the maximum bound of the input field. If they match, the key must be rejected. Well, not quite. What if the user presses the back-space key? This is a special case that should not be blocked, regardless of the current length of the data model. Of course, it is easy to write code that recognizes this particular key and suppresses the usual check. Unfortunately, this is not the only special case. Suppose the programmer chooses to bind some other key or keys to actions that affect the content of the text field? How about if the programmer binds CTRL-U so that it clears the text field? In this particular case, if the user typed 10 characters into a field that accepts 10 characters and then pressed CTRL-U, this would be seen as an illegal 11th character and suppressed before it can clear the input field. Should you look for this key combination and write special code for that, too? Because the programmer can, in fact, bind arbitrary keys to arbitrary actions (as you'll see in "Keymaps and Key Bindings" on page 86), it is impossible to hard-wire all of the exceptions into the key event code.

Even if you feel comfortable with creating a bounded text field that doesn't allow custom key bindings that could cause you trouble, there are still other problems to deal with. What happens if the programmer decides to initialize the field by calling the setText method? Suppose the initial value is more than 10 characters long. Should this be allowed? Clearly, it should not. However, this operation does not involve key events, so the key listener, no matter how carefully it is coded, cannot intervene to prevent it. The only possible recourse is to override the JTextField setText method and add the check there, adding a little more code to plug another leak. This is surely not a good design principle.

Unfortunately, even with all of this sticking plaster there is still another problem. As you know, all the Swing text components allow you to paste text from the system clipboard. Suppose the clipboard contains a 100-character string and the user clicks in your text field, and then presses CTRL-V, or whichever key sequence corresponds to the paste action in the selected look-and-feel. What will happen is that all 100 characters will be pasted into the text component's data model via its insertString method, bypassing the key event handler and the (presumably overridden) setText method. In fact, you can't really get around this without overriding the paste method of JTextComponent. Again, this is possible, but the complexity is now surely becoming unacceptable for such a simple feature.

Using the Document Model

The most elegant way to validate the proposed content of a text field was actually touched upon in the previous paragraph—when data is pasted into a text component, it is copied directly to the data model. In fact, anything being entered into the text field is also ultimately written to the data model, whether it comes from the keyboard, the clipboard, or via `setText`. In implementation terms, any text insertion is performed in the `Document insert-String` method, so this is the obvious common place to check what is being placed in the model and to take the appropriate action. Furthermore, this approach also ensures that only appropriate document and undoable edit events are generated, because these events reflect exactly what happens to the model.

Core Note

I am not trying to imply that all custom text components should be implemented by subclassing `PlainDocument` *or some other* `Document` *class. For the examples in this section, this is, indeed, the simplest thing to do. However, there are cases in which you can't add all the extra functionality by modifying the model alone. When this is true, despite the complications outlined previously, you will have to do more work in the text component itself. For an example of this, see "A Text Field with Look-Ahead" on page 73.*

Let's see how this might work in practice by looking at the implementation of a subclass of `JTextField` that allows only a fixed number of characters to be typed into it. In terms of the data model, this translates to there being an upper limit on the number of characters in the model. If anything that gets into the model goes via `insertString`, it is obviously possible to check that the allowed capacity won't be exceeded by the `String` passed to `insert-String` by adding appropriate code to that method. Listing 1-5 shows a subclass of `PlainDocument` with an overridden `insertString` method that implements this policy.

Because the aim is to create a model that can be used in conjunction with a `JTextField`, this model is derived from `PlainDocument`, the document type used by `JTextField` (and, incidentally by `JPasswordField` and `JText-Area`). The first two constructors allow you to create a `BoundedPlainDocu-ment` with a specific limit, or to set the limit later using the `setMaxLength` method. The third constructor accepts a maximum length and some initial data in the form of an object of type `AbstractDocument.Content`. This is, in fact, an interface rather than a class. Up to now, we have assumed that the Document implementation actually stores the data, but this is not quite true. The responsibility for storing the data is delegated to a separate class that implements the Content interface. Swing has two such classes, String-Content and GapContent.

**Listing I-5 A Text Component Data Model
              with Limited Capacity**

```java
package AdvancedSwing.Chapter1;

import javax.swing.text.*;

public class BoundedPlainDocument extends PlainDocument {
    public BoundedPlainDocument() {
        // Default constructor - must use setMaxLength later
        this.maxLength = 0;
    }

    public BoundedPlainDocument(int maxLength) {
        this.maxLength = maxLength;
    }

    public BoundedPlainDocument (
            AbstractDocument.Content content,int maxLength) {
        super(content);
        if (content.length() > maxLength) {
            throw new IllegalArgumentException(
                "Initial content larger than maximum size");
        }
        this.maxLength = maxLength;
    }

    public void setMaxLength(int maxLength) {
        if (getLength() > maxLength) {
            throw new IllegalArgumentException(
                "Current content larger than new maximum size");
        }

        this.maxLength = maxLength;
    }
```

**Listing 1-5 A Text Component Data Model
with Limited Capacity (continued)**

```java
public int getMaxLength() {
    return maxLength;
}

public void insertString(int offset, String str,
    AttributeSet a)
        throws BadLocationException {
    if (str == null) {
        return;
    }


    // Note: be careful here - the content always has a
    // trailing newline, which should not be counted!
    int capacity = maxLength + 1 - getContent().length();
    if (capacity >= str.length()) {
        // It all fits
        super.insertString(offset, str, a);
    } else {
        // It doesn't all fit. Add as much as we can.
        if (capacity > 0) {
            super.insertString(offset, str.substring(0,
                                capacity), a);
        }

        // Finally, signal an error.
        if (errorListener != null) {
            errorListener.insertFailed(this, offset,
                                str, a);
        }
    }
}

public void addInsertErrorListener(
                        InsertErrorListener l) {
    if (errorListener == null) {
        errorListener = l;
        return;
    }
    throw new IllegalArgumentException(
        "InsertErrorListener already registered");
}
```

**Listing I-5 A Text Component Data Model
          with Limited Capacity (continued)**

```
public void removeInsertErrorListener
        (InsertErrorListener l) {
   if (errorListener == l) {
      errorListener = null;
   }
}

public interface InsertErrorListener {
   public abstract void insertFailed
      (BoundedPlainDocument doc,
       int offset, String str, AttributeSet a);
}

protected InsertErrorListener errorListener;
                // Unicast listener
protected int maxLength;
}
```

The first of these classes stores the content as a character array that grows as the content's size increases. The character array always maps exactly the model's content, so that when data is inserted in the middle the characters at and above the insertion point need to be copied to their new locations to allow new data to be added. Similarly, when anything is deleted, the characters above the deleted region need to be copied down to occupy the newly freed space. GapContent is a more sophisticated class that tries to minimize data copying when content is added or removed by allowing a single gap to exist in the data. The gap is moved around as necessary to preserve the illusion of a contiguous span of characters. Unless you intend to implement your own Content class, you won't need to delve into the details of the implementation of these classes. By default, the Swing Document classes use GapContent to store their data.

Core Note

In Swing 1.0, StringContent was the only Content implementation available.

Most of the code in Listing 1-5 is straightforward and should be readily understandable. When new content is passed to the insertString method, the available space in the model is computed by subtracting the number of characters already in the model from the maximum capacity. Note that the model always includes a trailing newline, which is not counted in our maximum length, so the calculation takes this into account. If the available capacity exceeds the length of the `String` to be inserted, the insertion is legal and the superclass `insertString` method is called to carry it out. `Bounded-PlainDocument` does not, of course, need to care about how the data is actually stored because it can simply delegate everything apart from checking the total length to `PlainDocument`. Removing data from the model is also not a particular concern for this class, because this operation can never cause the maximum size to be exceeded. Therefore, the `remove` method of `Plain-Document` doesn't need to be overridden here.

The only design issue of any interest is what to do when the insertion operation is not legal. When the user is typing into a text field that uses this model, each call to `insertString` will be passed a `String` containing exactly one character. Obviously, this character will not be added to the model. There are, however, two other things to consider:

- What should happen if the `String` has more than one character and there is room for some, but not all, of its content? This might happen if the data is coming from the clipboard or the `setText` method.
- Should there be any direct feedback to the user when insertion fails and how can this feedback be generated?

As far as the first point is concerned, there are two possible approaches: either that part of the data that could fit in the model should be added and the rest discarded, or the entire operation should be ignored. Which you choose is largely a matter of taste or the requirements of your particular application. For complete flexibility, you could make this behavior a configurable property of the control and make the decision when the issue arises in the `insertString` method. The implementation shown in Listing 1-5 chooses to add as much data as will fit and discard the rest. It is, of course, a simple matter to change this to adopt the alternative policy.

The second issue is slightly more difficult to deal with. Looking at this from the user's point of view, there must be some feedback when the text field fills up, otherwise if users are typing without looking at the screen, they may not be aware that not all the characters being typed are actually getting into the text field. The best thing to do is probably to generate a short beep to alert the user to the problem. This could be done directly from the `insert-String` method, because the AWT `Toolkit` class includes a method that allows you to cause a short beep. However, in design terms this is not very desirable. After all, `BoundedPlainDocument` is concerned only with storing data—it is an MVC model class. User feedback is not a model issue—it is the view's job to let the user know what is happening; the model's duty is only to make sure that the view has the information needed to keep the user up-to-date.

Instead of hard-coding a beeping action into the model, this example defines an interface called `InsertErrorListener` with a single method (`insertFailed`) that will be called when some (or all) of the characters passed to `insertString` did not fit in the model. The idea is that the view will use the `addInsertErrorListener` method to connect an implementation of `BoundedPlainDocument.InsertErrorListener` to the model and provide whatever feedback is appropriate to the user when its `insertFailed` method is called. In practice, only the text field that hosts this model is likely to need to be notified of insertion problems, so only one listener is allowed. You can, of course, change this if your requirements turn out to be different. As you can see, if the `insertString` method cannot add all the data it is given to the model, it checks whether there is a listener registered and calls its `insertFailed` method if there is one.

That's all there is to the model itself. Listing 1-6 shows a subclass of `JTextField` that uses `BoundedPlainDocument` to create a text field with limited capacity.

Listing I-6 A Fixed-Length Text Input Field

```
package AdvancedSwing.Chapter1;

import javax.swing.*;
import javax.swing.text.*;
import java.awt.Toolkit;

public class BoundedTextField extends JTextField
      implements BoundedPlainDocument.InsertErrorListener {
   public BoundedTextField() {
      this(null, 0, 0);
   }

   public BoundedTextField(String text, int columns,
                           int maxLength) {
```

```
┌─────────────────────────────────────────────────────────────┐
│ Listing 1-6  A Fixed-Length Text Input Field (continued)     │
└─────────────────────────────────────────────────────────────┘
```

```java
      super(null, text, columns);

      if (text != null && maxLength == 0) {
         maxLength = text.length();
      }
      BoundedPlainDocument plainDoc =
                  (BoundedPlainDocument)getDocument();
      plainDoc.setMaxLength(maxLength);

      plainDoc.addInsertErrorListener(this);
   }

   public BoundedTextField(int columns, int maxLength) {
      this(null, columns, maxLength);
   }

   public BoundedTextField(String text, int maxLength) {
      this(text, 0, maxLength);
   }

   public void setMaxLength(int maxLength) {
      ((BoundedPlainDocument)getDocument()).setMaxLength(
                  maxLength);
   }

   public int getMaxLength() {
      return ((BoundedPlainDocument)
                  getDocument()).getMaxLength();
   }

   // Override to handle insertion error
   public void insertFailed(BoundedPlainDocument doc,
                  int offset, String str, AttributeSet a) {
      // By default, just beep
      Toolkit.getDefaultToolkit().beep();
   }

   // Method to create default model
   protected Document createDefaultModel() {
      return new BoundedPlainDocument();
   }
```

Listing 1-6 A Fixed-Length Text Input Field (continued)

```
// Test code
public static void main(String[] args) {
    JFrame f = new JFrame("Bounded Text Field Example");
    BoundedTextField tf = new BoundedTextField(10, 32);
    JLabel l = new JLabel("Type up to 32 characters: ");
    f.getContentPane().add(tf, "East");
    f.getContentPane().add(l, "West");
    f.pack();
    f.setVisible(true);
  }
}
```

Again, this code is very easy to understand. `BoundedTextField` extends `JTextField`, so it inherits most of its functionality from `JTextField`. There is a choice of constructors that allow you to specify or default various parameters, the most important of which is the text field's maximum capacity, which can be given to a constructor or set later using the `setMaxLength` method. However it is set, this value is passed directly to the data model.

For this component to work properly, it must have `BoundedPlainDocument` as its data model. All the constructors end up calling the second constructor in Listing 1-6, which first invokes the `JTextField` constructor. One of the things that this constructor does is to create the data model by calling the `createDefaultModel` method. In `JTextField`, this returns an instance of `PlainDocument`. Here, it is overridden to create a `BoundedPlainDocument` instead. Thus, when the `JTextField` constructor returns, the `BoundedTextField` has a `BoundedPlainDocument` as its model and it can then proceed to set the maximum length of the model from the value passed to whichever constructor was used. If no value was given, the `setMaxLength` method will need to be called later.

The only other special behavior required of `BoundedTextField` is to connect some code that handles the failure to insert data. As you can see, `BoundedTextField` directly implements the `BoundedPlainDocument.InsertErrorListener` interface, so it simply registers itself to be notified of any errors. If the user tries to insert too much text into the text field, its `insertFailed` method will be called and the user will get audible feedback. If you want to do something other than this, you can change this behavior by subclassing `BoundedTextField` and overriding this method.

The `BoundedTextField` class includes a `main` method that allows us to see how it works in practice. If you type the command

```
java AdvancedSwing.Chapter1.BoundedTextField
```

a window containing a text field that will accept up to 32 characters will appear, as shown in Figure 1-11.

Figure 1-11   An input field with limited capacity.

Click in the input field and type as usual until you've typed 32 characters. Now try to add an extra character. You'll find that the character you type does not appear in the text field and you should also hear a beep. You don't have to try to add the character at the end of the field for this to work, of course. To demonstrate this, move the input cursor to the left and try again to type something. Once more, you'll hear a beep and what you typed will not be added to the text field. If you delete some characters from anywhere in the field, you'll find that you can now type again, but only until you reach the 32-character limit.

A more sophisticated test is to fill the text field as before, then select some of the text and type over it, replacing the selection with new characters. You'll find that you can insert as many characters as you selected and no more. Say you select four characters; you'll be able to replace them with four others, but not five. Also, if you substitute three characters for the original four, you'll find that you can add one more anywhere in the text field.

You can verify that pasting data from the clipboard works by selecting text from another window and pasting it into the `BoundedTextField`. Provided its capacity is not reached, whatever you paste will appear in the text field. However, if you try to paste in too much, the part that doesn't fit will be discarded and you'll hear a beep.

Creating a Numeric Input Control

Almost every application needs an input field that handles numbers. Creating such a field is simple, if you don't want too many frills. The simplest approach is just to use a `JTextField` and attach an `ActionListener`. When the user presses RETURN, the `ActionListener` retrieves the content of the text field and tries to convert it to a number. If this fails, there would usually be some feedback to the user, typically a beep. These days, however, input fields are expected to be a good deal smarter than this. A properly implemented numeric input field would check each character as the user typed it, making sure that it was valid. If the user attempts to type something that would not be acceptable in its current context, it should be rejected immediately, with the usual feedback.

Checking for Valid Numbers

Implementing a smart numeric text field is very similar to the example shown in Listings 1-6 and 1-7. Each character entering the model needs to be checked. In this case, however, the checks are a little more sophisticated than simply ensuring that there is room in the model for the next character. Each time the user types something, the whole content of the input field needs to be looked at, to see if it still constitutes a valid number. This is no simple task—it isn't as easy as ensuring that each character is in the range 0 through 9. Consider the following points.

- Some input fields might be restricted to integers, while others will need to deal with floating point numbers. In the latter case, it would be legal to type a decimal point, whereas this would not be acceptable in an integer field. However, only one decimal point should be allowed, so it is necessary to check not only what is being typed, but also the rest of the input field to see if there is already a decimal point.
- In some contexts, negative numbers are allowed. A simple numeric input field would implement this by allowing the user to type a minus sign as the first character of the input field and reject this key if it were typed anywhere else. However, as you'll see, this is not always sufficient.
- The issue of presentation is important for many applications. For example, it is often useful to be able to use group separators so that it is easier to see the exact magnitude of a number. When group separators are in use, an input field containing the value one million might show the string 1,000,000. An intelligent numeric input field would allow (but not require) the user to type the separators and would be able to insert them as necessary when the user finished typing.

In fact, the representation of a number is very locale-dependent and application-dependent. In some places, the decimal separator is a period while in others it is a comma. Some applications use the traditional minus sign to indicate a negative number, while others use a more complex representation. For example, in a financial application, the following might be legal inputs:

```
$1,345,623.89
($1,345,623.89)
```

The first number represents a positive amount, the dollar sign being merely decorative as far as the application is concerned, while the second is negative, indicated by the surrounding parentheses. From these two examples, you can see that detecting a negative number is not as simple as looking for a minus sign as the first character. Here, for example, you need to ensure that the number starts with (\$ and ends with), while a positive number must start with \$. More complex conventions are, of course, possible.

Fortunately, you don't have to write code that parses input strings like the ones shown above because the code already exists in the `DecimalFormat` class in the `java.text` package. To use this class, you create a `DecimalFormat` object that describes how you want your numbers to look. You can then use the object to create a string representation of the number that adheres to your specification, or you can supply a string that contains a number in that format and have it translated into the equivalent `Long` or a `Double`. When parsing a string into a number, `DecimalFormat` uses some of the information in the formatting string, but doesn't insist that the string strictly conforms to it. As an example, suppose you want the user to type a number that uses group separators around each block of three numbers and displays two places after the decimal point. To do this, you pass the following format string to `DecimalFormat`:

```
#,###.##
```

Each # represents an optional decimal digit, the comma represents the group separator, and the period represents the decimal point. In any given locale, the group separator may or may not be a comma, the decimal point need not be a period, and the numeric digits need not be 0 through 9. When using a `DecimalFormat` configured like this, if you supply it a `Double` with value `12345678.978`, it would produce the string:

```
12,345,678.98
```

As you can see, the group separators have been added in the appropriate places and the decimal part has been rounded to two places, as required by the format. However, when parsing an input string, more leniency is shown. The group separators, for example, don't need to be supplied and, even if they are present, they don't need to be in the correct places. The user could type any of the following to get the same value:

```
1234,56,78.98
1,234,5678.98
12,345,678.98
12345678.98
```

Implementing the Model—Outline

The simplest way to create a numeric text field with the capabilities that you saw in the previous paragraph is to implement a model that uses the `DecimalFormat` class to specify what constitutes a valid number. Whenever new content is added to the model, from the keyboard or elsewhere, the model content would be parsed by the `DecimalFormat` object to ensure that it is valid. This would, of course, allow the programmer to specify what constitutes a valid number by creating a suitable `DecimalFormat` object, instead of hard-coding the rules into the model. The resulting numeric text field, which will use the model, would be extremely flexible and portable from locale to locale as well as being usable in various different types of application.

Well, that's the theory at least. The implementation is actually a little more complex than that. Ideally, you would want to implement the model's `insertString` method along these lines:

- Merge the text being inserted with that already in the model.
- Parse the resulting text using the model's `DecimalFormat` object.
- If it is not valid, reject it.
- If it is valid, insert it in the model.

Let's look at why this might not work. Suppose the model is configured with a `DecimalFormat` that requires the use of a - sign as the first character to indicate a negative number and a period as the decimal point, and that the user wants to type the value -1.3 into the control. When the - has been typed, the `insertString` method will be called with this single character. Because there is nothing in the model yet, a string consisting of just the - sign is passed to the `DecimalFormat parse` method. Unfortunately, this method accepts only complete numbers, so it rejects the - because it isn't valid. According to the algorithm shown previously, the user's keystroke will not be added to the model. In other words, there is no way, under these conditions, for the user to type a negative number. This isn't the only problem, however. It turns out that even positive numbers don't always work either. If the user tries to type 1.3, the 1 will be accepted (because it is a valid number), but the . will not be. This is because the `DecimalFormat` will be asked to parse 1., which it considers to be illegal.

How can this problem be solved? One possibility is to abandon the idea and write all the parsing code in the `insertString` method. This is not a very appealing possibility, though, because of the duplication of code between the `java.text` package and our input control. It also means that enhancements to the `DecimalFormat` class will not be picked up automatically. The alternative is to catch all of the cases that won't work and ignore the parsing errors that result when the input control is in one of these states. In the two cases shown before, the content would be parsed. When the error occurs, the `insertString` method would check to see whether it was a real error or a transient one that will be corrected when the user types more into the control. The details of this are a little complicated, but the task is manageable as you can see from the implementation in Listing 1-7.

Listing 1-7 A Document that Accepts Numeric Input

```
package AdvancedSwing.Chapter1;

import javax.swing.text.*;
import java.text.*;

public class NumericPlainDocument extends PlainDocument {
    public NumericPlainDocument() {
        setFormat(null);
    }

    public NumericPlainDocument(DecimalFormat format) {
        setFormat(format);
    }

    public NumericPlainDocument(AbstractDocument.Content
            content, DecimalFormat format) {
        super(content);
        setFormat(format);

        try {
            format.parseObject(content.getString(0,
                            content.length()), parsePos);
        } catch (Exception e) {
            throw new IllegalArgumentException(
                    "Initial content not a valid number");
        }

        if (parsePos.getIndex() != content.length() - 1) {
            throw new IllegalArgumentException(
                    "Initial content not a valid number");
```

Listing 1-7 A Document that Accepts Numeric Input (continued)

```
      }
  }

  public void setFormat(DecimalFormat fmt) {
     this.format = fmt != null ? fmt :
           (DecimalFormat)defaultFormat.clone();

     decimalSeparator =
                 format.getDecimalFormatSymbols().
                 getDecimalSeparator();
     groupingSeparator =
                 format.getDecimalFormatSymbols().
                 getGroupingSeparator();
     positivePrefix = format.getPositivePrefix();
     positivePrefixLen = positivePrefix.length();
     negativePrefix = format.getNegativePrefix();
     negativePrefixLen = negativePrefix.length();
     positiveSuffix = format.getPositiveSuffix();
     positiveSuffixLen = positiveSuffix.length();
     negativeSuffix = format.getNegativeSuffix();
     negativeSuffixLen = negativeSuffix.length();
  }

  public DecimalFormat getFormat() {
     return format;
  }

  public Number getNumberValue() throws ParseException {
     try {
        String content = getText(0, getLength());
        parsePos.setIndex(0);
        Number result = format.parse(content, parsePos);
        if (parsePos.getIndex() != getLength()) {
           throw new ParseException(
                 "Not a valid number: " + content, 0);
        }

        return result;
     } catch (BadLocationException e) {
        throw new ParseException("Not a valid number", 0);
     }
  }
```

Listing 1-7 A Document that Accepts Numeric Input (continued)

```java
public Long getLongValue() throws ParseException {
   Number result = getNumberValue();
   if ((result instanceof Long) == false) {
      throw new ParseException("Not a valid long", 0);
   }

   return (Long)result;
}

public Double getDoubleValue() throws ParseException {
   Number result = getNumberValue();
   if ((result instanceof Long) == false &&
         (result instanceof Double) == false) {
      throw new ParseException("Not a valid double", 0);
   }

   if (result instanceof Long) {
      result = new Double(result.doubleValue());
   }

   return (Double)result;
}

public void insertString(int offset, String str,
                         AttributeSet a)
            throws BadLocationException {
   if (str == null || str.length() == 0) {
      return;
   }

   Content content = getContent();
   int length = content.length();
   int originalLength = length;

   parsePos.setIndex(0);

   String targetString = content.getString(0, offset) +
         str + content.getString(offset, length -
         offset - 1);
```

Listing 1-7 A Document that Accepts Numeric Input (continued)

```
// Create the result of inserting the new data,
// but ignore the trailing newline
// Parse the input string and check for errors
do {
    boolean gotPositive =
        targetString.startsWith(positivePrefix);
    boolean gotNegative =
        targetString.startsWith(negativePrefix);

    length = targetString.length();

    // If we have a valid prefix, the parse fails if
    // the suffix is not present and the error is
    // reported at index 0. So, we need to add the
    // appropriate suffix if it is not present at this
    // point.
    if (gotPositive == true || gotNegative == true) {
        String suffix;
        int suffixLength;
        int prefixLength;

        if (gotPositive == true && gotNegative == true) {
            // This happens if one is the leading part
            // of the other - e.g. if one is "(" and the
            // other "((" 
            if (positivePrefixLen > negativePrefixLen) {
                gotNegative = false;
            } else {
                gotPositive = false;
            }
        }

        if (gotPositive == true) {
            suffix = positiveSuffix;
            suffixLength = positiveSuffixLen;
            prefixLength = positivePrefixLen;
        } else {
            // Must have the negative prefix
            suffix = negativeSuffix;
            suffixLength = negativeSuffixLen;
            prefixLength = negativePrefixLen;
        }
```

Listing 1-7 A Document that Accepts Numeric Input (continued)

```
        // If the string consists of the prefix alone,
        // do nothing, or the result won't parse.
        if (length == prefixLength) {
           break;
        }

        // We can't just add the suffix, because part of
        // it may already be there. For example,
        // suppose the negative prefix is "(" and the
        // negative suffix is "$)". If the user has
        // typed "(345$", then it is not correct to add
        // "$)". Instead, only the missing part
        // should be added, in this case ")".
        if (targetString.endsWith(suffix) == false) {
           int i;
           for (i = suffixLength - 1; i > 0 ; i--) {
              if (targetString.regionMatches(length - i,
                     suffix, 0, i)) {
                 targetString += suffix.substring(i);
                 break;
              }
           }

           if (i == 0) {
              // None of the suffix was present
              targetString += suffix;
           }

           length = targetString.length();
        }
     }

     format.parse(targetString, parsePos);

     int endIndex = parsePos.getIndex();
     if (endIndex == length) {
        break;   // Number is acceptable
     }

     // Parse ended early
     // Since incomplete numbers don't always parse, try
     // to work out what went wrong.
     // First check for an incomplete positive prefix
```

Listing I-7 A Document that Accepts Numeric Input (continued)

```
        if (positivePrefixLen > 0 &&
            endIndex < positivePrefixLen &&
            length <= positivePrefixLen &&
            targetString.regionMatches(0, positivePrefix,
                                       0, length)) {
            break;       // Accept for now
        }

        // Next check for an incomplete negative prefix
        if (negativePrefixLen > 0 &&
            endIndex < negativePrefixLen &&
            length <= negativePrefixLen &&
            targetString.regionMatches(0, negativePrefix,
                                       0, length)) {
            break;     // Accept for now
        }

        // Allow a number that ends with the group
        // or decimal separator, if these are in use
        char lastChar =
                targetString.charAt(originalLength - 1);
        int decimalIndex =
                targetString.indexOf(decimalSeparator);
        if (format.isGroupingUsed() &&
            lastChar == groupingSeparator &&
            decimalIndex == -1) {
            // Allow a "," but only in integer part
            break;
        }

        if(format.isParseIntegerOnly() == false &&
            lastChar == decimalSeparator &&
            decimalIndex == originalLength - 1) {
            // Allow a ".", but only one
            break;
        }

        // No more corrections to make: must be an error
        if (errorListener != null) {
            errorListener.insertFailed(this, offset,
                                       str, a);
        }
        return;
    } while (true == false);
```

Listing 1-7 A Document that Accepts Numeric Input (continued)

```java
    // Finally, add to the model
    super.insertString(offset, str, a);
  }

  public void
        addInsertErrorListener(InsertErrorListener l) {
    if (errorListener == null) {
      errorListener = l;
      return;
    }
    throw new IllegalArgumentException(
          "InsertErrorListener already registered");
  }

  public void
      removeInsertErrorListener(InsertErrorListener l) {
    if (errorListener == l) {
      errorListener = null;
    }
  }

  public interface InsertErrorListener {
    public abstract void
          insertFailed(NumericPlainDocument doc,
          int offset, String str, AttributeSet a);
  }

  protected InsertErrorListener errorListener;
  protected DecimalFormat format;
  protected char decimalSeparator;
  protected char groupingSeparator;
  protected String positivePrefix;
  protected String negativePrefix;
  protected int positivePrefixLen;
  protected int negativePrefixLen;
  protected String positiveSuffix;
  protected String negativeSuffix;
  protected int positiveSuffixLen;
  protected int negativeSuffixLen;
  protected ParsePosition parsePos = new ParsePosition(0);
  protected static DecimalFormat defaultFormat =
              new DecimalFormat();
}
```

The constructors allow you to create a model initialized in various different ways. You can specify the initial content and the formatter to be used. If you don't specify a formatter, the constructor installs a default `DecimalFormat` whose characteristics depend on the locale in which the control is used. The `setFormat` method can be used to change the formatting object at any stage. However, changing the formatter while the control is in use is not recommended because it may be confusing to the user. In practice, this method is most likely to be used to configure the formatter shortly after the model is created, probably as part of the construction of a complete text field that uses it, such as the one that will be shown later in this section.

There are several important features of the formatter that the model implementation needs to be aware of. These are:

- The character used as the decimal separator (typically a period).
- The character used as the grouping separator (typically a comma).
- The prefix used to introduce positive numbers and its length.
- The suffix used to end positive numbers and its length.
- The prefix used to introduce negative numbers and its length.
- The suffix used to end negative numbers and its length.

For convenience, all these attributes are extracted and stored locally for use in the `insertString` method. It is important to understand how the prefixes and suffixes work. With normal conventions, a negative number is introduced by a minus sign and has no special terminator, while a positive number has no prefix or suffix. In this case, the formatter would be set as follows:

Positive prefix:	"" (empty string)
Positive suffix:	"" (empty string)
Negative prefix:	"-"
Negative suffix:	"" (empty string)

In this case, any string that does not start with a minus sign is considered to be a positive number. Now consider a different convention in which numbers are always expressed with a leading dollar sign and negative numbers start and end with brackets. You can create such a formatter by using the `Decimal-Format` `setNegativePrefix`, `setPositivePrefix`, `setNegativeSuffix`, and `setPositiveSuffix` methods, like this:

```
DecimalFormat f = new DecimalFormat();
f.setPositivePrefix("$");
f.setPositiveSuffix("");
f.setNegativePrefix("($");
f.setNegativeSuffix(")");
```

Now, every number must start with either (\$ or \$ and, furthermore, if it starts with (\$, it must end with). With this setting, the user can't just start by typing a number.

Core Note

Although this example won't implement it, in cases like this you could help the user by looking at the first key pressed and, if it is a number, adding the $ yourself. Similarly, if the user starts with (, you could add the $. This would be implemented in a subclass of `NumericPlainDocument` that would know the format being applied—it would not be appropriate to do this for all numeric text fields.

Implementing the Model—The `insertString` Method

Now let's look in detail at how the `insertString` method works. This method should simply insert the `String` that is passed to it into the model, provided that the characters in the `String` make sense in the context in which they are applied. To check their validity, `insertString` merges them with whatever is already in the model and passes the result to the formatter's `parse` method. If what is there is a valid number, `parse` will process the complete string and the `insertString` method will just insert the new data in the model. If the data does not look like a number, however, `parse` will return before it has scanned the whole string. This does not, as we know, mean that the data should be rejected. It just means that some more checking needs to be done to eliminate certain special cases. The `ParsePosition` object passed to `parse` records the location within the string at which parsing ended. Sometimes, however, this does not correspond to the location of the formatting error, as you'll see as you read through the description of the `insertString` method that follows.

Core Note

If you're not interested in the details of the `insertString` method, you can skip ahead to "Implementing the Numeric Text Field" on page 68. None of this code will teach you anything about Swing text components.

The first part of `insertString` deals with the handling of sign prefixes and suffixes. Here is the issue that it is trying to deal with. Suppose, as in this case, that all numbers must start with ($ and end with). Suppose also that the user has typed ($4 so far. If you pass this to the formatter's `parse` method, you'll get an error, because it expects the opening negative prefix to be balanced with the corresponding suffix. To ensure that this string gets parsed properly, the suffix needs to be added. But what is the point of this? If you know that this number will fail for this reason, why bother compensating for it? The issue is that the `parse` method doesn't tell you exactly why the scan failed. In this case, the `ParsePosition` object would indicate a failure at position 0—the start of the string. That's not very useful—typing the string A would produce the same result. Because you can't distinguish lack of a suffix from any other error at position 0, the only way you can determine whether the number is valid is to add the suffix before invoking `parse`. This will allow `parse` to concentrate on other errors in the number.

Even doing that is not simple. First, you have to check whether there actually is a positive or negative prefix present and work out which it is. The obvious way to do this is to look at the start of the string. In the example we are using here, the positive prefix would be considered to be present if it started with $ and the negative prefix if it started with ($, so there is no ambiguity. However, what if the positive prefix were (+ and the negative prefix (and the user types (+4? In this case, simply looking at the start of the string would indicate that both prefixes are present. To remove the ambiguity, if both prefixes appear to be present, we take it that the longer of the two is actually in use. This correctly chooses the positive prefix.

When you've worked out the correct prefix, you just select the corresponding suffix and add it. That works for the case you've seen so far, but it isn't always the right thing to do. At some stage, the user will get as far as actually typing the suffix. Now it wouldn't be correct to add all of the suffix. Returning to our original example, if the user has typed ($4), the whole suffix has been supplied, but the logic so far would have us add the suffix again, giving ($4)). To avoid this, we do the obvious thing: look at the end of the string and work out whether some of the suffix has been added. If it has, all that is necessary is to append the rest of the suffix. If the negative suffix were)-, and the user had typed ($4), only the - would now be added.

Once the matter of a balancing suffix has been dealt with, the modified string can be passed to the `parse` method. If the number between the prefix and suffix (if they exist) is valid, `parse` will complete normally. However, if there is anything wrong with the number, you need to work out what it is and decide whether it is a real error or just the result of the user not having typed enough of the number yet for it to be valid.

There are several possibilities:

- The user has typed some, but not all, of the positive or negative prefix.
- Grouping is in use and the user has just typed the grouping separator.
- The user has just typed the decimal separator.

Recognizing the first case is simple because both prefixes are known. Care needs to be taken if one of the prefixes is the empty string, because every string starts with an empty string. If the start of a nonempty prefix is present, and the string consists entirely of that segment, the `parse` error should be ignored and the string inserted into the model. Note that, in these cases, because the prefix is incomplete, it won't have been recognized by the processing carried out before the `parse` method, so the corresponding suffix won't have been appended.

The other two cases are just as straightforward. A string that ends in a decimal or grouping separator is not parsed as valid so, for example, the strings `4.` or `4,` are not seen as legal and return an error. It looks like you can recognize this by checking the last character in the string, but a little care is needed. Consider what happens when `($4.` is typed in by the user. Because this string starts with a negative prefix, it is amended to `($4.)` before being presented to the `parse` method and now the decimal separator does not appear at the end of the string! The code actually checks the character that was at the end of the string before the suffix was appended.

Even this is not the end, though. There can only be one decimal separator in a number. The `parse` method will detect that `($4.4.)` is illegal and it will indicate that the second period is in error. To avoid letting this through, the code also checks whether there are any more decimal separators in the number and rejects the number if there are. Finally, if grouping is in use, the grouping separator can only be used to the left of the decimal separator—in other words, `($3.123,` is not valid. Again, `parse` will indicate that the `,` is in error, as it would with `($3,.` To reject the first and accept the second, the code checks whether there is a decimal separator and, if there is, it is an error.

Retrieving the Model Value

Having dealt with the issue of checking the model's input to ensure that it is valid, the remaining facility that is required is to extract the value as a number. The `getNumberValue`, `getLongValue`, and `getDoubleValue` methods are provided to return the value as a `Number`, a `Long`, or a `Double` as appropriate. The `getNumberValue` method uses the formatter's `parse` method (which returns a `Long` object if the content represents a value without a fractional part or a `Double` if it does not) and just returns whatever `parse` returns. However, even though the user input is carefully checked, the value in the model might still not be a valid number. For example, if the user types (\$ and presses `RETURN`, `parse` will fail. In this case, `getNumberValue` will throw a `ParseException`.

If you want the field content as a `Long` or a `Double`, you can use `getLongValue` or `getDoubleValue`. These methods both use `getNumberValue` to get the value as a `Number`, and then do the appropriate conversion: `getDoubleValue` returns the value directly if it is a `Double`, or creates a new `Double` if it is a `Long`. However, `getLongValue` is slightly different: If the result is a `Long`, it returns it, but if it is a `Double`, it throws a `ParseException` because converting the `Double` to a `Long` would result in a loss of information.

Implementing the Numeric Text Field

With the model implemented, it is a simple matter to wrap it with a suitable subclass of `JTextField` to produce a numeric text field, as shown below in Listing 1-8.

Listing 1-8 A Numeric Text Field

```
package AdvancedSwing.Chapter1;

import javax.swing.*;
import javax.swing.text.*;
import java.awt.*;
import java.awt.event.*;
import java.text.*;

public class NumericTextField extends JTextField
      implements NumericPlainDocument.InsertErrorListener {
   public NumericTextField() {
      this(null, 0, null);
   }
```

Listing 1-8 A Numeric Text Field (continued)

```java
public NumericTextField(String text, int columns,
            DecimalFormat format) {
    super(null, text, columns);

    NumericPlainDocument numericDoc =
            (NumericPlainDocument)getDocument();
    if (format != null) {
        numericDoc.setFormat(format);
    }

    numericDoc.addInsertErrorListener(this);
}

public NumericTextField(int columns,
            DecimalFormat format) {
    this(null, columns, format);
}

public NumericTextField(String text) {
    this(text, 0, null);
}

public NumericTextField(String text, int columns) {
    this(text, columns, null);
}

public void setFormat(DecimalFormat format) {
            ((NumericPlainDocument)
            getDocument()).setFormat(format);
}

public DecimalFormat getFormat() {
            return ((NumericPlainDocument)
            getDocument()).getFormat();
}

public void formatChanged() {
    // Notify change of format attributes.
    setFormat(getFormat());
}
```

Listing 1-8 A Numeric Text Field (continued)

```java
// Methods to get the field value
public Long getLongValue() throws ParseException {
        return ((NumericPlainDocument)
        getDocument()).getLongValue();
}

public Double getDoubleValue() throws ParseException {
        return ((NumericPlainDocument)
        getDocument()).getDoubleValue();
}

public Number getNumberValue() throws ParseException {
        return ((NumericPlainDocument)
        getDocument()).getNumberValue();
}

// Methods to install numeric values
public void setValue(Number number) {
    setText(getFormat().format(number));
}

public void setValue(long l) {
    setText(getFormat().format(l));;
}

public void setValue(double d) {
    setText(getFormat().format(d));
}

public void normalize() throws ParseException {
    // format the value according to the format string
    setText(getFormat().format(getNumberValue()));
}

// Override to handle insertion error
public void insertFailed(NumericPlainDocument doc,
                int offset, String str,
                AttributeSet a) {
    // By default, just beep
    Toolkit.getDefaultToolkit().beep();
}
```

Listing 1-8 A Numeric Text Field (continued)

```java
// Method to create default model
protected Document createDefaultModel() {
    return new NumericPlainDocument();
}

// Test code
public static void main(String[] args) {
    DecimalFormat format =
            new DecimalFormat("#,###.###");
    format.setGroupingUsed(true);
    format.setGroupingSize(3);
    format.setParseIntegerOnly(false);

    JFrame f = new JFrame("Numeric Text Field Example");
    final NumericTextField tf =
            new NumericTextField(10, format);

    tf.setValue((double)123456.789);

    JLabel lbl = new JLabel("Type a number: ");
    f.getContentPane().add(tf, "East");
    f.getContentPane().add(lbl, "West");

    tf.addActionListener(new ActionListener() {
        public void actionPerformed(ActionEvent evt) {
            try {
                tf.normalize();
                Long l = tf.getLongValue();
                System.out.println("Value is (Long)" + l);
            } catch (ParseException e1) {
                try {
                    Double d = tf.getDoubleValue();
                    System.out.println("Value is
                                    (Double)" + d);
                } catch (ParseException e2) {
                    System.out.println(e2);
                }
            }
        }
    });
    f.pack();
    f.setVisible(true);
}
}
```

A `NumericTextField` wraps a `NumericPlainDocument`. Its constructors allow you to specify various different parameters to initialize the model, including the formatter and the initial content in the form of a `String`. It also allows you to change the format after the text field has been created (using `setFormat`), or to have the model update its view of its format if some aspect of it has changed (the `formatChanged` method). To create a numeric text field in which grouping is used but fractions are not, you might do the following:

```
DecimalFormat f = new DecimalFormat();
f.setGroupingUsed(true);       // Use ","
f.setGroupingSize(3);          // 3 digits between ","
f.setParseIntegerOnly(true);   // Only integers: no decimal point
NumericTextField tf = new NumericTextField(10, f);
```

If, later, you want to set a nondefault negative suffix or prefix, you might do this:

```
f.setNegativePrefix("(");
f.setNegativeSuffix(")");
t.formatChanged();
```

It is unlikely that you would want to do this, but the facility exists nevertheless.

The `NumericTextField` also has pass-through methods that allow you to get the numeric value out of the model by calling the model's `getNumberValue`, `getDoubleValue`, and `getLongValue` methods. The `setValue` methods allow you to change the value in the model by supplying a new value as a `Number` (which could be a `Long` or a `Double`) or a primitive `long` or `double`. You can also change the value by invoking `setText`, which is inherited from `JTextField` and accepts a `String` value, which would, of course, be parsed and checked by the model's `insertString` method.

The last public method of interest is the `normalize` method. This causes the field's content to be read and formatted by the model's formatter, and then written back to the model. This method causes the text field's content to be displayed in the canonical format specified when it was created. For example, suppose the formatter was created with the formatting string `#,###.##`. The parser does not insist that the decimal separators are present as the number is typed and, if they are typed, it does not require them to be in the correct places. As a result, the user could type something untidy like `1,2,3,4,5,67` or the shorthand `123456`. Calling `normalize` would cause either of these to be changed to `1,234,567` and written back to the text field. This would normally be done after the user presses RETURN, to tidy up the field's display content.

The `NumericTextField` implementation includes a `main` method that displays a `NumericTextField` and lets you type into it. When you press RETURN, its `ActionListener` calls `normalize` to put the text field content into its canonical form and then calls `getLongValue` to extract the number typed as a `Long`. If this fails, it is assumed that the number has a fractional part and `getDoubleValue` is called. If both of these fail, the number must be incorrectly formatted and an error message is printed.

To try this example, use the command:

```
java AdvancedSwing.Chapter1.NumericTextField
```

The field is initialized with the value `123456.789` supplied as a `double`. Because the implementation of `setValue` uses the formatter to produce the corresponding `String` for insertion into the model, the representation you see in the text field (see Figure 1-12) includes the group separator.

Figure 1-12   Using the `NumericTextField` class.

You can verify that the text field works as it should by trying to type illegal characters, such as letters, or attempting to supply more than one decimal point. Illegal values should not appear in the text field and cause a beep to alert you to the fact that your keystroke has been ignored. If you press RETURN, the value that you typed into the input field will be printed. Here are some examples:

```
Value is (Double)-123456.789
Value is (Double)-4.7
Value is (Long)-4
```

Notice that a `Double` is returned when the number has a fractional part and a `Long` when it does not.

A Text Field with Look-Ahead

Now that you've seen two custom text fields that rely for their functionality on specialized data models, let's look at another way to provide additional functionality. What we want to do this time is to build a text field that has the ability to "look ahead" and guess what the user is trying to type as each key is pressed. When it has a good guess to offer, it would display the guess in the text field, allowing the user to accept it immediately. If the guess is wrong, the user would be allowed to continue typing, providing more letters for the text field to use as the basis for another guess.

This type of input field is useful in cases in which the user is typing one value from a (possibly long) set of legal possibilities, such as the name of somebody in the same organization. If the names of all a company's employees are held centrally, it might be reasonable to have the input field match the user's keystrokes to names in the employee database and bring up the name of the best match available. With a little more sophistication, you could add a fuzzy matching algorithm that allowed users to match names that sound like the one they have typed part of. Of course, we're not going to cover all of that in this section. The text field that will be implemented here will be open-ended—it will delegate the job of turning the user's keystrokes into a suitable guess to another class that can be plugged in as appropriate. To demonstrate, we'll also provide a plug-in class that offers a guess from an array of possible choices.

To begin with, let's look at how the look-ahead text field works in practice. To try it out, type the following command:

```
java AdvancedSwing.Chapter1.LookAheadExample
```

This creates a frame with an input field, pre-configured with the following short list of words:

aback	abacus	abandon	abashed
abate	abdomen	abide	ability
baby	back	backache	backgammon

This set of words is chosen to demonstrate how the look-ahead process works. Click in the input field and press "a." Immediately, the text field looks at the list of possible words, matches the first entry, "aback," and displays it—see Figure 1-13.

Figure 1-13 A text field with look-ahead.

Notice that the cursor appears after the letter a and that the part of the word that was added by the look-ahead process, back, is selected. The reason for selecting the added text is to allow the user to easily delete it if it is wrong:

Pressing the `backspace` key now would clear the extra text and leave the cursor where it is. On the other hand, if you continue to type, the text field continues to make guesses as to what it is you are trying to type. The next two letters, `b` and `a`, match all the possibilities in the configured word list. If you now type `n`, the content of the text field changes to `abandon`, with the letters `d`, `o`, and `n` selected. Now if you type any letter other than `d`, the text field runs out of guesses and just lets you continue typing without intervening any more.

You'll notice also that no guessing takes place when you use the backspace or delete key, but once you start typing other keys, you get new guesses. For example, if you delete everything but the first two characters, you'll be left with `ab`. Now press `d` and you'll be offered `abdomen`. Delete the `d` (which actually takes two keystrokes) and type `i` and the content changes to `abide`.

Now that you've seen the control working, let's examine the implementation. The first design decision to make is where the look-ahead functionality belongs. Up to now, the clever code has been in the text component's model and it is perfectly possible to add code to the model that would provide most of the features that you've just seen. However, there is one small problem—how to arrange for the text added by the look-ahead to be selected for easy deletion? As you know, the model deals only with holding the text field's content—it cannot select text. Selection is managed by the text component itself, in response to operations on the caret. There is no mechanism in the text components for the model to directly dictate where the caret is and therefore what is selected. The only logical place to add this feature, therefore, is in the text component. The example shown in Figure 1-13 uses a subclass of `JTextField` called `LookAheadTextField`, the implementation of which is shown in Listing 1-9.

Listing 1-9 A Text Field with Look-Ahead

```
package AdvancedSwing.Chapter1;

import javax.swing.*;
import javax.swing.text.*;
import java.awt.event.*;

public class LookAheadTextField extends JTextField {
    public LookAheadTextField() {
        this(0, null);
    }
```

Listing I-9 A Text Field with Look-Ahead (continued)

```
public LookAheadTextField(int columns) {
   this(columns, null);
}

public LookAheadTextField(int columns,
             TextLookAhead lookAhead) {
   super(columns);
   setLookAhead(lookAhead);
   addActionListener(new ActionListener() {
      public void actionPerformed(ActionEvent evt) {
         // Remove any existing selection
         setCaretPosition(getDocument().getLength());
      }
   });
   addFocusListener(new FocusListener() {
      public void focusGained(FocusEvent evt) {
      }

      public void focusLost(FocusEvent evt) {
         if (evt.isTemporary() == false) {
            // Remove any existing selection
            setCaretPosition(getDocument().getLength());
         }
      }
   });
}

public void setLookAhead(TextLookAhead lookAhead) {
   this.lookAhead = lookAhead;
}

public TextLookAhead getLookAhead() {
   return lookAhead;
}

public void replaceSelection(String content) {
   super.replaceSelection(content);

   if (isEditable() == false || isEnabled() == false) {
      return;
   }
```

Listing 1-9 A Text Field with Look-Ahead (continued)

```
        Document doc = getDocument();
        if (doc != null && lookAhead != null) {
            try {
                String oldContent =
                        doc.getText(0, doc.getLength());
                String newContent =
                        lookAhead.doLookAhead(oldContent);
                if (newContent != null) {
                    // Substitute the new content
                    setText(newContent);

                    // Highlight the added text
                    setCaretPosition(newContent.length());
                    moveCaretPosition(oldContent.length());
                }
            } catch (BadLocationException e) {
                // Won't happen
            }
        }
    }

    protected TextLookAhead lookAhead;

    // The TextLookAhead interface
    public interface TextLookAhead {
        public String doLookAhead(String key);
    }
}
```

A `LookAheadTextField` is associated with an implementation of the interface `LookAheadTextField.TextLookAhead`, which provides the code that knows how to map from the text typed by the user to a suitable guess as to what the user intends. This interface has only one method:

```
public String doLookAhead(String key);
```

The `key` argument supplies the text that the user has typed so far. Using this information and any internal state it retains, the `doLookAhead` method chooses a candidate word and returns it. The returned `String` is used to fill the text field, unless `null` is returned, when it is assumed that the content of the text field does not correspond to any word that the look-ahead mechanism recognizes. In this case, whatever the user has typed is left in the input field, unmodified. An object that implements the `TextLookAhead` interface can be provided to the constructor, or set later using the `setLookAhead` method.

All of the useful work is actually carried out in the `replaceSelection` method. The `replaceSelection` implementation that all text components inherit from `JTextComponent` first removes anything in the component that is selected, and then adds whatever is in the `String` argument that it is given to the document at the position that was occupied by the start of the selection. If nothing was selected initially, the text is added at the initial position of the caret. In either case, the caret is moved to the end of the inserted text.

To catch all the user input as it is typed, the `replaceSelection` method is overridden. The user's input is first merged into the existing text by using the superclass implementation. At this point, the text component contains what it would have contained had the look-ahead not been implemented. This text is then extracted from the model using the `Document getText` method, and then passed to the `doLookAhead` method of the configured `TextLookAhead` object. If `null` is returned, there is no guess to replace the user's typing with, so nothing more is done.

If a `String` is returned, however, it is used to replace the text component's content by passing it to the `setText` method, which writes whatever it is given directly to the model, without invoking the `replaceSelection` method again. The final step is to highlight the part of the returned `String` that was added to the key that was passed in. To achieve this, the extra characters are selected by first placing the caret at the end of the new content, and then moving it forward so that it is after the last character that the user typed. The act of placing the caret using `setCaretPosition` and then moving it with `moveCaretPosition` creates a selection covering the text between those two locations. Placing the caret at the end and then moving it backward both creates the selection and leaves the caret in the correct location for the user to continue typing should the result of the look-ahead be incorrect.

There is one final piece of the text field that needs to be implemented. If the user types several characters and the look-ahead returns whatever the user was trying to type, the user will probably press RETURN or move the keyboard focus elsewhere. At this point, the text field still has the part of the text added by the look-ahead mechanism selected, which looks untidy. To get around this, an `ActionListener` is added that will be activated when the RETURN key is pressed and a `FocusListener` is added to handle loss of focus. In both cases, the caret will be moved to the end of the text field, clearing the selection. Note that the `FocusListener` clears the selection only if the loss of focus is permanent. A permanent loss of focus occurs when the focus is moved to another component in the same window. If the user moves the focus to another window, a temporary focus change occurs and the focus will return to the text field when the user brings the window that it is part of back to the foreground. In this case, the selection should not be cleared and the caret should remain where it is.

The final piece of the puzzle is the `TextLookAhead` object. You can implement any algorithm that you need for guessing what the user is trying to type. The look-ahead algorithm used in the example you have just seen is a very basic one—it just looks through a set of `Strings` for one that starts with whatever is already in the text field. Nevertheless, this provides a template for writing other, more complex, variations that might require, for example, a database search. You can see the implementation, in a class called `String-ArrayLookAhead`, in Listing 1-10.

Listing 1-10 A Simple Look-Ahead Implementation

```java
package AdvancedSwing.Chapter1;

import javax.swing.*;
import javax.swing.text.*;

public class StringArrayLookAhead implements
                LookAheadTextField.TextLookAhead {
   public StringArrayLookAhead() {
      values = new String[0];
   }

   public StringArrayLookAhead(String[] values) {
      this.values = values;
   }

   public void setValues(String[] values) {
      this.values = values;
   }

   public String[] getValues() {
      return values;
   }

   public String doLookAhead(String key) {
      int length = values.length;
```

Listing 1-10 A Simple Look-Ahead Implementation (continued)

```
        // Look for a string that starts with the key
        for (int i = 0; i < length; i++) {
            if (values[i].startsWith(key) == true) {
                return values[i];
            }
        }

        // No match found - return null
        return null;
    }

    protected String[] values;
}
```

This class is configured with an array of `Strings`, passed to the constructor or via the `setValues` method. The work is done by `doLookAhead`, which searches through the array for a `String` that starts with the characters of the `String` passed to it. Obviously, for a production implementation, you would probably want to make this more efficient by using a faster searching algorithm. The `LookAheadTextField` used in the example used in this section is actually initialized as follows:

```
StringArrayLookAhead lookAhead =
            new StringArrayLookAhead(values);
LookAheadTextField tf = new LookAheadTextField(
            20, lookAhead);

// Code omitted

// The possible look-ahead values

public static String[] values = new String[] {
    "aback", "abacus", "abandon", "abashed", "abate",
    "abdomen", "abide", "ability",
    "baby", "back", "backache", "backgammon"
};
```

Text Actions and Keyboard Mappings

So far, you've seen how the text component's model works and how to replace it in order to impose some constraint on what the user can type into the component. The next piece of the text component architecture that we'll look at is the MVC controller part, specifically the piece of the controller that handles keyboard input; as noted earlier, the controller also separately deals with mouse and focus events, which are directed to the caret.

As far as the controller is concerned, there are actually two types of key-stroke: those that result in the key typed being stored in the model and those that result in some action within the component. Keystrokes that fall into the latter category are usually a single character used in conjunction with the CTRL or ALT key and so can be considered keyboard shortcuts. The keyboard shortcuts that are associated with a text component depend on the text component itself, the editor kit that the text component is using, and on the look-and-feel being used. The operations that a text component can perform are referred to as *actions*; these actions are made accessible to the user through *keyboard mappings*. For example, all the text components support copy, cut, and paste actions, but the key combinations that produce these actions vary depending on which look-and-feel is installed. Table 1-4 shows the default mappings for these actions.

Table 1-4 Keyboard Mappings for the Copy, Cut, and Paste Actions			
	Metal	*Windows*	*Motif*
Copy	CTRL+C	CTRL+C	CTRL + INSERT
Cut	CTRL+X	CTRL+X	SHIFT + DELETE
Paste	CTRL+V	CTRL+V	SHIFT + INSERT

Text Actions

The complete set of actions for a text component is the union of the actions supported by the editor kit and by the text component itself. Usually, the editor kit supplies the bulk of the available actions and the text component adds a small number of actions specific to itself. Because all the standard text components use the DefaultEditorKit or one derived from it, they all have a common set of editing operations that are provided by actions implemented by the DefaultEditorKit class.

Every action, whether it is provided by an editor kit or by a text component, is implemented as a class derived from the abstract base class Text-Action, which is derived from the AbstractAction class. Text actions, therefore, all implement the Swing Action interface. As a result, they can be called upon to do whatever they are supposed to do (for example, paste some text from the clipboard) by invoking their `actionPerformed` methods. Later in this chapter, you'll see how a simple text action is implemented.

The `TextAction` class has only two public and two protected methods of its own:

```
public abstract class TextAction extends AbstractAction {
    public TextAction(String name);
    public static final Action[] augmentList(Action[]
            list1, Action[] list2);
    protected final JTextComponent
            getTextComponent(ActionEvent e);
    protected final JTextComponent getFocusedComponent();
}
```

The constructor associates a human-readable name with the text action. This name can be used as the text that would appear if this action were posted on a menu or a toolbar. The `getTextComponent` and `getFocused-Component` methods are both used within the implementation of a text action to determine which text component the action should be performed on. You'll see how this works in "Implementing Overwrite Mode in a Text Field" on page 104.

Editor kits and text components both have a `getActions` method that returns an array of `Action` objects representing the complete set of actions that they implement. The text component `getActions` method is usually implemented as a call to the static `TextAction` method `augmentList`, merging the set of actions that the specific text component provides with those provided by `JTextComponent`, which simply pretends to support the set of actions provided by its installed editor kit. The set of actions implemented by `DefaultEditorKit`, and therefore available from all text components, is shown in Table 1-5.

The name in the first column of Table 1-5 is a `String` value by which the action is known. The editor kit or text component will usually declare a symbolic name that maps to each specific action. These names are part of the public API of the component. The paste action, for example, can be referred to using the constant value `DefaultEditorKit.pasteAction`. The actual object that implements this operation can be found by invoking the `get-Actions` method of a text component and searching the returned array of `Action` objects for one whose name is `DefaultEditorKit.pasteAction`. Usually, however, you won't need to do this, because text actions are usually used directly only when mapping them to keystrokes, a process that requires the action's symbolic name rather than the object reference itself.

Table 1-5 Text Actions Implemented by DefaultEditorKit	

Name	*Action*
caret-backward	Moves the caret backward one character.
beep	Causes a beep.
caret-begin	Moves the caret to the start of the document.
caret-begin-line	Moves the caret to the start of the current line.
caret-begin-paragraph	Moves the caret to the start of the current paragraph.
caret-begin-word	Moves the caret to the start of the current word.
caret-down	Moves the caret down a line.
caret-end	Moves the caret to the end of the document.
caret-end-line	Moves the caret to the end of the current line.
caret-end-paragraph	Moves the caret to the end of the current paragraph.
caret-end-word	Moves the caret to the end of the current word.
caret-forward	Moves the caret forward one character.
caret-next-word	Moves the caret to the start of the next word.
caret-previous-word	Moves the caret to the start of the previous word.
caret-up	Moves the caret up by one line.
copy-to-clipboard	Copies the currently selected text onto the system clipboard.
cut-to-clipboard	Deletes the text that is currently selected and places it on the system clipboard.
default-typed	Inserts the last key typed in the document model.
delete-next	Deletes the character that immediately follows the caret.

Table 1-5 Text Actions Implemented by `DefaultEditorKit` (continued)	
Name	*Action*
`delete-previous`	Deletes the character immediately before the caret.
`insert-break`	Inserts a newline into the document.
`insert-content`	Places the keystroke that caused this action into the document.
`insert-tab`	Inserts a tab in the document.
`page-down`	Moves the caret down one page.
`page-up`	Moves the caret up one page.
`paste-from-clipboard`	Pastes the content of the system clipboard into the document immediately before the current caret position, deleting anything currently selected.
`select-all`	Selects the entire document.
`select-line`	Makes the current line into the selection.
`select-paragraph`	Makes the current paragraph into the selection.
`select-word`	Makes the current word into the selection.
`selection-backward`	Moves the caret backward one position, extending the current selection.
`selection-begin`	Extends the selection to the start of the document.
`selection-begin-line`	Extends the selection to the start of the current line.
`selection-begin-paragraph`	Extends the selection to the start of the current paragraph.
`selection-begin-word`	Extends the selection to the start of the current word.
`selection-down`	Moves the caret down one line and moves the selection with it.

Table 1-5 Text Actions Implemented by `DefaultEditorKit` (continued)	
Name	**Action**
`selection-end`	Extends the selection to the end of the document.
`selection-end-line`	Extends the selection to the end of the current line.
`selection-end-paragraph`	Extends the selection to the end of the current paragraph.
`selection-end-word`	Extends the selection to the end of the current word.
`selection-forward`	Moves the caret forward one position, extending the current selection.
`selection-next-word`	Extends the selection to the start of the next word.
`selection-previous-word`	Extends the selection to the start of the previous word.
`selection-up`	Moves the caret up one line and moves the selection with it.
`set-read-only`	Makes the editor read-only.
`set-writable`	Switches the editor into read-write mode.

The more complex `StyledEditorKit` inherits all the actions provided by `DefaultEditorKit` and supplies an extra set of operations that are appropriate for text components that handle text with more complex attributes, such as `JTextPane` and `JEditorPane`. These extra operations are listed in Table 1-6.

The individual text components may define their own specific actions that are additional to the ones supplied by their editor kits. In fact, of the standard Swing components, only `JTextField` uses this facility, to add an action called `notify-field-accept`, which posts an `ActionEvent` to all registered `ActionListeners`. This action, which is inherited by `JPasswordField`, is used when the user presses RETURN, to notify listeners that the user has finished typing into the field. In the next section, you'll see exactly how this action is activated by the RETURN key and later you'll find out how to disable it if necessary.

Table 1-6 Text Actions Supplied by `StyledEditorKit`	
Name	*Action*
`font-family-SansSerif`	Select a Sans Serif font.
`font-family-Monospaced`	Select a monospaced font.
`font-family-Serif`	Select a Serif font.
`font-size-8`	Set font size to 8 points.
`font-size-10`	Set font size to 10 points.
`font-size-12`	Set font size to 12 points.
`font-size-14`	Set font size to 14 points.
`font-size-16`	Set font size to 16 points.
`font-size-18`	Set font size to 18 points.
`font-size-24`	Set font size to 24 points.
`font-size-36`	Set font size to 36 points.
`font-size-48`	Set font size to 48 points.
`font-bold`	Toggle bold attribute on and off.
`font-italic`	Toggle the italic attribute on and off.
`font-underline`	Toggle the underline attribute on and off.
`left-justify`	Left-justify paragraph(s).
`center-justify`	Center paragraph(s).
`right-justify`	Right-justify paragraph(s).

Keymaps and Key Bindings

The actions that a text component defines for itself or inherits from its editor kit are accessible directly to the programmer, but they can't be used by the user unless mappings, examples of which were shown in Table 1-4, are created between individual actions and keystrokes. The establishment of these particular mappings allows the user to access the cut, copy, and paste features of a text component by simply pressing CTRL+X, CTRL+C, or CTRL+V (or the corresponding keystrokes in the selected look-and-feel) when the text component has the focus. In this section, you'll see the data structures that hold the keyboard mapping information and how the mappings themselves are created.

The KeyBinding and KeyMap Classes

Two classes are used to create and maintain key-to-action mappings—KeyBinding and KeyMap. The first of these is more properly called JText-Component.KeyBinding because it is a static inner class of JTextCompo-nent. Its function is simply to map the specification of a key, or combination of keys, to the name of a text component action. Here is its definition:

```
public static class KeyBinding {
   public KeyStroke key;
   public String actionName;
   public KeyBinding(KeyStroke key, String actionName) {
}
```

The KeyStroke object specifies the keys that the user will use to activate the corresponding action. The KeyStroke class has a static method called getKeyStroke that returns an appropriate object given a keycode name and the modifier keys that must be pressed along with the key. The actionName argument is the name of the action as specified in the public API of the text component or its associated editor kit. Here, for example, is how you would create a KeyBinding object that would request the mapping of the default editor kit's paste action to the key sequence CTRL+V:

```
KeyBinding binding = new KeyBinding(
        KeyStroke.getKeyStroke(KeyEvent.VK_V,
                InputEvent.CTRL_MASK),
        DefaultEditorKit.pasteAction);
```

The KeyBinding object does not actually create a keyboard mapping—it is used in the process of building the complete set of mappings for a component, which is held in a Keymap object. Keymap is an interface, defined as follows:

```
public interface Keymap {
   public String getName();
   public Action getAction(KeyStroke key);
   public KeyStroke[] getBoundKeyStrokes();
   public Action[] getBoundActions();
   public KeyStroke[] getKeyStrokesForAction(Action a);
   public boolean isLocallyDefined(KeyStroke key);
   public void addActionForKeyStroke(KeyStroke key, Action a);
   public void removeKeyStrokeBinding(KeyStroke keys);
```

```
public void removeBindings();
public Action getDefaultAction();
public void setDefaultAction(Action a);
public Keymap getResolveParent();
public void setResolveParent(Keymap parent);
}
```

A keymap essentially contains mappings of `KeyStroke` objects to `Action` objects, while the `Action` object is usually a `TextAction` (although, in fact, it need not be). As the user presses keys, each single key press and its associated modifiers (the states of the `SHIFT`, `CTRL`, and `ALT` keys) is used to build a `KeyStroke` object that is then used to search the text component's keymap. If a corresponding `KeyStroke` is found, the associated `Action` is performed. If no mapping is found, the keymap's *default* action, if there is one, is used instead. You'll see what the default action does later in this section.

Keymaps are actually hierarchical in nature; any keymap can be created with another keymap as its parent, or a parent can be associated with it later using the `setResolveParent` method. The set of all keymaps in an application is maintained by `JTextComponent`. When the `JTextComponent` class is first loaded, it creates the first `Keymap` object, which contains the default action and a set of mappings of keys to the standard actions provided by the `DefaultEditorKit`, as shown in Table 1-7. This `Keymap` is known as the *default* `Keymap`.

Table 1-7 Keyboard Mappings in the Default Keymap

Keys	Action
VK_BACK_SPACE	DefaultEditorKit.deletePrevCharAction
VK_DELETE	DefaultEditorKit.deleteNextCharAction
VK_RIGHT	DefaultEditorKit.forwardAction
VK_LEFT	DefaultEditorKit.backwardAction

Creating Individual Keymaps

To create a new keymap, the `JTextComponent` addKeymap method is used:

```
public static Keymap addKeymap(String name, Keymap parent);
```

A new keymap initially has no key bindings of its own, but it does inherit those of its parent. Many keymaps, including the ones created for the standard Swing text components, have the default keymap as their direct parent. As a result, the key mappings shown in Table 1-7 are available in all of these keymaps (and hence in all Swing components). A keymap can have a name, which must be unique within an application. Given the name, you can find the corresponding keymap using the following static `JTextComponent` method:

```
public static Keymap getKeymap(String name);
```

The name of the default keymap is available in the static field `JTextComponent.DEFAULT_KEYMAP`, so you can get a reference to the default keymap and use it to create a new keymap called `MYKEYMAP` as follows:

```
Keymap defaultKeymap =
    JTextComponent.getKeymap(JTextComponent.DEFAULT_KEYMAP);
Keymap myKeymap =
    JTextComponent.addKeymap("MYKEYMAP", defaultKeymap);
```

This new keymap contains only the mappings shown in Table 1-7.

The name given to a keymap is visible to the entire application and can be given to the `getKeymap` method to get a reference to it. If you want to create a private and anonymous keymap, you can do so by supplying a null name:

```
Keymap privateKeymap =
    JTextComponent.addKeymap(null, defaultKeymap);
```

Such a keymap is accessible only through the reference stored in the variable `privateKeymap`.

Creating Keymaps for Text Components

As you've seen, a `Keymap` contains mappings from `KeyStrokes` to `Actions`, while `KeyBindings` map `KeyStrokes` to action *names*. When keys are pressed, the text component uses its `Keymap` to determine what action to take, not the `KeyBindings`. To build a `Keymap` from a set of `KeyBindings`, you need a way to obtain the `Action` corresponding to a given action name, which is specified in the `KeyBinding`, such as `DefaultEditorKit.paste-Action`. However, there is no simple way to do this: The `Actions` are usually created internally by editor kits and components. Only the names are publicly available, which is why `KeyBinding` objects are used to specify the required key mappings for a component. The only way to map a name to an `Action`, in order to create an entry in a `Keymap`, is to call the `JTextComponent` or `EditorKit getActions` method, which returns an array containing all the `Actions` that it supports. Each `Action` has an associated name, which can be obtained using its `getValue` method. Here, for example, is a code extract that prints the names of all the `Actions` supported by `JTextField`:

```
public JTextField tf = new JTextField();
Action[] actions = tf.getActions();
for (int i = 0; i < actions.length; i++) {
   System.out.println(actions[i].getValue(Action.NAME));
}
```

Given a set of `KeyBinding` objects, it is possible to construct a `Keymap` by searching the list of `Actions` for one with the name of each action in the `KeyBinding` list, and then using the `addActionForKeyStroke` method to add an entry to the `Keymap`:

```
public void addActionForKeyStroke(KeyStroke key, Action a);
```

This is something of a long-winded process, especially if you want to install a set of mappings in a keymap, which is usually the case. For example, all the Swing text components have mappings for the full set of actions supported by `DefaultEditorKit` (see Table 1-5). To make it easier to build the key mappings for a text component, `JTextComponent` has a convenience method called `loadKeymap`, defined as follows:

```
public static void loadKeymap(Keymap map,
    KeyBinding[] bindings, Action[] actions);
```

This method *adds* to the keymap supplied, as its first argument, a mapping corresponding to each binding in the second argument. The third argument is the list of `Actions` that are searched for whose names match the ones specified in the array of `KeyBinding` objects. If no suitable `Action` is found in the `actions` array for any of the bindings, no corresponding mapping is added; this is not considered to be an error. Because key bindings are look-and-feel specific, as you can see from Table 1-4, the keymap for each standard text component is installed by its UI class when the component is created. If the look-and-feel is switched at any time, a new keymap is created to reflect the bindings appropriate for the new look-and-feel.

Keeping a dedicated keymap for each text component would be expensive, because, unless the programmer takes special steps to customize individual components, the keymaps for all instances of `JTextField`, for example, are the same. Because of this, each text component *type* shares a common keymap; only one instance of this keymap is created and it is installed in every instance of that component. It follows that there are separate keymaps created for each of `JTextField`, `JPasswordField`, `JTextArea`, `JTextPane`, and `JEditorPane`, making a total of five keymaps no matter how many of these components exist within the application.

Core Note

Actually, each look-and-feel creates its own keymap for a particular component type, so there will actually be five keymaps for each look-and-feel that the application has used. In the rest of this chapter, for the sake of brevity, we'll assume that only one look-and-feel is in use, so there will be one keymap per component type.

You can get and set the keymap for a specific component *instance* using the following `JTextComponent` methods:

```
public void setKeymap(Keymap map);
public Keymap getKeymap();
```

Each of the per-component type keymaps is, of course, stored by `JText-Component` and can be retrieved without having an instance of that component by invoking the static `getKeymap` method and passing it the name given to `addKeymap` when it was created. The names used for the keymaps created for the standard text components are actually the names of the UI classes associated with those components. That is, the keymap for `JTextField` when the Metal look-and-feel is in use is stored with the name "`MetalTextFieldUI`," the one for `JTextArea` under the name "`BasicTextAreaUI`" (because the Metal look-and-feel uses the common UI class for `JTextArea`, whereas it extends `BasicTextFieldUI` to create `MetalTextFieldUI` for `JTextField`) and so on. Thus, you can get a reference to the keymap shared by all the `JTextFields` in the Metal look-and-feel like this:

```
Keymap map = JTextComponent.getKeymap("MetalTextFieldUI");
```

or like this, assuming that the Metal look-and-feel is selected:

```
JTextField tf = new JTextField();
Keymap map = tf.getKeymap();
```

Whichever method you choose, you get exactly the *same* reference returned, because there is only one keymap shared by all `JTextField` objects for a given look-and-feel. The second method is more convenient because you don't need to know which look-and-feel is selected to retrieve the keymap, or to understand the algorithm used to create the name.

Resolving Key Bindings

As noted earlier, when the user types something into a text component, the key code and modifiers from the `KeyEvent` are used to create a `KeyStroke` object, which is then used to search the component's keymap for a corresponding `Action`. If no mapping is found for the `KeyStroke`, the search continues with the keymap's resolving parent, set when the keymap was created by the `addKeymap` method (or later using `setResolveParent`). This process continues until a mapping is found or until there are no more parents to search.

As an example, consider what happens when the `backspace` key is pressed in a `JTextArea`. The keymap for this component actually consists of a `Keymap` created by the `JTextArea` UI class to map a subset of the actions of `DefaultEditorKit` and a reference to the default keymap as its resolving parent, which contains the mappings shown in Table 1-7. A `KeyStroke` object for the `VK_BACK_SPACE` key (with no modifiers) is built and searched for in the `JTextArea`'s keymap. Because this doesn't contain an entry for this `KeyStroke`, the search continues in the default keymap, where a mapping to the `DefaultEditorKit deletePrevCharAction` will be found and used to implement the effect of the `backspace` key. The standard text components all have a two-level keymap like this, by default. As you'll see shortly, you can add extra levels to a component's keymap to change the way it reacts to selected keys.

The Default Keyboard Action

If the process of resolving a `KeyStroke` does not produce a mapping, the `Keymap`'s *default* action is used. The default action can be obtained by calling the `Keymap`'s `getDefaultAction` method. Every `Keymap` can have a default action, but none is required to have one. In fact, a `Keymap` has no default action unless you assign one to it using the `setDefaultAction` method, or it inherits one from its resolving parent. The default `Keymap` has a default action that inserts the key that the user typed into the text component at the current location of the caret. This is, in fact, how data gets into a text component. Because the `Keymaps` used by the standard text components all have the default `Keymap` as their resolving parents, you can change the way in which most keys are handled for *every* text component by installing a different default action in this `Keymap`. Alternatively, you can modify the handling of input characters for a specific component *type* (for example, for all `JTextAreas`) by changing the default action of the `Keymap` for that component type, because the newly installed default action will override the one in the default `Keymap`.

Disabling the RETURN Key in a Text Field

The `Keymap` for `JTextField` (and `JPasswordField`) has an entry that maps the RETURN key to an action (called `notify-field-accept`) that generates an `ActionEvent` to inform listeners that the content of the input field is valid. Sometimes, however, you won't need to use this event and, in many cases, the fact that this mapping exists can cause problems. Let's look at a simple example that demonstrates the problem.

Suppose you have a frame that contains a form-like layout consisting of several text fields, in which the user is expected to fill in all the fields on the form and press a button to have the form processed. Typically, you would have an OK button and a Cancel button at the bottom of the form and the first input field would have the input focus when the frame appears. An experienced user would want to drive this form by using the TAB key to move between the fields and then pressing RETURN when the form is filled, as an alternative to clicking the OK button by moving the mouse over it or using the TAB key to move to the button and activating it with the space bar. The difference between these two approaches can be very annoying for the user if some of the fields have default values that are acceptable, because in the latter case, to submit the completed form the user might have to press the TAB key several times to reach the OK button.

In this situation, you would want to make the OK button the *default button* for its containing frame. The default button can be activated by pressing the RETURN key, without needing to give it the keyboard focus. This looks like the right thing to do, because the OK button would then be activated no matter how many fields the user changes before the form content is correct and no matter where the input focus happens to be. Unfortunately, the default button does not work when there are `JTextFields` in the frame and one of them has the focus. The reason for this is that the RETURN key is seen first by the focused `JTextField`, which has an action registered for it in its keymap that would just generate an `ActionEvent` from the text field. In this situation, of course, you are unlikely to be using the `ActionEvent`, because the user will be moving between fields using the TAB key, so this event is not going to be delivered to any listeners. If you are going to take the trouble to process fields as the user completes them, you will probably use a `FocusListener`, which will be activated as the user moves out of each field and into the next one.

Removing the RETURN key from the Keymap

What you need to do in this case is to remove the text field's mapping for the RETURN key. If you can do this, the RETURN key won't be swallowed by the text field and will get passed instead to the default button, which will be activated to signal the completion of the form. Listing 1-11 shows the most straightforward implementation of this idea.

Listing 1-11   Changing the Text Field Keymap

```java
package AdvancedSwing.Chapter1;

import javax.swing.*;
import javax.swing.text.*;
import java.awt.event.*;

public class PassiveTextField1 extends JTextField {

    public static void main(String[] args) {
        JFrame f = new JFrame("Passive Text Field");
        f.getContentPane().setLayout(
                    new BoxLayout(f.getContentPane(),
                    BoxLayout.Y_AXIS));
        final JTextField ptf = new JTextField(32);
        JTextField tf = new JTextField(32);
        JPanel p = new JPanel();
        JButton b = new JButton("OK");
        p.add(b);
        f.getContentPane().add(ptf);
        f.getContentPane().add(tf);
        f.getContentPane().add(p);

        Keymap map = ptf.getKeymap(); // Gets the shared map
        KeyStroke key =
                KeyStroke.getKeyStroke(KeyEvent.VK_ENTER, 0);
        map.removeKeyStrokeBinding(key);

        ActionListener l = new ActionListener() {
            public void actionPerformed(ActionEvent evt) {
                System.out.println("Action event
                                from a text field");
            }
        };
        ptf.addActionListener(l);
        tf.addActionListener(l);
```

Listing 1-11 Changing the Text Field Keymap (continued)

```
        // Make the button the default button
        f.getRootPane().setDefaultButton(b);
        b.addActionListener(new ActionListener() {
            public void actionPerformed(ActionEvent evt) {
                System.out.println("Content of text field: <"
                    + ptf.getText() + ">");
            }
        });
        f.pack();
        f.setVisible(true);
    }
}
```

This example creates two text fields and a button, which is made the default button for the frame. The difference between the two text fields is that an extra operation is performed on the top one before it is displayed. Here is the code that performs that operation:

```
Keymap map = ptf.getKeymap();    // Gets the shared map
KeyStroke key = KeyStroke.getKeyStroke(KeyEvent.VK_ENTER, 0);
map.removeKeyStrokeBinding(key);
```

This code gets the text field's keymap, builds a `KeyStroke` object that corresponds to the RETURN key being pressed, and then removes whatever mapping is attached to the RETURN key using the `Keymap removeKeyStroke-Binding` method. This should result in the text field at the top of the form having no mapping for the RETURN key. If you run this example using the command

```
java AdvancedSwing.Chapter1.PassiveTextField1
```

you'll get the layout shown in Figure 1-14.

Figure 1-14 Disabling the RETURN key in a text field.

First, type something in the upper text field and press RETURN. When you do so, the OK button will change its appearance to show that it has been activated, and you'll see the content of the text field printed in the window from which you started the example program. This message was, as you can see from the code, printed from an event handler connected to the button, not to the text field. As you can also see from Listing 1-11, there is also an Action-Listener associated with the text field. The fact that the message that it would print if were activated does not appear demonstrates that the text field is not generating an event when the RETURN key is pressed and this is confirmed by the fact that the RETURN key is successfully activating the default button.

So far, all seems well. However, there is a side effect. The other text field has not had its keymap changed, or so you might think. Certainly, there has been no explicit modification of its keymap. However, if you type some text into it and press RETURN, you'll find that it behaves in the same way as the other text field—the button fires and the text field's ActionListener is not activated. What has happened here is that the keymap retrieved by the code in the main method is a *shared* keymap used by all text fields. Changing that keymap makes the same change for every JTextField using that keymap— in other words, for all JTextFields that do not have a private keymap that your application explicitly installed and that does not depend on the shared JTextField keymap. If your application never needs to use the JText-Field's ActionEvent, this is probably a side effect you can live with. However, it is not satisfactory as a general solution.

Creating a Replacement Keymap

Because the simple solution isn't completely satisfactory, perhaps it would be better to create an entirely new keymap for our text field. The new keymap would need to have all the same mappings as the standard JTextField, except for the case of the RETURN key. Creating such a keymap is not very difficult. Unfortunately, you can't clone keymaps because the Keymap interface does not include a clone operation, but you can arrange to copy a keymap, keystroke by keystroke, and in doing so, you can omit the mapping for the RETURN key.

When is the appropriate time to create the new keymap? Because the keymap will be derived from the one used by JTextField, you can't create it until the JTextField keymap has been initialized, which happens during construction of the JTextComponent part of the JTextField object. If we create a derived class of JTextField, then after the JTextField constructor has been executed, its keymap will be valid and we could extract it (using getKeymap), create a slightly modified version, and then install the new one using setKeymap. Creating a new component is more convenient than adding a few lines of code to change the keymap, as was done in Listing 1-11, because it encapsulates the operation as part of a new type of object that the programmer can use without needing to know how it works.

However, this would only be a partial solution. The new component has a keymap that won't react to the RETURN key. However, what happens if the application allows the user to switch from one look-and-feel to another? Because the key mappings are look-and-feel dependent, they will be switched as part of the changeover from one look-and-feel to another. When this happens, the new keymap that was installed in the constructor will be replaced by a keymap for JTextField, with the mapping for RETURN installed. To work around this problem, you need to catch this change of keymap and install a modified keymap instead. Fortunately, this case is easy to detect because a switch of look-and-feel first sets the component's keymap to null (as the old look-and-feel is switched out) and then to a non-null value as the new keymap is installed. These operations are performed by calling the setKeymap method, which is also called to install the initial keymap during construction. If you add the code to modify the keymap to setKeymap and only make modifications when the installed keymap is null, you won't need to add code to the constructor and the keymap changes will persist over a switch of look-and-feel. Listing 1-12 shows the implementation details.

Listing 1-12 Creating a New Keymap for a Text Component

```
package AdvancedSwing.Chapter1;

import javax.swing.*;
import javax.swing.text.*;
import java.awt.event.*;

public class PassiveTextField2 extends JTextField {
    public PassiveTextField2() {
        this(null, null, 0);
    }

    public PassiveTextField2(String text) {
        this(null, text, 0);
    }
```

**Listing 1-12 Creating a New Keymap for a Text
              Component (continued)**

```java
public PassiveTextField2(int columns) {
   this(null, null, columns);
}

public PassiveTextField2(String text, int columns) {
   this(null, text, columns);
}

public PassiveTextField2(Document doc,
                         String text, int columns) {
   super(doc, text, columns);
}

public void setKeymap(Keymap map) {
   if (map == null) {
      // Uninstalling keymap.
      super.setKeymap(null);
      sharedKeymap = null;
      return;
   }

   if (getKeymap() == null) {
      if (sharedKeymap == null) {
         // Initial keymap, or first
         // keymap after L&F switch.
         // Generate a new keymap
         sharedKeymap = addKeymap(null,
                     map.getResolveParent());
         KeyStroke[] strokes = map.getBoundKeyStrokes();
         for (int i = 0; i < strokes.length; i++) {
            Action a = map.getAction(strokes[i]);
            if (a.getValue(Action.NAME) ==
                      JTextField.notifyAction) {
               continue;
            }
            sharedKeymap.addActionForKeyStroke(
                      strokes[i], a);
         }
      }
      map = sharedKeymap;
   }
   super.setKeymap(map);
}
```

Listing 1-12 Creating a New Keymap for a Text Component (continued)

```
protected static Keymap sharedKeymap;

// Test method
public static void main(String[] args) {
   JFrame f = new JFrame("Passive Text Field");
   f.getContentPane().setLayout(new BoxLayout(
               f.getContentPane(),
               BoxLayout.Y_AXIS));
   final PassiveTextField2 ptf =
               new PassiveTextField2(32);
   JTextField tf = new JTextField(32);
   JPanel p = new JPanel();
   JButton b = new JButton("OK");
   p.add(b);
   f.getContentPane().add(ptf);
   f.getContentPane().add(tf);
   f.getContentPane().add(p);

   ActionListener l = new ActionListener() {
      public void actionPerformed(ActionEvent evt) {
         System.out.println("Action event from a
                            text field");
      }
   };
   ptf.addActionListener(l);
   tf.addActionListener(l);

   // Make the button the default button
   f.getRootPane().setDefaultButton(b);
   b.addActionListener(new ActionListener() {
      public void actionPerformed(ActionEvent evt) {
         System.out.println("Content of text field: <"
               + ptf.getText() + ">");
      }
   });
   f.pack();
   f.setVisible(true);
}
}
```

The code to copy the keymap is shown in the `setKeymap` method. The keymap for `JTextField` consists of two parts—the default keymap and the part that contains the usual key mappings for the actions handled by `DefaultEditorKit` plus the extra action for the RETURN key, which has the default keymap as its resolving parent. To create the new keymap, the second of these two parts is copied into a new keymap, which also has the default keymap as its resolving parent. The code that clones the keymap is very straightforward. The first step is to create an empty keymap with the default keymap as its parent, using the `addKeymap` method. Then, the set of bound keystrokes from the `JTextField` map is obtained and the action for each keystroke is copied into the new keymap using the `addActionForKeyStroke` method. The action associated with the RETURN key, recognized by comparing the name in each of the `Action` objects with the name used by `JText-Field`, is not copied during this process. The resulting keymap is functionally identical to the one used by `JTextField`, except that it does not handle the RETURN key. Finally, the new keymap is installed.

If this code executed every time `setKeymap` were called when the installed keymap is `null`, we would end up with a modified keymap for every instance of this new component, because the first keymap installed in every such component satisfies this criterion. To avoid this overhead, what we actually need to do is create a new (shared) keymap the first time `setKeymap` is called when the installed keymap is `null`. On subsequent `setKeymap` calls, the shared keymap already created would be used. This would be fine, except that it wouldn't recognize a switch of look-and-feel. Fortunately, during a look-and-feel switch, all the keymaps are set to `null` before being reloaded, so we can use the occurrence of a `setKeymap(null)` call as a trigger to clear the reference to the shared keymap, so that it will be recreated the next time a real keymap is loaded.

If you run this example using the command

```
java AdvancedSwing.Chapter1.PassiveTextField2
```

you'll get the same layout as was shown in Figure 1-14, but now the results are different. Type some text in the upper text field, which has the new key-map, and press RETURN. As before, the default button will activate and the text that you typed will appear in the window from which you started the example. Now, if you type something in the lower field, which is an unmodified `JTextField`, and press RETURN, the default button does not fire and you get the message "Action event from a text field," which is printed in the text field's `ActionListener`, showing that the lower `JTextField` still generates an `ActionEvent`.

Another Method—Intercepting the RETURN *key*

Before leaving this example, there is one more way of achieving the same effect that we'll show you. So far, we've tried to unmap the RETURN key by adjusting the component's keymap. It seems that removing the mapping for a key in this way is not a simple operation because of the shared nature of key-maps, so what about an implementation that doesn't interfere with the key-map at all? This would avoid all the problems that you saw in the previous two sections. To see how this is possible, let's look at how keys are handled by the text components.

When a key is pressed, the JComponent processKeyEvent method is called. This tries to deal with the key by passing it to various methods, as follows:

1. If the Swing focus manager is installed, pass it to the focus manager.
2. If the key has not been consumed, pass it to the process-KeyEvent of java.awt.Component, which will result in it being dispatched to registered KeyListeners.
3. If the key has still not been consumed, pass it to the JComponent processComponentKeyEvent method.
4. Finally, if processComponentKeyEvent did not consume the key, look for a mapping in the KeyStroke registry.

The Swing text components map keys to actions in step 3 of the process, whereas the default button mechanism is part of the KeyStroke registry, which appears at step 4. This is why the RETURN key is seen by the key map-ping mechanism first and why mapping RETURN to a no-operation instruction (NO-OP) within the text components would not work—the fact that there is a mapping of any kind, even one that simply discards the key, would cause JTextComponent to consume the RETURN key in step 3.

However, this sequence also holds the key to solving the problem of pre-serving the RETURN key so that the default button can grab it. If, at step 3, we could arrange for the key not to be consumed, it would survive to step 4 and the default button would work. And this is easy to arrange—just override the JTextComponent processComponentKeyEvent method and return immedi-ately when the RETURN key is received, instead of allowing the key mapping code to handle it. This has the same effect as unmapping the key, but none of the complications that you saw before. The implementation is shown in List-ing 1-13.

Listing 1-13 Ignoring Mapped Keys Without Changing
              the Keymap

```java
package AdvancedSwing.Chapter1;

import javax.swing.*;
import javax.swing.text.*;
import java.awt.event.*;

public class PassiveTextField extends JTextField {
    public PassiveTextField() {
        this(null, null, 0);
    }

    public PassiveTextField(String text) {
        this(null, text, 0);
    }

    public PassiveTextField(int columns) {
        this(null, null, columns);
    }

    public PassiveTextField(String text, int columns) {
        this(null, text, columns);
    }

    public PassiveTextField(Document doc, String text,
                            int columns) {
        super(doc, text, columns);
    }

    public void processComponentKeyEvent(KeyEvent evt) {
        switch (evt.getID()) {
        case KeyEvent.KEY_PRESSED:
        case KeyEvent.KEY_RELEASED:
            if (evt.getKeyCode() == KeyEvent.VK_ENTER) {
                return;
            }
            break;

        case KeyEvent.KEY_TYPED:
            if (evt.getKeyChar() == '\r') {
                return;
            }
            break;
        }
```

```
Listing 1-13  Ignoring Mapped Keys Without Changing
              the Keymap (continued)
```

```
        super.processComponentKeyEvent(evt);
    }

    // Test method
    public static void main(String[] args) {
        // Unchanged from Listing 1-12: not shown
    }
}
```

As with the previous example, the constructors of this class just mimic those of JTextField so that you can use a PassiveTextField interchangeably with JTextField. The important part of this object is the processComponentKeyEvent method. As you can see, it works slightly differently depending on the type of event received. KEY_PRESSED and KEY_RELEASED events carry a key code for each key, while the KEY_TYPED event contains the Unicode character for the key, not the key code. As a result, the test for the RETURN key needs to be slightly different for these two cases, but the action taken when it is detected is the same—just return without consuming it. All other keys are passed to the superclass processComponentKeyEvent method, which uses the installed keymap to handle them and will consume them if there is a valid mapping. To verify that this works, use the command:

```
java AdvancedSwing.Chapter1.PassiveTextField
```

You should see the same results as you saw with the previous example.

Whether you prefer this simple implementation or the one in Listing 1-12 is a matter of taste. Certainly, the code in Listing 1-13 is the much simpler of the two and it is far easier to understand. It also has the virtue of being independent of look-and-feel switching. From the purist's point of view, however, it may not be so desirable, because it works by subverting the text components' key mapping mechanism rather than working with it to achieve the desired effect. The difference between these solutions would become less clear-cut if you wanted to take this example a step further and suppress several actions from the keymap. To pursue the solution shown in Listing 1-13 would mean expanding the switch statement to test for each individual key, with the consequent performance overhead for every key that you type. By contrast, the approach taken in Listing 1-12 has no additional overhead after you install the correct keymap.

Implementing Overwrite Mode in a Text Field

The last example in this section demonstrates several aspects of the text component architecture that you've seen in this chapter. When you type text into the standard Swing components, the characters that you type are inserted at the location of the caret, moving existing content, if any, to the right to make room. The only way to replace text with something new is to manually delete it with the BACKSPACE or DELETE key, or to select the characters that you want to remove and then type the replacement text. In some cases, it would be more convenient to switch to a mode in which the characters that you type directly overwrite those already in the text field. Although the Swing text controls do not provide this facility, you can implement it using techniques that you have already seen in this chapter.

To provide a usable overwrite feature, you need to do three things:

1. Implement the mechanics of the overwrite mode in the control itself. That is, arrange for each new character to replace the one to the right of the cursor instead of being placed before it.
2. Arrange for the user to be able to toggle between insertion and overwriting. This should be a global setting, so that all the text fields that are capable of overwrite are in the same mode, to avoid confusing the user.
3. Provide some way to indicate to the user whether a text field is in insert or overwrite mode.

Each of these three aspects will be described separately next.

Implementing the Overwrite Capability

You've already seen that there are two ways to control what happens when the user types into a text control: You can override the model `insertString` method and implement a different policy within the document model itself, or you can reimplement the `JTextComponent` `replaceSelection` method. You have seen examples of both techniques in this chapter. Either of these methods could be used to implement an overwrite mode, but there is a good reason for choosing one over the other.

Suppose you chose to add this functionality in the model's `insertString` method. To do this, you would create a custom document type derived from `PlainDocument` and override `insertString` so that it would either insert the text at the given offset if the model is in insert mode, or first remove the required number of characters from the model and then insert the new content in its place if it is in overwrite mode. The number of characters to be removed would be the length of the replacement string, or the number of characters between the start offset and the end of the model if that is smaller. The code to do this is very simple; here's an example implementation:

```
public void insertString(int offset, String str,
                         AttributeSet a) throws
                         BadLocationException {
    if (overwriting == true) {
        int length = str.length();
        int overlapSize = getLength() - offset;
        int overwriteSize = length <= overlapSize ? length :
                                      overlapSize;

        if (overwriteSize > 0) {
            remove(offset, overwriteSize);
        }
    }

    super.insertString(offset, str, a);
}
```

This would work in almost all cases. However, it falls short in one respect. Consider what happens when the user selects a range of characters from the text field and then types a single replacement character. Let's take an example to illustrate the point. Suppose that the control contains the following (not very original) text:

abcdefgh

and that the user selects the letters d, e, and f, and then types 1. What should the result be? In a normal text field that supports only direct insertion, the selected text would be removed and replaced by the 1, so that the control would then contain:

abc1gh

In a control with overwrite turned on, the user would expect the same result—in other words, replacement of selected text should take precedence over the use of the overwrite mode. Now let's see what happens if you choose to implement the overwrite mode in the control's data model, as shown before.

The process of replacing the text is actually performed in two steps. First, the selected text is removed using the model's remove method. Second, the new text is inserted at the caret location by calling insertString. In this case, if the control contains the string `abcdefgh`, and then after the `remove` method is called, the model would contain

`abcgh`

and the caret would be positioned before the letter `g`. Next, the `insert-String` method is called to insert the single-character string `1` at offset 3. Using the implementation shown before (or any equivalent implementation), one character would be removed from the model to make room for the `1`, which would then be inserted in its place. The control would then contain the text

`abc1h`

which is not what the user would expect to see.

The problem with this approach is that the `insertString` method is not aware of the `remove` operation that precedes it. Because it is written to replace characters rather than move them out of the way, it does this even when it really shouldn't.

The alternative to this is to put the overwrite functionality in the `JText-Component replaceSelection` method instead. This is a much better solution, because `replaceSelection` is responsible for the complete operation—both removing the selected text, if any, and inserting the new text. Because of this, it can arrange to perform an overwrite operation only if there is no text selected for removal. The details are shown in Listing 1-14.

Listing 1-14 A Text Control That Supports Overwriting of Existing Content

```
package AdvancedSwing.Chapter1;

import javax.swing.*;
import javax.swing.text.*;
import java.awt.*;
import java.awt.event.*;

public class OverwritableTextField extends JTextField {
    public OverwritableTextField() {
        this(null, null, 0);
    }
```

**Listing 1-14 A Text Control That Supports Overwriting
of Existing Content (continued)**

```java
public OverwritableTextField(String text) {
   this(null, text, 0);
}

public OverwritableTextField(int columns) {
   this(null, null, columns);
}

public OverwritableTextField(String text, int columns) {
   this(null, text, columns);
}

public OverwritableTextField(Document doc,
                             String text,
                             int columns) {
   super(doc, text, columns);
   overwriteCaret = new OverwriteCaret();
   super.setCaret(overwriting ?
             overwriteCaret : insertCaret);
}

public void setKeymap(Keymap map) {
   if (map == null) {
      super.setKeymap(null);
      sharedKeymap = null;
      return;
   }

   if (getKeymap() == null) {
      if (sharedKeymap == null) {
         // Switch keymaps. Add extra bindings.
         removeKeymap(keymapName);
         sharedKeymap = addKeymap(keymapName, map);
         loadKeymap(sharedKeymap, bindings,
                 defaultActions);
      }
      map = sharedKeymap;
   }
   super.setKeymap(map);
}
```

Listing 1-14 A Text Control That Supports Overwriting
of Existing Content (continued)

```java
public void replaceSelection(String content) {
    Document doc = getDocument();
    if (doc != null) {
        // If we are not overwriting, just do the
        // usual insert. Also, if there is a selection,
        // just overwrite that (and that only).
        if (overwriting == true &&
                getSelectionStart() == getSelectionEnd()) {

            // Overwrite and no selection. Remove
            // the stretch that we will overwrite,
            // then use the usual code to insert the
            // new text.
            int insertPosition = getCaretPosition();
            int overwriteLength = doc.getLength() -
                                  insertPosition;
            int length = content.length();

            if (overwriteLength > length) {
                overwriteLength = length;
            }

            // Remove the range being overwritten
            try {
                doc.remove(insertPosition, overwriteLength);
            } catch (BadLocationException e) {
                // Won't happen
            }
        }
    }

    super.replaceSelection(content);
}

// Change the global overwriting mode
public static void setOverwriting(boolean overwriting) {
    OverwritableTextField.overwriting = overwriting;
}

public static boolean isOverwriting() {
    return overwriting;
}
```

**Listing 1-14 A Text Control That Supports Overwriting
of Existing Content (continued)**

```
// Configuration of the insert caret
public void setCaret(Caret caret) {
    insertCaret = caret;
}

// Allow configuration of a new
// overwrite caret.
public void setOverwriteCaret(Caret caret) {
    overwriteCaret = caret;
}

public Caret getOverwriteCaret() {
    return overwriteCaret;
}

// Caret switching
public void processFocusEvent(FocusEvent evt) {
    if (evt.getID() == FocusEvent.FOCUS_GAINED) {
        selectCaret();
    }
    super.processFocusEvent(evt);
}

protected void selectCaret() {
    // Select the appropriate caret for the
    // current overwrite mode.
    Caret newCaret = overwriting ?
                    overwriteCaret : insertCaret;

    if (newCaret != getCaret()) {
        Caret caret = getCaret();
        int mark = caret.getMark();
        int dot = caret.getDot();
        caret.setVisible(false);

        super.setCaret(newCaret);

        newCaret.setDot(mark);
        newCaret.moveDot(dot);
        newCaret.setVisible(true);
    }
}
```

Listing 1-14 A Text Control That Supports Overwriting
             of Existing Content (continued)

```
protected Caret overwriteCaret;
protected Caret insertCaret;

protected static boolean overwriting = true;

public static final String toggleOverwriteAction =
                   "toggle-overwrite";

protected static Keymap sharedKeymap;
protected static final String keymapName =
                   "OverwriteMap";
protected static final Action[] defaultActions = {
                   new ToggleOverwriteAction()
};

protected static JTextComponent.KeyBinding[] bindings = {
   new JTextComponent.KeyBinding(
        KeyStroke.getKeyStroke(KeyEvent.VK_INSERT, 0),
        toggleOverwriteAction)
};

// Insert/overwrite toggling action
public static class ToggleOverwriteAction
                   extends TextAction {
   ToggleOverwriteAction() {
      super(toggleOverwriteAction);
   }

   public void actionPerformed(ActionEvent evt) {
      OverwritableTextField.setOverwriting(
              !OverwritableTextField.isOverwriting());
      JTextComponent target = getFocusedComponent();
      if (target instanceof OverwritableTextField) {
         OverwritableTextField field =
                   (OverwritableTextField)target;
         field.selectCaret();
      }
   }
}
```

> **Listing 1-14 A Text Control That Supports Overwriting of Existing Content (continued)**

```
    public static void main(String[] args) {
    JFrame f = new JFrame("Overwrite test");

    OverwritableTextField tf =
                new OverwritableTextField(20);
    f.getContentPane().add(tf, "North");
    tf = new OverwritableTextField(20);
    f.getContentPane().add(tf, "South");

    f.pack();
    f.setVisible(true);
  }
}
```

Listing 1-14 shows a control called `OverwritableTextField`, derived from `JTextField`, that does everything that `JTextField` can do and also implements a toggle to allow the user to overwrite existing text or to insert new text. The state of the toggle is a static boolean called `isOverwriting` that can be set using the static `setOverwriting` method. Because this is a static attribute, all instances of `OverwritableTextField` are either in insert mode or overwrite mode at any given time. Initially, overwriting is selected for the entire application.

The details of the overwrite operation are contained in the `replace-Selection` method. If the control is in insert mode, there is no need to do anything special, so the `replaceSelection` method of `JTextField` is invoked directly. This is also true if there is a non-empty selection, which is detected by calling the `getSelectionStart` and `getSelectionEnd` methods and testing for inequality, which indicates that some text has been selected. If the control is in overwrite mode and there is no selection, it is necessary to overwrite existing text with the new content, by first removing it and then adding the replacement characters.

In the simplest case, all that is necessary to determine how much text to remove from the control is to get the length of the text string passed to `replaceSelection` and remove that many characters. This doesn't work, however, if the replacement string is longer than the number of characters left after the insertion point. For example, suppose the model contains the string

abcdefg

and the `replaceSelection` method is called with the caret at offset 5 (that is, before the letter `f`) and with three characters to insert. According to the simple algorithm in the last paragraph, we would want to remove three characters from offset 5 to replace them with the three new characters. However, there are only two characters in the model after offset 5 and attempting to remove three would cause the `Document` remove method to throw a `BadLocationException`. Obviously, the correct thing to do is to remove the smaller of the number of characters in the replacement string and the number of characters between the caret position and the end of the model. This is exactly what the `replaceSelection` method in Listing 1-14 does. The most common case in which this happens, of course, is when the user is adding text to the end of a text field, when there would be no characters left to remove. In this special case, having the control in overwrite mode is no different from having insert mode selected. Once the characters to be replaced have been removed, the new text can be inserted by calling the original `replaceSelection` method. Because there is no selection and the caret is not moved by the `remove` operation, this will just insert the new text in the correct place.

Switching Between Insert and Overwrite Modes

The `OverwritableTextField` provides the static methods `setOverwriting` and `isOverwriting` to enable its operating mode to be set and read. The user, of course, cannot call either of these methods, so how is it possible for the user to change the mode to overwrite or insert? The obvious way to do this is to map the `INSERT` key so that it calls the `setOverwriting` method with the appropriate value to select the required mode. For consistency with existing user interface models, in this implementation the `INSERT` key behaves as a toggle, flipping all the `OverwritableTextFields` in the application into insert mode the first time it is pressed, into overwrite mode the next time, and so on.

You already know that to map a key so that it performs some operation on a text component you need to add an entry to the text component's keymap. In this case, we need to map the `INSERT` key to some action that calls the static `setOverwriting` method. You've already seen how to change existing keymaps. Here, we want to take the keymap for `JTextField`, which `OverwritableTextField` will inherit, and add a single entry to it, without affecting the `JTextField` keymap. To do this, we create a new keymap that has the `JTextField` keymap as its resolving parent and add the mapping for the `INSERT` key to it. This activates the new mapping and makes the mappings for `JTextField` available within the new control without changing the mappings for `JTextField` itself. The code that implements the creation of the keymap is shown in the `setKeymap` method in Listing 1-14. As with the example shown in Listing 1-12, the new keymap is created here so that the mapping is preserved even if the application's look-and-feel is changed. Care is taken to create only a single copy of the new keymap, because it can be shared by all instances of `OverwritableTextField`. The single copy of the keymap is held in the static variable `sharedKeymap`. It is created and installed in the control when `setKeymap` is called, but only if there is no keymap currently installed. This allows the programmer to override the default keymap with another one by explicitly calling `setKeymap`.

How is the action for the `INSERT` key added to the keymap and mapped to the code that switches the operating mode of the control? Here is the code that creates the keymap:

```
public void setKeymap(Keymap map) {
    if (map == null) {
        super.setKeymap(null);
        sharedKeymap = null;
        return;
    }

    if (getKeymap() == null) {
        if (sharedKeymap == null) {
            // Switch keymaps. Add extra bindings.
            removeKeymap(keymapName);
            sharedKeymap = addKeymap(keymapName, map);
            loadKeymap(sharedKeymap, bindings, defaultActions);
        }
        map = sharedKeymap;
    }
    super.setKeymap(map);
}
```

The extra key binding is added by the `loadKeymap` call. When this method is invoked, the new keymap will not have any bindings of its own, and will inherit the bindings of `JTextField` (because the argument to this method, `map`, will be the keymap being installed for `JTextField` and the new map is created with this map as its resolving parent). The `loadKeymap` method creates a keymap entry for each item in the `bindings` array mapping the `KeyStroke` in each entry to the corresponding `Action` in `defaultActions`, using the `Action` name to provide the linkage. Here is how `bindings` and `defaultActions` are defined:

```
public static final String toggleOverwriteAction =
                            "toggle-overwrite";

protected static JTextComponent.KeyBinding[] bindings = {
    new JTextComponent.KeyBinding(
        KeyStroke.getKeyStroke(KeyEvent.VK_INSERT, 0),
                            toggleOverwriteAction)
};

protected static final Action[] defaultActions = {
                            new ToggleOverwriteAction()
};
```

Both arrays contain just one entry. The bindings entry maps the INSERT key (with no modifier keys pressed) to an Action called "toggle-over-write," while the defaultActions array contains a reference to a single Action implemented in the class ToggleOverwriteAction. Actions on text components are always implemented by extending the abstract class Text-Action, which is derived from the Swing AbstractAction class. Here is how ToggleOverwriteAction is implemented:

```
public static class ToggleOverwriteAction extends TextAction
{
    ToggleOverwriteAction() {
        super(toggleOverwriteAction);
    }

    public void actionPerformed(ActionEvent evt) {
        OverwritableTextField.setOverwriting(
            !OverwritableTextField.isOverwriting());
        JTextComponent target = getFocusedComponent();
        if (target instanceof OverwritableTextField) {
            OverwritableTextField field =
                            (OverwritableTextField)target;
            field.selectCaret();
        }
    }
}
```

The constructor gives the Action a name—in this case, the Action will be called "toggle-overwrite"; as noted above, this name connects this Action to the key binding for the INSERT key, so the loadKeymap method will arrange for the actionPerformed method of this object to be invoked if the

INSERT key is pressed when the keyboard focus is directed to any `Overwrit-`
`ableTextField` that has the keymap created earlier.

Core Note

If you are curious about how this mapping works, here are the details. All
`Keymaps` *returned by* `addKeymap` *are instances of the inner class*
`JTextComponent.DefaultKeymap`, *which contains a* `Hashtable`
that is initially empty. When `loadKeymap` *is called, it takes the*
`Action` *name from a* `bindings` *entry and looks for the* `Action` *in the*
`defaultActions` *array with that name, which will locate the ref-*
erence to the single `ToggleOverwriteAction` *object held in the*
`defaultActions` *array. It then creates an entry in the* `Hashtable`
with the `KeyStroke` *from the* `bindings` *entry as the key and the*
`ToggleOverwriteAction` *reference as the data stored under*
that key. Later, when the `INSERT` *key is pressed in an*
`OverwritableTextField`, *the* `processComponentKeyEvent`
method builds the corresponding `KeyStroke` *object and uses it to access*
the `Hashtable` *in the keymap. Because two* `KeyStrokes` *are equal if*
the keys are the same and the modifiers are the same, this will find the
`ToggleOverwriteAction` *object. The* `Action` *is then performed by*
invoking that object's `actionPerformed` *method.*

The last piece of the puzzle is how to implement the `actionPerformed`
method. This method has to do everything necessary to switch all the `Over-`
`writableTextFields` between insert and overwrite modes. Because this
state is held as a static member, changing it simply entails using the static
method `isOverwriting` to get the current setting as `true` or `false` (in
which `true` represents overwrite mode and `false` insert mode), flipping it
and writing it back with `setOverwriting`. This simple operation changes the
state for all instances of the control, which read the state from the static
member `overwriting` when necessary.

This is not quite all that the `actionPerformed` method does, however.
The rest of the code is responsible for switching the caret between the shape
used when the text field is in insert mode and an alternative used to indicate
that overwriting is selected. This aspect of the `actionPerformed` method is
discussed in the next section.

Switching the Cursor

To provide a different caret for insert and overwrite modes, you need to do the following:

1. Allow two different caret objects to be configured.
2. Set the correct caret for the current mode and switch the caret when the mode changes.
3. Provide the implementation of a custom caret, at least for the overwrite case.

The first of these is easy to provide: `OverwritableTextField` inherits the `setCaret` method from `JTextComponent`. This method will be called (from the `JTextField` UI class for the active look-and-feel) when the object is constructed to install the usual single-line caret that you see in all the Swing text components. This caret will continue to be used when the control is in overwrite mode. As you can see from Listing 1-14, the `setCaret` method is overridden to store a reference to this caret in the instance variable `insertCaret`. This is necessary because a different caret will be installed when the mode is switched and it will be necessary to restore the original one when the control is reverted to insert mode. To configure a new caret for use in overwrite mode, the `setOverwriteCaret` method is provided. This method just stores the caret in the instance variable `overwriteCaret` for later use.

To select a particular caret, the `setCaret` method of `JTextComponent` is invoked. When should this method be called? There are two occasions when it is necessary to install a caret:

- When the control is created, the caret appropriate for the initial mode should be installed.
- When the mode is changed, the old caret should be removed and the new one activated.

The initial caret is installed at the end of the `OverwritableTextField` constructor, based on the setting of the `overwrite` flag. The caret installed is either the standard one installed from the look-and-feel class, or the overwrite caret. Because the overwrite caret cannot be customized before the constructor completes, a default overwrite caret, the implementation of which you'll see shortly, is used if the text field starts in overwrite mode (which is the default).

Core Note

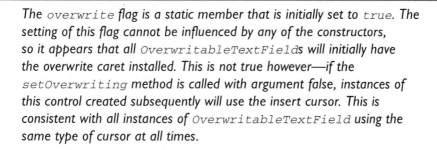

The `overwrite` *flag is a static member that is initially set to* `true`*. The setting of this flag cannot be influenced by any of the constructors, so it appears that all* `OverwritableTextField`*s will initially have the overwrite caret installed. This is not true however—if the* `setOverwriting` *method is called with argument false, instances of this control created subsequently will use the insert cursor. This is consistent with all instances of* `OverwritableTextField` *using the same type of cursor at all times.*

Handling the change of mode from insert to overwriting and vice versa is more difficult. This happens when the user presses the INSERT key when the focus is directed at one of the (possibly many) OverwritableTextFields in the application. Obviously, it is simple enough to change the caret of the OverwritableTextField that receives the INSERT key—you'll see the code that does this in the actionPerformed method of the keymap's ToggleOverwriteAction, shown above. When this action is triggered, there is no information available within the event that indicates to the actionPerformed method which control was the target of the action. However, it needs this information in order to change its caret. This is a common problem for all actions activated from a keymap and it is solved by code in JTextComponent that remembers which is the active text component, defined as the text component that currently has the input focus. JTextComponent tracks all focus events for all text components and remembers which text component last received the focus. The static getFocusedComponent method can be used to get a reference to the active component. Having obtained this reference, the actionPerformed method of the ToggleOverwriteAction switches the caret by calling the selectCaret method of the currently active OverwritableTextField, if the current text field is indeed an OverwritableTextField.

Core Note

Under normal circumstances, when the `ToggleOverwriteAction` *is activated, the active text component should be an* `OverwritableTextField`*. This will not be the case, however, if a programmer incorrectly bound this action in the keymap of a different text component. The explicit test in the* `actionPerformed` *method avoids a* `ClassCastException` *that would otherwise occur if this mistake were made.*

The `selectCaret` method chooses the appropriate caret for the component's operating mode. If this differs from the caret currently installed, the current one is replaced by the new one. Care is needed when installing a new caret in case there is currently a selection within the text field. When you install a caret using the `JTextComponent` `setCaret` method, it is positioned at the start of the text field and any existing selection is cleared. This is not user-friendly; The caret should remain in its current location and any existing selection should be preserved. To arrange for this, the current mark and dot positions are saved and then restored using the `setDot` and `moveDot` method. The first of these re-establishes the original mark, while the second resets the original dot position and, by moving the caret away from the mark, recreates the selection. This also works if there was no selection, because in this case the mark and dot positions would have been the same.

It is simple, then, to deal with changing the caret of the active `Overwritable-TextField`, because it is directly involved in the mode-switching operation. However, it is also necessary to do the same for all of the other `OverwritableTextFields`. One way to achieve this would be to keep track of all such objects and process all of them during a mode switch. However, this would be time-consuming and inefficient if a large number of these objects were in use.

There is, in fact, a better way to handle this. A text component's caret appears only when it has the focus and, furthermore, the only caret that can be used is the one in the focused text component. Therefore, it is possible to delay selecting the correct caret for an `OverwritableTextField` until it actually gets the focus. At this point, the `selectCaret` method can be called and if the caret that corresponds to the value of the `overwrite` attribute is not the same as the currently selected caret, the new one will be installed. With this approach, when the mode is switched, only those `Overwritable-TextFields` that are used after the switch will actually have their caret changed. To make this possible, `OverwritableTextField` overrides the `processFocusEvent` method of `Component` and calls `selectCaret` when it gains the focus, as you can see in Listing 1-14.

Implementing a Custom Caret

The last piece of the `OverwritableTextField` is the custom caret that will be used when the control is in overwrite mode. In this section, you'll see how the overwrite caret that the control installs by default is implemented. Because this caret can be changed using the `setOverwriteCaret` method, you can use the same mechanism used here to create your own custom overwrite caret to replace the default one.

Before looking at the implementation of the caret, let's see how it works. If you type the following command

```
java AdvancedSwing.Chapter1.OverwritableTextField
```

you'll see a window that contains two `OverwritableTextField`s stacked one above the other, as shown in Figure 1-15. When the window first appears, the upper text field, which has the focus, has the overwrite caret selected. You can see that it is not the same as the single-line insert caret—it looks like a small black blob. If you type a few characters into the text field, the caret moves to the right, staying ahead of the text. Now move the caret to the left by a few characters using the mouse or the arrow keys and you'll see that, as it moves over the text, the caret blob surrounds the character that it is placed over and the color of that character changes to contrast with that of the caret (see Figure 1-15). You'll also notice that the width of the caret adjusts automatically to match the width of the character that it is placed over.

Figure 1-15   A text field with a custom caret.

Next, with the caret over some text, type a few more characters. Now you'll see that the new text overwrites the existing text instead of being inserted to the left of the caret and that the caret moves so that it is positioned over the next character to be replaced. If you want to contrast this with the behavior of the usual insert caret, press the INSERT key and you'll find that the caret changes and that the text field is now in insert mode, as you can verify by typing more characters. Press the INSERT key again to switch back to overwrite mode and notice that the caret becomes a blob again. With overwrite mode selected, press the TAB key and the caret will move to the second text field. Because all the `OverwritableTextField`s are always in the same mode, the caret in the second text field will also be the overwrite caret. To see that this is true, press INSERT again and the caret in the lower text field will switch back to insert mode; if you now press TAB, the focus moves to the upper text field, which will display an insert cursor.

Every caret implements the `Caret` interface, defined in the Swing text package. There is a concrete implementation of this interface in the class `DefaultCaret`, which provides the single-line caret that appears in all the standard text components. The simplest way to implement your own caret is to extend this class and override the two methods that deal with managing the cursor's on-screen appearance—the `paint` and `damage` methods.

When the caret moves, the region of the text component underneath its old location is repainted so that the caret disappears. The caret is then responsible for redrawing itself at its new location. To arrange for this to happen, `DefaultCaret` calls its own `damage` method, which is responsible for determining which part of the text component should be repainted to cause the cursor to appear and then calls the text component's `repaint` method to cause the painting operation to occur. The `damage` method is given a `Rectangle` that indicates the new position of the caret; because only the actual caret implementation knows its own shape, the width of this `Rectangle` will not correspond to the size of the caret itself—only the x and y and `height` members of the `Rectangle` object can be trusted—the `height` member reflects the height of the drawing area of the text field. When the text component is painted, the `paint` code in its UI class will notice that the damaged area includes the location occupied by the caret and will call the caret's `paint` method to have it draw itself. That's how the caret painting mechanism works. Now let's look at how this is implemented for the default overwrite caret used by the `OverwritableTextField`, shown in Listing 1-15.

Listing 1-15 A Custom Caret

```
package AdvancedSwing.Chapter1;

import javax.swing.text.*;
import javax.swing.plaf.*;
import java.awt.*;

public class OverwriteCaret extends DefaultCaret {
    protected synchronized void damage(Rectangle r) {
        if (r != null) {
            try {
                JTextComponent comp = getComponent();
                TextUI mapper = comp.getUI();
                Rectangle r2 = mapper.modelToView(comp,
                                            getDot() + 1);
                int width = r2.x - r.x;
                if (width == 0) {
                    width = MIN_WIDTH;
                }
```

Listing 1-15 A Custom Caret (continued)

```
                comp.repaint(r.x , r.y, width, r.height);
                // Swing 1.1 beta 2 compat
                this.x = r.x;
                this.y = r.y;
                this.width = width;
                this.height = r.height;
            } catch (BadLocationException e) {
            }
        }
    }

    public void paint(Graphics g) {
        if(isVisible()) {
            try {
                JTextComponent comp = getComponent();
                TextUI mapper = comp.getUI();
                Rectangle r1 = mapper.modelToView(comp,
                                                getDot());
                Rectangle r2 = mapper.modelToView(comp,
                                                getDot() + 1);
                g = g.create();
                g.setColor(comp.getForeground());
                g.setXORMode(comp.getBackground());
                int width = r2.x - r1.x;
                if (width == 0) {
                    width = MIN_WIDTH;
                }
                g.fillRect(r1.x, r1.y, width, r1.height);
                g.dispose();
            } catch (BadLocationException e) {
            }
        }
    }

    protected static final int MIN_WIDTH = 8;
}
```

The overwrite caret is a rectangular blob with two characteristics that determine how the `damage` and `paint` methods are implemented:

1. The width of the caret is variable and matches that of the character that it appears over.

2. Because the caret appears over the text instead of between the characters, it must be drawn in such a way that it contrasts with both the characters in the text field and its background.

The first point is very important for the `damage` method. Ideally, this method should arrange for a region of the text component the width of the cursor to be repainted. This means that the width of the character under the caret needs to be known for the `damage` method to do its job properly. The coordinates of the left side of the caret are passed to the `damage` method in its `Rectangle` argument. To compute the width, you need to know the coordinates of the next character. This can be done by using the text component UI class's `modelToView` method, as shown in Listing 1-15:

```
Rectangle r2 = mapper.modelToView(comp, getDot() + 1);
```

The `getDot` method returns the model offset of the character under the caret. Hence, `getDot() + 1` corresponds to the offset of the character after the cursor and the line above will store the coordinates of that character in the `Rectangle r2`. The rest of the damage method calculates the width of the area to be repainted. Notice that if the computed width is zero, the repaint width is set to 8 pixels. This ensures that an 8-pixel caret will be shown when the text component is empty and when the caret is at the extreme right end of the text component.

The `paint` method uses similar logic to recalculate the size and location of the caret block; because it isn't given the caret position as an argument, it calls `modelToView` twice to get the offsets of both sides of the caret. Once the bounds and location of the caret are known, the block is colored by using the `Graphics fillRect` method, filling it with the foreground color. The `Graphics` object is switched into XOR mode while filling the rectangle, so that the color of the text under the caret, which was drawn in the component's foreground color, is switched to that of the component's background to make it visible.

Summary

This chapter covers just about all you need to know about the basic Swing input fields, `JTextField` and `JTextArea`. Starting with a brief overview of the Swing text controls, we moved on to look at their basic architecture, which we'll make much use of in the next four chapters of this book. By exploiting the separation between the graphical user interface (GUI) component and the `Document` model that lies behind it, we were able to create several powerful custom components that offer facilities that you'll be able to use in real-world applications, including text fields that accept only a limited number of characters and the ability to help the user by providing a look-ahead feature that can minimize typing when there is a fixed set of possible acceptable values, as is often the case in form-based applications. Finally, we saw how to create a custom caret and use a keymap to change characteristics of a text component in response to key presses that are not passed to the `Document` model.

USING JTEXTPANE

Topics in this Chapter

- Attributes and Styles
- Style Contexts
- Paragraph and Character Attributes
- Displaying Icons and Attributes in `JTextPane`

Chapter 2

I n the last chapter, you saw how the text components store the text that they draw and how to subclass the `PlainDocument` class used by `JTextField` to implement various forms of input validation. `Plain-Document` is a very simple text model that is sufficient for a component that uses a single font and two colors, but the `Document` interface itself also allows you to associate attributes with arbitrary ranges of content within the model, a facility that can be exploited by using the `JTextPane` and `JEditorPane` controls.

In this chapter, you'll see exactly what the attributes that you can store in the model represent and how the `JTextPane` allows you to specify the attributes that should be associated with an arbitrary run of text. With this knowledge, you'll be prepared for the next chapter, which looks at the `View` classes that determine how the attributes themselves are interpreted and translate them into font, color, and positioning information as the text component is rendered onto the screen. The material in this chapter also forms the groundwork for Chapter 4, which covers `JEditorPane`, the most powerful Swing text component and the one that makes full use of the features that you'll see in this chapter.

Documents with Attributes

If you refer to the class hierarchy shown in Figure 1-1, you'll see that there are two controls, JEditorPane and JTextPane, which we didn't say much about in the previous chapter. JEditorPane is, in fact, a powerful editor that can be fitted with an arbitrary editor kit and a corresponding document class to enable you to view or edit documents that are represented in well-known or proprietary external formats, and that also contains colored text, text in multiple fonts, embedded images, and much more. The other control, JTextPane, is a subclass of JEditorPane that can be used to create multifont and multicolored areas of text under direct program control. Chapter 4 is devoted almost entirely to looking at the facilities provided by JEditorPane and at how you can use it to display Web documents encoded in HTML. JEditorPane and JTextPane rely on the same infrastructure of classes that represent the organization of text and the associated font and color changes that cannot be handled by the simpler text components. In this section, you'll see how the text attributes are specified, using JText-Pane as the host component.

Attributes, Styles, and Style Contexts

The simple PlainDocument class that you saw in the previous chapter is only capable of managing plain text. The more complex text components use a more sophisticated model that implements the StyledDocument interface. StyledDocument is a subinterface of Document that contains methods for manipulating attributes that control the way in which the text in the document is displayed. The Swing text package contains a concrete implementation of StyledDocument called DefaultStyledDocument that is used as the model for JTextPane and is also the base class from which more specific models, such as the HTMLDocument class that handles input in HTML format, can be created. To make full use of DefaultStyledDocument and JText-Pane, you need to understand how Swing represents and uses attributes.

Attributes, Attribute Sets, and Styles

In Swing, an attribute is simply a key with an associated value. Usually, the key is an object that contains a String that acts as a human-readable name for the attribute. The value can be an object of any type, but it is typically an object of a type that matches the aspect of the text component that the attribute relates to. For example, an attribute that controls color would naturally have a value of type `java.awt.Color`. Although in theory the name of an attribute and its value can both be of any type, there is a standard set of attributes that are all recognized by the Swing text components. These attributes, together with the type and meaning of their associated values, are listed in Table 2-1. Attributes that apply at the paragraph level are denoted `P` and character attributes `C`.

Table 2-1 Standard Text Component Attributes

Name	*Value Type*	*P/C*	*Meaning*
`Alignment`	`Integer`	`P`	Specifies the text alignment. The value is an `Integer` derived from one of the following int constants: `ALIGN_LEFT`, `ALIGN_RIGHT`, `ALIGN_CENTER`, `ALIGN_JUSTIFED`
`Background`	`Color`	`C`	The background color.
`BidiLevel`	`Integer`	`C`	Specifies the direction of bi-directional text.
`Bold`	`Boolean`	`C`	Specifies whether text is to be rendered in bold (value `true`).
`ComponentAttribute`	`Component`	`C`	A `Component` to be rendered inline with the text flow.
`ComposedTextAttribute`	`AttributedString`	`C`	Includes composed text in the text flow.

Table 2-1 Standard Text Component Attributes (continued)

Name	Value Type	P/C	Meaning
FirstLineIndent	Integer	P	The extra indent to be used for the first line of a paragraph, specified in points.
FontFamily	String	C	The name of a font family.
FontSize	Integer	C	The font size, in points.
Foreground	Color	C	The foreground color.
IconAttribute	Icon	C	An Icon to be included in the text flow.
Italic	Boolean	C	Specifies whether text is to be rendered in italics (value true).
LeftIndent	Integer	P	The size of the left paragraph indent, in points.
LineSpacing	Integer	P	The amount of extra vertical space to allocate between text lines.
RightIndent	Integer	P	The size of the right paragraph indent, in points.
SpaceAbove	Integer	P	The space to leave above a paragraph, in points.

Table 2-1 Standard Text Component Attributes (continued)			
Name	*Value Type*	*P/C*	*Meaning*
SpaceBelow	Integer	P	The space to leave below a paragraph, in points.
StrikeThrough	Boolean	C	Causes a line to be drawn through the text, when true.
Subscript	Boolean	C	When true, tags the associated text as a subscript, rendering it in a smaller font and in subscript position.
Superscript	Boolean	C	When true, marks the text as a superscript, rendering it in a smaller font and in superscript position.
TabSet	TabSet	P	Specifies the tab positions for a range of text.
Underline	Boolean	C	When true, causes the text to be underlined.

Attribute Sets

Although there is a set of standard attributes, there is no single Swing class or interface that represents an attribute. Instead, attributes exist only as members of a collection in a class that implements the AttributeSet interface, which is defined as follows:

```
public interface AttributeSet {
    public int getAttributeCount();
    public Object getAttribute(Object key);
    public boolean isDefined(Object attrName);
    public boolean isEqual(AttributeSet attr);
```

```
public AttributeSet copyAttributes();
public Enumeration getAttributeNames();
public boolean containsAttribute(Object name,
                                 Object value);
public boolean containsAttributes(AttributeSet
                                  attributes);
public AttributeSet getResolveParent();
public interface FontAttribute {}
public interface ColorAttribute {}
public interface CharacterAttribute {}
public interface ParagraphAttribute {}
public static final Object NameAttribute;
public static final Object ResolveAttribute;
}
```

Attribute sets, like keymaps, are hierarchical—that is, every attribute set can have a resolving parent that can be searched for attributes if they are not found in the original set. This allows attribute sets to be built by taking an existing one and then applying local changes to it by creating a new set and assigning the original one as its resolving parent. The new attribute set would contain only the attributes whose values need to differ from those in the existing set (or which do not exist in the existing set) and does not replicate the complete attribute set. The `AttributeSet getResolveParent` method returns the resolving parent of a set of attributes.

You can get the value of an individual attribute using the `getAttribute` method. As you can see, this method takes the attribute's name as its argument and returns its value as an `Object`. To interpret the value, you have to cast it to an object of the correct type. For example, if `attrSet` is a reference to an `AttributeSet`, the following code gets the value of the foreground color attribute:

```
Color fgColor =
    (Color)attrSet.getAttribute(StyleConstants.Foreground);
```

If the attribute set does not contain the foreground color attribute, `null` is returned. This method looks first in the attribute set itself; if the attribute is not defined there, it looks next in the set's resolving parent. This process continues until the attribute is found or until an attribute set without a resolving parent is reached. Note, however, that not all the methods in the `AttributeSet` interface look in both the attribute set and its resolving ancestors. Specifically, the following methods look only in the attribute set itself:

- `getAttributeCount`
- `getAttributeNames`
- `isDefined`
- `isEqual`

The `getAttributeCount` method counts only the locally defined attributes, while `getAttributeNames` returns an `Enumeration` of the names of those same attributes. The `isDefined` method returns `true` if the given attribute is defined in the attribute set itself (that is, it would not be necessary to search the resolving parent to find a value for the attribute). Because this does not involve the resolving parent, it is possible for `isDefined` to return `false` and `getAttribute` to return a non-`null` value for the same attribute. Finally, `isEqual` returns `true` if the number of attributes in the set being addressed is the same as the number in the set given as the argument *and* the attributes in both sets have the same names and the same values.

The `copyAttributes` method returns another attribute set that has the same values as the target set, but whose values will not change. In fact, it is possible for `copyAttributes` to return the same attribute set as it was given, if that attribute set is immutable—you'll see shortly what constitutes a mutable attribute set. The `containsAttribute` method returns `true` if the attribute set (or any of its resolving parents) contains the named attribute and the attribute has the given value. Similarly, `containsAttributes` returns `true` if all the attributes in the `AttributeSet` given as its argument are present in the target attribute set and have the same values. An important point to note about this is that the list of attributes to be checked is obtained by invoking `getAttributeNames` on the set given as the argument, so the attributes in the resolving parent of that set are not considered. The resolving parent of the attribute set to which `containsAttributes` is applied is used, however, to retrieve values for comparison.

The `AttributeSet` interface defines two attributes of its own, which are used internally. `NameAttribute` is the name of an attribute, the value of which is considered to be the name of the set of attributes. You'll see how this feature is used in the discussion of styles later in this chapter. `Resolve-Attribute` stores the resolving parent of the attribute set. The fact that these attributes exist should, however, be treated as an implementation detail because there are more portable ways to obtain the same information. For example, the resolving parent of an attribute set can be obtained using the `getResolveParent` method; that is, both

```
(AttributeSet)attr.getAttribute(
    AttributeSet.ResolveAttribute)
```

and the preferred alternative

```
attr.getResolveParent()
```

return the same value. `AttributeSets` with names are usually `Styles`, which have an explicit method to retrieve the name, as you'll see shortly.

AttributeSet also defines four nested interfaces that have no methods. These interfaces are markers that are used to tag the names of attributes that can be used in specific ways. For example, classes that represent the names of attributes that operate at the character level all implement the Character-Attribute interface. You'll see more about this in the discussion of the StyleConstants class later in this chapter.

Mutable Attribute Sets

The AttributeSet interface presents a read-only view of a set of attributes because there are no methods that allow you to create new attributes, remove attributes, or change the value of an existing attribute. The Mutable-AttributeSet interface is an extension of AttributeSet that allows you to change the content of the set or the values of individual attributes. Here is how it is defined:

```
public interface MutableAttributeSet extends AttributeSet {
    public void addAttribute(Object name, Object value);
    public void addAttributes(AttributeSet attributes);
    public void removeAttribute(Object name);
    public void removeAttributes(Enumeration names);
    public void removeAttributes(AttributeSet attributes);
    public void setResolveParent(AttributeSet parent);
}
```

The addAttribute method adds a single attribute to a MutableAttribute-Set with the special case that if the named attribute is already defined in the target set, its value is just changed to the new supplied value. Similarly, add-Attributes adds all the attributes from the AttributeSet given as the argument to the MutableAttributeSet to which it is applied. The remove-Attributes methods allow you to remove a collection of attributes that can be specified in three different ways. Finally, the setResolveParent method changes the resolving parent of a MutableAttributeSet. This operation is not present in the AttributeSet interface because it can have the effect of changing which attributes are defined, as well as possibly modifying the apparent values of attributes not defined locally in the attribute set itself.

Styles and StyleContexts

Although there is a complete implementation of the MutableAttributeSet interface in the SimpleAttributeSet class in the Swing text package, often you won't directly create objects that implement MutableAttributeSet. The most common way to get such an object is to use the StyleContext class to create a Style object. Style is yet another interface, derived from

`MutableAttributeSet`, that adds a couple of extra features of its own. The only implementation of `Style` in the text package is provided by the class `NamedStyle`, which is an inner class of `StyleContext`. Here is the definition of the `Style` interface:

```
public interface Style extends MutableAttributeSet {
    public String getName();
    public void addChangeListener(ChangeListener l);
    public void removeChangeListener(ChangeListener l);
}
```

`Style` adds to `MutableAttributeSet` the ability to associate a name with a set of attributes and to listen for changes to the attributes or their values. The addition of the `getName` method is really only a cosmetic touch, however, because `SimpleAttributeSet` defines the name of the attribute that holds the name and `MutableAttributeSet` allows you to set or read the name via the `addAttribute` and `getAttribute` methods; `getName` is just a convenience method that hides the underlying implementation.

The useful thing about a `Style` is that you can easily obtain a `Style` from an instance of the `StyleContext` class, and once you have one you can use it to control the way in which a text component's contents are rendered. Here are the public methods of the `StyleContext` class:

```
public StyleContext();
public AttributeSet addAttribute(AttributeSet old,
                                 name, value);
public AttributeSet addAttributes(AttributeSet old,
                                  AttributeSet attr);
public void addChangeListener(ChangeListener l);
public Style addStyle(String name, Style parent);
public Color getBackground(AttributeSet attr);
public static StyleContext getDefaultStyleContext();
public AttributeSet getEmptySet();
public Font getFont(AttributeSet attr);
public Font getFont(String family, int style, int size);
public FontMetrics getFontMetrics(Font f);
public Color getForeground(AttributeSet attr);
public static Object getStaticAttribute(Object key);
public static Object getStaticAttributeKey(Object key);
public Style getStyle(String nm);
public Enumeration getStyleNames();
public void readAttributes(ObjectInputStream in,
                           MutableAttributeSet a);
public static void readAttributeSet(ObjectInputStream in,
                                    MutableAttributeSet a);
public void reclaim(AttributeSet a);
```

```
public static void registerStaticAttributeKey(Object key);
public AttributeSet removeAttribute(AttributeSet old,
                                    Object name);
public AttributeSet removeAttributes(AttributeSet old,
                                     AttributeSet attrs);
public AttributeSet removeAttributes(AttributeSet old,
                                     Enumeration names);
public void removeChangeListener(ChangeListener l);
public void removeStyle(String nm);
public String toString();
public void writeAttributes(ObjectOutputStream out,
                            AttributeSet a);
public static void writeAttributeSet(ObjectOutputStream out,
                                     AttributeSet a);
```

StyleContext is essentially a repository for Styles. Let's look at the StyleContext methods that you'll use most often. The other methods are mainly for internal use and won't be discussed here.

You can create a new Style using the StyleContext addStyle method, passing a name to be associated with the Style and a resolving parent, either of which can be null. If you pass a null name, then the returned Style is anonymous and can't be found using the getStyle method. If you supply a null resolving parent, the new attribute set will not have a resolving parent from which to fetch attributes that it does not define itself. The name should be unique within the StyleContext that was used to create the Style; if you use the same name a second time, the new Style replaces the original. When a Style is created, it has its name and resolving parent attributes set from the parameters passed to addStyle. If either (or both) of these parameters was null, the corresponding attribute will not be set. As a result, a newly created Style will have zero, one, or two initial attributes in addition, of course, to the attributes that it inherits from its resolving parent, if it has one.

Given a name, you can find the corresponding Style using the getStyle method (which returns null if there is no Style with the given name in the StyleContext) and you can list the names of all the Styles in the context that have non-null names using getStyleNames. Finally, you can delete a Style, by name, using removeStyle.

The getBackground, getForeground, and the two getFont methods are useful for translating attributes into Abstract Window Toolkit (AWT) resources without having to understand how the attributes are implemented. These methods can also be overridden to change the way in which these same attributes are interpreted. As an example, consider this variant of the getFont method:

```
public Font getFont(AttributeSet attr);
```

The default implementation of this method looks for font characteristics (that is, the font family name, the font size, and the font type) in the given `AttributeSet` and returns a `Font` that has these characteristics. By overriding this method, you can arrange for certain changes to be made to the returned `Font` to suit the style of the particular type of document with which your `StyleContext` is associated. You might use this, for example, to provide a rough-and-ready way to view a document that doesn't show bold or italic font or reflect changes to the font size, by arranging for the `getFont` method to always return the same plain font with a fixed font size. This is not, however, the only reason for providing these methods in the `StyleContext`. Both variants of the `getFont` method provide a potential performance improvement by caching `Fonts`, allowing a speedy lookup based on the font's attributes.

Inserting Text into a `JTextPane`

Up to this point, the discussion of attributes and `Styles` has been a little abstract. In this section, you'll see how `Styles` can be used to change the way in which a text component renders its content. The first example that you'll see demonstrates how to apply a `Style` to create a heading that stands out from its associated text. To keep things simple, the code in this example will be good enough to create the desired effect, but it won't show you the most effective solution to this particular problem. In the second example, we'll make several improvements and introduce some new concepts that help when you need to create more structured documents or use the same `Styles` in more than one text component within an application.

Creating StyleContexts

As you know, to create a `Style`, you need a `StyleContext`. There are two ways to create a `StyleContext` that can be used with a `JTextPane`. The simplest way to achieve this is just to create a `JTextPane`:

```
JTextPane pane = new JTextPane();
```

When you create a `JTextPane`, it is initialized with a `DefaultStyledDocument`, which has its own `StyleContext`. Note that there is no way to get a reference to the `StyleContext` from a `DefaultStyledDocument`, so when you directly create the `JTextPane`, you cannot use the `StyleContext` `addStyle` method to add `Styles` to it. However, `JTextPane` has a convenience method that allows you to indirectly manipulate the underlying

`StyleContext` without having an explicit reference to it, as does `Default-StyledDocument`. Hence, you can create a `Style` called `MyStyle` using either the `JTextPane` `addStyle` method:

```
Style myStyle = pane.addStyle("MyStyle", null);
```

or the `addStyle` method of `DefaultStyledDocument`:

```
DefaultStyledDocument doc = pane.getStyledDocument();
Style myStyle = doc.addStyle("MyStyle", null);
```

If you need a reference to the `StyleContext`, you will need to explicitly create it, associate it with a `DefaultStyledDocument`, and then create a `JTextPane` that uses the `DefaultStyledDocument`:

```
StyleContext sc = new StyleContext();
DefaultStyledDocument doc = new DefaultStyledDocument(sc);
JTextPane pane = new JTextPane(doc);
```

When you use this approach, you can, if you want, arrange to share the same `StyleContext` between several `DefaultStyledDocuments`:

```
StyleContext sc = new StyleContext();
JTextPane pane1 = new JTextPane(
                        new DefaultStyledDocument(sc));
JTextPane pane2 = new JTextPane(
                        new DefaultStyledDocument(sc));
```

The context in this case is shared between the two text panes, so that `Styles` added to it are available in both `DefaultStyledDocuments` and in both text panes. If you simply create a `JTextPane` using its default constructor, however, the `DefaultStyledDocument` that comes with it has its own, private `StyleContext` that is not shared.

Adding Styles to a StyleContext

Having created a `StyleContext`, your next step is to add some `Styles` to it. In the first example in this section, the intention is to make a heading stand out from its associated text. To do this, we'll use a `Style` that produces red text in a bold, 16-point Serif font. Creating the `Style` is a simple matter. Here's the code:

```
Style heading2Style = sc.addStyle("Heading2", null);
```

This line creates a new `Style` with the name "Heading2" with no resolving parent. At this point, the new `Style` does not contain any attributes that would affect any text that it might later be applied to. In fact, all it contains is an attribute recording its name. To achieve the font and color changes needed to produce the desired effects, the following attributes must be added (refer to Table 2-1 for a complete list of the standard attributes):

Foreground color:	Red
Font Size:	16
Font Family:	Serif
Bold:	True

Style inherits the `addAttribute` method from its super-interface `MutableAttributeSet`. This method can be used to install the required attributes, as follows:

```
heading2Style.addAttribute(StyleConstants.Foreground,
                           Color.red);
heading2Style.addAttribute(StyleConstants.FontSize,
                           new Integer(16));
heading2Style.addAttribute(StyleConstants.FontFamily,
                           "serif");
heading2Style.addAttribute(StyleConstants.Bold,
                           new Boolean(true));
```

At this point, the text pane has a document without any content. The last step is to add the text to the model and then apply the `Style` to the heading. As you'll see in the next section, there are several ways to add text and attributes to a `JTextPane`. For now, we'll take the simplest possible approach and add the text and attributes separately. The easiest way to install the text is to use the `insertString` method of the underlying `DefaultStyledDocument`, as you saw in the previous chapter:

```
doc.insertString(0, text, null);
```

The attributes are also added directly to the model, this time using the `setParagraphAttributes` method of `DefaultStyledDocument`, which is defined as follows:

```
public void setParagraphAttributes(int offset, int length,
                                   AttributeSet attr,
                                   boolean replace);
```

Here's the code that applies the `Style` to the heading:

```
doc.setParagraphAttributes(0, 1, heading2Style, false);
```

You'll see exactly what the arguments to this method mean in the next section. The complete listing of this example is shown in Listing 2-1 and produces the result shown in Figure 2-1. You can try this example by typing the command:

```
java AdvancedSwing.Chapter2.StylesExample1
```

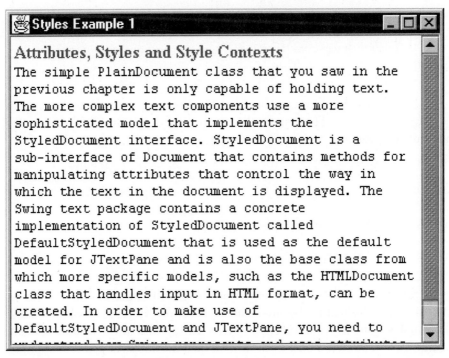

Figure 2–1   Using a style to highlight a text heading.

Listing 2-1 Using a Style

```
package AdvancedSwing.Chapter2;

import javax.swing.*;
import javax.swing.text.*;
import java.awt.*;

public class StylesExample1 {
    public static void main(String[] args) {
        JFrame f = new JFrame("Styles Example 1");

        // Create the StyleContext, the document and the pane
        StyleContext sc = new StyleContext();
```

Listing 2-1 Using a Style (continued)

```java
final DefaultStyledDocument doc =
                    new DefaultStyledDocument(sc);
JTextPane pane = new JTextPane(doc);

// Create and add the style
final Style heading2Style = sc.addStyle("Heading2",
                                    null);
heading2Style.addAttribute(StyleConstants.Foreground,
                        Color.red);
heading2Style.addAttribute(StyleConstants.FontSize,
                        new Integer(16));
heading2Style.addAttribute(StyleConstants.FontFamily,
                        "serif");
heading2Style.addAttribute(StyleConstants.Bold,
                        new Boolean(true));

try {
    SwingUtilities.invokeAndWait(new Runnable() {
        public void run() {
            try {
                // Add the text to the document
                doc.insertString(0, text, null);
                // Finally, apply the style to the heading
                doc.setParagraphAttributes(0, 1,
                        heading2Style, false);
            } catch (BadLocationException e) {
            }
        }
    });
} catch (Exception e) {
    System.out.println("Exception when
                    constructing document: " + e);
    System.exit(1);
}

f.getContentPane().add(new JScrollPane(pane));
f.setSize(400, 300);
f.setVisible(true);
}
```

Listing 2-1 Using a Style (continued)

```
public static final String text =
        "Attributes, Styles and Style Contexts\n" +
        "The simple PlainDocument class that you
            saw in the previous " +
        "chapter is only capable of holding text.
            The more complex text " +
        "components use a more sophisticated model
            that implements the " +
        "StyledDocument interface. StyledDocument is
            a sub-interface of " +
        "Document that contains methods for
            manipulating attributes that " +
        "control the way in which the text in the
            document is displayed. " +
        "The Swing text package contains a concrete
            implementation of " +
        "StyledDocument called DefaultStyledDocument
            that is used as the " +
        "default model for JTextPane and is also the
            base class from which " +
        "more specific models, such as the HTMLDocument
            class that handles " +
        "input in HTML format, can be created. In order
            to make use of " +
        "DefaultStyledDocument and JTextPane, you need
            to understand how " +
        "Swing represents and uses attributes.\n";
}
```

Notice that the code that installs the text and the attributes is not executed directly by the `main` method; instead, it is run on the event thread. Swing components are not thread-safe and, as a result, you should update them only from the AWT event thread, by arranging for all code that accesses them to be run as the result of an event from the user interface or, as here, using the `SwingUtilities invokeAndWait` method. However, if you look at the `javadoc` pages for `AbstractDocument` and `DefaultStyledDocument`, you'll see that they say that both `insertString` and `setParagraphAttributes` are thread-safe. So why use `invokeAndWait` here?

Strictly speaking, you don't need to go to all that trouble in this simple case. However, it is as well to be careful when updating the text components outside the event thread, because even though some methods are marked as thread-safe, they don't always do what you might expect unless you invoke them from the event thread. In particular, operations that implicitly move the caret don't always work unless you call them from the event thread. For example, if you are using the `replaceSelection` method of `JTextCompo-nent` to add several pieces of text one after the other, you only get the correct effect if you invoke it from the event thread, because only then does it move the insertion point to the end of the text you last inserted, which is where it would need to be to add the next chunk. If the caret were not moved, the text would be inserted into the document in the wrong order. To avoid unexpected problems of this kind, it is good practice to use the event thread at all times and the appearance of the extra code in Listing 2-1 is intended to remind you of this.

Type-Safe Attribute Handling with `StyleConstants`

When the attributes were added to the heading style in Listing 2-1, a set of name-value pairs were passed to the `addAttribute` method, which simply installed them in the `Style`. Because the `addAttribute` method views both the attribute name and its value as `Objects`, no checks are performed to verify that the value type matches that of the attribute. For example, the foreground color was set as follows:

```
heading2Style.addAttribute(StyleConstants.Foreground,
                           Color.red);
```

However, we could have incorrectly written the following:

```
heading2Style.addAttribute(StyleConstants.Foreground,
                           new Integer(6));
```

Although this looks nonsensical, the compiler won't detect any problem with this statement and it won't fail when it is executed either. If you do this, however, you *will* encounter an exception, but not until the text component is made visible. At this point, the view objects are created and the one that will render the heading will try to get its foreground color from its associated attributes, using the `StyleContext getForeground` method. This method looks for the `StyleConstants.Foreground` attribute in the attribute set that it is given and casts the `Object` that it gets back to a `Color`. Of course, because the actual value stored was of type `Integer`, this results in a `Class-CastException`.

To remove the possibility of errors like this, you can make use of a set of static convenience methods defined by the `StyleConstants` class that make it possible to apply type-checking to the code that sets the predefined attributes at compilation time. `StyleConstants` also has a similar collection of methods that retrieve the same attributes. The complete set of these methods is shown in Table 2-2.

Table 2-2 Convenience Methods to Set and Retrieve Attributes

```
public static int getBidiLevel(AttributeSet a);

public static void setBidiLevel(MutableAttributeSet a, int o)

public static Component getComponent(AttributeSet a)

public static void setComponent(MutableAttributeSet a,
                                Component c)

public static Icon getIcon(AttributeSet a)

public static void setIcon(MutableAttributeSet a, Icon c)

public static String getFontFamily(AttributeSet a)

public static void setFontFamily(MutableAttributeSet a,
                                 String family)

public static int getFontSize(AttributeSet a)

public static void setFontSize(MutableAttributeSet a, int s)

public static boolean isBold(AttributeSet a)

public static void setBold(MutableAttributeSet a, boolean b)

public static boolean isItalic(AttributeSet a)

public static void setItalic(MutableAttributeSet a, boolean b)

public static boolean isUnderline(AttributeSet a)

public static void setUnderline(MutableAttributeSet a,
                                boolean b)

public static boolean isStrikeThrough(AttributeSet a)

public static void setStrikeThrough(MutableAttributeSet a,
                                    boolean b)

public static boolean isSuperscript(AttributeSet a)

public static void setSuperscript(MutableAttributeSet a,
                                  boolean b)

public static boolean isSubscript(AttributeSet a)
```

Table 2-2 Convenience Methods to Set and Retrieve Attributes (continued)

```
public static void setSubscript(MutableAttributeSet a,
                                boolean b)

public static Color getForeground(AttributeSet a)

public static void setForeground(MutableAttributeSet a,
                                 Color fg)

public static Color getBackground(AttributeSet a)

public static void setBackground(MutableAttributeSet a,
                                 Color fg)

public static float getFirstLineIndent(AttributeSet a)

public static void setFirstLineIndent(MutableAttributeSet a,
                                      float i)

public static float getRightIndent(AttributeSet a)

public static void setRightIndent(MutableAttributeSet a,
                                  float i)

public static float getLeftIndent(AttributeSet a)

public static void setLeftIndent(MutableAttributeSet a,
                                 float i)

public static float getLineSpacing(AttributeSet a)

public static void setLineSpacing(MutableAttributeSet a,
                                  float i)

public static float getSpaceAbove(AttributeSet a)

public static void setSpaceAbove(MutableAttributeSet a,
                                 float i)

public static float getSpaceBelow(AttributeSet a)

public static void setSpaceBelow(MutableAttributeSet a,
                                 float i)

public static int getAlignment(AttributeSet a)

public static void setAlignment(MutableAttributeSet a,
                                int align)

public static TabSet getTabSet(AttributeSet a)

public static void setTabSet(MutableAttributeSet a,
                             TabSet tabs)
```

As well as enforcing compile-time type checking, these methods also make it simpler to set and retrieve attributes whose values can be expressed using primitive types by allowing you to supply the value as a primitive rather than by creating a wrapper object. For example, the `FontSize` attribute requires an attribute of type `Integer`, as was shown in Listing 2-1:

```
heading2Style.addAttribute(StyleConstants.FontSize,
                        new Integer(16));
```

However, the corresponding `StyleConstants` method allows you to use an `int` instead:

```
public static void setFontSize(MutableAttributeSet a, int s)
```

and, similarly, the `getFontSize` method returns an `int` instead of an `Integer`. Finally, the example that we saw at the start of this section, namely,

```
heading2Style.addAttribute(StyleConstants.Foreground,
                        Color.red);
```

could be more safely written like this:

```
StyleConstants.setForeground(heading2Style, Color.red);
```

Another advantage you get by using these methods is that the accessors all return a default value if the attribute is not actually defined in the attribute set. The defaults are shown in Table 2-3. If you used the `AttributeSet` `getAttribute` method instead, you would have to check whether the return value is `null` and supply your own default when it is.

Instead of directly setting the attributes in the heading style used in Listing 2-1, it is better to use the `StyleConstants` convenience methods from Table 2-2. Here is how the heading style would be created using these methods:

```
final Style heading2Style = sc.addStyle("Heading2", null);
StyleConstants.setForeground(heading2Style, Color.red);
StyleConstants.setFontSize(heading2Style, 16);
StyleConstants.setFontFamily(heading2Style, "serif");
StyleConstants.setBold(heading2Style, true);
```

If you look at the source code for the `StyleConstants` class, you'll see another feature of this class that could be used to provide compile-time and run-time type safety when using attributes. The constant value `StyleConstants.Foreground`, which represents the name of the foreground color attribute, (see Table 2-1) is defined as follows:

```
public static final Object Foreground =
                CharacterConstants.Foreground;
```

Table 2-3 Default Attribute Values	
Bidi Level	0
Component	null
Icon	null
FontFamily	"monospaced"
FontSize	12
Bold	false
Italic	false
Underline	false
StrikeThrough	false
Superscript	false
Subscript	false
Foreground	Color.black
Background	Color.black
FirstLineIndent	0
RightIndent	0
LeftIndent	0
LineSpacing	0
SpaceAbove	0
SpaceBelow	0
Alignment	ALIGN_LEFT
TabSet	null

The value on the right side of this expression is another constant, declared by `CharacterConstants`, an inner class of `StyleConstants`. Here is how this constant is defined:

```
public static class ColorConstants implements
    AttributeSet.ColorAttribute,
    AttributeSet.CharacterAttribute {
```

```
    public static final Object Foreground =
                        new ColorConstants("foreground");

    // Definitions of other values omitted
}
```

From this code extract, you can see that `ColorConstants.Foreground` is an instance of the `ColorConstants` class and, therefore, implements the `AttributeSet.ColorAttribute` interface.

Because `StyleConstants.Foreground` is initialized with this value, it also implements that interface. The same is true of the value `StyleConstants.Background`. Because of this, it is possible to check at runtime whether a proposed attribute name is valid in a context that expects a color attribute using code like this:

```
Object attributeName = StyleConstants.Foreground;
    // Initialize
if (attributeName instanceof AttributeSet.ColorAttribute) {
    // It is valid
else {
    // Not a color attribute
}
```

If you examine the source code for the `StyleConstants` class, you'll find that all the attributes listed in Table 2-1 are declared using similar constructions, so they all implement one or more of the four marker interfaces in the `AttributeSet` interface that you saw earlier in this chapter.

Paragraph Attributes, Character Attributes, and Logical Styles

In the example you have just seen, attributes were applied to the header text using the `setParagraphAttributes` method of `DefaultStyledDocument`. This is one of three methods in the `StyledDocument` interface that allow you to apply attributes:

```
public void setLogicalStyle(int offset, AttributeSet attrs);
public void setParagraphAttributes(int offset, int length,
                    AttributeSet attrs, boolean replace);
public void setCharacterAttributes(int offset, int length,
                    AttributeSet attrs,boolean replace);
```

Each of these methods supplies a start offset and a new set of attributes. The last two also have a length argument and a replace flag. The interpretation of the offset and length arguments depend on the method being used.

Both `setLogicalStyle` and `setParagraphAttributes` work at the paragraph level, where a paragraph is defined as a range of text terminated by a newline character. In the example shown in Listing 2-1, the heading represents one paragraph and the rest of the text is another. When you invoke `setLogicalStyle`, the operation applies to the whole of the paragraph that contains the specified offset. In the case of `setParagraphAttributes`, the new attributes are applied to the paragraph that contains the initial offset, the paragraph at offset (`offset + length - 1`) and to every paragraph in between. To apply the `Heading2` style to the heading alone, the `setParagraphAttributes` call in Listing 2-1 specifies a start offset of 0 and a length of 1. Even though the length is given as 1 character, the `Heading2` style is applied to the whole paragraph, not just its first character.

By contrast, `setCharacterAttributes` affects only the *exact* range of offsets specified by its arguments. In the case of Listing 2-1, had the `setParagraphAttributes` call been replaced by `setCharacterAttributes` with the same arguments, only the first character of the heading would have been affected.

The `replace` flag indicates whether the supplied attributes should be merged with any existing attributes (when `false`) or should completely replace them (when `true`). If, for example, a paragraph already has attributes that specify, say yellow foreground and underlining on, and `setParagraphAttributes` is invoked with a `Style` that specifies a red foreground and with `replace` set to `false`, the paragraph attributes will change to underlining on and red foreground. If, on the other hand, `replace` were true, the underlining and foreground attributes would be removed and then the new foreground attributes applied, resulting in red text with no underlining.

Attribute Hierarchy

The attribute applied by `setLogicalStyle`, `setParagraphAttributes`, and `setCharacterAttributes` form a resolving hierarchy. A logical style is intended to be a broad-brush set of attributes that might apply to an entire document. For example, you might want every paragraph to have the same left and right margins and the same default font. To achieve this, you would set a logical style on the document before adding any text to it. As text is added, new paragraphs inherit the logical style of the preceding paragraph, so these attributes would be propagated through the entire document.

Having set the logical style, you can use `setParagraphAttributes` to add extra attributes to a particular paragraph or to a group of paragraphs, to augment or override the logical style settings for these paragraphs. Finally, you can change the formatting for character ranges within a paragraph (or even across paragraph boundaries) using the `setCharacterAttributes` method.

The hierarchical nature of styles is illustrated by the next example, which improves upon the one shown in Listing 2-1. Here, we're going to use a logical style to set global attributes, a paragraph style to change the way in which the heading is rendered, and character attributes to affect the formatting of individual words.

If you look back at Figure 2-1, you'll see that the text starts at the left side of the control and ends at the right edge (at least when word wrapping doesn't force it to end earlier). In this example, a left and right margin are going to be added to introduce some space between the text and the sides of the control. Also, the first line of the paragraph will have extra indentation. These attributes can be thought of as a style that applies to the whole document, not just to the first non-heading paragraph, so it will be applied as a logical style. We'll also take the opportunity to set the font size, style, and family for the whole document in the logical style.

Core Note

You'll see later that there is more than one way to control the default font and the foreground color for those parts of a document that don't have attributes that explicitly specify them. For now, we'll set them in the logical style.

The heading, as in the first example, will be in a larger, bold font and will be drawn in red. In this example, it will also be arranged so that it starts a little to the left of the text, but not quite up against the left side of the control. This entails overriding the logical style, which would move the heading to the right by the amount of the left margin plus the extra first-line indent, because the heading is a paragraph to which the document's logical style applies. This change will, however, be effective only for the heading.

Finally, the text font in Listing 2-1 was a 12-point monospaced font that was selected by default, because no explicit attributes were applied to the text. In this example, we're going to use a 12-point proportional font as the default throughout the document (except in the heading), but we're also going to highlight the words that correspond to Swing class names by using the original monospaced font for those words. To make them stand out even more, they'll also be drawn in green. Because this extra formatting applies to very specific ranges of text, it will be applied as character attributes. The details can be found in Listing 2-2 and the result you can see for yourself using the command

```
java AdvancedSwing.Chapter2.StylesExample2
```

is shown in Figure 2-2.

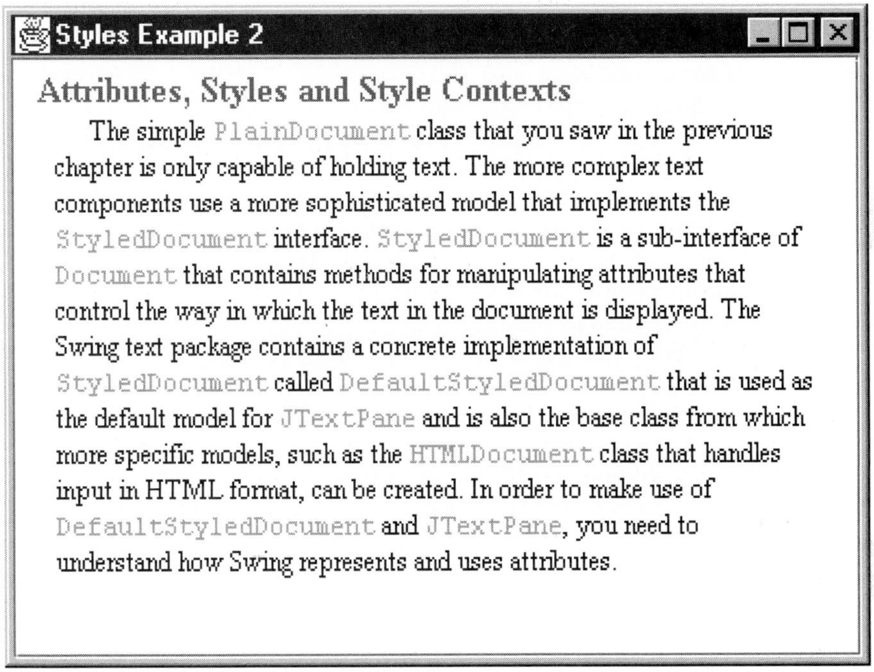

Figure 2-2   Using logical styles, paragraph, and character attributes.

Listing 2-2 A Style Hierarchy

```
package AdvancedSwing.Chapter2;

import javax.swing.*;
import javax.swing.text.*;
import java.awt.*;

public class StylesExample2 {
    public static void main(String[] args) {
        JFrame f = new JFrame("Styles Example 2");
```

Listing 2-2 A Style Hierarchy (continued)

```
// Create the StyleContext, the document and the pane
StyleContext sc = new StyleContext();
final DefaultStyledDocument doc =
      new DefaultStyledDocument(sc);
JTextPane pane = new JTextPane(doc);

// Create and add the main document style
Style defaultStyle =
      sc.getStyle(StyleContext.DEFAULT_STYLE);
final Style mainStyle =
      sc.addStyle("MainStyle", defaultStyle);
StyleConstants.setLeftIndent(mainStyle, 16);
StyleConstants.setRightIndent(mainStyle, 16);
StyleConstants.setFirstLineIndent(mainStyle, 16);
StyleConstants.setFontFamily(mainStyle, "serif");
StyleConstants.setFontSize(mainStyle, 12);

// Create and add the constant width style
final Style cwStyle =
      sc.addStyle("ConstantWidth", null);
StyleConstants.setFontFamily(cwStyle, "monospaced");
StyleConstants.setForeground(cwStyle, Color.green);

// Create and add the heading style
final Style heading2Style =
      sc.addStyle("Heading2", null);
StyleConstants.setForeground(heading2Style,
                             Color.red);
StyleConstants.setFontSize(heading2Style, 16);
StyleConstants.setFontFamily(heading2Style, "serif");
StyleConstants.setBold(heading2Style, true);
StyleConstants.setLeftIndent(heading2Style, 8);
StyleConstants.setFirstLineIndent(heading2Style, 0);

try {
    SwingUtilities.invokeAndWait(new Runnable() {
        public void run() {
            try {
                // Set the logical style
                doc.setLogicalStyle(0, mainStyle);
```

Listing 2-2 A Style Hierarchy (continued)

```
                    // Add the text to the document
                    doc.insertString(0, text, null);

                    // Apply the character attributes
                    doc.setCharacterAttributes(49, 13,
                                            cwStyle, false);
                    doc.setCharacterAttributes(223, 14,
                                            cwStyle, false);
                    doc.setCharacterAttributes(249, 14,
                                            cwStyle, false);
                    doc.setCharacterAttributes(286, 8,
                                            cwStyle, false);
                    doc.setCharacterAttributes(475, 14,
                                            cwStyle, false);
                    doc.setCharacterAttributes(497, 21,
                                            cwStyle, false);
                    doc.setCharacterAttributes(557, 9,
                                            cwStyle, false);
                    doc.setCharacterAttributes(639, 12,
                                            cwStyle, false);
                    doc.setCharacterAttributes(733, 21,
                                            cwStyle, false);
                    doc.setCharacterAttributes(759, 9,
                                            cwStyle, false);

                    // Finally, apply the style to the heading
                    doc.setParagraphAttributes(0, 1,
                                        heading2Style, false);
                } catch (BadLocationException e) {
                }
            }
        });
    } catch (Exception e) {
        System.out.println("Exception when
                        constructing document: " + e);
        System.exit(1);
    }

    f.getContentPane().add(new JScrollPane(pane));
    f.setSize(400, 300);
    f.setVisible(true);
}
```

Listing 2-2 A Style Hierarchy (continued)

```
public static final String text =
        "Attributes, Styles and Style Contexts\n" +
        "The simple PlainDocument class that you saw in
                the previous " +
        "chapter is only capable of holding text. The more
                complex text " +
        "components use a more sophisticated model that
                implements the " +
        "StyledDocument interface. StyledDocument is a
                subinterface of " +
        "Document that contains methods for manipulating
                attributes that " +
        "control the way in which the text in the
                document is displayed. " +
        "The Swing text package contains a concrete
                implementation of " +
        "StyledDocument called DefaultStyledDocument
                that is used as the " +
        "default model for JTextPane and is also the
                base class from which " +
        "more specific models, such as the HTMLDocument
                class that handles " +
        "input in HTML format, can be created. In order
                to make use of " +
        "DefaultStyledDocument and JTextPane, you need
                to understand how " +
        "Swing represents and uses attributes.\n";
}
```

The first style to be created is the logical style that will apply to the whole document, which contains global settings for the font, the left and right paragraph margins, and the extra indentation for the first line of each paragraph. Notice how this style is actually created:

```
Style defaultStyle = sc.getStyle(StyleContext.DEFAULT_STYLE);
final Style mainStyle = sc.addStyle("MainStyle",
                                        defaultStyle);
```

Every `StyleContext` is initially created with a single empty `Style` called the default style installed in it. If you need only one style and you don't want to create your own, you can simply apply the attributes you want to the default style. As you'll see in "The Default Style" on page 163, the default style has special significance for documents that don't apply their own logical style. The global logical style that will be applied to this document has the default style of its resolving parent. Because this example doesn't add any attributes to the default style, it won't affect the way in which the text in this example is rendered; you'll see the benefit of using the default style as the resolving parent of a global logical style in "The Default Style" on page 163.

Because the logical style is applied before any text is added, it will be propagated to every paragraph in the document, even though logical styles apply only at the paragraph level. This would not happen if you added the text and then set the logical style for the first paragraph, however. Such a change would apply the logical style only to the first paragraph.

Next, the character style that will be applied to Swing class names in the main text is created. We want these words to be green and to be drawn in the same font size as the other words in the text, but with a monospaced type face, so this `Style` has explicit settings for the foreground color and font family. Notice that it does not specify values for the font size or the bold and italic attributes that also have an effect on font selection. These attributes would be inherited from the paragraph style that this style will override. Finally, the heading style is created. The code here is very similar to that shown in Listing 2-1, except that it now uses the `StyleConstants` convenience methods for type safety (and improved readability) and sets two extra attributes that control the left margin and the first-line indentation.

Having created the attributes, the next step is to apply them to the text. The logical style is applied first, so that it affects all of the text, as noted earlier. After adding the text, paragraph attributes are applied to the heading and finally character attributes are added to specific ranges of the main text. Notice that applying character attributes in this way is very inconvenient. Because the `DefaultStyledDocument` methods require the offset and length of the area to be affected by an attribute change, it is necessary to manually work out the correct offset and length values when writing the code. This is, of course, also true for paragraph attributes. In "A Simpler Way to Apply Attributes" on page 166, you'll see a much more usable way to apply attributes that doesn't require you to hard-code offsets and lengths.

With the attributes in place, let's now look at exactly how they control the way in which the text is rendered. Attributes are interpreted by the view objects that draw the text onto the screen, about which we'll say much more in the next chapter. An attribute is used only if the view is coded to use it; the standard views look for font and color information and other attributes such as underline, subscript, superscript, and strikethrough. Attributes are handled hierarchically, in the following order of precedence, with highest precedence first:

1. Character attributes
2. Paragraph attributes
3. Logical style

Core Note

This is the conventional order. As you'll see in "More on Attribute Hierarchy" on page 156 it is possible to create a slightly different attribute resolution hierarchy. Unless you explicitly change it, however, the order of precedence shown above applies.

Let's first look at the header. In this case, there are no character attributes to consider, so only the paragraph attributes and the logical style can affect the way in which it is drawn. Consider how the following attributes are obtained:

- Font
- Foreground color
- Left indent
- Right indent
- First-line indent

The font and foreground colors are explicitly specified in the paragraph attributes for the heading, so they are taken from there. This also applies to the left indent and the first-line indent; the values for these attributes override the ones in the logical style. The right indent, however, is not specified in the Heading2 style, but there is a value for it in the document's logical style. Therefore, the heading will have the same right indent as the rest of the document, but a different font, foreground color, left indent, and first-line indent. What about attributes like underline? This attribute is not specified in any of the styles applied to the document. When a specific value for an attribute does not appear anywhere in the attribute hierarchy, the default value shown in Table 2-3 applies. In this case, the text will not be underlined because the default for the underline attribute is false.

Now let's look at the second paragraph, which contains the main body of the document. This paragraph is covered by the same logical style as the heading, which means that it will have the document-wide left and right indents of 16 points and an extra first-line indent of 16 points (for a total indent of 32 points on the first line of the paragraph). The font is also determined by the logical style. The foreground color is, however, not specified at all in the logical style. Because there are no paragraph attributes applied to this text, you might be wondering how the foreground color for this paragraph is determined. In the last paragraph, we said that attributes for which there is no value specified take their value from the default specified in Table 2-3, so the foreground color should be black. This does, in fact, match what you see. However, for the foreground color (and, in fact, the font), the story is a little more involved than this. We'll postpone further discussion of this topic for now to avoid complicating this example too much—you'll find the complete truth in "More on Attribute Hierarchy" on page 156.

Finally, some regions of the second paragraph have specific character attributes applied. Where this is the case, the character attributes take precedence over both the paragraph attributes and the logical style. As a result, for the words affected by these attributes, the foreground color will always be green and the font family will be monospaced. The actual font is, however, determined by the combination of the following attributes:

- Family
- Size
- Bold
- Italic

In this example, the first of these is determined by the character attributes. The font size is obtained from the logical style. The bold and italic attributes are not specified anywhere, so they take the default values (both `false`) shown in Table 2-3. As a result, applying the character attributes changes only the font face, as you would expect from the definition of the style.

Before leaving this example, you can see for yourself proof that the logical style is propagated from paragraph to paragraph even when it is not explicitly applied to a new paragraph. To see this, with the example in Listing 2-2 running, click with the mouse somewhere in the second paragraph, for example, before the words "The Swing text package." Now press RETURN. This splits the text where the caret was positioned, creating a new paragraph, as shown in Figure 2-3.

Notice that the new paragraph has all the same attributes as the original paragraph—the same left and right indent and the first line also has the additional first-line indent. Because these attributes were specified in the logical style, this demonstrates that the logical style applied to the original first paragraph also applies to the second paragraph. How about adding text that wasn't originally in the control? You can try this by clicking at the end of the text and creating another new paragraph by pressing RETURN, and then typing some text of your own. Again, the logical style will be applied to this completely new paragraph. This, of course, mimics exactly what happens when the original text was added in Listing 2-2. In fact, propagation of attributes in this way is not restricted to the logical style; Paragraph attributes and character attributes in effect at the text insertion point are also inherited by the new text.

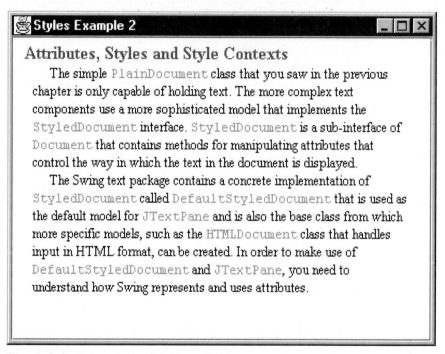

Figure 2–3   Propagation of the logical style.

More on Attribute Hierarchy

Now that you've seen how character and paragraph attributes and logical styles can be used, it's time to look a bit more closely at how they actually work. Some of what has been said so far in this chapter is, in fact, the truth, while not being the whole truth. To avoid complicating things too quickly, some details have been passed over. In this section, you'll find out the whole truth about attributes and logical styles.

First, let's look more closely at the relationship between paragraph attributes and logical styles. We've said that you would want to use a logical style to apply document-wide characteristics such as margin spacing and font that should apply everywhere, except where there should be exceptions. We also said that you can apply paragraph attributes to create entire paragraphs in which the styles are partially or completely different, but should be confined entirely to the individual paragraphs that they are explicitly applied to. From this simple and logical description, you might think that a document has one logical style that is used everywhere to look up attributes that are not supplied at the paragraph (or character) level and that each paragraph has its own separate set of attributes. This impression would apparently be borne out by the examples you have seen so far, in which the logical style was applied once by calling `setLogicalStyle` and then seemed to take effect everywhere.

In fact, though, this is not the case. The logical style is actually a paragraph-level concept: When you apply a logical style, it takes effect only for the paragraph whose offset is given in the `setLogicalStyle` call. Why, then, do the earlier examples work? Why do all the paragraphs in those documents seem to have the same logical style applied to them? The reason that this happens has already been mentioned at the end of the last section—when you add new text to a document, certain attributes get propagated. Let's see why this is.

When you create a `DefaultStyledDocument`, it is not completely empty; It actually has a single newline character in it. In Listing 2-1, immediately after creating the document we applied a logical style. In reality, this applied the logical style to the single paragraph consisting of the initial newline. At this point, the newline occupies offset 0 of the document. Next, we inserted the document's text at offset 0. When we did this, the text was actually being inserted before the original newline and therefore into the (empty) first paragraph of the document. Because of this, it picked up the logical style that was assigned to the paragraph that it was being inserted into. To see exactly what happens, type the following command:

```
java AdvancedSwing.Chapter2.StylesExample3
```

This example is a cut-down version of Listing 2-1, in which the logical style is applied and then the text added. No paragraph or character attributes are overlaid on the text. When this has been done, the `AbstractDocument` method `dump` is called to print a representation of the model in the window in which you started this example. Here is what you should see:

```
<section>
    <paragraph
      resolver=NamedStyle:MainStyle {
            family=serif,RightIndent=16.0,
            name=MainStyle,LeftIndent=16.0,
            resolver=AttributeSet,
```

```
                   size=12,FirstLineIndent=16.0,nrefs=1 }
     >
       <content>
          [0,38][Attributes, Styles and Style Contexts
]
     <paragraph
       resolver=NamedStyle:MainStyle {family=serif,
            RightIndent=16.0,
            name=MainStyle,LeftIndent=16.0,
            resolver=AttributeSet,
            size=12,FirstLineIndent=16.0,nrefs=1}
     >
       <content>
          [38,835][The simple PlainDocument class that you ...]
     <paragraph
       resolver=NamedStyle:MainStyle {family=serif,
            RightIndent=16.0,
            name=MainStyle,LeftIndent=16.0,
            resolver=AttributeSet,
            size=12,FirstLineIndent=16.0,nrefs=1}
     >
       <content>
          [835,836][
]
```

Core Note

The order in which the attributes within the styles are displayed by the dump method is not the same in JDK 1.1 and Java 2. You should, however, see the same attributes as those shown above with whichever version you are using, even if the order does not match.

The words section, paragraph, and content in angle brackets refer to different levels of document storage. In a `DefaultStyledDocument`, everything is held within a single section; each paragraph is encapsulated at the paragraph level and actual text is held at the content level. These levels are nested, so the paragraphs are all contained within the single section and the content items are nested within their respective paragraphs.

Core Note

The structures that are shown above are referred to as elements. You'll see more about elements in Chapter 3.

You can see that this document has three paragraph elements, even though we actually only added two paragraphs corresponding to the header and the main body text. The last of these three paragraphs was created because there are two adjacent newline characters—the one at the end of the String that was used to initialize the document (refer to Listing 2-1) and the one that was initially present in the model. In fact, we could have left off the last newline when creating the model, which would have avoided creating this redundant paragraph (and saved a trailing blank line on the screen). The important thing about these three paragraphs is that they all have the same attributes. The attributes are shown after the word paragraph inside the angle brackets. This demonstrates that the attributes applied to the empty paragraph that was initially present are propagated to content added inside that paragraph, even if this content consists of more than one paragraph. In this case, you can see that the logical style has been applied to each paragraph in the document.

The result would have been very different, however, had we reversed the order of operations and added the text before applying the logical style, like this:

```
// Add the text to the document
doc.insertString(0, text, null);

// Set the logical style
doc.setLogicalStyle(0, mainStyle);
```

The result of this change can be seen by typing the command:

```
java AdvancedSwing.Chapter2.StylesExample4
```

This time, the content of the model is slightly different:

```
<section>
  <paragraph
    resolver=NamedStyle:MainStyle
        {FirstLineIndent=16.0,family=serif,
         RightIndent=16.0,name=MainStyle,
         resolver=AttributeSet,
         LeftIndent=16.0,size=12,nrefs=1} }
  >
```

```
        <content>
          [0,38][Attributes, Styles and Style Contexts
]
    <paragraph
      resolver=NamedStyle:default {name=default,nrefs=1}
    >
        <content>
          [38,835][The simple PlainDocument class that you ...]
    <paragraph
      resolver=NamedStyle:default {name=default,nrefs=1}
    >
        <content>
          [835,836][
]
```

As you can see, there are still three paragraphs, but now only the first has the logical style with the extra left and right indentations applied to it. The other two have a default set of attributes that is actually empty. This makes it clear that the propagation of logical style took place as the new text was added—the logical style applied to the first paragraph has *not* been applied to the other two paragraphs.

The second thing to be aware of is the relationship between logical style and paragraph attributes. You know that both of these attribute sets are applied at the paragraph level, so what is the difference? Actually, the logical style of a paragraph is just the resolving parent of its paragraph attributes. This, of course, explains why both sets of attributes apply at the paragraph level and why the logical style has lower precedence than the paragraph attributes themselves. This has three consequences:

1. If you create a set of attributes with another set as its resolving parent, then assign them as paragraph attributes; any logical style that had been applied to that paragraph will be lost and replaced by the attributes in the resolving parent.

2. If you create a set of attributes without a resolving parent and apply them to a paragraph using `setParagraphAttributes` with the `replace` argument `true`, the logical style assigned to that paragraph, if any, will be lost.

3. If you assign a set of attributes to a paragraph and then call `setLogicalStyle` on the same paragraph, the attributes passed with the `setLogicalStyle` call will replace any attributes that might have been in the original resolving parent of the paragraph attributes, if there was one.

All these consequences are obvious once you realize that the logical style is just a formal way of thinking of the resolving parent of the paragraph attributes. In fact, you can see that this is the case by looking at the last piece of program output. Here, the first paragraph has an attribute called `resolver`, which points to the style named `MainStyle`, which was assigned as the logical style for this paragraph. Also of interest is the fact that the resolver for the other two paragraphs is a style called `default`. In fact, when you first create a `DefaultStyledDocument`, a `Style` called the default style is created and assigned as the logical style for the first paragraph. In "The Default Style" on page 163, you'll see that this has some interesting consequences.

Let's clarify the relationship between paragraph attributes and the logical style by looking at some code extracts that illustrate some of the points listed earlier. First, let's create three styles:

```
Style defaultStyle = sc.getStyle(StyleContext.DEFAULT_STYLE);
final Style mainStyle = sc.addStyle("MainStyle",
                                    defaultStyle);
StyleConstants.setLeftIndent(mainStyle, 16);
StyleConstants.setRightIndent(mainStyle, 16);
StyleConstants.setFirstLineIndent(mainStyle, 16);
StyleConstants.setFontFamily(mainStyle, "serif");
StyleConstants.setFontSize(mainStyle, 12);

Style para1Style = sc.addStyle("Para1Style", null);
StyleConstants.setBold(para1Style, true);

Style para2Style = sc.addStyle("Para2Style", para1Style);
StyleConstants.setItalic(para2Style, true);
```

The `MainStyle` style is the same one that we've used before. The style `Para1Style` has the bold attribute set to `true`. The style `Para2Style` has `Para1Style` as its resolving parent (because the `Para1Style` style is passed as the second argument of the `addStyle` call that creates it) and also has the italic attribute set to `true`. Now suppose that you create a document with one paragraph of text already added and do the following:

```
doc.setLogicalStyle(0, mainStyle);
doc.setParagraphAttributes(0, 1, para2Style, false);
```

After the `setLogicalStyle` call, the paragraph attributes for the document's only paragraph has `MainStyle` as its resolving parent, so the attributes in this style would now apply to that paragraph. Now, when the `setParagraphAttributes` call completes, the attributes from `Para2Style` are applied to the paragraph. Because this contains its own resolving parent attribute, the resolver for this paragraph will now be `Para1Style`. In other words, text in this paragraph will be rendered in italics (from `Para1Style`) and bold (from `Para2Style`), but the left and right indentation and the other attributes from `MainStyle` will no longer apply.

Now let's reverse the order of the two statements above:

```
doc.setParagraphAttributes(0, 1, para2Style, false);
doc.setLogicalStyle(0, mainStyle);
```

Now, after the first line has been executed, the paragraph will have bold and italics applied because its paragraph attributes are `Para2Style`, which produces italics, and its resolving parent, `Para1Style`, provides the bold attribute. In effect, `Para1Style` is the logical style for this paragraph. However, after the `setLogicalStyle` call completes, `MainStyle` becomes the resolving parent for the first paragraph, so the bold attribute is lost and is replaced by the left and right indent (and other attributes) from `MainStyle`. The italic attribute will remain.

Now consider this sequence:

```
doc.setLogicalStyle(0, mainStyle);
doc.setParagraphAttributes(0, 1, para1Style, false);
```

After the `setLogicalStyle` call, the first paragraph has `MainStyle` as its logical style. The second line applies `Para1Style` as the first paragraph's attributes. Because `Para1Style` was created like this:

```
final Style para1Style = sc.addStyle("Para1Style", null);
StyleConstants.setBold(para1Style, true);
```

it has no resolving parent attribute, so the logical style `MainStyle` is not replaced when `Para1Style` is applied. This is the usual way of applying paragraph attributes. Now look at this variation:

```
doc.setLogicalStyle(0, mainStyle);
doc.setParagraphAttributes(0, 1, para1Style, true);
```

In this case, `setParagraphAttributes` is called with the `replace` argument set to `true`. When this happens, the existing attributes for the paragraph are cleared before the new ones are added. The clearing operation includes the resolving parent attribute. As a result, when these two lines of code have been executed, the paragraph has only the `Para1Style` attributes applied to it—the text is rendered in bold, but does not have the indents from `MainStyle`. The moral of this is clear: do not use `setParagraphAttributes` with `replace` set to `true` if you want to preserve the existing logical style.

The Default Style

As you saw earlier, every `StyleContext` contains the default style. This style is initially assigned as the logical style for a `DefaultStyledDocument` when it is created, so that if you don't explicitly set a logical style for the document, or override it by setting a paragraph style that has its own resolving parent, the default style will be the logical style for the whole document. This can be very useful, because the default style is treated differently from all the other styles in a document's `StyleContext` when the `DefaultStyledDocument` is plugged into a `JTextPane`. Specifically, the foreground color and font attributes in the default style are automatically changed whenever `setForeground` or `setFont` are invoked on the `JTextPane` itself. Note, however, that the default style does not initially contain a foreground color or any font settings, so it will use the default attributes implied by Table 2-3, that is:

Foreground	black
Font Family	Monospaced
Font Size	12
Bold	False
Italic	False

These attributes are changed only when `setFont` or `setForeground` is invoked. As an example, refer to Listing 2-1. Here, no specific logical style was set, so the default style is the logical style for every paragraph in the document shown in that example. Therefore, the attributes for the text in the second paragraph can be changed by invoking `setFont` and `setForeground`. You can see this by typing the command

```
java AdvancedSwing.Chapter2.StylesExample5
```

This program is the same as the one shown in Listing 2-1, except that the font and foreground color have been changed as follows (the changes are shown in bold):

```
// Add the text to the document
doc.insertString(0, text, null);

// Finally, apply the style to the heading
doc.setParagraphAttributes(0, 1, heading2Style, false);

// Set the foreground and font
pane.setForeground(Color.blue);
pane.setFont(new Font("serif", Font.PLAIN, 12));
```

The result of running this example is shown in Figure 2-4. If you compare this with Figure 2-1, you'll notice that the text is now rendered in a proportional font instead of the original monospaced font that was used in Figure 2-1. The text color has also changed from black to blue, but it is not possible to see that in the gray-scale figure shown in Figure 2-4.

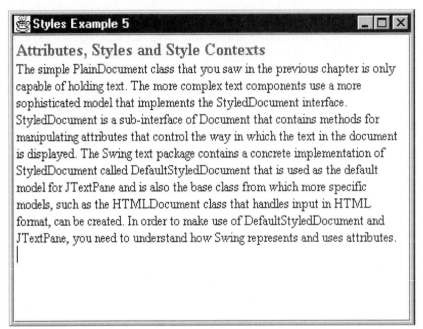

Figure 2–4   Effect of font and foreground changes on the default style.

This automatic updating of the default style doesn't necessarily produce any benefit if you assign your own logical style to the document, as we did in Listing 2-2. However, the logical style assigned in that example was carefully constructed so that its resolving parent was the StyleContext's default style:

```
// Create and add the main document style
Style defaultStyle = sc.getStyle(StyleContext.DEFAULT_STYLE);
final Style mainStyle = sc.addStyle("MainStyle",
                                    defaultStyle);
```

The reason for this may not have been obvious to you at the time. Now, however, you should be able to see that, by constructing the document's logical style in this way, the foreground color and any font attributes that are not overridden in the MainStyle itself will come from the default style and will be updated when the JTextPane setForeground and setFont methods are called. Suppose we took the example code from Listing 2-2 and added the following two lines:

```
// Set the foreground color and change the font
pane.setForeground(Color.pink);
pane.setFont(new Font("Monospaced", Font.ITALIC, 24));
```

You can see the results of this change using the command

```
java AdvancedSwing.Chapter2.StylesExample6
```

The JTextPane that this example produces is shown in Figure 2-5.

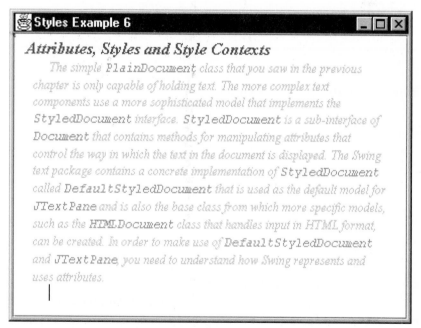

Figure 2-5 Inheriting from the default style.

The code change would imply that the text should now be rendered in a pink, 24-point, monospaced, italic font. The text is, in fact, pink but you can see from Figure 2-5 that it is not in a monospaced font and not 24-point. It is, however, in italics. The explanation for this is simple. The setFont and set-Foreground methods update the default style so that the foreground attribute is pink, the italic attribute is true, the font family is Monospaced, and the font size is 24 points. However, the MainStyle itself overrides the font family (to Serif) and the font size (to 12). Only the foreground color and the `italic` attribute from the default style are actually used to render the text.

In summary, `setFont` and `setForeground` affect the text in a `JTextPane` only if the logical style in the `JTextPane` is defaulted, or if the logical style(s) applied have the default style as resolving parent. As well as this, the logical style must not be disabled by installing paragraph styles that have their own resolving parent, unless the resolving parent is itself the default style or resolves through it.

Core Note

This behavior is implemented by the user interface (UI) class for
`JTextPane`. *It does not work for* `JEditorPane`.

A Simpler Way to Apply Attributes

The `DefaultStyledDocument` methods that have been used so far in connection attributes have all required you to specify the portion of the document to which they should be applied in the form of an offset and, possibly, a length. As you saw in Listing 2-2, however, this can be inconvenient because it requires you to manually calculate the required offset and length, a tedious task that may have to be repeated if you add or remove text. Fortunately, there is a simpler way to add attributes to a `JTextPane`, using the following four methods:

```
public void setLogicalStyle(Style s);
public void setParagraphAttributes(AttributeSet
                                    attr, boolean replace);
public void setCharacterAttributes(AttributeSet
                                    attr, boolean replace);
public void replaceSelection(String content);
```

The first three of these look the same as the `DefaultStyledDocument` methods that you've already seen in this chapter. The important difference is that they do not specify a document position, or an offset. This also applies to `replaceSelection`, which is inherited from `JTextComponent` and was used in the last chapter to insert text into components derived from `JTextField`. The fact that you don't need to directly specify a location is the reason these methods are so much more convenient to use than those that directly manipulate the underlying document.

These methods all operate on the portion of the document that is currently selected. The exact behavior varies slightly from method to method, as follows:

- `setLogicalStyle` and `setParagraphAttributes` operate on each paragraph between the beginning and the end of the selected range. Thus, for example, if the selection begins somewhere in paragraph A, covers paragraphs B and C, and ends somewhere in paragraph D, the attributes or style will be applied to all four paragraphs in their entirety, because paragraph attributes and styles operate at the paragraph level and cannot be applied to part of a paragraph.
- The `setCharacterAttributes` method operates on the exact range covered by the selection, no matter how many paragraphs it straddles.
- The `replaceSelection` method removes any text that is currently selected and installs the text supplied as its argument in its place. It also applies attributes to the new text—where it gets these from will be covered shortly.

What happens if there is no selection? In this case, the result is slightly different:

- `setLogicalStyle` and `setParagraphAttributes` apply to the single paragraph that contains the caret.
- The `setCharacterAttributes` method does not affect the document itself. Instead, the attributes are applied to a hidden set of attributes called the *input attributes*.
- The `replaceSelection` method inserts its text immediately after the caret location.

The input attributes affected by the `setCharacterAttributes` method are maintained by `JTextPane`. They are applied, as character attributes, to all text inserted using the `replaceSelection` method, whether this text replaces an existing selection or is inserted at the caret location. Paragraph attributes and logical styles that apply to the inserted or replaced text are not, of course, affected by the use of input attributes.

Both `setParagraphAttributes` and `setCharacterAttributes` have a `replace` argument that determines whether the supplied attributes will be merged with those already present or will completely replace them. You've already seen how this works in connection with the related `DefaultStyled-`

`Document` methods. In the case of `setCharacterAttributes`, there is a small difference when no text is selected because the attributes will then be used to change the input attribute set instead of being applied to the document itself. As you might expect, if `replace` is `false`, the new attributes are merged into the existing input attributes, while if `replace` is `true` the input attribute set is cleared and then initialized from the new attributes.

There is one more aspect of the management of the input attribute set that you need to be aware of: when you move the caret, the input attributes are set to the character attributes that apply at the caret's new location. If you think about it, this is the natural thing to do, as a simple example will show. Referring to Figure 2-2, consider any of the highlighted words in the text in the second paragraph. Each of these words is highlighted by applying character attributes that change the color and force the use of a monospaced font. If you were to move the caret into one of these words, you would want whatever you type to have the same color and font, so that it appears that you are just adding more text to the highlighted word. If, in fact, you run that example again and try this out, you'll find that this is exactly what happens. This works because when you move the caret to the middle of the word, the input attributes are cleared and then take on the foreground color and the monospaced font assigned in the active character attributes. As you type, the new text is inserted using `replaceSelection`, which, as described above, applies the attributes from the input attribute set to the content that it is adding. Another consequence of this is that, if you move the caret to a location that does not have character attributes applied, the input set is cleared. You'll see another case in which the input attributes are affected as a side effect of another operation in "Inserting Icons and Components" on page 177.

Let's now look at an example that demonstrates how to make use of these methods to simplify the addition of attributes to text within a `JTextPane`. This example creates a text component that looks just like the one shown in Figure 2-2, but does so by using a framework that you'll be able to reuse with different text and different attributes. The code in Listing 2-2 combined the code and the text together because of the need to know the correct offsets and lengths for the text to which the character attributes should be applied. This example, in contrast, uses a formal mechanism to describe the text together with its associated attributes, so that this data can be held independently from the code, which just has to know how to interpret the data.

Before looking at the code, let's see how the data itself is represented. As you've already seen, a document can be represented as a set of paragraphs, each of which may have its own logical style and/or paragraph attributes. Within each paragraph, the content can be broken down into pieces, or *runs*, of contiguous text that have the same character attributes applied to them. For each paragraph, then, you need to be able to specify a set of paragraph attributes and the content that it should contain. The content consists of a series of runs, in which each run is a sequence of characters and an associated set of character attributes. If a paragraph does not need specific paragraph attributes, they should not need to be supplied. Similarly, a run that does not need attributes over and above the attributes that it will inherit from its containing paragraph need not have any character attributes specified.

To represent these two cases, we invent classes called `Paragraph` and `Run` defined as follows:

```
public static class Run {
    public Run(String styleName, String content) {
        this.styleName = styleName;
        this.content = content;
    }

    public String styleName;
    public String content;
}

public static class Paragraph {
    public Paragraph(String styleName, Run[] content) {
        this.styleName = styleName;
        this.content = content;
    }

    public String styleName;
    public Run[] content;
}
```

Core Note

These two classes are declared as `static` because they are inner classes of the class used to implement the complete example that you'll see in Listing 2-3. Because they don't need access to the state of their containing class, it is logical to declare them as `static`.

The `Run` class contains the text, specified as a `String` and the name of the `Style` that will be applied, as character attributes, to the text. If no character attributes are required, the `Style` name should be supplied as `null` when invoking the constructor. Here is how you would typically create some text that has the `Style` called `cwStyle` applied to it:

```
new Run("cwStyle", "DefaultStyledDocument");
```

while the following text will use only the attributes assigned to its containing paragraph:

```
new Run(null, "The simple ");
```

Similarly, a `Paragraph` specifies paragraph attributes and an array of `Run` objects that make up the content of the paragraph. If the paragraph attributes are supplied as `null`, no paragraph attributes are supplied, which means that the paragraph will inherit the document's logical style if there is one. The code that uses these classes to create a `JTextPane` with the supplied text and the appropriate attributes applied is shown in Listing 2-3.

Listing 2-3 Using `JTextPane` Methods to Insert Text and Apply Attributes

```
package AdvancedSwing.Chapter2;

import javax.swing.*;
import javax.swing.text.*;
import java.awt.*;

public class StylesExample7 {
    public static void createDocumentStyles(StyleContext sc) {
        Style defaultStyle =
                sc.getStyle(StyleContext.DEFAULT_STYLE);

        // Create and add the main document style
        Style mainStyle = sc.addStyle(mainStyleName,
                                      defaultStyle);
        StyleConstants.setLeftIndent(mainStyle, 16);
        StyleConstants.setRightIndent(mainStyle, 16);
        StyleConstants.setFirstLineIndent(mainStyle, 16);
        StyleConstants.setFontFamily(mainStyle, "serif");
        StyleConstants.setFontSize(mainStyle, 12);
        // Create and add the constant width style
        Style cwStyle = sc.addStyle(charStyleName, null);
        StyleConstants.setFontFamily(cwStyle, "monospaced");
        StyleConstants.setForeground(cwStyle, Color.green);
```

```java
    // Create and add the heading style
    Style heading2Style = sc.addStyle(heading2StyleName,
                                      null);
    StyleConstants.setForeground(heading2Style,
                                 Color.red);
    StyleConstants.setFontSize(heading2Style, 16);
    StyleConstants.setFontFamily(heading2Style, "serif");
    StyleConstants.setBold(heading2Style, true);
    StyleConstants.setLeftIndent(heading2Style, 8);
    StyleConstants.setFirstLineIndent(heading2Style, 0);
  }

  public static void addText(JTextPane pane,
                             StyleContext sc,
                             Style logicalStyle,
                             Paragraph[] content) {
    // The outer loop adds paragraphs, while the
    // inner loop adds character runs.
    int paragraphs = content.length;
    for (int i = 0; i < paragraphs; i++) {
      Run[] runs = content[i].content;
      for (int j = 0; j < runs.length; j++) {
        pane.setCharacterAttributes(
          runs[j].styleName == null ?
                  SimpleAttributeSet.EMPTY :
                  sc.getStyle(runs[j].styleName), true);
        pane.replaceSelection(runs[j].content);
      }
      // At the end of the paragraph, add the logical
      // style and any overriding paragraph style and
      // then terminate the paragraph with a newline.
      pane.setParagraphAttributes(
                       SimpleAttributeSet.EMPTY, true);

      if (logicalStyle != null) {
        pane.setLogicalStyle(logicalStyle);
      }
      if (content[i].styleName != null) {
        pane.setParagraphAttributes(
              sc.getStyle(content[i].styleName), false);
      }
```

**Listing 2-3 Using `JTextPane` Methods to Insert Text
and Apply Attributes (continued)**

```
        pane.replaceSelection("\n");
   }
}

public static void main(String[] args) {
   JFrame f = new JFrame("Styles Example 7");

   // Create the StyleContext, the document and the pane
   final StyleContext sc = new StyleContext();
   final DefaultStyledDocument doc =
                              new DefaultStyledDocument(sc);
   final JTextPane pane = new JTextPane(doc);

   // Build the styles
   createDocumentStyles(sc);
   try {
      // Add the text and apply the styles
      SwingUtilities.invokeAndWait(new Runnable() {
         public void run() {
            // Add the text
            addText(pane, sc, sc.getStyle(mainStyleName),
                     content);
         }
      });
   } catch (Exception e) {
      System.out.println("Exception when constructing
                        document: " + e);
      System.exit(1);
   }


   f.getContentPane().add(new JScrollPane(pane));
   f.setSize(400, 300);
   f.setVisible(true);
}

// Style names
public static final String mainStyleName = "MainStyle";
public static final String heading2StyleName =
                                    "Heading2";
public static final String charStyleName =
                                    "ConstantWidth";
```

Listing 2-3 Using `JTextPane` Methods to Insert Text
and Apply Attributes (continued)

```java
// Inner classes used to define paragraph structure
public static class Run {
    public Run(String styleName, String content) {
        this.styleName = styleName;
        this.content = content;
    }

    public String styleName;
    public String content;
}

public static class Paragraph {
    public Paragraph(String styleName, Run[] content) {
        this.styleName = styleName;
        this.content = content;
    }

    public String styleName;
    public Run[] content;
}

public static final Paragraph[] content =
                                    new Paragraph[] {
    new Paragraph(heading2StyleName, new Run[] {
        new Run(null, "Attributes, Styles and
                Style Contexts")
    }),
    new Paragraph(null, new Run[] {
        new Run(null, "The simple "),
        new Run(charStyleName, "PlainDocument"),
        new Run(null, " class that you saw in the
                        previous " +
            "chapter is only capable of holding text. " +
            "The more complex text components use a
                        more " +
            "sophisticated model that implements the "),
        new Run(charStyleName, "StyledDocument"),
        new Run(null, " interface. "),
        new Run(charStyleName, "StyledDocument"),
        new Run(null, " is a sub-interface of "),
        new Run(charStyleName, "Document"),
```

Listing 2-3 Using `JTextPane` **Methods to Insert Text
and Apply Attributes (continued)**

```
              new Run(null, " that contains methods for
                              manipulating attributes " +
                    "that control the way in which the text
                              in the " +
                    "document is displayed. The Swing text
                              package " +
                    "contains a concrete implementation of "),
              new Run(charStyleName, "StyledDocument"),
              new Run(null, " called "),
              new Run(charStyleName, "DefaultStyledDocument"),
              new Run(null, " that is used as the default
                              model for "),
              new Run(charStyleName, "JTextPane"),
              new Run(null, " and is also the base class
                              from which " +
                    "more specific models, such as the "),
              new Run(charStyleName, "HTMLDocument"),
              new Run(null, " class that handles input in
                              HTML format, can be " +
                    "created. In order to make use of "),
              new Run(charStyleName, "DefaultStyledDocument"),
              new Run(null, " and "),
              new Run(charStyleName, "JTextPane"),
              new Run(null, " you need to understand how
                              Swing represents " +
                    "and uses attributes.")
          })
      };
  }
```

The `createDocumentStyles` and `main` methods contain much of the code that was originally in the `main` method in Listing 2-2. The creation of the `Styles` that will be used in this example has been broken out into a separate method so that you can more clearly see how the whole process works and to make it easier for you to reuse this code for your own purposes. The `Styles` that are created by `createDocumentStyles` are, however, the same as the ones created in Listing 2-2. Notice, though, that in this case references to the `Styles` themselves are not kept—they are simply local variables within the createDocumentStyles method. This is because the Styles will be referred to by name when the text is added, whereas in Listing 2-2 the Style references were used. The reason for this difference is modularity: In a real application, the Styles might be created by a piece of common code that is shared among many applications and would reside in a different class from the one that holds the text and creates the JTextPane. When the Styles are created in a separate class, the original Style references are not readily available to code that would subsequently need to use them. They can, however, be obtained from the document's StyleContext by using the getStyle method, which requires the name of the Style, and this is how the references are recovered as they are needed.

The key to this example is the addText method, which is called after the Styles have all been created. This method is supplied with references to the JTextPane, the StyleContext, a global logical style to use, and the document content, in the form of an array of Paragraph objects. If a global logical style is not required, the logical style argument can be null.

The addText method consists of two nested loops that build the document from scratch. Each iteration of the outer loop processes a single Paragraph and applies its paragraph attributes and the logical style, if there is one. The inner loop handles the array of Run objects for the Paragraph currently being built. Each Run installs some content and may have associated character attributes applied. That's the big picture—now let's look at the details.

First, let's consider the inner loop, which deals with the array of Run objects that make up a single paragraph. Because the paragraph text must be installed as a contiguous sequence of characters, it is convenient to use the replaceSelection method, which adds text at the current location of the caret and then advances the caret to the end of what it inserted. To install the text for the entire paragraph, it is only necessary to loop over the entries in the Paragraph's content array calling replaceSelection for the text in each Run object in the array.

The other aspect of adding the text for a paragraph is arranging for the correct character attributes to be applied. As you know, replaceSelection automatically adds the attributes in the input attribute set as character attributes when it adds or replaces text, so it is only necessary to make sure that the input attribute set is correct before replaceSelection is called. Each Run has its own, optional, set of character attributes that apply to all the text in the Run. The attributes in each Run are independent of those of adjacent Runs, so we want to set the input attributes from those in the Run before each invocation of replaceSelection and we also want to replace any attributes that were placed in the input set by the previous call of `setChar-acterAttributes`. This is achieved using the following line of code (from `addText`):

```
pane.setCharacterAttributes(
    runs[j].styleName == null ? SimpleAttributeSet.EMPTY :
    sc.getStyle(runs[j].styleName), true);
```

Because there is no selection, this call affects the content of the input attribute set. The `replace` argument is `true` to remove from the input set any attributes installed by the previous call. The attribute set itself is obtained by taking its name, from the `Run` object, and resolving it through the `Style-Context`. If no character attributes are to be applied, the name is passed as `null`. It is not acceptable in this case just to skip setting the input attributes, because that would leave whatever was installed by the previous `setCharac-terAttributes` call in the input set. Instead, an empty set of attributes is supplied. This empty set is applied to the input attributes after any existing attributes have been removed as a result of setting `replace` to `true`. This, of course, leaves an empty attribute set.

The inner loop, then, creates a complete paragraph and installs the required character attributes. The job of the outer loop is to create a complete paragraph. Building a paragraph consists of installing the text, and then applying the logical style and the paragraph attributes, if either is required, and finally terminating the paragraph by adding a newline character. As with the character attributes, however, it is important to be careful about resetting attributes as each paragraph is installed. As you saw earlier, if you add one paragraph after another, the new paragraph inherits the earlier one's paragraph attributes (which may include its logical style). This is definitely not required here, so the first step is to clear any existing paragraph attributes by calling `setParagraphAttributes` passing an empty attribute set and with `replace` set to `true`. Now, we need to apply the logical style and the actual paragraph attribute for the current paragraph, by calling `setLogicalStyle` and `setParagraphAttributes`, this time passing the attributes in the current `Paragraph` object and with `replace` set to `false`, to avoid removing the logical style.

Note that the sequence used in Listing 2-3 works for all combinations of logical style and paragraph attributes, as summarized here.

`Logical Style == null,` `paragraph attributes == null`	Neither set should be applied. As you can see from Listing 2-3, this is what happens.

`Logical Style != null,` `paragraph attributes == null`	Only the logical style should be applied.
`Logical Style == null,` `paragraph attributes != null`	The paragraph attributes are applied—no logical style.
`Logical Style != null,` `paragraph attributes != null`	Both logical style and paragraph attributes should be applied, with the paragraph attributes having precedence over the logical style.

The last case is the most interesting one, because it contains a subtle point of ordering. As you can see from Listing 2-3, when both a logical style and paragraph attributes are supplied, `setLogicalStyle` is called before `setParagraphAttributes`. Usually the order of these calls does not matter, because the two attribute sets are usually distinct. However, as you saw earlier, it is possible for the paragraph attributes to have their own resolving parent. When this is the case, the attributes in the resolving parent should be used instead of those in the logical style. For this to happen, the paragraph attributes must be added *after* the logical style, because the logical style is installed as the resolving parent of the paragraph attributes—applying the logical style after the paragraph attributes would lose the paragraph attributes' resolving parent.

If you try the example in Listing 2-3 using the command

```
java AdvancedSwing.Chapter2.StylesExample7
```

you'll get the same result as you saw in Figure 2-2. However, this example is much more flexible because you can change what is displayed by simply modifying the data in the `content` array. In fact, there is no real reason for the code and data to reside in the same class—that was done here only for convenience.

Inserting Icons and Components

As well as using attributes to control the way in which text is rendered, you can also use them to include images (in the form of `Icons`) or AWT and Swing components inline with the document text. The easiest way to do this is to use the following `StyleConstants` convenience methods:

```
public static void setComponent(MutableAttributeSet a,
                                Component c)
public static void setIcon(MutableAttributeSet a, Icon c)
```

Once you've got an attribute set with a `Component` or an `Icon` installed, you simply apply it, as character attributes, to a range of text to have the `Component` or `Icon` appear at that location. When you do this, the text to which the attributes have been applied is not displayed (at least not by the standard views—you could write your own view to make use of the text, perhaps as a caption), so it is usual to supply a single space in the document where the `Icon` or `Component` is located. Another way to include a `Component` or an `Icon` is to make use of a couple of convenience methods provided by `JTextPane`:

```
public void insertComponent(Component c)
public void insertIcon(Icon c)
```

These methods insert the `Component` or `Icon` at the current location of the caret, replacing any content that is currently selected. In both cases, a space is added to the document content and the appropriate attributes are then applied to it. These two methods are simple to use, but they have the side effect of clearing the text pane's input attribute set before and after the object is inserted, so care may be needed if you are using these methods in conjunction with `replaceSelection`, which applies character attributes from the input set.

We'll demonstrate how to add a `Component` to a text pane by adding an illustration to the example that we've been developing in this chapter. We could put an illustration into a document by creating an `ImageIcon` and adding that, but instead we'll use a `JLabel`, because that allows us to easily add a caption below the diagram. For the diagram itself, we use a GIF file that contains a screen shot of this example at an earlier stage of its development.

To add the `Component` itself, we need a `Style` that contains the `Component` attribute. To separate the diagram from the text that precedes it, we also create a paragraph style that adds 16 points of space above it and place the `Component` on its own in this paragraph.

The first step is to create these two `Styles` by adding the following code to the `createDocumentStyles` method shown in Listing 2-3:

```
// Create and add the Component style
Class thisClass =
        AdvancedSwing.Chapter2.StylesExample8.class;
URL url = thisClass.getResource("images/Style8img.gif");
ImageIcon icon = new ImageIcon(url);
JLabel comp = new JLabel("Displaying text with attributes",
                  icon, JLabel.CENTER);
comp.setVerticalTextPosition(JLabel.BOTTOM);
```

```
comp.setHorizontalTextPosition(JLabel.CENTER);
comp.setFont(new Font("serif", Font.BOLD | Font.ITALIC, 14));
Style componentStyle = sc.addStyle(componentStyleName, null);
StyleConstants.setComponent(componentStyle, comp);

// The paragraph style for the component
Style compParagraphStyle = sc.addStyle(compParaName, null);
StyleConstants.setSpaceAbove(compParagraphStyle,
                      (float)16.0);
```

The first part of this code creates a Uniform Resource Locator (URL) for the image file, relative to the class file for the example. This URL is used to create an `ImageIcon`, which then becomes part of the `JLabel`, together with the diagram's caption. By setting the vertical and horizontal text position attributes, we arrange for the text to appear below the diagram. The last step is to use `addStyle` to create a new `Style` and the `StyleConstants` `setComponent` method to create the attribute needed to display the `JLabel`. The paragraph style contains only an attribute that adds the necessary vertical space above the content of the paragraph. The names of these two styles are constant strings, defined as follows:

```
public static final String componentStyleName = "Component";
public static final String compParaName = "CompPara";
```

The last thing we need to do is to place the `Component` in its own paragraph. We don't need to add any more code to achieve this, because the `addText` method can add any `Style` to either a paragraph or a run of text. To place the diagram in its own paragraph at the end of the document, we just add the following `Paragraph` to the end of the `content` array:

```
new Paragraph(compParaName, new Run[] {
          new Run(componentStyleName, " ")
})
```

You can see how this works using the command

```
java AdvancedSwing.Chapter2.StylesExample8
```

The result is shown in Figure 2-6.

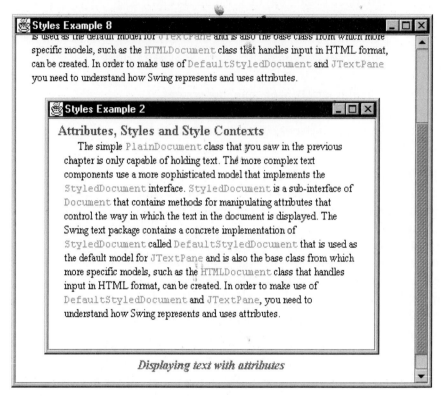

Figure 2-6 A document with an embedded component.

Summary

JTextPane is a very flexible component that you can use to display text with multiple fonts and colors when the simple JTextArea is not sufficient. In practice, as we have seen, JTextPane requires quite a lot of programming if you want to make the best possible use of it. In the course of explaining how this component works, we've shown you how the Swing Document model holds the color, font, and other information in the form of AttributeSets and Styles and the way in which attributes applied at the paragraph level relate to those that cover character ranges. In reality, you'll probably find it easier in many cases to use JEditorPane, which is fully described in Chapter 4, when you want to render formatted text. In the next chapter, we take a look at another aspect of the Swing text architecture—the Views that determine how a component's content are rendered.

TEXT
COMPONENTS
WITH
CUSTOM VIEWS

Topics in this Chapter

- The Element Hierarchy
- Document Views
- View Factories
- Tab Handling
- Creating Customized Views
- Custom Highlighters
- Using Customized Views to Build Clever Input Fields

Chapter 3

I n the first two chapters of this book, you've seen how the document content is stored in the model associated with a text component and how it is possible to store attributes that determine how the text is rendered on the screen. In this chapter, you'll see that the attributes that were discussed in Chapter 2, which exist at both the character and paragraph level, are actually stored in a hierarchy of "elements" that map out the various structures within the document. Once we've described the element structure, we'll move on to look at the last major piece of the Swing text component architecture—the collection of View classes that use the information stored in the content model, the element structure, and the attributes to determine how the text should actually appear on the screen. In the second part of this chapter, we'll show you several techniques for creating enhanced text components by implementing custom Views, including a powerful text component that allows you to specify how its content should be rendered using a separately supplied formatting string.

Customized Document Views

The document content and the associated attributes in its model specify what the text component should display and how it should display it, but the job of rendering the text is actually performed by various *view* objects that know how to interpret the document content. The views are responsible for laying out the text on the screen, arranging it into paragraphs, performing word wrapping, supplying margins, and changing color as appropriate. If the standard views do not meet your needs, you can create views of your own that perform custom rendering. To do this, you need to understand how attributes are stored in the document model. In this section, we'll look at how the attributes are represented, and then we'll see an example of a custom view.

How Attributes Are Stored

As you saw in the last chapter, the data in a text component is held in the `Document`, but that's not all that the `Document` stores. Holding the data alone is not sufficient, even for the simpler text components. The content of a `JTextArea`, for example, is divided into lines separated by newline characters, so it is necessary to remember not only the text, but also where the line boundaries are. In the case of `JEditorPane` and `JTextPane`, as you saw in the last chapter, the text is arranged into paragraphs and can have arbitrary formatting associated with it. Instead of trying to embed the structural information into the storage used to hold the text, the `Document` implementations supplied with the Swing text package maintain a parallel structure of *elements* that organizes the text into lines or paragraphs and provides the storage for the associated attributes. The details of the element structure vary from component to component. Let's look first at the structures used by `JTextField` and `JTextArea`.

The Element Structure of the Simple Text Components

The element structure of a text component can be seen by using the dump method of `AbstractDocument`, which sends a readable representation of it to a given output stream:

```
public void dump(PrintStream out);
```

If you type the following command:

```
java AdvancedSwing.Chapter3.TextFieldElements
```

you'll see a text field with a single line of text appear. In the window from which you started the program, you'll see the following output:

```
<paragraph>
  <content>
    [0,33][That's one small step for man...]
<bidi root>
  <bidi level
    bidiLevel=0
  >
    [0,33][That's one small step for man...]
```

The first part of this output (up to the string "`<bidi root>`") shows the elements that form the logical structure of the text field. The rest of the output is the structure used when there is bi-directional text in the document; bi-directional text is discussed in Chapter 5. A document can have an arbitrary number of different hierarchy structures layered over it, but the standard `Document` implementations support only two. If you want to add extra hierarchies that map the content in different ways, you can do so, but you must provide a way to store the location of the root of each hierarchy. Usually, you would do this by subclassing `Plain-Document` or `DefaultStyledDocument` and overriding the following method:

```
public Element[] getRootElements();
```

The `PlainDocument` and `DefaultStyledDocument` classes imple-ment this method to return an array with two entries, the first of which points to the usual element structure that we'll discuss in this section, and the second to the bi-directional text information. If you need extra hierarchies, you should return an array that contains the two standard entries and your own private ones. The standard `Document` implementa-tions also provide the following convenience methods:

```
public Element getDefaultRootElement();
public Element getBidiRootElement();
```

which obtain the same hierarchy information directly, without assuming the order of entries in the array returned by `getRootElements`.

Let's concentrate on the main element structure that is shown in the first part of the program ouput that you have just seen. What this output shows is that a text field consists of a single paragraph, within which there is a single piece of content that represents all the text that was added to the text component, including a trailing newline.

Core Note

The newline was not supplied by the code that created the text field—it was added by the `Document` *implementation. If a newline had been included in the text inserted in the component by the* `setText` *method, the document would contain two newlines. In fact, you can add more than one line of text to a* `JTextField` *and it will display them much like a* `JTextArea` *would. It isn't really intended to be used in this way, however, so it is recommended that you restrict yourself to a single line of text.*

Elements are hierarchical. A *content* element is always the lowest level of the hierarchy and the only one that can reference actual character data. A *paragraph* element represents the next level of the hierarchy; its only job is to contain one or more content elements. In the case of `JTextField`, the model contains a single paragraph element, which in turn contains a single content element. `JTextArea` uses a very similar element structure, as you can see by typing the command:

```
java AdvancedSwing.Chapter3.TextAreaElements
```

This example creates a `JTextArea` with two lines of text, separated by a newline. Here is what the output looks like in this case:

```
<paragraph>
  <content>
    [0,33][That's one small step for man...]
  <content>
    [33,61][One giant leap for mankind.]
<bidi root>
  <bidi level
    bidiLevel=0
  >
    [0,61][That's one small step for man...
           One gia...]
```

Ignoring the bi-directional text elements, you can see that this is just a logical extension of the elements structure used for `JTextField`: The whole document is represented by a single paragraph element, which contains two content elements, one for each line of text. The data in each content element includes its terminating newline. Another way to look at this is to show the hierarchy pictorially, as in Figure 3-1.

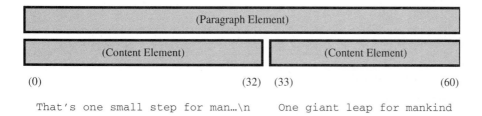

Figure 3-1 Element hierarchy for a JTextArea.

Here, you can see more clearly the fact that the paragraph element is the parent of the two content elements and that the content elements map directly to text within the model. There is no overlap between the text in the first content element and that in the second. This element hierarchy is created and maintained by the Document implementation. The particular structure used for JTextField and JTextArea is determined by the PlainDocument class, which is the model used by both of these components. As you'll see later, it is slightly different from the structures used by JEditorPane and JTextPane. However, the idea of a hierarchy of elements is common to both PlainDocument and DefaultStyledDocument, which manages the element structure for the more complex text components.

It is important to realize that the element structure is not constrained by or directly related to the way in which the text will actually appear on the screen. Putting this more clearly, a single content element in a JTextArea corresponds to a single line of text. However, a line of text (in this sense) does not have to be rendered on a single screen line. If the text component is performing wrapping, a single content line may actually be spread over more than one line on the screen. The job of mapping content lines to screen lines is performed by the View objects that you'll see later in this chapter. To see an example of this, try the following command:

```
java AdvancedSwing.Chapter3.TextAreaElements2
```

This example creates a text area in which word wrapping is enabled but which is too narrow for either line of text to be shown in its entirety in the horizontal space available. Because word wrapping is enabled, the lines wrap at the right edge of the component and continue on the next line, so that four screen lines are used to display the two lines of text (see Figure 3-2). The element structure, however, is exactly the same as that shown in Figure 3-1—two content elements within a single paragraph. Enabling wrapping, then, changes the way in which the element structure is used by the View objects, but does not change the element structure.

Figure 3-2   JTextArea with word wrapping.

Elements and Element Types

The previous section mentioned content and paragraph elements, but these terms are simply convenient tags that reflect the way in which these specific element types are used. In regard to classes and interfaces, all elements are implementations of the Element interface, which is defined by the Swing text package (javax.swing.text). Real elements are all instances of Leaf-Element or BranchElement, which are inner classes of AbstractDocument that implement the Element interface These two classes are derived from the abstract base class AbstractDocument.AbstractElement. Here is the definition of the Element interface:

```
public interface Element {
    public Document getDocument();
    public Element getParentElement();
    public String getName();
    public AttributeSet getAttributes();
    public int getStartOffset();
    public int getEndOffset();
    public int getElementIndex(int offset);
    public int getElementCount();
    public Element getElement(int index);
    public boolean isLeaf();
}
```

The getDocument method returns a reference to the Document of which the element is a part. Because elements exist in a hierarchy, the getParent-Element method can be used to find the parent of the element to which it is applied. In terms of Figure 3-1, the paragraph element is the parent of the two content elements. Invoking `getParentElement` on either of the content elements would return a reference to the paragraph element, while invoking it on the paragraph element would return `null`, because it has no parent. The `getName` method returns a `String` that describes the type of the element. The values most commonly returned from this method are:

`AbstractDocument.ParagraphElementName`	"paragraph"
`AbstractDocument.ContentElementName`	"content"
`AbstractDocument.SectionElementName`	"section"
`AbstractDocument.BidiElementName`	"bidi level"
`StyleConstants.ComponentElementName`	"component"
`StyleConstants.IconElementName`	"icon"

As you can see, you can use this method to determine whether an element represents a paragraph or the content of a paragraph. Of the other four element types, the section, icon, and component elements are used by `JEditorPane` and `JTextPane`, as you'll see in "Elements and JTextPane" on page 191, and the bidi level element is used to manage bi-directional strings and appears only in the bi-directional hierarchy of elements that you have seen when looking at the element structure of both `JTextField` and `JTextArea`. You'll see more about bi-directional strings in Chapter 5.

The `getAttributes` method returns the attributes associated with an element; attributes are not much used by the simple text components, so we'll postpone discussion of how they fit into the element structure until later.

The `getStartOffset` and `getEndOffset` methods return the start and end offsets of the content of the text component with which the element is associated. Because elements are hierarchical, more than one element may contain a particular offset but only one content element (in a given hierarchy) will map to any specified offset. That offset will also be within the start and end offset range of the containing paragraph. If you refer to the element hierarchy for the `JTextArea` shown in the output from the `TextAreaElements` example (and represented pictorially in Figure 3-1), you'll see that the start and end offsets for each content element are displayed in square brackets. The first line occupies offsets 0 through 33, including its trailing newline, while the second line has start offset 33 and end offset 61. Notice that the end offset is one larger than the offset of the last character in the element's range, so that the end offset of the first line is the same as the start offset of the second. The start and end offsets of the paragraph element, which are not shown by the `AbstractDocument` dump method, are 0 and 61, respectively, but the last offset occupied by a real character is 60. Thus, the offset range of the paragraph contains the union of the offset ranges of its child content elements.

The `getElementIndex`, `getElementCount`, `getElement`, and `isLeaf` methods are used to map between an element hierarchy and the document content. When applied to an element, these methods return information as known by that element. The `getElementIndex` method returns the ordinal of the child element that contains the given document offset. To see what this means, refer to Figure 3-1. If the call

```
getElementIndex(34);
```

is made on the paragraph element, it would return the index 1 because it contains two content elements, numbered 0 and 1, in which the element with index 0 covers offsets 0 through 32 (inclusive) and the element with index 1 corresponds to offsets 32 through 60. Applying this call to either of the content elements, however, would return -1, because content elements are at the lowest level of the hierarchy and so do not contain other elements. In terms of classes, a content element is an instance of the `AbstractDocument.LeafElement` class, while paragraphs are instances of `AbstractDocument.BranchElement`. A `BranchElement` is a container that can hold one or more `LeafElements`, but also appears as a fully fledged element in its own right.

Core Note

Keep in mind the distinction between the two kinds of elements types that we are discussing here. On the one hand, there are two fundamental classes that are used to represent all the elements within a `Document` *(*`BranchElement` *and* `LeafElement`*). These types are of importance when the element structure is being built, but not when it is being interpreted as the text component is being rendered by* `View` *objects. The* `View` *objects make use of the second type of element classification—the* `String` *returned by the* `getName` *method, which represents a logical way of distinguishing different types of element. Section, paragraph, content, and bidi elements are logically different from the viewpoint of* `View`s, *but they are not all implemented by different Java classes.*

The `getElementCount` method returns the number of child elements that a given element has. For `LeafElements`, like the two content elements in Figure 3-1, this always returns 0. For the paragraph `BranchElement` in the same diagram, this method would return the value 2.

The `getElement` method returns the child whose index is supplied as its argument. If applied to a `LeafElement`, this method always returns `null`. In Figure 3-1, this method would return a reference to the leftmost content element if called with argument 0 and to the rightmost element when called with argument 1. Other indices do not map to existing child elements and return the value `null`. The `isLeaf` method indicates whether the element to which it is applied could *not* contain child elements, returning `true` for a `LeafElement` and `false` for a `BranchElement`. Note that `isLeaf` *always* returns `false` for a `BranchElement`, even if it actually has no child elements when the method is invoked.

Elements and `JTextPane`

With the basic concepts underlying elements covered, let's now look at how the element structure is built by `DefaultStyledDocument`. Because this class is used by both `JEditorPane` and `JTextPane`, what you'll see in this section applies to both of these components even though, for brevity, we'll refer exclusively to `JTextPane` throughout. As before, we'll examine the element structure by using a representative example and looking at the results produced by the `AbstractDocument` `dump` method. You can run this example using the command:

```
java AdvancedSwing.Chapter3.TextPaneElements
```

This command produces quite a lot of output in the command window from which it was started. Because the `dump` call in this example writes to the program's standard output, you can easily capture the results in a file using shell redirection. For example,

```
java AdvancedSwing.Chapter3.TextPaneElements > filename
```

With the appropriate choice of *filename*, this works for both UNIX and DOS. The result will look something like this:

```
<section>
  <paragraph
    bold=true
    resolver=NamedStyle:MainStyle
    {resolver=AttributeSet,name=MainStyle,
                RightIndent=16.0,size=12,family=serif,
```

```
    LeftIndent=16.0,FirstLineIndent=16.0,nrefs=1}
      name=Heading2
      foreground=java.awt.Color[r=255,g=0,b=0]
      size=16
      family=serif
      LeftIndent=8.0
      FirstLineIndent=0.0
   >
      <content>
         [0,38][Attributes, Styles and Style Contexts]
   <paragraph
      resolver=NamedStyle:MainStyle
{resolver=AttributeSet,name=MainStyle,
             RightIndent=16.0,size=12,family=serif,
             LeftIndent=16.0,FirstLineIndent=16.0,nrefs=1}
   >
      <content>
        [38,49][The simple ]
      <content
        name=ConstantWidth
        foreground=java.awt.Color[r=0,g=255,b=0]
        family=monospaced
      >
        [49,62][PlainDocument]
      <content>
        [62,223][ class that you saw in the previous chap...]
      <content
        name=ConstantWidth
        foreground=java.awt.Color[r=0,g=255,b=0]
        family=monospaced
      >
        [223,237][StyledDocument]
      <content>
        [237,249][ interface. ]
      <content
        name=ConstantWidth
        foreground=java.awt.Color[r=0,g=255,b=0]
        family=monospaced
      >
        [249,263][StyledDocument]
      <content>
        [263,286][ is a sub-interface of ]
      <content
        name=ConstantWidth
        foreground=java.awt.Color[r=0,g=255,b=0]
        family=monospaced
```

```
>
  [286,294][Document]
<content>
  [294,475][ that contains methods for manipulating ...]
<content
  name=ConstantWidth
  foreground=java.awt.Color[r=0,g=255,b=0]
  family=monospaced
>
  [475,489][StyledDocument]
<content>
  [489,497][ called ]
<content
  name=ConstantWidth
  foreground=java.awt.Color[r=0,g=255,b=0]
  family=monospaced
>
  [497,518][DefaultStyledDocument]
<content>
  [518,557][ that is used as the default model for ]
<content
  name=ConstantWidth
  foreground=java.awt.Color[r=0,g=255,b=0]
  family=monospaced
>
  [557,566][JTextPane]
<content>
  [566,639][ and is also the base class from which m...]
<content
  name=ConstantWidth
  foreground=java.awt.Color[r=0,g=255,b=0]
  family=monospaced
>
  [639,651][HTMLDocument]
<content>
  [651,733][ class that handles input in HTML format...]
<content
  name=ConstantWidth
  foreground=java.awt.Color[r=0,g=255,b=0]
  family=monospaced
>
  [733,754][DefaultStyledDocument]
<content>
  [754,759][ and ]
<content
 name=ConstantWidth
```

```
      foreground=java.awt.Color[r=0,g=255,b=0]
      family=monospaced
   >
      [759,768][JTextPane]
   <content>
      [768,834][ you need to understand how Swing repres...]
 <paragraph
   resolver=NamedStyle:MainStyle
{resolver=AttributeSet,name=MainStyle,
           RightIndent=16.0,size=12,family=serif,
           LeftIndent=16.0,FirstLineIndent=16.0,nrefs=1}
   name=CompPara
   SpaceAbove=16.0
 >
   <component
     $ename=component
     name=Component
     component=javax.swing.JLabel[,0,0,0x0,invalid,hidden,
           alignmentX=0.0,alignmentY=null,
           border=,flags=0,
           maximumSize=,minimumSize=,preferredSize=,

   defaultIcon=javax.swing.ImageIcon@685ee635,disabledIcon=,

   horizontalAlignment=CENTER,horizontalTextPosition=CENTER,
           iconTextGap=4,labelFor=,
           text=Displaying text with attributes,

 verticalAlignment=CENTER,verticalTextPosition=BOTTOM]
   >
      [834,835][ ]
   <content
     name=Component
   >
      [835,836][ ]
 <paragraph
   resolver=NamedStyle:MainStyle
{resolver=AttributeSet,name=MainStyle,
           RightIndent=16.0,size=12,family=serif,
   LeftIndent=16.0,FirstLineIndent=16.0,nrefs=1}
   name=CompPara
   SpaceAbove=16.0
 >
   <content>
      [836,837][ ]
```

```
<bidi root>
  <bidi level
    bidiLevel=0
  >
    [0,837][Attributes, Styles and Style Contexts Th...]
```

The first thing to notice is that this document starts with a new element type called *section*. All DefaultStyledDocument element hierarchies are wrapped in a section element, whose only job is to act as a container for paragraph elements. The second difference between this hierarchy and the ones you have already seen is the way in which paragraph elements are used. In the JTextArea, the whole document is contained in a single paragraph element and each line is a content element. When DefaultStyled-Document is used, however, a paragraph corresponds more closely to what you would think of as a paragraph in a word processor such as Microsoft Word—a paragraph is a continuous run of text that ends with (and includes) a newline character. In other words, a paragraph element is used in a JTextPane where a content element would have been used with JTextArea.

If that is the case, what are content elements used for? In a Default-StyledDocument, a single content element maps the longest possible run of text that has the same set of character attributes, which is often smaller than a single line of text. In the simplest case, if you create a JTextPane with one line of text and no attributes, you'll get a single section element that contains a paragraph element wrapped around one content element that maps all the text. As soon as you add character attributes, the content elements are broken up at the boundaries between which the attributes are applied.

The document shown in Figure 3-6 has four paragraphs—the heading, the text, the paragraph containing the diagram, and a paragraph at the end of the document containing the newline that was created automatically for us by DefaultStyledDocument. If you refer to the program output shown above, you should be able to find the paragraph elements for each of these. Each element has its own associated attribute set, the content of which is shown when it is nonempty. Consider the heading paragraph, the first one in the document. Here is what the paragraph element looks like:

```
<paragraph
    bold=true
    resolver=NamedStyle:MainStyle
{resolver=AttributeSet,name=MainStyle,
            RightIndent=16.0,size=12,family=serif,
            LeftIndent=16.0,FirstLineIndent=16.0,nrefs=1}
```

```
      name=Heading2
      foreground=java.awt.Color[r=255,g=0,b=0]
      size=16
      family=serif
      LeftIndent=8.0
      FirstLineIndent=0.0
  >
      <content>
        [0,38][Attributes, Styles and Style Contexts]
```

The attributes are shown immediately after the paragraph tag. If you refer to Listing 2-2 in Chapter 2, you'll see that these are exactly the attributes that were encoded into the `Heading2` style. You'll also see two attributes that we didn't install by name—the `name` attribute, whose meaning is obvious, and the `resolver` attribute. The `resolver` attribute was discussed in the previous chapter—it points to the attribute set's resolving parent which, in this case, is called `MainStyle`. As you'll remember, this is the logical style for the document and it is linked to the `Heading2` style in this way because it was applied to the paragraph using the `setLogicalStyle` method. The `dump` method actually shows the content of the resolving parent attribute set and, as you can see, these attributes correspond exactly to the logical style created in Listing 2-3. This paragraph contains only one content element because the heading doesn't have any explicit character attributes applied to it.

Now let's look at the start of the next paragraph. The element structure that corresponds to part of the first line of this paragraph is shown next.

```
<paragraph
    resolver=NamedStyle:MainStyle
{resolver=AttributeSet,name=MainStyle,
          RightIndent=16.0,size=12,family=serif,
          LeftIndent=16.0,FirstLineIndent=16.0,nrefs=1}
  >
    <content>
      [38,49][The simple ]
    <content
      name=ConstantWidth
      foreground=java.awt.Color[r=0,g=255,b=0]
      family=monospaced
  >
      [49,62][PlainDocument]
    <content>

      [62,223][ class that you saw in the previous chap...]
```

```
<content
   name=ConstantWidth
   foreground=java.awt.Color[r=0,g=255,b=0]
   family=monospaced
 >
   [223,237][StyledDocument]
<content>
   [237,249][ interface. ]
<content
   name=ConstantWidth
   foreground=java.awt.Color[r=0,g=255,b=0]
   family=monospaced
 >
   [249,263][StyledDocument]
```

First, notice that the paragraph attributes don't contain a `name` attribute, but they do have a `resolver` attribute. In fact, if you look back at Listing 2-3, you'll see that this paragraph was created by adding an empty paragraph attribute set and the logical style. An empty attribute set has no attributes at all, not even `name` and `resolver` attributes, which explains why there is no `name` attribute present. The `resolver` attribute was added when `setLogicalStyle` was called and, again, you can see that the attributes shown are those of the global logical style created in this example.

Within this paragraph, there are many content elements. In fact, each time the character attributes change, there is a new content element. The first content element corresponds to the words "`The simple.`" It uses the paragraph attributes and has no explicit character attributes applied to it (refer to the `content` array in Listing 2-3 to see where character attributes are applied), but the next word, "`PlainDocument`" was rendered in green and with a constant-width font. Because it has different character attributes, it has its own content element, to which the extra attributes that were applied to it in Listing 2-3 are attached. Similarly, the next run of text has no character attributes and so needs yet another content tag, with an empty character attribute set. Both of these elements inherit all the attributes stored in their parent element.

Toward the end of the document you'll see the elements that are involved in representing the diagram, which is a `JLabel` included in the document using the `Component` attribute. When the element structure was created, a *component* element was added to represent the place at which the diagram should be rendered. A component element is just a leaf element whose name has been set to "`component`"—in all other respects, it is the same as a content element. The attributes in this element include the original component attribute that points to the Component and the content associated with it is the space that was added and to which the component attribute was applied. If an Icon had been installed in the document, an *icon* element would have been used instead.

You'll notice that the component element has an attribute called $ename that has the value "component." This attribute is actually the name of the element—it is the value that would be returned by the Element method getName. Elements store their names within their associated attribute set. If you're wondering why the paragraph, content, and section elements don't have a $ename attribute, it's because this attribute is not included in an attribute set by default; BranchElement returns "paragraph" and LeafElement returns "content" from the getName method if the attribute set does not define $ename. A section element is implemented by the SectionElement inner class of DefaultStyledDocument and returns "section" from its getName method. Therefore, these three types do not need to define $ename attribute.

Core Note

SectionElement is a subclass of BranchElement, because it is required to act as a container for ParagraphElements.

Views: Rendering the Document and Its Attributes

The document model contains both the raw text and the structural elements needed to reproduce the content of a text component in the way that the programmer expects. The model does not, however, directly determine how the component appears on the screen. This job is done by view objects, which interpret the element structure to lay out the text in paragraphs and lines and apply colors, fonts, and other effects as specified by the attributes held within the elements. In this section, we'll show you how the standard components map view objects onto the underlying model, and then we'll look at how to create your own views to enhance the rendering of text fields and JText-Pane. The techniques that you'll see in this section will be shown in the context of specific text components, but they are generic and can therefore be used with all of the text controls.

The Basic Views

There is a set of standard views used by the Swing text components, the most common of which were shown in Table 1-2 in Chapter 1. These views are created slightly differently by the simpler text components and the more complex ones. Let's start by looking at views in general and at the view structure of JTextField and JTextArea in particular to see how the views map onto the element structure shown in the previous section.

Views and the View Hierarchy

There are basically two types of views—those that act as containers and those that simply render text or other content. This makes views analogous to AWT components, some of which are also containers. The similarity also extends to the way in which views are handled because, for example, a view may be asked for its preferred size and will subsequently be given a rectangular area within which to work and within which it must render its content. Unlike AWT, however, there are no separate layout managers that you can assign to "container" views; the view contains the code that does the work that would fall to a layout manager.

Views are linked to elements and, like the element structure, the view structure is hierarchical. In the simplest possible case, one view object would map a single element, but this does not always happen—sometimes, a single element has more than one view associated with it. However, no view is ever associated with more than one element. A consequence of this is that the region of text covered by a single basic view (that is, a view that is not a container) only ever has one set of attributes, because an element only has a single (logical) attribute set. For reference, Table 3-1 lists the most important of the standard views in the Swing text package and indicates which is a container and which is a basic view and the text component with which they are associated.

Core Note

In this chapter, the term "basic view" will be used to refer to a view that is not a container.

Table 3-1 Swing Text Views by Type

View	Type	Text Component
BoxView	Container	Generic
CompositeView	Container	Generic
ComponentView	Basic	JEditorPane/JTextPane
FieldView	Basic	JTextField
IconView	Basic	JEditorPane/JTextPane
LabelView	Basic	JEditorPane/JTextPane
LabelView.LabelFragment	Basic	JEditorPane/JTextPane
ParagraphView	Container	JEditorPane/JTextPane
ParagraphView.Row	Container	JEditorPane/JTextPane
PasswordView	Basic	JPasswordField
PlainView	Basic	JTextArea
TableView	Container	JEditorPane/JTextPane
TableView.TableRow	Container	JEditorPane/JTextPane
TableView.TableCell	Container	JEditorPane/JTextPane
TableView.ProxyCell	Basic	JEditorPane/JTextPane
WrappedPlainView	Container	JTextArea
WrappedPlainView.WrappedLine	Basic	JTextArea

Notice that some of the views in Table 3-1 are inner classes of other views. For example, the container view `ParagraphView` has an inner class called `ParagraphView.Row`, which is also a container view. These inner class views are used to manage a smaller part of the element to which the main view is mapped. You'll see how this works when we look at specific examples later in this section.

The class hierarchy of the standard views is shown in Figure 3-3. For clarity, this diagram does not show the inner classes. Notice that all the container views are derived from `BoxView`, which is a subclass of `CompositeView`. `CompositeView` implements the methods that are required to host child views with no specific spatial relationship between them, while `BoxView` organizes its children either horizontally or vertically. `ParagraphView` is, in turn, a specialized form of `BoxView` that arranges lines in a vertical configuration to form a paragraph. You'll see examples shortly that show how specific container and child views are used by some of the text components to achieve the expected text layout.

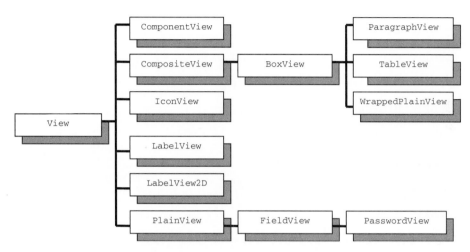

Figure 3-3   The Swing text view class hierarchy.

The *View* Class

All views are derived from the abstract class `View`, the methods and constants of which are shown in Table 3-2. As you can see from the constructor, to create a `View`, you must have an element with which it will be associated. Usually, a particular `View` subclass will be associated with a specific type of element. `Views` are created by a `ViewFactory`, which knows how to create the appropriate `Views` for the types of elements that are contained within the document that it is working on behalf of.

Table 3-2 Methods and Constants of the View Class

```
public View(Element elem)

public View getParent()

public void setParent(View parent)

public Document getDocument()
```

Table 3-2 Methods and Constants of the View Class (continued)

```
public View(Element elem)

public int getStartOffset()

public int getEndOffset()

public Element getElement()

public AttributeSet getAttributes()

public Container getContainer()

public ViewFactory getViewFactory()

public boolean isVisible();

public float getAlignment(int axis)

public int getViewCount()

public View getView(int n)

public abstract float getPreferredSpan(int axis)

public float getMinimumSpan(int axis)

public float getMaximumSpan(int axis)

public int getResizeWeight(int axis)

public void setSize(float width, float height)

public Shape getChildAllocation(int index, Shape a)

public void preferenceChanged(View child, boolean width,
    boolean height)

public abstract void paint(Graphics g, Shape allocation)

public int getNextVisualPositionFrom(int pos,
    Position.Bias b, Shape a, int direction,
    Position.Bias[] biasRet) throws BadLocationException

public abstract Shape modelToView(int pos, Shape a,
    Position.Bias b) throws BadLocationException

public Shape modelToView(int p0, Position.Bias b0, int p1,
    Position.Bias b1, Shape a) throws BadLocationException
```

Table 3-2 Methods and Constants of the View Class (continued)

```
public View(Element elem)

public abstract int viewToModel(float x, float y, Shape a,
     Position.Bias[] biasReturn);

public void insertUpdate(DocumentEvent e, Shape a,
     ViewFactory f)

public void removeUpdate(DocumentEvent e, Shape a,
     ViewFactory f)

public void changedUpdate(DocumentEvent e, Shape a,
     ViewFactory f)

public View breakView(int axis, int offset, float pos,
     float len)

public View createFragment(int p0, int p1)

public int getBreakWeight(int axis, float pos, float len)

public int getResizeWeight(int axis)

public static final int BadBreakWeight = 0;

public static final int GoodBreakWeight = 1000;

public static final int ExcellentBreakWeight = 2000;

public static final int ForcedBreakWeight = 3000;

public static final int X_AXIS = HORIZONTAL;

public static final int Y_AXIS = VERTICAL;
```

The `setParent` and `getParent` methods respectively set and retrieve the `View` that lies above the target `View` in the view hierarchy. The parent of a `View` is set as the hierarchy is being constructed, which usually happens when content is being added to the document.

The `getDocument`, `getStartOffset`, `getEndOffset`, `getElement`, `get-Container`, and `getViewFactory` methods all return attributes of the `View`. The start and end offsets will sometimes be the corresponding offsets of the element that the `View` is mapping, but this need not be the case, because sometimes more than one `View` will be used to span a single element. The offsets associated with a `View` are always bounded by the offset range of the element and, furthermore, no more than one non-container `View` covers a given offset range. The `getElement` method returns the mapped element, while `getContainer` returns the text component that is hosting the view. This can be used, for example, to get back to the `JTextField` or `JTextPane` from within a `View`. You'll see why this is useful when looking at some example `View` implementations later in this chapter.

The `getViewFactory` method returns the `ViewFactory` that created the `View`. Because only one `ViewFactory` is used to produce all the `View`s for a particular component, the default implementation of this method just delegates to its parent on the assumption that the `View` at the root of the hierarchy will know how to locate the `ViewFactory` that created it. You'll find out more about this in "View Factories" on page 211.

The `getAttributes` method returns the `View`'s associated `AttributeSet`. These attributes are typically the attributes of the element that the `View` is mapping and are obtained directly from the element by default. You can, of course, create your own `View` objects that return a different `AttributeSet` that may or may not be related to those of the underlying element. You'll see in Chapter 4 that this technique is used by the `View`s used to render HTML.

The `isVisible` method returns `true` if the `View` is visible and `false` if it is not. All of the standard `View`s in the text package just use the default implementation of this method, which always returns `true`. Some of the `View`s in the HTML package, however, override this and can claim to be invisible. When a `View` is not visible, screen space is not allocated for it to draw its content into.

The `getAlignment` method takes an argument that specifies whether alignment along the x-axis (`View.X_AXIS`) or the y-axis (`View.Y_AXIS`) is being requested. As with AWT and Swing components, the alignment value ranges from 0.0 to 1.0 and specifies the relative location of the `View`'s alignment point along the specified axis. A y-axis alignment value of 0.0 places the alignment point at the top of the `View` and 1.0 places it at the bottom. Similarly, an x-axis alignment of 0.0 aligns the left side of the `View` with the alignment points of other `View`s and 1.0 moves the alignment point to the right-hand side. By default, this method returns 0.5 for both axes, which has the effect of centering the `View` within whichever container it is placed. Often, a container `View` will be interested only in the alignment in a single direction. For example, when a `ParagraphView` is laying out a row, it is interested only in the y-axis alignment, to determine how to place its child `View`s relative to the baseline of each row within the paragraph. Figure 3-4 shows an example in which a `ParagraphView` is being used to lay out two lines of content, different parts of which have their own specific alignment requirements.

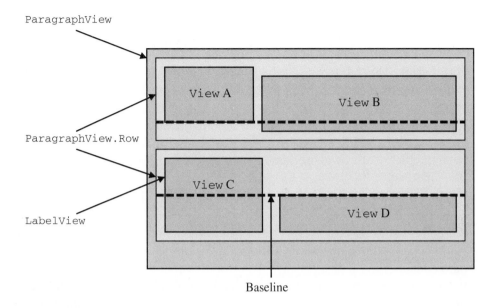

Figure 3-4 A view hierarchy with differing alignments.

The figure shows the ParagraphView, which places each line of content into a ParagraphView.Row subview and arranges them one above the other. Within each row, the pieces of content are placed horizontally. You can think of the ParagraphView as a box that lays out children along the y-axis, while a ParagraphView.Row is a box that lays out subviews along the x-axis. In fact, this is exactly how it works, because both ParagraphView and Paragraph-View.Row are derived from BoxView, which can be constructed to manage either a vertical (View.Y_AXIS) or a horizontal (View.X_AXIS) configuration. Within each row, there are views that render content. In the case of a JText-Pane, these would probably be instances of LabelView. The vertical position-ing of these content views is controlled by the value returned by getAlignment(View.Y_AXIS. The view labeled View A has its alignment point at its lower edge and so this edge is placed along the baseline. To achieve this, the getAlignment method would return 1.0. View B, by con-trast, has its alignment point part way between its upper and lower edge, nearer the bottom than the top. The alignment value of this view would be something between 0.5 and 1.0, depending on how much of the view appears below the baseline. In Figure 3-4, the y-alignment of View B is probably around 0.8. In the second row, View C is centered on the baseline because its y-axis alignment is 0.5, while `View` D is aligned with its upper edge on the baseline, because its alignment is 0.0.

In practice, the standard views don't allow their alignments to be easily customized. The `LabelView`, which renders text for `JTextPane`, uses the ratio of the total height of the font to its descent to determine the y-alignment. This places the `View` baseline in the same place as the font baseline, so that the correct amount of space is allocated to draw the descenders for those characters in the font that have them. To change this behavior, you would have to create your own subclass of `LabelView` and override its `getAlignment` method.

The `getViewCount` and `getView` methods are used by `View`s that act as containers and allow the set of child `View`s to be accessed. Because these methods exist in all `View`s, every `View` can be a container, so theoretically you could code a container `View` without subclassing `CompositeView`, the standard container in the text package. You would probably only do this, however, if you need to create a container `View` that has special requirements that cannot be obtained by subclassing `CompositeView`. The default `View` implementations of these methods return 0 and `null`, respectively.

The next three methods, `getPreferredSpan`, `getMinimumSpan`, and `getMaximumSpan`, are equivalent to the AWT component `getPreferredSize`, `getMinimumSize`, and `getMaximumSize` methods, except that they deal only in one dimension at the time. Each method takes an argument (either `View.X_AXIS` or `View.Y_AXIS`) that specifies the direction for which the span is required. The values returned from these methods are used by the parent container `View` to decide how large it needs to be to accommodate its child views. The functionality provided by layout managers in respect of AWT and Swing components is coded directly into the container `View`s and so cannot be changed by plugging in a different layout policy. This is not usually an issue, however, because the layout requirements of pieces of a text component are more clearly defined than those of graphical user interface (GUI) components.

Notice that these three methods all return values of type `float`, not `int`. The intention is that size measurements will be made in points instead of pixels, so you can render documents in a way that is not dependent on the resolution of your screen or your printer. To make this work, it is sometimes necessary to return fractional point counts. In practice, however, in both JDK 1.1 and Java 2, the text components map points directly to pixels, so it is common to see code that casts the returned value of these methods directly to `int`s.

The getResizeWeight method is used to indicate whether a View would like to be resized if necessary to fit available space. If this method returns 0, the View will always be rendered at its preferred size and the getMinimum-Span method will return the same value as getPreferredSpan.

The setSize method is invoked by a View's immediate parent to inform it of the dimensions of the space allocated to it. In response to this, a container View will usually determine the new layout of its children, which will result in their setSize method being called. Noncontainer Views usually do nothing when this method is called because their main function is simply to paint their content, which will happen when the child View's paint method is invoked later.

The getChildAllocation method is implemented only by container views and returns the space allocated to a child view, given by its index number. In a noncontainer View, this method returns null. The ordering of views is dependent on a particular container; for example, ParagraphView orders rows from top to bottom, so that index 0 corresponds to the top row of the paragraph, index 1 to the next row down, and so on. By contrast, Paragraph-View.Row builds a horizontal layout in which index 0 is the leftmost component, index 1 the next to the right, and so forth. The second argument to this method and the return value are both of type Shape. Shape is an interface defined by the AWT package that can represent a graphical object with any kind of outline. Given a Shape, you can use the getBounds method to get the smallest Rectangle that completely surrounds the shape. The standard text Views all deal with rectangular areas, so the Shape argument to this method (and to all the other methods that specify a Shape) will always be a Rectangle when the standard Views are in use. The Shape argument of get-ChildAllocation is actually the region allocated to the View. This value can be used to dynamically compute the area that corresponds to the given child, if this information is not stored within the container View.

The preferenceChanged method of a container View is called by a child View when the width or height of that child might have changed because of, for example, a change of font within the region that the View covers. The width and height values indicate which direction might have changed its preferred span, while the child argument specifies the child making the call. Not all container Views need the information provided by the child argument, so it is often supplied as null.

The paint method is, as its name suggests, where the View renders it contents given a Graphics object to draw into and a Shape that describes the area allocated to the View. Usually, a container View like Paragraph-

View will implement the paint method by calling the paint method of each of its children. This process may continue if there are several levels of nested Views. Eventually, the paint method of a content-rendering View will be invoked and something will be drawn on the screen (or on the printer). You'll see typical implementations of the paint method in the examples later in this chapter.

The getNextVisualPositionFrom method is typically used when moving the cursor up, down, left, or right. The pos argument is the offset within the document of the current location of the cursor, while direction, which takes one of the values SwingConstants.NORTH, SOUTH, EAST, or WEST, specifies which way the cursor is moving. The return value is the offset within the model that corresponds to the new location of the cursor. Because this method is applied to a particular View that maps only a part of the model, it is possible that the target location is not within the element that the View maps. For example, because a LabelView covers part or all of a single line of text, the result of moving the cursor up (NORTH) or down (SOUTH) will always be to move it out of the current View. If the new location is not within the bounds of the View, -1 is returned. When this happens, the parent View is responsible for redirecting the request to a more appropriate child View. Consider, for example, the situation shown in Figure 3-5. This figure shows the Views for a simple document containing a single paragraph with three lines of text as they would be if the document were rendered within a JTextPane. Each line of text is held within a ParagraphView.Row and, within that, a Label-View. The LabelView is directly associated with the content of the model, whereas the other Views are containers. Suppose the cursor is currently located immediately before the number 2 in the second row and the cursor up key is pressed. To determine where to move, the getNextVisualPosi-tionFrom method will be called on the LabelView that contains the text for the second row. The cursor should move up to the 1 in the row above. However, LabelView cannot return a meaningful position when asked to move North because, as you can see from Figure 3-5, this is bound to take it outside the area that it covers. Instead, it returns -1. The ParagraphView.Row object for the second row sees this result and also returns -1 to the enclosing ParagraphView. The ParagraphView responds to this by passing the request to the ParagraphView.Row for the top row (the one before the row that it just tried), which does contain the desired location.

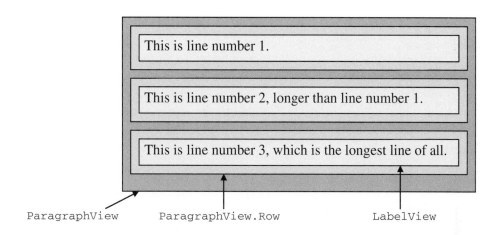

This is line number 1.

This is line number 2, longer than line number 1.

This is line number 3, which is the longest line of all.

ParagraphView   ParagraphView.Row   LabelView

Figure 3-5   Determining the next visual position within a `View`.

Even such simple operations as moving the cursor left or right need not imply that the model position is just incremented or decremented because, for example, the model may contain content that a particular `View` does not actually display. In cases like this, moving the cursor forward one location might involve increasing the `pos` value by four if there are three intervening model locations that are not displayed. The two `Bias` arguments are used in conjunction with the bi-directional text support that will be described in Chapter 5.

The `modelToView` and `viewToModel` methods map directly between model positions and `View` locations. Because the way in which a `View` renders the model content is `View` specific, only the `View` can know how to map from a screen location to the position in the model that supplied the character or other information rendered at that location. For this reason, a `viewToModel` request is usually processed by the `View` that actually drew the content at the position given by the `x` and `y` values supplied. Similarly, the first form of the `modelToView` method is delegated to the `View` at the location corresponding to the `pos` argument. When the second form of `modelToView` is used, all `View`s in the range `p0` to `p1` are consulted by calling their `modelToView(int pos, Shape a, Position.Bias b)` method, and a `Shape` corresponding to the total area covered by that range is created as the union of all the `Shape`s corresponding to the child `View`s. This, for example, could be used to obtain a `Rectangle` covering two lines of a paragraph as the union of the `Rectangle`s of the individual lines. You'll see typical implementations of both `modelToView` and `viewToModel` in "Custom Views and Input Fields" on page 282.

The `insertUpdate`, `removeUpdate`, and `changedUpdate` methods are called when a change takes place within the document that falls within the area mapped by the `View`. Typically, these methods respond by creating or deleting `Views` or by changing the attributes associated with an existing `View`. The arguments to all of these methods are a `DocumentEvent` that describes the change to the document, a `Shape` that specifies the space allocated to the receiving `View`, and the `View-Factory` that is being used to create the `Views` for the text component displaying the document. This factory is used to create new `Views` if necessary.

The `breakView` and `getBreakWeight` methods are used to organize runs of text (and other content if necessary) into units that can fit on the current line. As you'll see later, paragraphs are built from rows whose width is bounded by the width of the space allocated to the text component. The preferred width of the text within a particular `Element` may bear no relation to the space available to render it. If the content of the `Element` is too wide to fit within the space available on the current row, it must be split at an appropriate point and some of the content moved to the next row. The `breakView` method has the job of creating a `View` that maps as much of the `Element` as will fit in what remains of the current row; layout then continues on the next row with the balance of the `Element`. If the `Element` is large, this splitting process may continue over several rows. The `getBreakWeight` method determines how favorable it is to break the `View` that it is applied to at the offset given by the `pos` argument. Some `Views` (such as `IconView` and `ComponentView`) cannot be broken, so return the value `BadBreakWeight`. Text views prefer to be broken at white space boundaries and return `ExcellentBreakWeight` if the proposed location coincides with white space and `GoodBreakWeight` otherwise. Some `Views` require a mandatory break after they have been rendered and return `Forced-BreakWeight` to indicate this. Splitting usually occurs along the x-axis, but could (at least theoretically) happen along the y-axis if a text component were being rendered in an environment that had a notion of page size, in which case it would be necessary to split a `ParagraphView` so that it was wholly contained within the available space on the current page. Although the framework exists to support this, the current implementation of `ParagraphView` does not split itself on the y-axis. If you need this functionality, you will have to create a custom view derived from `ParagraphView`. An example of a custom `Paragraph-View` is shown later in this chapter.

While splitting a `View` into fragments is most often required because of space constraints, another reason for doing so is the presence of bi-directional text. When an `Element` contains text that flows in both directions, it is mapped by a set of `Views` that each render only in one direction. The `createFragment` method is used to create a `View` fragment that covers a uni-directional chunk of content.

View Factories

You've already seen that there are several different types of `View`s that render different types of content. In fact, the same content type can be managed by a different `View` type within different text components. For example, plain text in a `JTextField` is mapped by a `FieldView`, by a `PasswordView` in `JPasswordField`, by a `PlainView` or a `WrappedPlainView` in `JTextArea`, and by a `LabelView` in `JTextPane`. The allocation of the appropriate view for a particular type of content is performed by a `ViewFactory`; Different text components use different implementations of the `ViewFactory` to create the correct type of `View` for their particular circumstances.

`ViewFactory` is, in fact, an interface with just one method:

```
public interface ViewFactory {
    public View create(Element elem);
}
```

The `create` method is supposed to instantiate a `View` object that can map some or all of the `Element` given as its argument. Some `ViewFactory` imple-mentations (such as that for `JTextField`) only have a single `View` type (`FieldView`) and so always return an object of that type. More complex com-ponents use various different `View` types and typically look at the name of the `Element` (returned by its `getName` method) to decide which subclass of `View` to use. In a `JTextPane`, for example, a content `Element` is mapped by a `LabelView`, while a component `Element` is mapped by a `ComponentView`. The `create` method is usually an `if` statement that compares the element's name to a fixed set of valid names to decide which type of `View` to return. It is equally valid, however, to use the attributes associated with the `Element` (or any other criterion) as well as (or instead of) the name to determine the `View` type. This approach is taken by `JEditorPane` when it is displaying HTML, as you'll see in Chapter 4.

Where does the `ViewFactory` come from? There are two ways in which a text component can obtain a `ViewFactory`: from its `EditorKit` or from its UI delegate. When the `View` hierarchy for a component is being built, the `modelChanged` method of the component's UI delegate is called. Unless you write a custom delegate that overrides it, this method is provided by the class `javax.swing.plaf.basic.BasicTextUI`, which gets the `ViewFactory` from the `getViewFactory` method of an inner class called `RootView` that is always at the top of the `View` hierarchy for *every* text component. The get-`ViewFactory` method of `BasicTextUI.RootView` first calls the `getEditor-`

`Kit` method of the `JTextComponent` that the `View`s are to be associated with, and then calls the editor kit's `getViewFactory` method. If this method returns a factory, it is used to create all the `View`s for that component. If, instead, it returns `null`, the UI delegate will provide the `ViewFactory` by supplying a suitable `create` method.

In terms of the standard text components, the three simpler ones, `JText-Field`, `JPasswordField`, and `JTextArea`, all use the `DefaultEditorKit`, which does not supply a `ViewFactory` (its `getViewFactory` method returns `null`), so the `ViewFactory` for each of these components is implemented in their UI delegate class. By contrast, `JTextPane` uses `StyledEditorKit` (or a custom subclass of `StyledEditorKit`), which does provide a `ViewFactory` that knows how to map elements from `DefaultStyledDocument`. `JEditor-Pane` can use any editor kit, but that editor kit must supply a view factory, because `BasicEditorPaneUI` does not override the `BasicTextUI` `create` method, which returns `null` when asked for a `View` for any kind of element. The relationship between the standard Swing text components and their view factories is summarized in Table 3-3.

Table 3-3 Text Components and View Factories

Component	Source of View Factory
JTextField	BasicTextFieldIU
JPasswordField	BasicPasswordFieldUI
JTextArea	BasicTextAreaUI
JTextPane	From editor kit
JEditorPane	From editor kit

Because a `ViewFactory` creates a `View` based on the type of each `Element` that it finds in the document, it is clear that there must be a close connection between the `ViewFactory` and the `Document` class that is plugged into the text component. The factories in the UI delegates for the simple text components can, for example, return only `View` objects for the `Element` types created by `PlainDocument`, which is the `Document` model used by these components. If you create a subclass of `PlainDocument` that you want to use with any of these components, you must either restrict yourself to using the same element types as `PlainDocument` or you will have to extend the `ViewFactory` in the UI delegate class so that it can provide `Views` for your specialized element types. You'll see how to create a custom `ViewFactory` and a custom `View` for `JTextField` in "Custom Views and Input Fields" on page 282.

The View Hierarchies of `JTextField` and `JTextArea`

The discussion so far has been a little academic, so let's make it more concrete by looking at specific examples. We'll start by creating a class that can be used to display the hierarchy of `Views` within a component. Once we've got this, we'll use it to look at the internals of some of the five text components in the Swing package, starting with `JTextField`.

Looking at the View Hierarchy

As you've already seen, all the `Views` that map a single component form a hierarchy, rooted from a single `View` called the root view. You can obtain a reference to this `View` by calling the `getRootView` method of `BasicTextUI` and then using the `getViewCount` and `getView` methods that you saw in Table 3-3 to find all the children, grandchildren, and later descendants of the root view. Using these methods, it is a simple matter to create a method that will recursively descend the complete view hierarchy for an instance of any text component and display a representation of all the `Views` that have been created, much as we were able to do for the `Element` structure within the document model earlier in this chapter. You can see an implementation of this in Listing 3-1.

Listing 3-1 A Text Pane with Automatic Scrolling

```
package AdvancedSwing.Chapter3;

import javax.swing.*;
import javax.swing.text.*;
import java.io.*;

public class ViewDisplayer {
    public static void displayViews(JTextComponent comp,
                                    PrintStream out) {
```

Listing 3-1 A Text Pane with Automatic Scrolling (continued)

```
        View rootView = comp.getUI().getRootView(comp);
        displayView(rootView, 0, comp.getDocument(), out);
    }

    public static void displayView(View view, int indent,
                                   Document doc,
                                   PrintStream out) {
        String name = view.getClass().getName();
        for (int i = 0; i < indent; i++) {
            out.print("\t");
        }

        int start = view.getStartOffset();
        int end = view.getEndOffset();
        out.println(name + "; offsets [" + start + ", " +
                    end + "]");
        int viewCount = view.getViewCount();
        if (viewCount == 0) {
            int length = Math.min(32, end - start);
            try {
                String txt = doc.getText(start, length);
                for (int i = 0; i < indent + 1; i++) {
                    out.print("\t");
                }
                out.println("[" + txt + "]");
            } catch (BadLocationException e) {
            }
        } else {
            for (int i = 0; i < viewCount; i++) {
                displayView(view.getView(i), indent + 1,
                            doc, out);
            }
        }
    }
}
```

The `ViewDisplayer` class contains two static methods, either of which could be used to look at some or all of the `View` structure within a text component. The first of these methods, `displayViews`, is the more useful of the two. It takes as arguments a reference to a text component and a `PrintStream`, to which it sends its output. This method uses the

`JComponent getUI` method to locate the text component's UI delegate (which will always be a subclass of `javax.swing.plaf.TextUI`) and then calls its `getRootView` method to locate the root of the hierarchy. It uses the second public method, `displayView`, to print a representation of the root `View` and its child `Views`. This method is recursive; Each time it calls itself, it increments the indent argument by one, so that the hierarchical structure of the `Views` that it encounters can be clearly seen. So that you can easily relate the various `Views` to the parts of the document model that they map, the `displayView` method displays not only all the `View` objects that it finds, but also up to the first 32 characters of the `Element` within the document model that each `View` maps.

Views and *JTextField*

Let's now use the `ViewDisplayer` class to examine the `Views` that are used by the simplest text component of all, the one-line `JTextField`. Earlier in this chapter, you saw how simple the `Element` structure of this component is. For ease of comparison with the `View` hierarchy, here are the `Elements` that are created for a `JTextField` that contains the text "That's one small step for man…":

```
<paragraph>
  <content>
    [0,33][That's one small step for man...]
```

Core Note

For clarity, we're not going to show the elements attached to the "Bidi" root in this section because they do not relate directly to the `View` hierarchy in any of the examples that you'll see here. Bi-directional text is discussed in Chapter 5.

To see the `View` hierarchy for this text component, use the command:

```
java AdvancedSwing.Chapter3.TextFieldViews
```

The output from this command should look like this:

```
javax.swing.plaf.basic.BasicTextUI$RootView; offsets [0, 33]
   javax.swing.text.FieldView; offsets [0, 33]
         [That's one small step for man...]
```

The first thing to notice about this is that it is very simple: there is a single root view, implemented by the `BasicTextUI.RootView` class that maps the whole text field. Contained within the root view is a single `FieldView`, which also maps the whole text field. You'll see that the offset range for the `FieldView` exactly matches that of the content and paragraph elements seen in the `Document` representation. In this case, the `ViewFactory` for the `JTextField` returned a `FieldView` when its `create` method was called with the paragraph element as its argument. Because a `JTextField` is only supposed to hold a single line of text, you would see this exact structure in any `JTextField`, no matter how large its content and whether all the content could appear on the screen at the same time. In fact, if the width of the `JTextField` is constrained so that it cannot display all the characters in the model, the `FieldView` arranges for the content to appear to scroll left and right as the user types or drags the mouse inside the text field's visible area. Because this is just a matter of presentation, the model is not aware that any of this is happening. If you're interested, you can see some of the details of the scrolling mechanism in "Custom Views and Input Fields" on page 282.

The mapping between the simple element hierarchy of `JTextField` and the corresponding `View` hierarchy is shown pictorially in Figure 3-6.

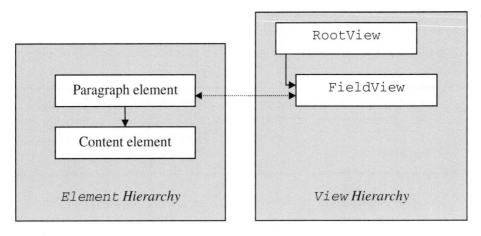

Figure 3-6 The `View` and `Element` hierarchies for `JTextField`.

An obvious question that arises from Figure 3-6 is why there is no `View` object corresponding to the content element on the left side of the diagram. Simply put, there isn't a `View` object for this element because it isn't needed—the paragraph element maps all the text, so the `View` object for the paragraph can render everything. There is slightly more to it than this, however, as you'll see when looking at the `View` structure for `JTextArea`.

JTextArea: Nonwrapping and Wrapping Views

The `View` structure for a `JTextArea` is very similar to that of `JTextField`, but there are two slightly different cases to consider. Let's look at the simple case first. As you saw earlier in this chapter, the element structure of a `JTextArea` that contains two lines of text looks like this:

```
<paragraph>
  <content>
    [0,33][That's one small step for man...]
  <content>
    [33,61][One giant leap for mankind.]
```

If you type the command

```
java AdvancedSwing.Chapter3.TextAreaViews
```

you'll see the `View` hierarchy that corresponds to this model structure:

```
javax.swing.plaf.basic.BasicTextUI$RootView; offsets [0, 61]
    javax.swing.text.PlainView; offsets [0, 61]
        [That's one small step for man...]
```

As you can see, as with the `JTextField`, there is only one `View` covering all the content, despite the fact that there are two content elements and the fact that the text covers two lines. Here, as before, the `View` maps the paragraph element, not the content element, and it is responsible for displaying all the data. This `JTextArea` does not have line wrapping turned on, so if you narrow the window so that the text no longer fits, it will just be clipped to the right. If you do this within 30 seconds of running the example, the `View` structure will be printed again and, not surprisingly, you'll see that it doesn't change as a result of the text area being narrowed. This situation changes, however, in the next example in which line wrapping *is* enabled. You can run this example with the following command:

```
java AdvancedSwing.Chapter3.TextAreaViews2
```

This text area is exactly the same as the previous one, except that it has line wrapping turned on. The element structure is not affected by this change, but the `View` hierarchy changes:

```
javax.swing.plaf.basic.BasicTextUI$RootView; offsets [0, 61]
    javax.swing.text.WrappedPlainView; offsets [0, 61]
        javax.swing.text.WrappedPlainView$WrappedLine;
                                              offsets [0, 33]
```

```
        [That's one small step for man...]
  javax.swing.text.WrappedPlainView$WrappedLine;
                                     offsets [33, 61]
        [One giant leap for mankind.]
```

As before, the paragraph element maps to a `WrappedPlainView`, but this time each content element has a corresponding `WrappedPlain-View.WrappedLine` object. `WrappedLine` is an inner class of `Wrapped-PlainView`; its job is to render one line of text, wrapping it at the right margin of the text component if necessary. If you narrow the window within 30 seconds of starting this example, you'll see that the text does indeed wrap (as shown in Figure 3-2), but the `View` structure does not change. Therefore, the `WrappedLine` `View` may need to draw text that covers more than one line on the screen. The `View` and `Element` structures for this `JTextArea` are shown in Figure 3-7.

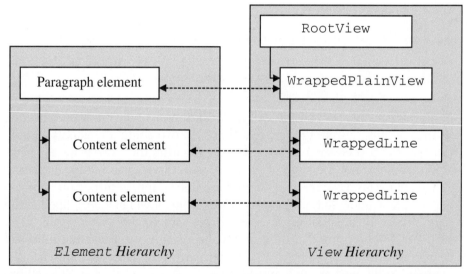

Figure 3-7   The `View` and `Element` hierarchies for `JTextArea` with line wrapping.

How does this more complex `View` hierarchy get built? So far, all we've said about building the `View` hierarchy is that the create method of the `View-Factory` is called to manufacture `Views` corresponding to elements in the model. However, you've just seen this work in two different ways. In the case of the `JTextField` and the nonwrapping `JTextArea`, only one `View` is created, despite the fact that there are two content elements and, in fact, these `Views` correspond to the paragraph element that wraps all the model content, rather than the content elements themselves. By contrast, when line wrapping is turned on, the View structure changes—there is still a top-level View that is associated with the paragraph element, but now there are two more, one for each content element. What is it that causes this difference in the View structure? To see how this happens, let's look at how the second of these structures is built.

To build the View structure, the getViewFactory method of the Root-View is called (from the UI delegate's modelChanged method) to get the ViewFactory and then the factory's create method is called, passing it the root element of the document hierarchy as its argument. The View returned by this call is installed as the only child of the RootView of the component and no more create calls are made from the modelChanged method. In the case of a JTextArea with line wrapping enabled, the initial create call results in the creation of a WrappedPlainView object that maps the paragraph element given to it. When this View is connected to the RootView, its setParent method is called to establish a backward reference from the WrappedPlainView to the RootView. As you can see from the class hierarchy diagram in Figure 3-3, WrappedPlainView is derived from BoxView, which is a subclass of CompositeView. The setParent method of WrappedPlainView is actually inherited from CompositeView. As well as saving the reference to its parent (by passing it to the setParent method of View), this method also invokes a method called load-Children, which is defined as follows:

```
protected void loadChildren(ViewFactory f);
```

Although there is a default implementation of this method in Composite-View, WrappedPlainView overrides it. The WrappedPlainView implementation loops over all the child elements of the paragraph element that it is associated with and creates a WrappedLine View for each of them. Each of these Views is installed as a child of the WrappedPlainView and is associated with a single content element, producing the structure shown in Figure 3-7. It is important to note that, although the basis for this mechanism, namely the loadChildren method, is part of the CompositeView class, the exact details of the implementation are a part of WrappedPlainView. Hence, other container Views can use different policies to create and install child Views as necessary. Furthermore, because this functionality is part of CompositeView and all container Views are derived from CompositeView, every container has the opportunity to create the necessary child views when its setParent method is called and can do so simply by overriding the loadChildren method of CompositeView. This same mechanism is exploited by the Views used by JTextPane to create the more complex hierarchies that you'll see later in this chapter.

What about the simpler structure that was created for both `JTextField` and `JTextArea` when line wrapping was turned off? In these two cases, the process is initially identical—the `create` method of the component's `View-Factory` is called and passed the root element of the model. In the case of `JTextField`, this results in the creation of a `FieldView` object, which becomes the child of the `RootView` (see Figure 3-6). As before, the connection between the `FieldView` and `RootView` is made by calling the `set-Parent` method of `FieldView`. Unlike `PlainView`, however, `FieldView` is not derived from `CompositeView`; in fact, the `setParent` method of `Field-View` is inherited from `View` and no method equivalent to `loadChildren` is called from the `View` `setParent` method. As a result, no child `Views` are created for the `FieldView` and the hierarchy remains as shown in Figure 3-6. The nonwrapping `JTextArea` case is almost identical. Here, the `create` method of the `JTextArea` `ViewFactory` creates a `PlainView` if line wrapping is not enabled (instead of a `WrappedPlainView`). `PlainView` is actually the superclass of `FieldView` and it behaves in the same way so, again, no children are created. The final `View` hierarchy for a `JTextArea` without line wrapping is the same as that shown in Figure 3-6, except that a `PlainView` replaces the `FieldView`.

The Views Used with `JEditorPane` and `JTextPane`

Because `JEditorPane` and `JTextPane` support a wider range of facilities than the components we looked at in the previous section, you won't be surprised to discover that they use a more complex `View` structure to provide this extra functionality. The `View` structure of `JEditorPane` is, in fact, completely customizable—because you can plug any editor kit into it and you can also supply your own `Document` class, the attributes that `JEditorPane` can support are completely open-ended. As a result, the editor kits used with `JEditorPane` will almost certainly need to define their own custom `Views` that either extend the standard `Views` to provide extra features or implement completely new functionality. The Swing package comes with support for documents encoded in either Hypertext Markup Language (HTML) or Rich Text Format (RTF); HTML use its own implementation of `Document` and both types supply their own editor kit. At the time of writing, the HTML editor kit, which is discussed in the next chapter, uses several custom `Views`, but the RTF editor kit does not.

`JTextPane` is more constrained than `JEditorPane`, because you can only install a `Document` that implements the `StyledDocument` interface and an editor kit that extends `StyledEditorKit`. This doesn't, of course, mean that you can't have a `JTextPane` configured in such a way as to use custom attributes or new `View` objects—in fact, you'll see two examples of this in the next section. It does mean, however, that customized `JTextPanes` are more likely to use the standard `Views` than customized `JEditorPanes`. In this section, you'll see the `View` structure of `JTextPane` and how it differs from that of `JTextArea` and `JTextField`. We'll use this `View` structure to demonstrate general principles that also apply to `JEditorPane`, so that you'll be in a better position to properly use the Swing HTML support and, more importantly, to extend it if necessary.

A Typical *JTextPane* View Hierarchy

As we did in the previous section, we'll explain the `JTextPane` `View` structure by showing you the `Views` that correspond to an example that you saw earlier in this chapter. If you type the command

```
java AdvancedSwing.Chapter3.TextPaneViews
```

and wait for a short time, you'll see the `View` structure that corresponds to the example shown in Figure 3-6. Because this is a fairly complex example, the `View` structure is relatively large, so it would be a good idea to redirect the output to a file, especially if you're working in an environment (such as DOS) that doesn't provide much scrolling in the shell window. Although there is quite a lot of output, if you look carefully at it you'll find that it is pretty repetitive and that there are only a few basic constructs that are used many times over. Here, for example, is a snapshot of the start of the `View` structure:

```
javax.swing.plaf.basic.BasicTextUI$RootView; offsets [0, 837]
   javax.swing.text.BoxView; offsets [0, 837]
      javax.swing.text.ParagraphView; offsets [0, 38]
         javax.swing.text.ParagraphView$Row; offsets [0, 38]
            javax.swing.text.LabelView; offsets [0, 38]
               [Attributes, Styles and Style Con]
      javax.swing.text.ParagraphView; offsets [38, 834]
         javax.swing.text.ParagraphView$Row; offsets [38, 114]
            javax.swing.text.LabelView; offsets [38, 49]
               [The simple ]
            javax.swing.text.LabelView; offsets [49, 62]
               [PlainDocument]
            javax.swing.text.LabelView$LabelFragment;
                                        offsets [62, 114]
               [ class that you saw in the previ]
```

If you examine the rest of the output, you'll find that it consists of repeated passages that all look very much like this (with the exception of the first two lines, which are not repeated). The last part is slightly different, because there is an embedded Component in the document—we'll look at that later. Here is the element structure that corresponds to this part of the View hierarchy:

```
<section>
  <paragraph
    bold=true
    resolver=NamedStyle:MainStyle
{resolver=AttributeSet,name=MainStyle,
            RightIndent=16.0,size=12,family=serif,
            LeftIndent=16.0,FirstLineIndent=16.0,nrefs=1}
    name=Heading2
    foreground=java.awt.Color[r=255,g=0,b=0]
    size=16
    family=serif
    LeftIndent=8.0
    FirstLineIndent=0.0
  >
    <content>
      [0,38][Attributes, Styles and Style Contexts]
  <paragraph
    resolver=NamedStyle:MainStyle {resolver=AttributeSet,
            name=MainStyle,
            RightIndent=16.0,size=12,family=serif,
            LeftIndent=16.0,FirstLineIndent=16.0,nrefs=1}
  >
    <content>
      [38,49][The simple ]
    <content
      name=ConstantWidth
      foreground=java.awt.Color[r=0,g=255,b=0]
      family=monospaced
    >
      [49,62][PlainDocument]
    <content>
      [62,223][ class that you saw in the previous chap...]
```

As usual, the View hierarchy starts with a RootView. The first *real* View is, in this case, a BoxView. As you can see by looking at the offsets, the BoxView covers all the document content and, in fact, is created because of the Section element that always wraps the element structure created by DefaultStyledDocument. The job of a BoxView is to arrange its children in a straight line, either horizontally or vertically depending on the axis passed as an argument to its constructor:

```
public BoxView(int axis);    // View.X_AXIS or View.Y_AXIS
```

When created to map a `Section` element, `BoxView` arranges its children vertically, making sure that their alignment points are lined up on a vertical straight line. This behavior is, in fact, just like that of the Swing `Box` container when created with constructor `BoxLayout.Y_AXIS`, and it results in all the paragraphs being laid out one above the other. The element structure next shows two paragraphs covering offsets 0 through 37, and 38 through 833; in terms of Figure 3-6, these correspond to the heading and the main body of the text, which ends just before the embedded diagram. Because the text attributes vary over the span of these two paragraphs, many different elements are used to represent their content. As you know, each paragraph has its own `paragraph` element, within which there is a `content` element for each run of text that shares the same attributes. Thus, for example, the `paragraph` element for the heading has a single `content` element, while the extract of the element structure for the main body text shown above has three, because the word "PlainDocument" is shown in red and in a monospaced font, whereas the rest of the text in this range, some before and some after this word, uses the attributes installed at the paragraph level.

As we said earlier, under normal circumstances, each element in the element hierarchy will tend to map to one `View`. To see how this works for `JTextPane`, look first at the `View` structure created for the first paragraph. The `paragraph` element causes the creation of a single `ParagraphView` object that maps the entire `paragraph` element. `ParagraphView` is a subclass of `BoxView` that lays out its children vertically; every paragraph in a `JTextPane` is represented by a single `ParagraphView`. This `ParagraphView` has one child of type `ParagraphView.Row` that also covers the whole paragraph because, in this case, the paragraph fits on a single screen line. This `View`, in turn, has a `LabelView` that again maps all of the paragraph's content—in this case, the text "Attributes, Styles, and Style Contexts." This is not quite a one-to-one mapping between elements and `View`s! What exactly is going on here?

As we said before, a `ParagraphView` maps a complete paragraph and is capable, using features inherited from `BoxView`, of arranging its child `View`s one above the other. Because of this, it would be natural for each child of a `ParagraphView` to correspond to a single line of text as seen on the screen. However, the `content` elements that contain the text to be displayed do not, in general, correspond to single lines of text. In fact, the actual mapping between screen lines and element content is variable and depends on several factors, including the width of the area allocated to the text component, the font in use, and any indents assigned at the paragraph level. Because of this, there is not a one-to-one mapping between content elements and `Views` in `JTextPane`. To simplify its job, `ParagraphView` doesn't attempt to deal directly with `Views` such as `LabelView` that render text (or other content). Instead, it creates a set of child `Views` of type `ParagraphView.Row`, each of which maps a single line of text on the screen. Because it knows that each of these child `Views` exactly spans a single line, its only responsibility, after creating its children, is to make sure that they are lined up one above the other in the screen space allocated to the paragraph. You'll see how the child `Views` are created in "Paragraph Size, Line Layout, and Wrapping" on page 225.

Even though the first paragraph has only one line of text, it still needs the overhead of a `ParagraphView.Row View`, because `ParagraphView` deals only with children of this type. In fact, if you resized the window and made it narrow enough so that the heading would no linger fit on one line, the `ParagraphView` would create as many `ParagraphView.Row` `Views` as it needed to manage all the lines of heading text in the new arrangement. In the case shown above, the `ParagraphView.Row View` has a single `LabelView` child that maps all the text in the corresponding content element. `LabelView`'s job is to draw the actual text on the screen, using the correct font and the correct foreground color. It is also obliged to be able to determine the width of the text that it maps, and to translate from an offset within the part of the document that it is rendering to the location on the screen at which the text at that offset is being drawn, and vice versa.

The second paragraph has the same basic structure as the heading. Again, the paragraph element maps to a single `ParagraphView`, which has one `ParagraphView.Row` child for each actual line of text. Because this paragraph spans several lines, this particular `ParagraphView` has several `ParagraphView.Row` children; the extract above shows only the first `ParagraphView.Row` but, in fact, with the window width initially assigned to it and the fonts installed on my system, this paragraph actually has 10 `ParagraphView.Row`s allocated to it. Looking only at the first line of text (in Figure 3-6), the change of font and color part way through dictates that there will be three `content` elements involved in this row so, because one `View` can only map at most one element, you would probably expect to find that the `ParagraphView.Row` has three `LabelView` children. If you look at the extract of the `View` hierarchy shown earlier, you will, in fact, find that this `ParagraphView.Row` has three children, the first two of which are `LabelViews`. The last child is, however, not the same—it is an instance of an inner class of `LabelView` called `LabelView.LabelFragment`.

Why is the last child of a different type? As we said earlier, `Paragraph-View.Row` can only manage a single line of text. In fact, `Paragraph-View.Row` is derived from `BoxView` but, unlike `ParagraphView`, it arranges its children horizontally (so is created with constructor argument `View.X_AXIS`). As a result, it must have child `Views` that cover parts of the document that begin and end within the same screen line. In this case, the text that would be mapped by the third `LabelView` would not all fit on the line being managed by the `Row`, so a particular type of `View`, called `Label-View.LabelFragment` was created. This `View` is almost identical to `Label-View`, but doesn't map all of the elements that it is associated with.

Paragraph Size, Line Layout, and Wrapping

To understand exactly how and why the `LabelView.LabelFragment` was created, let's take a more detailed look at how `ParagraphView` and `ParagraphView.Row` create and manage their child `Views`. When a `ParagraphView` is first created, it has an associated `paragraph` element. At this stage, it doesn't know how much screen space will be allocated to it and, in fact, it will probably be asked for its preferred size before it is given an actual screen allocation to work with. Because working out its preferred size involves being able to measure the width of the text (and other objects) that it contains, it needs to create child `Views` (such as `LabelView`) that can do this job by working directly with the content elements in the model. `ParagraphView` itself, being a relatively simple container object, does not know how to perform measurement of text, so it must delegate this operation to its children.

As you know from our earlier description of `JTextArea`, shortly after a `View` is created, its `setParent` method is called. You also know that, for a container `View` derived from `CompositeView`, this results in the invocation of a method called `loadChildren` and that this method is the natural place to create a child's `Views`, if it requires any. This is, in fact, where `ParagraphView` creates a new set of `Views` that it will ultimately manage and, from what you have seen so far, you might expect these to be `ParagraphView.Row Views`. However, this is not what happens. Instead, the `loadChildren` method loops over all the child elements of the paragraph element that the `ParagraphView` maps and creates the appropriate `View` for each element, using the text component's associated `ViewFactory`. In the case of the second paragraph of the example that we are looking at in this section, all the child elements are `content` elements. For `JText-Pane`, the `ViewFactory` is implemented by the plugged-in editor kit, which, in the case of this example, is `StyledEditorKit`. When requested to return a `View` that maps a content element, it creates a `LabelView`.

Core Note

Throughout this section, we are assuming that a standard `StyledEditorKit` is plugged into the `JTextPane`. As noted earlier, any editor kit connected to a `JTextPane` must be derived from `StyledEditorKit`. It is, of course, possible to subclass `StyledEditorKit` and implement a custom `ViewFactory` that returns completely different custom, `View` objects. If you are working with a component that uses a customized editor kit and you need to enhance its `View` objects, you will need to look at its `create` method to see how it maps element types to `View`s, and then add your enhancements by subclassing those `View`s and reimplementing the `create` method in your own subclass of the editor factory. You'll see an example of this in "A Customized Paragraph View" on page 239.

Having created a set of `LabelView` objects, `ParagraphView` stores them all in a `Vector` that it refers to as its *layout pool*. This pool of `View`s is ordered in the same way as the content elements that they map but they do not appear as the direct children of the `ParagraphView`, because the `get-ViewCount` and `getView` methods do not allow them to be seen from outside the `ParagraphView` object. Shortly after this, the text component will probably be asked for some or all of its minumum, maximum, and preferred sizes, depending on the layout manager being used by the container in which the component is mounted. The appropriate sizes for a text component depend, of course, on how its `View`s render the component's content, so this request is passed to the `View` hierarchy. In this example, the `BoxView` at the top of the hierarchy will be asked, using `getPreferred-Span`, `getMinimumSpan`, and `getMaximumSpan`, for the horizontal and vertical spans that it requires. The `BoxView` computes its requirements by delegating this request to each of the `ParagraphView`s that it contains and using the results to compute its own requirement. For example, the vertical span for a `BoxView` that manages its children along the y-axis can be obtained by summing the vertical spans of each child. The preferred horizontal span of the same `BoxView` can be obtained by taking the maximum of the preferred spans of all its children and there is a similar algorithm in each direction for the minimum and maximum sizes.

So, how does a `ParagraphView` compute its own preferred, maximum, and minimum sizes? This is actually something of a chicken-and-egg problem because there is more than one way to lay out the text in a paragraph when line wrapping is enabled. If you were given some text to typeset, you would start at the top left of the space allocated and work across the top row, placing the words until you ran out of space and then move down to the next line and continue until you had no more words left. This, of course, presumes that you know how wide the paragraph is and, from this, you can arrive at a value for the height of the paragraph. However, if you don't know how wide your allocated space is, there are many ways in which you could lay out the words that it contains, ranging from placing everything on a single line to placing one word per line. What actually happens is that, when `ParagraphView` is asked for its preferred span along the x-axis, it goes through each child in its layout pool and asks it how much horizontal space it needs (again using `getPreferredSpan`, and so forth), and then adds the results together. To this, it adds any paragraph insets that have been set and returns the result. This corresponds to laying the entire paragraph out on a single line of the screen. Along the y-axis, only the sum of the top and bottom paragraph insets, if any, are returned. Often, this will mean that the paragraph's preferred height will be advertised as 0. The preferred size returned by a `JTextPane` is, therefore, not of much practical use.

Core Note

The basic algorithm used by `ParagraphView` *is also used by the simpler text components. However, both* `JTextField` *and* `JTextArea` *can be created with a specific number of rows and columns. These requests can, using the selected font, be transformed into a corresponding preferred size. If the number of rows and columns has been specified, the size calculated in this way is passed to the* `setSize` *method of* `RootView` *and then the* `getPreferredSpan` *method is called for each direction. This gives the* `View`s *for these components some clue as to how large a space they will have available. This is not possible for* `JTextPane` *or* `JEditorPane` *because there is no way to set a desired number of rows or columns for these components.*

When the preferred size has been returned, the text component will be allocated some space in its container. Eventually, the `setSize` method of the `RootView` will be called with the exact dimensions of the text component. Now, it is necessary to divide this space between the `View`s that want to use it. This task is done, step-by-step, by the various `View` objects in the hierarchy. First, `RootView` calls the `setSize` method of the top-level `View` in the hierarchy below it, which will be a `BoxView` in this case. The `BoxView` at the top of the hierarchy uses the size allocated to it to create allocations for each of its child `View`s, which will all be `ParagraphView`s, and then calls the `setSize` method of each with its actual size allocation.

Each `ParagraphView` now knows how much screen space it has to work with and has to allocate space for each line of text that it contains. As described earlier, it does this by allocating an inner class `ParagraphView.Row` object for each line of text. At this stage, the `ParagraphView` object knows the range of offsets that mark out the text (or other content) that it covers, but it does not know how many screen rows this will cover. In fact, this will not be known until all the rows have been individually laid out. What actually happens is that the `ParagraphView` creates a single `ParagraphView.Row` and tries to fit as much as it can into it. When the `ParagraphView.Row` is full, another one is created and so on, until all the content has been mapped.

Now let's look at how each `ParagraphView.Row` object is filled. At the outset, the `ParagraphView.Row` knows how wide the screen area that it can work with is and the start and end offsets of the content that it must map. In general, of course, any given `ParagraphView.Row` will only map the beginning of this offset range and return the rest for the next `ParagraphView.Row`. First, the `ParagraphView.Row` leaves space for the left inset of the paragraph that it is contained in, and then it gets the `View` for the element that it is mapping from the layout pool by using the offset of the element as the key. To determine how much space this `View` needs, one of two methods is called. If the `View` supports embedded tabs, its `getTabbedSpan` method is called, otherwise `getPreferredSpan` is used. Both of these methods have access to the content that they are rendering, because a `View` is created with an associated element. If the width required to render the `View` is less than that remaining in the row, the `View` is just added directly to the `ParagraphView.Row` and its width deducted from the available space. Then, the `getBreakWeight` method of the `View` is called and, if this returns `ForcedBreakWeight` (or any larger value), the `ParagraphView.Row` is considered filled and a new `Row` will be started for the `View` associated with the next element.

In general, however, a point will be reached at which there is insufficient space for the current `View` in the row being built. At this point, the `View` will already have been added to the `ParagraphView.Row`. To make maximum use of the space available, the `View` must be split so that as much as possible of the element that the `View` is mapping can be rendered in the current row. This situation is shown in Figure 3-8.

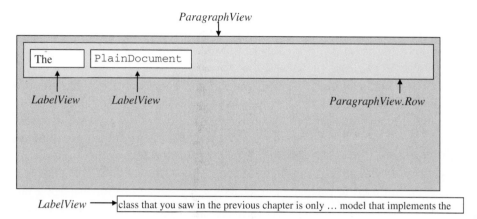

Figure 3-8 Laying out Views in a paragraph row.

Here, the first two elements have each been mapped by LabelView objects. At this point, the ParagraphView.Row is only partly full. However, as you can see by looking back at the element structure of this document, the next element contains 161 characters from offset 62 in the model. Not surprisingly, with the font size in use this won't fit in the space left to the ParagraphView.Row. However, the fact that the View wouldn't fit wasn't known when it was created and added to the layout pool, so the LabelView mapping this text already exists—it is shown at the bottom of Figure 3-8. As described earlier, all Views have a method called breakView that is used to create a smaller View that maps part of the same element but will fit in a given smaller space, declared as follows:

```
public View breakView(int axis, int offset, float pos, float len)
```

The parameters passed to this method are:

axis	The axis along which the break is to occur. In this case, where a ParagraphView.Row is being populated, this will have the value View.X_AXIS.
offset	The starting offset within the document of the View fragment being created. When ParagraphView is the container that is responsible for the splitting, this is always the start offset of the View being split.
pos	The distance from the start of the ParagraphView.Row at which the new View will be placed. In this example, this value will be the sum of the left indentation of the paragraph plus the length of the two Views already in place.
len	The amount of space into which the broken View must fit. This is the amount of space left in the current ParagraphView.Row, less the padding required for the right indentation of the paragraph, if any.

The breakView method is supposed to return another View that starts at the given offset and that will fit in the space given by len. Ideally, this View should occupy as much as possible of the remaining space in the Paragraph-View.Row. In the case of LabelView, the breakView method uses a convenience method called Utilities.getBreakLocation that calculates the optimal location within the text at which to break. This method takes into account the current font and expands tabs, and then tries to break between word boundaries. The pos argument to breakView is useful when expanding tabs, because it gives the starting distance from the left of the Paragraph-View.Row at which the text being rendered will start, which can be a factor in the algorithm used to calculate tab locations. The provisions for managing tabs within the Swing text components are described in "Handling Tabs" on page 233.

Once the optimal offset has been determined, a LabelView.LabelFragment object is created, mapping the same element as the original, from the start offset of that View through to the offset corresponding to the location in the text at which the break should occur. This fragment is then used to fill out the ParagraphView.Row, but the View being replaced (the one that was too wide for the remaining space) remains in the layout pool. You can see the final layout of the ParagraphView.Row in Figure 3-9.

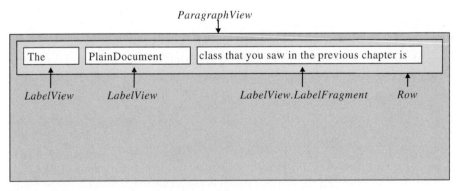

Figure 3-9 Using a View fragment to fill a row.

That takes care of the first line of text—what happens now? After the last View in the ParagraphView.Row has been created, the layout code in Para-graphView gets the offset of the start of the next ParagraphView.Row by calling getEndOffset on the last View of the ParagraphView.Row just completed. This gives the correct starting offset for the first View in the new ParagraphView.Row, whether the last View was fragmented. As with the previous ParagraphView.Row, the offset is used to find a child View from the layout pool. If the last View was split, this will find the same View that was processed at the end of the last `Row`. In response to this situation, the `ParagraphView` creates another fragment from the `View` in the layout pool. This time, the fragment is trimmed at the front with respect to the original `View`—that is, its start offset is different from that of the original `View`, but its end offset is the same. This `View` fragment (in this example, a `Label-View.LabelFragment`) is then added as the first item of the new `ParagraphView.Row`. At this point, the same process as detailed above is followed. In the example that we're looking at here, however, with the default window size created by the example code that we're using, there is going to be an immediate problem. Let's look at what has happened so far.

In the first `ParagraphView.Row` of this paragraph, there are three `Views`:

- A `LabelView` covering offsets 38 through 48 (inclusive).
- A `LabelView` covering offsets 48 through 61.
- A `LabelView.LabelFragment` for offsets 62 through 121.

This last fragment maps part of the element from offsets 62 through 222, replacing the `LabelView` for those offsets that were originally created and placed in the layout pool. At the start of the second `ParagraphView.Row`, the initial offset is 122, which is the end offset of the previous `View`.

Core Note

Recall that the end offset stored in `Views` and elements is one more than the last offset actually covered by the object. However, the end offsets in the previous list and in the descriptions in this section refer to the actual last offset and so are one less than the value returned by the `getEndOffset` method.

This offset is used to access the layout pool, which will result in the `Label-View` for offsets 62 to 222 being returned again. Because the starting offset for the next `View` does not match that of the one in the layout pool, a new fragment is created covering offsets 62 to 222 and is added to the `ParagraphView.Row`. The next step is to measure the width of this `View` to determine how much space is left in the `ParagraphView.Row`. Unfortunately, the 160 characters left in this `View` won't fit in the width allocated to the text component, so this `View`, which is already a fragment, needs to be fragmented again and the resulting fragment is placed in the `Paragraph-View.Row` instead of the original fragment. The original fragment is now no longer referenced and will be garbage collected some time later.

Now we move on to the third row. On my system, the `View` fragment in the second row would cover offsets 62 to 121, so the starting offset for the third row is 122. Again, this offset is used to index the layout pool and again the `View` for offsets 62 through 222 is returned. Once more, this `View` is fragmented to cover offsets 123 to 222 and placed in the new `Paragraph-View.Row` but again it is too wide for the screen, so a second fragmentation occurs, resulting in a fragment for offsets 123 to 207 and the `Paragraph-View.Row` is filled. For the fourth `ParagraphView.Row`, the start offset is 208, which is, of course, still in the bounds of the same `View` in the layout pool. Again, a fragment is created for offsets 208 to 222 and placed in the fourth `ParagraphView.Row`. This time, the remaining characters do not fill up the screen, so no further fragmentation is needed. The end offset of this `View` becomes the start offset for the next operation. Now, offset 223 is presented to the layout pool. This is beyond the offset of the `View` that we have been using for the last three rows and so a new `View` is extracted and the process begins again and continues until all the elements in the document have been mapped. You can see the complete result by examining the output of the `Text-PaneViews` example that we have been using in this section.

A Few Minor Details

The description that you've just read is accurate but, for simplicity, a few small details were left out. Let's clear them up now. There are two things that we didn't fully describe:

- How the view to be fragmented is chosen.
- What happens if the view to be fragmented doesn't support fragmentation.

Core Note

With few exceptions, the code used in the Swing releases for Java Developer's Kit (JDK) 1.1 is identical to that used with Java 2. However, the text components sometimes have Java 2-specific code. Because there isn't room in this book to discuss both implementations, some of the low-level details that are described here are specific to the JDK 1.1 implementation. Although the details differ slightly for Java 2, the basic principles remain the same. In fact, the `View` hierarchies, which are the important part, are identical in JDK 1.1 and Java 2—only the precise details of text measurement and the way in which the `View` fragments are created changes for Java 2. This is also true of the discussion of tab handling in the next section.

Let's look at these two in order. In the last section, we implied that the `View` to be fragmented was always the last one added to the `Paragraph-View.Row` and, in fact, this happened to always be the case, but it need not have been so. In fact, when a `ParagraphView.Row` is full, `ParagraphView` walks down all the `Views` in that `ParagraphView.Row` and calls its `get-BreakWeight` method. As described earlier, larger values returned from this method indicate that it is more favorable to break that `View`. A `View` that cannot be fragmented would return a number no larger than `BadBreakWeight`. At the end of the `ParagraphView.Row`, the `View` with the largest return value from `getBreakWeight` is selected and then its `breakView` method is called to determine where in that `View` the break will actually be made. In the example used in this section, all the `Views` are `LabelViews` or `LabelView` fragments and they all return the same value from `getBreakWeight`. As a result, the last one encountered is chosen to be fragmented.

What about a `View` that cannot be fragmented? In most cases, no attempt will be made to fragment such a `View`, because it should return `BadBreak-Weight` from `getBreakWeight` and another `View` should be chosen instead. However, if the `View` completely fills the `ParagraphView.Row`, or if all the `Views` in the `ParagraphView.Row` return `BadBreakWeight` and this is the last `View` in the `ParagraphView.Row`, it will be the only candidate for fragmentation and its `breakView` method will be called. A `View` that cannot be fragmented returns itself (that is, this) from `breakView`. As a result, no fragmentation takes place and the original `View` is placed in the `Paragraph-View.Row`. This will mean that the `ParagraphView.Row` will be wider than the space allocated to the text component and so the component's content will be drawn outside its allocated space. Such a case is, of course, rare. It is only likely to occur if you include a `Component` or an `Icon` in the text flow, because these objects have fixed widths and they cannot be split over more than one `ParagraphView.Row`. This will not corrupt the area outside the component, however, because the `Graphics` object used to draw it is clipped at the component's boundaries.

Handling Tabs

As far as the Swing text components are concerned, there are two aspects to tab handling:

1. How the tab positions are specified.
2. How the tabbing is implemented by the `Views`.

In this section, we'll look first at the two possible ways to specify tab positions, and then we'll describe how the standard `Views` interpret the tabbing information.

Specifying Tab Positions

The simplest way to specify tab positions is not to bother, in which case the tabbing mechanism implemented by the `Views` used by `JTextPane` provides tabs at 72-pixel intervals. The alternative is to use a `TabSet` object, which allows you complete control over where tab stops are placed and what happens when a `TAB` character is encountered. A `TabSet` is a collection of `TabStop` objects, each of which specifies a single tab position. The association between a `TabSet` and its `TabStops` is made when the constructor is invoked:

```
public void TabSet(TabStop[] tabStops)
```

Once a `TabSet` has been created, it is immutable—you cannot change the tabbing information in any way. For the tabbing to operate properly, the `TabStop` objects must be passed to the constructor in left-to-right order. At the time of writing, the constructor does not perform any sorting if the tab stops are not correctly ordered. `TabSet` is a simple class that has only a small number of methods:

```
public TabStop getTab(int index)
public TabStop getTabAfter(float location)
public int getTabCount()
public int getTabIndex(TabStop stop)
public int getTabIndexAfter(float location)
public String toString()
```

These methods should be self-explanatory. The most useful of them is `getTabAfter`, which can be used to find the next `TabStop` given the current location of the cursor or the current insertion point while expanding tabs during `View` creation. Given a `TabStop`, the actual location of the corresponding tab can be obtained using its `getPosition` method.

The `TabStop` class is a little more complex than `TabSet`. Here are its constructors and its significant methods:

```
public TabStop(float position)
public TabStop(float position, int align, int leader)
public int getAlignment()
public int getLeader()
public float getPosition()
```

The simplest form of `TabStop` just specifies a tab location in the form of an offset from the left side of the text component's visible area. As noted earlier, when creating a `TabSet`, the locations associated with the `TabStops` in the array supplied to the `TabSet` constructor must be in ascending order. You can, if you wish, supply two extra attributes for a `TabStop`—alignment and leader. The possible values for the leader attribute are shown in Table 3-4.

Table 3-4 `TabStop` Leader Values	
LEAD_NONE	The space between the tab and the tab stop is left empty.
LEAD_DOTS	Fill the space from the tab location to the tab stop with dots.
LEAD_HYPHENS	Fill the space from the tab location to the tab stop with hyphens.
LEAD_UNDERLINE	Underline the space from the tab location to the tab stop
LEAD_THICKLINE	Draw a thick underline beneath the space from the tab location to the tab stop.
LEAD_EQUALS	Fill the space from the tab location to the tab stop with equals signs.

If you don't specify a value for leader, LEAD_NONE is assumed. The other values are useful for creating certain types of tabular display. For example, if you want to build something that looks like a contents page, you might set a single tab stop near to the right side of the page and then set the leader value to LEAD_DOTS. Then, if the text were installed like this:

```
Preface [TAB]i
Chapter 1[TAB]1
Chapter 2[TAB]21
```

and so on, then the resulting display might be something like this:

```
Preface..................i
Chapter 1..............1
Chapter 2..............21
```

Core Note

This feature looks very useful but, at the time of writing, the leader value, which was initially intended to help support the rendering of RTF files, is not actually implemented. As a result, whatever leader value you supply, the effect is the same as if you had used LEAD_NONE.

The possible values for alignment are listed in Table 3-5.

Table 3-5 `TabStop` Alignment Values

`ALIGN_LEFT`	Text following the tab starts at the tab stop location.
`ALIGN_RIGHT`	Text after the tab, up to the following tab, or the next newline, is aligned to end at the location supplied in this `TabStop`.
`ALIGN_CENTER`	Text after the tab, up to the following tab, or the next newline, is arranged to be centered on the location of this `TabStop`.
`ALIGN_DECIMAL`	Text after the tab, up to the next tab, newline, or decimal separator, is aligned to the end location specified in this `TabStop`. If the text after the tab consists of or contains a number (or other text) that contains a decimal separator, the effect of using this alignment value is to place all the decimal points in a vertical straight line.
`ALIGN_BAR`	Currently treated as `ALIGN_LEFT`.

At the time of writing, `ALIGN_BAR`, which has a specific meaning for RTF files, is treated as `ALIGN_LEFT`. If you don't specify an alignment value when constructing a `TabStop`, `ALIGN_LEFT` is assumed.

If you want to specify tabs using a `TabSet`, you must create a `TabSet` object and apply it to a paragraph or a range of paragraphs as a paragraph attribute or as part of a logical style. To simplify this task, the `Style-Constants` class provides the convenience method `setTabSet`:

```
public static void setTabSet(MutableAttributeSet attrs,
                             TabSet tabs)
```

Here's an example that provides tab positions 72, 160, and 220 points from the left side of a text component:

```
TabStop[] tabStops = new TabStop[] {
  new TabStop(72.0f),
  new TabStop(160.0f),
  new TabStop(220.0f)
};
TabSet tabSet = new TabSet(tabStops);
StyleConstants.setTabSet(attrs, tabSet);
```

Views and Tab Expansion

Tab expansion is triggered by the presence of TAB characters in a text component's content. Even though content is usually interpreted and rendered by basic Views like LabelView, tabs are actually expanded only by an object that implements the TabExpander interface. In the Swing text package, tab expansion is not performed directly by the methods that are usually used to draw text such as Utilities.drawTabbedText (which you'll see later in this chapter). Instead, these methods are passed a reference to a TabExpander, which is used to perform the expansion as required. The TabExpander interface has only one method:

```
public interface TabExpander {
    public float nextTabStop(float x, int tabOffset);
}
```

The return value from this method is the location of the next tab stop. The first argument is the x position along the line at which the TAB character was encountered. The second argument is the offset within the document model of the TAB character. How the next tab stop is determined depends entirely on the TabExpander implementation; this interface is implemented by three classes in the standard text package, as summarized in Table 3-6.

Table 3-6 Views That Implement Tab Expansion

PlainView	Used by JTextArea when line wrapping is not enabled. Provides tabs separated by a fixed distance determined by the PlainDocument.tabSizeAttribute property of the document being viewed. By default, this property is set to 8 and is measured in units of the letter "m" in the font used by the text component. If the letter "m" in the font is 9 pixels wide and the PlainDocument.tabSizeAttribute property is set to 10, then tab stops occur at 90-pixel intervals starting from the left edge of the text component. TabSets cannot, of course, be used with JTextArea, so this implementation does not handle them.
WrappedPlainView	Used by JTextArea when line wrapping is enabled. Uses the same implementation as PlainView.

Table 3-6 Views That Implement Tab Expansion (continued)	
ParagraphView	This is a complete implementation for JTextPane and JEditorPane that uses the TabSet property of the paragraph that it is mapping if it is set. If this property is not set, tabs are deemed to occur at 72-point intervals.

Basic views, such as LabelView, delegate tab expansion to their containing ParagraphView. Because JTextField and JPasswordField both use Views derived from PlainView, tab expansion in these components is the same as in JTextArea. If tabs occur in text being rendered by a View that does not support tab expansion, the TAB character is replaced by a space.

Handling Embedded Icons and Components

Icons and Components in documents are mapped by two dedicated Views—IconView and ComponentView, both of which are relatively simple. The main job of IconView is to arrange for the Icon to draw itself into the area allocated to it within the text component. Because the Icon-View inherits from its base class (View) a paint method that receives the width and height of the allocated area and a Graphics object to draw with, it is a simple matter to map this call to a call on the Icon's paint-Icon method. The only other important job that the IconView performs is to return the preferred span of the object in each direction, by asking the Icon how much space it needs.

ComponentView is much the same as IconView except that it manages an arbitrary Component (almost certainly a JComponent) instead of an Icon. Most of the View methods that ComponentView directly implements are delegated directly to the Component. Table 3-7 summarizes the implementation of these methods.

Table 3-7 Implementation of View Methods by ComponentView	
paint	Sizes the Component to the area allocated to the ComponentView and makes it visible if it is not. This will make the Component paint itself. If it was already visible, the Component will get its own paint call automatically.

Table 3-7	Implementation of View Methods by `ComponentView` (continued)
`getPreferredSpan` `getMinimumSpan` `getMaximumSpan`	These three methods use the `getPreferredSize`, `getMinimumSize`, and `getMaximumSize` methods of the `Component` and return the width or height depending on the `axis` argument.
`getAlignment`	Delegates to the `Component` methods `getAlignmentX` or `getAlignmentY` depending on the `axis` argument.
`setSize`	Changes the `Component`'s size to match the supplied width and height. This is always done in the AWT event thread, even if this method is invoked in a different thread.
`setParent`	This method adds the `Component` to the text component that it is a part of, establishing the AWT parent/child `Container`/`Component` relationship. If the `Component` has already been added to a `Container`, it is first removed from that `Container`. These operations are always performed in the AWT event thread.

A Customized Paragraph View

After a lengthy and somewhat academic discussion of `View`s, it's time to put what we've learned to some practical use by creating a couple of `View`s that you can use to enhance your applications. The first example we're going to look at is a custom `ParagraphView` that you can use with `JTextPane` to highlight text that needs to stand out from its surroundings. If you use only the standard features of `JTextPane`, your options for highlighting text are limited to changing the font, changing the color, or using underlining. Here, we'll show you how to make a paragraph stand out by changing its background color and adding a border of your choosing around the paragraph. In fact, with the implementation that you'll see here, you'll be able to use these effects separately or together, according to your requirements. Before we start looking at how to implement this feature, let's look at what it looks like when applied to the `JTextPane` example you saw in the last chapter (Figure 2-3). That example consisted of a heading and a single paragraph of text to which limited formatting had been applied at the paragraph and character level to emphasize specific words. If you type the command

```
java AdvancedSwing.Chapter3.ExtendedParagraphExample
```

you'll see the same text, but now the main text is surrounded by an etched border and the background is filled with gray, as shown in Figure 3-10.

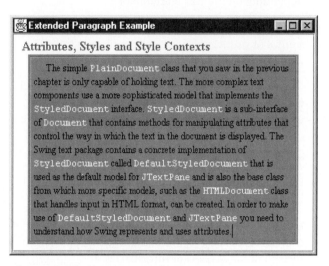

Figure 3-10   A custom `ParagraphView`.

While you've got this example running, resize the window in various ways and observe what happens to the paragraph highlighting: Whether you make the window narrower or wider, taller or shorter, the border and the color fill reshape themselves so that they always neatly fit around the text. Notice also that the colored area is indented away from both sides of the component and that there is a space between the border and the text that it wraps. As you'll see, all of this is provided by the `View` that we're going to create and it can all be controlled by applying the appropriate attributes to the paragraph.

Anatomy of the Extended `ParagraphView`

Before looking at the new `View`, let's review the structure of the existing `ParagraphView` and how the attributes that you can assign at the paragraph level are interpreted. Figure 3-11 shows a standard `ParagraphView`. The main function of `ParagraphView` is to organize the text that it contains into rows and to draw them onto the surface of the text component. The shape of the paragraph is controlled in part by the width of the component, but there are a few attributes that you can use to modify the behavior slightly.

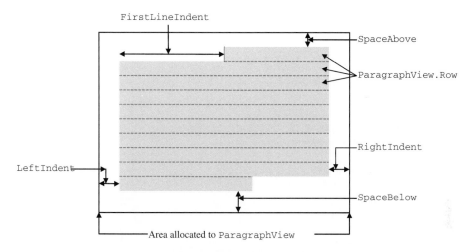

Figure 3-11 ParagraphView and its attributes.

The SpaceAbove and SpaceBelow attributes determine how much room is left above and below the paragraph and, similarly, the LeftIndent and RightIndent attributes control the left and right margins. Finally, the first line of text in the paragraph may have extra indentation, specified using FirstLineIndent. You've seen these attributes in use in the examples shown earlier in this chapter. In effect, these attributes create an inset area around the paragraph text that is under the management of the Paragraph-View but is not available for use by the paragraph's child Views. This is, in itself, very much like having a border around the paragraph contents. Because the ParagraphView is able to create this blank area, you can deduce without even looking at its source code that it should be fairly simple to make it draw a border around itself. In fact, the only real problem to be solved as far as rendering the modified View is concerned is actually drawing the border, because ParagraphView is already able to ensure that the text that it contains does not stretch all the way to the edges of its allocated space. If this were not true, we would have a much harder job. In fact, as you'll see when we look at the implementation later in this section, the ability to specify insets around a paragraph is inherited by ParagraphView from CompositeView.

Given that we can arrange to draw a border around the paragraph, there are two ways in which this could be done. Figure 3-12 shows one possible choice. In this diagram, we've added a border around the outside of the area allocated to the paragraph and also painted the paragraph's background (another feature that will be added by our custom View). With this implementation, the paragraph insets are interpreted as the distance of the paragraph text from the inside of the border.

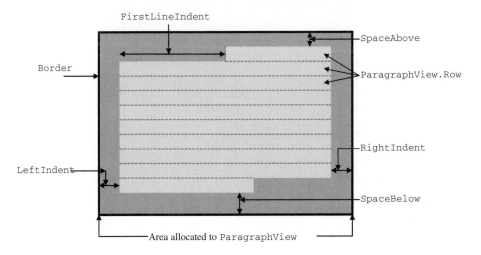

Figure 3-12 A `ParagraphView` with a border: choice 1.

This is, of course, a perfectly acceptable way to provide this feature, but it isn't particularly pleasing. The main problem with this approach is that the paragraph background is filled in all the way to the edge of the text component—there's no margin any more. Under some circumstances, this may be what you want, but because this implementation gives you no choice, it's not as good as the alternative, which is shown in Figure 3-13.

In this case, the paragraph insets are used to create a margin around the outside of both the border and the painted area. If you want, you can remove these insets by setting the associated paragraph attributes to zero and you'll get back to something like Figure 3-12. In most cases, though, you'll probably want insets around the paragraph so that it is flush with the rest of the content. Given that the paragraph insets are now applied around the outside of the border, why does Figure 3-13 show a blank area between the border and the text? This blank space is a feature of the border and it is totally under your control. The border shown in Figure 3-13 is actually a compound border, composed of a lined border on the outside and an empty border on the inside. The empty border creates the space between the edge of the paragraph and the text. As you'll see, you can install any kind of border around our extended paragraph, so the exact spacing, if any, and the relationship between the border and the spaced area, is entirely up to you. As a result, you could, if you wanted, arrange for the text to be flush against the lined part of the border and add extra space outside. The external space is still part of the paragraph, so it would have its background filled if a filled background is specified.

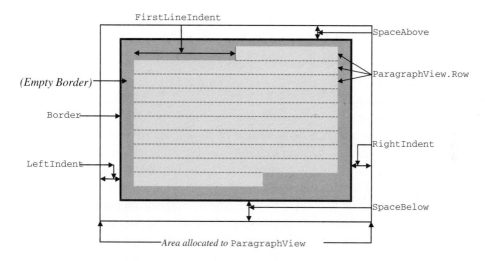

Figure 3-13 A `ParagraphView` with a border: choice 2.

Incidentally, it's worth noting that you can't use the theoretical implementation shown in Figure 3-12 to produce the effect shown in Figure 3-13 by adding an empty border on the outside of the lined border, because the filled area extends to the edges of the paragraph which, in Figure 3-12, extend to the limits of the component, so the background fill would reach outside the border area. Although it could be considered a matter of taste, we'll implement the alternative shown in Figure 3-13.

Specifying the Border and the Background Color

Our new paragraph is going to be able do two things that existing ones don't:

1. Optionally fill its background with a specified color.
2. Optionally draw an arbitrary border around itself.

By now, it should be evident that both of these things should be specified as paragraph attributes. If you look back to Table 2-1 in the last chapter, you'll see that there is already an attribute defined for background color, but it is a character attribute. Because we want to apply a background color at the paragraph level, we'll need to create a new paragraph-level attribute.

We will also need a new attribute to specify the border that we want to be drawn around the paragraph. The existing attributes are all defined in the `StyleConstants` class; because we can't add new attributes to this class, we do the next best thing and create a derived class called `Extended-StyleConstants` to define our new attributes. Listing 3-2 shows the implementation of this class.

Core Note

We could cheat and use the existing character-level `Background` *attribute as a paragraph attribute, because none of the* `Views` *in the standard Swing text package fill their background. This would be a mistake, however, because you might want to implement a* `View` *that could change the background of a range of characters. If you applied this attribute as a character attribute to a run of characters in a paragraph that also used the* `Background` *attribute at the paragraph level, the character attribute would override the one at the paragraph level for the length of that character run. This usually would not be a problem. For example, if you had a paragraph with the* `Background` *attribute set to yellow within which there was a character run with* `Background` *set to black, the black background would override the yellow paragraph background for that part of the paragraph. Is this a problem? Not if you're only going to use solid colors, because you could say that, logically, the yellow background is painted first and gets over-painted with black. So what does it matter that the yellow background was lost? This reasoning is correct in JDK 1.1. However, in Java 2, the Java2D package gives you the possibility of using colors that are not solid—in other words, you could conceive of the possibility of a background applied to the character run that allowed the paragraph background color to be partly visible through gaps. This isn't possible with the current definition of the* `StyleConstants` `setBackground` *method, which only accepts a solid color, but nothing prevents you from adding another method, in a class like* `ExtendedStyleConstants`, *that would overload* `setBackground` *to accept a Java2D textured background as the* `Background` *attribute and then implementing the* `View` *support for it. In this case, you would certainly want the paragraph background color to be defined by a different attribute.*

Listing 3-2 Declaring a New Attribute

```java
package AdvancedSwing.Chapter3;

import javax.swing.text.*;
import javax.swing.border.Border;
import java.awt.Color;

public class ExtendedStyleConstants {
    public ExtendedStyleConstants(String name) {
        this.name = name;
    }

    public String toString() {
        return name;
    }

    /**
     * The border to be used for a paragraph.
     * Type is javax.swing.border.Border
     */
    public static final Object ParagraphBorder =
                ExtendedParagraphConstants.ParagraphBorder;

    /**
     * The background to be used for a paragraph.
     * Type is java.awt.Color
     */
    public static final Object ParagraphBackground =
                ExtendedParagraphConstants.ParagraphBackground;

    /* Adds the border attribute */
    public static void setParagraphBorder
                            (MutableAttributeSet a, Border b) {
        a.addAttribute(ParagraphBorder, b);
    }

    /* Gets the border attribute */
    public static Border getParagraphBorder(AttributeSet a) {
        return (Border)a.getAttribute(ParagraphBorder);
    }
```

Listing 3-2 Declaring a New Attribute (continued)

```
    /* Adds the paragraph background attribute */
    public static void setParagraphBackground
                            (MutableAttributeSet a, Color c) {
      a.addAttribute(ParagraphBackground, c);
    }

    /* Gets the paragraph background attribute */
    public static Color getParagraphBackground(AttributeSet a) {
      return (Color)a.getAttribute(ParagraphBackground);
    }

    /* A typesafe collection of extended paragraph attributes */
    public static class ExtendedParagraphConstants
                        extends ExtendedStyleConstants
      implements AttributeSet.ParagraphAttribute {
      /**
       * The paragraph border attribute.
       */
      public static final Object ParagraphBorder =
                        new ExtendedParagraphConstants(
                        "ParagraphBorder");

      /**
       * The paragraph background attribute.
       */
      public static final Object ParagraphBackground =
                        new ExtendedParagraphConstants(
                        "ParagraphBackground");

      private ExtendedParagraphConstants(String name) {
        super(name);
      }
    }

    protected String name;        // Name of an attribute
  }
```

The `ExtendedStyleConstants` class, like `StyleConstants`, is a base class within which we can define new attributes in a type-safe way. An `ExtendedStyleConstants` attribute has a name that can be used to recognize it when you dump the model of a document to which it is applied; like those of all the standard attributes, this name has no other direct use within the Swing text framework. The border attribute is a constant instance of the inner class `ExtendedParagraphConstants`, accessible via the name `ExtendedStyleConstants.ParagraphBorder`, by analogy to all the other Swing text attributes. The `ExtendedParagraphConstants` class extends `ExtendedStyleConstants` and implements the interface `Attribute-Set.ParagraphAttributes`. The first of these two circumstances makes `ExtendedParagraphConstants` recognizable (to any code that wishes to check) as an instance of `ExtendedStyleConstants` and the second indicates that it is an attribute that applies at the paragraph level. The `Paragraph-Background` attribute is declared in the same way.

Core Note

This roundabout way of declaring attributes looks a little convoluted and slightly cumbersome. The fact is that you don't actually have to go to all this trouble to create new attributes, because nothing in the Swing text package checks that the attributes that are used are actually of the required generic types, unless you use the `StyleConstants` *convenience methods, which require the specific type to be correct. There is no explicit check, for example, that attributes applied at the paragraph level implement* `AttributeSet.ParagraphAttributes`. *Nevertheless, for consistency, we follow the same pattern used by* `StyleConstants` *to create these attributes.*

As well as defining the attributes, methods that allow them to be added to or retrieved from an attribute set are required. Like the similar methods in `StyleConstants`, these are not strictly necessary; they do, however, make code that uses these attributes slightly more readable as well as providing a measure of type safety. The implementation of all four methods is trivial—adding an attribute maps directly to the `MutableAttributeSet` `add-Attribute` method, while the accessor methods use `getAttribute`. If an accessor method is used to retrieve the paragraph border or background color when it hasn't been set, `null` is returned. Because applying either of these attributes to a paragraph is optional (and, moreover, using one does not imply using the other), it is not an error for either `getParagraphBack-ground` or `getParagraphBorder` to return `null`.

A New *ViewFactory*

Having defined a couple of new attributes, the next problem is to somehow arrange for them to affect the way in which the paragraph to which they are applied is rendered. To change the way in which paragraphs are drawn, you need to use a custom `View` that understands the new attributes and arranges for an instance of it to be created for every paragraph in the document. As you know, the mapping between element types in the model and `Views` is determined by the text component's `ViewFactory`, which is determined either by the plugged-in editor kit or the component's UI delegate. In the case of `JTextPane`, the editor kit supplies the `ViewFactory`, so to arrange for a new `View` to be used to map paragraph elements, we have to create a new editor kit with a suitable `ViewFactory`.

`JTextPane` requires that its editor kit be derived from `StyledEditorKit`. Because of this, our custom editor kit will be created by extending `Styled-EditorKit`. Because the only enhancement we need to make is the `View-Factory`, we need only to override the `getViewFactory` method, which is called from the `JTextPane`'s UI delegate. The implementation of the new editor kit, called `ExtendedStyledEditorKit`, is shown in Listing 3-3.

Listing 3-3 A Customized Editor Kit

```
package AdvancedSwing.Chapter3;

import javax.swing.*;
import javax.swing.text.*;

public class ExtendedStyledEditorKit extends
                                        StyledEditorKit {
   public Object clone() {
      return new ExtendedStyledEditorKit();
   }

   public ViewFactory getViewFactory() {
      return defaultFactory;
   }

   /* The extended view factory */
   static class ExtendedStyledViewFactory implements
                                        ViewFactory {
      public View create(Element elem) {
         String elementName = elem.getName();
         if (elementName != null) {
            if (elementName.equals(
```

Listing 3-3 A Customized Editor Kit (continued)

```
                    AbstractDocument.ParagraphElementName)) {
                return new ExtendedParagraphView(elem);
            }
        }

        // Delegate others to StyledEditorKit
        return styledEditorKitFactory.create(elem);
    }
  }

  private static final ViewFactory styledEditorKitFactory =
                (new StyledEditorKit()).getViewFactory();
  private static final ViewFactory defaultFactory =
                new ExtendedStyledViewFactory();
}
```

The new `ViewFactory` is declared as a static inner class of our custom editor kit and a single instance is created when the class is first loaded. The `getViewFactory` method simply returns a reference to this shared instance. The `ViewFactory` only has a single method, which creates the `Views` for each type of element in the associated document. In the `create` method, we look at the element name to determine the type of `View` to return. If the element represents a paragraph, the appropriate thing to return is an instance of our new `View` class, `ExtendedParagraphView`, the implementation of which you'll see later. For all the other element types, we want to delegate to the `ViewFactory` for `StyledEditorKit` rather than copy all its code into our own `create` method. To delegate to `StyledEditorKit`'s `ViewFactory`, we get a reference to it in our static initializer. However, because the `getViewFactory` method is not static, we need to create a `StyledEditorKit` object to invoke it. The overhead of this is small and is incurred only once in the lifetime of any application that uses our editor kit. Moreover, the `StyledEditorKit` that we create in the static initializer will be garbage collected some time after the initializer completes.

Before looking at the implementation of `ExtendedParagraphView`, it's worth considering whether an alternative `ViewFactory` implementation is possible. As it stands now, every paragraph in the document has an `ExtendedParagraphView` associated with it, whether it uses either of our new attributes. As an alternative, perhaps we could have the `create` method look for these attributes and return an `Extended-ParagraphView` for a paragraph in which they are present and an ordinary `ParagraphView` otherwise. The problem with this is what should be done if the paragraph border or paragraph background attributes are added after the `View` structure has been created. When this happens, it would be necessary to replace the `ParagraphView` by an `ExtendedParagraphView`. However, if applying these attributes is the only change made to the document (that is, the actual document content does not change at the same time), the `View` structure is not automatically rebuilt and, as a result, the affected paragraph would continue to be rendered by a `ParagraphView`. Extra code would need to be added to react to certain attribute changes by installing an `ExtendedParagraphView`, complicating the implementation.

Implementing the New `ParagraphView`

The last piece we need to implement is the new `ParagraphView`. Because this class has to do everything that the existing `View` does, we create it by extending `ParagraphView`. We need to add two features:

- Filling the background with the paragraph background color if the paragraph has the `ParagraphBackground` attribute applied to it.
- Drawing a border around the paragraph if the `ParagraphBorder` attribute has been used.

As we said earlier, and as Figure 3-13 shows, the background fill will be applied to the region inside the paragraph insets. To determine the size of the area to be filled, we need to get the insets that have been applied to the paragraph. These insets are actually held by `CompositeView`, one of the superclasses of `ExtendedParagraphView`, which provides the methods `getLeftInset`, `getRightInset`, `getTopInset`, and `getBottomInset` to allow access to them. The inset values are set when the `View` is created by calling the protected method `setPropertiesFromAttributes`, which obtains any values that it needs from the paragraph attributes attached to the element that the `View` maps and caches them internally for faster access. This method is subsequently called only when something happens that would invalidate the cached values, such as the application of changed attributes. Because `ExtendedParagraphView` has two extra attributes, it makes sense to override `setPropertiesFromAttributes` to cache the values of these two attributes at the same time as the paragraph insets are being set.

The other method of `ParagraphView` that we'll need to override is `paint`. The paint method of a container `View` usually does not actually `paint` anything; like the `paint` method of the AWT `Container` class, its normal job is just to arrange for its child `Views` to draw themselves by invoking their `paint` methods. In the case of `ParagraphView`, its usual function is to loop over all the `Row Views` that it contains and have them draw themselves directly onto their assigned part of the area assigned to the paragraph. This results in each line of text being drawn on the screen, from the top of the paragraph to the bottom. The `ExtendedParagraphView paint` method still needs to do this, of course, but it also needs to fill the appropriate rectangular area of the paragraph with the background color if it is set and also draw the paragraph border, if there is one. After doing this, it can delegate the job of drawing the paragraph content to the usual `ParagraphView paint` method.

Because our `View` is such a simple one, we don't need to override any other methods. You can see the implementation of the `ExtendedParagraphView` class in Listing 3-4.

Listing 3-4 A Custom `ParagraphView`

```
package AdvancedSwing.Chapter3;

import javax.swing.*;
import javax.swing.text.*;
import javax.swing.border.*;
import java.awt.*;

public class ExtendedParagraphView extends ParagraphView {
    public ExtendedParagraphView(Element elem) {
        super(elem);
    }

    // Override ParagraphView methods
    protected void setPropertiesFromAttributes() {
        AttributeSet attr = getAttributes();
        if (attr != null) {
            super.setPropertiesFromAttributes();
            paraInsets = new Insets(getTopInset(),
                    getLeftInset(), getBottomInset(),
                    getRightInset());
```

Listing 3-4 A Custom `ParagraphView` (continued)

```
      border =
              ExtendedStyleConstants.getParagraphBorder(attr);
      bgColor =
          ExtendedStyleConstants.getParagraphBackground(attr);
      if (bgColor != null && border == null) {
         // Provide a small margin if the background
         // is being filled and there is no border
         border = smallBorder;
      }

      if (border != null) {
         Insets borderInsets = border.getBorderInsets(
                              getContainer());
         setInsets((short)(paraInsets.top +
            borderInsets.top),(short)(paraInsets.left +
            borderInsets.left),(short)(paraInsets.bottom +
            borderInsets.bottom),(short)(paraInsets.right +
            borderInsets.right));
      }
   }
}

public void paint(Graphics g, Shape a) {
   Container comp = getContainer();
   Rectangle alloc = new Rectangle(a.getBounds());

   alloc.x += paraInsets.left;
   alloc.y += paraInsets.top;
   alloc.width -= paraInsets.left + paraInsets.right;
   alloc.height -= paraInsets.top + paraInsets.bottom;

   if (bgColor != null) {
      Color origColor = g.getColor();
      g.setColor(bgColor);
      g.fillRect(alloc.x, alloc.y, alloc.width,
               alloc.height);
      g.setColor(origColor);
   }

   if (border != null) {
      // Paint the border
      border.paintBorder(comp, g, alloc.x, alloc.y,
                        alloc.width, alloc.height);
   }
   super.paint(g, a);    // Note: pass ORIGINAL allocation
}
```

```
┌─────────────────────────────────────────────────────┐
│ Listing 3-4  A Custom ParagraphView (continued)       │
└─────────────────────────────────────────────────────┘
     // Attribute cache
     protected Color bgColor;
                   // Background color, or null for transparent.
     protected Border border;    // Border, or null for no border
     protected Insets paraInsets;   // Original paragraph insets

     protected static final Border smallBorder =
                   BorderFactory.createEmptyBorder(2, 2, 2, 2);
}
```

Setting the Paragraph Insets

The first of the two overridden methods we'll look at is `setProperties-FromAttributes`, which is called when the `View` is created and whenever any change to the attributes occurs. The first thing that this method does is obtain the paragraph attributes that apply to it by calling the `getAttributes` method. This method is implemented by the `View` class (see Table 3-2) and just returns the attributes associated with the paragraph element that the `ExtendedParagraphView` maps. Of course, if this method were called within a `View` that was associated with a content element, it would return the attributes associated with the character run that the element represents, not those assigned to the surrounding paragraph. After obtaining the paragraph's attribute set, it then invokes the `setPropertiesFromAttributes` method on its superclass, which allows the `ParagraphView` to extract and cache the following paragraph attributes:

- SpaceAbove
- SpaceBelow
- LeftIndent
- RightIndent
- FirstLineIndent
- Alignment
- LineSpacing

The first four of these attributes determine the space to be left around the filled area and the outside of the border, if it exists. The `ParagraphView` obtains and saves these values by calling the `CompositeView setParagraphInsets` method, which stores the insets in *private* instance members of the `CompositeView` superclass of the `ExtendedParagraphView` object. Although these attributes are held in private members, you can still get access to them using the `CompositeView getTopInset, getBottomInset` (and so forth) methods, so it is a simple matter to work out how much space to leave around the outside when filling the paragraph background in the paint method. Unfortunately, if we are going to use a paragraph border, life is not so simple. The issue with this is that the border will take up space inside the area allocated for the paragraph insets. The code that lays out the text of the paragraph by creating Row objects computes the space available by subtracting the sum of the left and right insets (obtained using the CompositeView getLeftInset and getRightInset methods) from the horizontal space allocation. If there is a border present, however, the left and right border insets needs to be taken account of to avoid drawing text over the border. The simplest way to obtain this effect is to add the border insets to the initial paragraph insets, so that code that calls methods like getLeftInset and getRightInset will retrieve values that take all the unusable space into account. This is exactly what the setPropertiesFromAttributes method in Listing 3-4 does. After obtaining the paragraph insets, it uses the ExtendedStyleConstants convenience methods that were shown in Listing 3-2 to retrieve the paragraph background and paragraph border attributes. If a paragraph border has been defined for this paragraph, its size is obtained by calling its getBorderInsets method and new paragraph insets are set for the paragraph using the CompositeView setInsets method, adding together the existing paragraph insets and those of the border. This step ensures that the text will be properly laid out inside the border area.

There are two points of interest in this code that should be carefully noted. First, note that we save a copy of the original paragraph insets in the instance variable paraInsets. This is necessary because the paint method needs to fill the background and place the border with respect to the original paragraph insets, which can no longer be obtained from the CompositeView methods that were used earlier. These insets could be obtained from the paragraph attributes, but it is faster to cache them in this way. The second point of interest is a small matter of presentation. If the paragraph is configured with background fill but no border, the text within the paragraph would be drawn from the left edge of the filled area, which looks ugly. To improve matters, if a background fill is specified but no border, we add a small border inset to move the text away from the edges of the filled area. This doesn't cause an empty border to be drawn; instead it works by giving the code that lays out the Rows a restricted space to work in that does not include a small region just inside the filled area. The effect is, of course, the same as if a small empty border had been requested. If a paragraph border is used, we don't supply any extra margin because the programmer is expected to create a border that includes any margins that the programmer deems fit, as you'll see shortly in the example code that demonstrates ExtendedParagraphView.

Painting the Paragraph

Once the paragraph insets have been dealt with, the `paint` method is simple to implement. The `Shape` argument describes the area allocated to the paragraph. The bounding rectangle of this area is retrieved by using the `get-Bounds` method and, because we are going to change the position and size of this rectangle, we create a new one to avoid any side effects that might be caused by changing the original.

Core Note

The JDK documentation does not specify whether the `Shape getBounds` *method returns a* `Rectangle` *that can be mutated. Because* `Shape` *is an interface that could be implemented by many classes, it isn't safe to assume that you get a private* `Rectangle` *each time you call* `getBounds`*. Even if you find this to be the case for one implementation of* `Shape`*, it may not be true for another. Hence, the safest approach is to create your own* `Rectangle`*.*

Having obtained the bounding rectangle of the paragraph, the next step is to use the original paragraph insets that were saved in the `set-PropertiesFromAttributes` and use them to adjust the bounding rectangle so that it bounds the space to be filled with background color and which will mark the outer boundaries of the border. If a paragraph background color has been specified, the `Graphics fill-Rect` method is called to fill the area inside the paragraph and border insets. Similarly, if a paragraph border has been configured, it is drawn by calling its `paintBorder` method and passing it a description of the outer boundary of the paragraph area, a `Graphics` object to draw with, and a reference to the text component, obtained using the `View get-Container` method. Some borders use this argument to obtain properties (such as the colors and fonts) from the component that they are drawing on so that you don't need to specify border drawing colors every time you create a border. With `JTextPane`, however, this is not always a useful property, because the background color of the `JText-Pane` is not always the one relevant to the border. Indeed, in this case, it would not always be of much use, because if the border were being drawn on a filled area, it would need to use colors that contrast with the fill color, not with the background color of the `JTextPane`. In cases like this, you should create the border with suitable colors rather than allow it to choose its colors when it is drawn.

Having filled the background and drawn the border, the last step is to call the superclass `paint` method, which does the usual work of rendering the paragraph's text. Note that the `Shape` passed to this method is the original `Shape`, which corresponds to the complete paragraph space allocation and is not restricted to the inside of the border. This is the correct thing to do, because the `ParagraphView paint` method takes into account the paragraph insets (which now include the border) when drawing and so will not draw over the border or outside the filled area.

Using the *ExtendedParagraphView*

At the beginning of this section, you saw an example that shows you how a paragraph rendered by the `ExtendedParagraphView` looks (see Figure 3-10). This example was based on the example code that was developed earlier in this chapter, so we're not going to repeat all the code here (and you can find it in the sample code on the CD-ROM that accompanies this book). In this example, we create a new style that incorporates both a background fill and a paragraph border, like this:

```
// Create and add the extended para styles
Style paraStyle = sc.addStyle(paraStyleName, null);
Color bgColor = Color.gray;
ExtendedStyleConstants.setParagraphBackground(paraStyle,
                                              bgColor);
ExtendedStyleConstants.setParagraphBorder(paraStyle,
        BorderFactory.createCompoundBorder(
        BorderFactory.createEmptyBorder(2, 2, 2, 2),
        BorderFactory.createCompoundBorder(
        BorderFactory.createEtchedBorder(
        bgColor.brighter(), bgColor.darker()),
        BorderFactory.createEmptyBorder(4, 4, 4, 4))));
```

This code uses the `setParagraphBackground` and `setParagraph-Border` convenience methods of `ExtendedStyleConstants` to add the relevant attributes to a new style. In this case, the paragraph will be filled in gray. The border is slightly more complex. Fundamentally, this is an etched border that is drawn using colors that are slightly lighter and darker than the background fill applied to the paragraph. As noted earlier, many of the borders in the Swing package (including the etched border) can deduce suitable drawing colors when they are painting themselves by referring directly to the component that they are being drawn on. This is, of course, an example in which this doesn't work because the `JTextPane` has a white background and a black foreground, whereas the filled area is gray. For this reason, the etched border is given specific colors to use.

The configured border is, in fact, two compound borders nested one inside the other. On the outside, there is a 2-pixel wide empty border that leaves a small gap between the etch and the boundary of the colored area. This is followed by the etched border. Finally, inside the etched area, we add another empty border, which, in this case, leaves a 4-pixel space between the drawn part of the border and the text that it surrounds. If this had not been added, the left side of text would be abutted to the border. The border insets obtained in the `setPropertiesFromAttributes` method are those of the compound border, which is the sum of the insets of all three borders.

The only other important change needed to make the extended paragraph attributes usable is to change the editor kit that the `JTextPane` uses by adding the following code (highlighted in bold) in the `main` method:

```
// Create the StyleContext, the document and the pane
final StyleContext sc = new StyleContext();
final DefaultStyledDocument doc =
                              new DefaultStyledDocument(sc);
final JTextPane pane = new JTextPane(doc);
pane.setEditorKit(new ExtendedStyledEditorKit());
```

With this change in place, our modified `ViewFactory` will be used and will create an `ExtendedParagraphView` object for every paragraph in the document, instead of a `ParagraphView`. Finally, the border and background fill are applied to the main text by specifying the name that corresponds to the paragraph style show previously in the `Paragraph` object for the main text:

```
public static final Paragraph[] content = new Paragraph[] {
   new Paragraph(heading2StyleName, new Run[] {
       new Run(null, "Attributes, Styles and Style Contexts")
   }),
   new Paragraph(paraStyleName, new Run[] {
       new Run(null, "The simple "),
       new Run(charStyleName, "PlainDocument"),
```

Highlighting and Highlighters

In the development of ExtendedParagraphView, we glossed over one important point. To see what the problem is, run the example program again using the command:

```
java AdvancedSwing.Chapter3.ExtendedParagraphExample
```

With the example running, create a selection by clicking somewhere with the mouse and dragging over the text you want to select. You'll see that the selection appears, highlighted in the usual selection color, as shown in Figure 3-14. You probably won't be surprised by this, but if you refer to Figure 1-10 in Chapter 1, you'll see that the selection highlighter is drawn on the background of the component, before the Views get a chance to draw the text and other content. This means that the selection will be drawn and then the Extended-ParagraphView will fill the paragraph's background. This should obscure the selection, so you shouldn't be able to see it, yet the selection still appears.

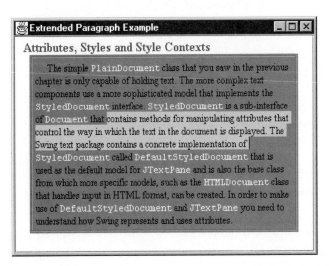

Figure 3-14   A custom ParagraphView with text selected.

What actually happens is exactly what was described in the last paragraph, but there's one more operation that gets performed that we haven't yet told you about. There are two kinds of highlighters—*ordinary* and *layered*. Ordinary highlighters are drawn directly on the background of the component, as shown in Figure 2-10, by the painting code in BasicTextUI, just before the Views' paint methods are called. In contrast, layered highlighters are drawn by the text-rendering Views before they carry out their own drawing. The selection appears in this example because the default highlighter used to draw the selection is actually a layered highlighter and is drawn by the LabelViews that render the paragraph's text. Had this not been the case, the implementation of ExtendedParagraphView would have had to avoid painting the paragraph background over the selection. In this section, we'll discuss highlighters in more detail and show you how to use a custom highlighter to do more than simply show selected text.

The *Highlighter* and *HighlightPainter* Interfaces

Every highlighter implements the Highlighter interface defined in the javax.swing.text package. Highlighter consists of a relatively small set of methods and two nested interfaces:

```
public interface Highlighter {
    public void install(JTextComponent c);
    public void deinstall(JTextComponent c);
    public void paint(Graphics g);
    public Object addHighlight(int p0, int p1,
                              HighlightPainter p)
                              throws BadLocationException;
    public void removeHighlight(Object tag);
    public void removeAllHighlights();
    public void changeHighlight(Object tag, int p0, int p1)
                              throws BadLocationException;
    public Highlight[] getHighlights();

    public interface HighlightPainter {
        public void paint(Graphics g, int p0, int p1,
                         Shape bounds, JTextComponent c);
    }

    public interface Highlight {
        public int getStartOffset();
        public int getEndOffset();
        public HighlightPainter getPainter();
    }
}
```

The install and deinstall methods are used to connect a Highlighter to a JTextComponent and to subsequently break the association. A Highlighter is associated with only one text component at a time and would usually save a reference to that component in the install method, for later use. The `paint` method requests that the `Highlighter` draw all its highlights on its related text component, using the `Graphics` object passed as its argument to perform the rendering. We'll say more about how highlight painting is performed later.

A `Highlighter` can actually support several highlighted areas at the same time, each of them represented internally by an object that implements the `Highlighter.Highlight` interface. New highlights are added using the `addHighlight` method, which is given the start and end offsets of the part of the text component's model to which the highlight is to be applied and an object that can perform the painting of that highlight. There is no need for different highlights connected to a single `Highlighter` to use the same painter, because the painter to be used is stored along with the offsets. This method returns an `Object` of unspecified type, which the caller of `addHighlight` can use to remove the highlight later using the `removeHighlight` method, or to change the start and/or end offset of the highlighted area using `changeHighlight`. You should not make any assumption about the type of the `Object` returned by `addHighlight`. The `removeAllHighlights` method, as its name suggests, removes all the highlights associated with a `Highlighter`. In the case of the default `Highlighter` used by the Swing text components, this method is called each time a `Highlighter` is installed into a text component, so that `Highlighters` can be reused without accidentally carrying over highlights from one text component to another one. Finally, the `getHighlights` method returns an array of objects that all implement the `Highlight` interface. Each of these objects represents one highlight that has been added to the `Highlighter`. The parameters associated with a `Highlight` can be obtained using its `getStartOffset`, `getEndOffset`, and `getPainter` methods. You'll see how these methods, and many of the `Highlighter` methods, are typically used in the example shown later in this section (Listing 3-6).

Every highlight is actually drawn by an object that implements the `HighlightPainter` interface, which has only a `paint` method. The `paint` method of `Highlighter` actually renders its highlights by looping through them and calling the `paint` method of the `HighlightPainter` associated with each of them. The Swing text package provides a single implementation of the `Highlighter.HighlightPainter` interface (called `DefaultHighlighter`) that renders highlights by drawing a block of solid color over the area of the text component used to display the portion of the model between the two offsets (`p0` and `p1`) given to its `paint` method. This highlighter is the one that draws the selection that you see when you drag the mouse over some text, or move the cursor with the SHIFT key pressed. Later in this section, you'll see how to implement a custom highlighter that is slightly more inter-esting than the default one.

Core Note

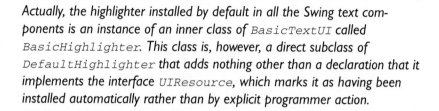

Actually, the highlighter installed by default in all the Swing text com-ponents is an instance of an inner class of BasicTextUI *called* BasicHighlighter. *This class is, however, a direct subclass of* DefaultHighlighter *that adds nothing other than a declaration that it implements the interface* UIResource, *which marks it as having been installed automatically rather than by explicit programmer action.*

The *LayeredHighlighter* Class

As well as the Highlighter interface, the Swing text package also contains an abstract class called LayeredHighlighter, which is defined as follows:

```
public abstract class LayeredHighlighter implements Highlighter {
    public abstract void paintLayeredHighlights(Graphics g, int
                          p0,int p1,
                          Shape viewBounds,
                          TextComponent editor,
                          View view);
    static public abstract class LayerPainter
                      implements Highlighter.HighlightPainter {
        public abstract Shape paintLayer(Graphics g, int p0,
                          int p1,Shape viewBounds,
                          JTextComponenteditor,
                          View view);
    }
}
```

This class claims to implement the Highlighter interface but does not actually provide implementations of any of its methods; this simply obliges any concrete subclass of LayeredHighlighter to implement the High-lighter methods and ensures that a LayeredHighlighter can be treated as a Highlighter. Such a subclass must also implement the paintLayered-Highlights method.

A layered highlighter is simply a highlighter that can support layered highlights as well as nonlayered highlights. In implementation terms, the difference between a layered highlight and a nonlayered highlight is that the former uses a layered highlight painter, that is, a painter that is derived from the inner class LayeredHighlighter.LayerPainter, while the latter uses a nonlayered highlight painter. A layered highlighter is capable of supporting layered highlights because it provides the `paintLayeredHighlights` method as well as the `paint` method used to draw nonlayered highlights.

Here's a summary of the way in which highlights are drawn from within the `paint` method of `BasicTextUI`:

- The `Highlighter` is obtained from the host text component using its `getHighlighter` method. At this stage, nothing has yet been drawn on the component.
- `BasicTextUI`'s `paint` method calls the `paint` method of the `Highlighter`. This is a request to draw any nonlayered highlights that have been added to the `Highlighter`. It implements this by looping through all its installed highlights and calling the `paint` method of all those that have a painter that is *not* derived from `LayeredHighlighter.LayerPainter`.
- The top level `View` is asked to paint itself. This ripples down through all the nested `View`s, which all have their `paint` methods called at the appropriate times. If a `View` supports the rendering of layered highlights, before it renders the text that it maps it gets the text component's `Highlighter` and checks whether it is derived from `LayeredHighlighter`. If it is, it calls the `Highlighter`'s `paintLayeredHighlights` method. This causes the layered highlighter to loop through all of its highlights and call the `paintLayer` method of all those that have highlight painters derived from `LayeredHighlighter.LayerPainter`—that is, the layered highlights. The `View` then proceeds with its normal rendering activity.

The following `View`s support layered highlights by invoking the `paintLayeredHighlights` method at the appropriate time:

- `ImageView` (in the HTML package)
- `LabelView`
- `PasswordView`
- `PlainView`
- `WrappedPlainView`

Because the `LayeredHighlighter.LayerPainter` interface actually extends `Highlighter.HighlightPainter`, it follows that a layered highlight painter must have both a `paintLayer` and a `paint` method, so it could also, theoretically, be treated as a nonlayered highlight. The default Swing highlighter is derived from `LayeredHighlighter`, so it supports both layered and nonlayered highlights. The default highlight painter is also a layered highlight painter. This means that the selection highlight is actually drawn as a layered highlight, which, as noted earlier, is why selection rendering still works with `Views` like `ExtendedParagraphView` that would obscure a nonlayered highlight by filling their backgrounds.

Creating a Custom Highlighter

Now let's illustrate all the theory that you've seen so far with a simple example of a custom `Highlighter`. A common feature of a text viewer or editor is the ability to search for a string. When the string has been located, the program usually highlights one or all the instances that it has found. This is an obvious application for a `Highlighter`.

There are two separate parts to the solution of this problem—implementing the `Highlighter` and writing the code that searches the text for a string and decides which parts of the text should be highlighted. These parts are quite distinct and are connected only by the `Highlighter` interface that the searching code uses to add highlights where necessary. In fact, the searching code doesn't need to know which `Highlighter` is being used, so there is no requirement for us to implement a special `Highlighter` to provide a solution to this problem—we do only for the purposes of illustration.

An Underlining Highlighter

As you know, the default `Highlighter` works by drawing a solid colored rectangle on the background of the areas that it highlights, so if you use this `Highlighter`, all the regions that you highlight will look just like selected text does. In the case of our word search program, if you selected some text and then performed a word search, it would be impossible to distinguish the results of the search from text that had been selected. There are four ways to address this problem:

1. Remove any text selection before performing a search.
2. Use the default `Highlighter` but create the highlights by using a different `HighlightPainter` that works just like the default one, but draws rectangles in a different color.
3. Use the default `Highlighter` but create the highlights by using a new `HighlightPainter` that makes the text stand out in some other way.
4. Use a custom `Highlighter` and a custom `HighlightPainter`.

The first solution would certainly get rid of the ambiguity problem, but it wouldn't be very user friendly. The second solution is both workable and easy to implement. Because the `Highlighter addHighlight` method requires that you specify a `HighlightPainter` (even if you are going to use the default one), using this solution is as simple as creating a variant of the default painter with your chosen color, like this:

```
Highlighter.HighlightPainter painter = new
          DefaultHighlighter.DefaultHighlightPainter(Color.red);
```

and then using this painter when adding a new highlight:

```
Highlighter highlighter = textPane.getHighlighter();
highlighter.addHighlight(startOffset, endOffset, painter);
```

in which `textPane` is a reference to the `JTextPane` containing the text being highlighted. The only reason for not taking this approach is that it doesn't demonstrate how to implement a new `Highlighter`!

The last two solutions do, however, involve creating something new. The third solution uses a custom `HighlightPainter` in conjunction with whichever `Highlighter` is installed when the text component is created. Because the visual aspects of highlights are determined entirely by the `HighlightPainter`, implementing this approach would be sufficient to show you how to create highlights that are something other than a solid block of color. Creating a custom `HighlightPainter` does not oblige you to create a new `Highlighter`—any `HighlightPainter` can be used with the default `Highlighter`, or with any other `Highlighter`, so the fourth solution is strictly overkill. Nevertheless, we choose to adopt this solution to demonstrate how to create both your own `Highlighter` as well as a new `HighlightPainter`. Another reason for taking this approach is to enable us to implement our new `HighlightPainter` as an inner class of its own `Highlighter`, which, although not at all necessary, keeps the implementation close to that of the `DefaultHighlightPainter` in the Swing text package.

Core Note

Do not be misled by this into assuming that you must implement a new `Highlighter` *each time you create a new* `HighlightPainter`. *It is perfectly acceptable to implement a freestanding* `HighlightPainter` *that is not part of any* `Highlighter`.

The new `HighlightPainter` that we are going to implement will underline the text that it is attached to instead of drawing a solid block of color behind the text. Although this might sound simple, as you'll see there are some assumptions that need to made about the way in which the underlying Views render the text that they map. The Highlighter will primarily be a wrapper class for the new HighlightPainter; to allow it to have some added value, we implement an overloaded addHighlight method that supplies an underlining Highlight-Painter, thus making it slightly easier to apply underlines if you use this Highlighter instead of the default one.

Core Note

If you look at Table 2-1 in Chapter 2, you'll see that there is a standard attribute called Underline that can be used to underline blocks of text. So why create a HighlightPainter that can do the same thing? While in many cases you would use the Underline attribute to underline text as a permanent change, a Highlighter is usually used to give temporary emphasis to a block of text. Using attributes for this purpose is more cumbersome, because you have to apply and remove the attributes yourself, whereas a Highlighter takes care of drawing a highlight given only the range of offsets to which it should apply. Directly manipulating the underlying attributes is more complex because you need to be careful to properly restore the previous attributes when the highlighting is removed. In the case of underlining highlights, if the affected text was already underlined, you would need to remember that the underlining attribute should not be removed if the highlight is removed. Finally, using attributes to create a temporary display effect would not be appropriate if the text component contained data loaded from a file (such as an HTML file) that might be written back to the file, because the modified attributes would then be stored as part of the permanent external representation, which is probably not a desirable side effect.

The implementation of our custom Highlighter, called Underline-Highlighter, and the more useful painter is shown in Listing 3-5.

Listing 3-5 A Custom Highlighter

```
package AdvancedSwing.Chapter3;
import javax.swing.text.*;
import java.awt.*;

public class UnderlineHighlighter extends
                                DefaultHighlighter {
    public UnderlineHighlighter(Color c) {
```

Listing 3-5 A Custom Highlighter (continued)

```
    painter = (c == null ? sharedPainter :
            new UnderlineHighlightPainter(c));
}

// Convenience method to add a highlight with
// the default painter.
public Object addHighlight(int p0, int p1)
            throws BadLocationException {
    return addHighlight(p0, p1, painter);
}

public void setDrawsLayeredHighlights(boolean newValue) {
    // Illegal if false -
    // we only support layered highlights
    if (newValue == false) {
        throw new IllegalArgumentException(
            "UnderlineHighlighter only draws
            layered highlights");
    }
    super.setDrawsLayeredHighlights(true);
}

// Painter for underlined highlights
public static class UnderlineHighlightPainter extends
                    LayeredHighlighter.LayerPainter {
    public UnderlineHighlightPainter(Color c) {
        color = c;
    }

    public void paint(Graphics g, int offs0, int offs1,
                Shape bounds, JTextComponent c) {
        // Do nothing: this method will never be called
    }

    public Shape paintLayer(Graphics g, int offs0,
            int offs1, Shape bounds,
            JTextComponent c, View view) {
        g.setColor(color == null ? c.getSelectionColor() :
            color);

        Rectangle alloc = null;
        if (offs0 == view.getStartOffset() &&
```

Listing 3-5 A Custom Highlighter (continued)

```
            offs1 == view.getEndOffset()) {
            if (bounds instanceof Rectangle) {
                alloc = (Rectangle)bounds;
            } else {
                alloc = bounds.getBounds();
            }
        } else {
            try {
                Shape shape = view.modelToView(
                        offs0, Position.Bias.Forward,
                        offs1, Position.Bias.Backward,
                        bounds);
                alloc = (shape instanceof Rectangle) ?
                    (Rectangle)shape : shape.getBounds();
            } catch (BadLocationException e) {
                return null;
            }
        }

        FontMetrics fm = c.getFontMetrics(c.getFont());
        int baseline = alloc.y + alloc.height -
                            fm.getDescent() + 1;
        g.drawLine(alloc.x, baseline, alloc.x +
                alloc.width, baseline);
        g.drawLine(alloc.x, baseline + 1, alloc.x +
                alloc.width, baseline + 1);

        return alloc;
    }

    protected Color color;    // The color for the underline
}

// Shared painter used for default highlighting
protected static final
            Highlighter.HighlightPainter sharedPainter
            = new UnderlineHighlightPainter(null);

// Painter used for this highlighter
protected Highlighter.HighlightPainter painter;
}
```

Implementing the `UnderlineHighlighter`

Let's look first at the `UnderlineHighlighter` class. This class extends and inherits most of its behavior from the standard `Highlighter` (`DefaultHighlighter`). Because of this, it automatically implements the `Highlighter` interface and is an instance of `LayeredHighlighter`, which allows it to handle both layered and nonlayered highlights without the need for any new code to be added. The only useful additional feature of this class is the overloaded `addHighlight` method, which allows the programmer to create highlights that use the underlining highlight painter without having to directly create an instance of that painter. In other words, the method

```
public void addHighlight(int startOffset, int endOffset);
```

can be used instead of the more usual

```
public void addHighlight(int startOffset, int endOffset,
                     Highlighter.HighlightPainter painter);
```

to add underlining highlights. The implementation of this method is, as you might expect, trivial—it just invokes the three argument `addHighlight` method of its superclass, passing through the offsets and a reference to an underlining `HighlightPainter` created in the constructor. In fact, as you'll see shortly, the underlining painter allows you to specify the color that it will use to draw the underline, which can be given as `null` to indicate that the component's selection highlight color should be used. The color to be used for underline highlights created using the `UnderlineHighlighter` `addHighlight` method is passed as an argument to the `UnderlineHighlighter` constructor. If this argument is `null`, a single painter shared by all `UnderlineHighlighters` that are created in this way, can be used; a private painter is created if a specific color is requested.

The only `DefaultHighlighter` method that `UnderlineHighlighter` overrides is `setDrawsLayeredHighlights`. As you know, if this method is called with argument `false`, all highlights drawn by the target `Highlighter` are treated as nonlayered, even if the `HighlightPainters` that they use are layered painters. For reasons that will shortly become clear, it is not acceptable to disable the layered painting of underlining highlights, so this method is overridden to throw a runtime exception if an attempt is made to do this by invoking it with argument `false`. Calling this method with argument `true` is harmless and does not cause an exception. Because the constructor of the class `LayeredHighlighter` (from which `UnderlineHighlighter` is descended) switches on layered highlighting by default, it is guaranteed that `UnderlineHighlighter` will always draw highlights configured with layered painters as layered highlights.

The *UnderliningHighlightPainter*

Now let's look at the highlight painter, which is the most useful and interesting part of this example. The painter is implemented as an inner class of `UnderlineHighlighter` called `UnderlineHighlight-Painter` and is derived from the abstract class `LayeredHigh-lighter.LayerPainter`, which means that it will be a layered highlight painter. Because its superclass is completely abstract, `UnderlineHighlightPainter` does not inherit any behavior and is obliged to implement both of the abstract methods of its super-class—the `paintLayer` method declared by `LayerPainter` and the `paint` method of the `Highlighter.HighlightPainter` interface that `LayerPainter` claims to implement. These methods should con-tain the code that provides, respectively, the layered and nonlayered highlighting functionality of the painter.

Let's look at the `paintLayer` method first. This method is called from the `paint` method of any `View` that supports layered highlights and is responsible for drawing the part of a single highlight that over-laps the space allocated to the `View`. If a single highlight crosses more than one `View`, it will be drawn in pieces as a result of separate invocations of `paintLayer` from each affected `View`. The `paint-Layer` method is defined like this:

```
public Shape paintLayer(Graphics g, int offs0, int offs1,
                    Shape bounds, JTextComponent c, View view)
```

and the parameters are as follows:

`Graphics g`	A `Graphics` context covering the visible part of the host text component.
`int offs0, offs1`	The model offsets of the start and end of the part of the highlight that intersects this `View`.
`Shape bounds`	The bounds of the area occupied by the `View` that contains the highlight being rendered.
`JTextComponent c`	The text component that contains the highlight. This argument is usually used to get global state, such as the color that should be used to draw the highlight which, in the case of the default selection highlighter and the underlining highlighter implemented in this section, is taken from the component's selection color.

| `View view` | The `View` on which the highlight is being rendered. |

The return value of this method is a `Shape` that represents the actual area of the `View` over which the highlight was rendered. To see how these arguments are used, let's look at a typical example.

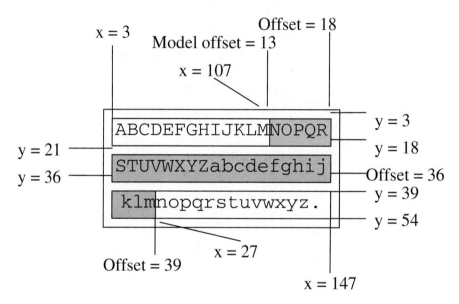

Figure 3-15   Highlights and `Views`.

Figure 3-15 shows a `JTextPane` containing a single paragraph of text split over three lines. As you know from the discussion of `Views` earlier in this chapter, the text will be rendered by three `Views` of type `LabelView.LabelFragment`; these `Views` are represented in Figure 3-15 by the three boxes inside a larger box, which represents the `JText-Pane`. The shaded area represents one contiguous highlight, which extends from model offset 13 to offset 39. Although we are implementing a highlighter that underlines the text that it is associated with, in Figure 3-15 we represent the highlight as a shaded area for clarity.

To draw the complete highlight, the `paintLayer` method of the highlight painter will be invoked three times, once for each `View` that intersects the highlighted region. The first call draws the part of the highlight from model offset 13 to offset 18. The `Graphics` object for this call, as for the other two, will have its origin at the top left of the component and will cover the visible part of the JTextPane. If the component were mounted in a JScrollPane, some of the component might not be visible and the top left of the visible area might not correspond to the origin of the JTextPane or to the origin of the Graphics object. These complications are not, however, relevant to the highlight paint-Layer method because all the coordinates it deals with are relative to the origin of the JTextPane, which makes them independent of the effects of scrolling.

For the first call, the parameters to paintLayer (other than the Graphics object and the JTextComponent arguments, which are the same on all three calls) are:

```
offs0 = 13, offs1 = 18, Shape = (x = 3, y = 3, width = 144,
                         height = 15), View = top View
```

Similarly, the parameters for the other two calls are:

```
offs0 = 18, offs1 = 36, Shape = (x = 3, y = 21, width = 144,
                         height = 15), View = middle View
offs0 = 36, offs1 = 39, Shape = (x = 3, y = 39, width = 144,
                         height = 15), View = bottom View
```

Notice that the offsets for all three calls are limited to the area covered by the highlight, whereas the Shape that is passed in is the bounding rectangle for the View, which will never be smaller than the part of the highlight being rendered on each call.

Now let's look at what needs to be done to draw the underline that represents the highlight. To draw a line, we need to select the correct color into the Graphics object, and then call drawLine with the coordinates of the start and end points of the line to be drawn. Selecting the correct color is simple—the appropriate color is given as an argument to the constructor of the UnderlineHighlightPainter. If this value is supplied as null, the color is obtained from the host text component, a reference to which is passed to the paintLayer method. You can see the code that gets and selects the color at the beginning of the paint-Layer implementation in Listing 3-5.

To determine where to draw the underline, it is necessary to convert the start and end offsets of the highlighted region to coordinate positions on the surface of the text component. This is exactly the job performed by the View modelToView method. In Listing 3-5, we use a variant of modelToView that takes two offsets and returns a Shape that represents the screen area between them. For the three Views shown in Figure 3-15, the three Shapes returned would represent the shaded areas; they would be `Rectangles` with the following positions and dimensions:

Top View:	x = 107, y = 3, width = 40, height = 15
Middle View:	x = 3, y = 21, width = 144, height = 15
Bottom View:	x = 3, y = 39, width = 24, height = 15

in which, for simplicity, we have assumed the use of a monospaced font in which each character occupies 8 pixels horizontally and is 15 pixels high and that a gap of 3 pixels is left between `Views`. In the special case in which the highlighted area covers the entire `View`, there is no need to call `modelToView` to obtain the correct `Shape`—we can just use the one passed to `paintLayer`, which represents the space allocated to the `View`, as shown in Listing 3-5.

The `Shape` thus obtained gives the x coordinates for both ends of the underline, as you can see by comparing the values shown above with the coordinates in Figure 3-15. What about the y coordinate? This is slightly more difficult. To draw a line beneath some text, you need to know where the baseline of that text is placed within its bounding box, which depends partly on the metrics of the font in use and on the code that does the drawing, which could place the baseline anywhere within the bounding box. Assuming that the height of the font and the height of the bounding box are the same, the usual location of the baseline would be a distance from the bottom of the bounding box equal to the descent value of the font in use. This is, in fact, the way in which the methods in the Swing text package that handle the drawing of text for the standard `Views` work. The implementation of `paintLayer` in Listing 3-5 assumes that this is how the baseline location is determined and draws two lines just below the assumed text baseline.

Core Note

Some of the methods that handle the drawing and placement of text for `LabelView` *and similar* `View`s *are described later in this chapter.*

That's all there is to the `paintLayer` method, so what about `paint`? If you look at Listing 3-5, you'll see that the `paint` method has no implementation at all. This is because, as we said earlier, we have restricted the `UnderlineHighlightPainter` to draw only layered highlights. Because it can't legally be used to draw nonlayered highlights, it does not require a real implementation of the `paint` method. But why did we place this restriction in the first place?

The reason for this restriction is the fact that the `paint` method receives much less information about the layout of the text component than the `paintLayer` method does. We've just seen that to place the underline properly, it is necessary to make some assumptions about the way in which the text rendering `Views` draw the text that they contain. In fact, we also made the assumption that the text that needs to be underlined in the `paintLayer` method all appears on a single line and, as long as we use the standard `Views` used with `JTextPane`, this will be true. Now consider what happens when nonlayered highlights are being drawn. Layered highlights are rendered by `Views`, but nonlayered highlights are drawn directly onto the background of the text component from `paint` method of `BasicTextUI`. At this level, there is no direct visibility of any of the `Views`—the `paint` method sees only the drawing space allocated to the text component, with no clue as to how the text, or other elements such as images and inline components, are laid out within that area. Suppose, then, that a highlight is added that would cover an area of a text component such as that shown as the shaded area in Figure 3-16.

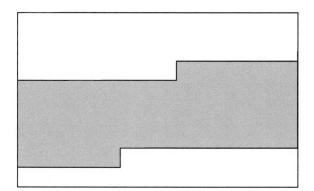

Figure 3-16   Drawing a nonlayered highlight.

This diagram looks a little bare—you can't see where the text is or even where the individual line of text might appear. This is intentional—when the `paint` method of a `HighlightPainter` is called, this is exactly how the text component will look (except that the shading won't be there either). The fact that a highlight has been created to cover the part of the model that will be drawn within the shaded area doesn't give any information at all about how much text, if any, will appear in that region. If you had to draw the underlines that the underlining `Highlighter` would need to draw in Figure 3-16, where would you place them? You could assume that the initial part of the shaded area represents a line of text and draw it just below the baseline for that stretch and the same assumption could be made about the last piece. What about the rectangular section in the middle? How many lines of text appear here? To even make a guess at where the underlines should be drawn, you would need to assume that all the text lines are of equal height, which need not be true. Even assuming that there is any text in this area is not safe—the whole area could be occupied by an image. If this were a layered highlight, however, the drawing would be done by the `Views` that cover the area. The `Views` reflect the actual layout of text and other objects, removing the need to guess about that, and they also know whether they should draw a highlight at all. The standard `View` that renders inline images (`IconView`), for example, does not draw rendered highlights so, if an embedded image is surrounded by text and an underlining highlight is applied to all the text, the underline would not be drawn across the image.

This example illustrates that it is not always possible to create a highlight painter for a nonlayered highlighting effect. The problems that we have seen with the underlining painter do not exist for the default selection highlighter, which only needs to fill one, two, or three rectangular areas with a solid color and therefore does not need to concern itself with how the text component's content is organized within the highlighted area.

Using the Highlighter

Having implemented the highlighter, let's now demonstrate how to use it in the context of a simple example program. In this example, we're going to load the content of a plain text file into a `JTextPane` and allow the user to specify a search string. Every occurrence of this string that appears in the file will be underlined by adding a highlight drawn by the `UnderlineHighlight-Painter`. There are several aspects of this example that are not directly related to the use of the highlighter; to avoid getting bogged down in irrelevant detail, we'll gloss over most of the implementation and focus mainly on how the highlighting is done. You can try this example using the command

```
java AdvancedSwing.Chapter3.HighlightExample filename
```

in which *filename* is the full name of the file to be read. When the program starts, you'll see a `JTextPane` containing the file's content with an input field just below it. If you type a word from the input file (or even a part of a word) into the input field and press RETURN, you should see all occurrences of that word underlined, as shown in Figure 3-17. The display will scroll, if necessary, to show the first instance found.

```
Highlight example                    _ □ ×
package AdvancedSwing.Chapter4;

import javax.swing.*;
import javax.swing.event.*;
import javax.swing.text.*;
import java.awt.*;
import java.awt.event.*;
import java.io.*;

public class HighlightExample {
        public static void main(String[] args) {
                if (args.length != 1) {

System.out.println("Please supply the name of a
file");
                        System.exit(1);
                }

                JFrame f = new JFrame("Highlight
example");
                final JTextPane textPane = new
JTextPane();

Enter word: jframe
```

Figure 3-17 A word search program using underlining highlights.

The code for this example is shown in Listing 3-6. The only code of any interest in the main method appears toward the end, where listeners are added to both the input field and the Document in the JTextPane. The listener attached to the input field is activated when the user types a search string and presses return. It uses a package private class called WordSearcher, which we will look at shortly, to actually perform the search and apply the underline highlights. The DocumentListener is called when the content of the JTextPane changes and its job is to research the text for occurrences of the search string. This is necessary, because changing the content might add or remove occurrences of that string. For example, in the case shown in Figure 3-17, if the user started editing the displayed file content and typed the word JFrame somewhere, this listener would immediately underline it. On the other hand, if the user deleted a character from a highlighted instance of the word JFrame, that instance would no longer match the search string and the highlight should be removed. This functionality is actually all part of the WordSearcher class rather than the DocumentListener—the listener simply arranges for the search to be performed from scratch whenever the Document content changes.

**Listing 3-6 A Word Search Program Using a
              Custom Highlighter**

```
package AdvancedSwing.Chapter3;

import javax.swing.*;
import javax.swing.event.*;
import javax.swing.text.*;
import java.awt.*;
import java.awt.event.*;
import java.io.*;

public class HighlightExample {
    public static void main(String[] args) {
        if (args.length != 1) {
            System.out.println("Please supply the name
                               of a file");
            System.exit(1);
        }
        JFrame f = new JFrame("Highlight example");
        final JTextPane textPane = new JTextPane();
        textPane.setHighlighter(highlighter);
        JPanel pane = new JPanel();
        pane.setLayout(new BorderLayout());
        pane.add(new JLabel("Enter word: "), "West");
        final JTextField tf = new JTextField();
        pane.add(tf, "Center");
        f.getContentPane().add(pane, "South");
        f.getContentPane().add(new JScrollPane(textPane),
                               "Center");

        try {
           textPane.read(new FileReader(args[0]), null);
        } catch (Exception e) {
           System.out.println("Failed to load file " +
                              args[0]);
           System.out.println(e);
        }
        final WordSearcher searcher =
                             new WordSearcher(textPane);

        tf.addActionListener(new ActionListener() {
           public void actionPerformed(ActionEvent evt) {
              word = tf.getText().trim();
```

Listing 3-6	A Word Search Program Using a Custom Highlighter (continued)

```
                int offset = searcher.search(word);
                if (offset != -1) {
                    try {
                        textPane.scrollRectToVisible(
                            textPane.modelToView(offset));
                    } catch (BadLocationException e) {
                    }
                }
            }
        });

        textPane.getDocument().addDocumentListener(
            new DocumentListener() {
                public void insertUpdate(DocumentEvent evt) {
                    searcher.search(word);
                }

                public void removeUpdate(DocumentEvent evt) {
                    searcher.search(word);
                }

                public void changedUpdate(DocumentEvent evt) {
                }
            });

        f.setSize(400, 400);
        f.setVisible(true);
    }

    public static String word;
    public static Highlighter highlighter =
                    new UnderlineHighlighter(null);
}

// A simple class that searches for a word in
// a document and highlights occurrences of that word
class WordSearcher {
    public WordSearcher(JTextComponent comp) {
        this.comp = comp;
        this.painter =
            new UnderlineHighlighter.UnderlineHighlightPainter
                                        (Color.red);
```

Listing 3-6 A Word Search Program Using a
Custom Highlighter (continued)

```java
   }

   // Search for a word and return the offset of the
   // first occurrence. Highlights are added for all
   // occurrences found.
   public int search(String word) {
      int firstOffset = -1;
      Highlighter highlighter = comp.getHighlighter();

      // Remove any existing highlights for last word
      Highlighter.Highlight[] highlights =
                              highlighter.getHighlights();
      for (int i = 0; i < highlights.length; i++) {
         Highlighter.Highlight h = highlights[i];
         if (h.getPainter() instanceof
            UnderlineHighlighter.UnderlineHighlightPainter) {
            highlighter.removeHighlight(h);
         }
      }

      if (word == null || word.equals("")) {
         return -1;
      }

      // Look for the word we are given - insensitive search
      String content = null;
      try {
         Document d = comp.getDocument();
         content = d.getText(0,
                             d.getLength()).toLowerCase();
      } catch (BadLocationException e) {
         // Cannot happen
         return -1;
      }

      word = word.toLowerCase();
      int lastIndex = 0;
      int wordSize = word.length();

      while ((lastIndex = content.indexOf(word,
                                   lastIndex)) != -1) {
         int endIndex = lastIndex + wordSize;
```

Listing 3-6 A Word Search Program Using a
             Custom Highlighter (continued)

```
        try {
            highlighter.addHighlight(lastIndex, endIndex,
                                    painter);
        } catch (BadLocationException e) {
            // Nothing to do
        }
        if (firstOffset == -1) {
            firstOffset = lastIndex;
        }
        lastIndex = endIndex;
    }

    return firstOffset;
}

protected JTextComponent comp;
protected Highlighter.HighlightPainter painter;
}
```

The relevant part of this example is in the WordSearcher class, which is created with its associated JTextComponent as the only argument to its constructor. During construction, the WordSearcher object creates an UnderlineHighlightPainter, which it will use to add highlights to ranges of characters with the text component that match its search string. Note that only one highlight painter is constructed no matter how many highlights are actually added because HighlightPainters do not hold any state that relates to individual highlights and so can be shared. In this case, the underlines will be drawn in red. The real work of the WordSearcher object is carried out in the search method, which is passed a search string. The implementation shown here is a case-insensitive search; a more useful class would add a case-sensitive search and the ability to match only on entire words and would add to the WordSearcher class properties that could be set to enable these features. Such complications would not, however, clarify the use of highlighters.

The first thing that the search method does is remove from the installed Highlighter any highlights that it added last time it was called. The quickest way to remove all highlights from a Highlighter is to use the removeAllHighlights method, but that is usually overkill because, for one thing, it would also remove the highlight corresponding to any text that is currently selected, which might not be appropriate.

Core Note

A more realistic search example would probably confine its search to the selected region if there is one and search the whole Document *if there is not. Again, to avoid complicating the example with features that do not relate directly to* Highlighter*s, this functionality is not implemented here.*

To avoid losing unrelated highlights, the search method removes only those that are rendered with the UnderlineHighlightPainter, by using the Highlighter getHighlights method to get an array of the current highlights and walking down it checking the object type of the painter of each highlight in the returned array, which is obtained by calling the Highlight getPainter method.

Having cleared unrequired highlights, the text is searched for matches with the given search string. When a match is found, a new highlight is added by calling the addHighlight method of the text component's installed Highlighter, passing the start and end offset of the matching character range to specify the region to be highlighted and the shared UnderlineHighlight-Painter to do the highlight painting. Note that this method uses whichever Highlighter is currently installed in the text component—it does not need to install an UnderlineHighlighter because, as we said earlier, you can use the UnderlineHighlightPainter with any Highlighter.

Notice that when you add a highlight to a Highlighter, you supply the start and end offsets as integers, not as Position objects (see Chapter 1 for a description of Positions). This means that the highlight does not automatically track changes in the document. If you allow the user to edit the document content in such a way that the start or end offset of a highlight would need to change to remain attached to its associated text, you must arrange to respond to this by changing each affected highlight appropriately. In this example, we achieve this by performing the search from scratch in response to any change in the document (see the DocumentListener in the main method), partly because this is the simplest thing to do and partly because the changes might change the number of highlights required, as described earlier.

There is actually a subtlety in the implementation of the search method that is not related to Highlighters but which is worth mentioning here. Note that the search is done by extracting the content of the text component in the form of a String, using the following code:

```
String content = null;
try {
   Document d = comp.getDocument();
   content = d.getText(0, d.getLength()).toLowerCase();
} catch (BadLocationException e) {
   // Cannot happen
   return -1;
}
```

You might wonder why you can't just use the apparently more convenient `getText` method provided by `JTextPane`, (which is inherited from `JEditorPane`), like this:

```
String content = comp.getText();
```

In some cases, this would work. However, if the file loaded into the `JTextPane` used carriage return/line feed pairs as line delimiters (as is usually the case on the Windows platform), you won't get the results you expect. Consider the example of a file that contains two lines of text, as follows:

```
import javax.swing.*;\r\n
import javax.swing.text.*;\r\n
```

When this is loaded into the `JTextPane`, the fact that the `\r\n` sequence was used as the line separator is recorded as a property of the `Document` and, when `getText` is subsequently called, both the carriage return and newline characters are written out between each pair of lines. Hence, for this file, `getText` would return the following `String`:

```
import javax.swing.*;\r\nimport javax.swing.text.*;\r\n
```

This is the `String` that is used for the search, so if a search for the word `import` were performed, it would be found at offsets 0 and 23. Accordingly, highlights would be applied covering model offsets 0 through 5 and 23 through 28. Unfortunately, this is not the correct result, because the `Document` does not contain the `\r` characters. As a result, the content of the model actually amounts to this:

```
import javax.swing.*;\nimport javax.swing.text.*;\n
```

So although the first highlight is properly placed, the second will result in the string, `mport` being underlined. The carriage returns and new lines are written back by the `JEditorPane getText` method because of the property set on the `Document` when its content was loaded. The `Document getText` method does not do this, however, so it leads to the correct results. This subtlety should be borne in mind any time you need to relate offsets in a `Document` to those in the file from which it was loaded.

Custom Views and Input Fields

The `ExtendedParagraphView` that you saw earlier in this chapter was relatively simple, but it allowed us to look at the steps needed to add custom rendering to a text component. Now that you've seen the basic principles, in this section you'll see how to apply them to create a specialized input field that can be used to provide visual cues to the user as to what the format of the data being input into the field should be. Although the component that we'll create will be fairly general in scope, to stay focused on what we are trying to achieve, we'll use a particular application of this input field when describing the implementation. Our aim will be to produce a text component that can accept a telephone number of fixed length as its input. The feature of this component that requires a custom `View` is the fact that it will display the characters in the telephone number together with characters added to make the user's input look like a telephone number, even though those extra characters will not be stored in the text field and will not be returned to the application program when it uses the `getText` method to extract the text field's contents. Using a `View` is the natural way to achieve this kind of effect, because what we are trying to do is present some data to the user in a natural way, without changing the nature of the data. In many ways, you can consider a `View` to be analogous to the renderers that are used by other Swing components like `JTree`, `JTable`, `Jlist`, and `JComboBox`. `View`s are a little more complex to create, but not unacceptably so.

The Formatted Text Field

Creating a new `View` that renders the content of a text field in a particular way is not the only thing you have to do to make the `View` useful. As you saw when we looked at the `ExtendedParagraphView`, the `View` needs a `ViewFactory` that will create instances of it as appropriate. The `ViewFactory` is provided either by a text component's editor kit or by its UI delegate class, so it follows that we'll need to customize one or other of those as well. Furthermore, if the `View` needs to be configured in any way for particular circumstances, we'll probably need a new text component with methods that can be used to pass the configuration information to the `View` and we might even need to use a specialized `Document` to impose constraints on the data that the user can supply, if any are needed.

Our formatted text field will be a subclass of `JTextField`, called `FormattedTextField`, to which the programmer can attach some formatting instructions that control how the characters that the user types should be displayed. The job of the `View` will be to use these instructions when the text field's content is painted on the screen. For example, if the text field were to be used for the input of a telephone number, you might want the phone number with digits `1234567890` to be displayed as follows:

```
(123)-456-7890
```

whereas a field used to display a stock code number would need the following format for the same number:

```
12-345-6-7890
```

The characters that have been added to make the value more readable to the user supplying the input will not be stored in the model because they are of no use to the application that will eventually use them, perhaps to dial a modem or to look up the associated stock item in an orders database. These characters are provided to the text field as a configurable property that can be set by the programmer. To keep this example simple, we'll assume that the characters appear in the same order in both the model and when being displayed. However, with a little more work, you could modify this example to make it possible to specify a more complex mapping between the model and the `View`.

The simplest way to specify the manner in which the data should be displayed is to use a `String` in which a particular character represents a character from the model. For example, if the character * were used for this purpose, the two display formats shown earlier might be specified as follows:

```
(***)-***-****
**-***-*-****
```

This has the drawback that whichever character is chosen as a place marker for the model content could not appear in the formatted string. So instead of taking this simple approach, we'll use a slightly more complex representation that adds a mask to the formatting specification. The mask takes over the job of specifying where the model data should appear. With this approach, the telephone number field might have the following format and mask fields, where the formatting field is shown first:

```
(...)-...-....
(***)_***_****
```

Wherever the * character appears in the mask field, the corresponding character in the format string will be replaced with the character from the model. When the text field has no real data in it, the format string is copied directly to the screen, so you can use the positions that will be filled with model data to give visual cues to the user as to where the characters being typed will appear. In the example shown above, the places reserved for the digits of the telephone number will be filled with periods. By contrast, the characters in the mask that are not in the * locations are not important—they just have to be there to align the * characters properly.

Because we need to specify two character strings to define the way in which the text in the input field will be formatted, we'll create a dedicated class that contains both strings and, because this class is only of use with this text field (or subclasses thereof), we'll define it as an inner class of `FormattedTextField`. The implementation of `FormattedTextField` and the inner class, called `FormatSpec`, is shown in Listing 3-7.

Listing 3-7 A Formatted Input Field

```java
package AdvancedSwing.Chapter3;

import javax.swing.*;
import javax.swing.text.*;
import java.awt.*;
import AdvancedSwing.Chapter2.BoundedPlainDocument;

public class FormattedTextField extends JTextField {
    public FormattedTextField() {
        this(null, null, 0, null);
    }

    public FormattedTextField(String text, FormatSpec spec) {
        this(null, text, 0, spec);
    }
```

Listing 3-7 A Formatted Input Field (continued)

```java
public FormattedTextField(int columns, FormatSpec spec) {
    this(null, null, columns, spec);
}

public FormattedTextField(String text, int columns,
                          FormatSpec spec) {
    this(null, text, columns, spec);
}

public FormattedTextField(Document doc, String text,
                          int columns, FormatSpec spec) {
    super(doc, text, columns);
    setFont(new Font("monospaced", Font.PLAIN, 14));
    if (spec != null) {
        setFormatSpec(spec);
    }
}

public void updateUI() {
    setUI(new FormattedTextFieldUI());
}

public FormatSpec getFormatSpec() {
    return formatSpec;
}

public void
        setFormatSpec(FormattedTextField.FormatSpec
        formatSpec) {
    FormatSpec oldFormatSpec = this.formatSpec;
    // Do nothing if no change to the format specification

    if (formatSpec.equals(oldFormatSpec) == false) {
        this.formatSpec = formatSpec;

        // Limit the input to the number of markers.
        Document doc = getDocument();
        if (doc instanceof BoundedPlainDocument) {
            ((BoundedPlainDocument)doc).setMaxLength(
                            formatSpec.getMarkerCount());
        }
```

Listing 3-7 A Formatted Input Field (continued)

```
            // Notify a change in the format spec
            firePropertyChange(FORMAT_PROPERTY,
                               oldFormatSpec, formatSpec);
        }
    }

    // Use a model that bounds the input length
    protected Document createDefaultModel() {
        BoundedPlainDocument doc =
                                    new BoundedPlainDocument();

        doc.addInsertErrorListener(
            new BoundedPlainDocument.InsertErrorListener() {
            public void insertFailed(BoundedPlainDocument doc,
                                      int offset,
                               String str, AttributeSet a) {
                // Beep when the field is full
                Toolkit.getDefaultToolkit().beep();
            }
        });
        return doc;
    }

    public static class FormatSpec {
        public FormatSpec(String format, String mask) {
            this.format = format;
            this.mask = mask;
            this.formatSize = format.length();
            if (formatSize != mask.length()) {
                throw new IllegalArgumentException(
"Format and mask must be the same size");}
            for (int i = 0; i < formatSize; i++) {
                if (mask.charAt(i) == MARKER_CHAR) {
                    markerCount++;
                }
            }
        }

        public String getFormat() {
            return format;
        }
```

Listing 3-7 A Formatted Input Field (continued)

```
    public String getMask() {
        return mask;
    }

    public int getFormatSize() {
        return formatSize;
    }

    public int getMarkerCount() {
        return markerCount;
    }

    public boolean equals(Object fmt) {
        return fmt != null &&
                (fmt instanceof FormatSpec) &&
                ((FormatSpec)fmt).getFormat().equals(
                        format) &&
                ((FormatSpec)fmt).getMask().equals(mask);
    }

    public String toString() {
        return "FormatSpec with format <" + format + ">,
                                mask <" + mask + ">";
    }

    private String format;
    private String mask;
    private int formatSize;
    private int markerCount;
    public static final char MARKER_CHAR = '*';
  }

  protected FormatSpec formatSpec;
  public static final String FORMAT_PROPERTY = "format";
}
```

Let's first look at `FormatSpec`. `FormatSpec` is a simple class that stores the format and masks strings for the text field. The constructor verifies that the two strings are the same length and throws an exception if they are not. This check, although not strictly necessary from a design point of view, simplifies the code in the custom `View` that works with the format specification, at the possible cost of requiring extra spaces to be provided in the mask or format field if they were, for some reason, not naturally of the same length. Note that the *marker* character that is used to indicate which positions in the mask should be replaced by characters from the model is fixed. You could make this another parameter to the constructor but, because this character only appears in the mask and not in the string drawn on the screen, there is little to be gained by doing this and it would add extra complication to the View class. FormatSpec defines accessors for the format and mask fields and a method that counts the number of marker positions in the mask. There's also an implementation of the equals method (inherited from Object) that allows two FormatSpec objects to be compared. As you might expect, a pair of FormatSpecs are considered equal if they have the same format string and the same mask string. You'll see how these methods are used later

The FormattedTextField class is also very simple. It is derived from JTextField, so it has all the normal text field methods and its constructors allow access to all the constructors of its superclass. With the exception of the default constructor, however, they all require a FormatSpec to be specified. In fact, the FormatSpec can be given as null, in which case FormattedText-Field will behave as an expensive version of JTextField. The FormatSpec supplied to the constructor is applied using the setFormatSpec method, which can also be called directly if the default constructor was used or in the unlikely event that the format or mask string needs to be changed after the text field has been created. This method does two important things. First, it counts the number of markers in the mask. This is necessary to limit the number of characters that the user can type into the text field to the same number as there are markers. Because characters that do not correspond to markers will not be displayed, it would be confusing to user if they were allowed to continue typing once all the marker slots in the input field were filled. In the telephone number example shown earlier, for example, there are 10 markers, allowing a 10-character telephone number to be displayed. Once the user has typed 10 characters, no more will be displayed (and no more are valid), so they should be ignored and, preferably, the user should get feedback to indicate this. To enforce this restriction, FormattedText-Field overrides the JTextComponent createDefaultModel method and installs a BoundedPlainDocument, the implementation of which you saw in Chapter 1, as its model. When the FormatSpec is configured, the number of markers in the mask is used to set the number of characters allowed in the model, as you can see from the implementation of the setFormatSpec method. An error handler is also installed in the model so that the user will hear a beep if too many characters are typed.

The second function of `setFormatSpec` is to fire a `Property-ChangeEvent` when the `FormatSpec` is installed for the first time or if it is changed to a new value. To ensure that the event is fired only if the format is actually changing, the new and old values are compared using the `equals` method of `FormatSpec`, which returns `false` if neither the format string nor the mask have changed. If a genuine change has occurred, a `Property-ChangeEvent` is sent to all registered listeners, notifying both the new and old values. This behavior is very common in Swing components. One reason for doing this is to make it easier to treat `FormattedTextField` as a Java-Bean and configure it from a integrated development environment (IDE) or application builder, although to support this properly you would have to add a customizer class that allowed the IDE to configure the `FormatSpec` value. In the case of this component, the more important motivation for this event is to notify its `ViewFactory` that the `FormatSpec` has been changed, as you'll see shortly.

One other detail to notice is the fact that the `FormattedTextField` constructor installs a monospaced font by default. Using a monospaced font in place of a proportional font in this type of control is preferable, because it stops the fixed elements of the field's content moving around as the user types. Returning to the example of the telephone number, if the positions that will be occupied by digits of the telephone number are initially set to "." as shown previously, the string displayed in the field will initially be very narrow if a proportional font is used, because a period takes up very little space. As the user types, the periods will be replaced by wider characters and the field content will expand. If a constant width font is used, the total width of the input string will be the same no matter how many characters the user has typed, which is more natural. You can, of course, override the initial choice of font if you wish by installing your own using the `setFont` method inherited from `Component`.

The `ViewFactory`

As you know, there are two places that a text component might find a `View-Factory`—either in its editor kit or in its UI delegate class. Because it is derived from `JTextField`, `FormattedTextField` will be created with an instance of `DefaultEditorKit`, which does not supply a `ViewFactory` so, like `JTextField`, it would get its `ViewFactory` from its UI delegate. While we could create and install a subclass of `DefaultEditorKit` that included a `ViewFactory` suitable for `FormattedTextField`, much as was done (with `StyledEditorKit`) for the customized `ParagraphView` you saw in the last section, in this case we'll take the opportunity here to show you how to create a custom `ViewFactory` within a text component's UI delegate.

Being derived from `JTextField`, `FormattedTextField` would naturally be given whichever UI delegate the selected look-and-feel would install for `JTextField`. To install a different UI delegate, you have two choices:

1. Change the `UIDefaults` table for the installed look-and-feel to install an instance of your UI delegate for every `FormattedTextField`.

2. Explicitly install an instance of the UI delegate by overriding the `updateUI` method that `FormattedTextField` inherits from `JTextField`.

Either of these techniques will work and there is very little to choose between them, so we arbitrary elect to use the second. If you look at Listing 3-7, you'll see that the `updateUI` method creates an instance of a class called `FormattedText-FieldUI` and installs it as the UI delegate. This method is called whenever the selected look-and-feel is changed. As you can see, this will ensure that our private UI delegate is installed whichever look-and-feel is selected. Because the UI delegate will contain the `ViewFactory`, it is important that changing the look-and-feel does not result in a different delegate being installed, because the behavior of the `FormattedTextField` would revert to that of `JTextField` if this were to happen.

Placing the `ViewFactory` in the UI delegate is relatively simple, as you'll see, but, because the selected UI delegate is now independent of the selected look-and-feel, any look-and-feel specific behavior of `JTextField` will be lost. Our implementation will use the UI delegate from the Metal look-and-feel. This is a good choice, because Metal is always present when Swing is installed; if we had chosen instead to extend the Windows UI delegate, you would only be able to use the `FormattedTextField` on Windows platforms. An alternative solution is to subclass `BasicTextFieldUI`, which is the super-class of all the UI delegates used for `JTextField`. This class is, like the Metal UI delegate, always installed. This wouldn't cost very much in terms of loss of functionality by comparison to using the Metal UI delegate, because the only thing that Metal adds to `BasicTextFieldUI` is setting a different back-ground color depending on whether the text control is editable. In fact, there isn't very much difference in the behavior of a simple text field whichever look-and-feel is being used. The Windows UI delegate selects the field con-tent when the text field gets the focus and both Windows and Motif use slightly different `Caret` implementations. In the unlikely event that these dif-ferences are critical to your application, you might prefer the approach of customizing the editor kit instead.

To implement a custom `ViewFactory`, all we need to do is override the `create` method, which is inherited from `BasicTextFieldUI`. `Formatted-TextField` will use the same basic `View` hierarchy as `JTextField`, which was shown in Figure 3-6, except that the `FieldView` used by `JTextField` will be replaced by a custom `View` that we'll call `FormattedFieldView`. The code for the `create` method is shown in Listing 3-8, along with the rest of the UI delegate implementation.

Listing 3-8 The `FormattedTextField` UI delegate

```
package AdvancedSwing.Chapter3;

import javax.swing.*;
import javax.swing.text.*;
import javax.swing.plaf.*;
import javax.swing.plaf.metal.*;
import java.beans.*;

public class FormattedTextFieldUI extends MetalTextFieldUI
            implements PropertyChangeListener {
    public static ComponentUI createUI(JComponent c) {
        return new FormattedTextFieldUI();
    }

    public FormattedTextFieldUI() {
        super();
    }

    public void installUI(JComponent c) {
        super.installUI(c);

        if (c instanceof FormattedTextField) {
            c.addPropertyChangeListener(this);
            editor = (FormattedTextField)c;
            formatSpec = editor.getFormatSpec();
        }
    }

    public void uninstallUI(JComponent c) {
        super.uninstallUI(c);
        c.removePropertyChangeListener(this);
    }
```

Listing 3-8 The `FormattedTextField` UI delegate (continued)

```
public void propertyChange(PropertyChangeEvent evt) {
    if (evt.getPropertyName().equals(
                FormattedTextField.FORMAT_PROPERTY)) {
        // Install the new format specification
        formatSpec = editor.getFormatSpec();

        // Recreate the View hierarchy
        modelChanged();
    }
}

// ViewFactory method - creates a view
public View create(Element elem) {
    return new FormattedFieldView(elem, formatSpec);
}

protected FormattedTextField.FormatSpec formatSpec;
protected FormattedTextField editor;
}
```

Note that the UI delegate registers itself to receive `PropertyChange-Events` from its host `FormattedTextField` when it is installed and removes itself from the listener list when it is uninstalled. This allows it to receive notification of changes to the `FormatSpec`, which would affect the way in which the field's contents should be drawn. When this event is received, the new `FormatSpec` is retrieved and stored. Because the `View` needs to know the `FormatSpec`, when a change occurs it is necessary to inform the `View`. The simplest way to do this is to recreate the complete `View` hierarchy by calling the `modelChanged` method, which is inherited from `BasicTextUI`. This method is usually called when a new `Document` is installed (not in response to content insertion or removal which are notified directly to the `View`). The `modelChanged` method creates a new `View` hierarchy to replace any existing one. During this process, the `FormattedTextFieldUI create` method will be called and a `FormattedFieldView` with the new `FormatSpec` will be created. This is, in fact, the same mechanism that builds the initial `View` hierarchy for any text component. In this case, of course, the hierarchy is very flat, consisting only of the standard `RootView` and the custom `FormattedField-View`. In most cases, the `FormatSpec` will be set when the component is created and never changed, so this process will only happen once.

A Custom `FieldView`

`FormattedFieldView` will, not surprisingly, be derived from `FieldView`. To do its job, this `View` (like all `Views`) requires a reference to the `Element` that it will map and also to the `FormatSpec` that it will use to determine how the content should be displayed. As you saw in the implementation of the `View-Factory` in Listing 3-8, references to both of these are available when the `View` is created and are passed as arguments to its constructor.

The custom paragraph `View` that you saw in the previous section was relatively simple—it didn't have to override many of the `View` methods because the implementations it inherited from `ParagraphView` were suitable and did not need to be extended or modified. This time, though, we are not going to be so lucky. Our `View` will have to take full responsibility for the following:

- Determining its preferred width and height.
- Drawing itself onto the screen.
- Mapping a position in the `View` to the corresponding location in the model.
- Mapping a model position to the location within the `View` at which it is drawn.

Returning the appropriate preferred width and height means overriding the `getPreferredSpan` method. We can't use the implementation of this method provided by `FieldView` because it assumes that the `View` is displaying exactly what is in the model and computes the required width accordingly. We can, however, delegate to the `FieldView` for the height calculation. For similar reasons, the `FieldView` paint method is not directly usable. In fact, the `paint` method is, at least logically, where most of the differences between `FieldView` and `FormattedFieldView` appear because the reason for implementing `FormattedFieldView` is simply to render the model content differently than it is by `FieldView`. In fact, as you'll see, the `Formatted-FieldView` paint method is very simple—most of the code that is specific to `FormattedFieldView` appears in other methods, inherited from `FieldView` and from its superclass `PlainView`, that are called from within the `paint` method.

The mapping between model and view locations (and vice versa) is done in the `modelToView` and `viewToModel` methods. `FieldView` provides implementations for both of these methods, but we can't use them because we will be adding characters from the format string that don't appear in the model so, for example, in the case of the telephone field example, if the text field looks like this:

(789)-012-3456

and the user clicks between the digits 1 and 2, the `viewToModel` method should return the value 5, because the cursor will be occupying position 5 in the model, even though it is in position 8 on the screen. Performing this mapping requires access to the `FormatSpec`, which indicates how the characters on the screen map to those in the model. A similar process is performed to map from a model location to the place in the `View` where that character will be displayed.

Initialization and State

The complete implementation of the `FormattedFieldView` is shown in Listing 3-9. As you can see, this is quite a bit more complex than the last example we looked at, so we'll examine the code in pieces, starting with the constructor. As you already know, the constructor is passed a reference to the `Element` that the `View` will map and the `FormatSpec` to be used. The `Element` reference is saved for later use, but the `FormatSpec` is not saved because it is more useful, for performance, reasons, to extract information from it that can be used directly as needed. The constructor allocates three `Segment` objects, which will be used as follows:

`contentBuff`   Used to hold the content of the text field as it will be displayed. Initially, this contains the format field from the `FormatSpec`; as the user types characters into the model, they will be transferred into this buffer in the correct locations as determined by the mask field.

`measureBuff`   This segment points to a character array that is used in the process of determining the desired width of the text component.

`workBuff`   This object is a scratch area that points to a region of the text field while it is being painted. You'll see exactly how this object is used when the painting mechanism is described.

A `Segment` object maps a portion of a character array, a reference to which is held in its `array` member. The `offset` and `count` fields indicate a contiguous region of the character array that typically corresponds to a range of positions within the text component's model. Directly creating a `Segment` object, as shown in the `FormattedFieldView` constructor, allocates the `Segment` object but not the character array, which is logically separate from the `Segment`. The three `Segments` created in the constructor, therefore do not initially point to any associated data. There are two ways to connect a `Segment` to some data:

1. Directly set the array, offset, and count members to point to some portion of an existing character array.

2. Call the `Document getText` method with an offset, length, and `Segment` object as arguments.

When you use the second of these methods, you cannot make any assumptions about the returned value of the `offset` argument in the `Segment` object. Even if you ask for a part of the document starting at offset 0, you cannot assume that the offset value in the `Segment` object will be returned as 0. Furthermore, for efficiency, whenever possible the `getText` method initializes the `Segment` object to point directly into the content of the model, so the returned character array should be considered to be read-only. In this example, you'll see cases in which the `Segment` is initialized by calling `getText` and other instances in which the `Segment` is manually set to point to a character array that is not part of the document model.

Listing 3-9 A Custom Text `FieldView`

```
package AdvancedSwing.Chapter3;

import javax.swing.text.*;
import javax.swing.event.*;
import java.awt.*;

public class FormattedFieldView extends FieldView {
    public FormattedFieldView(Element elem,
                FormattedTextField.FormatSpec formatSpec) {
        super(elem);

        this.contentBuff = new Segment();
        this.measureBuff = new Segment();
        this.workBuff = new Segment();
        this.element = elem;
```

Listing 3-9 A Custom Text FieldView (continued)

```
        buildMapping(formatSpec);     // Build the model ->
                                      // view map

        createContent();    // Update content string
}

// View methods start here
public float getPreferredSpan(int axis) {
    int widthFormat;
    int widthContent;

    if (formatSize == 0 || axis == View.Y_AXIS) {
        return super.getPreferredSpan(axis);
    }

    widthFormat = Utilities.getTabbedTextWidth(measureBuff,
            getFontMetrics(), 0, this, 0);
    widthContent = Utilities.getTabbedTextWidth(contentBuff,
            getFontMetrics(), 0, this, 0);

    return Math.max(widthFormat, widthContent);
}

public Shape modelToView(int pos, Shape a,
                Position.Bias b)
                throws BadLocationException {
    a = adjustAllocation(a);
    Rectangle r = new Rectangle(a.getBounds());
    FontMetrics fm = getFontMetrics();
    r.height = fm.getHeight();

    int oldCount = contentBuff.count;

    if (pos < offsets.length) {
        contentBuff.count = offsets[pos];
    } else {
        // Beyond the end: point to the location
        // after the last model position.
        contentBuff.count = offsets[offsets.length - 1] + 1;

    }

    int offset = Utilities.getTabbedTextWidth(contentBuff,
            metrics, 0, this, element.getStartOffset());
```

Listing 3-9 A Custom Text `FieldView` **(continued)**

```
        contentBuff.count = oldCount;

        r.x += offset;
        r.width = 1;

        return r;
    }

    public int viewToModel(float fx, float fy, Shape a,
                    Position.Bias[] bias) {
        a = adjustAllocation(a);
        bias[0] = Position.Bias.Forward;

        int x = (int)fx;
        int y = (int)fy;
        Rectangle r = a.getBounds();
        int startOffset = element.getStartOffset();
        int endOffset = element.getEndOffset();

        if (y < r.y || x < r.x) {
            return startOffset;
        } else if (y > r.y + r.height || x > r.x + r.width) {
            return endOffset - 1;
        }

        // Given position is within bounds of the view.
        int offset = Utilities.getTabbedTextOffset(contentBuff,
                getFontMetrics(), r.x, x, this,
                startOffset);
        // The offset includes characters not in the model,
        // so get rid of them to return a true model offset.
        for (int i = 0; i < offsets.length; i++) {
            if (offset <= offsets[i]) {
                offset = i;
                break;
            }
        }

        // Don't return an offset beyond the data
        // actually in the model.
        if (offset > endOffset - 1) {
            offset = endOffset - 1;
        }
        return offset;
    }
```

Listing 3-9 A Custom Text `FieldView` (continued)

```
public void insertUpdate(DocumentEvent changes,
                         Shape a, ViewFactory f) {
  super.insertUpdate(changes, adjustAllocation(a), f);
  createContent();    // Update content string
}

public void removeUpdate(DocumentEvent changes,
                         Shape a, ViewFactory f) {
  super.removeUpdate(changes, adjustAllocation(a), f);
  createContent();    // Update content string
}
// End of View methods

// View drawing methods: overridden from PlainView
protected void drawLine(int line, Graphics g, int x,
                        int y) {
  // Set the colors
  JTextComponent host = (JTextComponent)getContainer();
  unselected = (host.isEnabled()) ?
              host.getForeground() :
                host.getDisabledTextColor();
  Caret c = host.getCaret();
  selected = c.isSelectionVisible() ?
              host.getSelectedTextColor() : unselected;

  int p0 = element.getStartOffset();
  int p1 = element.getEndOffset() - 1;
  int sel0 =
  ((JTextComponent)getContainer()).getSelectionStart();
  int sel1 =
  ((JTextComponent)getContainer()).getSelectionEnd();

  try {
      // If the element is empty or there is no selection
      // in this view, just draw the whole thing in one go.
      if (p0 == p1 || sel0 == sel1 ||
              inView(p0, p1, sel0, sel1) == false) {
          drawUnselectedText(g, x, y, 0,
                              contentBuff.count);
          return;
      }

      //   There is a selection in this view. Draw up to
      //   three regions:
      //   (a) The unselected region before the selection.
      //   (b) The selected region.
```

Listing 3-9 A Custom Text `FieldView` **(continued)**

```
        //  (c) The unselected region after the selection.
        //  First, map the selected region offsets to be
        //  relative to the start of the region and
        //  then map them to view offsets so that they take
        //  into account characters not present in the model.
        int mappedSel0 = mapOffset(Math.max(sel0 - p0, 0));
        int mappedSel1 = mapOffset(Math.min(sel1 - p0,
                                            p1 - p0));

        if (mappedSel0 > 0) {
            // Draw an initial unselected region
            x = drawUnselectedText(g, x, y, 0, mappedSel0);
        }
        x = drawSelectedText(g, x, y, mappedSel0,
                             mappedSel1);

        if (mappedSel1 < contentBuff.count) {
            drawUnselectedText(g, x, y, mappedSel1,
                               contentBuff.count);
        }
    } catch (BadLocationException e) {
        // Should not happen!
    }
}

protected int drawUnselectedText(Graphics g, int x, int y,
        int p0, int p1) throws BadLocationException {
    g.setColor(unselected);
    workBuff.array = contentBuff.array;
    workBuff.offset = p0;
    workBuff.count = p1 - p0;
    return Utilities.drawTabbedText(workBuff, x, y, g,
                                    this, p0);
}

protected int drawSelectedText(Graphics g, int x,
        int y, int p0, int p1) throws BadLocationException {
    workBuff.array = contentBuff.array;
    workBuff.offset = p0;
    workBuff.count = p1 - p0;
    g.setColor(selected);
    return Utilities.drawTabbedText(workBuff, x, y, g,
                                    this, p0);
}
```

Listing 3-9 A Custom Text `FieldView` **(continued)**

```
// End of View drawing methods

// Build the model-to-view mapping
protected void buildMapping(
      FormattedTextField.FormatSpec formatSpec) {
   formatSize = formatSpec != null ?
      formatSpec.getFormatSize() : 0;

   if (formatSize != 0) {
      // Save the format string as a character array
      formatChars = formatSpec.getFormat().toCharArray();

      // Allocate a buffer to store the formatted string
      formattedContent = new char[formatSize];
      contentBuff.offset = 0;
      contentBuff.count = formatSize;
      contentBuff.array = formattedContent;

      // Keep the mask for computing
      // the preferred horizontal span, but use
      // a wide character for measurement
      char[] maskChars =
            formatSpec.getMask().toCharArray();
      measureBuff.offset = 0;
      measureBuff.array = maskChars;
      measureBuff.count = formatSize;

      // Get the number of markers
      markerCount = formatSpec.getMarkerCount();

      // Allocate an array to hold the offsets
      offsets = new int[markerCount];

      // Create the offset array
      markerCount = 0;
      for (int i = 0; i < formatSize; i++) {
         if (maskChars[i] ==
            FormattedTextField.FormatSpec.MARKER_CHAR) {
            offsets[markerCount++] = i;

            // Replace marker with a wide character
            // in the array used for measurement.
```

Listing 3-9 A Custom Text `FieldView` **(continued)**

```
                maskChars[i] = WIDE_CHARACTER;
            }
        }
    }
}


// Use the document content and the format
// string to build the display content
protected void createContent() {
    try {
        Document doc = getDocument();
        int startOffset = element.getStartOffset();
        int endOffset = element.getEndOffset();
        int length = endOffset - startOffset - 1;

        // If there is no format, use the raw data.
        if (formatSize != 0) {
            // Get the document content
            doc.getText(startOffset, length, workBuff);

            // Initialize the output buffer with the
            // format string.
            System.arraycopy(formatChars, 0,
                            formattedContent, 0,
                            formatSize);

            // Insert the model content into
            // the target string.
            int count = Math.min(length, markerCount);
            int firstOffset = workBuff.offset;

            // Place the model data into the output array
            for (int i = 0; i < count; i++) {
                formattedContent[offsets[i]] =
                        workBuff.array[i + firstOffset];
            }
        } else {
            doc.getText(startOffset, length, contentBuff);
        }
    } catch (BadLocationException bl) {
        contentBuff.count = 0;
    }
}
```

Listing 3-9 A Custom Text `FieldView` **(continued)**

```
// Map a document offset to a view offset.
protected int mapOffset(int pos) {
   pos -= element.getStartOffset();
   if (pos >= offsets.length) {
      return contentBuff.count;
   } else {
      return offsets[pos];
   }
}


// Determines whether the selection intersects
// a given range of model offsets.
protected boolean inView(int p0, int p1, int sel0,
                         int sel1) {
   if (sel0 >= p0 && sel0 < p1) {
      return true;
   }

   if (sel0 < p0 && sel1 >= p0) {
      return true;
   }

   return false;
}  protected char[] formattedContent;
                     // The formatted content for display
protected char[] formatChars;
                     // The format string as characters
protected Segment contentBuff;
                     // Segment pointing to formatted
                     // content
protected Segment measureBuff;
                     // Segment pointing to mask string
protected Segment workBuff;
                     // Segment used for scratch purposes
protected Element element;
                     // The mapped element
protected int[] offsets;
                     // Model-to-view offsets
protected Color selected;
                     // Selected text color
protected Color unselected;
                     // Unselected text color
protected int formatSize;
                     // Length of the formatting string
```

> **Listing 3-9 A Custom Text** `FieldView` **(continued)**

```
    protected int markerCount;
                        // Number of markers in the format

    protected static final char WIDE_CHARACTER = 'm';
}
```

Having allocated the `Segment` objects, the constructor invokes two initialization methods. The first of these, `buildMapping`, performs setup tasks that need to be carried out whenever the `FormatSpec` changes. Because a new `FormattedFieldView` is created whenever this occurs, this method is actually used only once during the `View`'s lifetime. By contrast the other method, `createContent`, is called during construction and also every time the model's content is changed in any way.

Let's look first at `buildMapping`. This method performs two functions:

1. It initializes the `Segment` objects.
2. It uses the `FormatSpec` object to create a mapping from model position to the location in the `View` at which the corresponding character should be displayed.

The first step is to get the format string from the `FormatSpec` in the form of a character array and save a reference to it for later use in the `formatChars` field. This reference will be used in the `createContent` method as the starting point from which to build the representation of the model as it will appear in the text field. Next, a new character array is allocated to hold the constructed view of the model data and the `Segment` object `contentBuff` is initialized to point to it. Initially, this buffer will not have any useful content, but it is large enough to hold the content of the model formatted according to the `FormatSpec`. The length of this array is the same as the length of the format string (and also the same length as the mask). Having dealt with the formatting string, the next step is to handle the mask. A copy of the mask, in the form of a character array, is obtained from the `FormatSpec` and the `Segment` object `measureBuff` is set up to point to it. As you'll see later, this object is used when determining the preferred width of the `View`. Next, the `buildMapping` method allocates an array of integers called `offsets` that has as many entries as there are markers in the mask. Then, it loops over all the characters in the mask doing two things. First, it checks each character looking for mask characters that indicate locations that will be occupied by the characters from the model. As each of these is found, the next entry in the offsets array is filled with the offset of the marker down the mask (and hence the offset from the start of the formatting string). Then, once the locations occupied by the markers have been recorded, their actual content is no longer important and the positions in the character array that corresponded to markers are filled with the lowercase letter m, which is a wide character in most fonts. You'll see the reason for this in the next section.

To clarify what the buildMapping method has done, let's look at how the various pieces of state information would be set up from a FormatSpec corresponding to the telephone number example that we've been using throughout this section. In this case, the format and mask fields would be set up by the programmer as follows:

```
(...)-...-....
(***)_***_****
```

The formatChars field will first be initialized with a reference to a character array that contains the characters of the format string, the first of the two strings shown above. Then, a character array with 14 characters will be created and the contentBuff Segment object initialized to point to it, with code equivalent to the following

```
contentBuff.array = new char[14];
contentBuff.offset = 0;
contentBuff.count = 14;
```

Note that this array does not yet have any useful content. The measure-Buff object is then set up to point to a copy of the mask in which all the marker positions have been replaced by the letter m. Here is how it will look:

```
measureBuff.arrray is a character array containing
```
$$" (mmm) -mmm-mmmm"$$
```
measureBuff.offset = 0;
measureBuff.count = 14;
```

Finally, the offsets array is initialized to map from model location to the position in the view at which the corresponding character will appear. In the case of this example, the offsets array will have 10 entries (because there are 10 markers in the mask field) and will be set up as follows:

offsets[0] = 1	offsets[1] = 2	offsets[2] = 3	offsets[3] = 6	offsets[4] = 7
offsets[5] = 8	offsets[6] = 10	offsets[7] = 11	offsets[8] = 12	offsets[9] = 13

In other words, the first character in the model will appear at offset 1 in the view, the second at offset 2, the third at offset 3, the fourth at offset 6, and so on. Taking a concrete example of how the `offsets` array would be used when the text control is being drawn, suppose the model contained the first five digits of a telephone number, like this:

```
98765
```

For display purposes, the digit 9 would be placed at position `offsets[0]`, that is, position 1, within the text view. This is as you would expect, because position 0 is occupied by the opening parenthesis of the pair that surrounds the first three digits. Similarly, the digit 8 appears at offset 2 and the digit 7 at offset 3. The next two digits, 6 and 5, would be placed at offsets 6 and 7 respectively, because of the intervening close parentheses and the hyphen. Positions for which the model does not yet contain data are occupied by the characters that were specified in the original format string, so this is how the text component would look at this stage:

```
(987)-65.-....
```

To verify this, you can try out the `FormattedTextField` by typing the command:

```
java AdvancedSwing.Chapter3.FormattedTextFieldExample
```

This simple program creates a text field formatted to look like the telephone number example that we've been using in this chapter. Here is the snippet of code that created this text field:

```
final FormattedTextField tf = new FormattedTextField();
FormattedTextField.FormatSpec formatSpec =
        new FormattedTextField.FormatSpec(
                "(...)-...-....",
                "(***)-***-****");
tf.setFormatSpec(formatSpec);
```

If you type the digits 98765, you'll see that the text field is indeed drawn as was suggested above, as Figure 3-18 shows. If you now press RETURN, the content of the text field's model will be displayed in the window in which you started the program. You should see the following output:

```
Field content is <98765>
```

which demonstrates that the extra formatting characters (the parentheses, the hyphens, and the periods) are not held in the model, even though they are being displayed.

Figure 3-18   A `FormattedTextField` displaying a telephone number.

The other method called from the constructor, `createContent`, is the method that builds the text for the `View` from the model content and the information saved by `buildMapping`. This method is called when the `View` is first created and each time the model content changes. It extracts the data from the model and builds the formatted content in the character array pointed at by `contentBuff`, which was allocated by `buildMapping`. You can see how this is done by looking at the code near the end of Listing 3-9.

The first step is to work out how many characters have been inserted into the portion of the model mapped by this `View`. In practice, while this `View` is being used by `FormattedTextField`, it will map the whole model so we could just get the number of characters by calling the `Document getLength` method. However, in this implementation we make the `View` slightly more general, and more like the other `View`s in the text package, by using the start and end offsets of the element that the `View` maps to determine the number of characters to be rendered. In the case of `FormattedTextField`, this will give the same result as calling `getLength`. Having obtained the length, we call the `Document getText` method to get the characters. As you saw in Chapter 1, there are two variants of `getText`, one of which returns the content in a `String` and another that uses a `Segment`. The second of these is usually the more efficient of the two, so we make use of it here, passing it the `workBuff Segment` object that was allocated by the constructor. When this method returns, the `array` field of `workBuff` points to a character array that contains the model data, while the `offset` and `count` fields indicate which part of the array actually holds the data.

The process of building the formatted result is very simple. First, the output buffer is initialized with a copy of the format string. This is done by copying the character array `formatChars`, saved by the `buildMapping` method, to the array pointed to by the `contentBuff Segment`, which was also allocated by `buildMapping`. At this stage, `contentBuff` contains an image of the original format string. In the case of the telephone number example, it would look like this:

```
(...)-...-....
```

The next step is to copy the characters from the model into their correct locations in `contentBuff`. This is done using the offsets array created by `buildMapping`. The process terminates as soon as the number of characters in the model, or the number of characters indicated by the number of markers in the mask, whichever is the smaller, has been copied. While the user is typing into the field, the copy will finish when the model data is exhausted. In fact, because a `BoundedPlainDocument` is installed as the default model and then set to limit the number of characters to the number of markers in the mask, it should not be possible to have more characters in the model than markers, so a simple test against the marker count should be sufficient. However, the programmer is at liberty to install a different model or to change the maximum length constraint on the `BoundedPlainDocument`. In either case, it is possible to create a control that can hold more characters than the mask in the `FormatSpec` requires. To protect against this possibility, the loop that copies the characters checks both possible terminating conditions. This will have the effect of not displaying data in the model that does not have a corresponding marker position.

Note carefully how the data is copied from the model into the output buffer:

```
int count = Math.min(length, markerCount);
int firstOffset = workBuff.offset;

// Place the model data into the output array
for (int i = 0; i < count; i++) {
  formattedContent[offsets[i]] = workBuff.array[i +
                                            firstOffset];
}
```

The important point to note about this is the array index used when accessing the source character array pointed to by the `workBuff` `Segment`. As we said earlier, you cannot assume that the useful data in the array starts at index 0; because of this, the initial offset (obtained from the `offset` field) is used as the starting point of the copy. The target location of the copy is obtained, as explained earlier, by extracting the correct offset from the `offsets` array.

When `createContent` is complete, the character array pointed to by `contentBuff` contains the text that should be displayed as the text control's content. Because this method is called when the control is initially created and whenever the user inserts or deletes characters from the control, this ensures that `contentBuff` is always up to date, so painting the content of the control is just a matter of drawing the text in `contentBuff`. Because the text control is likely to be painted at least as often as its content changes, it is more efficient to build the text to be displayed as each change occurs than it would be to do so just before each `paint` operation.

Determining the Preferred Span of the Text Field

The preferred size of a text component is actually determined by its UI delegate, which uses the `View` hierarchy to calculate how much space is needed in each direction. Each `View` can implement the `getMinimumSpan`, `getPreferredSpan`, and `getMaximumSpan` methods to indicate preferences and constraints that exist on its width and height. In the case of `Formatted-FieldView`, implementations of all three of these methods will be inherited from its superclasses. The inherited `getMinimumSpan` and `getMaximumSpan` methods come from `View` and return `0` and `Integer.MAX_VALUE` respectively, for both the width and the height. These values are acceptable, so there is no need to override these methods. The `getPreferredSpan` method, however, is inherited from `FieldView`. If called with argument `Y_AXIS`, this method returns the height of the selected font, which is also acceptable for `FormattedFieldView`. However, the preferred horizontal span for `FieldView` is the width needed to draw the characters stored in the model. Because `FormattedFieldView` will usually display more characters than exist in the model, this would usually not yield the correct result. Therefore, it is necessary to override `getPreferredSpan` to provide a more accurate preferred width.

How should we work out the preferred width of the `View`? The simplest possible way would be to take advantage of the fact that the number of characters that can be displayed in the `View` is limited to the length of the formatting string. Using this information, we could multiply the maximum number of characters by the width of a single character in the selected font to obtain the maximum width of the input field. This would work very well, and would give a constant value for the result that could be calculated once and returned on each call to `getPreferredSpan`, were it not for the following two points:

- The programmer is not forced to use a constant-width font, even though the `FormattedTextField` installs one by default. If, instead, a proportional font were used, the initial size calculation could produce a result that differed greatly from the width required when the field is fully populated with user input. In the case of the telephone field, the format string would be much narrower in a proportional font than the complete telephone number, because the periods that appear when the control is created are not nearly as wide as the digits that will replace them.

- Although it isn't very likely, the format string could legitimately include TAB characters. If you create a JTextField and initialize it with a String that includes a TAB character, the text field will act on it, even though you can't type a TAB into the field unless you arrange for the focus manager to pass TABs directly to the text field instead of moving the focus to the next component. This behavior should, at least by default, be preserved by FormattedTextField. This makes it harder to calculate the width of the View. If a monospaced font is used, the width will still be constant even if there are TABs, but it is no longer a simple matter of multiplying the width of one character in the font by the number of characters in the formatting string.

Because of these issues, it isn't possible to guess the correct width for the View. In fact, just working out the maximum width of the formatting string isn't always good enough. If a proportional font is in use, the width of the data in the control at any given time depends entirely on the characters that have been typed. Ideally, the first value returned from getPreferredSpan would be large enough to accommodate the longest string that could ever appear in the text field. Because of the possibility of TAB characters, it is almost impossible to work out in advance the maximum possible width, so we take the following approach when asked for the preferred width of the View:

1. Measure the width of the formatting string with wide characters in place of the locations that will be occupied by characters from the model.

2. Measure the actual width of the current content of the View.

3. Return the larger of these two widths.

Although this may sound complicated, it is actually fairly simple. To start with, we already have all the necessary information available. The string whose width is measured in step 1 is actually created during initialization, because, as described earlier, we take a copy of the formatting string, substitute an "m" in all the locations that will be filled from the model and initialize the Segment object measureBuff to point to it. This is exactly the string that we need to measure in step 1. As for step 2, the string we need here is exactly the current state of the data to be displayed in the View. This string is maintained by the createContent method and is pointed to by the contentBuff object.

Given that we have the necessary strings available, how do we calculate their lengths? Usually, you measure the width of strings using the FontMetrics stringWidth method, but that won't work here because the strings might contain TAB characters. Because the TAB characters can be expanded in ways that depend on the TabExpander that happens to be installed, in general the only way to get the correct width is to actually perform the TAB expansion and work out how wide the resulting string would be. Fortunately, the text package contains a class called Utilities that includes a method that does this job for you:

```
public int getTabbedTextWidth(Segment s, FontMetrics metrics,
                   int x, TabExpander e, int startOffset)
```

All the arguments required by this method are easily available from within the getPreferredSpan method. The first argument is the Segment that points to the string to be measured; this will be measureBuff for the first measurement and contentBuff for the second.

Core Note

The fact that this method, like some others in the Utilities class that you'll see later, uses Segment objects is the main reason for using them in the implementation of this View.

The FontMetrics are available from the FormattedTextField. In fact, FieldView, from which FormattedFieldView is derived, has a convenience method that obtains the FontMetrics from whichever text component it is mapping. The third argument is the x position of the start of the string to be measured. This value is passed to the TabExpander, the fourth argument. This is necessary, because if, for example, tab stops are placed at fixed offsets along the View, the effect of any TABs that might be present in the string will depend on where the string starts. The last argument is the offset within the document of the start of the string, which will always be 0 in this case. PlainView implements the TabExpander interface. Because Formatted-FieldView is derived from FieldView, which is a subclass of PlainView, this implementation is inherited by FormattedFieldView, so the Tab-Expander argument is supplied simply as this and the start offset of the text within the document is not actually used by this implementation.

Mapping from *View* Location to Model Position

The mapping from `View` location to model position in a component that performs custom rendering is not something that can be done by generic code in the component—it can only be done by the `View`. The most obvious case in which this mapping is needed is when the user clicks inside the component with the mouse. This action causes the caret to move to the location of the mouse click. As you already know, however, the caret's location is actually specified by its position within the model. What actually happens when the user attempts to move the caret using the mouse is the following:

1. The mouse press is detected by the text component's installed `Caret`, which is registered as a `MouseListener` of the text component.
2. The `Caret mousePressed` method gets the new mouse location from the `MouseEvent` and converts it to a model location by calling the `viewToModel` method of the text component's UI class. This call is directed to the `viewToModel` method of the `View` that contains the mouse location.
3. Having obtained the model location, the `Caret` position is changed by passing the location to the `Caret`'s `setDot` method.

The process of converting a `View` offset to the corresponding model location is not a simple one. One obvious reason for this is that the component may be using a proportional font, so it isn't possible to work out where the caret should be by taking the x position from the `MouseEvent` and dividing it by the width of a single character. Another complication is the possibility of the presence of `TAB` characters, which, in general, occupy more than one character position on the screen. In fact, though, both of these problems are taken care of by the `viewToModel` method of `FieldView`, which `Formatted-FieldView` inherits. So why do we need to implement our own `viewToModel` at all?

The inherited `viewToModel` method works by using the `Utilities get-TabbedTextOffset` method, which you'll see shortly. Loosely speaking, this method takes a character array, a `FontMetrics` object, and an offset and returns the number of characters in the array that lie to the left of the given offset. As an example, suppose that a constant-width font in which each character occupies eight points is in use and that the text component contains the string:

`FormattedFieldView`

If the `getTabbedTextOffset` method is called with this text, the `Font-Metrics` object for the constant-width font and the offset is 16, it would return the value 2, because each character occupies eight points. This would correspond to the user clicking the mouse between the characters o and r; you can easily see that 2 is the correct model offset for this `View` position. This is fine for `FieldView`, because it only displays characters that are in the model. Now suppose that `FormattedFieldView` is in use and the text component shows the following content:

```
(123)-456-7890
```

Suppose also that the `FormatSpec` that we have been using in our telephone number example is applied and that the same 8-point constant-width font is being used. If the user now clicks the mouse between the digits 1 and 2, the `View` offset 16 will still be obtained from the `MouseEvent` and, consequently, `getTabbedTextOffset` would still return the answer 2. However, this is not the correct model offset because it includes the opening parenthesis, which is not part of the model. In fact, the correct model offset in this case is 1, because there is only one character from the model to the left of the mouse location. For this reason, we have to implement our own `viewTo-Model` method that works in the same way as that of `FieldView`, and then converts the value returned by `getTabbedTextOffset` to take account of the extra characters in the format string that are not in the model.

The `FormattedFieldView` implementation of `viewToModel` is shown in Listing 3-9. Let's ignore for now the first two lines of this method, which read:

```
a = adjustAllocation(a);
bias[0] = Position.Bias.Forward;
```

This first of these two statements takes account of another complication that `FormattedFieldView` shares with `FieldView` that we'll deal with at the end of this section, while the second is another consequence of handling bi-directional text, which is discussed in Chapter 5. This method first converts the given `View` location from the floating-point values that are passed in to the `ints` that are required by the methods in the `Utilities` class, and then gets the bounding rectangle of the space allocated to the `View`. For the sake of simplicity, let's assume for now that this rectangle corresponds to the visible area of the text component on the screen (as we'll see later, this is not always true). The first check to be made is that the `View` location is actually within the bounding rectangle of the component's visible area. If the `View` location is to the left of or above the bounding rectangle, and then it is taken as being before the first character in the model—in other words, the corresponding model offset will be the start offset of the `Element` within the model that is mapped by this `View`. On the other hand, if the `View` location is below or to the right of the bounding rectangle, it is taken as indicating the last valid offset in the mapped `Element`. Usually, however, the coordinates passed to this method will map to a position that lies somewhere between these two extremes. Having verified that this is the case, we get the model location, as described earlier, by invoking `getTabbedTextOffset`, a method of the `javax.swing.text.Utilities` class that is declared as follows:

```
public static final int getTabbedTextOffset(Segment s,
                        FontMetrics metrics,
                        int x0, int x, TabExpander e,
                        int startOffset)
```

This method looks very similar to the `getTabbedTextWidth` method that we used earlier in this example. In fact, in many ways these methods are the reverse of each other; while `getTabbedTextWidth` returns the width of a given string, `getTabbedTextOffset` is given a size and returns the answer to the question "How much of this string occupies this much horizontal space?" The first argument is a `Segment` object that points to the string being measured, in the form of a character array. In this example, the string is the text being displayed by the `FormattedFieldView`, which is always pointed to by the `contentBuff` object. The second, fifth, and sixth arguments should also be familiar from the description of `getTabbedTextWidth`—they refer to the `FontMetrics` for the font being used by the `FormattedTextField`, the object to be used to expand tabs, which, as before, will be the `Formatted-FieldView` itself and the starting offset of the text within the model, which is used by the `TabExpander`.

That leaves the third and fourth arguments, which are both obviously the x coordinates of two points. The first is the x coordinate of the `View`'s bounding rectangle, measured relative to the space occupied by the text component. Usually, this would be zero because `FormattedTextField` only has one real `View` that displays all of its content and so occupies all of its screen space; as we'll shortly see, this isn't always true. For `View`s such as `LabelView` that are used by more complex text components, the bounding rectangle can correspond to any area of the space occupied by the component because a `Label-View` can cover part of a line of text that need not begin at the left side of the component, so this argument need not be zero even in the simplest of cases. The second x coordinate is that of the `View` location whose model offset is required, measured from the same origin as the first x coordinate. In the simple case of a mouse click in a `FormattedTextField`, this will be the x coordinate from the `MouseEvent`. Figure 3-19 shows this pictorially for the less trivial case of a `LabelView` in a `JTextPane`.

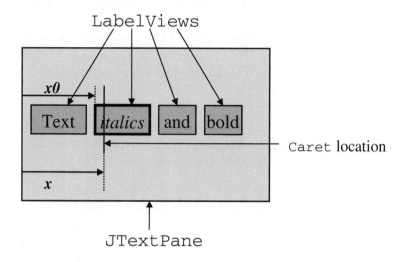

Figure 3-19   Offsets passed to the `getTabbedTextOffset` method.

Here, you can see the `Views` that correspond to a single line of text rendered on a `JTextPane`. Because there are several attribute changes within the line, each section has its own `LabelView` that maps an `Elements` with a particular set of attributes. Let's suppose that the user clicks to place the `Caret` between the letters i and t of the word `italics`, as shown by the vertical line in the diagram. Initially, the `viewToModel` method of the `JText-Pane` UI delegate is called, which passes the request to the `RootView` `viewToModel` method. The `RootView` locates the `ParagraphView` that contains the location at which the user clicked and calls its `viewToModel` method. This process continues through the `ParagraphView.Row` containing the mouse location and finally reaches the `LabelView` that actually draws the text `italics`. At this point, the `Shape` passed to the `viewToModel` method (the third argument) is the box that bounds the area occupied by the `Label-View` (shown with bold edging in Figure 3-19) and the coordinates passed as the first two arguments are the x and y values of the point where the mouse was clicked, relative to the `JTextPane`. In other words, the x coordinate supplied to the `LabelView modelToView` method is the value shown as x in Figure 3-19, while the bounding box of the `View` has the x coordinate shown as x0. These designations are the same as those used in the definition of `get-`

`TabbedTextOffset` above. However, in the case of `FormattedFieldView`, the bounding box covers the whole line, so the x0 value is 0. In effect, the `getTabbedTextOffset` method is asked to return the offset of the model location that is (x - x0) points from the left edge of the `View`'s bounding box.

The actual algorithm used by `getTabbedTextOffset` is not important to the rest of this discussion; in fact, it operates by working along the characters that it is given, adding the width of each (taken from the `FontMetrics` object passed in) to the initial offset (x0) until the resulting offset is equal to or greater than the target offset x. When this occurs, the number of characters needed to reach this point, added to the `startOffset` argument, is the required model offset and becomes the return value, unless the given offset is nearer to the next character, in which case the offset of the next character is returned. For example, suppose that, in Figure 3-19, the user clicked somewhere in the middle of the letter a in `italics`. If the mouse click is nearer to the t than to the l, the offset returned is that of the a (that is, the offset of the position between t and a), whereas if it is closer to the l, the offset of l is returned. There is, in fact, another variant of `getTabbedTextOffset` with an additional `boolean` argument called `round`, which can be supplied as `true` if the rounding described here is to be performed, or `false` if the location before the given offset is required (that is, rounding down).

The return value from `getTabbedTextOffset`, then, is the number of characters that lie to the left of the given `View` location. As we said earlier, though, for `FormattedFieldView`, this is not the final answer, because not all these characters are in the model. What we need is to map the number of characters in the view to the number of model characters that appear in that segment of the view. This mapping is, fortunately, very simple to perform. Let's look again at our telephone number example, which has the following format string:

(. . .) - . . . - . . . .

As you know, the dots are the locations that will be occupied by characters from the model. Now, if the user clicks between the first and second dots, there will be two characters in the view in front of the `Caret`, so the offset returned by `getTabbedTextOffset` will be 2. However, as you can see, there is only one model character before this location, so the correct return value for `viewToModel` would be 1. To see how to convert the value 2 to the correct value, recall that the `offsets` array created by `FormattedFieldView` maps model offset to offset with the format string. This is exactly the reverse of the mapping that is required for `viewToModel`, so we can map the `getTabbed-TextOffset` value to the correct value by iterating through the `offsets` array until we find an entry that contains an offset greater than that returned by getTabbedTextOffset. When we have located this entry, the correct return value is the index in the offsets array of the *previous* entry. Looking again at our telephone example, the offsets array in this case looks like this:

Index	*Offset*
0	1
1	2
2	3
3	6
4	7
5	8
6	10
7	11
8	12
9	13

Walking down the array, you can see that the first entry containing an offset greater than 2 is the one with index 2. Therefore, the correct return value for viewToModel would be $(2 - 1) = 1$. Similarly, if the user clicked after the first dot in the second group (the fourth dot overall), getTabbedTextOffset would return the value 7, which would map to 4 according to the earlier table. This is, of course, the correct result. However, there is another complication. What happens if the user clicks to the right of the last dot? In this case, getTabbedTextOffset returns the value 14, because all 14 characters are now to the left of the click point. There is, however, no entry in the offsets table that is larger than 14. When this happens, the largest possible model offset is returned as the model offset. As a consequence of this, the Caret will actually be placed to the right of the last dot—so the user cannot move the Caret into a location further right than the last actual character from the model. Similarly, because model offset 0 corresponds to display offset 1, the Caret cannot actually be moved to the left of the first character in the model, which will be just after the opening parenthesis in the telephone number example. Another consequence of the way the `viewToModel` method works is that the user cannot move the `Caret` further to the right than the space occupied by characters from the model, even though there will be characters from the mask there. Thus, for example, if only the first three digits of a telephone number have been typed, it will not be possible to move the `Caret` beyond the third digit, either using the mouse or the arrow keys on the keyboard.

Finally, let's return to the first line of the `viewToModel` method that have so far omitted to describe:

```
a = adjustAllocation(a);
```

To see what this line achieves, start the telephone number example again by typing the command

```
java AdvancedSwing.Chapter3.FormattedTextFieldExample
```

and then resize the window horizontally to make the space allocated to the telephone number smaller. As you do this, the space reserved for the rightmost part of the number will be clipped, leaving only the start of the input field in view. Now start typing numbers into the input field. As you do so, everything works as normal until you reach the right side of the visible area, at which point the content scrolls to the left to make room for further input, as shown in Figure 3-20.

Figure 3-20   Scrolling in a `FormattedTextField`.

The scrolling occurs as characters are entered into or removed from the text field, by the `insertUpdate` and `removedUpdate` methods of `FieldView`, which are inherited by `FormattedFieldView`. As the content of the input field changes, the `getPreferredSpan` method is invoked to determine how wide the visible area would need to be to hold all the characters that it should display. `JTextField` contains a `BoundedRangeModel` that holds the preferred size of the control as the maximum value and the size of the area allocated to the control on the screen is usually held in the extent. The value of the `BoundedRangeModel` is set as the `Caret` moves so that the correct portion of the component is visible; as the `BoundedRangeModel`'s value is changed, the control is repainted. Painting the control causes the `View`'s `paint` method to be called. It is this method that actually determines which part of the text component's content will actually be displayed. As you'll see later, the FormattedFieldView paint method, like that of FieldView, uses the values held in the BoundedRangeModel to decide which characters to render on the screen.

The scrolling also affects the view-to-model mapping, of course. Look again at Figure 3-20. Suppose the user now clicks the mouse a little way in (say 16 pixels) from the left side of the FormattedTextField. In the earlier discussion, we assumed that the text would actually be aligned with its start at the left side of the visible area, so that a distance of 16 pixels would correspond to, say, two characters from the start of the text field's content. Here, though, that logic plainly does not work—the 16 pixels should be, perhaps, two characters from the start of the visible text content. To map this to an actual model offset, you need to know how many characters have been moved out of view to the left of the visible area. In fact, when a proportional font is in use, it is difficult to know how many characters have been lost—you can't just work out how many characters on the screen are to the left of the cursor and add that to what is not on view.

To solve this problem, the FormattedFieldView viewToModel method starts by calling adjustAllocation, which it inherits from FieldView. This method does two things:

- Gets the actual height of the area assigned to the View (its bounding rectangle) and compares it to the View's preferred height. If these are not the same, the y component of the View's bounding rectangle and its height are adjusted so that it has the preferred height and is vertically centered in the component's allocated screen area. So, for example, if the content of a FormattedTextField is being drawn with a font that requires a vertical space of 17 pixels but the component is 31 pixels high, the bounding box will be changed so that it starts 7 pixels from the top of the screen area and its height is 17 pixels. On the other hand, if the actual screen area allocated is only 13 pixels, the bounding box is still changed to be 17 pixels high, but now it will start 2 pixels above the upper boundary of the screen area, which will result in the text being clipped at the top and the bottom. In either case, however, the text is vertically centered.

- Gets the width of the bounding rectangle and compares it to the View's preferred width. If the bounding rectangle is not smaller than the preferred width, the bounding box is adjusted so that the text is centered or right- or left-aligned depending on the horizontal alignment specified using the `setHorizontalAlignment` method of the text control. On the other hand, if the preferred width of the text is larger than the actual width, the visible rectangle is adjusted to fit around the text, placing the location indicated by the `BoundedRangeModel`'s value at the left side of the screen area occupied by the component. This will usually result in the x value of the bounding rectangle becoming negative.

To see how this works and how calling this method helps the `viewToModel` method return the correct model offset when some of the control's content has been scrolled of the screen, let's look at a couple of examples. First, consider the simple case in which the screen space is larger than the area required to draw the control's content and suppose also that the text control has right-alignment specified. In this case, the text area is vertically centered and moved to the right of the screen area, as shown in Figure 3-21. In this figure (and the next), the shaded area represents the bounding rectangle of the `Shape` that will be returned by `adjustAllocation`, while the area with the bold border is the `Shape` that was passed to it—that is, the area allocated to the `View` on the screen.

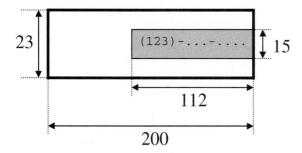

Figure 3-21   Adjusting a `View`'s allocation: case 1.

In Figure 3-21, the `View` is only partly populated, because the user has only supplied the first three characters of the telephone number; however, because of the formatting string, the rendered text still requires the full 112 pixels horizontally and 17 vertically. In this case, the text control is 200 pixels wide and 23 pixels high, leaving extra room in each direction. When the `viewToModel` method is called, the `Shape` passed to it will describe the text component, less some space reserved for insets. A typical bounding rectangle for this shape would be:

```
x = 2, y = 2, width = 196, height = 19
```

The `adjustAllocation` method would change this bounding rectangle to allocate extra vertical space equally above and below the `View` and place the text horizontally according to the text component's horizontal alignment, which, in this case, will move the text to the right side of the visible area. When `adjustAllocation` completes, it returns a `Shape` whose bounding rectangle is the following:

```
x = 86, y = 3, width = 112, height = 17
```

This arrangement leaves 3 pixels above and below the `View`, 86 pixels to the left of it, and 2 to the right (as margin space). Now suppose the reason for entering this method is that the user has clicked with the mouse between the digits 1 and 2. As we'll see, the `adjustAllocation` method is called when the `View`'s `paint` method is executed, so the `View` will have drawn itself with the same bounding rectangle and the digits will appear in the locations shown in Figure 3-21. Assuming a monospaced font in which each character occupies 8 pixels horizontally, the mouse event will have an x value of 102, because it is given relative to the actual bounds of the text component. We discovered earlier that the `viewToModel` method computes the number of characters to the left of the cursor by calling `getTabbedTextOffset`, passing it the x coordinate of the left edge of the bounding box as argument x0 and that of the `View` location to be converted (in this case the position of the mouse) as the x value. The model offset is then computed as the number of characters needed to span (x - x0) pixels horizontally. In this example, x is 102 and x0 is 86, so the value that `getTabbedTextOffset` will use is 16, which, of course, corresponds to two characters in the font in use here. Note that this arithmetic works only because the `adjustAllocation` method changes the bounding rectangle to match the actual location of the text, not that of the actual `View`.

Now let's look at the situation shown in Figure 3-20. Here, the container that the text component is mounted in has been narrowed so that there is not enough room for it to be allocated its preferred space. Not only that, but the user has typed the same three digits, causing the `Caret` to move to the right. As the `Caret` moves, it causes the content of the text control to scroll so that it remains visible, by changing the value field of the text control's `Bounded-RangeModel`. Figure 3-22 shows another example of this.

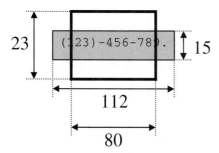

Figure 3-22 Adjusting a View's allocation: case 2.

Here, the user has typed nine digits of the telephone number into a narrowed text field which, in this case is 80 pixels wide, and then scrolled the display so that the first digit and the opening parenthesis are obscured by the left side of the control. The scrolling effect is actually achieved by setting the value of the BoundedRangeModel to 16. Because the preferred width of the View is still 112 pixels, that leaves 16 pixels, or two characters, that are also not visible to the right.

When the viewToModel method is called, the bounding rectangle of the Shape that it receives would be:

```
x = 2, y = 2, width = 76, height = 19
```

When the preferred span is larger than the width of the bounding rectangle, the adjustAllocation method does not take into account the horizontal text alignment specified by the setHorizontalAlignment method of JTextField. Instead, it reshapes the bounding rectangle so that its width matches the preferred width of the content and places the position that corresponds to the value of the BoundedRangeModel at the left of the visible area. In this case, the value of the BoundedRangeModel is 16, so the x coordinate of the bounding rectangle will be changed to –16, making the Shape that adjustAllocation returns look like this:

```
x = -16, y = 3, width = 112, height = 17
```

In terms of the calculation used in the viewToModel method, if the user clicks with the mouse at the left edge of the visible area shown in Figure 3-22, between the digits 1 and 2 in the rendered string, the x value passed to getTabbedTextOffset will be 0 and the x0 value will be –16. The pixel offset that it calculates will therefore be (0 - (-16)) = 16, which is equivalent to two characters, so once again the correct result is obtained.

Mapping from the Model to the `View`

The `modelToView` method translates a position within the model to the corresponding location within the `View`. As you might expect, it is essentially the reverse of `viewToModel`. Neglecting first of all the scrolling complications that pose the same problems here as they did for `viewToModel`, let's look at how a model position can be translated to the correct `View` location.

In a simple text field with a monospaced font, to calculate the `View` position for the character at model offset n, you would simply multiply n by the width of a character in the font. However, for our `View` this is an oversimplification for two reasons:

- There isn't a one-to-one mapping between characters in the model and the characters being displayed in the `View`. For example, in the case of the telephone number display field, the digit at offset 0 in the model is not the first character displayed on the screen—an open parenthesis appears before it.
- In general, the font will not be monospaced, so a simple multiplication does not work. This problem also exists for the normal `FieldView`, from which `FormattedFieldView` is derived.

Solving both of these problems is not difficult. To address the first problem, you need to know where in the `View` a given character from the model will be displayed. This information is readily available from the `offsets` array, which, as you saw earlier, maps directly from model offset to the position that the given character will occupy in the formatted string. In the telephone number example, the `offsets` array tells us that the first digit occupies offset 1 within the displayed string, so to find the actual offset of the start of this character in the `View`, we have to compute the width of the first character in the character array pointed to by the `contentBuff` Segment object. Similarly, the fourth model character (that is, the character at model offset 3) will be displayed in position 6 in the rendered string; to get its `View` offset, we need to measure the total width of characters 0 through 5 of `contentBuff`. The width of a contiguous range of characters can be obtained from the `getTabbedTextWidth` method of the `Utilities` class, which you saw when we discussed getting the preferred width of the `View`. If you look at the implementation of the `modelToView` method in Listing 3-9, you'll see both the translation of the model offset to an offset within `contentBuff` and the use of `getTabbedTextWidth` to get the width of the portion of the text that precedes the given location.

The offset that `getTabbedTextWidth` returns will be relative to the beginning of the string in the `View`, so it's absolute position relative to the text component is obtained by adding this offset to the x coordinate of the `View`'s bounding box. The `modelToView` method is actually supposed to return a `Shape` that corresponds to the `View` location; by convention, the returned `Shape` is a `Rectangle` whose height is the same as that of the `View`'s bounding box and whose width is 1 pixel; the x and y coordinates are those of the top left corner of the imaginary rectangle drawn to the left of the character in question. You can see how this `Rectangle` is constructed at the end of the `modelToView` method.

Finally, let's look at the effect of scrolling on this method. Most of the algorithm that has been described is actually independent of the scrolling—the calculation of the offset of the required position from the start of the string does not depend on where the string is positioned within the component's display area. As with the `viewToModel` method, though, it looks like things go wrong if the text field is made smaller so that not all the content is visible and the user places the `Caret` in such a way as to force the telephone number to be scrolled to the left. Fortunately, however, the same solution as we used for `viewToModel` also works for `modelToView`—all that is required is to call `adjustAllocation` at the beginning of the method. Let's look at the example shown in Figure 3-22 again to see why this is so. In this case, the leftmost two characters of the formatted string have scrolled out of view to the left. When `modelToView` is entered, the bounding rectangle of the `Shape` that describes the text component's allocated area looks like this:

```
x = 2, y = 2, width = 76, height = 19
```

If the `modelToView` method were now called with model offset 2, we would need to return the `View` offset of the position before the digit 3 (refer to Figure 3-22). Ignoring the effect of `adjustAllocation`, the algorithm outlined earlier would first find the position within the rendered string of the digit in model position 2, which would be 3, then calculate the length of the first three characters of the rendered text using `getTabbedTextWidth`. Assuming the usual fixed-width font with 8 pixels per character, this would give a `View` offset of 24, which would be correct if the `View` had not been scrolled. However, as we saw in the discussion of `viewToModel`, in this case `adjustAllocation` changes the bounding rectangle to the following:

```
x = -16, y = 3, width = 112, height = 17
```

We also know that the `Shape` returned by `modelToView` has its x coordinate determined by adding the x coordinate of the bounding box to the offset returned by `getTabbedTextWidth`. This calculation results in a final x coordinate of (-16 + 24) = 8, which is the width of one character. If you look back to Figure 3-22, you'll see that the digit 3 is, indeed, one character to the right of the left boundary of the component's visible area, so this result is correct. In fact, you should be able to see that this algorithm also works if a proportional font is in use and that it also works if the text component is wider than the `View`'s preferred width, as shown in Figure 3-21.

Drawing the Field Content—Overview

The most obvious duty of a `View` is to paint a representation of the portion of the model that it maps onto the area of the screen allocated to its host control. Now that you've seen some of the issues surrounding the mapping between model and `View` locations, the process of drawing the model's content onto the screen will be simpler to understand. Painting the control can be thought of as first locating the correct screen position for the first character to be drawn, and then rendering each character from `contentBuff` in the order in which they are stored. This is, however, not so straightforward in the case shown in Figure 3-22, because only a subset of the rendered telephone number is visible but, if you followed the descriptions of the `viewToModel` and `modelToView` methods, you should be able to see that we can use the same technique here to compensate for the scrolling effect.

Before we look in detail at how the actual painting occurs, let's step back and take an overview of how the process works. The `paint` method of a `View` is called whenever some part of the region covered by that `View` is damaged and needs to be redrawn, or is being drawn for the first time. The `paint` method of a content-rendering `View` like `FormattedFieldView` will, in fact, always be invoked from the `paint` method of its parent container `View`. In more complex text components like `JTextPane`, there may be several levels of nesting before a primitive `paint` method is called; not all of the `paint` methods that are called along the way will contain any real drawing logic. The `paint` method of `ParagraphView`, for example, doesn't draw anything—it just arranges for the `paint` methods of all of its child `View`s to be called. By contrast, the `ExtendedParagraphView` that you saw earlier in this chapter has a `paint` method that does have real drawing logic, because it may need to paint its background or draw a border.

A `View`'s paint method is declared as follows:

```
public void paint(Graphics g, Shape allocation);
```

It is important to understand the relationship between the `View`, the text component, the `Graphics` object, and the `Shape` that describes the `View`'s allocated region of the screen space used by the text component. Because text fields are so simple in structure, let's look at these relationships in the context of the more complex JTextPane. Here, text is usually rendered by a LabelView. Each text run has its own dedicated LabelView, so these objects could be required to map any part of the JTextPane's allocated space. Consider, for example, the View structure shown in Figure 3-23, which you first saw at the beginning of this discussion on Views.

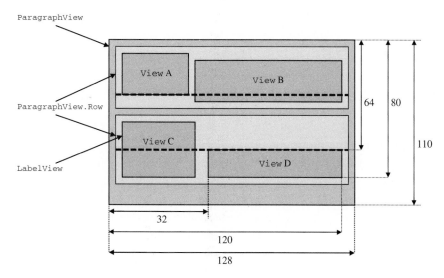

Figure 3-23 A typical View structure.

Here you see a JTextPane with two rows of text, each of which requires two LabelViews to map its contents. To draw this JTextPane, the paint method of the ParagraphView will be called with a Graphics that covers the entire text component and with a matching allocation. In this case, where the component is 128 pixels wide and 110 pixels high, the Graphics and allocations passed to the ParagraphView paint method will be configured like this:

Graphics clip rectangle: `x = 0, y = 0, width = 128, height = 110`

Shape bounding rectangle: `x = 3, y = 3, width = 122, height = 104`

As you can see, the bounding rectangle of the allocated area for the ParagraphView covers the whole area of the component, less a small outside margin. The ParagraphView will not do any drawing—instead, it will call the paint method of the upper ParagraphView.Row, followed by the paint method of the lower ParagraphView.Row. Each of these Views is itself a container that will just call the `paint` methods of the left and then the right `LabelView` object that they each contain. The `LabelView` paint methods will therefore be called in the order A, B, C, and finally D—it is here where the actual drawing work gets done. Let's look at the `paint` method of the `Label-View` marked D. The `paint` method of this `LabelView` will be called with `Graphics` and `Shape` arguments that are initialized like this:

Graphics clip rectangle:	`x = 0, y = 0, width = 128, height = 110`
Shape bounding rectangle:	`x = 32, y = 64, width = 88, height = 16`

The important things to note here are the following:

1. The `Graphics` clip rectangle covers the entire host text component, even though the `paint` method is required only to draw the part of the component that its content should occupy.

2. The bounding rectangle corresponds to the area that the `View` actually occupies. Its coordinates are specified relative to the parent text component.

As a result of this, the `paint` method of any `View` could draw anywhere on the surface of the text component, but usually it would change the `Graphics` object's clipping area to match the region that has been allocated to it to prevent accidental drawing outside of its own area. This is especially important for `FormattedFieldView` (and the standard `FieldView`), because of the way in which the scrolling of text within the `View` is handled, as you'll see shortly.

Before implementing the `paint` method for `FormattedFieldView`, we need to look at the corresponding method of its superclass, to see if there is anything useful that can be inherited. In fact, the `paint` method of `Field-View` does almost nothing other than call the `paint` method of its own super-class, `PlainView`. This latter method actually contains the core of the drawing logic used by `JTextArea`, `JtextField`, and `JPasswordField`. It works like this:

1. Using the `Shape` passed as its second argument, a modified one is obtained by calling the package private method `adjust-PaintRegion`. The bounding rectangle of the `Shape` returned from this method is used throughout the rest of the `paint` method.

2. The font attribute of the `Graphics` context passed as the first argument is set from the font of the host text component and its `FontMetrics` are obtained. Because getting the metrics for a font can be a relatively expensive operation, they are cached when first acquired and a new set is obtained only if the font is changed.

3. Two package private fields called `selected` and `unselected` are initialized to contain the text color to be used for text in the selected region of the component and text outside that region, respectively. The unselected color is usually just the foreground color of the text component but, if the component is disabled (because `setEnabled(false)` has been called on it), the disabled text color (set using the `JTextComponent setDisabled-TextColor` method) is used instead. The selected color depends on whether the selection is visible. The `Caret`, and the selection highlighting that is provided if you drag the `Caret` using the mouse, can be made invisible by calling the `Caret` method `setSelectionVisible(false)`. If the selection is visible (which is the default), the color set using the `setSelected-TextColor` method of `JTextComponent` is used; otherwise text in the selected region is drawn in the same color as unselected text.

4. Finally, a loop is performed with each pass handling one line of text. For each line, any layered highlights that apply to that line are drawn, followed by the text, which is actually rendered using a protected method called `drawLine`.

If `FormattedFieldView` did not provide its own `paint` method, it would simply inherit that of `PlainView`, plus the small additional task performed by `FieldView`'s paint method, which sets the clipping rectangle of the `Graph-ics` context to restrict drawing operations to the area bounded by the `Shape` that describes the space allocated to the `View`. To decide whether to take this course or to implement a new `paint` method, we need to examine how much of the inherited code is useful for `FormattedFieldView` and what changes need to be made to provide the extra functionality of this `View`. Let's look at the above list, point-by-point.

The first action, calling the package private method `adjustPaintRegion`, may not at first seem to be useful. This step certainly cannot be directly over-ridden from a subclass outside of the `javax.swing.text` package; however, the actual implementation of `adjustPaintRegion` that would be used by

`FormattedFieldView` is actually inherited from `FieldView` (which *is* in `javax.swing.text` and so can override the `adjustPaintRegion` method of `PlainView`). This method calls the protected method `adjustAllocation`, which we made much use of while implementing both `viewToModel` and `modelToView`. As we'll see later, it is as essential to use `adjustAllocation` from within the `paint` method as it was within the other two, so the invocation of `adjustPaintRegion` is useful. The second action, setting the font of the `Graphics` object, clearly also applies to `FormattedFieldView` and the caching of font metrics is just as useful to our `View` as it is to both `FieldView` and `PlainView`.

The third action, however, is not of any benefit to `FormattedFieldView`, because this step sets the values of two package private fields. These fields are used in the various drawing methods implemented by `PlainView`, which are invoked from its `drawLine` method. These fields cannot, of course, be accessed from a class that is not in the `javax.swing.text` package, so they could not be used by the custom drawing code that will need to be implemented for `FormattedFieldView`. When drawing the formatted string that represents the content of our `View`, we will certainly need to use different text colors, exactly as `PlainView` does and, in fact, if the `selected` and `unselected` fields of `PlainView` were protected or had protected or public accessors, we could make use of their values directly. Because this is not the case, we will need to shadow these fields with our own copies that are initialized to the same values.

The last of the four actions is, of course, the most interesting because it is here that the text control's content is drawn. `PlainView` is written to work with a multiline component like `JTextArea` and so it has a loop that processes a single line of text at a time, but it works just as well for the single line `JTextField` and for our `FormattedTextField`. From the point of view of `FormattedFieldView`, the automatic handling of layered highlights is beneficial if the programmer decides to create a subclass of `FormattedTextField` that uses a layered highlight, while the fact that `drawLine` is called to render a single line of text gives us a handy override point to install our own functionality. Here is the how `PlainView` defines the `drawLine` method:

```
protected void drawLine(int lineIndex, Graphics g, int x,
                        int y)
```

For a single-line component, this method will be called once, with `lineIndex` set to 0. The `Graphics` object will be the same object passed to the `paint` method, but by now clipped to the area allocated to the `View`, while x and y will usually (but not always, as you'll see shortly) be the coordinates allocated to the top left corner of the `View`. The `PlainView` implementation of this method just gets the content of the model that corresponds to the `View`'s offset range and draws it at the given coordinates using the `Graphics` object, taking care to handle `TAB` characters correctly. This, of course, is the area in which `FormattedFieldView` differs from both `FieldView` and `PlainView`: `FormattedFieldView` cannot simply draw the characters from the model—instead, it needs to draw the formatted version of the model, a cached copy of which is stored in its `contentBuff` `Segment` object.

There are at least two ways in which the `FormattedFieldView` drawing functionality could be implemented. The most obvious way would be to override the `paint` method, thereby short-circuiting all the code that has just been described, and handle everything ourselves. This would involve writing code that performs the useful parts of the four actions listed earlier and reusing little or none of the `PlainView` drawing code. At the other extreme, we could avoid overriding the `paint` method and just provide our own implementation of `drawLine`. Which of these approaches is better? There is no simple answer to this question. Overriding the `paint` method has the advantage of putting `FormattedFieldView` in direct control of how it is drawn and places the code in one place where it might be easier to maintain. It does, however, mean that there will be some avoidable duplication of code. Overriding the `drawLine` method maximizes code reuse at the cost of a small sacrifice in maintainability and a small performance cost because of extra method calling overhead and the fact that the code to obtain the selected and unselected foreground text colors (see action 3 above) is executed in `PlainView`'s `paint` method and then a copy of that code will run in our `drawLine` implementation.

Because there is little to choose between these two possibilities, `FormattedFieldView` is implemented to use the `paint` method of `FieldView` and override the `drawLine` method to handle the drawing. If you prefer the alternative, it is a relatively simple exercise to override the `paint` method instead and place all the drawing logic there. If you are going to do this, however, remember that you'll need to do the following things before rendering the text:

- Call `adjustAllocation` to take care of the case in which the context of the field has been scrolled.
- Clip the `Graphics` object to restrict drawing to the `View`'s allocated area.
- Draw any layered highlights that are in the `View`.

Implementing the `drawLine` Method

In principle, all the `drawLine` method needs to do is render the text from `contentBuff` into the `View`'s visible area using the `Graphics` object that is passed to it. The task should be particularly easy, because the text package's Utilities class contains a useful method that handles the actual text drawing for you:

```
public static final int drawTabbedText(Segment s, int x, int y,
    Graphics g, TabExpander e, int startOffset)
```

We first saw this method in "Handling Tabs" on page 233. As you can see, it conveniently takes a Segment object as the source of the characters to be drawn, a Graphics object to draw into and the x and y coordinates of the starting location. All of these values are passed as arguments to drawLine or are readily available. Similarly, the TabExpander argument can be supplied as this, because FormattedFieldView inherits the implementation of this interface from PlainView. Finally, the startOffset argument is the offset of the first character to be drawn. Usually, this would be the offset of the first character within the element of the model that this View maps. However, for our View there are characters to be drawn that are not actually in the model, so this offset will actually be the offset of a character within contentBuff and will initially be set to 0. This argument is actually used to determine the distance to the next TAB location in case there should be TAB characters to be drawn, as described earlier in this chapter. The drawTabbedText method returns the x value of the first pixel following the end of the string that it renders, which is useful for drawing several blocks of text placed end-to-end.

With this reasoning, the drawLine method would appear to be as simple as this:

```
protected void drawLine(int line, Graphics g, int x, int y) {
    Utilities.drawTabbedText(contentBuff, x, y, g, this, 0);
}
```

Unfortunately, it isn't quite that easy. What this simple implementation neglects is the possibility that some or all the text in the component might be selected. If this is the case, the selection highlight (that is, the background) will already have been drawn, but it is usual for the foreground color of selected text to be different from that of unselected text, if only to ensure that the selected text contrasts properly with the highlighted background that it is drawn over. The drawTabbedText method draws using the color selected into the Graphics object passed to it, so to arrange for the correct color to be used, you need to call drawTabbedText with different colors selected depending on whether it is rendering text that is selected or not. There are several possible cases:

- None of the text is selected.

- The selection extends from the start of the component to the end.
- The selection extends from the start of the component to somewhere in the middle.
- The selection extends from somewhere after the start of the component and reaches the end.
- The selection starts after the start of the component but does not reach the end.

The first case is the simplest, because this could be implemented by just using `drawTabbedText`. The next three cases are really special cases of the last one, but all of them can be considered as being of the form:

- A leading section that is not selected.
- A middle section that is selected.
- A trailing section that is not selected.

In all but the fourth case, one or more of these sections is empty. To implement the `drawLine` method with an arbitrary selection, we need a method, which we'll call `drawUnselectedText`, that can draw part of the text in the unselected foreground color and another called `drawSelectedText` that draws in the unselected color. Other than the foreground color that they use, however, these methods will be identical. Here is the implementation of `drawUnselectedText`, extracted from Listing 3-9:

```
protected int drawUnselectedText(Graphics g, int x, int y,
          int p0, int p1) throws BadLocationException {
    g.setColor(unselected);
    workBuff.array = contentBuff.array;
    workBuff.offset = p0;
    workBuff.count = p1 - p0;
    return Utilities.drawTabbedText(workBuff, x, y, g, this, p0);
}
```

This method assumes that an instance variable called `unselected` has been initialized with the color to be used for text that has not been selected; a similar variable called `selected` will also be set to the selected text foreground color at the start of the `drawLine` method, as you'll see later. The `Graphics` argument is the one passed to `drawLine`, while x and y are the coordinates of the location on the text baseline at which this segment of text should start. The `drawTabbedText` method requires a `Segment` object in which the `array` field points to the character array containing the text, the `count` field is the number of characters to be drawn and the `offset` field is the offset into the array of the first character to be rendered. The range of characters from the `Segment` passed as the argument to `drawUnselected-Text` is given by the arguments `p0` and `p1`, which represent the beginning and end of the range respectively. To convert this to the form required by `drawTabbedText`, we use a second `Segment` object (held in the instance variable `workBuff`), which is set so that its `array` member points to the base of the formatted character array while its `offset` and `count` fields correspond to the range between offsets `p0` and `p1`. When the drawing has been done, `drawUnselectedText` returns the pixel offset of the end of the drawn string, which can be used to place the next piece of text.

Let's take an example that shows how the `drawUnselectedText` and `drawSelectedText` methods work. Figure 3-24 shows a `FormattedText-Field` fully populated with a telephone number, with part of the field selected. As you can see, the selected text has been drawn in white so that it contrasts with the selection highlight.

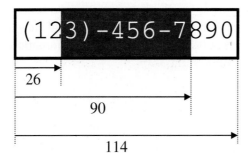

Figure 3-24   Drawing the content of `FormattedFieldView`.

Assuming the usual 2-pixel insets, the `drawLine` method will, in this case, be called with the x = 2 and y = 2, corresponding to the top left of the rectangle in which the text should be drawn. The `contentBuff` `Segment` object will contain all the text to be drawn and will therefore point to an array containing 14 characters—its `offset` field will be 0 and `count` will be 14. Drawing the first part this field requires a call to the `drawUnselectedText` method. The important parameters of this call will be:

x = 2

```
y = 2
p0 = 0
p1 = 3
```

because the drawing operation starts at the beginning of the allocated area and should draw the first three characters from `contentBuff`. This would result in `drawTabbedText` being invoked with a `Graphics` object in which the drawing color is that for unselected text, x and y values as shown earlier, and the `Segment` object `workBuff`, which will point to the same character array used by `contentBuff`, set up with an `offset` of 0 and a `count` of 3. Assuming a fixed-width font in which each character occupies 8 pixels horizontally, the value returned from `drawUnselectedText` after drawing the first three characters would be 26, which accounts for the three characters and the initial inset of 2 reflected in the value of the x parameter that `drawUnselectedText` was called with.

Next, the selected text needs to be drawn by calling `drawSelectedText`, which takes the same set of arguments as `drawUnselectedText`. For this call, they will be set as follows:

```
x = 26
y = 2
p0 = 3
p1 = 11
```

These parameters cause `drawTabbedText` to be invoked with x = 26, y = 2, and the `workBuff` object set up with `offset` 3 (from p0) and `count` 8 (from p1 - p0). Therefore, 8 characters will be drawn in the selected text foreground color, which `drawSelectedText` will select into the `Graphics` object and the returned pixel offset will be 90 (the initial offset of 26, plus 8 characters each spanning 8 pixels). Finally, the trailing unselected part will be drawn with another call to `drawUnselectedText`, this time with arguments

```
x = 90
y = 2
p0 = 11
p1 = 14
```

which will select the unselected text color into the `Graphics` object and again invoke `drawTabbedText`, the return value of which will be 114.

You can see how these calls are made and exactly how the parameters for each call are constructed by looking at the implementation of the `drawLine` method in Listing 3-9, which is repeated here for ease of reference.

```
// View drawing methods: overridden from PlainView
protected void drawLine(int line, Graphics g, int x, int y) {
```

```
// Set the colors
JTextComponent host = (JTextComponent)getContainer();
unselected = (host.isEnabled()) ?
      host.getForeground() : host.getDisabledTextColor();
Caret c = host.getCaret();
selected = c.isSelectionVisible() ?
      host.getSelectedTextColor() : unselected;

int p0 = element.getStartOffset();
int p1 = element.getEndOffset() - 1;
int sel0 =
     ((JTextComponent)getContainer()).getSelectionStart();
int sel1 =
     ((JTextComponent)getContainer()).getSelectionEnd();

try {

      // If the element is empty or there is no selection
      // in this view, just draw the whole thing in one go.
      if (p0 == p1 || sel0 == sel1 ||
                  inView(p0, p1, sel0, sel1) == false) {
         drawUnselectedText(g, x, y, 0,
                              contentBuff.count);
         return;
      }

      // There is a selection in this view. Draw up
      // to three regions:
      // (a) The unselected region before the selection.
      // (b) The selected region.
      // (c) The unselected region after the selection.
      // First, map the selected region offsets to be relative
      // to the start of the region and then map them to view
      // offsets so that they take into account characters not
      // present in the model.
      int mappedSel0 = mapOffset(Math.max(sel0 - p0, 0));
      int mappedSel1 = mapOffset(Math.min(sel1 - p0,
                                    p1 - p0));

      if (mappedSel0 > 0) {
            // Draw an initial unselected region
            x = drawUnselectedText(g, x, y, 0, mappedSel0);
      }
      x = drawSelectedText(g, x, y, mappedSel0, mappedSel1);

      if (mappedSel1 < contentBuff.count) {
```

```
                drawUnselectedText(g, x, y, mappedSel1,
                                contentBuff.count);
        }
    } catch (BadLocationException e) {
        // Should not happen!
    }
}
```

The first part of this method initializes the instance variables `selected` and `unselected` to the appropriate colors. This code will also be found in the `paint` method of `PlainView` and would also need to be included in any over-ridden implementation of `paint` because, as noted earlier, the `PlainView` copies of these fields are package private and hence not accessible to code in `FormattedFieldView`. The next step is to find out whether there is any text selected and, if so, whether the selection intersects the part of the text component mapped by this `View`. To do this, we get the offset range of the part of the model that corresponds to this `View` from the element that the `View` is associated with (which was passed to the `FormattedFieldView` constructor and stored in an instance variable), and then get the range of offsets for the selected region from the host component. Given these two ranges, it is simple to work out whether they overlap; the code for this test is in the method `inView`, which is shown in Listing 3-9.

Core Note

In the case of `FormattedTextField`, *there will only ever be one leaf* `View`, *so the* `FormattedFieldView` *will always map all the document content. That being the case, being careful to check both that there is a selection and that it overlaps the region mapped by the* `View` *looks like overkill, because it would be good enough just to check whether a nonempty selection exists. Making the extra check, however, allows you to make use of* `FormattedFieldView` *should you write a more general text component that needs this functionality but also uses more than one* `View` *to map its content.*

If there is no selection within the area covered by the `View`, all the content can be drawn in a single call to `drawUnselectedText`, passing the start offset as 0 and the end offset as the number of characters in `contentBuff`. In fact, this is likely to be the most common path through the `drawLine` method. When there is a selection, the rest of the code in `drawLine` calls `draw-UnselectedText` to draw the initial unselected part, `drawSelectedText` for the selected region, and finally `drawUnselectedText` to render the unselected portion at the end. As described earlier, some of these calls will be skipped if they are not required.

There is only one subtle point in this code that we have not yet mentioned. Remember that the getSelectionStart and getSelectionEnd methods return the location of the start and end of the selected region in terms of model offsets, but the drawSelectedText and drawUnselectedText methods deal in terms of offsets into contentBuff. These offsets do not match, as you can see by looking again at Figure 3-24. In this example, the selection start and end offsets as returned by getSelectionStart and getSelectionEnd are 2 and 7 respectively, but the offsets required by the drawing methods are 3 and 11. Before we can use the selection offsets, they need to be mapped to the correct values for the View. This mapping is performed by the mapOffset method, the implementation of which is shown in Listing 3-9. As you can see by looking at the code, getting from the model offset to the View offset is very simple and it is a problem we have already solved—the mapping we need is exactly that provided by the offsets array, so all that is required is to use the model offset as an index into offsets to retrieve the required View position.

Now that you've seen all the code in the FormattedFieldView class, there is one last point to be cleared up. The description of the drawLine method so far has made the simplifying assumption that the text in the View has not been scrolled to the left as a result of the space allocated to the component being too narrow to accommodate its content. When we discussed the viewToModel and modelToView methods, we saw that it was necessary to adjust our calculations to cater for the possibility that the View had been scrolled and that we could do this by simply invoking the adjustAllocation method of FieldView before attempting either mapping. The effect of calling adjustAllocation was to change the bounding rectangle of the Shape that described the area allocated to the View to compensate for the scrolling, so that the simple algorithms for mapping between model and view that work when the content has not been scrolled also work when scrolling has taken place. In fact, the same trick also works when painting the View—if adjustAllocation is called and the Shape that it returns is used as the basis for drawing, everything will work whether the View has been scrolled and whichever part of the View should be visible will appear in the component on the screen. If you look back a few pages to the description of the PlainView paint method, which we chose not to override, you'll see that adjustAllocation is actually called at the start of the painting process from the package private adjustPaintRegion method, so the bounding rectangle of the View will already have been modified to take the scrolling into account before drawLine is invoked. The x and y values that are passed to drawLine are taken from the adjusted bounded rectangle, so any changes that `adjust-Allocation` method made will affect `drawLine`. As an example, let's look again at the case that we examined in connection with the `viewToModel` method and shown in Figure 3-22. In this example, the user has typed a complete telephone number and scrolled the display so that the `Caret` is located between the first and second digits of the number, so that the opening parenthesis and the first digit are out of view. In this situation, when `paint` is called, the `Shape` that it receives will have the bounding rectangle:

```
x = 2, y = 2, width = 76, height = 19
```

We know from the earlier discussion that `adjustAllocation` will change this rectangle to the following:

```
x = -16, y = 3, width = 112, height = 17
```

As a result of this, when our `drawLine` method is called, the initial x coordinate will be –16 instead of 2. However, the origin of the `Graphics` context will *not* be changed, so the `drawTabbedText` method (called by either `draw-SelectedText` or `drawUnselectedText`) will start rendering the control's content 16 pixels to the left of the visible area, which is outside the clipping rectangle of the `Graphics` object. Therefore, the first two characters of the field will not be displayed—the leftmost character that you'll see will be the one rendered at x coordinate 2, which will be the third character in the text area. This, of course, creates the effect of scrolling the text to the left by two characters.

Summary

In this chapter, you saw the element structure of the various Swing text components, from the simple `JTextField` and `JTextArea` to the more complex `JTextPane` and `JEditorPane`. The element structure organizes the underlying content into paragraphs and also delineates regions of the document that share exactly the same rendering attributes.

Corresponding to each element within the document are one or more `View` objects that are responsible for drawing the content of that element on the screen. You saw that different text components used different `View`s to obtain the rendering behavior that they require, including such features as tab expansion and line wrapping. We also showed you how to enhance text components by creating new highlighters and your own custom `View`s that present data in a way that is suitable for your application.

JEDITORPANE
AND
THE SWING HTML
PACKAGE

Topics in this Chapter

- Displaying and Saving HTML, RTF, and Plain Text

- Asynchronous Page Loading

- Converting Between Different Document Formats

- The HTML Document Model

- Loading and Parsing HTML

- Handling Hypertext Links

- Style Sheets and Views

- Dynamically Changing HTML in a `JEditorPane`

Chapter 4

I n Chapter 2, you saw how to use the JTextPane control to display text with multiple fonts and colors and how to embed images and other active content into it. To use JTextPane in this way, you need to do quite a lot of programming, manually setting up both the text and the corresponding attributes. Although this might be acceptable in some applications, perhaps because the text to be displayed is fixed at compile time or the algorithm used to apply the attributes is a simple one that is based on the text itself, for more complex text layouts it quickly becomes unwieldy. What you actually need is a way to store the text and the attributes together so that the attributes can be applied as the text is read into the component. From the development and maintenance point of view, it would be even simpler if the storage format were easily readable and editable by a human or could be created and manipulated by a tool that can be used without the need for much (or any) programming ability.

There are, of course, several file formats that meet this requirement. Hypertext Markup Language (HTML), for example, is a very well known and popular way to represent complex document layouts that encapsulates the text (and other content) along with a representation of the attributes used to render it. Although many people will create HTML pages manually (and this could be considered to be a form of programming), these days there are plenty of HTML editors that let you create a Web page using HTML without needing to understand the format of the Web page itself. These editors ultimately write their output to a text file that can be loaded into a browser. This sounds like an ideal way to provide input to a `JTextPane`. All you need is some software that reads HTML and converts it into the sort of `Document` model that you saw in Chapter 2. In fact, Swing has a component that can do just that. `JEditorPane` is a superclass of `JTextPane` that provides the ability to plug in software that knows how to read external document formats and convert what it reads into the appropriate `Document` model for `JEditorPane` to display. Furthermore, Swing provides plug-in document readers that allow `JEditorPane` to read and display documents encoded in HTML and Rich Text Format (RTF) as well as in plain text. In this chapter, we'll first look at the general features of `JEditorPane` and show how to use it to display different types of document. We'll then look at how the various classes that a `JEditorPane` is made up of combine to make it possible for it to handle different input formats and, finally, we'll take an in-depth look at Swing's HTML support and show you how to customize it and make best use of its features.

The `JEditorPane` Control

The basic design of `JEditorPane` makes it a very simple component to use for the common task of loading and displaying a page of HTML or a plain text document. In fact, as we'll demonstrate, it's as simple as creating a `JEditorPane` and passing it a pointer to the document that you want to load, in the form of a URL.

A Simple HTML Viewer

Figure 4-1 shows a simple example of a `JEditorPane` displaying a Web page downloaded directly from the Internet.

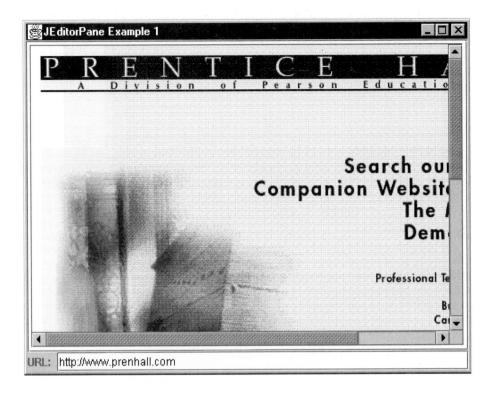

Figure 4-1   Using `JEditorPane` to display a Web page.

You can try this example out by typing the command

```
java AdvancedSwing.Chapter4.EditorPaneExample1
```

and then typing the URL of the Web page you'd like to view in the text field at the bottom of the frame. In this case, the Prentice Hall home page has been loaded from the URL `http://www.prenhall.com`. If you load this page and compare it with what you see in a real Web browser, you'll probably find it hard to see the difference. In fact, very little code was needed to create this mini HTML viewer, as you can see from Listing 4-1.

Most of the code in Listing 4-1 is concerned with creating the frame and adding the label and the `JTextField` that allows you to type a Uniform Resource Locator (URL)—only a few lines are directly concerned with `JEditorPane` itself. First, the `JEditorPane` is created using its default constructor, which loads an empty document, as you can see when the program starts. The next line ensures the pane's editing capabilities are turned off—the reason for which you'll see later in this chapter when we look in detail at the

HTML support built into JEditorPane. Nothing else of any interest happens until you press the RETURN key in the JTextField. At this point, the URL of the Web page you want to see is read from the input field and passed to the JEditorPane setPage method. That's all you need to do to make it load an HTML page.

**Listing 4-1 A Simple HTML Viewer Implemented
              Using JEditorPane**

```
package AdvancedSwing.Chapter4;

import java.awt.*;
import java.awt.event.*;
import java.io.*;
import javax.swing.*;
import javax.swing.text.*;

public class EditorPaneExample1 extends JFrame {
    public EditorPaneExample1() {
        super("JEditorPane Example 1");
        pane = new JEditorPane();
        pane.setEditable(false);        // Read-only
        getContentPane().add(new JScrollPane(pane), "Center");

        JPanel panel = new JPanel();
        panel.setLayout(new BorderLayout(4, 4));
        JLabel urlLabel = new JLabel("URL: ", JLabel.RIGHT);
        panel.add(urlLabel, "West");
        textField = new JTextField(32);
        panel.add(textField, "Center");

        getContentPane().add(panel, "South");

        // Change page based on text field
        textField.addActionListener(new ActionListener() {
            public void actionPerformed(ActionEvent evt) {
                String url = textField.getText();
                try {
                    // Try to display the page
                    pane.setPage(url);
                } catch (IOException e) {
                    JOptionPane.showMessageDialog(pane,
```

Listing 4-1 A Simple HTML Viewer Implemented
          Using JEditorPane (continued)

```
                new String[] {
                    "Unable to open file",
                    url
                }, "File Open Error",
                JOptionPane.ERROR_MESSAGE);
            }
        }
    });
    }

    public static void main(String[] args) {
        JFrame f = new EditorPaneExample1();

        f.addWindowListener(new WindowAdapter() {
            public void windowClosing(WindowEvent evt) {
                System.exit(0);
            }
        });
        f.setSize(500, 400);
        f.setVisible(true);
    }

    private JEditorPane pane;
    private JTextField textField;
}
```

Initializing a *JEditorPane*

There are several ways to load a JEditorPane with some content and arrange for it to be displayed. The most obvious way is to use one of the following three constructors:

```
public JEditorPane(String url) throws IOException
public JEditorPane(URL url) throws IOException
public JEditorPane(String type, String text)
```

The first two constructors both load a document given its URL, either in the form of a String or as a URL object. If you pass the URL in the form of a String, JEditorPane attempts to create the corresponding URL object for you and throws an IOException if the String is not a valid representation of a URL. Given a valid URL object, the document is loaded from its source, which may be a local file or a Web server somewhere; if an error occurs while the data is being read, an IOException is again the result. The fact that these constructors require a URL does not imply that only HTML files can be loaded—you need to use a URL no matter what type of data is in the file being read, be it HTML, RTF, plain text, or a private format of your own.

The third constructor allows you to load text from a String variable. This might be useful if you wanted to display some HTML that you create dynamically or load independently from some external source. In this case, the type argument tells JEditorPane how to interpret the text; if it's encoded in HTML, the type would be passed as "text/html." You'll see more shortly about how the document type is established for the other constructors and how it is used.

If, as in Listing 4-1, you don't know the URL of the document you want to load when the JEditorPane is created, you can use the default constructor instead. In this case, the component is initialized with an empty Document that will allow it to display plain text. There are several ways to load content into an existing JEditorPane. If you want to load some fixed text, you can simply use the setText method:

```
public void setText(String t);
```

If you haven't already loaded a Document into the JEditorPane, the contents of the String argument will be treated as plain text. If, however, the component is already loaded with some content or you have explicitly installed an EditorKit and a Document for some other type, the text will be considered to be of the same type as that for which the component is currently initialized. This means, for example, that if you load an HTML page into a JEditorPane and then replace its content using setText, the String will be expected to be formatted in HTML. This is not, however, a common way to load a JEditorPane and, if you use it, you will probably want to explicitly set the content type so that the String is interpreted properly. You'll see how to do that shortly.

Core Note

The setText method completely replaces the content of the JEditorPane by installing a new Document. Because of this, it makes no sense to create a JEditorPane, manually install a DefaultStyledDocument to which you apply a logical style, and then use setText to add the text. You might try this approach to create a component in which all the text is displayed in a 15-point, italic font, for example, by creating an empty document and setting a logical style containing this font, expecting it to apply to the text subsequently installed using setText. This would fail, however, because the setText method would remove the original Document and so lose the attributes in the logical style. If you want to set the model content without losing the logical style, you can use the Document insertString method to install the text.

The most common way to open a document in `JEditorPane`, and the one shown in Listing 4-1, is to use one of the `setPage` methods:

```
public void setPage(String url) throws IOException
public void setPage(URL url) throws IOException
```

These methods look the same as two of the constructors shown previously and, in fact, they are directly called from the constructors that they mirror. As before, if there is a problem with the URL or an error occurs while reading the data, an `IOException` is thrown.

Content Type and Editor Kit Selection

The most powerful feature of `JEditorPane` is that it can adapt itself to be able to display and edit many kinds of data by plugging in the appropriate `Editor-Kit` and the corresponding `Document` model. You've already seen this in action in the simple Web browser example in the last section, where an `EditorKit` and a model suitable for handling HTML were installed automatically. How does `JEditorPane` know the type of data that it is working with and how does that determine the helper classes that it installs? There are actually several ways for `JEditorPane` to find out which document type it is handling:

1. By explicit installation of an editor kit.
2. From the `setContentType` method.
3. Automatically from its input source.

These three mechanisms are actually three different levels of application programming interface (API), starting with the most primitive level and working up to the most abstract. Let's look at how each of them works.

Installation of an Editor Kit

To do its job properly, `JEditorPane` needs to be configured with the right `EditorKit` and the correct `Document` implementation for the type of data that it is handling. There is a tight binding between the `EditorKit` and the `Document` classes that it can handle. This is reflected in the fact that `Editor-Kit` has a method called `createDefaultDocument` that can be used to obtain an instance of the appropriate `Document` type for a given `EditorKit`. Thus, to obtain a consistent set of classes for `JEditorPane`, it is sufficient to create the right `EditorKit` for the type of data that you want it to display and use the `JEditorPane` `setEditorKit` method to install it. When you do this, a new `Document` of the correct type will automatically be used. Table 4-1

shows the correlation between the type of content to be displayed, the
`EditorKit` and the `Document` class required.

Table 4-1 Mapping from Content Type to Editor Kit and Document Class		
Content Type	*Editor Kit*	*Document Class*
Plain text	`PlainEditorKit`	`Plain Document`
RTF	`RTFEditorKit`	`DefaultStyleDocument`
HTML	`HTMLEditorKit`	`HTMLDocument`

Core Note

As described earlier, when the `setEditorKit` method is invoked, a new empty `Document` of the type shown in the table will be installed. If you need to install a custom `Document` type, you can either follow `setEditorKit` invocation with an explicit call to `setDocument`, or you can subclass the editor kit and override its `createDefaultDocument` method to return an instance of your `Document` class instead of the default one. To make this work, you'll need to change the mapping from content type to editor kit so that your editor kit is used instead of the usual one. You'll see how this mapping is done in "The `setContentType` Method" on page 351.

Let's look at a simple example of how this works. Earlier, we said that you could use the `setText` method to install some text into a `JEditorPane`. If you simply create a `JEditorPane` using its default constructor and then call `setText`, the text that you pass will be interpreted as plain text and displayed with no special formatting. Suppose instead that you wanted to pass a `String` containing HTML and have it displayed as if it had been loaded into a Web browser. One way to achieve this is to create a `JEditorPane` using the default constructor, invoke `setEditorKit` to install an HTML editor kit, and then use `setText` to supply it with some HTML to format. You can see this process in action by typing the following command:

```
java AdvancedSwing.Chapter4.EditorPaneExample2
```

This example creates a frame with a `JEditorPane` and a `JTextArea` into which you can type some text to be installed into the `JEditorPane`, as shown in Figure 4-2.

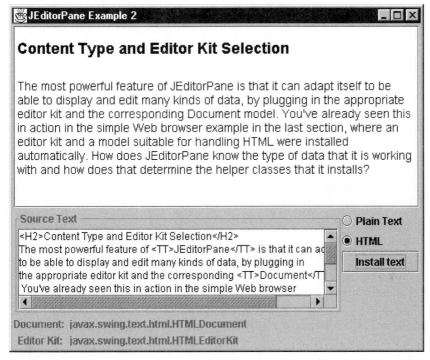

Figure 4-2 Using `JEditorPane` to display HTML and plain text.

As well as the text area, the lower half of the frame displays the type of `Document` and the editor kit that are currently installed in the `JEditor-Pane`. Because the `JEditorPane` was created using its default constructor, it starts with a `PlainDocument` and a `PlainEditorKit` installed. If you now type some text into the text area and press the option button (also known as a radio button) labeled `Install text`, the text that you typed will appear in the `JEditorPane`, exactly as you typed it, because both text components are working with plain text. If you now select the option button marked `HTML`, two things will happen. First, the document type and editor kit at the bottom of the frame will change to `HTMLDocument` and `HTMLEditorKit` respectively and, second, the content of the `JEditorPane` will disappear.

What happened here? Here's the code that is connected to the option buttons in this example:

```
ActionListener radioButtonListener = new ActionListener() {
    public void actionPerformed(ActionEvent evt) {
        JRadioButton b = (JRadioButton)evt.getSource();
        String type = ((b == plainButton) ? "text/plain":
                            "text/html");
        final EditorKit kit =
                    pane.getEditorKitForContentType(type);

        SwingUtilities.invokeLater(new Runnable() {
            public void run() {
                pane.setEditorKit(kit);
            }
        });
    }
};
```

When either of the buttons is pressed, the `actionPerformed` method is executed in the Abstract Window Toolkit (AWT) event thread. This method looks at the source of the event to decide whether to switch to HTML or plain text: Here, the variable `plainButton` contains a reference to the option button used to select plain text, so it can be used to determine which of the two buttons was pressed. Based on this, the `JEditorPane getEditorKit-ForContentType` method is called with argument `text/plain` or `text/html`. You'll find out more about this method later in this section, but it should be obvious that this call is getting a reference to an editor kit suitable for handling plain text or HTML, respectively. Having obtained the editor kit, it is installed by calling the `setEditorKit` method.

Core Note

Because a large part of the code for this example is concerned only with setting up the user interface, to save space the complete listing is not shown here—only the code relevant to this discussion is included. If you want to look at the complete example, you can find it on the CD-ROM that accompanies this book.

When a new editor kit is installed, the `Document` associated with the previous one will no longer be appropriate, because each editor kit requires its own specific `Document` subclass. In this case, when the `HTMLEditorKit` is installed, it creates an empty `HTMLDocument`, which replaces the `PlainDocument` used by the `PlainEditorKit`, causing the loss of all its content. This is why the `JEditorPane` becomes empty after the change from plain text to HTML.

Now, if you press the `Install text` button one more time, the text from the `JTextArea` will be installed into the `JEditorPane` again. Here is the code that is executed when the button is pressed:

```
installButton.addActionListener(new ActionListener() {
    public void actionPerformed(ActionEvent evt) {
        // Get the text and install it in the JEditorPane
        SwingUtilities.invokeLater(new Runnable() {
            public void run() {
                pane.setText(textArea.getText());
            }
        });
    }
});
```

This code simply uses the setText method of JEditorPane to install the new text. This time, because an HTMLDocument and HTMLEditorKit are installed, the text is interpreted as HTML rather than as plain text. In Figure 4-2, the text typed into the text area contained HTML markup and, as you can see, the header text, which was surrounded by H2 tags, has been rendered differently from the rest of the text and appears in a paragraph of its own, set off from the body of the text. If you were now to press the Plain Text option button, the PlainEditorKit and PlainDocument would be installed and the HTML would disappear from the upper display. Pressing Install text again would show the HTML tags and the text as it appears in the JTextArea.

Core Note

In the earlier code extract, the setEditorKit method is not invoked directly. Instead, the SwingUtilities invokeLater method is called to arrange to have it executed after the actionPerformed method returns. As you know, you can only safely update Swing components from within the AWT event thread. However, this code was already in the event thread, so there was no reason to postpone the call to setEditorKit to ensure thread safety. The reason for deferring it is to make the user interface (UI) appear slightly more responsive. When the option button is pressed, its appearance changes to reflect the fact that it has been activated; in fact, its background changes to gray, but the black dot that indicates that it has been selected doesn't appear until the action associated with it has been carried out. Changing the editor kit can take a relatively long time. If this operation were carried out in the actionPerformed method, the user would see the option button in its transitional state for a discernible amount of time. By deferring this operation, the option button is allowed to redraw itself in its final state before the editor kit is switched, which gives the user the impression of a more responsive application.

The only aspect of this example that you haven't yet seen is how the labels showing the editor kit and document type get updated. You might expect the code that changes the editor kit in response to a change in the state of the option buttons to extract the new values and update the labels but, as you can see from the code presented earlier, that isn't how it happens. In fact, both the editor kit and the Document are bound properties of the JEditorPane, so changes can be detected by registering for PropertyChangeEvents, which is how this example works. Here is the code that responds to these events:

```
// Listen to the properties of the editor pane
pane.addPropertyChangeListener(new PropertyChangeListener() {
    public void propertyChange(PropertyChangeEvent evt) {
        String prop = evt.getPropertyName();
        if (prop.equals("document")) {
            docLabel.setText(evt.getNewValue().getClass().getName());
        } else if (prop.equals("editorKit")) {
            kitLabel.setText(evt.getNewValue().getClass().getName());
        }
    }
});
```

You may have noticed that when it is displaying plain text, JEditorPane uses an editor kit called JEditorPane.PlainEditorKit (which, because of the way in which inner class names are constructed, will actually appear as JEditorPane$PlainEditorKit). This might surprise you, because in Chapter 1 we said that the text components use DefaultEditorKit when handling plain text. In fact, this *is* the case for JTextField, JPasswordField, and JTextArea, but not for JEditorPane. The reason for the difference is the ViewFactory. As you saw in Chapter 3, every text component needs a ViewFactory, which is supplied either by its editor kit or its UI class. For the simple text components, the ViewFactory is part of the UI class, so DefaultEditorKit does not provide one. Because it can, theoretically, handle any type of document, it is not possible for JEditorPane's UI class to supply a fixed ViewFactory, because the Views required will depend entirely on the type of document being rendered. JEditorPane expects its editor kit to supply a ViewFactory that can manufacture Views appropriate to its associated document type. Because DefaultEditorKit does not supply a ViewFactory, JEditorPane cannot use it directly. PlainEditorKit is, in fact, a subclass of DefaultEditorKit that overrides only the getViewFactory method to return a ViewFactory that creates a WrappedPlainView for every Element in the document.

The `setContentType` Method

The example you have just seen demonstrates that you can arrange for the display capabilities of `JEditorPane` to be changed according to the type of document that you want it to handle by using the `setEditorKit` method. Setting the editor kit, however, requires you to know which editor kit to use for your document type. If you are using one of the types for which `JEditorPane` has built-in support, you can avoid having to hard-code this information in your application by using the higher-level `setContentType` method:

```
public final void setContentType(String type);
```

This method maps the `type` argument to the correct editor kit and installs it by invoking `setEditorKit`, as was shown in the earlier example. In fact, it uses the same technique as you saw in that example to perform the mapping from type to editor kit. So what is the `type` argument and how does the `getEditorKitForContentType` method use it to obtain an editor kit? The `type` argument has the following format:

```
MIME-type ; parameters
```

The optional *parameter* section is a space- or comma-separated list of values of the form `key = value`, most of which, if they are present at all, are not directly used by `JEditorPane`. You'll see later in this chapter how you can use the parameter list to specify the character encoding of the document's data. The interesting part of the content type is the first part, which specifies the document's data type in the form of a MIME (Multi-purpose Internet Mail Extensions) type description. MIME document types are specified in two parts—a type and a subtype. The complete set of valid MIME types is forever growing; you can find out all about MIME by reading the Internet RFCs (Request For Comments) numbered 2045 through 2049, which you can find on the Internet at the following URL: `http://ds.internic.net/rfc/rfc2045.txt` and so on.

`JEditorPane` comes with built-in mappings from four MIME types to the editor kits needed to support documents of that type, as shown in Table 4-2. This table is, of course, very similar to Table 4-1, which showed the mapping from content type name to the editor kit and the corresponding `Document` class.

Table 4-2 Mapping from MIME Type to Editor Kit

MIME Type	Editor Kit
text/plain	PlainEditorKit
text/rtf	RTFEditorKit
application/rtf	RTFEditorKit
text/html	HTMLEditorKit

As you can see, there are actually two MIME types that correspond to an RTF document. These default mappings are installed automatically when a JEditorPane is created. There are several methods that can be used to create new mappings or retrieve existing ones:

```
public EditorKit getEditorKitForContentType(String type)
public void setEditorKitForContentType(
              String type, EditorKit k)
public static EditorKit createEditorKitForContentType(
              String type)
public static void registerEditorKitForContentType(
              String type, String classname)
public static void registerEditorKitForContentType(
              String type, String classname,
              ClassLoader loader)
```

At first glance, it looks like there is duplicate functionality here. For example, getEditorKitForContentType and createEditorKitForContentType both return an EditorKit given a content type in the form of a String. In fact, there is a three-level scheme for holding the mapping between type and editor kit, as shown in Figure 4-3.

At the bottom of the diagram is the editor kit type registry, which stores in a Hashtable the mapping from the content type to the fully qualified class name of the class that implements the editor kit for that type of content. For example, it might have an entry mapping the MIME type text/html to the class name javax.swing.text.html.HTMLEditorKit. The registry is initialized with a hard-coded default set of mappings equivalent to those shown in Table 4-2, installed using the static method register-EditorKitForContentType. This method has two variants, one of which includes a ClassLoader argument. In fact, the editor kit type registry consists of two Hashtables, one mapping content type to class name and one mapping content type to the ClassLoader required to load the editor kit class. When no `ClassLoader` is given, no entry is made in the second `Hashtable`. Both of these `Hashtables` are held as static data, so there is only one copy shared by all `JEditorPanes`.

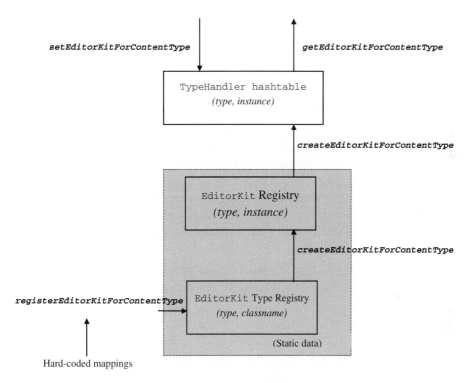

Figure 4-3 The `EditorKit` registry.

When `JEditorPane` (or other code) needs an `EditorKit`, it calls the `getEditorKitForContentType` method, which looks first in the `Type-Handler Hashtable`, shown at the top of Figure 4-3. This table maps from content type to an instance of an `EditorKit`. Unlike the editor kit type table, there is one copy of the `TypeHandler` table for each `JEditorPane` instance. This table is initially empty, so `getEditorKitForContentType` will not find the required `EditorKit` there. As a result, it invokes the static method `createEditorKitForContentType`, which looks in yet another `Hashtable`—the `EditorKit` registry shown in the middle of Figure 4-3. Like the `EditorKit` *type* registry, this is a static member of `JEditorPane`, so it is a shared resource. Again, this table is initially empty, so the required `EditorKit` won't be found here either. Finally, `createEditorKitForContentType` uses the

MIME type to access the EditorKit type registry (at the bottom of Figure 4-3) to find the required EditorKit's class name and the corresponding ClassLoader if applicable. If the MIME type is known, the required class is loaded (using the ClassLoader if one is configured) and an instance of the class is loaded into the static EditorKit registry, with the MIME type as the key.

Now that the EditorKit registry has an instance of the EditorKit, createEditorKitForContentType creates a copy of it (using its clone method) and returns it to getEditorKitForContentType, which stores it in the TypeHandler table. Subsequent calls to getEditorKitForContentType on the *same* JEditorPane object with the same content type will return the *same* EditorKit from the TypeHandler table. If, however, this method is invoked on a different JEditorPane, it won't find the entry in its TypeHandler table because this table is not shared. Instead, it will call createEditorKitForContentType, as before. This time, however, an instance of the correct EditorKit will be found in the static EditorKit registry and a new cloned copy will be returned and stored in the second JEditorPane's TypeHandler table.

The result of this is that, in the case of HTML, for example, a single HTMLEditorKit (let's call it instance A) will be loaded into the static EditorKit registry the first time any JEditorPane needs to display an HTML document. A cloned copy of this EditorKit (instance B) will then be loaded into that JEditorPane's TypeHandler table and will also be installed in the JEditorPane. If the document type of the same JEditorPane is changed to some other type and then back to HTML, the same EditorKit (instance B) will be used again. If another JEditorPane needs to display an HTML document, it won't find an HTMLEditorKit in its own TypeHandler table, but it will find instance A in the shared EditorKit registry and will clone it, creating instance C, which it will place in its TypeHandler table and use it to load the HTML document. Subsequent calls to retrieve an HTML-EditorKit in this second JEditorPane will also retrieve instance C.

If you want to add your own custom EditorKit for use with a private document type, you can do so by installing a mapping from the content type of your document to the name of your custom EditorKit's class in the EditorKit type registry. This would make the new document type available to all JEditorPanes in the application. For example, if you implement an EditorKit in the class com.mycom.text.MyType for a new type of document to which you assign the MIME type application/x-my-type, you can make it globally available like this:

```
JEditorPane.registerEditorKitForContentType(
        "application/x-my-type",
        "com.mycom.text.MyTypeEditorKit");
```

Core Note

Actually, if you are using Java 2, you will need to use the form of the
`registerEditorKitForContentType` *that specifies the*
`ClassLoader` *to use instead of the simpler form shown here, which is*
sufficient only in Java Development Kit (JDK) 1.1. The more complex form
works both for JDK 1.1 and Java 2. You'll see later why this is necessary.

You can arrange for this `EditorKit` to be loaded using `setContentType`:

```
JEditorPane pane = new JEditorPane();
pane.setContentType("application/x-my-type");
```

This doesn't, of course, install the appropriate `Document` class, which you
will need to implement and install an instance of using `setDocument`. On the
other hand, if you want to make this `EditorKit` available in one specific
`JEditorPane`, you can use the `setEditorKitForContentType` method
instead. To do this, you will need to have created the `JEditorPane` and an
instance of the `EditorKit`:

```
JEditorPane pane = new JEditorPane();
EditorKit myKit -= new MyTypeEditorKit();
pane.setEditorKitForContentType("application/x-my-type", myKit);
pane.setContentType("application/x-my-type");
```

Configuration from the Input Source

You've now seen two different ways to determine the `EditorKit` and `Docu-
ment` installed into a `JEditorPane`—you can either call `getEditorKitFor-
ContentType` and install the returned `EditorKit`, or you can use the more
convenient `setContentType` method, which performs those two steps for
you. Either way, you need to have the content type of the document that you
need to display in the form of a MIME description. If you look back to Listing 4-1, however, you won't see any evidence of a MIME type being used.
The only line of code in that example that loads content into the `JEditor-
Pane` is this one:

```
pane.setPage(url);
```

The `setPage` method is given only a URL. Using this, it reads the file to
be loading using the `URLConnection` class in the `java.net` package. `URL-`

Connection has a method called getContentType that returns the MIME type of the file that it is reading. The means by which it determines the MIME type depends on exactly how the file is being read. If the file being retrieved from a Web server using the HTTP protocol, the content type will be determined by the Web server and will be returned as part of the HTTP header information. Web servers are typically configured to recognize content types based on the suffix of the name of the actual file being read so that, for example, files whose names end with .htm or .html are expected to hold HTML. For such files, the Web server would return the content type text/html. In other cases, such as when the file is on the local file system and is not retrieved via a Web server, the process of determining the file type might also involve looking at the filename suffix for certain well-known cases. If this doesn't work, another common technique is to look for easily recognized patterns stored at the start of the file's data. Graphic Interchange Format (GIF) files, for example, start with the characters G, I, and F in that order.

Core Note

The workings of the URLConnection *class and Java networking in general are beyond the scope of this book. If you want to find out more about these topics, I recommend that you read* Core Java 2, Volume 2: Advanced Features, *by Cay Horstmann and Gary Cornell, which discusses networking in detail.*

However the content type is determined, the setPage method retrieves it from the URLConnection and passes it to setContentType to initialize the JEditorPane with the correct EditorKit.

Loading Document Content

You've seen how JEditorPane selects and installs the appropriate EditorKit and you've also seen a couple of ways to load the document data itself. In fact, as with the EditorKit, there are several layers of API involved in document loading and you need to be able to choose the one most appropriate to your circumstances. In this section, we'll show you all the different possibilities and how they relate to each other.

The JEditorPane examples that you've seen so far both have editing disabled, so that the document content cannot be changed. However, as its name suggests, you can use JEditorPane as an editor for whichever type of document it contains. If you allow the user to change the document, you'll also need to be able to write the amended content out in a form appropriate to the original document encoding, which could mean writing out HTML tags. In this section, you'll also see how to arrange for JEditorPane to write data to an output stream.

Document Loading

So far in this chapter, you have seen three different ways to load a Document into a JEditorPane:

- At construction time, passing a URL object or a URL specification.
- Using the setPage method, passing a URL or a URL specification.
- Using the setText method, providing the content directly in the form of a String.

These three ways of initializing a JEditorPane are not all independent of each other. There is a hierarchy of methods that can be used to load some content; which one you choose will depend in part on the form in which you have the data and also on the current state of the JEditorPane. Using setText, for example, requires that you first obtain the data in the form of a String and that you already have the appropriate EditorKit selected. Figure 4-4 shows the relationship between the various methods involved in setting up a JEditorPane.

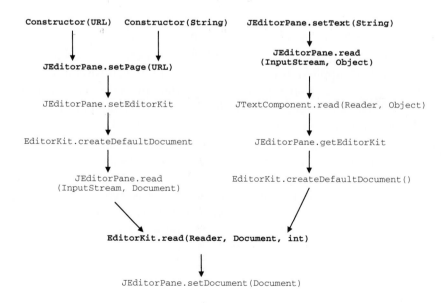

Figure 4-4 JEditorPane document loading methods.

Figure 4-4 shows the flow of control from the point at which you invoke a method that changes the content of the component up to the point at which the new `Document` object is installed. To keep the diagram simple, not all the methods that get called are shown—only the more important ones have been included. All the methods shown in the diagram are part of the public API of `JEditorPane` or `EditorKit`; the ones that you might reasonably want to use directly are highlighted in bold for ease of reference.

Much of what happens in the upper part of the diagram should already be familiar to you, because we have already seen the use of both `setPage` and `setText` to install text. Loading a page using the constructor is the same as creating a `JEditorPane` with the default constructor and then explicitly invoking `setPage`. At the next level down, however, there are a couple of things that haven't been covered yet in this chapter. Ultimately, all text loading passes through a method called `read`, either in `JEditorPane` or its superclass `JTextComponent`. There are three slightly different versions of the `read` method:

- `void read(InputStream in, Document doc)`
  `throws    IOException`
- `public void read(InputStream in, Object obj)`
  `throws    IOException`
- `public void read(Reader reader, Object obj)`
  `throws    IOException`

The way in which the first of these works is fairly obvious from its parameter list—the content is read from the given `InputStream` and used to populate the `Document` supplied as the second argument, which is then installed into the `JEditorPane`. Notice that you can't directly access this method, because it has package scope, which is why it is not highlighted in Figure 4-4 as being a useful override point or a useful method to invoke. The other two variants, however, are slightly different. The second form still requires a document source in the form of an `InputStream`, but expects an `Object` instead of a `Document` as its second argument. The third form is identical, except that it takes a `Reader` as its input source. What is the actual type of the `Object` argument supplied to both these methods and how is it used? It turns out that the second method is simply a wrapper around the third one that first takes special action if the `Object` argument is an `HTMLDocument` and the `JEditorPane` has an `HTMLEditorKit` installed. If this is the case, it directly loads the HTML from the `InputStream` into the `HTMLDocument`, just as if the first variant had been invoked. Otherwise, it creates a `Reader` from the `InputStream` (by wrapping it with an `InputStreamReader`, which maps an

8-bit incoming byte stream into a 16-bit Unicode character stream) and invokes the third read method, which is actually implemented by JTextComponent.

The JTextComponent read method creates a new Document of the type expected by the installed EditorKit, and then uses the Reader it is passed to get the data to install into it. The Object argument is simply stored as a property of the Document called Document.StreamDescriptionProperty. How this is used (if at all) depends on the actual Document implementation itself. As you'll see later, HTMLDocument interprets this property as the base URL from which to resolve relative URL references within the HTML page that it is loading.

Core Note

All the read *methods take their input from either an 8-bit* InputStream *or a Unicode-based character source accessed via a* Reader. *If the constructor or the* setPage *method are used to load a new document, the* URLConnection getInputStream *method is used to get the* InputStream *that the* read *method needs. What about the* setText *method, which is given the document content in the form of a* String? *Fortunately, the* java.io *package includes a class called* StringReader *that allows a* String *to be viewed as a Unicode character stream: The* setText *method creates a* StringReader *with the supplied document text as its source and calls the third variant of* read *shown earlier. You can find out more about the* java.io *package in* Core Java 2, Volume 1: Fundamentals, *by Cay Horstmann and Gary Cornell.*

All three of the read methods assume that you have already initialized the JEditorPane with an EditorKit suitable for the type of document being read; in addition, the first method requires you to have a Document of the correct type, whereas the other two will create a new Document of the appropriate type for you. As you can see if you refer to Figure 4-4, these methods all end up invoking an EditorKit method called read, which is defined as follows:

```
public void read(Reader reader, Document doc, int offset)
            throws IOException, BadLocationException
```

This method is where the work of loading the document and building the Element structure with the appropriate attributes actually gets done. What happens in this method depends on the actual EditorKit being used. Here's what the three editor kits supplied with Swing actually do:

`DefaultEditorKit` and `JEditorPane.PlainEditorKit`	These `EditorKits` expect to read plain, unformatted text straight into a `PlainDocument`. Therefore, there is very little to do other than read the data stream and insert it directly into the model using the `insertString` method. However, conventions for marking the end of a line of text vary from platform to platform. UNIX platforms delimit lines with a single newline character (`\n`), whereas DOS and Microsoft Windows use the two-character carriage return/newline sequence (`\r\n`). The text components avoid the complication of having to cope with both conventions by replacing a `\r\n` pair with a single `\n` before inserting the text into the model. To mark the content as having been processed in this way, the document property `EndOfLineStringProperty` is set to the `String` value `\r\n`. If this mapping was not performed, this property will have the value `null`.
`HTMLEditorKit`	This editor kit expects to read HTML from its input source. As it reads the HTML, it parses it into tags and builds an `HTMLDocument`. The details of this are covered in detail in "The Swing HTML Package" on page 392.
`RTFEditorKit`	Reads the input source and interprets it as Rich Text Format. You can use this editor kit to load documents saved from Microsoft Word or WordPad, as long as they were specifically saved in RTF format.

The `offset` argument theoretically causes the text to be loaded into the `Document` at the specified location, moving any existing content at that position to make room for it. When this method is called indirectly from the higher-level methods shown in Figure 4-4, the `offset` is always given as zero, implying that the content will be loaded at the start of the model (and in most cases this is academic because the model is initially empty). If you directly invoke the `EditorKit read` method, however, you can specify a non-zero offset provided that it does not lie beyond the current end of the model (an offset equal to the current size of the model is, of course, valid).

Core Alert

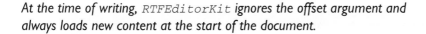

At the time of writing, `RTFEditorKit` ignores the offset argument and always loads new content at the start of the document.

At this point, you've seen almost all there is to know about the mechanics of loading text into a `JEditorPane`. While this might have been academically interesting, you could be forgiven for wondering whether there was any real point in looking at the details of this process when the higher-level API seems to work well enough in most cases. The reason for taking such a close look at the mechanics of the `Document` loading process is that it makes it easier to understand the next three topics in this chapter—loading `Document` content asynchronously, handling input that is not encoded in your system's default character set, and handling RTF documents. Even though the basic API that you saw earlier in this chapter will allow you to make use of the first two of these features without having to worry about what goes on "under the hood," having a proper understanding of the `Document` loading process will help when it comes to going beyond what is possible using the supplied API alone.

Asynchronous Page Loading

Figure 4-4 implies that the `setPage` method loads a new `document` into the `JEditorPane` synchronously, so that the `document` is completely loaded when `setPage` returns control to its caller. This is not always true, however, as you can see by typing the command:

```
java AdvancedSwing.Chapter4.EditorPaneExample3
```

When this example program starts, you'll see a blank `JEditorPane` and a text field into which you can type the URL of a file to load. There is an example HTML file to load in the same directory as the example programs for this chapter. If you installed the examples in the directory `c:\Advanced-Swing\Examples`, then you can load this file using the URL:

```
file:///c:\AdvancedSwing\Examples\AdvancedSwing\Chapter4\
    EditorPaneExample2.html
```

When you press RETURN, you'll see that the field labeled "State" changes to "Loading" and shortly afterward to "Loaded." At the same time, the "Type" field shows that the type of the loaded file is "text/html." However, at this point the JEditorPane will still be blank—it will take a few seconds for the HTML page to completely load, at which point your screen will look something like Figure 4-5.

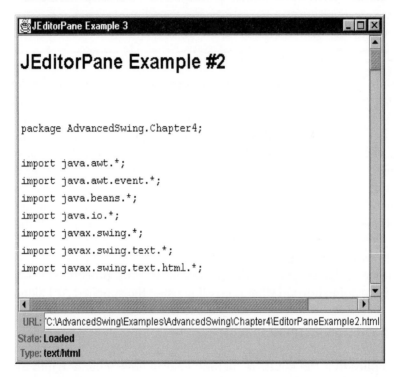

Figure 4-5 JEditorPane asynchronous page loading.

You can see the code that handles the event generated when you press the RETURN key in Listing 4-2. Ignoring the details for now, you can see that fundamentally all that happens here is that the label of the "State" field is set to "Loading…," the URL for the file to be loaded is obtained from the text field and passed to the setPage method and, finally, when the setPage method returns, the "State" field's label is changed to "Loaded" and the "Type" field is set to the loaded document's content type.

The fact that the document is not completely loaded when setPage returns demonstrates that at least some of the processing initiated by set-Page is carried out asynchronously. Here's what actually happens.

Listing 4-2 Demonstrating Asynchronous Page Loading with
`setPage`

```
// Change page based on text field
textField.addActionListener(new ActionListener() {
    public void actionPerformed(ActionEvent evt) {
        String url = textField.getText();
        try {
            // Try to display the page
            loadingState.setText("Loading...");
            loadingState.paintImmediately(0, 0,
                    loadingState.getSize().width,
                    loadingState.getSize().height);
            loadedType.setText("");
            loadedType.paintImmediately(0, 0,
                    loadedType.getSize().width,
                    loadedType.getSize().height);
            pane.setPage(url);

            loadingState.setText("Loaded");
            loadedType.setText(pane.getContentType());
        } catch (IOException e) {
            JOptionPane.showMessageDialog(pane,
                new String[] {
                    "Unable to open file",
                    url
                }, "File Open Error",
                JOptionPane.ERROR_MESSAGE);
            loadingState.setText("Failed");
        }
    }
});
```

---

1. When `setPage` is called, it gets a `URLConnection` to the file to be loaded and uses its `getContentType` method to obtain the content type of the document to be read. In this case, the content type will be `text/html`.

2. The `JEditorPane` is switched to the right mode for loading the document by calling `setContentType`. As you know, this selects the correct `EditorKit` and installs the appropriate `Document` type, which, in this case, will be an `HTMLDocument`.

3. If the `Document` is a subclass of `AbstractDocument`, its `getAsynchronousLoadPriority` method is called. This

method returns an integer that determines whether the document will be loaded synchronously or asynchronously. If the value returned from this method is negative, the document will be loaded synchronously and will complete before setPage returns. Otherwise, loading will be asynchronous.

4. If asynchronous loading is required, the new document is installed into the JEditorPane (by calling setDocument); at this point, the Document will be empty so the JEditorPane will remain blank. Then, a new thread is created. This thread uses the EditorKit read(InputStream in, Document doc) method to load the document from the InputStream corresponding to the URLConnection opened in step 1 of this process. The dispatching priority of this thread is set to the value returned by the getAsynchronousLoadPriority method.

5. Having created the background loading thread and started it, setPage returns to its caller.

Whether the document will have completely loaded when setPage returns depends entirely on the value returned by the getAsynchronous-LoadPriority method. The implementation of this method in Abstract-Document looks for a Document property called AsyncLoadPriority whose value is expected to be of type java.lang.Integer. By default, this property is not set, in which case getAsynchronousLoadPriority will return -1 and synchronous loading will be used. There are two ways to arrange for asynchronous loading to take place

- Implement and use a Document subclass that overrides the getAsynchronousLoadPriority method to return a non-negative value.

- Setting the AsyncLoadPriority property of the Document to be loaded to a non-negative value using the AbstractDocument setAsynchronousLoadPriority method.

The second of these two methods is more convenient than the first, because you don't need to subclass the Document implementation for the type of content being loaded. The HTMLEditorKit in the Swing HTML package is the only one of the standard EditorKits that supports asynchronous loading, which it does by calling setAsynchronousLoadPriority in its createDefaultDocument method. As a result, all HTML pages are loaded asynchronously (with thread dispatching priority 4 in the current implementation), while all other types load synchronously.

Although asynchronous loading is usually a useful feature because it allows the user interface to continue to be responsive while a page loaded from a slow network is still loading, it can have its drawbacks. Suppose you want to know when the new page has finished loading, perhaps because you want to count the number of words in the document or do something more complex such as display a list of the links that it contains in a separate pane. If the document were loaded synchronously, you could scan the document counting the words or looking for links immediately after the `setPage` method returns, but this won't work for HTML documents. In an example shown earlier, you saw how to extract the content type of a document being loaded by registering a `PropertyChange-Listener` for a bound property of the `JEditorPane` called `document` and calling the `JEditorPane` `getContentType` method in the listener's `propertyChange` method. Unfortunately, you can't use that technique in this case because the `HTMLDocument` is installed before page loading begins, so your listener will be called long before the page has loaded. Fortunately, there is another `JEditorPane` bound property, called `page` that holds the URL of the currently loaded page. This property changes when page loading is complete, so you can use the `Property-ChangeEvent` that this property generates to receive notification that the HTML document has been read and the `Document` structure and attributes have been completely built.

Core Note

This property is set for all types of documents, not just for HTML documents, so this technique can be used whenever the `setPage` method is called to load a document. It also works whether the document was loaded synchronously or asynchronously.

To demonstrate the use of this property, suppose you want to display a busy cursor while a page is being loaded. If you display this cursor just before the `setPage` method is called and revert to the previous cursor when it returns, you won't get the right effect if asynchronous loading is used because, as you saw above, `setPage` returns long before the page is properly displayed. The correct approach is to register a `PropertyChangeListener` for the `page` property and switch the cursor back when this property changes, as shown in Listing 4-3.

Listing 4-3 Using the `Page` Property to Detect the End of
            Document Loading

```java
package AdvancedSwing.Chapter4;

import java.awt.*;
import java.awt.event.*;
import java.beans.*;
import java.io.*;
import java.net.*;
import javax.swing.*;
import javax.swing.text.*;

public class EditorPaneExample4 extends JFrame {
    public EditorPaneExample4() {
        super("JEditorPane Example 4");

        pane = new JEditorPane();
        pane.setEditable(false);    // Read-only
        getContentPane().add(new JScrollPane(pane), "Center");

        // Build the panel of controls
        JPanel panel = new JPanel();

        panel.setLayout(new GridBagLayout());
        GridBagConstraints c = new GridBagConstraints();
        c.gridwidth = 1;
        c.gridheight = 1;
        c.anchor = GridBagConstraints.EAST;
        c.fill = GridBagConstraints.NONE;
        c.weightx = 0.0;
        c.weighty = 0.0;

        JLabel urlLabel = new JLabel("URL: ", JLabel.RIGHT);
        panel.add(urlLabel, c);
        JLabel loadingLabel = new JLabel(
                                    "State: ", JLabel.RIGHT);
        c.gridy = 1;
        panel.add(loadingLabel, c);
        JLabel typeLabel = new JLabel("Type: ", JLabel.RIGHT);
        c.gridy = 2;
        panel.add(typeLabel, c);

        c.gridx = 1;
        c.gridy = 0;
```

Listing 4-3 Using the `Page` Property to Detect the End of
             Document Loading (continued)

```java
c.gridwidth = 1;
c.weightx = 1.0;
c.fill = GridBagConstraints.HORIZONTAL;

textField = new JTextField(32);
panel.add(textField, c);
loadingState = new JLabel(spaces, JLabel.LEFT);
loadingState.setForeground(Color.black);
c.gridy = 1;
panel.add(loadingState, c);
loadedType = new JLabel(spaces, JLabel.LEFT);
loadedType.setForeground(Color.black);
c.gridy = 2;
panel.add(loadedType, c);

getContentPane().add(panel, "South");

// Change page based on text field
textField.addActionListener(new ActionListener() {
    public void actionPerformed(ActionEvent evt) {
        String url = textField.getText();

        try {
            // Check if the new page and the old
            // page are the same.
            URL newURL = new URL(url);
            URL loadedURL = pane.getPage();
            if (loadedURL !=
                    null && loadedURL.sameFile(newURL)) {
                return;
            }
            // Try to display the page
            textField.setEnabled(false);
                    // Disable input
            textField.paintImmediately(0, 0,
                    textField.getSize().width,
                    textField.getSize().height);
            setCursor(Cursor.getPredefinedCursor(
                    Cursor.WAIT_CURSOR));
                    // Busy cursor
            loadingState.setText("Loading...");
            loadingState.paintImmediately(0, 0,
```

Listing 4-3 Using the `Page` Property to Detect the End of
            Document Loading (continued)

```
                        loadingState.getSize().width,
                        loadingState.getSize().height);
          loadedType.setText("");
          loadedType.paintImmediately(0, 0,
                        loadedType.getSize().width,
                        loadedType.getSize().height);
          pane.setPage(url);

          loadedType.setText(pane.getContentType());
        } catch (Exception e) {
          System.out.println(e);
          JOptionPane.showMessageDialog(pane,
            new String[] {
                "Unable to open file",
                url
            }, "File Open Error",
            JOptionPane.ERROR_MESSAGE);
          loadingState.setText("Failed");
          textField.setEnabled(true);
          setCursor(Cursor.getDefaultCursor());
        }
      }
    });

    // Listen for page load to complete
    pane.addPropertyChangeListener(
                        new PropertyChangeListener() {
      public void propertyChange(PropertyChangeEvent evt) {
        if (evt.getPropertyName().equals("page")) {
          loadingState.setText("Page loaded.");
          textField.setEnabled(true);
                            // Allow entry of new URL
          setCursor(Cursor.getDefaultCursor());
        }
      }
    });
  }
  public static void main(String[] args) {
    JFrame f = new EditorPaneExample4();
    f.addWindowListener(new WindowAdapter() {
      public void windowClosing(WindowEvent evt) {
```

Listing 4-3   Using the `Page` Property to Detect the End of
                  Document Loading (continued)

```
            System.exit(0);
      }
   });
   f.setSize(500, 400);
   f.setVisible(true);
}

private static final String spaces = "                  ";
private JEditorPane pane;
private JTextField textField;
private JLabel loadingState;
private JLabel loadedType;
}
```

The two areas of interest in this listing are the `actionPerformed` method of the `ActionListener` attached to the `JTextField`, and the `PropertyChangeListener`. The `actionPerformed` method is similar to the one shown in Listing 4-2, but there are a couple of important differences:

1. A URL object is created from the filename typed into the input field. This URL is compared with the URL of the object currently loaded in the `JEditorPane` and, if they match, the load is not performed.

2. Before `setPage` is called, the `JTextField` is disabled to prevent further user input and the cursor is switched to the platform-specific `WAIT_CURSOR`.

The second of these two differences is the motivation behind this example because it provides the user with feedback regarding the state of the application. The other change looks like a simple optimization but, in fact, there is slightly more to it than that. To see why this change is necessary, look at the `propertyChange` method, which is called when a bound property of the `JEditorPane` changes. In this example, this method checks whether the `page` property has been changed and, if it has, it reverts the cursor to the default and re-enables the `JTextField`, reversing the steps taken by the `actionPerformed` method. A `Property-ChangeEvent` for the `page` property is generated when the `setPage` method completes the loading of a page, either synchronously or asynchronously.

However, the event will be generated only if the page being loaded is *not* the same as the current one. In fact, the `setPage` method won't even start loading a page that is already installed. Because of this, if we hadn't checked in advance that the page was about to change, the state changes made in the `actionPerformed` method would never be reversed because the `propertyChange` method would not be called.

If you try this example using the command

```
java AdvancedSwing.Chapter4.EditorPaneExample4
```

and then type the same URL into the text field as you used with the last example, you should see that the input field is disabled and the cursor changes as soon as you press the RETURN key. These changes are reversed only when the page has completely loaded and the status changes to reflect that.

Character Set Handling

As you've seen, all operations that cause content to be loaded into a `JEditorPane` eventually result in an invocation of the underlying `EditorKit`'s `read` method. This method has two variants, one of which uses an `InputStream` as the input source, the other using a `Reader`. At a slightly higher level, `JEditorPane` also has a pair of `read` methods that take input from either an `InputStream` or a `Reader`. As mentioned previously, if you supply an `Input-Stream` as the source to the `JEditorPane read` method, it will be converted to a `Reader` by wrapping it with an `InputStreamReader` object. The conversion from an 8-bit `InputStream` to a Unicode character `Reader` is necessary because the Swing text package works internally only with 16-bit Unicode character encodings.

The file systems of most computer systems in the world do not store text files in Unicode format; instead, they use a more compact 8-bit encoding such as ASCII, or the ISO Latin-1 superset of ASCII that also includes many special characters not available with ASCII itself. The actual encoding of characters used on a particular system depends on the language requirements of the users of that system. Because 256 different values is nowhere near enough to simultaneously handle all the character sets in use today, there are many standard 8-bit encodings that encompass various character sets in use around the world. For example, in Western Europe, the usual encoding used on the Windows platform goes by the name of "Cp1252," or the slightly more descriptive "Windows (Western Europe) Latin-1." If you are in Russia, however, you might find that your files are encoded using "Cp1251," otherwise known as "Windows Cyrillic." Both of these encodings have the capacity to represent 256 different characters, but a given 8-bit value in Cp1251 does not necessarily stand for the same character as it does in Cp1252. The same situation exists for other encodings. In other words, there is no global one-to-one mapping between the 8-bit value stored in a file on a computer system and the actual real-world character that it represents—what you understand by a byte with value `0xC0` depends on where you are in the world.

Unicode, however, uses a 16-bit encoding and so can handle far more characters—65536, to be precise. Because of its larger capacity, Unicode assigns a unique value to each character in all the languages that it supports, so, for example, there is a reserved Unicode value for each and every Cyrillic character, which differs from the values used by any ASCII character or by any character in the Windows Latin-1 character set. Whereas the interpretation of the 8-bit encoding `0xC0` is locale-dependent, each 16-bit Unicode character has only one possible interpretation.

Now let's look at this from the perspective of the problem faced by `JEditorPane` or its `EditorKits`. When you use the `setPage` method to load a Web page or an ordinary file into a `JEditorPane`, it opens a `URLConnection` to the Web server that owns the page or to the local file system and reads the data using the stream returned by the `URLConnection getInputStream` method. As its name suggests, this method actually returns an `InputStream`, so the data delivered from the remote system or the local file system will be represented in some 8-bit encoding. But which 8-bit encoding? To convert the incoming `InputStream` to the corresponding `Reader` that can deliver the corresponding 16-bit Unicode characters, `JEditorPane` uses an `Input-StreamReader`. This class has two constructors:

```
public InputStreamReader(InputStream in);
public InputStreamReader(InputStream in, String encoding);
```

An `InputStreamReader` created using the first constructor assumes that its input is provided in the default encoding of the platform that it is running on. On a Windows system in the United Kingdom, an object constructed in this way would expect to receive a byte stream encoded according to the Cp1252 encoding scheme, while an object instantiated from the same code in Russia would assume it was receiving a Cp1251-encoded input stream. If the input stream encoding matches the expectation of the `InputStreamReader`, the correct Unicode characters will be read into the `JEditorPane`. If it does not, however, the results will be wrong.

The second constructor is more general. Instead of using the local encoding, it allows you to specify the particular encoding that the input stream uses, using one of the well-known encoding names recognized by the `java.io` package, a full list of which can be found in the documentation that accompanies the JDK. Not surprisingly, Cp1251 and Cp1252 are legal values for this parameter.

The problem is, given an `InputStream`, how can you tell which encoding it is using? Unfortunately, without further information, you can't. If you pass it an `InputStream`, `JEditorPane` just assumes that it will be fed characters in the Latin-1 (8859_1) encoding, which is the appropriate default for the United States and will work perfectly well in Western Europe too, as long as some of the special characters used in some European languages are not encountered. As long as you're only using the `JEditorPane` to load documents held on your own system or on other systems that use the same encoding, you'll probably never notice any problem. But this really is quite restrictive if you're going to be loading pages over the Internet, because those pages could have come from anywhere. If you load a page from a Web server in Russia, you'd better be prepared to handle Cyrillic characters encoded according to Cp1251. But how can you do this if `JEditorPane` can't tell which character set it is receiving? There is a way to arrange for `JEditorPane` to use an `Input-StreamReader` configured for the correct encoding, but it requires cooperation on the part of the owner of the Web site from which you are reading an HTML page.

The only way to change the encoding that the `JEditorPane` uses is to supply it as a part of the content type that gets passed to the `setContent-Type` method. As noted earlier, the content type has the format:

```
MIME type ; parameters
```

The only parameter that `setContentType` recognizes (at the time of writing) is `charset`, which takes a character encoding as its value. Using this method, you might arrange for Cp1251 encoding to be used with the following call:

```
pane.setContentType("text/html;charset=Cp1251");
```

The call to `setContentType` takes place in the `JEditorPane` `setPage` method and uses the content type returned from the `URLConnection` `getContentType` method. If you're loading a local file (using the *file:* protocol prefix), the content type will never contain a `charset` parameter, because the Sun™ implementation of the code that reads local files just guesses the content type from the filename and returns a bare MIME type. If you are reading an HTML page (or some other content) from a Web server, the `charset` parameter will not be included unless you can arrange for the Web server to return it. However, there is a way to do that.

HTML provides a tag called META that contains information about the document itself rather than actually contributing to its content. This tag has an attribute called `HTTP-EQUIV`, which can be used to name an HTTP header field that will be set by the Web server to the value of the accompanying content attribute. You can use this to have `JEditorPane` change its encoding to Cp1251 (the Cyrillic character encoding) by placing the following tags at the top of the Web page:

```
<HTML>
<HEAD>
<META HTTP-EQUIV="Content-Type" content="text/html; charset=cp1251">
<TITLE>Document Title</TITLE>
</HEAD>
<BODY>
<!-- Content goes here -->
</BODY>
</HTML>
```

The `HTTP-EQUIV` tag causes the Web server to replace its usual `Content-Type` header with the following:

```
Content-Type: text/html; charset=cp1251
```

Now, the `URLConnection getContentType` method will return the value

```
text/html; charset=cp1251
```

which will be passed to `setContentType` and cause the Cp1251 encoding to be selected. Obviously, you can't require that all Web page authors include a `META` tag with the proper `HTTP-EQUIV` attribute. However, Web browsers are in the same position as `JEditorPane`—they also need to know how the Web page is encoded. Because of this, you'll find that most Web pages that need to specify a particular character encoding will do so and, in fact, most commercial HTML editors will supply the correct `META` tag automatically, without the owner of the Web site needing to be aware of it.

The `META` tag that you have just seen works because the Web browser replaces its usual `Content-Type` header with the one supplied by the `HTTP-EQUIV` attribute. What about when you load an HTML file locally using a URL that starts with *file:*? When you do this, there is no Web browser involved—the file is read straight from the local disk: As we said earlier, its content type will be `text/html` and the character set will be assumed to be 8859-1. Nevertheless, this arrangement still works for local files, even though there is no Web browser to set up the correct HTTP headers and nothing reading the local file that expects to see them. This clever trick is actually performed by the HTML parsing code in the Swing HTML package that we'll be looking very closely at later in this chapter. Here's how it works.

When a `file:` URL is used, the HTML page is read from the local disk and the encoding is, indeed, initially set to 8859-1. As the file content is read, it is passed to a parser in the HTML package, which scans the HTML tags and builds the corresponding `Document` model with the appropriate text package attributes. As it does this, it will encounter the `META` tag and its `HTTP-EQUIV` attribute and extract the content type and the new character set. If a `charset` parameter is found in the new content type, the parser throws a `ChangedCharSetException`, which is caught by the `JEditorPane` `read` method that originally initiated the process of reading the file. When it receives this exception, it extracts the name of the new encoding and uses it to create a new `InputStreamReader` with the proper encoding. The part of the `Document` model that has been built so far is then discarded and the HTML page is read again from the beginning, this time with the proper translation into Unicode being performed. A property called `IgnoreCharsetDirective` with value `true` is set on the `Document` to prevent this process repeating itself forever as a result of the `META` tag being read again on the second pass through the Web page.

The need to set the proper encoding arises only if you use the `setPage` method or one of the lower-level `JEditorPane` `read` methods that take an `InputStream` as the data source. If you are working at such a low level and you already know the correct encoding, you can construct your own `Reader` with the correct encoding from the `InputStream` (using the second `InputStreamReader` constructor shown earlier) and call the `read` method with your `Reader`. The `setText` method, of course, does not need to concern itself about character encoding issues, because its input source is, by definition, a `String` consisting of Unicode characters, so no translation is necessary.

Loading RTF Documents

The examples that you've seen so far in this chapter and the discussion surrounding them have centered exclusively on the use of plain text or HTML documents but, as you know, `JEditorPane` can handle any document type for which it has an `EditorKit` and a `Document` class available. The third type of document for which the Swing text package provides support is RTF, which is understood by, among other things, Microsoft Word and the simpler Wordpad editor found on the Windows platform. Loading an RTF file into a `JEditorPane` does not require any special code or different action on the part of the user. Among the examples that accompany this book is an RTF file that you can load using the same command as you used to view an HTML file:

```
java AdvancedSwing.Chapter4.EditorPaneExample4
```

and then typing a URL that corresponds to the file into the input field. If you installed the example code in the directory `c:\Advanced-Swing\Examples`, the appropriate URL would be:

```
file:///c:\AdvancedSwing\Examples\AdvancedSwing\
   Chapter4\LM.rtf
```

When you press RETURN, the RTF document will be loaded and should look something like Figure 4-6. At the time of writing, the RTF support in the Swing text package is not complete. One problem with it is visible here—the document that you have loaded actually contains an image, but the RTF package doesn't display it. Hopefully, this situation will improve in later Swing releases.

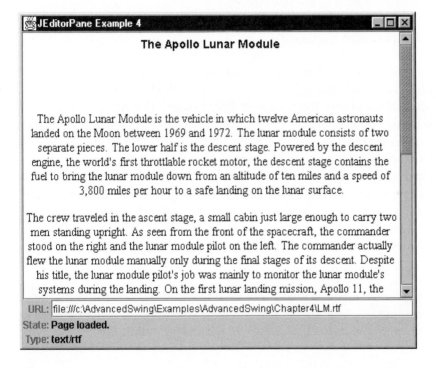

Figure 4-6 Viewing an RTF document with JEditorPane.

Core Note

There was a bug in Swing 1.1 and early versions of Java 2 that prevented JEditorPane from loading RTF files. If, when you try to load LM.rtf you get an exception with the message "RTF is an 8-bit format," you should install a later version of Swing or a more up-to-date Java 2 release, such as version 1.2.2 or later.

Saving Document Content

So far, we have only used JEditorPane to display documents but, as its name suggests, it can also be used as a document editor. To use a component as an editor requires three things:

- It must be capable of loading documents from an external source.
- It must be possible to make changes to the loaded representation of the document.
- There must be a way to store the updated state to the original location or to another file.

You've just seen that JEditorPane supports the first of these via its read method, the setText method, or the setPage method and via the read methods of the EditorKit for the document being loaded. Because JEditorPane is derived from JTextComponent, once it has been loaded with some content and a Document created, you can use the usual editing capabilities to modify the content. You can, for example, use the cursor keys to move the caret around the screen and insert, delete, and modify text. You can also copy, delete, and paste text between the JEditorPane and the clipboard. All these capabilities are available if you make the JEditorPane editable, which is the default state.

JEditorPane provides a write method that allows you to save its current state to an external location, defined as follows:

```
public void write(Writer out) throws IOException
```

This method, which is actually inherited from JTextComponent, writes all of the current Document model to the file (or whatever else) that the Writer argument corresponds to. This brings up a couple of questions:

- In what format is the output written?
- How is it possible to save RTF files, which do not work well with the 16-bit data paths that Writers represent?

Document Output Format

When you save the content of a JEditorPane, it is actually written out by the installed EditorKit, in the format appropriate for that EditorKit. In other words, an HTML file is written out as HTML and a plain text file as plain text. While it might be obvious that you can read a plain text file into a JEditorPane and write it back without losing any information, for file formats that contain internal formatting and other attributes that are not directly displayed, it is not so clear that the process of saving the content will not lose any information. For example, HTML uses tags to encode font and color changes. When the HTML document is loaded, those tags affect the attributes that are stored within the Document and cause the appropriate effects on the screen. However, there are often several different ways to write the HTML to achieve a particular effect. Is the exact HTML preserved when it is written back out?

Core Note

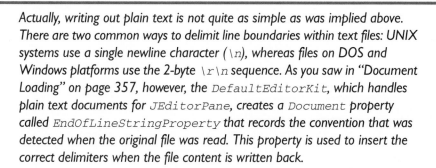

Actually, writing out plain text is not quite as simple as was implied above. There are two common ways to delimit line boundaries within text files: UNIX systems use a single newline character (\n), whereas files on DOS and Windows platforms use the 2-byte \r\n sequence. As you saw in "Document Loading" on page 357, however, the DefaultEditorKit, which handles plain text documents for JEditorPane, creates a Document property called EndOfLineStringProperty that records the convention that was detected when the original file was read. This property is used to insert the correct delimiters when the file content is written back.

The HTMLEditorKit writes out HTML that preserves what it displays on the screen. In most cases, the HTML you get will be very close to that which was in the original file. As you'll see later in this chapter, the HTML tags from the original input source are preserved within the Document, making it possible to produce a fairly accurate reproduction of the original file. However, the exact file layout is not necessarily preserved—the indentation, for example, is not likely to be the same in the output file as it was in the file originally read, but comments that appear in the input file will be retained and written to the output file in their original locations.

You can see an example of this by typing the following command:

```
java AdvancedSwing.Chapter4.EditorPaneExample6
```

This program is similar to the examples that you have already seen in this chapter, apart from the fact that it expects you to supply a filename rather than a URL and it also has a Save button. Furthermore, if the file that you load into the JEditorPane was writable, the JEditorPane itself has editing enabled. In the same directory as the example program is a simple HTML file that you can use to see how the tags from the source file are affected when they are written back out.

Core Note

You can find the source code for this example on the book's CD-ROM. We'll look at the code that implements the action performed by the Save *button later in this chapter.*

The content of this HTML file is as follows:

```
<HTML>
<HEAD>
<TITLE>JEditorPane HTML Example</TITLE>
</HEAD>
<BODY>
<!-- A preserved commment -->
<H1>JEditorPane HTML Example</H1>
<P>
This example shows that
<FONT COLOR="red" SIZE=+1>HTML attributes </FONT>
are preserved by <TT>JEditorPane</TT>.
<!-- End of text -->
</BODY>
</HTML>
```

To load this file into the JEditorPane, type its filename (*not* URL) into the input field and press RETURN. If you installed the examples from the CD-ROM into the directory c:\AdvancedSwing\Examples, the appropriate filename to type would be:

```
c:\AdvancedSwing\Examples\AdvancedSwing\Chapter4\
    EditorPaneExample6.html
```

In this example, you type a filename, not a URL, because the file is going to be modified when you've made some changes to it, so a local filename, not the URL of a resource somewhere on the other side of the Internet, is required. Nevertheless, the example still has to convert this filename to a URL so that JEditorPane can use it. For the sake of readers using JDK 1.1, if you look at the source code on the CD-ROM you'll see that it performs the conversion like this:

```
String fileName = textField.getText().trim();
File file = new File(fileName);
absolutePath = file.getAbsolutePath();
String url = "file:///" + absolutePath;
URL newURL = new URL(url);
```

In other words, convert the content of the text field to an absolute path name and put `file:///` in front of it, and then pass the result to the URL constructor. In Java 2, the `File` class has a convenience method that does this job for you. If you're using Java 2, you can replace the above with this:

```
String fileName = textField.getText().trim();
File file = new File(fileName);
URL newURL = file.toURL();
```

The result of loading this file is shown in Figure 4-7.

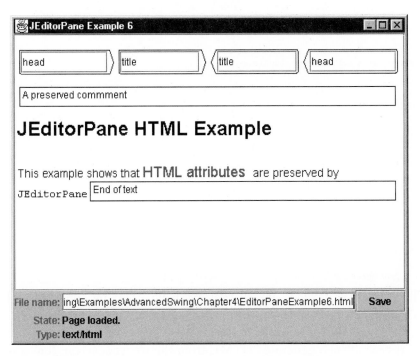

Figure 4-7   Viewing an HTML document with editing enabled.

Because the original document was writable, the example code makes the `JEditorPane` editable. As you can see, this makes a major difference to the way in which the HTML document is displayed. As well as the rendered HTML, you can also see tags from the HTML that would not normally be seen, including the HEAD and TITLE tags and the comments, which appear in

boxes in positions reflecting their actual locations in the source file. If you
now press the Save button, the JEditorPane write method will be called to
write the document content back to the file system. So that you can easily see
the changes that are made as a result of reading the document into the
JEditorPane and writing it back out again, the output filename is the same
as the input name but with the suffix .save added. The result of saving this
particular document is shown below.

```
<html>
   <head>
   <title>JEditorPane HTML Example  </title>
   </head>


   <body>
      <!-- A preserved commment -->


      <h1>
         JEditorPane HTML Example
      </h1>
      <p>
       This example shows that <font color="red"
size="+1">HTML attributes </font> are preserved by
<tt>JEditorPane</tt><!-- End of text -->

      </p>
   </body>
</html>
```

You'll notice that the tags are all preserved, but their indentation (and
case) is not and that the comments are also retained. These changes occur
because the document is actually written out by the write method of the
HTMLEditorKit, which generates HTML from the HTMLDocument that was
built when the file was read. If you add or delete some text within the
JEditorPane and save the content again, you'll find that your updates are
reflected in the HTML that is written to the output file. There is only one
JEditorPane write method, which requires a Writer, but the abstract base
class EditorKit requires the implementation of two lower-level write
methods:

```
public void write(Writer out, Document doc, int pos, int len)
                    throws IOException, BadLocationException
```

```
public void write(OutputStream os, Document doc, int pos, int len)
            throws IOException, BadLocationException
```

These more primitive APIs theoretically allow you to write out only a portion of a document, although not all implementations actually support this—in particular, the RTFEditorKit ignores the pos and len arguments and simply creates an external representation of the entire document.

The JEditorPane write method maps directly to the first of the Editor-Kit write methods shown earlier. There is no way to use the second method via JEditorPane, but we'll show an example that uses it in the next section. Whether you write out the document content from the JEditorPane or directly from the EditorKit, you need to create a Writer corresponding to the file or other object that you would like to direct the output to. This sounds simple, but actually there is a catch awaiting the unwary. Suppose you want to write the content of the JEditorPane to a file on your local system, as the example program you previously saw does. It looks like the simplest thing in the world to achieve this—just create a FileWriter:

```
FileWriter writer = new FileWriter(fileName);
pane.write(writer);
writer.close();
```

The problem here, though, is the same as the one we explored in "Character Set Handling" on page 370. All files are held in some 8-bit encoding, to which the Writer must translate the Unicode from the JEditorPane's Document model. You saw earlier that it is possible to create a Reader that accepts an encoding name and an InputStream as parameters, and performs the translation implied by the encoding on the data from the InputStream. A FileWriter actually creates an OutputStream, which is an 8-bit data channel, but uses the platform's default encoding when writing to it. This may not be what you want. If it isn't, you can take the more complex route of constructing your own Writer by wrapping an OutputStreamWriter around a suitable OutputStream. When you create the OutputStream, you can specify the encoding that you require. For example, to create a Writer that encodes in Windows Cyrillic, the following code can be used:

```
Writer writer = new OutputStreamWriter(
            new FileOutputStream(fileName), "cp1251");
```

That only leaves the problem of knowing which encoding to use. Unfortunately, the JEditorPane doesn't help here. When the document was loaded, it will have been assumed to be in the local encoding (unless you created your own Reader with a different encoding and called the appropriate read method), but if the document contained HTML, for example, the encoding may have changed as a result of an HTTP-EQUIV tag that supplied the CHARSET attribute. Although the JEditorPane sees this and changes its internal encoding, there is currently no way to get this information from outside the JEditorPane. Therefore, at least for the present, you either have to be content with saving the data in your platform's local encoding, or you need to allow the user to specify the encoding when saving content from a JEditorPane.

Saving RTF Files

Saving RTF documents from JEditorPane is not straightforward because of the 8-bit nature of the encoding that RTF uses. If you try to invoke the JEditorPane write method when an RTF document is installed, you'll get an exception with an error message informing you that RTF is an 8-bit format. Nevertheless, you can still save an RTF document by using the lower-level RTFEditorKit write method, which accepts an OutputStream as an argument. In fact, EditorPaneExample6 does just that. To try this out, load an RTF document by typing the filename

```
c:\AdvancedSwing\Examples\AdvancedSwing\Chapter4\LM.rtf
```

into the input field and pressing RETURN, and then pressing the Save button. This creates a file called LM.rtf.save in the same directory as the original. If you edit the document in the JEditorPane before you save it, the changes you make will be reflected in the output file. This example is able to save both HTML and RTF files, even though one format requires you to use a raw OutputStream and to save via the EditorKit, while the user uses a Writer and can be saved from JEditorPane. The distinction between these two is made in the ActionListener that handles events from the Save button, the implementation of which is shown in the code extract in Listing 4-4.

Listing 4-4 Saving RTF Documents

```
saveButton.addActionListener(new ActionListener() {
    public void actionPerformed(ActionEvent evt) {
        try {
            String type = pane.getContentType();
            OutputStream os = new BufferedOutputStream(
                    new FileOutputStream(file + ".save"));
            pane.setEditable(false);
            textField.setEnabled(false);
            saveButton.setEnabled(false);
```

Listing 4-4 Saving RTF Documents (continued)

```
        f.setCursor(Cursor.getPredefinedCursor(
                                Cursor.WAIT_CURSOR));

        Document doc = pane.getDocument();
        int length = doc.getLength();
        if (type.endsWith("/rtf")) {
            // Saving RTF - use the OutputStream
            try {
                pane.getEditorKit().write(
                                os, doc, 0, length);
                os.close();
            } catch (BadLocationException ex) {
            }
        } else {
            // Not RTF - use a Writer.
            Writer w = new OutputStreamWriter(os);
            pane.write(w);
            w.close();
        }
    } catch (IOException e) {
        JOptionPane.showMessageDialog(pane,
            new String[] {
                "Unable to save file",
                file.getAbsolutePath(),
            }, "File Save Error",
            JOptionPane.ERROR_MESSAGE);
    }
    pane.setEditable(file.canWrite());
    textField.setEnabled(true);
    saveButton.setEnabled(file.canWrite());
    f.setCursor(Cursor.getDefaultCursor());
    }
});
```

This code creates a new file to which the document will be written by using a `FileOutputStream`, and then wraps it in a `BufferedOutputStream` for improved performance. The resulting `OutputStream` can be used directly if the document in the `JEditorPane` is RTF and, if it is not, it can be used instead to create an `OutputStreamWriter` that can be given to the `JEditor-Pane write` method. The choice between these two is made here by examining the installed document's content type—if the string returned by the

JEditorPane getContentType method ends in /rtf, the document is assumed to be RTF. Other ways to achieve the same thing would be to check whether the JEditorPane is using an RTFEditorKit or an RTFDocument. A minor drawback of these techniques, however, is that this code would have a runtime dependency on one of these classes, which would cause the RTF support to be loaded into your Java VM as a result of saving an HTML file or a plain text file. The implementation shown earlier avoids this possibility.

Notice that, as mentioned in the previous section, if it is necessary to create a Writer, the OutputStreamWriter constructor that does not accept an encoding name is used, because there is no way to know the proper encoding without user intervention. In a production application, if this were an issue you would need to prompt the user for the correct encoding to use.

Core Note

If you load and save the file LM.rtf from the examples installed from the CD-ROM, you'll notice that the saved file is much smaller than the original—3K compared to an initial size of 700K! The reason for this is that the current implementation of RTF does not handle images, which is why the image isn't visible when you load the document. Because the image isn't part of the loaded RTFDocument, it doesn't get written back to the output file.

Document Type Conversion

Because JEditorPane has built-in support for a number of document types, it is reasonable to wonder whether it is possible to use it as a means of converting one document format to another. An example of this might be to load an HTML document and save it in RTF. The basis for this question is the fact that the loading process converts the source format into an internal representation that has some level of commonality over all the supported formats. Each EditorKit also has a write method that can translate this internal form to the external format that it knows about.

The answer to this question is that, in general, reliable document conversions are not possible. Although the result of loading an HTML document is similar to that obtained when loading the same content from an RTF files each document type has many private attributes that can be interpreted properly only by its own EditorKit. You'll see in the next section that the HTML support makes extensive use of private attributes to represent HTML tags from the input file. These attributes would be incomprehensible to the

RTF `EditorKit`. As a result, if you write the content of a document using an `EditorKit` other than the one that loaded it you will, at best, get a poor representation of the original, perhaps containing only plain text.

You can experiment with the various document conversions available by using a modified version of the previous example that allows you to load from and save into any of the supported document formats. To try out this example, type the command:

```
java AdvancedSwing.Chapter4.EditorPaneExample7
```

This application looks the same as the previous one, except that it has a set of radio boxes that allow you to chose the format in which you want to save the output document, as shown in Figure 4-8.

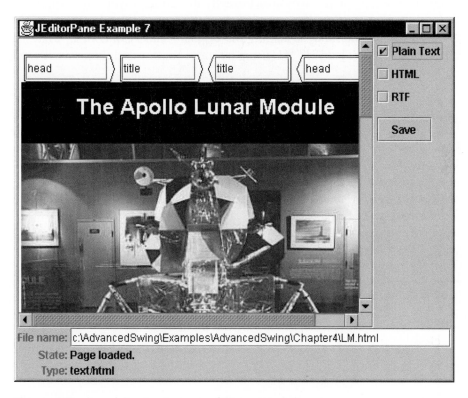

Figure 4-8 An application that saves files in various formats.

After loading a document, select the format in which you would like to save it and press the `Save` button. The result of saving the document is written to the program's standard output, so if you intend to look closely at what is generated, you might want to redirect the standard output to a file when you start the program, like this:

```
java AdvancedSwing.Chapter4.EditorPaneExample7 >
    c:\temp\savedfile
```

In Figure 4-8, we've loaded an HTML page that you can find in the examples on the CD-ROM. If you have installed the examples in the usual location, you can load this file by typing the following into the filename field:

```
c:\AdvancedSwing\Examples\AdvancedSwing\Chapter4\LM.html
```

If you save this in plain text, you'll get simply the text, grouped into paragraphs. Saving it in HTML produces an almost perfect representation of the original—the tags themselves aren't exactly the same, as you saw earlier, but the result of reloading the saved document into a Web browser or the JEditorPane is the same as loading the original. This is, of course, what you might expect if you load HTML using HTMLEditorKit and then save it using the same EditorKit.

Saving the HTML as RTF loses the image (as it would even if the document had been in RTF format originally) and some of the color and font formatting. The reason for the somewhat inaccurate conversion to RTF is that HTML documents do not store all their attributes in the same way as you saw in Chapter 2, so there are fewer attributes available for the RTF generator (which only understands the ones shown in Chapter 2) to look at. You'll see how the attributes implied by the HTML tags are actually stored later in this chapter.

The code that implements the Save button in this example is shown in Listing 4-5.

Listing 4-5 Saving in Different Formats

```
button.addActionListener(new ActionListener() {
   public void actionPerformed(ActionEvent evt) {
      Writer w = null;
      OutputStream os = System.out;
      String contentType;
      if (plain.isSelected()) {
         contentType = "text/plain";
         w = new OutputStreamWriter(os);
      } else if (html.isSelected()) {
         contentType = "text/html";
         w = new OutputStreamWriter(os);
```

Listing 4-5 Saving in Different Formats (continued)

```
      } else {
         contentType = "text/rtf";
      }

      EditorKit kit =
            pane.getEditorKitForContentType(contentType);
      try {
         if (w != null) {
            kit.write(w, pane.getDocument(),
            0, pane.getDocument().getLength());
            w.flush();
         } else {
            kit.write(os, pane.getDocument(),
               0, pane.getDocument().getLength());
            os.flush();
         }
      } catch (Exception e) {
         System.out.println("Write failed");
      }
   }
});
```

When the button is pressed, the target content type is obtained by checking the state of the radio boxes. The content type is used to get the appropriate `EditorKit` by calling the `JEditorPane getEditorKitFor-ContentType` method, and then the document content is written out by calling the `EditorKit write` method passing it the installed `Document`. Note that, as ever, there is special code here that handles writing out RTF, which requires an `OutputStream` instead of a `Writer`; writing RTF uses the standard output stream directly, whereas it is wrapped with an `OutputStreamWriter` for the other content types. Notice that it is not necessary to install the `EditorKit` for the output format into the `JEditorPane` to have it write its output and, in fact, doing so would lose the content of the loaded `Document` because the `JEditorPane setEditor-Kit` method creates a new, empty `Document`, as you have already seen.

You should experiment with loading documents of all three types and saving them in each of the other formats. An interesting case arises when you load a plain text or RTF document and try to save it in HTML. The `HTMLEditorKit` has special code that detects that the `Document` it is working with is not an `HTMLDocument` and, when this happens, it tries to create a reasonable copy of the original using the attributes stored at the character and paragraph level by the code that created the Document. In the case of a plain document, there will be no attributes to reproduce, so only the usual header and body tags along with paragraph tags to break the text at newline boundaries are written out. With RTF, though, the effect is different. You can see this by loading the LM.rtf file that was used earlier in this chapter and then saving it as HTML. The saved file starts like this:

```html
<html>
  <head>
    <style>
      <!--
        p.Default Paragraph Font {
          underline:;
          italic:;
          bold:normal;
        }
        p.heading 1 {
          RightIndent:0.0;
          SpaceBelow:12.0;
          LeftIndent:0.0;
          SpaceAbove:3.0;
          FirstLineIndent:0.0;
        }
        p.Normal {
          LeftIndent:0.0;
          FirstLineIndent:0.0;
          RightIndent:0.0;
        }
        p.H4 {
          RightIndent:0.0;
          SpaceBelow:13.0;
          LeftIndent:0.0;
          SpaceAbove:6.5;
          FirstLineIndent:12.0;
        }
      -->
    </style>
  </head>
  <body>
    <p class=heading 1>
      <font style="color: #000000; font-size: 14;
                              font-family: Arial; ">
      <b>The Apollo Lunar Module</b>
      </font>
    </p>
```

The header contains an HTML style sheet, which defines styles to be used with HTML tags later in the document. You can see an example of this at the end of the extract shown earlier, in which the text between the start and end paragraph tags has the "heading 1" style applied to it. This style is defined by the style sheet to have a particular amount of spacing before and after the text and no special indentation. The styles in the style sheets are created from the `Styles` in the `Document` that the HTML writer is given to process (refer to Chapter 2 for a full discussion of `Styles` and `StyleContexts`). In this case, the `Styles` will have been created by the RTF reader to represent the formatting in the original RTF file.

The automatic creation of a style sheet from a `StyleContext` also works (after a fashion) for documents that you handcraft using `JTextPane` and gives you a way to save them in external form. Because `JTextPane` is a subclass of `JEditorPane`, everything that we have discussed in this chapter applies also to `JTextPane`. To demonstrate the point, type the following command:

```
java AdvancedSwing.Chapter4.EditorPaneExample8
```

This command runs a slightly modified version of an example that was shown in Chapter 2 (see Figure 2-6 for the original application), consisting of a `JTextPane` containing a `Document` with several custom `Styles` applied to it, which looks like Figure 4-9. This version was created simply by adding the same visual elements as were used in `EditorPaneExample7`, along with the code to handle the `Save` button that you saw in the discussion of that example. Because `JTextPane` is a subclass of `JEditorPane`, the same code continues to work with `JTextPane`.

Select HTML and press `Save` and you'll get an HTML page that more-or-less corresponds to the styling that was applied in the `JTextPane`. If you look at the output, you'll see that it again starts with an HTML style sheet:

```
<style>
   <!--
   p.MainStyle {
      LeftIndent:16.0;
      RightIndent:16.0;
      FirstLineIndent:16.0;
      family:serif;
      size:12;
   }
   p.CompPara {
      SpaceAbove:16.0;
   }
```

```
p.Heading2 {
   LeftIndent:8.0;
   foreground:java.awt.Color[r=255,g=0,b=0];
   FirstLineIndent:0.0;
   bold:true;
   family:serif;
   size:16;
}
p.ConstantWidth {
   foreground:java.awt.Color[r=0,g=255,b=0];
   family:monospaced;
}
p.Component {
   component:
   javax.swing.JLabel[,0,0,399x319,alignmentX=0.0,
       alignmentY=null,border=,flags=0,maximumSize=
       minimumSize=,preferredSize=,
       defaultIcon=javax.swing.ImageIcon@e5db8825,
       disabledIcon=,horizontalAlignment=CENTER,
       horizontalTextPosition=CENTER,iconTextGap=4,
       labelFor=,text=Displaying text with attributes,
       verticalAlignment=CENTER,verticalTextPosition=BOTTOM];
   }
   -->
</style>
```

Core Alert

*The output above was obtained using a beta release of Swing 1.1.1.
In the version of Java 2 available at the time of writing (version 1.2.2),
this example does not work due to a Swing bug—a* Null-
PointerException *occurs when the document is being saved
in HTML format and you'll just see a message that reads "Write failed."*

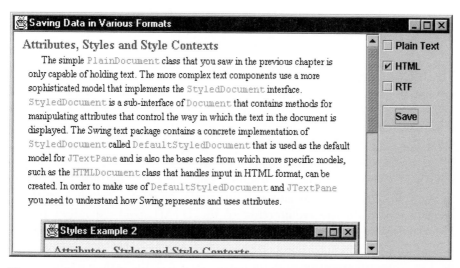

Figure 4-9   An application that uses `JTextPane` content in various formats.

Listing 2-3 in Chapter 2 showed most of the `Styles` that were created when building this `Document`, with the exception of the `Component` style that was added in the following example. If you compare the `Styles` in Listing 2-3 with those in the style sheet, you'll see that they match. Unfortunately, the style sheet is useless because the attributes held in the `Document` do not map to attributes recognized by HTML; if you load the page back into a browser, you'll get what looks like plain text arranged into paragraphs. If you want to use this feature to generate correct HTML from the content of a `JTextPane`, you'll either have to be prepared to edit the output to replace the names defined in the `StyleConstants` class with the attributes that are valid within style sheets or, better, create a subclass of `HTMLEditorKit` that has an HTML generator that maps to the correct attributes automatically.

Core Note

Ideally, this mapping should be performed by the standard `HTMLEditorKit` and perhaps in a future release of Swing this will be done.

The Swing HTML Package

The HTML package has been subject to frequent changes during the development of Swing and it continues to evolve even after the release of Swing as a fully supported product. One of the areas that has changed most noticeably is the subset of HTML that the package actually supports. Because the HTML specification itself is still expanding rapidly, it is likely that the Swing HTML package will continue to change to recognize more tags and to provide better support for some features that are currently not fully implemented. Because of this, what you'll find in this chapter is mainly intended to acquaint you with the architecture of the HTML package rather than to cover in great detail exactly what is and is not available. However, you will see how to find out which tags and attributes are recognized by the version of the package that you are using without having to search the source code.

The first part of this section looks at the various pieces that work together to turn the `JEditorPane` into a simple Web browser. You'll see how an HTML file is parsed and the how the tags and content are represented in the `Document` model and we'll look at the features of the `HTMLEditorKit`, which are currently somewhat limited. Having seen the storage mechanism, we'll then move on to look at how the `Document` is rendered by the HTML package's `Views` and how you can subclass them to adjust the way that a Web page is presented to suit your needs.

The HTML Document Model

As you've already seen in this chapter, when you load an HTML document into a `JEditorPane`, an `HTMLEditorKit` is created and installed. Like all editor kits, `HTMLEditorKit` creates a `Document` class that can handle the type of content that it is responsible for; in this case, an `HTMLDocument` will be created. Because `HTMLDocument` is derived from `DefaultStyledDocument`, the way in which HTML pages are stored within the `JEditorPane` is fundamentally very similar to the way in which the documents are stored that we saw in Chapter 2 when we looked at how to use `JTextPane` the content is mapped by an `Element` structure and the way in which the text should be rendered is described by attributes attached to those `Elements`. However, HTML is a fairly rich and flexible document description language, so there is quite a bit more complexity surrounding not only the way in which it is stored within the model, but also in the architecture of the HTML package itself. In fact, there are several classes that are involved in maintaining an HTML document that have no parallel in the simpler RTF package or the small set of classes used to display plain text. A complete picture of the most important of these classes and their relationships is shown in Figure 4-10.

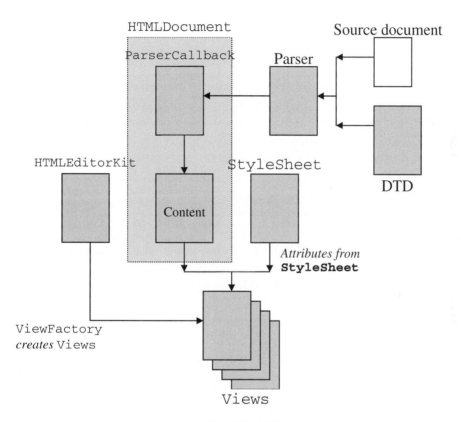

Figure 4-10 The components of an HTML document.

The collection of classes shown in Figure 4-10 is created and assembled by the HTMLEditorKit when its read method is called. In many cases, there are override points available that allow you to substitute your own implementation of some of the pieces. To make full use of the HTML package, you need to understand what all these classes are and how they interact with each other. Brief descriptions of each of them will be found in the sections that follow. When we've looked at each of the component parts, we'll then move on to examine in more detail the structure of the document model itself and how it differs from what we have seen so far.

The DTD

There have been several versions of HTML, the most recent of which, at the time of writing, is HTML 4.0. The official specification of HTML itself is maintained by the World Wide Web Consortium (W3C), and can be found on its Web site at `http://www.w3c.org`. Each version of HTML is specified by a *document type definition*, or DTD, which describes the legal elements of an HTML page and the way in which they can be combined. A DTD is written partly using a formal description language known as the Structured Generalized Markup Language (SGML) and partly with informal comments that add more detail to aid understanding. For example, here is how the HTML markup for a paragraph is defined in the HTML 3.2 DTD:

```
<!ELEMENT P - O (%text)*>
<!ATTLIST P
     align(left|center|right) #IMPLIED
     >
```

This short extract defines an element called P which has an associated set of possible attributes defined in the ATTLIST description. These two definitions are tied together by the common tag P, which is defined by the ELEMENT description to be the tag to be used within the HTML itself. The - following the P indicates that the start tag for this element is mandatory, while the O means that the corresponding end tag is optional. In practice, this says that a paragraph is introduced by a tag written like this:

```
<P>
```

and may be terminated by one that looks like this:

```
</P>
```

although the second of these tags may be omitted at the option of the person writing the HTML. The body of the paragraph is described by the rest of the element definition, namely:

```
(%text)*
```

The asterisk means zero or more instances of the item that precedes it, which in this case is whatever is meant by %text. This term is defined earlier in the DTD like this:

```
<!ENTITY % text "#PCDATA | %font | %phrase | %special | %form">
```

This definition is itself framed in terms of other definitions and the SGML term #PCDATA, which means Parsed Character Data. Parsed Character Data is a sequence of characters that may contain raw data that represents itself (such as ASCII characters) as well as other markup such as & which would be taken as an ampersand (&) character. The | character means OR, so this description says that text is made up of either PCDATA or whatever the DTD means by %font or %phrase or %special or %form. If you want to see how these terms are defined, you can find them in the DTD itself on the W3C Web site.

The ATTLIST specification describes the attributes that may accompany the paragraph tag. Attributes always appear within the angle brackets that surround the tag itself and are given in the form:

```
name = value
```

According to the DTD extract shown earlier, for a <P> tag, the only recognized attribute is called align and it can take one of the values left, center, or right, where (as always with HTML) case does not matter. The word #IMPLIED indicates that this attribute need not be specified, so either of the following would be valid:

```
<P>
<P ALIGN=LEFT>
```

Which of the alignment values is assumed when the alignment is not explicitly given is not specified by the DTD. If the keyword #REQUIRED were used in place of #IMPLIED, it would be mandatory to supply an explicit value for the align attribute and it would have to be one of the three possible values from the DTD.

Because HTML is defined in terms of a DTD, it makes sense to write software that interprets HTML in such a way that it can be driven directly by the DTD. That's exactly what happens in the HTML package. If you have Java 2 or Swing for JDK 1.1 installed on your machine, you'll find in the JAR file (swingall.jar or rt.jar depending on which JDK you are using) a file called javax/swing/text/html/parser/html32.bdtd, which contains a binary-encoded form of a DTD describing HTML. The encoding used in this file is a private one and, fortunately, you don't need to understand it to make full use of the HTML package. The version of the DTD that this encoding represents contains all the elements defined by HTML 3.2 and some extras that were not part of the official specification of that HTML version, such as the ability to define and use style sheets, a feature that has greatly influenced the design of the HTMLDocument class, as you'll see later.

Core Note

If you want to find out more about the binary encoding of the DTD file, the classes that are used to reading it are in the `javax.swing.text.html.parser` *package, the source code for which is included with Java 2 and with the Swing add-on package for JDK 1.1.*

The Parser and the `ParserCallback`

The binary DTD is used by an HTML parser, which reads HTML from a `Reader` and validates it against the rules contained in the DTD. The interface supplied by the parser is defined by the abstract class `HTMLEditor-Kit.Parser`, which contains only one method:

```
public static abstract class Parser {
    public abstract void parse(Reader r,
            ParserCallback cb, boolean ignoreCharSet)
            throws IOException;
}
```

The parser uses the DTD to validate the structure of the document, which is read through the `Reader` supplied as the first argument. However, nothing outside the parser itself knows or cares that it might be using a DTD to do its job, so you won't see any code that passes a particular DTD to the parser. The parser in the Swing text package is hard-coded to use the binary DTD for HTML 3.2 that is located in the `javax.swing.text.html.parser` package.

The `ParserCallback` given by the second argument is called as the HTML document is parsed. `ParserCallback` is an inner class of `HTML-EditorKit` that defines seven empty methods:

```
public static class ParserCallback {
    public void handleComment(char[] data, int pos) {
    }

    public void handleStartTag(HTML.Tag t,
                MutableAttributeSet a, int pos) {
    }

    public void handleEndTag(HTML.Tag t, int pos) {
    }

    public void handleSimpleTag(HTML.Tag t,
                MutableAttributeSet a, int pos) {
    }
```

```
public void handleText(char[] data, int pos) {
}

public void handleError(String errorMsg, int pos){
}

public void flush() throws BadLocationException {
}

}
```

The parser considers the pieces of an HTML document to be of five different types and it invokes the corresponding method of the `ParserCallback` class as each element type is encountered. A short description of each type follows.

Comments

The `handleComment` method is called when an HTML comment is encountered. Comments begin with the sequence `<!--` and are terminated with `-->`. These delimiters are not useful in the internal representation of the HTML document, so they are not passed when the `handleComment` method is called—only the text of the comment itself is given, in the form of an array of characters, including any spaces that follow the opening delimiter and precede the closing one. The `pos` argument gives the offset of the first character after the end of the comment, including the terminating delimeter. Thus, for example, if an HTML document started with the following sequence:

```
<!-- A comment -->
```

the `handleComment` method would be called with the characters " A comment " as the character array (note the leading and trailing space, which come from the text as typed into the document) and with the `pos` argument set to 18.

The current implementations of the parser and the DTD consider the body of the comment to be raw characters—they do not recognize embedded HTML tags and so there is no support for features that are hosted with HTML comments, such as JavaScript. You could, of course, provide this support yourself by capturing the output of the parser and performing further processing of comments. Complete support for JavaScript also requires extra work when handling most aspects of creating and displaying the `HTMLDocument`, one example of which is the extra attributes that are used with some HTML tags to invoke JavaScript functions when certain events occur. These attributes are not recognized by the HTML 3.2 DTD. Although adding Java-Script functionality to the HTML support provided by the Swing HTML package would be an interesting project, it is well beyond the scope of this book. You should, however, be able to work out how to add most of the extra facilities for JavaScript from the information in this section.

Start and End Tags

As mentioned in the discussion of the HTML DTD, many HTML tags come in pairs that start and end a section to which the markup specified by the tag applies. The parser calls the `handleStartTag` and `handleEndTag` methods as each element of the pair is encountered. A start tag and its matching end tag might be quite widely separated from each other and other markup may be encountered while the text between a start tag and its corresponding end tag is being processed. The HTML reader must, therefore, be prepared to stack tags and handle new tag pairs while the parser is searching for the matching end tag.

As with the `handleComment` method, the `pos` argument corresponds to the character after the tag. The other two arguments require a little more explanation. The first argument passed to both `handleStartTag` and `handleEndTag` is of type `HTML.Tag`, which describes the tag that has been encountered. There is one `HTML.Tag` constant for every tag recognized by the DTD. The tag constant that represents a paragraph break, for example, is called `HTML.Tag.P`. As well as containing the name of the tag (which is held in lowercase), the `HTML.Tag` object has two other attributes associated with it:

- The `causesBreak` attribute indicates whether this tag will cause a break in the text flow. This is true for tags such as `<P>`, but false for tags like `<FONT>` and `<B>` that simply change the formatting of the current text line.
- The `isBlock` attribute is true for a tag that starts a new block within the document. The `<P>` tag is an example for which this attribute is true, because it starts a block that is ended by the corresponding `</P>` tag, if there is one, or by the next `<P>` tag if `</P>` tags are not being used (which is usually the case).

The second argument passed to `handleStartTag` is `MutableAttribute-Set` that contains the HTML attributes that qualify the tag. Because closing tags do not have associated attributes, this argument is not used with `handleEndTag`. As an example of what is meant by an attribute in this context, consider the <FONT> tag, which can modify the size and color of the text that it bounds. A typical <FONT> tag might look like this:

```
<FONT COLOR=red SIZE=+1>
```

When the parser encounters this tag, it will call the `handleStartTag` method with the first argument set to `HTML.Tag.FONT`, while the second will be a reference to a `MutableAttributeSet` containing an attribute called `COLOR` with value `red` and another called `SIZE` with value `+1`. You'll see later in this section exactly how these attributes are encoded.

The parser keeps a stack of tags, which is added to as each opening tag is encountered. When a closing tag is detected, the entry for the opening tag is popped from the stack. However, it is common practice not to supply end tags where their presence can be inferred from context and the DTD permits this, as you saw earlier in the case of the `</P>` tag. In cases like this, the parser will internally generate the tag that has been omitted and invoke the `handleEndTag` method exactly as if the tag had been present in the input stream. The same is true of certain start tags, such as `<HTML>`, `<HEAD>`, and `<BODY>`, some or all of which are routinely omitted from HTML documents. This allows the code that handles the parsed document to be simpler, because it does not need to specifically cater for missing start or end tags.

Simple Tags

The `handleSimpleTag` method is called when the parser encounters a tag that is not part of a start/end pair. An example of a tag in this category is `<BR>`, which always appears on its own in a document—there is no corresponding `</BR>` tag. A simple tag may, however, have associated attributes so, in addition to the universal `pos` argument, the `handleSimpleTag` method is called with both an `HTML.Tag` object for the tag itself and a `MutableAttributeSet` for the qualifying HTML attributes.

Text

Anything that is not markup and is not a comment is considered to be text and is handled by calling the `handleText` method. Text can only legally appear where the DTD allows content of type `PCDATA`. Because text is described in this way, it may contain ordinary characters or character entities that specify characters in a manner that is independent of the character set in which the document is encoded, such as `&#38;` which, as noted earlier, signifies an ampersand. Ordinary characters are translated directly to Unicode by the `Reader` that handles the document input stream before it is seen by the parser, but character entities are not. Instead, these are detected by the parser and converted to the appropriate Unicode value before the `handle-Text` method is called.

A text run will be interrupted by the occurrence of any markup other than character entities: The text on either side of the markup will be delivered in separate invocations of `handleText`. For example, if the following sequence occurred in an HTML document:

```
This is <B>bold</B> text
```

`handleText` would be called three times, with an invocation of `handle-StartTag` for the `<B>` tag and `handleEndTag` when `</B>` is reached.

Errors

Parsing errors are reported via the `handleError` method, which passes a textual error message and the offset at which the error was detected. In some cases, HTML that does not strictly match the DTD is not reported as being in error, because there is quite a large number of Web pages that would not format properly if strict adherence to the DTD were enforced. This is consistent with the behavior of the more popular browsers, which generally tend to skip over markup that they don't understand. The Swing HTML package tries to correct common mistakes by introducing extra tags into the input stream or, in some cases, ignoring duplicate or invalid tags. When an error that cannot be automatically corrected or ignored is encountered, the `handleError` method is invoked. The default processing for this method (in `HTMLDocument.HTMLReader`) does nothing at all, so errors are not actually reported and parsing will continue. Whether further parsing will be useful will, as with all languages, depend on the nature and context of the error.

The *flush* Method

The last of the `ParserCallback` methods is the `flush` method, which is invoked once, when the parser reaches the end of its input stream, to notify the `ParserCallback` object that there is nothing more to parse. This method is present to allow the `ParserCallback` implementation to buffer whatever it creates from the results of parsing and to flush its cache of unprocessed items when the document has been completely read. An implementation is, of course, not obliged to buffer, but the default implementation in `HTMLDocument.HTMLReader` does provide this feature.

As it receives items from the parser, `HTMLReader` would like to create document `Elements` and attributes and insert them into the `HTMLDocument`, building up the model as the Web page is parsed. However, this is usually inefficient, especially if the `HTMLDocument` is already installed in a `JEditor-`

Pane (as it would be for the usual case of asynchronous loading via the
JEditorPane setPage method) because changes to the HTMLDocument
cause events that might kick off other processing. In particular, the Views
that render the document content will be notified of changes. This will cause
new Views to be created as the document is built and the screen to be
updated, if the component is visible. There is no real point in doing this in
most cases, so HTMLReader waits until it has a large set of document updates
and makes them all together, so that the Views redraw only relatively infre-
quently during the loading process. The flush method allows the HTML-
Reader to push any Elements that have not been created into the
HTMLDocument at the end of the process.

Core Note

*When the arrangement in Figure 4-10 is created from the
HTMLEditorKit read method (which will be the case unless you write
code to initialize the component), the HTMLReader will buffer
approximately 100 changes to the document before a real update occurs.
The number is only approximate because it is only checked when text is
being added.*

The Default Parser

The parser that is installed by default is obtained by invoking the
getParser method of HTMLEditorKit, which is invoked from the HTML-
EditorKit read method. This method returns an instance of the
class javax.swing.text.html.parser.ParserDelegator—in fact, a single instance of this class is created the first time the getParser method is
called and is shared by every copy of HTMLEditorKit that is subsequently created. This class is not the parser itself, however: Its only job is to load the DTD
and provide an implementation of the parse method required by the HTMLEdi-
torKit.Parser interface. The real parser resides in a class called
javax.swing.text.html.parser.DocumentParser. One instance of this class
is created each time the parse method of ParserDelagator is invoked—in
other words, a new copy is created each time an HTML document is parsed.
Having created the DocumentParser, the ParserDelagator parse method
simply delegates to the same method of DocumentParser, which has the same
signature as the parse method in the HTMLEditorKit.Parser interface.

If you want to supply your own parser, you must create a class that provides the parse method and calls the methods of the ParserCallback
object passed to the parse method as the HTML document is being scanned,

as outlined in this section. To arrange for your parser to be installed, you'll need to override the HTMLEditorKit getParser method and return a reference to your own parser instead of the default one. This, of course, requires you to implement a subclass of HTMLEditorKit. You'll see an example that installs a modified HTMLEditorKit in the next section. While this example won't actually create a new parser, you will see the code required to use a replacement editor kit.

Replacing the `ParserCallback`

By default, the HTMLDocument.HTMLReader class is used as the Parser-Callback. Under normal circumstances, you would not need to install your own ParserCallback but it is possible to use a different class by overriding the getReader method of HTMLDocument:

```
public HTMLEditorKit.ParserCallback getReader(int pos);
```

We'll make use of this facility to install an enhanced ParserCallback that allows us to see exactly what the parser does when it reads an HTML page. To do this, we'll create a thin layer of code that wraps the existing HTML-Reader class and, as each of the ParserCallback methods of this class is invoked, some debugging information will be printed and the call will be passed to the original HTMLReader implementation so that the JEditorPane continues to function normally. The code is shown in Listing 4-6.

Listing 4-6 Installing a Custom HTML Reader

```
package AdvancedSwing.Chapter4;

import javax.swing.*;
import javax.swing.text.*;
import javax.swing.text.html.*;
import java.io.*;

public class ReplaceReader {
    public static void main(String[] args) {
        JFrame f = new JFrame(
                        "JEditorPane with Custom Reader");
        JEditorPane ep = new JEditorPane();
        f.getContentPane().add(new JScrollPane(ep));
        f.setSize(400, 300);
        f.setVisible(true);
```

Listing 4-6 Installing a Custom HTML Reader (continued)

```java
        HTMLEditorKit kit = new HTMLEditorKit() {
            public Document createDefaultDocument() {
                HTMLDocument doc =
                    new CustomHTMLDocument(getStyleSheet());
                doc.setAsynchronousLoadPriority(4);
                doc.setTokenThreshold(100);
                return doc;
            }
        };
        ep.setEditorKit(kit);

        try {
            Document doc = ep.getDocument();
            doc.putProperty("IgnoreCharsetDirective",
                new Boolean(true));
            kit.read(new FileReader(args[0]), doc, 0);
        } catch (Exception e) {
            System.out.println(
                "Exception while reading HTML " + e);
        }
    }
}

class CustomHTMLDocument extends HTMLDocument {
    CustomHTMLDocument(StyleSheet styles) {
        super(styles);
    }

    public HTMLEditorKit.ParserCallback getReader(int pos) {
        return new CustomReader(pos);
    }

    class CustomReader extends HTMLDocument.HTMLReader {
        public CustomReader(int pos) {
            super(pos);
        }

        public void flush() throws BadLocationException {
            System.out.println("flush called");
            super.flush();

        }
        public void handleText(char[] data, int pos) {
            indent();
```

Listing 4-6 Installing a Custom HTML Reader (continued)

```
        System.out.println("handleText <" +
                    new String(data) + ">, pos " + pos);
        super.handleText(data, pos);
    }

    public void handleComment(char[] data, int pos) {
        indent();
        System.out.println("handleComment <"
                    + new String(data) + ">, pos " + pos);
        super.handleComment(data, pos);
    }

    public void handleStartTag(
            HTML.Tag t, MutableAttributeSet a, int pos) {
        indent();
        System.out.println(
            "handleStartTag <" + t + ">, pos " + pos);
        indent();
        System.out.println("Attributes: " + a);
        tagLevel++;
        super.handleStartTag(t, a, pos);
    }

    public void handleEndTag(HTML.Tag t, int pos) {
        tagLevel--;
        indent();
        System.out.println(
            "handleEndTag <" + t + ">, pos " + pos);
        super.handleEndTag(t, pos);
    }

    public void handleSimpleTag(
            HTML.Tag t, MutableAttributeSet a, int pos) {
        indent();
        System.out.println("handleSimpleTag <" + t + ">,
                        pos " + pos);
        indent();
        System.out.println("Attributes: " + a);
        super.handleSimpleTag(t, a, pos);
    }
```

Listing 4-6 Installing a Custom HTML Reader (continued)

```
        public void handleError(String errorMsg, int pos){
            indent();
            System.out.println("handleError <" + errorMsg +
                               ">, pos " + pos);
            super.handleError(errorMsg, pos);
        }

        protected void indent() {
            for (int i = 0; i < tagLevel; i++) {
                System.out.print(" ");
            }
        }

        int tagLevel;
    }
}
```

The mechanics of this example are very simple. To install a new `Parser-Callback`, we need to override the `HTMLDocument getReader` method, which requires us to implement a subclass of `HTMLDocument`. In this case, the subclass is called `CustomHTMLDocument` and, as you can see, it has an inner class called `CustomHTMLReader`, derived from `HTMLDocument.HTMLReader`, which overrides all the `ParserCallback` methods. In every case, the replacement method just prints its arguments and invokes the original code in its superclass so that the results of the parsing operation will be reflected in the `HTMLDocument` as usual.

The rest of the example code arranges for the `CustomHTMLDocument` to be installed in a `JEditorPane`. As you may recall, `HTMLEditorKit` creates an empty `HTMLDocument` when it is installed in a `JEditorPane`; to alter this behavior and have it use a `CustomHTMLDocument` instead, we subclass `HTML-EditorKit` and override its `createDefaultDocument` method to return an instance of our custom `Document`. This customized `HTMLEditorKit` will use a `CustomHTMLDocument` whenever it is connected to a `JEditorPane`. In this example, we explicitly create an instance of our `HTMLEditorKit` and install it using the `setEditorKit` method, and then invoke its `read` method to load an HTML page using a path name supplied on the program's command line. If you wanted to use this `HTMLEditorKit` to read a file over the Internet using `setPage`, you would need to arrange for it to be the default editor kit for handling files with MIME type `text/html`. To do this, you need to pass an instance of the editor kit to the `JEditorPane setEditorKitFor-ContentType` method that you saw earlier in this chapter:

```
ep.setEditorKitForContentType("text/html", kit);
```

To run the example, type the following command:

```
java AdvancedSwing.Chapter4.ReplaceReader pathname
```

where `pathname` is the full path name of an HTML page. If you have installed the example source code that accompanies this book in the directory `c:\AdvancedSwing\Examples`, you'll find a very simple HTML page that demonstrates some of the workings of the parser in the file

```
c:\AdvancedSwing\Examples\AdvancedSwing\Chapter4\
    ReplaceReader.html
```

This file contains the following (trivial) HTML:

```
<!-- A trivial HTML example -->

<H1>Level 1 Heading</H1>
<P align=center>
A paragraph with some <B>bold</B>
<FONT COLOR=red>red</FONT> text.
```

Here is the output generated by running the example with this HTML file:

```
handleComment < A trivial HTML example >, pos 31
handleStartTag <html>, pos 40
Attributes:
    handleStartTag <head>, pos 40
    Attributes:
    handleEndTag <head>, pos 40
    handleStartTag <body>, pos 40
    Attributes:
        handleStartTag <h1>, pos 40
        Attributes:
            handleText <Level 1 Heading>, pos 60
        handleEndTag <h1>, pos 60
        handleStartTag <p>, pos 80
        Attributes: align=center
            handleText <A paragraph with some >, pos 105
            handleStartTag <b>, pos 105
            Attributes:
                handleText <bold>, pos 113
            handleEndTag <b>, pos 113
            handleText < >, pos 131
            handleStartTag <font>, pos 131
```

```
        Attributes: color=red
            handleText <red>, pos 141
        handleEndTag <font>, pos 141
        handleText < text.>, pos 148
     handleEndTag <p>, pos 148
   handleEndTag <body>, pos 148
handleEndTag <html>, pos 148
handleSimpleTag <__EndOfLineTag__>, pos 148
Attributes: __EndOfLineString__=
```

```
flush called
```

This output illustrates several aspects of the parser that we mentioned earlier in this section. If you compare what the parser generates with the HTML
that it was given, you'll notice that despite the fact that the source document
did not contain <HTML>, <HEAD>, and <BODY> tags, the parser still called the
handleStartTag and handleEndTag methods just as if these tags had all
been specified. The entire document therefore appears to be bracketed by an
<HTML>, </HTML> pair and there is also an empty <HEAD> block. The fact that
these tags are fabricated by the parser means that the HTMLDocument implementation can assume that it will always see a certain minimum set of elements no matter what the original document actually looks like.

Looking a bit further down, you'll see how the parser handled the <H1>
tag. As you can see, it passed on the opening and closing tags as they occurred
and, in between, called handleText with the characters that make up the
actual text of the heading. All text is passed to the handleText method, so
there is nothing to distinguish heading text from the actual document content, except the context in which it was received. As you'll see later, the structure of the HTMLDocument that is created as a result of the method calls made
by the parser reflects the context in which each of these methods were
invoked.

This simple document contains only one paragraph of real content (if you
can call it that!). The start of the paragraph is marked with a <P> tag, which is
reflected by the parser calling handleStartTag. In typical lazy style, however, the optional closing tag (</P>) has been omitted, but the parser still
called handleEndTag as if it had been present, as you can see near the end of
the parser output. In fact, all the last three tags were invented by the parser.

How does this happen? Internally, the parser keeps a stack of tags. As a
new opening tag is detected, it is processed and then pushed onto the stack.
Even opening tags that aren't found in the document (such as <HTML> in this
case) are pushed onto the tag stack. When the corresponding end tag is
found, the original tag is popped off the stack. In some cases, though, end

tags are omitted and two consecutive start tags will be found together. For example, in a case like this:

```
<P>
First paragraph
<P>
```

the first `<P>` will be pushed onto the tag stack and the text will be processed. When the second `<P>` is encountered, the parser will check the stack and will see the original `<P>` there. Because paragraphs cannot be nested, the first `<P>` will be popped off the stack and `handleEndTag` will be called with `<P>` as the tag, thus simulating the occurrence of `</P>`. The second `<P>` will then be pushed and the process will continue. Because most HTML documents omit the `</P>` tag, this particular scenario occurs very frequently when parsing HTML documents.

When the end of the input document is reached, the tag stack should be empty, but the odds are that it is not, because most HTML documents leave out as many tags as they can get away with. In the case of this example, an `<HTML>` tag and a `<BODY>` tag are pushed onto the stack before any content is processed and these tags stay there until the corresponding end tag is found which, in this case, will not happen. As well as these tags, there also will be the `<P>` tag that marked the start of the only paragraph of content in the document. Because there is no further input to read, the parser pops any tags that are left on the stack and calls the `handleEndTag` method for each of them. This is why it appears from the parser output as if the document ended with the sequence:

```
</P>
</BODY>
</HTML>
```

none of which actually present in the document.

The text in this small document contains some markup that affects the way it will be formatted. The word `bold` will be rendered in bold because of the `<B>`, `</B>` tag pair, while the `<FONT>` tag will cause the word `red` to appear in red. The parser calls `handleStartTag` and `handleEndTag` once for each of these pairs of tags, with the content supplied in intervening invocations of `handleText`. The `handleStartTag` call for the `<FONT>` tag is more interesting because this call passes a non-empty `MutableAttributeSet`. As you can see from the parser output, the attributes from the parser exactly mirror the ones used with the tag—the attribute name is `color` and its value is `red`. You'll see later exactly how these attributes are stored in the `HTMLDocument` and how they are subsequently used by the `View` that will draw the text. If you look at the `handleStartTag` call for the `<P>` tag, you'll see that this call passed the `ALIGN=CENTER` attribute in the same way.

If we wanted text that was both bold and red, we would have nested the markup like this:

```
This is <B><FONT COLOR=red>bold and red</FONT></B> text
```

so that both attribute changes apply to the enclosed content. It is a common mistake to create plausible but incorrect markup like the following:

```
This is <B><FONT COLOR=red>bold and red</B></FONT> text
```

This is wrong because the `</B>` tag should appear after the `</FONT>`, unwinding the markup in the order in which it was applied. When the parser reads this sequence, it stacks the `<B>` and `<FONT>` tags, calling `handleStart-Tag` for both of them. When it reaches the `</B>` tag, it expects to find a `<B>` tag at the top of the stack, but instead it finds `<FONT>` and detects that the end tag `</FONT>` is missing. If the DTD specified that the `</FONT>` tag were optional then, as you saw with the `<P>` tag, the parser would assume the presence of `</FONT>` and just call `handleEndTag` with the tag argument set to `HTML.Tag.FONT`. Because this end tag is not optional, however, this is an error and the parser instead calls `handleError` with an error message that describes what has happened. You can see this by running the `ReplaceReader` command and passing it the filename `c:\AdvancedSwing\Examples\AdvancedSwing\Chapter4\ReplaceReader2.html` as its argument. This file contains the markup section shown previously. You may be surprised to find that the text actually appears as it was intended to—that is, the words `bold and red` are as they describe themselves and the word `text` is in black. The output from this command looks like this:

```
handleStartTag <html>, pos 9
Attributes:
   handleStartTag <head>, pos 17
   Attributes:
   handleEndTag <head>, pos 17
   handleStartTag <body>, pos 17
   Attributes:
      handleText <This is >, pos 28
      handleStartTag <b>, pos 28
      Attributes:
         handleStartTag <font>, pos 44
         Attributes: color=red
            handleText <bold and red>, pos 60
            handleError <end.missingfont??>, pos 60
         handleEndTag <font>, pos 60
```

```
        handleEndTag <b>, pos 60
        handleError <unmatched.endtagfont??>, pos 67
        handleText < text>, pos 81
    handleEndTag <body>, pos 81
handleEndTag <html>, pos 89
handleSimpleTag <__EndOfLineTag__>, pos 89
Attributes: __EndOfLineString__=
```

```
flush called
```

Immediately after the `handleText` call for the text `bold  and  red`, you can see the `handleError` call that reports the missing tag. To recover the situation, the parser calls `handleEndTag` anyway, effectively generating the `</FONT>` tag that it was expecting. The effect of this is to store correct HTML in the `HTMLDocument`. This is why the text is correctly rendered, despite the fact that the tags were in the wrong order. Next, `handleEndTag` is called for the `</B>` tag that started the error recovery sequence. Next, the parser finds the `</FONT>` tag that was expected earlier. This tag, too, is incorrect in the context in which the parser finds it, because the tag at the top of the stack is now `<BODY>`, not `<FONT>` so, as you can see, `handleError` is called again. Notice, however, that the two invocations of `handleError` are slightly different: the first declares a missing tag, while the second claims there is an unmatched end tag. However, both of these calls were made when the parser found an end tag for a tag that was not at the top of the tag stack, so why does it generate different errors for these two cases? This happens because when the parser finds an end tag that seems to be out of sequence, it looks down the tag stack to see if it can find the matching open tag. If it can, as would be the case with the `</B>` tag, it clears the tag stack up to the matched tag and generates a missing tag error. In the second case, however, there is no `<FONT>` tag on the stack, so a different error results.

The `HTMLDocument` class

Now that you've seen what the HTML parser does and how the results of the parsing operation are received by the `HTMLReader` class, it's time to look at how the parser's output is turned into a `Document`. The document class used when an HTML page is loaded into `JEditorPane` is `HTMLDocument`, which is derived from `DefaultStyledDocument`. We spent some time in Chapter 2 looking at the internals of `DefaultStyledDocument`, examining the `Elements` and `AttributeSets` that are created when you use `JTextPane` to create documents with a mixture of fonts, colors, and other components. All of this, of course, still applies to some degree to `HTMLDocument`, because it inherits the behavior and implementation of DefaultStyledDocument. However, as you'll see in this section, the way in which HTMLDocument uses the basic facilities offered by DefaultStyledDocument is quite different from the way that you saw when we looked at JTextPane in Chapter 2.

The Structure of an *HTMLDocument*

Before looking in detail at the internals of HTMLDocument, let's recap the document structure used by DefaultStyledDocument upon which that of HTMLDocument is based:

- The logical layout of the document is built using Elements.
- There are two Element subclasses that are used to build a tree structure reflecting a document's organization: LeafElements that hold the actual document content and BranchElements that permit nesting by holding references to other BranchElements or to LeafElements. A LeafElement cannot contain other Elements and is always the terminal Element of a branch of the tree.
- In practice, in DefaultStyledDocument a BranchElement typically represents a paragraph, while a LeafElement holds a run of text.
- Each Element can hold an AttributeSet that describes the way in which the text that it encloses should be rendered. The AttributeSet attached to a BranchElement contains paragraph-level attributes, while those at the LeafElement level are attached to the text covered by the element. The attributes are hierarchical, so that those associated with the LeafElement take precedence over the attributes in its containing BranchElement.
- The attributes directly describe the way in which the associated text will be rendered. For example, there are attributes that control the foreground color and font of the text and the margins of paragraphs.

To see how an HTMLDocument is structured, type the following command:

```
java AdvancedSwing.Chapter4.ShowHTMLDocument url
```

where *url* is the URL of an HTML page. A simple page that contains enough HTML to show most of the internals of HTMLDocument is included with the examples supplied with this book. If you installed these examples in the recommended location, the following URL will load the page:

```
file:///c:\AdvancedSwing\Examples\AdvancedSwing\Chapter4\
   SimplePage.html
```

The content of the model after the page has been loaded is displayed on standard output. Because there is quite a lot of output, you might want to redirect it to a file and view it using an editor. The content of this basic HTML page is shown here:

```
<HTML>
<HEAD>
<TITLE>Simple HTML Page</TITLE>
</HEAD>
<BODY>
<!-- An HTML comment -->
<H1>Level 1 heading</H1>
<P>
Standard paragraph with <FONT COLOR=red SIZE=+2>large red</
FONT>
text.
<P ALIGN=right>
Right-aligned paragraph.
<P>
<BL>
<LI>Bullet 1.
<LI>Bullet 2.
<LI>Bullet 3.
</BL>
<P>
A paragraph with an embedded
<IMG SRC="images/lemsmall.jpg" ALT="LEM image"> image.
</BODY>
</HTML>
```

As you can see, this is a very basic (and not very useful) HTML page, containing a heading, a couple of paragraphs of text, a bulleted list, and an embedded image. Nevertheless, it creates an HTMLDocument that is surprisingly large. Here is the output produced by ShowHTMLDocument for this page:

```
===== Element Class: HTMLDocument$BlockElement
Offsets [0, 161]
ATTRIBUTES:
  (name, html) [StyleConstants/HTML$Tag]
  ===== Element Class: HTMLDocument$BlockElement
  Offsets [0, 5]
  ATTRIBUTES:
    (name, p-implied) [StyleConstants/HTML$Tag]
```

```
===== Element Class: HTMLDocument$RunElement
Offsets [0, 1]
ATTRIBUTES:
 (name, head) [StyleConstants/HTML$Tag]
 [ ]
===== Element Class: HTMLDocument$RunElement
Offsets [1, 2]
ATTRIBUTES:
 (name, title) [StyleConstants/HTML$Tag]
 [ ]
===== Element Class: HTMLDocument$RunElement
Offsets [2, 3]
ATTRIBUTES:
 (name, title) [StyleConstants/HTML$Tag]
 (endtag, true) [HTML$Attribute/String]
 [ ]
===== Element Class: HTMLDocument$RunElement
Offsets [3, 4]
ATTRIBUTES:
 (name, head) [StyleConstants/HTML$Tag]
 (endtag, true) [HTML$Attribute/String]
 [ ]
===== Element Class: HTMLDocument$RunElement
Offsets [4, 5]
ATTRIBUTES:
 (name, content) [StyleConstants/HTML$Tag]
 [
]
  ===== Element Class: HTMLDocument$BlockElement
  Offsets [5, 161]
  ATTRIBUTES:
   (name, body) [StyleConstants/HTML$Tag]
    ===== Element Class: HTMLDocument$BlockElement
    Offsets [5, 7]
    ATTRIBUTES:
     (name, p-implied) [StyleConstants/HTML$Tag]
      ===== Element Class: HTMLDocument$RunElement
      Offsets [5, 6]
      ATTRIBUTES:
       (name, comment) [StyleConstants/HTML$Tag]
       (comment,  An HTML comment ) [HTML$Attribute/String]
       [ ]
      ===== Element Class: HTMLDocument$RunElement
      Offsets [6, 7]
      ATTRIBUTES:
       (name, content) [StyleConstants/HTML$Tag]
```

```
      [
]
    ===== Element Class: HTMLDocument$BlockElement
    Offsets [7, 23]
    ATTRIBUTES:
     (name, h1) [StyleConstants/HTML$Tag]
      ===== Element Class: HTMLDocument$RunElement
      Offsets [7, 22]
      ATTRIBUTES:
       (name, content) [StyleConstants/HTML$Tag]
      [Level 1 heading]
      ===== Element Class: HTMLDocument$RunElement
      Offsets [22, 23]
      ATTRIBUTES:
       (name, content) [StyleConstants/HTML$Tag]
      [
]
    ===== Element Class: HTMLDocument$BlockElement
    Offsets [23, 63]
    ATTRIBUTES:
     (name, p) [StyleConstants/HTML$Tag]
      ===== Element Class: HTMLDocument$RunElement
      Offsets [23, 47]
      ATTRIBUTES:
       (name, content) [StyleConstants/HTML$Tag]
      [Standard paragraph with ]
      ===== Element Class: HTMLDocument$RunElement
      Offsets [47, 56]
      ATTRIBUTES:
       (name, content) [StyleConstants/HTML$Tag]
       (font, size=+2 color=red ) [
          HTML$Tag/SimpleAttributeSet]
      [large red]
      ===== Element Class: HTMLDocument$RunElement
      Offsets [56, 62]
      ATTRIBUTES:
       (name, content) [StyleConstants/HTML$Tag]
      [ text.]
      ===== Element Class: HTMLDocument$RunElement
      Offsets [62, 63]
      ATTRIBUTES:
       (name, content) [StyleConstants/HTML$Tag]
      [
]
    ===== Element Class: HTMLDocument$BlockElement
    Offsets [63, 88]
```

```
    ATTRIBUTES:
     (name, p) [StyleConstants/HTML$Tag]
     (align, right) [HTML$Attribute/String]
      ===== Element Class: HTMLDocument$RunElement
      Offsets [63, 87]
      ATTRIBUTES:
       (name, content) [StyleConstants/HTML$Tag]
      [Right-aligned paragraph.]
      ===== Element Class: HTMLDocument$RunElement
      Offsets [87, 88]
      ATTRIBUTES:
       (name, content) [StyleConstants/HTML$Tag]
       [
]

    ===== Element Class: HTMLDocument$BlockElement
    Offsets [88, 90]
    ATTRIBUTES:
     (name, p) [StyleConstants/HTML$Tag]
      ===== Element Class: HTMLDocument$RunElement
      Offsets [88, 89]
      ATTRIBUTES:
       (name, bl) [StyleConstants/HTML$UnknownTag]
       [ ]
      ===== Element Class: HTMLDocument$RunElement
      Offsets [89, 90]
      ATTRIBUTES:
       (name, content) [StyleConstants/HTML$Tag]
       [
]

    ===== Element Class: HTMLDocument$BlockElement
    Offsets [90, 160]
    ATTRIBUTES:
     (name, ul) [StyleConstants/HTML$Tag]
      ===== Element Class: HTMLDocument$BlockElement
      Offsets [90, 100]
      ATTRIBUTES:
       (name, li) [StyleConstants/HTML$Tag]
        ===== Element Class: HTMLDocument$BlockElement
        Offsets [90, 100]
        ATTRIBUTES:
         (name, p-implied) [StyleConstants/HTML$Tag]
          ===== Element Class: HTMLDocument$RunElement
          Offsets [90, 99]
          ATTRIBUTES:
           (name, content) [StyleConstants/HTML$Tag]
          [Bullet 1.]
```

```
      ===== Element Class: HTMLDocument$RunElement
      Offsets [99, 100]
      ATTRIBUTES:
       (name, content) [StyleConstants/HTML$Tag]
       [
  ]
    ===== Element Class: HTMLDocument$BlockElement
    Offsets [100, 110]
    ATTRIBUTES:
     (name, li) [StyleConstants/HTML$Tag]
      ===== Element Class: HTMLDocument$BlockElement
      Offsets [100, 110]
      ATTRIBUTES:
        (name, p-implied) [StyleConstants/HTML$Tag]
        ===== Element Class: HTMLDocument$RunElement
        Offsets [100, 109]
        ATTRIBUTES:
         (name, content) [StyleConstants/HTML$Tag]
         [Bullet 2.]
        ===== Element Class: HTMLDocument$RunElement
        Offsets [109, 110]
        ATTRIBUTES:
         (name, content) [StyleConstants/HTML$Tag]
         [
  ]
    ===== Element Class: HTMLDocument$BlockElement
    Offsets [110, 160]
    ATTRIBUTES:
     (name, li) [StyleConstants/HTML$Tag]
      ===== Element Class: HTMLDocument$BlockElement
      Offsets [110, 122]
      ATTRIBUTES:
        (name, p-implied) [StyleConstants/HTML$Tag]
        ===== Element Class: HTMLDocument$RunElement
        Offsets [110, 120]
        ATTRIBUTES:
         (name, content) [StyleConstants/HTML$Tag]
         [Bullet 3. ]
        ===== Element Class: HTMLDocument$RunElement
        Offsets [120, 121]
        ATTRIBUTES:
         (name, bl) [StyleConstants/HTML$UnknownTag]
         (endtag, true) [HTML$Attribute/String]
         [ ]

      ===== Element Class: HTMLDocument$RunElement
```

```
                Offsets [121, 122]
                ATTRIBUTES:
                  (name, content) [StyleConstants/HTML$Tag]
                  [
  ]
            ===== Element Class: HTMLDocument$BlockElement
            Offsets [122, 160]
            ATTRIBUTES:
              (name, p) [StyleConstants/HTML$Tag]
                ===== Element Class: HTMLDocument$RunElement
                Offsets [122, 151]
                ATTRIBUTES:
                  (name, content) [StyleConstants/HTML$Tag]
                [A paragraph with an embedded ]
                ===== Element Class: HTMLDocument$RunElement
                Offsets [151, 152]
                ATTRIBUTES:
                  (name, img) [StyleConstants/HTML$Tag]
                  (src, images/lemsmall.jpg) [HTML$Attribute/String]
                  (alt, LEM image) [HTML$Attribute/String]
                  [ ]
                ===== Element Class: HTMLDocument$RunElement
                Offsets [152, 159]
                ATTRIBUTES:
                  (name, content) [StyleConstants/HTML$Tag]
                [ image.]
                ===== Element Class: HTMLDocument$RunElement
                Offsets [159, 160]
                ATTRIBUTES:
                  (name, content) [StyleConstants/HTML$Tag]
                  [
  ]
===== Element Class: HTMLDocument$BlockElement
    Offsets [160, 161]
    ATTRIBUTES:
      (name, p) [StyleConstants/HTML$Tag]
        ===== Element Class: HTMLDocument$RunElement
        Offsets [160, 161]
        ATTRIBUTES:
          (name, content) [StyleConstants/HTML$Tag]
          [
  ]
```

You should recognize the general structure from our earlier discussions of JTextPane in Chapter 2. Each element in the document is shown separately, with the indentation reflecting the nesting of elements. If you scan through the output, you'll notice that there are two different types of element, one of class `HTMLDocument.BlockElement`, the other `HTMLDocument.RunElement`. These are, in fact, the only element types used by `HTMLDocument`; the first is a `BranchElement` and the second a `LeafElement`. As their names suggest, the former basically represents a block within the original HTML document while the latter marks out actual renderable content.

If you work down from the top, you probably won't be surprised to see that the document opens with a `BlockElement`. This `Element` is the root of the document structure and contains everything else within it, as you can see from the range of offsets that it covers. Associated with this `Element` (and with every `Element`) is an `AttributeSet` that actually contains most of the useful information from the original HTML. In the case of the root element, there is only one attribute:

```
===== Element Class: HTMLDocument$BlockElement
Offsets [0, 161]
ATTRIBUTES:
 (name, html) [StyleConstants/HTML$Tag]
```

The attributes are displayed first by value and then by class. In this case, there is an attribute whose name is `name` with the value `html`. As you know, an attribute is just a key-value pair in which both the key and the value are `Object`s of some kind: In the representation shown here, what you see is the result of extracting both the attribute name and attribute value objects and applying the `toString` method to each of them. In fact, the attribute name is an object of type `javax.swing.text.StyleConstants`, while the class of the value is `javax.swing.text.html.HTML.Tag`. For clarity and to save space, we have removed the package prefix and only shown the class names themselves. The attribute that describes itself as `name` is the very same `StyleConstants.Name-Attribute` object that you were introduced to in "Attribute Sets" in Chapter 2, where we said it was the name of the `AttributeSet` that contained it; in a `Style`, it contains the name of the `Style` itself. In this context, the `Name-Attribute` is being used slightly differently. Instead of naming a `Style`, when it would have a `String` value associated with it, its value is instead of type `HTML.Tag`. Earlier in this section, we said that `Object`s of this type are the internal representation of an HTML tag and, in this case, the `NameAttribute` has the value `HTML.Tag.HTML`. In fact, this attribute represents the occurrence within the original page of the opening `<HTML>` tag. In general, when an HTML tag is encountered in the source Web page, it becomes an `Element` with an `AttributeSet` containing an attribute called `name` whose value is the `Object` representing that tag from the set of constant `HTML.Tag` objects defined by the class `javax.swing.text.html.HTML`.

The next couple of Elements look like this:

```
===== Element Class: HTMLDocument$BlockElement
  Offsets [0, 5]
  ATTRIBUTES:
   (name, p-implied) [StyleConstants/HTML$Tag]
    ===== Element Class: HTMLDocument$RunElement
    Offsets [0, 1]
    ATTRIBUTES:
     (name, head) [StyleConstants/HTML$Tag]
     [ ]
```

The first of these describes itself as p-implied, which means an implied paragraph. While an HTMLDocument is being built, an implied paragraph Element is usually generated as a substitute for a missing <P> tag. Here, however, it would be unusual to have a <P> tag directly after <HTML>. The only purpose that this tag appears to serve is to act as a container for the part of the HTMLDocument that precedes the <BODY> tag. The following Element represents the <HEAD> tag. In the case of this particular Web page, the <HEAD> tag was actually present but it need not have been—as you saw when we looked at the Parser, if this tag had not been found in the source document, the Parser would have synthesized one and this Element would have been inserted in the HTMLDocument anyway. In our simple Web page, the HEAD block contains only <TITLE>, the text of the title itself and the closing </TITLE> tag. The representation of this sequence in the HTMLDocument is the following:

```
===== Element Class: HTMLDocument$RunElement
    Offsets [1, 2]
    ATTRIBUTES:
     (name, title) [StyleConstants/HTML$Tag]
     [ ]
    ===== Element Class: HTMLDocument$RunElement
    Offsets [2, 3]
    ATTRIBUTES:
     (name, title) [StyleConstants/HTML$Tag]
     (endtag, true) [HTML$Attribute/String]
     [ ]
    ===== Element Class: HTMLDocument$RunElement
    Offsets [3, 4]
    ATTRIBUTES:
     (name, head) [StyleConstants/HTML$Tag]
     (endtag, true) [HTML$Attribute/String]
     [ ]
    ===== Element Class: HTMLDocument$RunElement
    Offsets [4, 5]
```

```
ATTRIBUTES:
  (name, content) [StyleConstants/HTML$Tag]
  [
]
```

The first `Element` in this set is not a `BlockElement`, but a `RunElement`, which usually indicates that it contains renderable content. In this case, though, the `RunElement` has an `AttributeSet` containing a `NameAttribute` with value `HTML.Tag.TITLE`, identifying it as the beginning of the document title. The title itself is not actually stored in the `Document`—as you can see, this `Element` is followed immediately not by the title text, but by another `Element` whose `NameAttribute` is `HTML.Tag.TITLE` representing the `</TITLE>` tag that follows the title text in the source page. Even though it has the same `NameAttribute` as that of the `Element` for the `<TITLE>` tag, you can tell that it represents a closing tag because it has a second attribute called `HTML.Attribute.ENDTAG` with the associated `String` value `true`.

At this point, we have to start being careful with our terminology. In the context of `DefaultStyledDocument`, when we use the term attribute, we mean a member of an `AttributeSet` such as `StyleConstants.Name-Attribute` or, in the case of `HTMLDocument`, `HTML.Tag.HTML`. In the context of HTML itself, though, the term attribute has a more precise meaning. Here, an attribute is a qualifier to an HTML tag. Like `DefaultStyledDocu-ment` attributes, HTML attributes are specified as name-value pairs, such as

```
ALIGN="CENTER"
```

where `ALIGN` is the HTML attribute and `CENTER` is its value. Each HTML tag has a set of valid HTML attributes that may be used with it, defined by the DTD. `Elements` in an `HTMLDocument` may have attributes whose names are `Objects` that represent HTML attributes, of which the `</TITLE>` tag is an example. Every end tag contains the `HTML.Attribute.ENDTAG` attribute to distinguish it from the corresponding opening tag. Just as the `javax.swing.text.html.HTML.Tag` class defines a set of constant `Objects` that represent all the HTML tags that it recognizes, there is also a corresponding set of `Objects` of type `HTML.Attribute` that represent the valid HTML attributes. The sets of HTML tags and HTML attributes defined in this class are both supersets of those in the HTML 3.2 DTD, because the current Swing HTML package can parse and represent (but not necessarily display) everything in HTML 3.2 as well as some extensions from HTML 4.0 (such as style sheets, a topic that will be covered later). Because we now have two different meanings for the word attribute in use at the same time, where it is not clear from the context which is meant, we will explicitly use the term HTML attribute where necessary. Just to confuse matters further, later in this chapter, you'll meet another use of the word attribute with another, slightly different meaning.

Returning to the content of the HTMLDocument, you may be wondering what happened to the document title text. It isn't stored as content within the model and it doesn't appear in the JEditorPane either, as you can see from Figure 4-11, which shows what this example Web page looks like when loaded using the ShowHTMLDocument application.

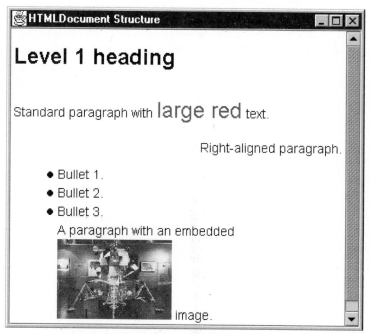

Figure 4-11   A simple HTML document loaded using JEditorPane.

In fact, when the HTMLReader is given the title text by the Parser, it stores it as a property of the document called Document.TitleProperty; if you want to use it to set the caption of the frame that the JEditorPane is installed in, you can use the following code to do so:

```
frame.setTitle((String)doc.getProperty(Document.TitleProperty));
```

Unfortunately, the Document properties are not bound properties, so it isn't possible to register a PropertyChangeListener to pick up the title as soon as it is known. Instead, you'll either have to wait until the document has been loaded or add this code to the ParserCallback using the technique you saw earlier.

The Element following the </TITLE> tag is a RunElement with the Name-Attribute set to HTML.Tag.CONTENT. This special tag value represents raw content from the HTML document itself; the original text is held in the Document at the offsets indicated by the `Element`. In this case, the text itself consists of a single newline character. This final tag completes the `<HEAD>` section of the document, as you can see from the indentation of the tags in the program output. The next `Element` is a `BlockElement` that encloses the document body; as you might expect by now, it has an associated `Name-Attribute` with value `HTML.Tag.BODY`.

The body of this HTML file begins with a single-line comment, delimited by the usual start and end comment tags. Although the start and end markers could be considered to be tags, the `HTMLDocument` doesn't store the comment as a start tag/content/end tag triplet. Instead, the entire comment is stored in one `Element`, which makes it easy for the `View` that will render this comment to access it. The `Element` for the comment looks like this:

```
===== Element Class: HTMLDocument$RunElement
      Offsets [5, 6]
      ATTRIBUTES:
       (name, comment) [StyleConstants/HTML$Tag]
       (comment,  An HTML comment ) [HTML$Attribute/String]
      [ ]
```

Notice that this `Element` has a `NameAttribute` with value `comment`, as you might expect, and also an attribute called `comment` with the comment string stored as its value. These are, in fact, different `Objects`—the first is an `HTML.Tag.COMMENT` and the second an `HTML.Attribute.COMMENT`. The HTML DTD does not define a `COMMENT` attribute—this is an additional attribute created for the purpose of storing the comment within an `HTML-Document`, just as the tag `HTML.Tag.CONTENT` was added to distinguish real document content from the internal representation of a tag and its accompanying HTML attributes. If you look at the offsets associated with this `Element`, you'll see that the comment isn't stored inline with the rest of the `Document` data—it is actually held as the value of the `COMMENT` attribute.

By contrast to the comment, the level 1 heading is not compressed into a second `Element`; instead, it is broken up into its constituent parts:

```
===== Element Class: HTMLDocument$BlockElement
    Offsets [7, 23]
    ATTRIBUTES:
     (name, h1) [StyleConstants/HTML$Tag]
      ===== Element Class: HTMLDocument$RunElement
      Offsets [7, 22]
      ATTRIBUTES:
       (name, content) [StyleConstants/HTML$Tag]
      [Level 1 heading]
      ===== Element Class: HTMLDocument$RunElement
```

```
    Offsets [22, 23]
    ATTRIBUTES:
     (name, content) [StyleConstants/HTML$Tag]
     [
]
```

The heading is created as a `BlockElement` labeled as `HTML.Tag.H1` wrapping a `RunElement` containing the heading text (the tag for which is, of course, `HTML.Tag.CONTENT`) and a terminating newline character. It might seem to be overkill to use a `BlockElement` for this purpose—why not use the same shortcut used for the comment and place the heading text in a single `RunElement` with name `HTML.Tag.H1` and the text stored as the value of another special attribute? The advantage of using a `BlockElement` for this is that it allows the heading to be made up of more than one run of text, yet still be rendered as heading text. This means that you can write something like this:

```
<H1>A heading with <I>italic</I> text</H1>
```

This particular heading would be split into three logical pieces—the text before the italicized region, the italicized part itself, and the text that follows it, all bounded by the `HTML.Tag.H1` `BlockElement`. The effect of bounding these three parts within a `BlockElement` is that all of them will be rendered with the drawing attributes (color, font, and so forth) appropriate for a level 1 heading, with the italics added as an extra for the word `italic` only. This actually works much like the paragraph and character level attributes that you saw in connection with `JTextPane` and `DefaultStyledDocument` in Chapter 2 where, in this case, the `BlockElement` is acting as a paragraph. You'll see more about how the drawing attributes are determined when we look at Style Sheets and `Views` later in this chapter.

The next section of output covers the first paragraph of text in the document:

```
===== Element Class: HTMLDocument$BlockElement
    Offsets [23, 63]
    ATTRIBUTES:
     (name, p) [StyleConstants/HTML$Tag]
      ===== Element Class: HTMLDocument$RunElement
     Offsets [23, 47]
     ATTRIBUTES:
      (name, content) [StyleConstants/HTML$Tag]
     [Standard paragraph with ]
      ===== Element Class: HTMLDocument$RunElement
     Offsets [47, 56]
     ATTRIBUTES:
      (name, content) [StyleConstants/HTML$Tag]
      (font, size=+2 color=red) [HTML$Tag/SimpleAttributeSet]
     [large red]
```

```
===== Element Class: HTMLDocument$RunElement
Offsets [56, 62]
ATTRIBUTES:
 (name, content) [StyleConstants/HTML$Tag]
[ text.]
===== Element Class: HTMLDocument$RunElement
Offsets [62, 63]
ATTRIBUTES:
 (name, content) [StyleConstants/HTML$Tag]
[
```

This part of the HTMLDocument is a paragraph, as indicated by the Block-View with the NameAttribute set to HTML.Tag.P, containing four RunElements, all of type HTML.Tag.CONTENT—in other words, real text from the original document. The first and the last two of these Elements are relatively uninteresting because they represent text drawn with whatever rendering attributes are applied to text within a paragraph. The second Element, though, is different, because it results from the following piece of HTML:

```
<FONT COLOR=red SIZE=+2>large red</FONT>
```

As you can see, the <FONT> and </FONT> tags do not have separate Elements within the model as other tags seem to. Instead, the <FONT> tag has been reduced to an attribute attached to the RunElement for the text that it affects. The value associated with this attribute is another AttributeSet (actually a SimpleAttributeSet) that contains the HTML attributes from the tag. Not surprisingly, although it is not shown that way here, there is one entry in this set for each HTML attribute, together with its value. In this case, the SimpleAttributeSet contains:

- an attribute with name HTML.Attribute.COLOR with the String value red.
- an attribute with name HTML.Attribute.SIZE with the String value +2.

Notice that the attribute in the original Element that represents <FONT> is actually of type HTML.Tag and not HTML.Attribute as you might have expected, because <FONT> is, after all, an HTML tag and not an HTML attribute. A similar thing would have happened to the following HTML sequence:

```
<I>italic text</I>
```

where the <I> tag would have been replaced by an attribute with the name HTML.Tag.I in the RunElement for the associated text.

The structure and content of the rest of the `HTMLDocument` follows a similar pattern and should now be readily understandable. You might find it interesting, though, to look at the structure of the bulleted list. As you would probably expect, the entire list resides within a `BlockElement`, within which each `<LI>` item has a child `Element` of its own. You may be surprised to see, though, that the `<LI>` `Elements` are themselves `BlockElements`, not `RunElements`. As with the heading text, the reason for this is that an `<LI>` tag may contain other markup—we could, for example, write

```
<LI> Bullet <FONT=RED>1</FONT>
```

and it is clear that a `BlockElement` would be needed to group together the pieces of this item.

Finally, the image at the end of the document is represented as a `RunElement` associated with a single character of data (which does not actually exist in the original HTML document itself and will not be drawn by the `View` that eventually renders the image):

```
===== Element Class: HTMLDocument$RunElement
          Offsets [151, 152]
          ATTRIBUTES:
           (name, img) [StyleConstants/HTML$Tag]
           (src, images/lemsmall.jpg) [HTML$Attribute/String]
           (alt, LEM image) [HTML$Attribute/String]
           [ ]
```

Here, the `RunElement` has a `NameAttribute` of `HTML.Tag.IMG` instead of `HTML.Tag.CONTENT`, so you can tell immediately that this `Element` does not represent text. The two HTML attributes that appeared in the Web page have become attributes in the associated `AttributeSet`, both of type `HTML.Attribute` and with `String` values. The value associated with the `ALT` attribute is, of course, the `String` from the original HTML, as is also the case with the `SRC` attribute. Here, though, the `SRC` attribute doesn't contain a full URL specification, because only a relative URL was supplied in the original HTML. When this image is displayed, it will be located by using the URL of the page itself as the base URL, together with the partial URL stored in the `SRC` attribute. The page URL is actually stored in the `HTMLDocument` as a document property called `Document.StreamDescriptionProperty` and, as you'll see later, it is used whenever a relative URL within the document needs to be resolved—typically when following the target of a hypertext link.

Supported HTML Tags and Attributes

The set of HTML tags and HTML attributes recognized by the Swing HTML package is ultimately determined both by the DTD and by the set of constant `HTML.Tag` and `HTML.Attribute` objects defined by the `javax.swing.text.html.HTML` class. You can find out what is supported by looking in the source code, or you can use the following static methods of the HTML class:

```
public static HTML.Tag[] getAllTags();

public static HTML.Attribute[] getAllAttributeKeys();
```

The example code that accompanies this book contains a simple program that invokes these two methods and prints the results, which you can run using the command

```
java AdvancedSwing.Chapter4.ListHTMLValues
```

The results obtained from this command using the version of Swing available at the time are summarized in Tables 4-3 and 4-4. If you are using a later version of Swing, you might want to run this command to check for extra tags and attributes.

Table 4-3 Recognized HTML Tags

a	address	applet	area	b	base	base-font	big
block-quote	body	br	caption	center	cite	code	dd
dfn	dir	div	dl	dt	em	font	form
frame	frameset	h1	h2	h3	h4	h5	h6
head	hr	html	I	img	input	isindex	kbd
li	link	map	menu	meta	noframes	object	ol
option	p	param	pre	samp	script	select	small
strike	s	strong	style	sub	sup	table	td
textarea	th	title	tr	tt	u	ul	var

Table 4-4 Recognized HTML Attributes

action	align	alink	alt	archive	background	bgcolor	border
cellpadding	cellspacing	checked	class	classid	clear	code	codebase
codetype	color	cols	colspan	comment	compact	content	coords
data	declare	dir	dummy	enctype	frameborder	halign	height
href	hspace	http-equiv	id	ismap	lang	language	link
lowsrc	marginheight	marginwidth	maxlength	method	multiple	name	nohref
noresize	noshade	nowrap	prompt	rel	rev	rows	rowspan
scrolling	selected	src	shape	shapes	size	standby	start
style	target	text	title	type	usemap	valign	value
valuetype	version	vlink	vspace	width			

Note, however, that the appearance of a tag or an attribute in these tables does not imply that the associated semantics are supported by the Swing HTML package. An example of this is the APPLET tag, which appears in Table 4-3 but which is not actually supported—if found, it will be included in the HTMLDocument but will have no effect on the rendering of the page in JEditorPane.

Loading Content into an HTMLDocument

Earlier in this chapter, we saw several example programs that loaded HTML pages for the purposes of displaying them in a JEditorPane. All those examples used either the JEditorPane setPage method or the lower-level read method of HTMLEditorKit. Although in many cases this is the most convenient way to load an HTML page, there are circumstances under which it is better to use a more direct approach. Suppose, for example, that you want to fetch an HTML page and scan through it looking for hypertext links to other pages, and then fetch the targets of those links and analyze those too, continuing the process until there are no further linked documents or some threshold is reached. A good reason for doing this would be to create an index of Web documents together with their titles and, perhaps, the first few lines of content, that could be used as the basis for a document search engine. If this is what you want to do, using JEditorPane would not be appropriate because you don't actually want to display the HTML at all. It would still be useful, however, to make use of the parsing capabilities of the Swing HTML package and of the structure of the HTMLDocument that it builds, which allows easy access to the content of the original page in a form that is appropriate for automated processes like scanning for tags or creating a document content summary. All this is possible using the facilities provided by the Swing HTML package and a little extra code that you'll see in this section and the two that follow.

A Class That Loads HTML

Let's start with the problem of loading a document without using a JEditorPane. As you've already seen, most of the mechanics of loading an HTML page are contained in the HTMLEditorKit read method, which is called either from either the read or the setPage method of JEditorPane. Here's the definition of the HTMLEditorKit read method:

```
public void read(Reader in, Document doc, int pos)
           throws IOException, BadLocationException
```

This method reads the content from the given `Reader` into the `Document` starting at location `pos`. It does this by connecting a `Parser` to a `ParserCallback` that will build the structure of the `HTMLDocument`. As you've seen, both the `Parser` and the `ParserCallback` are implemented in the Swing text package and the `read` method uses them by default. To create a class that can load HTML documents without using a `JEditorPane`, it seems that all you would need to do would be to call the `read` method of `HTMLEditorKit` directly, having first created an `HTMLDocument` instance to receive the parsed content and a `Reader` with access to the original document source. This sounds relatively straightforward, but there are two problems:

- A specific `Reader` reads bytes from an `InputStream` and converts it to Unicode characters according to the encoding of the data being delivered from the `InputStream`. To create the appropriate `Reader`, you need to know the encoding of the incoming data.
- The header block of an HTML page can contain an `HTTP-EQUIV` tag that specifies a character set for the body of the HTML page. This tag must be processed properly to read the page correctly.

We've already discussed how this problem is solved by `JEditorPane`. Initially, the source document is assumed to be in the encoding of the platform on which the `JEditorPane` is running, so a `Reader` suitable for that encoding is created. If the encoding changes as a result of an `HTTP-EQUIV` tag or because the Web server returns an encoding specification in the content type information that precedes the HTML itself, a `ChangedCharSetException` is thrown by the `Parser`. The result of this is that a new `Reader` is created, using the correct character encoding, and the input stream is read again from the beginning. The problem is that all of this logic is provided not by the `HTMLEditorKit` read method, but by `JEditorPane` itself. If you want to read documents without using `JEditorPane`, you have to implement something equivalent to this yourself.

Loading HTML is not, then, as simple as calling the `HTMLEditorKit` read method. If we're going to have to write additional code anyway, it's worth looking at what benefit the `HTMLEditorKit` gives us to determine whether it is worth calling its `read` method, or whether we should invoke the lower level interfaces directly. In fact, if you look at the `read` method, you'll find that all it does is the following:

- Gets a `Parser` by calling its own `getParser` method.
- Gets a `ParserCallback` by invoking the `getReader` method of `HTMLDocument`.
- Starts the parsing process by calling the `Parser parse` method, and passing it the `ParserCallback`, the `Reader`, and a `boolean` that indicates whether it should ignore changes of character encoding within the document.
- When parsing is complete, calls the `ParserCallback flush` method to cause it to finish building the `HTMLDocument`.

None of these steps requires access to state information held within the `HTMLEditorKit`, so it doesn't seem worthwhile creating an `HTMLEditorKit` instance for each `HTMLDocument` we want to load. Because there is very little code involved in the process outlined earlier, we might as well implement it ourselves and save the memory overhead of an `HTMLEditorKit` for each document being loaded. If you want to load several documents in parallel, this could be a significant saving.

Listing 4-7 shows the implementation of a class that can load HTML documents without using a `JEditorPane`.

Listing 4-7 A Free-Standing Loader for HTML Documents

```
package AdvancedSwing.Chapter4;

import java.io.*;
import java.net.*;
import java.util.*;
import javax.swing.text.*;
import javax.swing.text.html.*;

public class HTMLDocumentLoader {
    public HTMLDocument loadDocument(HTMLDocument doc,
                          URL url, String charSet)
                          throws IOException {
        doc.putProperty(Document.StreamDescriptionProperty, url);

        /*
         * This loop allows the document read to be retried if
         * the character encoding changes during processing.
```

Listing 4-7 A Free-Standing Loader for HTML Documents (continued)

```
    */
    InputStream in = null;
    boolean ignoreCharSet = false;

    for (;;) {
        try {
            // Remove any document content
            doc.remove(0, doc.getLength());

            URLConnection urlc = url.openConnection();
            in = urlc.getInputStream();
            Reader reader = (charSet == null) ?
                    new InputStreamReader(in) :
                    new InputStreamReader(in, charSet);

            HTMLEditorKit.Parser parser = getParser();
            HTMLEditorKit.ParserCallback htmlReader =
                                    getParserCallback(doc);
            parser.parse(reader, htmlReader, ignoreCharSet);
            htmlReader.flush();

            // All done
            break;
        } catch (BadLocationException ex) {
            // Should not happen - throw an IOException
            throw new IOException(ex.getMessage());
        } catch (ChangedCharSetException e) {
            // The character set has changed - restart
            charSet = getNewCharSet(e);

            // Prevent recursion by suppressing
            // further exceptions
            ignoreCharSet = true;

            // Close original input stream
            in.close();

            // Continue the loop to read with the correct
            // encoding
        }
```

Listing 4-7 A Free-Standing Loader for HTML
            Documents (continued)

```
      }

    return doc;
  }

  public HTMLDocument loadDocument(URL url,
                        String charSet)
                        throws IOException {
    return loadDocument(kit.createDefaultDocument(),
                        url, charSet);
  }

  public HTMLDocument loadDocument(URL url)
                        throws IOException {
    return loadDocument(url, null);
  }

  // Methods that allow customization of the parser and
  // the callback
  public synchronized HTMLEditorKit.Parser getParser() {
    if (parser == null) {
      try {
        Class c = Class.forName("javax.swing.text.html.
                              parser.ParserDelegator");
        parser = (HTMLEditorKit.Parser)c.newInstance();
      } catch (Throwable e) {
      }
    }
    return parser;
  }

  public synchronized HTMLEditorKit.ParserCallback
                    getParseCallback(
                    HTMLDocument doc) {
    return doc.getReader(0);
  }

  protected String getNewCharSet(
                        ChangedCharSetException e) {
    String spec = e.getCharSetSpec();
    if (e.keyEqualsCharSet()) {
      // The event contains the new CharSet
      return spec;
```

Listing 4-7 A Free-Standing Loader for HTML
Documents (continued)

```java
    }

    // The event contains the content type
    // plus ";" plus qualifiers which may
    // contain a "charset" directive. First
    // remove the content type.
    int index = spec.indexOf(";");
    if (index != -1) {
        spec = spec.substring(index + 1);
    }

    // Force the string to lower case
    spec = spec.toLowerCase();

    StringTokenizer st =
                new StringTokenizer(spec, " \t=", true);
    boolean foundCharSet = false;
    boolean foundEquals = false;
    while (st.hasMoreTokens()) {
        String token = st.nextToken();
        if (token.equals(" ") || token.equals("\t")) {
            continue;
        }
        if (foundCharSet == false &&
                foundEquals == false &&
                token.equals("charset")) {
            foundCharSet = true;
            continue;
        } else if (foundEquals == false &&
            token.equals("=")) {
            foundEquals = true;
            continue;
        } else if (foundEquals == true &&
            foundCharSet == true) {
            return token;
        }

        // Not recognized
        foundCharSet = false;
        foundEquals = false;
    }
```

Listing 4-7 A Free-Standing Loader for HTML
                Documents (continued)

```
        // No charset found - return a guess
        return "8859_1";
    }

    protected static HTMLEditorKit kit;
    protected static HTMLEditorKit.Parser parser;

    static {
        kit = new HTMLEditorKit();
    }
}
```

This class provides three methods, all called `loadDocument`, that can be used to parse an HTML page into an `HTMLDocument`:

```
public HTMLDocument loadDocument(HTMLDocument doc, URL url,
                        String charSet) throws IOException
public HTMLDocument loadDocument(URL url, String charSet)
                        throws IOException
public HTMLDocument loadDocument(URL url) throws IOException
```

The first of these three methods is the most generalized version and is the one that actually does all of the real work; the other two simply call the first one, supplying defaults for some of it arguments. If you use the first form, you can supply the `HTMLDocument` that you would like to have populated as well as the initial character encoding for the `Reader` that will be created to read the page, or `null` if you want to use the local platform default (which will usually be the case). Supplying your own `HTMLDocument` is useful if you want to use a non-standard style sheet, a topic that will be covered later in this chapter. Most often, though, you'll probably use one of the two simplified methods that require you to supply only the URL of the page to be read and the source character set in the case of the second method. The third method, of course, uses the native platform encoding.

The first thing that the `loadDocument` method does is to store the URL of the page within the document as a property called `streamDescriptionProperty`. As has been mentioned before, this property is used when resolving relative URLs that might be found within the page (for example, references to images from with `IMG` tags). It then enters a loop that contains the logic for actually reading the page into the HTMLDocument. Before explaining why there needs to be a loop here, let's examine the code that actually loads the document content:

```
// Remove any document content
doc.remove(0, doc.getLength());

URLConnection urlc = url.openConnection();
in = urlc.getInputStream();
Reader reader = (charSet == null) ?
  new InputStreamReader(in) :
  new InputStreamReader(in, charSet);

HTMLEditorKit.Parser parser = getParser();
HTMLEditorKit.ParserCallback htmlReader = getParserCallback();
parser.parse(reader, htmlReader, ignoreCharSet);
htmlReader.flush();
```

This code starts by removing any existing content from the HTMLDocument. In most cases, there won't actually be anything in the HTMLDocument, but there are two reasons for taking this step:

1. The HTMLDocument is created by the caller of this method. Although the caller will usually be one of the other loadDocument methods, which creates an empty HTMLDocument, it could be called directly from application code, so there is no guarantee that the document is initially empty.
2. This code is executed within a loop. On the second pass of this loop, as you'll see, the HTMLDocument might contain data left over from the first pass.

The next step is to create a Reader through which the document itself can be read, given the document's URL. This is a two-step process. First, a connection to the source of the document is obtained using the URL openConnection method. If the source is a Web server, this step will make a connection to the server across the network. If the file is on a local disk, the file will be opened at this point. In either case, the URLConnection object that is returned has an associated InputStream to the document that can be obtained using its getInputStream method.

The second step is to wrap the InputStream with the appropriate Reader so that the incoming bytes can be correctly converted to Unicode. As we've said, creating a Reader from an InputStream is done by using the InputStreamReader class, which requires an encoding name. If an encoding is supplied as an argument to the loadDocument method, it is used here. If it is null, then the platform's default encoding will be used. Conveniently, the `InputStreamReader` class has two constructors, one of which allows you to supply the encoding while the other uses the default, so the correct constructor is used depending on whether this method's `charSet` argument is `null`. As we'll see later, the `charSet` argument can be changed while the page is being read, but let's not worry about that now.

The last step is to create the `Parser` and the `ParserCallback` and call the `Parser`'s parse method to read the Web page into the `HTMLDocument`. Under normal circumstances, the `Parser` would be supplied by `HTMLEditorKit` and the `ParserCallback` by `HTMLDocument`. Here, though, we delegate the creation of both of these objects to methods of the `HTMLDocumentLoader` class. The intention is that you can subclass `HTMLDocumentLoader` if you want to provide your own implementations of either of these objects. Here is how both of these methods are implemented:

```
public HTMLEditorKit.Parser getParser() {
   if (parser == null) {
      try {
         Class c = Class.forName("javax.swing.text.html.
                              parser.ParserDelegator");
         parser = (HTMLEditorKit.Parser)c.newInstance();
      } catch (Throwable e) {
      }
   }
   return parser;
}


public HTMLEditorKit.ParserCallback getParserCallback() {
   return doc.getReader(0);
}
```

The code in the `getParser` method is basically the same as the code used by `HTMLEditorKit` itself, so if this method is not overridden, `HTMLDocumentLoader` will use the standard Swing HTML package `Parser`. Similarly, the `getParserCallback` method uses the default `ParserCallback` supplied by `HTMLDocument`, which it obtains by calling the `HTMLDocument getReader` method. Another way to use a custom `ParserCallback` is to pass the `loadDocument` method your own `HTMLDocument` subclass with an overridden `getReader` method that returns your custom HTML reader, as we did in Listing 4-6.

Finally, having created the `Parser` and `ParserCallback` objects, `loadDocument` calls the `Parser` parse method, giving it the `ParserCallback` and the `Reader` as arguments. The parsing takes place inside the method; when it's complete, control is returned and the `ParserCallback`'s `flush` method is invoked to complete the process of building the `HTMLDocument`. The `parse` method also has a third argument, a `boolean`, that is initially passed with value `false`. You'll see the purpose of this argument shortly. Assuming that all goes well, when the `flush` method returns, the loop that we referred to earlier is terminated and the `load-Document` method returns the `HTMLDocument` to its caller.

Now let's look at what might go wrong and why all this code is enclosed in a loop. There are a couple of error conditions that this code does not really attempt to handle. The first is the `BadLocationException` that, theoretically, could be thrown by the `flush` method. Many of the methods in the text package that deal with a `Document` declare that they throw this exception because badly-behaved code could supply them with an illegal document offset, or cause them to generate an illegal document offset. Because the code shown here cannot do that, this exception should never be seen, but the compiler requires us to deal with it anyway, so we simply rethrow it to the caller as an `IOException`. The other possible error that we can do nothing about in this method is a real `IOException`, which can be thrown by any method that directly or indirectly reads the page source—for example, the `parse` method. This error is not caught here, because there is no possible recovery action at this level. The caller of `loadDocument` is responsible for catching `IOException` and doing whatever is appropriate.

There is one other exception that can be thrown by the parse method—`ChangedCharSetException`. As we said earlier in this chapter, this exception is thrown by the `Parser` when it detects an `HTTP-EQUIV` tag that directly or indirectly specifies a character encoding for the HTML page. There are two ways that this can be specified:

```
<META HTTP-EQUIV="Charset" content="cp1251">
<META HTTP-EQUIV="Content-Type" content="text/html; charset=cp1251">
```

When either of these two alternatives is found, the `Parser` parse method throws an exception, unless its third argument is `true`. When we first call `parse` however, this argument has the value `false`, so the exception will be thrown and will be caught by `loadDocument`.

When this exception is thrown, the exception contains the correct encoding to be used to translate the document from a stream of bytes to Unicode. This translation is performed by the `Reader` that wraps the `InputStream` returned by the `URLConnection`. What we would like to do would be to change the `Reader`'s encoding, but this cannot be done. Instead, we have to create a new `Reader` and wrap it around the `InputStream`. Unfortunately, it isn't possible to do this with the original `InputStream` and guarantee correctness, because the `Reader` is allowed to buffer what it reads from the `InputStream` and the `Parser` can also buffer data. As a result, the `InputStream` will probably not be positioned correctly to make it possible to continue reading without the possibility of losing data. Instead, we have to create a new `InputStream` and a new `Reader` with the correct encoding. The only way to do this is to get a new URLConnection object by calling the URL openConnection method again.

If you look back at the main body of code in the loadDocument method, that is, the part in the try block in Listing 4-7, you'll see that we actually need to repeat all of it from the beginning. That, of course, is why this code is all contained in a loop. The first time it is executed, we may have the wrong character encoding. If we do, the ChangedCharSet-Exception is thrown, we extract the correct encoding, and then restart the loop from the beginning. Before doing this, though, we do two things. First, the charSet argument is changed to reflect the correct character set. This causes the correct Reader to be created on the second pass of the loop. Second, we change the boolean variable ignoreCharSet from false to true. This variable is passed as the third argument of the parse method and it instructs the Parser to ignore the HTTP-EQUIV directive as it reads the source. Because on the second pass of the loop the Parser will reread the document from the beginning, it will certainly find the HTTP-EQUIV directive again and would otherwise throw another ChangedCharSetException, causing this loop to continue indefinitely.

Core Note

The Parser *throws the exception when it sees an* HTTP-EQUIV *line that specifies content or charset—it doesn't bother to check whether the character set implies by the* HTTP-EQUIV *matches the one being used by the* Reader. *This means that there will be a redundant exception if the document being read has an* HTTP-EQUIV *line that specifies the same encoding as the platform's default encoding, or the one supplied to* loadDocument. *With the current design of the* Parser, *there is no way to avoid this. If you feel strongly about it, you can avoid it by implementing your own* Parser *and overriding the* getParser *method of* HTMLDocumentLoader. *You'll need to get the encoding of the* Reader *that is passed to the* parse *method, decode the* HTTP-EQUIV *tag to get the target encoding (using code like that shown next), and compare the two to decide whether to throw the exception. Unfortunately, the abstract class* Reader *does not have a method that allows you to get the encoding, because not all* Readers *need be derived from an* InputStream, *so the concept of an encoding does not always exist. You'll have to check that your* Reader *is derived from* InputStreamReader, *which has a* getEncoding *method to give you the encoding. If the* Reader *you are given is not derived from* InputStreamReader, *you won't be able to perform this check.*

The last point to make about the `HTMLDocumentLoader` class is the way in which it gets the new character encoding from a `ChangedCharSetException`. This code is not as simple as you might think it would be; to keep the details out of the `loadDocument` method, this code is placed in the separate `getNewCharSet` method, which takes a `ChangedCharSetException` as its argument and returns the new character encoding in `String` form. The reason that this code is relatively complex is that there are two ways to specify the character encoding in an `HTTP-EQUIV` line, as you saw earlier. In the simpler case, the new encoding is directly specified using the `charset` form, like this:

```
<META HTTP-EQUIV="Charset" content="cp1251">
```

When this form is found in the HTML page, the `ChangedCharSetException` contains the character encoding itself. The `ChangedCharSetException` class has a method called `keyEqualsCharSet`, which returns `true` in this case, and another method called `getCharSetSpec` that returns the character encoding, so in this simple case, the `HTMLDocumentLoader` `getNewCharSet` method just returns whatever `getCharSetSpec` returns.

In the other case, the `HTTP-EQUIV` tag contains the character encoding as part of a content-type specifier, like this:

```
<META HTTP-EQUIV="Content-Type" content="text/html;
                                    charset=cp1251">
```

In this case, the `keyEqualsCharSet` method returns `false` and `getCharSetSpec` contains the value of the `content` attribute, that is `text/html; charset=cp1251`. To get the character encoding, it is necessary to parse this string to find the `charset` attribute and extract its value. The somewhat tedious code to do this can be found in the `getNewCharSet` method. We're not going to discuss it any further here because it isn't particularly enlightening. It's worth noting that code to do this same job also exists in `JEditorPane` but we can't use it because it's in a private method. Even if it were in a public method, we wouldn't want to use it because the aim of `HTMLDocumentLoader` is to load HTML without requiring the creation of a `JEditorPane` instance.

It looks like we have created an HTML document loader without involving either `JEditorPane` or `HTMLEditorKit` but, if you look back at Listing 4-7, you'll see that this isn't quite true because one of the `loadDocument` methods contains a reference to an instance of an `HTMLEditorKit`:

```
public HTMLDocument loadDocument(URL url, String charSet)
        throws IOException {
    return loadDocument(
        (HTMLDocument)kit.createDefaultDocument(),
        url, charSet);
}
```

Here, `kit` is an `HTMLEditorKit`. However, it is a static member of the `HTMLDocumentLoader` class, so we only need to create one `HTMLEditorKit` no matter how many instances of `HTMLDocumentLoader` are created or how many times the `loadDocument` method is called. We call the `createDefaultDocument` method of `HTMLEditorKit` to obtain an `HTMLDocument` rather than directly creating one ourselves to ensure that the document has a properly initialized style sheet. As you'll see later in this chapter, the style sheet controls how the HTML page is rendered. If you do the obvious thing, that is

```
HTMLDocument doc = new HTMLDocument();
```

the document that you create will have an empty style sheet, with the result that headings, paragraphs, lists, and all other formatted elements in the document will not be rendered properly.

Loading Web Pages with and without *JEditorPane*

Now that we've created a class that can load an HTML page without involving `JEditorPane`, let's use it to compare two ways of doing the same thing. Earlier in this chapter, you saw an example that loaded HTML (or any other kind of content for which it has support) into a `JEditorPane` from a given URL. Here, we'll extend that example so that you have the option to either load the page directly into the `JEditorPane` or to perform an offline load using `HTMLDocumentLoader` and then slot the complete `HTMLDocument` into the `JEditorPane`. We'll also add some code that measures the time taken for each of these alternatives, so that we can decide whether there is anything to choose between these two approaches. The complete code for this program is shown in Listing 4-8.

Listing 4-8 Using Two Different Ways to Load HTML

```
package AdvancedSwing.Chapter4;

import java.awt.*;
import java.awt.event.*;
import java.beans.*;
import java.io.*;
import java.net.*;
```

Listing 4-8 Using Two Different Ways to Load HTML (continued)

```java
import javax.swing.*;
import javax.swing.text.*;
import javax.swing.text.html.*;

public class EditorPaneExample9 extends JFrame {
    public EditorPaneExample9() {
        super("JEditorPane Example 9");
        pane = new JEditorPane();
        pane.setEditable(false);    // Read-only
        getContentPane().add(new JScrollPane(pane),
            "Center");

        // Build the panel of controls
        JPanel panel = new JPanel();

        panel.setLayout(new GridBagLayout());
        GridBagConstraints c = new GridBagConstraints();
        c.gridwidth = 1;
        c.gridheight = 1;
        c.anchor = GridBagConstraints.EAST;
        c.fill = GridBagConstraints.NONE;
        c.weightx = 0.0;
        c.weighty = 0.0;

        JLabel urlLabel = new JLabel("URL: ", JLabel.RIGHT);
        panel.add(urlLabel, c);
        JLabel loadingLabel = new JLabel("State: ",
                                    JLabel.RIGHT);
        c.gridy = 1;
        panel.add(loadingLabel, c);
        JLabel typeLabel = new JLabel("Type: ",
                                    JLabel.RIGHT);
        c.gridy = 2;
        panel.add(typeLabel, c);
        c.gridy = 3;
        panel.add(new JLabel(LOAD_TIME), c);

        c.gridy = 4;
        c.gridwidth = 2;
        c.weightx = 1.0;
        c.anchor = GridBagConstraints.WEST;
        onlineLoad = new JCheckBox("Online Load");
```

Listing 4-8 Using Two Different Ways to Load HTML (continued)

```
panel.add(onlineLoad, c);
onlineLoad.setSelected(true);
onlineLoad.setForeground(typeLabel.getForeground());
c.gridx = 1;
c.gridy = 0;
c.anchor = GridBagConstraints.EAST;
c.fill = GridBagConstraints.HORIZONTAL;

textField = new JTextField(32);
panel.add(textField, c);
loadingState = new JLabel(spaces, JLabel.LEFT);
loadingState.setForeground(Color.black);
c.gridy = 1;
panel.add(loadingState, c);
loadedType = new JLabel(spaces, JLabel.LEFT);
loadedType.setForeground(Color.black);
c.gridy = 2;
panel.add(loadedType, c);
timeLabel = new JLabel("");
c.gridy = 3;
panel.add(timeLabel, c);


getContentPane().add(panel, "South");

// Change page based on text field
textField.addActionListener(new ActionListener() {
    public void actionPerformed(ActionEvent evt) {
        String url = textField.getText();

        try {
            // Check if the new page and the old
            // page are the same.
            URL newURL = new URL(url);
            URL loadedURL = pane.getPage();
            if (loadedURL != null &&
                    loadedURL.sameFile(newURL)) {
                return;
            }

            // Try to display the page
            textField.setEnabled(false);
```

Listing 4-8 Using Two Different Ways to Load HTML (continued)

```
        // Disable input
textField.paintImmediately(0, 0,
        textField.getSize().width,
        textField.getSize().height);
setCursor(Cursor.getPredefinedCursor(
        Cursor.WAIT_CURSOR));
        // Busy cursor
loadingState.setText("Loading...");
loadingState.paintImmediately(0, 0,
        loadingState.getSize().width,
        loadingState.getSize().height);
loadedType.setText("");
loadedType.paintImmediately(0, 0,
        loadedType.getSize().width,
        loadedType.getSize().height);

timeLabel.setText("");
timeLabel.paintImmediately(0, 0,
        timeLabel.getSize().width,
        timeLabel.getSize().height);

startTime = System.currentTimeMillis();

// Choose the loading method
if (onlineLoad.isSelected()) {
  // Usual load via setPage
  pane.setPage(url);
  loadedType.setText(pane.getContentType());
} else {
  pane.setContentType("text/html");
  loadedType.setText(pane.getContentType());
  if (loader == null) {
     loader = new HTMLDocumentLoader();
  }
  HTMLDocument doc = loader.loadDocument(
                         new URL(url));
  loadComplete();
  pane.setDocument(doc);
  displayLoadTime();
```

Listing 4-8 Using Two Different Ways to Load HTML (continued)

```
            }
          } catch (Exception e) {
            System.out.println(e);
            JOptionPane.showMessageDialog(pane,
               new String[] {
                   "Unable to open file",
                   url
                 }, "File Open Error",
                 JOptionPane.ERROR_MESSAGE);
             loadingState.setText("Failed");
             textField.setEnabled(true);
             setCursor(Cursor.getDefaultCursor());
           }
        }
    });

    // Listen for page load to complete
    pane.addPropertyChangeListener(
                       new PropertyChangeListener() {
        public void propertyChange(
                          PropertyChangeEvent evt) {
          if (evt.getPropertyName().equals("page")) {
            loadComplete();
            displayLoadTime();
          }
        }
    });
  }

  public void loadComplete() {
    loadingState.setText("Page loaded.");
    textField.setEnabled(true);    // Allow entry of
                                   // new URL
    setCursor(Cursor.getDefaultCursor());
  }

  public void displayLoadTime() {
    double loadingTime = ((double)(
        System.currentTimeMillis() - startTime))/1000d;
```

Listing 4-8 Using Two Different Ways to Load HTML (continued)

```
        timeLabel.setText(loadingTime + " seconds");
    }

    public static void main(String[] args) {
        JFrame f = new EditorPaneExample9();
        f.addWindowListener(new WindowAdapter() {
            public void windowClosing(WindowEvent evt) {
                System.exit(0);
            }
        });
        f.setSize(500, 400);
        f.setVisible(true);
    }

    static final String spaces = "                    ";
    static final String LOAD_TIME = "Load time: ";

    private JCheckBox onlineLoad;
    private HTMLDocumentLoader loader;
    private JLabel loadingState;
    private JLabel timeLabel;
    private JLabel loadedType;
    private JTextField textField;
    private JEditorPane pane;
    private long startTime;
}
```

This program is a development of one that you first saw in Listing 4-3 when we were looking at how to gain control when an HTML page finishes loading. Here, we have added a label that will display how long the loading process takes for each file loaded and a checkbox that allows you to select the loading method, as you can see in Figure 4-12. You can start this application using the command:

```
java AdvancedSwing.Chapter4.EditorPaneExample9
```

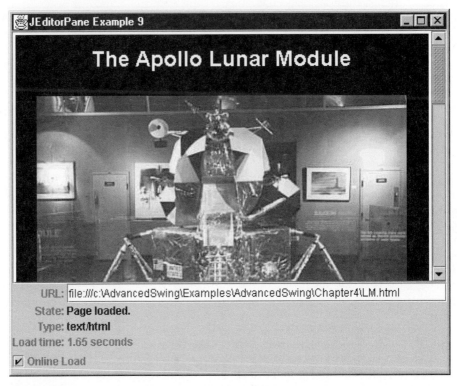

Figure 4-12 Loading HTML with and without using `JEditorPane`.

When the checkbox is in the selected state, as is the case in Figure 4-12, an online load is performed. That is to say, the file at the given URL is loaded directly into the `JEditorPane` using `setPage`. If the checkbox is unselected, the file is loaded offline using `HTMLDocumentLoader` and then connected to the `JEditorPane` using the `setDocument` method. The code that performs the loading is reproduced here:

```
startTime = System.currentTimeMillis();
// Choose the loading method
if (onlineLoad.isSelected()) {
   // Usual load via setPage
   pane.setPage(url);
   loadedType.setText(pane.getContentType());
} else {
   pane.setContentType("text/html");
   loadedType.setText(pane.getContentType());
   if (loader == null) {
      loader = new HTMLDocumentLoader();
   }
```

```
    HTMLDocument doc = loader.loadDocument(new URL(url));
    loadComplete();
    pane.setDocument(doc);
    displayLoadTime();
}
```

The first part of the `if` statement is the code from the original example that loads the file using `JEditorPane` `setPage` method. As you saw earlier in this chapter, when you use `setPage`, the loading takes place in a separate thread and you can get notification that the load is complete by registering a `PropertyChangeListener`. Because we want to measure the time taken to load the file in both the online and offline load cases, the start time is stored in the `startTime` member before the file is loaded. The total loading time is measured and displayed in the `displayLoadTime` method, which is called when the `PropertyChangeEvent` for the bound property `page` is delivered in the case of an online load and by a direct call for an offline load.

If the checkbox is not selected, an offline load is carried out. Here, we are going to assume that the file is HTML, so we directly set the content type in the `JEditorPane` and on the screen to `text/html`. Setting the `JEditorPane` content type selects and installs an `HTMLEditorKit`. We don't need to use this to perform the document load, but it will be needed when we finally connect the loaded document to the `JEditorPane`, so that the `HTMLDocument` is correctly interpreted and the right `Views` are used to display HTML (recall from Chapter 3 that the `Views` are created by a `ViewFactory` which, in the case of `JEditorPane`, is part of the `EditorKit`).

Performing the offline load is a simple matter. First, an `HTMLDocument` instance is created if one does not already exist. In this example, we'll only be loading one document at a time but, in fact, if you load documents in separate threads, a single `HTMLDocumentLoader` can be used to load as many documents as you like, because it doesn't store any per-document state that might be shared between its methods and the methods that create the `Parser` and the `Parser-Callback` are synchronized. Notice also that the default implementations of the `getParser` and `getParserCallback` methods create new `Parser` and `Parser-Callback` instances for each document loaded. If you override either of these methods to provide your own implementations of these objects, you should be careful to provide separate instances each time the method is called if you want to be able to load more than one document at a time.

Once the `HTMLDocumentLoader` object has been created, the document is loaded by calling the `loadDocument` method, passing the URL from the URL input field. Unlike the `JEditorPane` `setPage` method, `loadDocument` works synchronously in the thread in which it is invoked, so if you want to perform an asynchronous load you would need to create a separate thread and add your own mechanism to indicate when page loading is complete, if this is required. In this case, there is nothing to do while the page is being loaded, so the AWT event thread is used. When `loadDocument` returns, the `loadComplete` method and the `displayLoadTime` methods are called. These methods update the display to show that the page has been loaded and to show how long the operation took. To give a fair comparison with the online load case, before `displayLoadTime` is invoked, the newly loaded document is installed in the `JEditorPane` using its `setDocument` method.

To try this example out, type a URL into the URL field and press RETURN. By default, an online load (using `setPage`) is performed and, when the page has been loaded, the total time to complete loading is shown near the bottom of the window. You'll notice that the first time you load a file there is quite a long delay before anything seems to happen. Much of this time is spent loading and initializing classes that are being used for the first time. To eliminate this time from your measurements, you should load the same page several times and note how long each attempt takes. You can't do this directly, however, because `JEditorPane` will not load a page if it believes it has already been loaded. Also, the example code explicitly checks for an attempt to reload the same page because it relies on a `PropertyChangeEvent` for the page to re-enable the input field, and no such event will be generated when the page does not actually change. Instead, you will need to alternately load two (or more) files and record the times taken for each. Two suitable URLs are:

```
file:///c:\AdvancedSwing\Examples\AdvancedSwing\Chapter4\LM.html
file:///c:\AdvancedSwing\Examples\AdvancedSwing\Chapter4\SimplePage.html
```

assuming, as always, that you have installed the book's examples in the directory `c:\AdvancedSwing\Examples`. To properly compare online and offline loading, you should start the program and then load these two files several times with online loading selected, and then restart it, select offline loading, and repeat the process. Table 4-5 shows the results of a series of measurements on my laptop; all the times are given in seconds.

Table 4-5 Comparing Offline and Online Load Times for HTML Documents						
Online	LM.html	9.89	1.32	1.1	0.71	0.87	0.5
	SimplePage.html	1.48	0.72	0.61	0.71	0.44	0.66
Offline	LM.html	6.15	0.33	0.44	0.27	0.11	0.11
	SimplePage.html	0.60	0.33	0.33	0.06	0.11	0.11

As you can see, in all cases there is a large difference between the initial measurement and the ones that follow it, due to the time taken to load and initialize the HTML package classes. After this, the times are still slightly inconsistent, but you can see that the offline load times are much shorter than the corresponding times for online loading—even ignoring the single occasion on which offline loading reloaded `SimplePage.html` in 0.06 seconds, the best offline time for `LM.html` is almost five times shorter than the fastest online time, and the longest online time of 1.32 seconds compares to the longest offline time of 0.44 seconds—a factor of three improvement. Looking at `SimplePage.html`, the best online time here (0.44 seconds) is four times longer than the best achieved by offline loading (0.11 seconds), while the ratio of worst times is 0.72 seconds to 0.33—a factor of just over two.

The message from this experiment is that it is faster to load HTML using `HTMLDocumentLoader` rather than `setPage`. However, if all you need to do is load an HTML page on demand for a user to view, there are two caveats that you should bear in mind:

1. The gains to be made for a single read of a page, represented by the first column in Table 4-5, are not huge. These benefits increase for the second HTML page to be fetched because the required classes will already have been loaded and initialized by the VM. However, the time taken to load the second and subsequent pages is comparatively short and the difference may not be significant to the end user.

2. The `setPage` method automatically fetches the page in a separate thread so that the application will continue to respond to the user while the page is being read and formatted. To achieve the same effect with `HTMLDocumentLoader`, you need to create your own thread to do the loading, and then schedule the set-Document call to install it into the `JEditorPane` in the AWT event thread using the `SwingUtilities.invokeLater` method. Whether this is worthwhile depends on your application and the expectations of your users.

Using `HTMLDocument` to Analyze HTML

Using `HTMLDocumentLoader`, you can fetch an HTML page and parse it into an `HTMLDocument` without needing to display its content in a `JEditorPane`. One reason for doing this might be to analyze the content of the HTML to find hypertext links or to index its content in the same way that Web crawlers do. The structure of HTMLDocument makes it very simple to scan an HTML page to extract information, because the parser has done all the hard work of organizing the data for you. In particular, the tags and text content are separated from each other in the sense that the text is held in the HTMLDocument's content model, while the tags are stored as attributes of the elements that are mapped over the content. Therefore, you can independently extract plain text or search for specific tags or HTML attributes.

In this section, we'll see two examples that demonstrate how to load an HTML page and then extract information from it. In the first example, we'll load and display an arbitrary page and then walk through it looking for hypertext links. Any links that we find will be made available so that the user can select one and immediately jump to the target page. The second example will show how to manipulate both tags and text from the same document by finding all the HTML heading tags and extracting them, together with the associated heading text. We'll use this information to build a structure that shows how the headings are nested and display it in a JTree. We'll also arrange for selection events from the tree to cause the HTML page in the JEditorPane to scroll so that the selected heading is visible, making it very easy to navigate around the original document.

Searching for Hypertext Links

The basic feature that we're going to use to examine the structure of an HTMLDocument is a class called ElementIterator, which, as its name suggests, allows you to iterate over the Elements of a Document. ElementIterator is in the javax.swing.text package and works with any kind of Document, not just HTML. It has two constructors:

```
public ElementIterator(Element elem);
public ElementIterator(Document doc);
```

The first constructor creates an ElementIterator rooted at the given Element, while the second creates one that will scan the entire Document given as its argument. The basic idea is that each invocation of the next method returns the next Element in sequence:

```
public Element next();
```

There is also a previous method that allows you to reverse the traversal direction and a first method that returns to the start point. The iteration terminates when every Element below the starting point has been returned, at which point the next method will return null. A typical way to use ElementIterator to traverse a Document is as follows:

```
HTMLDocumentLoader loader = new HTMLDocumentLoader();
HTMLDocument doc = loader.loadDocument(url);
ElementIterator iter = new ElementIterator(doc);
```

```
Element elem;
while ((elem = iter.next()) != null) {
   // Process element "elem"
}
```

This small piece of code will load an HTML page from a Web server, parse it into an `HTMLDocument`, and then examine every tag that it contains (ignoring any errors). This simple loop is the basis of both of the examples in this section.

Core Note

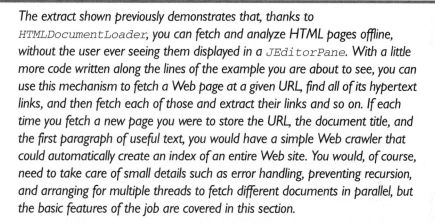

The extract shown previously demonstrates that, thanks to HTMLDocumentLoader, you can fetch and analyze HTML pages offline, without the user ever seeing them displayed in a JEditorPane. With a little more code written along the lines of the example you are about to see, you can use this mechanism to fetch a Web page at a given URL, find all of its hypertext links, and then fetch each of those and extract their links and so on. If each time you fetch a new page you were to store the URL, the document title, and the first paragraph of useful text, you would have a simple Web crawler that could automatically create an index of an entire Web site. You would, of course, need to take care of small details such as error handling, preventing recursion, and arranging for multiple threads to fetch different documents in parallel, but the basic features of the job are covered in this section.

Before we look at the code for this example, let's see how it works. If you start the program using the command

```
java AdvancedSwing.Chapter4.EditorPaneExample10
```

you'll see that it is the same as the last example we used, except that the URL text field has changed to a combo box. At the moment, there is nothing in the combo box pop-up window, but you can type a URL directly into the combo box editor field and, when you press ENTER, the page will be loaded as usual. If you have the Java 2 documentation loaded on your system, you can use the HTML pages that it contains for experimentation without incurring the delays of loading over the Internet. If you have the documentation installed in the directory `c:\jdk1.2.2\docs`, for example, a useful starting page can be found at

```
file:///c:\jdk1.2.2\docs\api\help-doc.html
```

After the page has been loaded, if you open the combo box you should find that it has been populated with hypertext links from the page that has just been loaded, as shown in Figure 4-13.

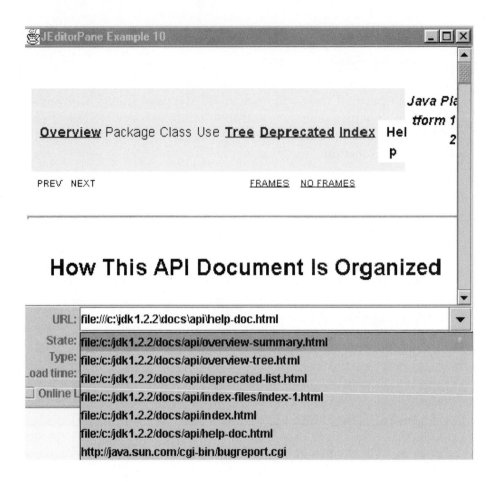

Figure 4-13   Extracting hypertext links from an HTML page.

If you now select a link from the combo box, the target page will be loaded and any links that it contains will replace those already in the combo box pop-up window.

As far as the implementation is concerned, most of this example is the same as the other similar programs that you have seen in this chapter. Scanning the loaded document for links and populating the combo box are activities that have been added to the code shown in Listing 4-9. A few minor changes were needed to replace the text field with a combo box, but we're not going to reproduce the entire listing here; if you are interested in seeing all of the code, you'll find it on the book's CD-ROM. Instead, we'll just look at how the list of hypertext links was created.

Listing 4-9 Extracting a List of Hypertext Links from an HTML
            Document

```
public URL[] findLinks(Document doc, String protocol) {
    Vector links = new Vector();
    Vector urlNames = new Vector();
    URL baseURL = (URL)doc.getProperty(
                        Document.StreamDescriptionProperty);
    if (doc instanceof HTMLDocument) {
        Element elem = doc.getDefaultRootElement();
        ElementIterator iterator = new ElementIterator(elem);

        while ((elem = iterator.next()) != null) {
            AttributeSet attrs = elem.getAttributes();
            Object link = attrs.getAttribute(HTML.Tag.A);
            if (link instanceof AttributeSet) {
                Object linkAttr = ((AttributeSet)link).
                            getAttribute(HTML.Attribute.HREF);
                if (linkAttr instanceof String) {
                    try {
                        URL linkURL = new URL(
                                    baseURL, (String)linkAttr);
                        if (protocol == null ||
                            protocol.equalsIgnoreCase(
                                    linkURL.getProtocol())) {
                            String linkURLName = linkURL.toString();
                            if (urlNames.contains(
                                        linkURLName) == false) {
                                urlNames.addElement(linkURLName);
                                links.addElement(linkURL);
                            }
                        }
                    } catch (MalformedURLException e) {
                        // Ignore invalid links
                    }
                }
            }
        }
    }

    URL[] urls = new URL[links.size()];
    links.copyInto(urls);
    links.removeAllElements();
    urlNames.removeAllElements();

    return urls;
}
```

The code that extracts the links from the document is contained in the
`findLinks` method, shown in Listing 4-9. This method takes a `Document` as
its argument along with an optional protocol specifier and returns an array of
URL objects, one for each link that it finds. In practice, this implementation
is only useful if the `Document` that it is passed is an `HTMLDocument`; if you
wish, you can make this dependency explicit by changing the type of the first
argument to `HTMLDocument` but you will, of course, have to check before calling this method that the document loaded into the `JEditorPane` is actually
HTML. With this implementation, this test is performed by `findLinks` and
an empty array of links is returned for anything other than HTML, which
would result in no links being inserted in the combo box.

The main body of this method is a loop that uses `ElementIterator` to
walk through the entire document, looking for hypertext links. How do we
identify a link? What we are looking for is a tag that originally looked something like this:

```
<A HREF="overview-summary.html">Overview</A>
```

Although it looks like a fully fledged HTML tag (and in fact that is exactly
what it is), `<A>` is not represented within `HTMLDocument` in the same way as
most other tags. In most cases, a tag becomes an `Element` in which the associated `AttributeSet` has the `HTML.Tag` value stored as the `NameAttribute`,
as you saw in "The Structure of an HTMLDocument" on page 411, but the
`<A>` tag is actually stored as an attribute of the text that it is associated with.
Here is how the `<A>` tag shown above would be stored in an `HTMLDocument`:

```
===== Element Class: HTMLDocument$RunElement
      Offsets [13, 21]
      ATTRIBUTES:
         (name, content) [StyleConstants/HTML$Tag]
         (a, href=overview-summary.html )
                  [HTML$Tag/SimpleAttributeSet]
      [Overview]
```

As you can see, the `Element` itself is a `RunElement` of type
`HTML.Tag.CONTENT` and it covers the characters Overview, which is the text
wrapped by the hypertext link. The `<A>` tag is to be found in the `Element`'s
`AttributeSet`; you can see that the type of this attribute is `HTML.Tag.A`, and
that its associated value is another set of attributes.

Locating hypertext links, then, is just a matter of looking for `Element`s that
have an attribute called `HTML.Tag.A`. If you look at Listing 4-9, you'll see that
this is exactly what it does, by getting the `AttributeSet` associated with each
`Element` that it finds and then calling `getAttribute` with `HTML.Tag.A` as

the argument. If this call returns an object of type `AttributeSet`, we have found a hypertext link.

Core Note

> *This code that performs this test is an example both of defensive programming and of a little shortcut that you will often find useful. First, note that in a correctly constructed `HTMLDocument`, if the `HTML.Tag.A` attribute is present, its value should always be an object of type `AttributeSet`. However, if a particular element does not contain an `HTML.Tag.A` attribute (which will be true for by far the majority of the `Element`s in the document, the `getAttribute` call will return `null`. As an alternative to this code, we could get away with the following:*

```
Object link = attrs.getAttribute(HTML.Tag.A);
if (link != null) {
    AttributeSet attrSet = (AttributeSet)link;
```

> *Technically, though, we are open to the possibility of a `ClassCastException` here because we haven't verified that the value of the `HTML.Tag.A` attribute is of the type that we expect. That's why the actual code looks like this:*

```
Object link = attrs.getAttribute(HTML.Tag.A);
if (link instanceof AttributeSet) {
    Object linkAttr = ((AttributeSet)link).getAttribute(
            HTML.Attribute.HREF);
```

> *Now we check the type of the returned object, which is the defensive aspect, but we don't verify that it isn't `null`. The slightly tricky part of this code is that this test is a side effect of `instanceof`—if the reference it is given is `null`, it returns `false` no matter what the type that it is being asked to check against happens to be. Whether you use this technique in your code is a matter of personal preference, but it can save you a small amount of code occasionally.*

The `AttributeSet` associated with an `HTML.Tag.A` object contains the HTML attributes that were specified along with the `<A>` tag in the HTML page. In the example you saw earlier, the `AttributeSet` would contain an attribute of type `HTML.Attribute.HREF` with an associated `String` value, which is the target of the link. As you can see from Listing 4-9, the next step is to extract this attribute and verify that it is a `String`. All that remains is to convert the link target to a URL and add it to the set of URLs that `find-Links` will return to its caller.

There are a couple of issues to deal with first, though. First, HTML links are often relative to the page that they are found in, as in the following case:

```
<A HREF="overview-summary.html">Overview</A>
```

Here, the link `overview-summary.html` would be interpreted by a Web browser in the context of the URL of the page itself, which, in this example, is `file:///c:\jdk1.2.2\docs\api\help-doc.html`, to produce the absolute URL

```
file:/// c:\jdk1.2.2\docs\api\ overview-summary.html
```

This is the URL that we need to return to the caller, because this is more convenient than returning a relative URL and requiring the caller to retain and use the URL of the original page when interpreting the set of hypertext links that the page contained. Fortunately, the `java.net.URL` class has a constructor that builds a URL from a relative URL string and the URL of the page from which that link was extracted:

```
URL(URL context, String spec);
```

To use this constructor, however, we need the URL of the original page. This information was not directly passed to the `findLinks` method but, as you saw earlier in this chapter, the base URL is stored with the `HTMLDocument` as the property `Document.StreamDescriptionProperty`. The value of this property is extracted at the start of the `findLinks` method and passed to the constructor of the URL class, together with the link from the document itself. This approach still works if the `<A>` tag contained an absolute link, like this:

```
<A HREF="www.phptr.com">Prentice Hall</A>
```

because the URL constructor will ignore the `context` argument when the `spec` is an absolute URL.

Every URL has an associated protocol, which determines the way in which the URL will be used. Web pages have the protocol `http` or, if they are stored on the local system, the alternative protocol `file`. Other protocols are also commonly found in HTML pages—for example, you can include a link that sends mail using the `mailto` protocol:

```
Send <A HREF="mailto:kt@topley.demon.co.uk">mail to
    the author</A>
```

Having constructed a URL, you can use the `getProtocol` method to get its protocol. The `findLinks` method has an argument that allows you to extract links of a specific protocol, ignoring all others. For example, calling findLinks with its second argument set to http will find all links to Web pages that are not on the local disk. If you pass this argument as null, all links will be returned, irrespective of their protocol. As you can see from Listing 4-9, the filtering is performed by simply extracting the protocol from the URL and comparing it (ignoring case) with the protocol supplied to findLinks.

The second issue we need to take care of in constructing the set of URLs to return is ensuring that we don't return any duplicates. As we find URLs, we add them to a Vector called links. The Vector class has a method called contains that allows you to check whether an element that you want to add is already present. Using this method, to ensure that we don't add a duplicate entry to the Vector we could write the following:

```
// linkURL is the new URL
if (!links.contains(linkURL)) {
    links.addElement(linkURL);
}
```

This looks fine, but there is a minor drawback here. The contains method works by comparing its argument to each entry in the Vector; it returns true when a match is found. The comparison is performed by calling the equals method of the object to be compared and passing it an item from the Vector. Both of these objects will be of type URL; the URL class overrides the equals method of java.lang.Object to perform the correct test for equality of two URLs which involves, for http URLs, checking that they refer to the same Internet host (that is, to the same Web server). However, this test is not as simple as a simple text comparison. Consider the case of the ACME company that hosts a Web server for PC sales on an Internet host called www.pcsales.acme.com. A typical URL served from this host might be

```
http://www.pcsales.acme.com/index.html
```

This company might also think that it may attract more customers by using another name for the same host, such as www.pcsales.com. This is, after all, a much more likely URL to come up with if you were guessing where to look for companies that sell PCs on the Internet. As a result, the following URL will also reach the same Web page on the same Web server:

```
http://www.pcsales.com/index.html
```

However, there is no way to see from the text forms of these URLs that they correspond to the same host. In fact, the only way to work out whether they are the same or not is to get the Internet Protocol (IP) addresses that correspond to these names and compare them. This is exactly what the URL `equals` method does. There is a problem with this, however, if your computer is set up to use the Domain Name Service to resolve host names to addresses and you are not connected to the network when you run these examples, because the code that performs the name lookup will be unable to connect to the Domain Name Service. On my laptop, this causes the program to hang forever. To enable you (and me) to run this example without being connected to the Internet, the `findLinks` method maintains a second `Vector` called `urlNames` that holds the URLs in `String` form, so that each entry looks like the one shown previously. Instead of checking in the `links` `Vector` to see whether it has found a duplicate link, it performs a simple name comparison with the items in the `urlNames` `Vector`. Of course, this is not technically correct because it will see `www.pcsales.acme.com` and `www.pcsales.com` as different Web servers, but it is good enough for this example and it solves the problem. If you want to use this code in a production application, you can choose whether you leave this workaround in or use the correct code.

When the `ElementIterator` next method returns `null`, all the `Elements` in the document will have been scanned and all the hypertext links loaded into the `links` `Vector`. Because it is usually easier and more efficient to manipulate an array than a `Vector`, `findLinks` completes its job by allocating an array of URL references of the right size and copying the contents of the links `Vector` into it. It was impossible to create an array of the right size at the beginning, of course, because the number of links that would be found was not known at that point.

Another Way to Scan for Tags

Before we leave this example, it's worth mentioning that `HTMLDocument` has a method called `getIterator` that we could have used to help us implement the search for hypertext links, which is defined like this:

```
public Iterator getIterator(HTML.Tag t);
```

Given a tag, this method returns an `Iterator` (actually an object of type `HTMLDocument.Iterator`) that allows you to traverse the whole document, but only processes `Elements` that are associated with the tag that you supply as its argument. Listing 4-10 shows a version of the `findLinks` method that uses this facility.

Listing 4-10 Another Way to Extract a List of Hypertext Links from an HTML Document

```java
public URL[] findLinks(Document doc, String protocol) {
    Vector links = new Vector();
    Vector urlNames = new Vector();
    URL baseURL = (URL)doc.getProperty(
                        Document.StreamDescriptionProperty);

    if (doc instanceof HTMLDocument) {
        HTMLDocument.Iterator iterator =
                ((HTMLDocument)doc).getIterator(HTML.Tag.A);
        for ( ;iterator.isValid(); iterator.next()) {
            AttributeSet attrs = iterator.getAttributes();
            Object linkAttr
                    = attrs.getAttribute(HTML.Attribute.HREF);
            if (linkAttr instanceof String) {
            try {
                URL linkURL = new URL(
                                    baseURL, (String)linkAttr);
                if (protocol == null ||
                    protocol.equalsIgnoreCase(
                                    linkURL.getProtocol())) {
                    String linkURLName = linkURL.toString();
                    if (urlNames.contains(linkURLName)
                                        == false) {
                        urlNames.addElement(linkURLName);
                        links.addElement(linkURL);
                    }
                }
            } catch (MalformedURLException e) {
                // Ignore invalid links
            }
            }
        }
    }

    URL[] urls = new URL[links.size()];
    links.copyInto(urls);
    links.removeAllElements();
    urlNames.removeAllElements();

    return urls;
}
```

If you compare this with Listing 4-9, you'll see that there aren't that many differences—all the important ones have been highlighted in bold. As you can see, the first difference is that we get an `Iterator` object from the `HTML-Document` instead of dealing directly with `Elements`—in fact, this code doesn't use `Elements` at all. The loop now calls the `next` method of the `Iterator` after checking that it is positioned over a valid tag by calling its `isValid` method. When the `Iterator` is created, it is automatically placed over the first occurrence of the tag that you specify, so you should only call `next` after you've processed the first tag. If the document does not contain an instance of the tag you are looking for, `isValid` will return `false` straight away, so the loop shown here will not execute at all.

The next difference is in how you get hold of the information provided by the `Iterator`. In Listing 4-9, the `next` method of `ElementIterator` returned us the next `Element`, which we used to extract the attributes and then look for the `<A>` tag. The `next` method of `Iterator`, however, is declared like this:

```
public void next();
```

So how do you get access to any information about the `Element` that the `Iterator` is positioned over? You can't get direct access to the `Element`, but `Iterator` does have three accessor methods that you can use:

```
public HTML.Tag getTag();
public int getStartOffset();
public AttributeSet getAttributes();
```

The `getTag` method just returns the tag that was used to create the `Iterator` while the `getStartOffset` method returns the start offset of the `Element` that the `Iterator` is currently looking at. The most useful method from the point of view of this example is `getAttributes`. This method does not return the `AttributeSet` of the `Element` that the tag has been found in—it actually returns the `Attribute-Set` associated with that tag. In other words, this returns the set of attributes that contains the `HTML.Attribute.HREF` attribute that has the hypertext link target so, as you can see from Listing 4-10, we invoke `getAttributes` on the `Iterator` itself and then look for this attribute in the returned `AttributeSet`. The rest of the code in this method is unchanged from Listing 4-9.

The choice between using `getIterator` as in Listing 4-10 and implementing the searching logic as we did in Listing 4-9 will depend on what you are trying to achieve. If you are searching for a single tag like `<A>` that is actually stored as an attribute name, you should be able to use `getIterator` and simplify your code a little. On the other hand, you can't use `getIterator` if you are looking for more than one tag or if the tag is stored as the value of the `NameAttribute` of the `AttributeSet`, as is often the case. Indeed, our next example is just such a case.

At the time of writing, there is another case in which you can't use the `getIterator` method. If the tag you want to search for is defined as a block tag, the `getIterator` method returns `null` because the code that handles this case has not yet been written. If you want to search for a block tag, you will need to check whether the version of Swing that you are using has this feature implemented. To check whether a tag is a block tag, call its `isBlock` method. For example,

```
HTML.Tag.A.isBlock()
```

returns `false`, but

```
HTML.Tag.H1.isBlock()
```

returns `true`.

Core Note

If you want to search a document for a particular tag or set of tags and you don't know how it is stored, the easiest thing to do is to create an HTML page that contains the tag and then look at it using the ShowHTMLDocument application that we used earlier in this chapter. This application loads the page into a JEditorPane and then writes the content of the HTMLDocument onto standard output, so you might want to redirect its output into a file, particularly if you are using a platform that doesn't allow you access to much of the output from the commands that you run (such as DOS).

Building a Hierarchy of Document Headings

Now let's look at a slightly more complex example. This time, we're going to traverse the document looking for all the heading tags—that is `H1`, `H2`, `H3`, `H4`, `H5`, and `H6`. Each time we find such a tag, we'll extract the heading text and we'll use this information to build a `JTree` that shows the heading hierarchy within the document. This example gives you the ability to present a quick overview of what's in a document. As an added bonus, we'll implement a listener that detects selections made on the tree and scrolls the displayed Web page so that the heading selected in the tree is visible in the `JEditorPane`. Although this sounds like quite a challenging example, there really isn't very much to it once you've worked out how to get the information you want from the `HTMLDocument`.

As we did last time, before looking at the code let's look at how the example itself works by typing the command:

```
java AdvancedSwing.Chapter4.EditorPaneExample11
```

When the program starts, you'll see that it looks almost the same as the last example, apart from the empty JTree displayed to the right of the JEditorPane. Type the URL of an HTML page into the combo box editor and press Enter to load it and, as before, the combo box will be populated with a list of links from the page. The tree will also be populated and will show the main headings from the document—in most cases, it will show the H1 tags but, if the document doesn't use any H1 tags it will show the H2 headings (or whatever the highest level of headings is). You'll also notice that the root node of the tree has the document's title associated with it. A good example that shows how this works is the Java 2 API Help page. which you can load by typing the URL

```
file:///c:\jdk1.2.2\docs\api\help-doc.html
```

if you have the Java 2 documentation installed in c:\jdk1.2.2\docs. Figure 4-14 shows the result of loading this page and then expanding the tree to its fullest extent.

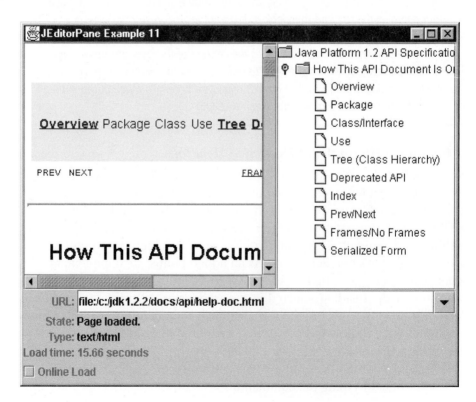

Figure 4-14   Creating a hierarchy of headings from an HTML document.

As before, we're not going to bore you with all of the details of creating the JTree and adding it to the layout; instead, we'll concentrate on the most interesting new pieces of code in this example. Here is the code that builds and installs a new heading hierarchy in the tree after the page has been loaded:

```
TreeNode node = buildHeadingTree(pane.getDocument());
tree.setModel(new DefaultTreeModel(node));
```

The real work is done in the `buildHeadingTree` method, which we'll see shortly. This method creates a `TreeNode` that represents the root of the document. Each heading tag will have its own `TreeNode`, which will be placed in the tree hierarchy in the appropriate place. When the `buildHeadingTree` method completes, it just returns the `TreeNode` for the root, which is used to create a new `DefaultTreeModel` that is then installed in the tree. Changing the `TreeModel` will cause the tree to redraw itself, so there is no need to call `repaint` explicitly. Incidentally, this example also creates a single instance of a `TreeModel` that contains only a root node and the associated text `Empty`, which is installed just before loading a new page so that the heading hierarchy of the old page is not left on display when the next page is being fetched and analyzed.

Every `TreeNode` in the tree returned by the `buildHeadingTree` method contains information relating to one heading. For the purposes of this example, we need to retain the following details for each heading:

- The heading text, for display purposes.
- The offset of the heading within the `Document` model, so that we can scroll the heading into view when the part of the tree that represents the heading's `TreeNode` is selected.
- The heading level, which is used when deciding where to place the `TreeNode` in the tree hierarchy and could also be used to render different heading levels with different fonts if we were to provide a custom renderer for the tree (although we don't actually go that far in this example).

One way to store this information would be to subclass `DefaultMutable-TreeNode` to include the required information and add instances of this subclass directly into the tree hierarchy. While this is a perfectly feasible approach, we don't use it here. Instead, we save all the header-related information in a separate class called `Header`. The tree is then built using `DefaultMutableTreeNode` objects in which the `Header` is stored as the user object of each node. This allows us to keep the header information separate from the tree, making the code that extracts headings from an `HTMLDocument` more reusable because it doesn't need to create an object that is specific to building a tree. The code that searches for headings is contained in a single method called `getNextHeading`, which requires an `HTMLDocument` and an `ElementIterator` as arguments; it calls the `ElementIterator`'s next method until it finds a header tag, then constructs a `Header` object and returns it. When the end of the document is reached, `null` is returned. None of this involves building `TreeNodes`. A typical way to use this method would look like this:

```
Element elem = doc.getDefaultRootElement();
ElementIterator iterator = new ElementIterator(elem);
Heading heading;

while ((heading = getNextHeading(doc, iterator)) != null) {
    // Use the Heading object referenced by "heading"
}
```

Inside the while loop, you can do anything appropriate with the `Heading` object. This code is, in fact, the skeleton around which the `buildHeadingTree` method used in this example is based. Before looking in more detail at how the tree is built, let's examine the `getNextHeading` method and the `Heading` class, which are the reusable pieces of this example.

The `Heading` class is a simple repository for a small amount of information. The three attributes that we need to store are passed to its constructor and there are accessor methods that can be used to retrieve them. In this example, there is no requirement to be able to change any of the attributes after the object has been created, so no mutator methods are provided. Listing 4-11 shows the implementation of this class.

**Listing 4-11   Storing the Attributes of a Document
                     Heading**

```
static class Heading {
    public Heading(String text, int level, int offset) {
        this.text = text;
        this.level = level;
        this.offset = offset;
    }

    public String getText() {
        return text;
    }
```

Listing 4-11 Storing the Attributes of a Document
                Heading (continued)

```
    public int getOffset() {
        return offset;
    }

    public int getLevel() {
        return level;
    }

    public String toString() {
        return text;
    }

    protected String text;
    protected int level;
    protected int offset;
}
```

Notice that we have provided a `toString` method that returns the heading text. This is done so that the tree will display the text of the heading when it renders each `TreeNode`. We'll revisit this point later in this section.

Now let's look at the implementation of the `getNextHeading` method. This method needs to do two things:

1. Given an `ElementIterator`, advance it until it finds the next heading tag.
2. Once a heading tag has been found, extract the text and build a `Heading` object.

Finding header tags is very similar to searching for hypertext links. However, we can't use the `getIterator` method because headings are not stored like the `<A>` tag—a heading tag actually creates a `BlockElement` with an `AttributeSet` in which the `NameAttribute` is `HTML.Tag.H1` in the case of `<H1>`, `HTML.Tag.H2` for `<H2>`, and so on. As noted earlier, `getIterator` does not work for block tags (at least not at the time of writing). The other reason we can't use `getIterator` (even if it worked for block tags) is that we need to search for six different tags and retrieve them all in their order of appearance within the document so that we can build the heading hierarchy properly. Because of this, we have to manually search for heading tags, as we did for hypertext links in Listing 4-9, by using the next method to advance the `Ele-mentIterator`, and then getting the `AttributeSet` from each `Element` and extracting the `NameAttribute`. If the `NameAttribute` is one of the tags `HTML.Tag.H1` through `HTML.Tag.H6`, the `Element` corresponds to a heading and the tag itself identifies the level of the heading. The process of identifying a heading and returning its level number (1 through 6) is implemented by the `getHeadingLevel` method:

```
public int getHeadingLevel(Object type) {
    if (type instanceof HTML.Tag) {
        if (type == HTML.Tag.H1) {
            return 1;
        }
        if (type == HTML.Tag.H2) {
            return 2;
        }
        if (type == HTML.Tag.H3) {
            return 3;
        }
        if (type == HTML.Tag.H4) {
            return 4;
        }
        if (type == HTML.Tag.H5) {
            return 5;
        }
        if (type == HTML.Tag.H6) {
            return 6;
        }
    }
    return -1;
}
```

This method accepts an `Object` of any kind and checks whether it corresponds to a header tag. If it does, it returns the corresponding heading level; otherwise, it returns -1. In this example, we will always invoke `getHeadingLevel` with the value of the `NameAttribute` from an `Element`. In fact, we'll call this method for every `Element` in the document and we'll use the return value to distinguish `Elements` that correspond to heading tags from all the other `Elements` within the document.

Using an `ElementIterator` in conjunction with the `getHeadingLevel` method allows us to identify all the headings. Now we need to get the text of the heading itself. This is not quite as simple as you might think because, as we said earlier, heading tags create `BlockElements`, so they don't actually contain the heading text. Instead, the text is distributed over one or more

RunElements that are the children of the heading's BlockElement. This arrangement is necessary to allow for formatting within the heading text. As an example, consider what would happen in the case of the following piece of HTML:

```
<H1>A header with <I>italic</I> text</H1>
```

The HTMLDocument created from an HTML page with this heading would contain the following sequence of Elements:

```
===== Element Class: HTMLDocument$BlockElement
    Offsets [3, 29]
    ATTRIBUTES:
     (name, h1) [StyleConstants/HTML$Tag]
     ===== Element Class: HTMLDocument$RunElement
     Offsets [3, 17]
     ATTRIBUTES:
      (name, content) [StyleConstants/HTML$Tag]
     [A header with ]
     ===== Element Class: HTMLDocument$RunElement
     Offsets [17, 23]
     ATTRIBUTES:
      (name, content) [StyleConstants/HTML$Tag]
      (font-style, italic) [CSS$Attribute/CSS$StringValue]
     [italic]
     ===== Element Class: HTMLDocument$RunElement
     Offsets [23, 28]
     ATTRIBUTES:
      (name, content) [StyleConstants/HTML$Tag]
     [ text]
     ===== Element Class: HTMLDocument$RunElement
     Offsets [28, 29]
     ATTRIBUTES:
      (name, content) [StyleConstants/HTML$Tag]
     [
]
```

The first Element is the BlockElement corresponding to the H1 tag—as you can see, its AttributeSet contains a NameAttribute whose value is HTML.Tag.H1. This Element has three children that contain respectively the text before the italicized part, the italicized word (together with the italic attribute stored as a CSS.Attribute object, which will be described in "Style Sheets and HTML Views" on page 483), and the text after the italicized word together with a fourth child that contains a newline. To get the heading text, we need to process all these Elements, extracting the text that they map from the Document model and concatenating it all. The complete implementation of the getNextHeading method is shown in Listing 4-12.

Listing 4-12 Locating Heading Tags in an HTMLDocument

```
public Heading getNextHeading(Document doc,
                              ElementIterator iter) {
    Element elem;

    while ((elem = iter.next()) != null) {
        AttributeSet attrs = elem.getAttributes();
        Object type = attrs.getAttribute(
                          StyleConstants.NameAttribute);
        int level = getHeadingLevel(type);
        if (level > 0) {
            // It is a heading - get the text
            String headingText = "";
            int count = elem.getElementCount();
            for (int i = 0; i < count; i++) {
                Element child = elem.getElement(i);
                AttributeSet cattrs = child.getAttributes();
                if (cattrs.getAttribute(
                              StyleConstants.NameAttribute) ==
                    HTML.Tag.CONTENT) {
                    try {
                        int offset = child.getStartOffset();
                        headingText += doc.getText(offset,
                            child.getEndOffset() - offset);
                    } catch (BadLocationException e) {
                    }
                }
            }
            headingText = headingText.trim();
            return new Heading(headingText,
                level, elem.getStartOffset());
        }
    }
    return null;
}
```

For each `Element` returned by the `ElementIterator`, `getNextHeading` extracts the `NameAttribute` and passes it to the `getHeadingLevel` method. If this method returns -1, the `Element` does not correspond to a heading and the iterator's next method is called to move on to the next `Element`. If there are no more `Element`s, `null` is returned. If the `Element` is a heading, the text is extracted from its `RunElement` children and merged into a single `String` and the trailing newline and any other white space at the beginning and end of the text are removed by calling the `String trim` method. Finally, a new `Header` object is created using the heading text, the heading level returned by `getHeadingLevel`, and the start offset of the heading's `BlockElement` returned to the caller.

Now let's look at the code that uses `getNextHeading` to build a heading hierarchy in a form that can be plugged directly into a `JTree`. You've already seen the outline of this method at the beginning of this section—it creates an `Element-Iterator` and repeatedly calls `getNextHeading` until the entire document has been traversed. As each `Header` object is returned by `getNextHeading`, it must be added to the hierarchy of `TreeNodes` to form the correct representation of the document's headings, reflecting the order in which they occur in the document and their relationship to each other as determined by their levels.

An HTML document has up to six levels of heading, ranging from `H1` at the top of the hierarchy to `H6` at the bottom. Let's consider a simple example of a document containing just headings and look at how we would want to structure the `TreeNodes` to properly reflect the document's content:

```
<H1>A: Level 1, number 1</H1>
<H2>B: Level 2, number 1</H2>
<H2>C: Level 2, number 2</H2>
<H4>D: Level 4, number 1</H4>
<H3>E: Level 3, number 1</H3>
<H1>F: Level 1, number 2</H1>
<H4>G: Level 4, number 2</H4>
```

For convenience, the text of each heading starts with a single letter that we'll use to refer to it in what follows. You'll notice that this is rather a disorganized document—usually you would not expect to see an `<H4>` tag follow an `<H2>` with no intervening `<H3>`, but there is nothing in the HTML specification to make this illegal, so we will need to cater for this possibility. You'll also notice that the last tag, an `<H4>`, directly follows an `<H1>`. Let's first change the layout to show how these headings actually relate to each other, using one level of indentation each time we move down a header level:

```
<H1>A: Level 1, number 1</H1>
   <H2>B: Level 2, number 1</H2>
   <H2>C: Level 2, number 2</H2>
       <H4>D: Level 4, number 1</H4>
       <H3>E: Level 3, number 1</H3>
<H1>F: Level 1, number 2</H1>
       <H4>G: Level 4, number 2</H4>
```

If you replace each line with a `TreeNode`, this is exactly how the `Tree-Nodes` should be connected, where the use of indentation signifies a parent-child relationship so that, for example, the `TreeNodes` for headings B and C will be sibling children of the `TreeNode` for heading A. The `TreeNode` for heading G will be a sibling of that for node A and both will be children of the root `TreeNode` (not shown here), which will contain the document's title instead of a heading. The `getNextHeading` method will return the headings in the order shown previously, reading from the top down. Each call will return a `Heading` object containing the header level (from 1 to 6). To build the tree, the `buildHeadingTree` method allocates a `DefaultMutable-TreeNode` for each `Heading` as it is returned and connects the two by making the `Heading` the user object of the `DefaultMutableTreeNode` by passing it to the constructor:

```
DefaultMutableTreeNode hNode =
            new DefaultMutableTreeNode(heading);
```

Now let's work out how to build the correct hierarchy. The first heading, at level 1, is easy to deal with—it is installed as a child of the root `TreeNode`. The next heading is also simple—because it is a level 2 heading and the previous heading was at level 1, it should be a child of the `TreeNode` for heading A. The problem is, however, how do we keep a reference to the `TreeNode` for heading A? We could remember the last `TreeNode` we created, but this won't always work—we don't always want to add a new `TreeNode` directly under the previous one, as is the case with heading C, which needs to be added beneath the `TreeNode` for heading A, not that of its predecessor (heading B). What we need to know, at any given time, is the location of the last `TreeNode` for each level of heading. To do this, we create an array of `TreeNode` references with one entry for each heading level and another for the root node. This gives us seven entries, with entry 0 corresponding to the root node and entries 1 through 6 for the six heading levels. You can see the code that implements this in Listing 4-13.

Listing 4-13 Building a Tree of Heading Tags

```
public TreeNode buildHeadingTree(Document doc) {
    String title =
        (String)doc.getProperty(Document.TitleProperty);
    if (title == null) {
        title = "[No title]";
    }
    Heading rootHeading = new Heading(title, 0, 0);
    DefaultMutableTreeNode rootNode =
                new DefaultMutableTreeNode(rootHeading);
```

Listing 4-13 Building a Tree of Heading Tags (continued)

```
    DefaultMutableTreeNode lastNode[] =
                    new DefaultMutableTreeNode[7];
    int lastLevel = 0;
    lastNode[lastLevel] = rootNode;

    if (doc instanceof HTMLDocument) {
        Element elem = doc.getDefaultRootElement();
        ElementIterator iterator = new ElementIterator(elem);
        Heading heading;

        while ((heading =
                    getNextHeading(doc, iterator)) != null) {
            // Add the node to the tree
            DefaultMutableTreeNode hNode =
                        new DefaultMutableTreeNode(heading);
            int level = heading.getLevel();

            if (level > lastLevel) {
                for (int i = lastLevel + 1; i < level; i++) {
                    lastNode[i] = null;
                }
                lastNode[lastLevel].add(hNode);
            } else {
                int prevLevel = level - 1;
                while (prevLevel >= 0) {
                    if (lastNode[prevLevel] != null) {
                        break;
                    }
                    lastNode[prevLevel] = null;
                    prevLevel--;
                }
                lastNode[prevLevel].add(hNode);
            }
            lastNode[level] = hNode;
            lastLevel = level;
        }
    }
    return rootNode;
}
```

The `lastNode` array holds the heading references. As you can see, the first entry in this array is initialized with the `DefaultMutableTreeNode` object for the document root. We also maintain a variable called `lastLevel` that records the level at which we last installed a heading—you'll see why this is required shortly. Let's see how the tree is built up using the `lastNode` array to determine where to place nodes as they are created.

At the start, every entry in `lastNode` (apart from entry 0) is `null` and `lastLevel` has value 0 (indicating that the document title has just been inserted). The first call to `getNextHeading` returns a heading at level 1. Because this is greater than the last installed level (because `lastLevel` is 0), we simply add its `TreeNode` object as a child of the root object—that is, a child of the `TreeNode` in array entry 0. We also need to record the fact that the last heading added at level 1 was heading A, so we set `lastNode[1]` to point to the `TreeNode` for heading A and change `lastLevel` to 1.

The next call to `getNextHeading` returns heading B at level 2. Again, this level is greater than the level recorded in `lastLevel`, so we add its `TreeNode` as a child of the `TreeNode` at `lastNode[lastLevel]`—that is the `TreeNode` for heading A—and then set `lastNode[2]` to the `TreeNode` for heading B (because this is a level 2 heading) and change `lastLevel` to 2. The third heading (heading C) is also at level 2, which is the same as `lastLevel`. Now the algorithm needs to be different—we can't add it to the last `TreeNode` we installed, because that was also a level 2 heading. What we need to do is place it under the `TreeNode` for the previous level 1 heading. We can get this directly from `lastNode[1]`, which refers to heading A. We also set `lastNode[2]` to the `TreeNode` for heading C and set `lastLevel` to 2 (which results in no change).

Heading D is at level 4, which is again greater then `lastLevel`. According to the reasoning we used for the last heading, we should add the `TreeNode` for this heading under that for the last level 3 heading, which we will find in `last-Node[3]`. However, there has not yet been a level 3 heading, so `lastNode[3]` is `null`. What we need to do here is work back up the hierarchy looking for a level 2 heading, or a level 1 heading if there is no level 2 heading, or the root node if there are no level 2 or level 1 headings. The code in Listing 4-13 implements this by looping up the `lastNode` array from the level of the heading that we want to insert the new heading under (level 3) until it finds a non-`null` entry. In this case, it will find that `lastNode[2]` is not `null` and that it contains the entry for heading C, so the `TreeNode` for heading D will be added as a child of the one for heading C. Finally, `lastNode[4]` will be set to point to heading D's `TreeNode` and `lastLevel` will be set to 4.

The next heading is a strange one—it is an `<H3>` following an `<H4>` that did not have a preceding `<H3>` of its own. Logically, you might think that the `<H3>` should appear higher in the hierarchy then the `<H4>` it follows, but this isn't going to be the case because the `<H4>` and the `<H3>` are both children of the heading C at level 2. In other words, the hierarchy that we will get will not be this:

```
<H2>C: Level 2, number 2</H2>
     <H4>D: Level 4, number 1</H4>
```

```
    <H3>E: Level 3, number 1</H3>
```

but this:

```
<H2>C: Level 2, number 2</H2>
    <H4>D: Level 4, number 1</H4>
    <H3>E: Level 3, number 1</H3>
```

If you think this is wrong, you could modify the code to introduce a "phantom" level 3 heading to act as the parent of heading D. However, without a lot of extra work, you won't be able to stop the JTree displaying your phantom heading, which doesn't really correspond to anything in the document.

Now let's follow through what happens when heading E is returned by getNextHeading. At this point, we have the following state:

```
lastNode[0] = the root TreeNode
lastNode[1] = TreeNode for heading A
lastNode[2] = TreeNode for heading C
lastNode[3] = null
lastNode[4] = TreeNode for heading D
lastLevel = 4
```

Heading E is at level 3, so we want to add it as the child of lastNode[2], which is the correct thing to do because lastNode[2] is the TreeNode for heading C. This corresponds to the hierarchy shown earlier. We now set lastNode[3] to point to the TreeNode for heading E and set lastLevel to 3, giving us this state:

```
lastNode[0] = the root TreeNode
lastNode[1] = TreeNode for heading A
lastNode[2] = TreeNode for heading C
lastNode[3] = TreeNode for heading E
lastNode[4] = TreeNode for heading D
lastLevel = 3
```

However, there is a potential problem with this. Suppose the next heading were an <H5>—in other words, we had the following sequence:

```
<H2>C: Level 2, number 2</H2>
<H4>D: Level 4, number 1</H4>
<H3>E: Level 3, number 1</H3>
<H5>E1: Level 5, number 1</H5>
```

It is obvious from this that the <H5> is actually a child of heading E at level 3, so the hierarchy should be set up like this:

```
<H2>C: Level 2, number 2</H2>
    <H4>D: Level 4, number 1</H4>
    <H3>E: Level 3, number 1</H3>
        <H5>E1: Level 5, number 1</H5>
```

However, according to the logic we used before, when we get a heading at level 5, we look first for a heading at level 4 and attach its `TreeNode` under it. As you can see, at this point `lastNode[4]` points to heading D, so according to this algorithm, the `TreeNode` for heading E1 would be added under that for heading D, giving this hierarchy:

```
<H2>C: Level 2, number 2</H2>
   <H4>D: Level 4, number 1</H4>
      <H5>E1: Level 5, number 1</H5>
   <H3>E: Level 3, number 1</H3>
```

This is obviously wrong, because it looks like heading E1 precedes heading E in the document. We should have added it under heading E. In fact, because heading E was higher in the hierarchy than heading D, it should have blocked access to heading D for all future headings—the paragraph that heading D is in has been effectively closed out by the appearance of heading E. We forgot to take account of this when updating the `lastNode` array. What we need to do is to set the `lastNode` entries for all the headings with a higher heading than the one we are inserting to `null` when we insert a heading at a numerically lower-level number than the previous one. This means that, after inserting heading E at level 3, we would `null` out the entries for headings 4, 5, and 6. In fact, we only need to `null` out the entries between our new level and `lastLevel`, because we know that there won't be any non-null `last-Node` entries after `lastNode[lastLevel]`. If we did this, the `lastNode` array would look like this after inserting heading E:

```
lastNode[0] = the root TreeNode
lastNode[1] = TreeNode for heading A
lastNode[2] = TreeNode for heading C
lastNode[3] = TreeNode for heading E
lastNode[4] = null
lastLevel = 3
```

Now if we encounter an `<H5>`, we see that `lastNode[4]` is null, so we move up to `lastNode[3]` which is non-null, and add its `TreeNode` beneath the `TreeNode` in `lastNode[3]`. In terms of this example, we would add the `<H5>` heading E1 directly under the `<H3>` heading E, which is the desired effect. If you look at Listing 4-13, you'll see that we do, indeed, `null` out the intervening entries in `lastNode` when the new heading level is less than `lastLevel`:

```
int prevLevel = level - 1;
while (prevLevel >= 0) {
   if (lastNode[prevLevel] != null) {
      break;
   }
   lastNode[prevLevel] = null;
```

```
        prevLevel--;
    }
    lastNode[prevLevel].add(hNode);
```

Of the remaining two headings (F and G), the level 1 heading is the same case as the <H3> following an <H4> and the final <H4> is the same as heading C because the level number is increasing.

Once the `TreeNode` hierarchy has been built, a new `DefaultTreeModel` is created and plugged into the `JTree` to cause the display to be updated. The tree renders each `TreeNode` using a default `TreeCellRenderer` that invokes the `toString` method of the node to get the text to display alongside its icon. When the tree nodes are `DefaultMutableTreeNodes`, as they are in this case, the `toString` method simply calls the `toString` method of the node's user object, which, as we saw earlier, is the `Header` object for the associated document heading. This returns the heading text that was collected and stored by `getNext-Heading`. The only case for which this is not true is the root node, the user object of which is a `String` containing the document title.

The last feature of this example that we'll look at is scrolling the `JEditorPane` to show the heading associated with a node in the tree. To do this, we create a `Tree-SelectionListener` and register it with the `JTree`, as shown in Listing 4-14.

Listing 4-14 Scrolling a Document Heading into View

```
tree.addTreeSelectionListener(new TreeSelectionListener() {
    public void valueChanged(TreeSelectionEvent evt) {
        TreePath path = evt.getNewLeadSelectionPath();
        if (path != null) {
            DefaultMutableTreeNode node =
                (DefaultMutableTreeNode)path.getLastPathComponent();
            Object userObject = node.getUserObject();
            if (userObject instanceof Heading) {
                Heading heading = (Heading)userObject;
                try {
                    Rectangle textRect =
                            pane.modelToView(heading.getOffset());
                    textRect.y += 3 * textRect.height;
                    pane.scrollRectToVisible(textRect);
                } catch (BadLocationException e) {
                }
            }
        }
    }
});
```

When the user selects a node, the `valueChanged` method is invoked and the `TreePath` object corresponding to the node is obtained from the event. The `TreePath` contains an entry for each `TreeNode` in the path from the root of the tree to the node that was selected, so we use `getLastPathComponent` to get a reference to the node that the user actually selected, which will be one of the `DefaultMutableTreeNode`s created by `buildHeadingTree`. To scroll the corresponding heading into view in the `JEditorPane`, we need the document offset of the heading that has been selected, which we get from the `Heading`, which is, of course, the `DefaultMutableTreeNode`'s user object. Having obtained the document offset, we convert it to a location within the `JEditorPane` using the `modelToView` method, and then invoke `scrollRectToVisible` to arrange for the scrolling to take place. Because the `Rectangle` returned by `scrollRectToVisible` is only tall enough to expose the heading line itself at the bottom of the `JScrollPane`, we change its y coordinate so that a point three lines below the heading is brought into view. The result of this is that the actual heading appears a little way up from the bottom of the `JScrollPane`'s viewport, allowing some of the text after the heading to be seen.

Note that having obtained the user object from the selected node, we check that it is a `Header` object before casting it and extracting the offset. This is necessary because the user object for the root node is not a `Header` object—it is a `String` containing the document title. If this test were omitted, we would get a `ClassCastException` when the user clicked on the document title next to the root node of the tree.

Hypertext Links

With the changes made to our simple HTML viewer during the development of the last two examples, we can now extract the headings from a document and allow the user to scroll immediately to a specific heading just by clicking on its node in the tree displayed to the right of the `JEditorPane`. The user can also activate any of the hypertext links in the document by selecting them from the combo box that is displayed below the `JEditorPane`. This is a useful option if the user wants to see all of the links in one place, but users expect to be able to activate hypertext links within the document itself by clicking on them. If you run the previous example again, find a hypertext link in the body of the document, and click on it, you'll find that nothing happens. In fact, when you click on a link an event is generated, but it is the programmer's job to catch the event and take the necessary action.

The event used to notify the activation of a hypertext link is a `HyperlinkEvent`. This event is generated by the `JEditorPane` in the following circumstances:

- When the user clicks on a hypertext link within the document. As with Web browsers, active links are underlined by default for easy identification.
- When the mouse moves over a hypertext link having not been over a link.
- When the mouse moves off a hypertext link.

To handle these events, you must register a `HyperlinkListener` using the `JEditorPane addHyperlinkListener` method. The `HyperlinkEvent` has a `getEventType` method that allows you to retrieve the event type; there are three possible return values, which correspond to the three events listed above:

- `HyperlinkEvent.EventType.ACTIVATED`
- `HyperlinkEvent.EventType.ENTERED`
- `HyperlinkEvent.EventType.EXITED`

Note that these values are *not* integers, so you can't code the event handler as a switch statement with cases based on the event type. Instead, you have to write an *if* statement that takes account of the three possible values, as shown in Listing 4-15.

Core Note

Versions of Swing earlier than Swing 1.1.1 Beta 2 (including the first customer release of Java 2) did not generate the ENTERED and EXITED events. If you have one of these Swing releases, some of the code you'll see in this section will not work on your system.

Listing 4-15 Handling `HyperlinkEvents`

```
pane.addHyperlinkListener(new HyperlinkListener() {
    public void hyperlinkUpdate(HyperlinkEvent evt) {
        // Ignore hyperlink events if the frame is busy
        if (loadingPage == true) {
            return;
        }
        if (evt.getEventType() ==
                    HyperlinkEvent.EventType.ACTIVATED) {
            JEditorPane sp = (JEditorPane)evt.getSource();
```

Listing 4-15 Handling `HyperlinkEvents` (continued)

```
            if (evt instanceof HTMLFrameHyperlinkEvent) {
               HTMLDocument doc = (
                            HTMLDocument)sp.getDocument();
               doc.processHTMLFrameHyperlinkEvent(
                  (HTMLFrameHyperlinkEvent)evt);
            } else {
               loadNewPage(evt.getURL());
            }
         } else if (evt.getEventType() ==
                        HyperlinkEvent.EventType.ENTERED) {
            pane.setCursor(handCursor);
         } else if (evt.getEventType() ==
                        HyperlinkEvent.EventType.EXITED) {
            pane.setCursor(defaultCursor);
         }
      }
   });
```

As well as the event type, a `HyperlinkEvent` has three other attributes:

- The event source, which can be retrieved using the `getSource` method. This is always the `JEditorPane` itself.
- The target URL in the form of a `java.net.URL` object. You can get the URL using the `getURL` method.
- A string description, to which you can get access using the `getDescription` method. This attribute is always the value of the `HREF` parameter for the link associated with the event.

The event handler shown in Listing 4-15 comes from another iteration of our ongoing example program. You can try this example by typing the command

```
java AdvancedSwing.Chapter4.EditorPaneExample12
```

This version of program looks exactly the same as the last one, but now the hypertext links have been activated. If you load a page with hypertext links in it, you'll notice three things:

1. If you move the mouse over an active link, the cursor changes to a hand cursor.
2. If you move the mouse away from the link, the cursor reverts to the usual default arrow cursor.
3. If you clink an active link, the target page is loaded.

There is a suitable HTML page in the examples for this chapter, which you can load using the URL

```
file:///C:\AdvancedSwing\Examples\AdvancedSwing\Chapter4\links1.html
```

All of this behavior is implemented in the `HyperlinkListener` shown in Listing 4-15. When the cursor moves over a link, you get an event with type `HyperlinkEvent.Event.ENTERED` and when it moves away from the link, you get the corresponding `Hyperlink.Event.EXITED` event. When these events are received, the cursor for the `JEditorPane` is switched to whatever the platform supplies for the predefined hand cursor or back to the default cursor, as appropriate. However, there is a small issue to beware of here. If you select a new document from the combo box pop-up window (or click a hypertext link in the document), a new page load is started and the cursor is changed to show that the application is busy. If you are performing an offline load, the page will actually be fetched in a background thread, leaving the AWT event thread free to continue with other work. In particular, mouse events will still be tracked and it would be possible to receive a `Hyper-linkEvent` while a page load is in progress. Naturally, we don't want to respond to these events because we want the wait cursor to remain displayed, so we invented a boolean variable called `loadingPage` that is set `true` when a page load begins and `false` when it ends. This variable is inspected at the top of the `HyperlinkListener`'s `hyperlinkUpdate` method; if it is `true`, the event is ignored. This also blocks handling of the other type of event—the one that is delivered when the user clicks on a hypertext link to load a new page. This, of course, is absolutely essential, because we don't want to start loading yet another page when we already have a page load in progress.

The code that is executed when a `HyperlinkEvent.Event.ACTIVATED` event is received is, perhaps, a little more complex than you might have expected. In fact, there are two types of `HyperlinkEvent`. A simple `Hyper-linkEvent` is delivered when the document in the `JEditorPane` is not a document that contains frames. For this type of document, switching to a new page means removing the old one completely and installing a new one. You've already seen the code to do this in the `actionPerformed` method of Listing 4-8. Because there is now more than one way to activate this code (from the combo box or via a hypertext link), we extracted it and placed it in a method of its own called `loadPage` which is used in Listing 4-15. If you need to see the details, the code is on the CD-ROM that accompanies this book.

When the document in the `JEditorPane` has frames, however, an `HTML-FrameHyperlinkEvent` is delivered instead of a `HyperlinkEvent`. `HTML-FrameHyperlinkEvent` is actually a subclass of `HyperlinkEvent` that contains an additional attribute called `target` that determines where the document will be loaded. This parameter takes one of the following values:

`_self`   The new document replaces the frame in which the original document resides.

`_parent`   The document replaces the parent of the current frame, which may be the entire HTML document, or another frame if the document contains frames within frames.

`_top`   The document replaces the whole document in the `JEditorPane`. This has the same effect as clicking a link in a document that did not have frames.

`name`   The new document is loaded into an existing frame within the current document called `name`.

Handling all these cases properly is not a simple matter. In fact, you need to know a lot about the internals of `HTMLDocument` and its `Views` to implement it at all. Fortunately, `HTMLDocument` provides a convenience method called `processHTMLFrameHyperlinkEvent` that does the job for us, so all we need to do to get the correct effect is to call it. This is what the code in Listing 4-15 does.

Note that we only check whether the event is an `HTMLFrameHyperlinkEvent` for the case in which a link is being activated. However, although the code does not clearly show this, within a frame of a frame document, all three event types are actually `HTMLFrameHyperlinkEvents`. The code in Listing 4-15 still works, however, because an `HTMLFrameHyperlinkEvent` *is* a `HyperlinkEvent`—we don't need any special checks for this case because we don't need to take different action as the mouse moves over a hypertext link when the document is in a frame.

You can try out the behavior of a framed document by loading the Java 2 Documentation index page, which is at URL

```
file:///c:\jdk1.2.2\docs\api\index.html
```

if you have installed the documentation in the directory `c:\jdk1.2.2\docs`. The result of loading this page is shown in Figure 4-15.

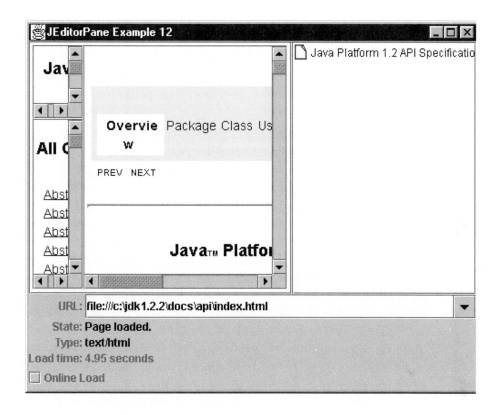

Figure 4-15 An HTML document with frames.

As you can see, this document consists of three frames, the largest containing the API document being viewed while the other two contain various sets of links to other parts of the API. If you select a link in the main document, you'll see that only the content of that frame changes. When you selected the link, an HTMLFrameHyperlinkEvent was delivered and the code in Listing 4-15 called the processHTMLFrameHyperlinkEvent convenience method provided HTMLDocument to replace only that frame.

If you look a little more closely at what is happening, however, you'll soon see that there are a few deficiencies in the current implementation of frame support that make it almost impossible to provide the same user interface when dealing with a framed document as we have achieved for a document without frames. The problems that exist at the time of writing, and the reasons that they exist, are summarized below.

Core Note

This description is based on Swing 1.1.1 with JDK 1.1.8 and Java 2 version 1.2.2. If you are using a later version of Swing or Java 2, you should check whether any of these shortcomings have been fixed.

- When you move the mouse over a hypertext link in a nonframed document, an event will be delivered from the JEditorPane in response to which the cursor will be changed to show a hand. If you try this with a framed document, however, this does not happen. You can see this immediately if you move the mouse over any of the links on any of the three frames in the Java 2 API index page. The reason for this is that frames within an HTML page are actually displayed by separate instances of JEditorPane. One new JEditorPane is created for each frame. In Figure 4-15, there are actually three JEditorPanes arranged over the top of the one created by the program itself. These JEditorPanes actually load what looks to them like a nonframed document (unless, of course, there is frame nesting, in which case these nested JEditorPanes may have other JEditorPanes nested inside themselves). When the mouse moves over a link in one of these documents, a HyperlinkEvent is generated by the nested JEditorPane, but it is not visible to our application because we did not register a HyperlinkListener on it. In fact, our application doesn't know anything about these hidden JEditorPanes (nor should it), so it is not feasible to register a listener with them. As a result, there is nothing to indicate that the cursor should be changed.

- When you clink on a hypertext link in a frame, the event goes to the nested JEditorPane. However, for this case, there is special code that redirects the event to the "outermost" JEditorPane, on which the application has its event registered. As a result, this event is seen by our application, even though the ENTERED and EXITED events that would have been used to change the cursor were not redirected to us. Because of this, our listener will pass the request to HTMLDocument, which works out which frame should be loaded and hence which JEditorPane is affected. Notice, though, that when the page load starts, the busy cursor is not shown. When we load an ordinary page, we change the cursor in the loadPage method and change it back when we get the

`PropertyChangeEvent` for the bound property `page`, which indicates that the background thread has finished fetching the page. If you look at Listing 4-15, you'll see that we don't change the cursor if we get an `HTMLFrameHyperlinkEvent`. The reason for this is that we wouldn't know when to switch it back! To do that, we would need to get the `PropertyChangeEvent`, but that, of course, is delivered not to our `JEditorPane`, but to the nested one into which the document is actually loaded. To make matters worse, we can't register a `PropertyChangeListener` with that `JEditorPane` for the duration of the load because the `HTMLFrameHyperlinkEvent` has a source object that indicates that it came from the application's `JEditorPane`, not the hidden one. Hence, there is no practical way for us to get a reference to the target `JEditorPane`.

• When you first load a framed document, the cursor changes to indicate that the frame is busy. When the page is loaded, the cursor changes back and the user can interact with the application again. Unfortunately, this happens long before the documents in each individual frame have finished loading. In an ideal world, the busy cursor should not be reset until all of the nested documents have been fetched, but it is very difficult to arrange for this to happen.

In fact, if you are prepared to do some research into the source code of the HTML package, you can come up with solutions to all the problems described earlier. However, they are complex and may not be portable from one version of Swing to the next, so we won't attempt to go into them here. Despite the minor problems that we've outlined, the Swing frame support is worth using if you must display an HTML page that has frames. If you are in control of the HTML pages that you display to your user, however, you might be well advised to avoid or minimize your use of frames for the time being.

Style Sheets and HTML Views

Having looked in some detail at `HTMLDocument`, now let's examine how the document content is actually rendered. Earlier in this chapter, we looked at the content of the `HTMLDocument` produced for a simple HTML page and noted that the attributes that were created for the `Elements` that reflect the HTML tags contained the tags themselves and any HTML attributes that accompanied those tags. These HTML attributes do not look anything like the attributes that you saw in connection with `JTextPane`, which directly encoded the color and font information used by the `Views` to render the text that corresponding `Element` mapped. Nevertheless, when an HTML document is loaded into a `JEditor-Pane`, the level 1 headings look different from the level 2 headings, which in turn do not look at all like the main body text. So how do the `Views` know how to render the document content if they don't have the appropriate attributes in the document `Elements`? The answer lies with style sheets, a topic that we'll look at in the first part of this section. When you've seen how the Swing HTML package handles style sheets, we'll conclude this section with a brief look at the HTML `Views` that do the actual text rendering.

Style Sheets

It used to be the case that the browser was completely in control of the way in which the various elements of an HTML page were rendered. There was no way, for example, for the author of the Web page to influence how the browser would represent a level 1 heading and, as a result, the precise appearance of headings and other elements of the page would vary from browser to browser. This was, in fact, in line with the original design aims of HTML—the Web page author was supposed to specify what should appear on the page and the browser would decide exactly how to represent it. However, with the widespread adoption of HTML as the *lingua franca* of the World Wide Web, the emphasis shifted from the ability to present data in an accessible fashion for the benefit of scientists, researchers, and programmers to the need to create eye-catching, professional-looking Web sites for commercial purposes. In this new environment, presentation became a major (and often the main) concern. Because HTML was not designed with precise control over presentation in mind, Web masters in charge of commercial Web sites had to resort to various techniques (or tricks) that stretched the capabilities of HTML and often relied on proprietary features of specific browsers to obtain the effects that they needed. This was not a situation that could be allowed to continue.

In response to the need for greater control over the way in which HTML is presented by browsers, the World Wide Web consortium (`www.w3c.org`) created a way for the Web developer to specify how the browser should render HTML elements. Instead of making major changes to HTML, W3C created a separate feature called *style sheets*. A style sheet effectively supplies attributes that are applied to headings, paragraphs, and text to change the way in which they appear. The mapping between HTML tags and the required attributes is specified as a set of rules, using a style sheet language. The style sheet language in common use today is called Cascading Style Sheets, usually abbreviated to CSS, the specification for which can be found on the W3C Web site. A full description of CSS and style sheets in general is beyond the scope of this book; instead, we'll confine ourselves to looking at a few simple examples that demonstrate the mechanism and how it influences the way in which HTML documents are rendered by JEditorPane. If you are already familiar with style sheets, you can skip the next section and continue from "HTML Attributes and View Attributes" on page 490.

Style Sheet Overview

There are three ways to use style sheets to change the appearance of an HTML document:

- By including a link to an external file containing a style sheet.
- By adding an inline style sheet in the HEAD block.
- Using attributes associated with individual HTML tags.

You can use any combination of these three mechanisms within a single document; if you use more than one of them, there are rules that determine which rules apply in the event of a clash. The fact that there is a hierarchical relationship between style rules specified in these three ways is the reason why the word "cascading" is used to describe the CSS style sheet language—rules cascade down from the most general level of specification (an external file) through the inline style sheet and finally to the tag-level overrides, with the tag-level rules having highest precedence. Let's look at a (contrived) example that uses all three techniques to see how styles sheets work and how rule clashes are resolved. Consider the HTML page shown in Listing 4-16.

Listing 4-16 Using Style Sheets with HTML

```
<HTML>
<HEAD>
<STYLE>
<!--
H1    {
    color: red;
    font-size: 36;
}
-->
</STYLE>
<LINK REL=STYLESHEET HREF="styles.css">
<TITLE>Document Title</TITLE>
</HEAD>
<BODY>
```

Listing 4-16 Using Style Sheets with HTML (continued)

```
<H1>Ordinary Heading 1</H1>
<H1 CLASS="Special">Special heading 1</H1>
<H1 STYLE="color: teal">Teal heading</H1>
<H2>Level two heading</H2>
<H3>Level three heading</H3>
<P>
Text in a paragraph body
<P CLASS="italicBold">
Text in a bold italic paragraph.
</BODY>
</HTML>
```

If you're not familiar with style sheets, some of the tags in this page may look unfamiliar to you. When rendered by Microsoft Internet Explorer 5.0, this page looks like Figure 4-16.

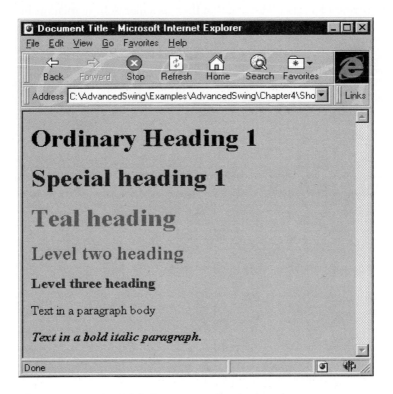

Figure 4-16 An HTML document with style sheets.

Although you can't see the colors of the text in this figure, it should be apparent that the various headings are colored and sized differently from each other. If you'd like to try loading this page on your own system, you'll find it in the file

```
c:\AdvancedSwing\Examples\AdvancedSwing\Chapter4\ShowCSS.html
```

assuming that you installed the example code in the directory `c:\Advanced-Swing\Examples`. Depending on how well your browser supports style sheets, you may or may not get the same result as that shown previously. Some older browsers (such as Netscape Version 3.0) don't have style sheet support at all, in which case the page will be processed exactly as if the style sheet information were not present.

Ignoring for the moment the tags in the header block, you can see that this page begins with three consecutive level 1 headings, all of which are rendered differently by the browser. The first heading appears with the browser's default color and font style, but may not use the same font size as level 1 headings on pages without style sheets. The next two headings, however, are displayed in blue and teal, respectively. What makes these heading as different? The first of them is declared as follows;

```
<H1 CLASS="Special">Special heading 1</H1>
```

The CLASS attribute refers to a style called `Special`, which is defined by the style sheet applied to this page. The presence of this attribute is what makes the heading color change from the default of black to blue. There are actually two styles sheets in operation here. The first of them is an inline style sheet in the header, bounded by `<STYLE>` tags:

```
<STYLE>
<!--
H1 {
    color: red;
    font-size: 36;
}
-->
</STYLE>
```

Within a style sheet, rules have the general form shown earlier. Each rule starts with the name of the tag to which it applies and is followed by the rule body in braces. Each entry in the body consists of a CSS attribute name, a colon, the value of the attribute, and a semicolon. In this case, the rule applies to all level 1 headings and changes their foreground color to red and their font size to 36. The complete set of CSS attribute names can be found in the CSS specification on the W3C Web site.

Inline styles can only be defined within the <HEAD> block of a Web page. To protect them from older browsers that do not recognize the STYLE tag, they are usually hidden within a comment, as shown in this example.

The second style sheet connected to this HTML page is in an external file referenced by the LINK tag, which must also appear in the header block:

```
<LINK REL=STYLESHEET HREF="styles.css">
```

This tag causes the browser to read the style sheet at URL styles.css, relative to the location of the original page. Placing styles in a separate file is a useful technique that can be used to give a uniform look-and-feel to a set of Web pages because the style of all of them can be changed by simply editing the single style sheet file. In this example, the file styles.css contains the following rules:

```
H1.Special {
    color: blue;
}

H2 {
    color: green;
/}

H3 {
    color: pink;
}

P.italicBold {
  font-style : italic;
  font-weight : bold;
}
```

The first rule in this file has the selector H1.Special, which selects level 1 headings in which the attribute CLASS has the value Special, as is the case with the second H1 tag in our example page. This rule is the reason for that heading being rendered in blue. The next two rules obviously change the foreground colors of level 2 and level 3 headings to green and pink, respectively, examples of which you can see in the Web page used in Figure 4-16, while the last rule affects paragraphs with class italicBold, changing the font style to italic and the weight to bold. In our example HTML page, this style is applied to the final paragraph:

```
<P CLASS="italicBold">
Text in a bold italic paragraph.
```

which, as you can see from Figure 4-16, is actually rendered in an italic bold font.

Rules specified in the header block of an HTML page, either inline or by inclusion from an external file, affect the entire Web page. You can, however, arrange for a style change to affect only a single instance of a tag by supplying an explicit STYLE attribute with that tag, like this example:

```
<H1 STYLE="color: teal">Teal heading</H1>
```

which changes the foreground color of that single level 1 heading to teal.

Sometimes a tag may be affected by more than one rule. This example has three rules that refer to level 1 headings—the local style applied to the single tag that you have just seen and the following two from style sheets in the header block:

```
H1 {
    color: red;
    font-size: 36;
}
H1.Special {
    color: blue;
}
```

The second of these rules applies only to level 1 headings with the CLASS attribute set to Special, but the first one applies to all level 1 headings. Both of these rules specify a change to the foreground color. When there is a clash, the more specific rule has preference, which results in headings tagged as Special being blue, not red. The font-size attribute, however, applies to all level headings, even those that do not take their foreground color from this rule. As a result, the font size of every level 1 heading will be 36, although this can be overridden by a STYLE attribute for individual tags. There are other cases in which the potential for ambiguity can arise—for example, it is possible to include more than one external style sheet by adding extra LINK tags to the header block. When this is the case, the rules in files included later take precedence over those included earlier (that is, the last definition wins). By contrast, though, styles defined in the <STYLE> block override those in external style sheets, whether or not they precede the LINK tag in the HTML page. Note, however, that selection only takes place for those parts of duplicate rule—other parts of an apparently overridden rule can still apply. As an example of this, suppose the following rule were added to the styles.css file included in our example HTML page:

```
H1 {
    color : yellow;
    text-decoration: underline;
}
```

On its own, this would change the foreground color of all level 1 headings to yellow and would underline the text in those headings. However, the page itself has the following rule in its inline style sheet, which appears to clash:

```
H1 {
    color: red;
    font-size: 36;
}
```

The rules in the inline style sheet will override those from external files, but only on an attribute-by-attribute basis so that the yellow color change in the external file will be hidden by the specification of red in the inline style sheet.The text-decoration attribute still applies, however, even though the rest of its rule has been overridden, with the result that all level 1 headings that do not have an explicit text-decoration specified in a local STYLE attribute and do not have a CLASS attribute indicating a style that changes this attribute will be underlined.

You now know enough about style sheets and CSS attributes to continue with our examination of how these features determine the way in which JEditorPane renders HTML. If you're interested in learning more about style sheets, I recommend Marty Hall's book *Core Web Programming*, which is also published by Prentice Hall.

HTML Attributes and View Attributes

Style sheets are the bridge from the HTML attributes stored in HTMLDocument and the way in which the content is rendered by the HTML Views. In fact, the Views map the HTML attributes to CSS attributes using a StyleSheet object associated with the HTMLDocument and use only the resulting CSS attributes for rendering; other than for this conversion process, the Views do not make use of HTML attributes at all. You can see the actual attributes that are used for rendering an HTML page by typing the following command:

```
java AdvancedSwing.Chapter4.ShowHTMLViews url
```

This program writes a representation of both the HTMLDocument and of the Views generated to display the document to standard output. You can use this to analyze the page shown in Figure 4-16 by specifying the URL

```
file:///c:\AdvancedSwing\Examples\AdvancedSwing\
    Chapter4\ShowCSS.html
```

Because there is likely to be quite a lot of output, you might want to redirect it to a file to avoid losing information.

Let's look at some of the Elements within the HTMLDocument and compare the attributes stored in the model with those used by the Views. Here, for example, is the Element structure corresponding to the first level 1 heading:

```
===== Element Class: HTMLDocument$BlockElement
    Offsets [25, 43]
    ATTRIBUTES:
     (class, Special) [HTML$Attribute/String]
     (name, h1) [StyleConstants/HTML$Tag]
     ===== Element Class: HTMLDocument$RunElement
     Offsets [25, 42]
     ATTRIBUTES:
      (name, content) [StyleConstants/HTML$Tag]
     [Special heading 1]
     ===== Element Class: HTMLDocument$RunElement
     Offsets [42, 43]
     ATTRIBUTES:
      (name, content) [StyleConstants/HTML$Tag]
      [
]
```

The Views corresponding to these Elements are as follows:

```
javax.swing.text.html.ParagraphView; offsets [25, 43]
        ATTRIBUTES:
     (margin-bottom, 10) [CSS$Attribute/CSS$LengthValue]
     (font-size, x-large) [CSS$Attribute/CSS$FontSize]
     (margin-top, 10) [CSS$Attribute/CSS$LengthValue]
     (name, h1) [StyleConstants/String]
     (font-weight, bold) [CSS$Attribute/CSS$FontWeight]
      javax.swing.text.ParagraphView$Row; offsets [25, 43]
            ATTRIBUTES:
      (margin-bottom, 10) [CSS$Attribute/CSS$LengthValue]
      (font-size, x-large) [CSS$Attribute/CSS$FontSize]
      (margin-top, 10) [CSS$Attribute/CSS$LengthValue]
      (name, h1) [StyleConstants/String]
      (font-weight, bold) [CSS$Attribute/CSS$FontWeight]
       javax.swing.text.html.InlineView; offsets [25, 42]
            ATTRIBUTES:
       [Special heading 1]

       javax.swing.text.html.InlineView; offsets [42, 43]
            ATTRIBUTES:
        [
]
```

It should be apparent that there is some similarity between this View hierarchy and the ones that we saw in Chapter 3 in connection with JTextPane. The level 1 heading has actually become a paragraph of its own mapped by a ParagraphView. Because the text fits on one line, the ParagraphView has a single child of type `ParagraphView.Row`, which in turn has a child of type `InlineView` that directly contains the heading text. Don't worry too much at this stage about what these `Views` are—we'll cover the `Views` used by the HTML `ViewFactory` in the next section.

Turning to the attributes, the only one of interest in the model is the `NameAttribute` with value `HTML.Tag.H1` in the first `Element`, which indicates a level 1 heading tag. Other than this, the model is remarkably devoid of attributes by comparison to the `Views`, which seem to be overloaded with them! The situation is not quite as bad as it might appear, however, because the `ParagraphView.Row` object inherits the `AttributeSet` of its parent `ParagraphView`, so we are actually seeing the same attributes twice. Where do all these attributes come from? The attribute tag for the level 1 heading obviously comes from the `Element`, but what about the others? These attributes are actually the standard CSS attributes for a level 1 heading as determined by this document's style sheet. When an `HTMLDocument` is created, it is initialized with a `StyleSheet` object that contains default CSS attributes for all HTML tags that need them. This `StyleSheet` is read from a plain text file that is included in the Java Active (JAR) .file from which the Swing classes are loaded. If you have the Swing source code installed on your system, you'll find it in a file called `default.css` in the `javax\swing\text\html` directory. Perhaps not surprisingly, it's written in CSS so it looks very much like the examples that we showed earlier. If you scan through the file, you'll find that it contains the following entry:

```
h1   {font-size: x-large;
      font-weight: bold;
      margin-top: 10;
      margin-bottom: 10}
```

These are, of course, exactly the attributes in the CSS attribute set that accompanies the `View` for the level 1 heading.

The attribute set for a `View` is created from the `Element`'s `AttributeSet` as follows:

- The `NameAttribute` is extracted and, if its value is of type `HTML.Tag` (which it should be), it is looked up in the `StyleSheet` to locate the rule containing the default CSS attributes for the tag. In the case of the level 1 heading shown previously, this is how the `font-size`, `font-weight`, `margin-top`, and `margin-bottom` attributes and their values are obtained.
- Any attributes whose keys are of type `HTML.Tag` are examined. If their associated values are of type `AttributeSet`, the accompanying attributes are translated one–by-one into CSS attributes and added to the `View`'s `AttributeSet`. You saw an

example of this type of HTML tag in "The Structure of an HTMLDocument" on page 411 where a `<FONT SIZE="+2" COLOR="red">` sequence was translated into an attribute of type `HTML.Tag.FONT` whose value was a `SimpleAttributeSet` containing attributes called `HTML.Attribute.SIZE` and `HTML.Attribute.COLOR` along with the values from the original HTML. In this case, the resulting CSS `AttributeSet` for the `View` will contain a `font-size` attribute and a `color` attribute. The tag itself is not required and does not appear in the `View` `AttributeSet`.

- Attributes of type `HTML.Attribute` are converted to the corresponding CSS attribute and their values are mapped to the appropriate CSS value. We'll say more about this process shortly.
- Attributes of type `CSS.Attribute` in the `Element`'s `AttributeSet` are copied over directly together with their values. No value translation is required in this case. You might find it surprising that the `Element AttributeSet` could contain an item of type `CSS.Attribute`—you'll see how this can come about in a moment.

Creating the `View AttributeSet` is a relatively expensive process, so the translated attributes are cached in the `View` and used during the rendering process. The translation process only occurs when the `View` is first created and when the `HTMLDocument` generates a `DocumentEvent` indicating that the HTML attributes for the `Element` that the `View` maps have changed.

Core Note

Actually, not all views bother with the translation from HTML to CSS attributes. As an example of this, the `View` that renders the HR tag uses the `HTML.Attribute.WIDTH` attribute if it is present. Instead of creating a new `AttributeSet` with CSS attributes, it just caches a reference to the `AttributeSet` in the `Element` itself. In other cases, the `View` converts the attributes but stores them in a private instance variable, so the `ShowHTMLViews` program that we used earlier will not be able to display them at all. `ImageView`, which renders inline images for the `IMG` tag is an example of this.

The actual translation from HTML attributes to CSS attributes is performed by a method in the class `javax.swing.text.html.CSS`, which uses a hash table that maps a key in the form of an HTML.Attribute to one or more CSS.Attribute types. The actual mapping performed is summarized in Table 4-6.

Table 4-6 Mapping from HTML to CSS Attributes		
HTML	*CSS*	*Value Mapping Type*
ALIGN	vertical-align, text-align, float	String Value
BACKGROUND	background-image	String Value
BGCOLOR	background-color	Color Value
BORDER	border-width	Length Value
CELLPADDING	padding	Length Value
CELLSPACING	margin	Length Value
COLOR	color	Color Value
FACE	font-family	Font Family Value
HEIGHT	height	Length Value
HSPACE	padding-left, padding-right	Length Value
MARGINWIDTH	margin-left, margin-right	Length Value
MARGINHEIGHT	margin-top, margin-bottom	Length Value
SIZE	font-size	Font Size Value
TEXT	color	Color Value
VALIGN	vertical-align	String Value
VSPACE	padding-bottom, padding-top	Length Value
WIDTH	width	Length Value

Although most HTML attributes map to a single CSS attribute, there are some that map to more than one. For example, the HSPACE attribute specifies the amount of space to leave to both the left *and* right of an image or a table. While HTML requires the same amount of space to be allocated on both sides of the object, the CSS specification allows you to specify the gap on each side individually via the `padding-left` and `padding-right` attributes. When converting an `HSPACE` attribute, a pair of `padding-left` and `padding-right` attributes will be generated, both specifying the same value.

Converting the attribute name is half of the process—it is also necessary to convert the associated value. In the `View AttributeSet`, an attribute value is stored as an instance of an inner class of `javax.swing.text.html.CSS`. The rightmost column of Table 4-6 shows the type of each HTML attribute that may be converted for storage in a `View AttributeSet`. The way in which this conversion is done for each of these types, and the class of the object in which it is stored, is summarized in Table 4-7. This table also describes how CSS attributes like `font-weight`, which may be created as a result of applying a CSS rule to an HTML tag, are stored. As an example, the usual CSS rule for the tag `H1` produces bold text, which is stored as the CSS attribute `CSS.Attribute.FONT_WEIGHT` with a value that represents `bold`. There is, however, no HTML attribute that directly converts to the CSS `font-weight` attribute, so it does not appear in Table 4-6.

Table 4-7 Mapping from HTML to CSS Attributes	
Border Style Value	The CSS `border-style` attributes take a string value from the set DASHED, DOTTED, DOUBLE, GROOVE, INSET, NONE, OUTSET, RIDGE, SOLID. The attribute is stored in an object of type `CSS.BorderStyle`, which contains both the string representation and a `type-safe` object that represents the border style. There is one such object for each of the legal styles.
Color Value	The color encoding for both HTML and CSS attributes is the same. If the color value starts with a #, the rest of the string (up to six characters) is treated as a red-green-blue (RGB) value encoded in hexadecimal so that, for example, #000000 is black. Otherwise, the color names `black`, `silver`, `gray`, `white`, `maroon`, `red`, `purple`, `fuchsia`, `green`, `lime`, `olive`, `yellow`, `navy`, `blue`, `teal`, and `aqua` are recognized, regardless of case. The color is converted to an instance of `java.awt.Color`, which is held inside a `CSS.ColorValue` that will be stored as the value of the CSS attribute.

Table 4-7	Mapping from HTML to CSS Attributes (continued)
Font Family Value	The font family is a string that is copied directly, except for the value monospace, which is converted to Monospaced. The string is stored in a CSS.FontFamily object from which it is retrieved at rendering time.
Font Size Value	A font size is stored in a CSS.FontSize object. If the font size begins with "+" or "-", it is taken as a numeric offset to the document's base font size, otherwise the value is assumed to be a valid number. The font size, or the result of adding an offset to the base font, must be in the range 0 to 6 inclusive. If the value is outside this range, it is forced to the nearest legal value. The resulting integer is stored in the CSS.FontSize object. During rendering, this integer is used as an index into a fixed array of integers that contains the values 8, 10, 12, 14, 18, 24, and 36, representing the actual font size in point.
Font Weight Value	A font weight is stored in a CSS.FontWeight object. The string values bold and normal are recognized and are stored as the numeric values 700 and 400 respectively. Alternatively, an explicit numeric value may be supplied. At rendering time, the value is used to determine whether to use a bold font; any value in excess of 400 selects a bold font, while any lower value uses a plain font.
Length Value	The length value in the HTML attribute is in the form of a string. It is stored in a CSS.LengthValue object. During rendering, the numeric value is extracted from the string. The numeric value may be followed by pt to signify a size in points.
String Value	The value of this attribute is stored unchanged, as a CSS.StringValue.

You can see how this works by looking at the View attributes that were stored for the level 1 heading in our example. Here is the complete View AttributeSet for this heading:

```
(margin-bottom, 10) [CSS$Attribute/CSS$LengthValue]
(font-size, x-large) [CSS$Attribute/CSS$FontSize]
(margin-top, 10) [CSS$Attribute/CSS$LengthValue]
(name, h1) [StyleConstants/String]
(font-weight, bold) [CSS$Attribute/CSS$FontWeight
```

As you can see, the attributes are all stored as objects of type CSS.Attribute and the value is stored in another object of a class that depends on the attribute type, as shown in Table 4-7.

As well as HTML attributes, it is also possible to find `StyleConstants` attributes in the `HTMLDocument` attribute set. The most common of these is, of course, `StyleConstants.NameAttribute` which contains the tag name, but it is possible to include other attributes, typically by applying actions of the `StyledEditorKit` to a range of text from the HTML document itself. Applying the `StyledEditorKit` `BoldAction`, for example, will include the `StyleConstants.Bold` attribute. Many of these `StyleConstants` attributes will be mapped to the corresponding CSS attribute in the `View`'s `Attribute-Set` as shown in Table 4-8.

Table 4-8 Mapping from `StyleConstants` Attributes to CSS Attributes

StyleConstants	**CSS**
Alignment	text-align
Background	background-color
Bold	font-weight
FirstLineIndent	text-indent
FontFamily	font-family
FontSize	font-size
Foreground	color
Italic	font-style
LeftIndent	margin-left
RightIndent	margin-right
SpaceAbove	margin-top
SpaceBelow	margin-bottom
StrikeThrough	text-decoration
Subscript	vertical-align
Superscript	vertical-align
Underline	text-decoration

Returning to our HTML page, the third level 1 heading looks like this:

```
<H1 STYLE="color: teal">Teal heading</H1>
```

and here's what this heading generates in the `HTMLDocument`:

```
===== Element Class: HTMLDocument$BlockElement
    Offsets [43, 56]
    ATTRIBUTES:
     (color, teal) [CSS$Attribute/CSS$ColorValue]
     (name, h1) [StyleConstants/HTML$Tag]
      ===== Element Class: HTMLDocument$RunElement
      Offsets [43, 55]
      ATTRIBUTES:
       (name, content) [StyleConstants/HTML$Tag]
      [Teal heading]
      ===== Element Class: HTMLDocument$RunElement
      Offsets [55, 56]
      ATTRIBUTES:
       (name, content) [StyleConstants/HTML$Tag]
       [
]
```

You can see that the attributes for the H1 tag contain the CSS attribute color with its associated value teal, from the `STYLE` clause in the heading tag. This example shows that it is possible to have attributes of type `CSS.Attribute` in the `HTMLDocument`. As we said earlier, these attributes are just copied directly to the `View`'s `AttributeSet`. Because of this, by using the `STYLE` attribute, you can often get more precise control over the way in which an HTML element is rendered. An example of this is the ability to individually specify top, left, bottom, and right margins around inline images using the CSS attributes `padding-top`, `padding-left`, and so on, whereas HTML provides only `VSPACE` and `HSPACE` which make the left and right padding amounts equal and similarly for the top and bottom. There are, in fact, several other cases in which CSS attributes are stored within the `Element` `AttributeSets`. Common examples are the `<B>` and `<I>` tags, which are not stored within the model as `HTML.Tag.B` and `HTML.Tag.I`—instead, the affected text run is allocated an `Element` of its own, with name `HTML.Tag.CONTENT`, and the CSS attribute `font-weight` with value `bold` or `font-style` with value `italic` are stored directly in the `Element`'s `AttributeSet`.

Changing an HTML Document's Style Sheet

You've seen that the mapping between HTML attributes and the CSS attributes used by the `Views` to display the contents of an HTML document is determined by the content of the `StyleSheet` object that is associated with the document. `HTMLDocument` has three constructors, two of which include a `StyleSheet` object as arguments:

```
public HTMLDocument();
public HTMLDocument(StyleSheet styles);
public HTMLDocument(Content c, StyleSheet s);
```

If you use the default constructor to create an `HTMLDocument`, you get an empty `StyleSheet`, which you will almost certainly need to populate yourself. `StyleSheet` is derived from the `StyleContext` class used by `HTMLDocument`'s superclass, `DefaultStyledDocument`, to hold `Styles`, so the empty `StyleSheet` actually has the default style that is associated with all instances of `DefaultStyledDocument`, which means that all text will be rendered using a default font and a default foreground color, both of which will track the font and foreground color associated with the `JEditorPane`. Neither `HTMLDocument` nor its superclasses has a method that allows the `StyleSheet` to be changed after the `HTMLDocument` has been created, which would seem to imply that you need to create the `StyleSheet` for an `HTMLDocument` in advance and that it thereafter cannot be changed. As we'll see, though, this is not the case.

If you use the `setPage` method to load content into a `JEditorPane`, the `HTMLDocument` for the page will be created by the `createDefaultDocument` method of `HTMLEditorKit`, which creates a default `StyleSheet` for you. This `StyleSheet` is initialized with the result of reading the `default.css` file referred to earlier in this section, which establishes a default set of rules for the attributes to be applied to HTML tags. This file is read only once and a single `StyleSheet` instance created from it, to which you can get a reference using the following method of `HTMLEditorKit`:

```
public StyleSheet getStyleSheet();
```

The result of this is that all `HTMLDocument`s share one copy of the default `StyleSheet`, which saves memory. However, what can you do if you want to use a different `StyleSheet` or if you want to make some adjustments to the default `StyleSheet` that will affect all instances of `HTMLDocument`, or make changes that affect only a single document? There are several approaches that you can take, which will be explained in the following sections. You only need to concern yourself with most of these techniques if you don't have direct control over the HTML pages that you are going to load but you want to enforce your own look-and-feel on them in some way. If you can change the HTML pages themselves, of course, the easiest thing to do would be to change them to reference a different external style sheet (using the LINK tag) or, for minor and isolated changes, add inline styles sheets or even insert STYLE attributes in the individual tags. Which of these techniques is appropriate depends on how many HTML pages you need to use and the extent of the change that you want to make. If you cannot change the pages themselves, you will need to apply style sheet modifications at the HTMLDocument level.

The Style Sheet Hierarchy

So far, we have described the StyleSheet mechanism rather loosely and you may have got, the impression that each HTMLDocument has only a single StyleSheet associated with it. This is not strictly true: There is only one StyleSheet *object* associated with any given HTMLDocument, but that StyleSheet may contain nested StyleSheets. This facility is required to make it possible to load multiple style sheets using several LINK tags within an HTML page. Let's look at an example to see exactly what happens. Suppose an HTML page starts with the following set of tags:

```
<HEAD>

<LINK REL="STYLESHEET" HREF="OrgStyles.css">

<LINK REL="STYLESHEET" HREF="JavaStyles.css">

</HEAD>
```

This set of tags imports what is presumably a global style sheet for an entire organization (from OrgStyles.css), followed by one that contains definitions for use within a specific team (from JavaStyles.css). Because later definitions override earlier ones, rules defined in the team style sheet will take precedence over those in the organization-wide one, which itself overrides rules in the default style sheet. If a particular style sheet does not define a rule for itself, it inherits that of its predecessor. Therefore, if OrgStyles.css defines rules for H1 and H2 tags but not for H3, and JavaStyles.css has a definition for H2 but not for H1 or H3, the style applied to H2 will be that specified in JavaStyles.css, the style for H1 will come from OrgStyles.css, and the H3 rule will be the one in the default style sheet. In terms of the StyleSheet associated with the HTMLDocument for this case, the situation is as shown in Figure 4-17.

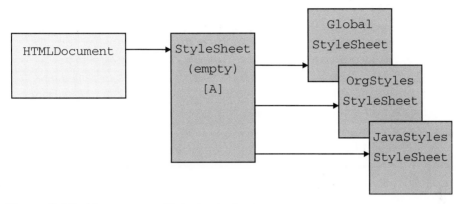

Figure 4-17 Management of linked style sheets.

The `StyleSheet` that's installed in the `HTMLDocument` (`[A]` in Figure 4-17) actually points to the set of linked style sheets, the first of which contains the default attributes loaded from the `default.css` file, which we will refer to here as the default style sheet. The `HTMLDocument` `StyleSheet` may also contain its own rules, which take precedence over those in the linked style sheets, including the default style sheet.

Installing a New Default StyleSheet

If the rules in the default style sheet do not suit the needs of your application, one possible approach is to install a completely new default style sheet in place of the one in the Swing JAR file. This style sheet is loaded by `HTMLEditorKit` the first time it needs to create an `HTMLDocument` and a reference to it is held as a static member variable called `defaultStyles`. All `HTMLDocuments` share a single instance of this style sheet, retrieved from `defaultStyles`, when they are created. You can change the reference held in `defaultStyles`, and therefore the default style sheet, using the `setStyleSheet` method:

```
public void setStyleSheet(StyleSheet ss);
```

The remaining problem is how to create the `StyleSheet` itself. One way to do this is to start with an empty sheet and add individual rules programmatically and we'll show you how to do this in "Making Changes to the Default StyleSheet" on page 505. A simpler approach is to create a text file containing the new style sheet and read that instead of the `default.css` file. Listing 4-17 shows a method that can be used to load a new default style sheet from an external file.

Core Note

In some circumstances, you may be able to modify the `default.css` *file and dispense with any programming. However, this is only likely to be possible in a development environment because it involves creating a new Swing JAR file with the modified version of* `default.css`, *or manipulating the* `CLASSPATH` *variable so that it finds an alternative version before looking in the JAR file. We're not going to cover those alternative mechanisms here.*

Listing 4-17 Loading a New Style Sheet

```
public StyleSheet loadStyleSheet(InputStream is)
            throws IOException {
    StyleSheet s = new StyleSheet();
    BufferedReader reader =
            new BufferedReader(new InputStreamReader(is));
    s.loadRules(reader, null);
    reader.close();
    return s;
}
```

To load a style sheet, you need to create a `StyleSheet` object and invoke its `loadRules` method, passing it a `Reader` corresponding to the style sheet file. In this case, the `loadStyleSheet` method is given an `InputStream` and converts it to a `Reader` by wrapping it first with an `InputStreamReader` and then with a `BufferedReader`, to achieve the best possible performance. The `loadRules` method is defined as follows:

```
public void loadRules(Reader in, URL ref) throws IOException
```

In our example, the second argument is passed as `null`, but you can supply a URL that corresponds to the original file. This URL is used to resolve any relative references to other styles sheets within the file being read. If the file does not contain any external references, you can give this argument the value `null`.

You can see how this works by typing the following command:

```
java AdvancedSwing.Chapter4.EditorPaneExample13
```

This program loads a drastically reduced style sheet that defines styles for the document body, the paragraph tag (<P>), the anchor tag (<A>), and for headings at level 1, 2, and 3:

```
body {
    font-size:          12pt;
    font-family:        Serif;
    margin-left:        0;
    margin-right:       0;
    color:              black
}


p {
    font-size:          14pt;
    font-family:        Serif;
    font-weight:        normal;
    margin-top:         12
}


h1 {
    font-size:          24pt;
    font-weight:        bold;
    color:              red;
    margin-top:         10;
    margin-bottom:      10
}


h2 {
    font-size:          16;
    font-weight:        bold;
    color:              blue;
    margin-top:         10;
    margin-bottom:      10
}


h3 {
    font-size:          medium;
    font-weight:        bold;
    font-style:         italic;
    text-decoration:    underline;
    color:              green;
    margin-top:         10;
    margin-bottom:      10
}
```

```
a {
  color:                  orange;
  text-decoration:        underline
}
```

If you type the URL of an HTML file into the URL field, you should see that the change in style sheet makes it look very different from the way it would look when loaded into a browser or using the other examples in this chapter. You can use the following URL to load a suitable HTML page:

```
file:///C:\AdvancedSwing\Examples\AdvancedSwing\Chapter4\links1.html
```

The level 1 headings will be in a 24-point, bold font, and will be colored red; level 2 headings will be blue; and the text for level 3 headings will be green, italicized, and underlined. Because all the formatting is specified by the style sheet, the effect of removing most of the rules is that much of the document reverts to default formatting using the rule associated with the <P> tag, which in this case is a 14-point Serif font.

Here's the code that actually loads the modified style sheet:

```
InputStream is = EditorPaneExample13.class.getResourceAsStream(
                               "changedDefault.css");
if (is != null) {
   try {
      StyleSheet ss = loadStyleSheet(is);
      editorKit.setStyleSheet(ss);
   } catch (IOException e) {
      System.out.println("Failed to load new default style sheet");
   }
}
```

The style sheet itself is in a file called `changedDefault.css` in the same directory as the class file for the example program; the `getResourceAsStream` method of `java.lang.Class` allows you to get an `InputStream` for this file given only its location relative the class file against which it is invoked. This method of locating a file does not require you to know exactly where your software has been installed on the system on which it is running. Alternatively, if you know the absolute file path of the style sheet file, you can use a `FileInputStream` instead:

```
InputStream is = new FileInputStream(fileName);
```

The `InputStream` is passed to the `loadStyleSheet` method shown in Listing 4-17, which creates a `StyleSheet` from the input file. This is then installed as the default style sheet by the following line of code:

```
editorKit.setStyleSheet(ss);
```

where `editorKit` is a reference to an instance of `HTMLEditorKit`. Note that, although the default style sheet is held as a static member of `HTMLEditor-Kit`, the method that sets it is not static, so you have to instantiate a copy of `HTMLEditorKit` to use it. It is important that you call this method *before* loading the first HTML page because, as noted earlier, `HTMLEditorKit` automatically loads its own default style sheet the first time it creates an `HTML-Document` if a custom style sheet has not been installed. Once you have installed your own style sheet, it will be attached to every `HTMLDocument`, as you can verify by loading other documents into the example program either by supplying the URL or following hypertext links.

Making Changes to the Default `StyleSheet`

Loading an entirely new style sheet is sometimes much more than you need to do—very often, all you'll want to do is make a few changes to the default styles. You can achieve this by using the `loadRules` method to import a set of changes from an external file into an existing `StyleSheet`. Where the rules being loaded conflict with those already in the `StyleSheet`, the new ones replace the old ones. To make your changes effective for all documents, just call the `HTMLEditorKit` `getStyleSheet` method to get the default style sheet (which will be loaded if necessary) and then call `loadRules` in the same way as was shown in Listing 4-17. Listing 4-18 shows how to modify an existing `StyleSheet` using the content of an external file.

Listing 4-18 Modifying an Existing Style Sheet

```
public void addToStyleSheet(StyleSheet s, InputStream is)
            throws IOException {
   BufferedReader reader =
            new BufferedReader(new InputStreamReader(is));
   s.loadRules(reader, null);
   reader.close();
}
```

The code here is almost identical to that shown in Listing 4-17, except that the new rules are loaded into the `StyleSheet` passed as the first argument rather than into a new `StyleSheet`. The code that installs the changes into the default style sheet is just as simple:

```
// Modify the default style sheet
InputStream is = EditorPaneExample14.class.getResourceAsStream(
                    "changedDefault.css");
```

```
if (is != null) {
   try {
      addToStyleSheet(editorKit.getStyleSheet(), is);
   } catch (IOException e) {
      System.out.println("Failed to modify default style sheet");
   }
}
```

Here, the `addToStyleSheet` method is called, passing it the default style sheet, obtained by invoking the `getStyleSheet` method of `HTMLEditorKit`. As with `setStyleSheet`, this is an instance method. The change is effective for all documents created after the changes have been installed, so you needn't invoke it right away if you want to have some documents loaded with the usual styles. Usually, however, you would use this code early on in your application. You can see how this differs from the previous example with the command

```
java AdvancedSwing.Chapter4.EditorPaneExample14
```

This example loads the same style sheet as shown previously, but styles in the default style sheet for which the file being read does not have a rule will be unaffected. In particular, the style sheet being loaded does not define the style for a level 4 heading. If you use the URL

```
file:///C:\AdvancedSwing\Examples\AdvancedSwing\Chapter4\links1.html
```

with both this example and the previous one, you'll see that the level 4 headings are rendered differently. This is because in the first example, the usual style for this heading level is removed as a result of replacing the default style sheet with our smaller one, whereas in the second example, because the level 4 style is not mentioned in the new style sheet, it is left unchanged.

Changing the `StyleSheet` for Individual Documents

The techniques we've used so far allow you to make global changes to the default style sheet. What should you do if you want to make style changes that are restricted to individual documents? As we've said, the style sheet mechanism supports multiple linked style sheets for a document, so you might think that the most natural way to make changes for a single document would be to create a new `StyleSheet`, read the rules into it using the code shown in Listing 4-17, and then link it into the document's global `StyleSheet`. However, at the time of writing, this is not possible because the `StyleSheet` methods that add and remove linked `StyleSheets`, which were public in earlier versions of Swing, and the instance variables that they control, have package scope and so are not accessible to application code. Instead, the only way to change the StyleSheet for an individual document is to modify the rules of the `StyleSheet` itself. If you refer to Figure 4-17, the StyleSheet labeled [A] is private to the HTMLDocument, so changes made here will not affect other documents. By constrast, the modifications we made in the previous two examples affected the default StyleSheet (at the top right of Figure 4-17), which is not private to the document.

There are two ways to change the document's private StyleSheet. The first is to use the addToStyleSheet method that you saw in Listing 4-18 to read a new set of rules into it from a file. To do this, you need to get a reference to the private StyleSheet, which is done using the getStyleSheet method of HTMLDocument. Here's an example that loads the rules from a file called fileName into the HTMLDocument referred to by the variable doc:

```
InputStream is = new FileInputStream(fileName);
StyleSheet ss = doc.getStyleSheet();
addToStyleSheet(ss, is);
```

Note carefully that we obtain the StyleSheet reference from HTMLDocument, not from HTMLEditorKit, which would return a reference to the default style sheet, and not from the private StyleSheet for this document.

An alternative way to add rules to a StyleSheet is to use the StyleSheet addRule method:

```
public void addRule(String rule);
```

The rule argument is written with CSS grammar and may, in fact, consist of any number of rules separated by white space. Here's an example that modifies the rules used to render level 1 headings and paragraphs:

```
StyleSheet s = doc.getStyleSheet();
  s.addRule(
  "h1 { color: teal; text-decoration: underline;
  text-style: italic }" +
  " p { color: blue; font-family: monospace }");
```

You can see the effect that this code has in practice using the command

```
java AdvancedSwing.Chapter4.EditorPaneExample15
```

As with the earlier examples in this chapter, this example allows you to choose between online and offline loading using the JEditorPane setPage method or our HTMLDocumentLoader class respectively. So that you can see that style sheet changes made this way do not apply to all documents, the code shown earlier has been added into the code that is executed after an HTML page loaded using HTMLDocumentLoader has been read into its HTMLDocument. As a result, if you load documents with the Online Load box checked, an unmodified style sheet will be used. If you clear the checkbox, HTMLDocumentLoader will be used and the document's StyleSheet will be modified. As a result, all level 1 headings will be colored teal, italicized, and underlined, while text formatted by the <P> tag will be blue and rendered in a monospaced font. The easiest way to see this effect is to leave the Online Load box checked and type the URL

```
file:///C:\AdvancedSwing\Examples\AdvancedSwing\Chapter4\links1.html
```

to load a page and display it using the default styles. Then, clear the Online Load box and click the link at the bottom of the page. This causes another page to be loaded with a modified style sheet, as a result of which the heading and text styles will change as described above.

This example works only because of the fact that the StyleSheet has the structure shown in Figure 4-17. In particular, it depends on the fact that the actual StyleSheet object installed in the HTMLDocument ([A] in Figure 4-17) is private to that document. If you allow the HTMLEditorKit to create the HTMLDocument, that will always be the case. However, when you use HTMLDocumentLoader (see Listing 4-7), you can create your own HTMLDocument or use a default one created by HTMLDocumentLoader. The code that creates the default document actually does so by invoking the createDefaultDocument method of HTMLEditorKit, which builds a StyleSheet with the appropriate structure. If you create an HTMLDocument of your own without using this method, you won't be able to apply the techniques shown in this section to it, because there is no way to create a StyleSheet like that in Figure 4-17 from application code. If the StyleSheet addStyleSheet method, which has package scope at the time of writing, is made public in the future, this situation will change. At present, if you want to modify a single document's style sheet, you can take one of the following approaches:

- Use HTMLDocumentLoader and allow it to create the HTMLDocument, and then apply your modifications to the style sheet after the loadDocument method returns.

- Use HTMLDocumentLoader, but pass it an HTMLDocument originally created using HTMLEditorKit's createDefaultDocument method.

- Use the JEditorPane setPage method and modify the style sheet in the PropertyChangeEvent handling code for the bound property page.

The last of these choices is not very useful, however, because by the time the PropertyChangeEvent is delivered to your application, some or all of the HTML page may already have been displayed in the JEditorPane using the original style sheet. Changing the style sheet in the event handler may well cause the text to be reformatted in full view of the user.

Finally, note that you can use the `addRule` method to make programmatic changes to any style sheet, so we could have used it when we showed you how to replace or make modifications to the default style sheet. Usually, however, it will be more convenient (and flexible) to take the approach we used in those cases and read replacement rules from an external file.

The HTML Views

In Chapter 3, we took a close look at the `Views` that are used to render the simpler text component and those managed by `StyledEditorKit` and saw how to customize them and to create new `Views` that change the appearance of the text component that they are installed in. When an HTML page is loaded in a `JEditorPane`, the `Views` that it uses are supplied by the `ViewFactory` of `HTMLEditorKit`. The basic design of the `Views` in the HTML package is the same as the ones that you saw in Chapter 3, except that many of them create a set of CSS attributes that are used for rendering instead of the attributes associated with the underlying document `Elements`. There are, as you might expect, more HTML `Views` than there are in the `javax.swing.text` package. Because these `Views` are very similar to the ones already described in Chapter 3, we're not going to take up much space describing them in detail here. A list of the HTML `Views`, the tags that they are connected with and a brief description of each of them appears in Table 4-9.

Table 4-9 Views in the HTML Package

View	Tags	Description
BlockView	`<BLOCKQUOTE>`, `<BODY>`, `<CENTER>`, `<DD>`, `<DIV>`, `<DL>`, `<HTML>`, `<LI>`, `<PRE>`	An HTML-specific subclass of the BoxView described in Chapter 3. This `View` lays out its children vertically, one above the other, and can provide a border if the appropriate CSS attributes are present in the associated CSS attribute set.

Table 4-9 Views in the HTML Package (continued)		
BRView	 	Maps the element by forcing a line break (see the description of ForcedBreakWeight under "Paragraph Size, Line Layout, and Wrapping" in Chapter 3 to see how this is achieved).
CommentView	<COMMENT>	Displays comments from the HTML file in an editable area surrounded by a box. This View is only visible when the associated JEditorPane is editable.
EditableView	N/A	Superclass of HiddenTagView. Not used directly.
FormView	<INPUT>, <SELECT>, <TEXTAREA>	A subclass of javax.swing.text.ComponentView that displays an appropriate component for the input tags of an HTML form. The component will be a JTextArea for <TEXTAREA> and a JList or JComboBox for <SELECT>, depending on whether the MULTIPLE attribute is defined and whether the SIZE attribute is present and greater than 1 (either of which causes a JList to be used). The <INPUT> tag causes one of several possible components to be used, depending on its TYPE attribute: • SUBMIT or RESET creates a JButton with the appropriate text displayed. • IMAGE creates a JButton displaying the image given by the SRC attribute. • CHECKBOX creates a JCheckBox. • RADIO creates a JRadioButton. • TEXT creates a JTextField. • PASSWORD creates a JPasswordField.

Table 4-9 Views in the HTML Package (continued)		
FrameSetView	<FRAMESET>	Manages a FRAMESET tag. Its job is to lay out its child FRAME or FRAMESET Views according to the number of rows and columns given by its ROWS and COLS attributes.
FrameView	<FRAME>	Manages a single frame within a FRAMESET. Each frame is implemented as an independent JEditorPane that can be loaded with its own HTML document. Hyperlink events from within the JEditorPane are handled by the FrameView. At the time of writing, ACTIVATED events are sent to the top-level JEditorPane so that the new document can be loaded. ENTERED and EXITED events are currently ignored (but this may change in later versions of Swing). The FrameView is responsible for drawing a border around the JEditorPane and supplying a JScrollPane, but placement and sizing of the frame is the responsibility of the FrameSetView.
HiddenTag-View	Unknown tags, <APPLET>, <AREA>, <HEAD>, <LINK>, <MAP>, <META>, <PARAM>, <SCRIPT>, <STYLE>, <TITLE>	This view is responsible for handling tags that do not normally cause anything visible to appear in the JEditorPane. When the JEditorPane is not editable, HiddenTagView is not visible. However, when it is editable, HiddenTagView displays the tag in a box containing an editable text field that allows the user to change the tag's content.
HRuleView	<HR>	Displays a horizontal line. Various attributes determine how wide and tall the line is and whether any vertical space is left above or below it.

Table 4-9   Views in the HTML Package (continued)

ImageView	<IMG>	Displays an image given by the SRC .attribute of the IMG tag. Images are loaded asynchronously and can be stored in a cache held at the HTMLDocument level for performance reasons. In practice, the caching is only done if a Dictionary to hold the cache is stored as a property of the HTMLDocument; there is currently no code that will create such a Dictionary. A border will be supplied around the image if the IMG tag appears within an <A> tag. If the image load fails, a suitable default icon is displayed. Another default icon is used while the image is in the process of being loaded.
InlineView	(Content)	This is the View that displays text from the HTML page. It is derived from the javax.swing. text.LabelView described in Chapter 3, so it inherits all its capabilities including the ability to display bi-directional text (described later in this book).
IsIndexView	<ISINDEX>	This View implements the ISINDEX tag by displaying a fixed prompt string ("This is a searchable index. Enter search keywords:"), followed by a JTextField. When the user enters some text and presses RETURN, a question mark followed by the value from the text field is appended to the page URL and the result passed to the setPage method, which should result in a query being performed by the Web server and the resulting page being loaded into the JEditorPane.

Table 4-9   Views in the HTML Package (continued)

LineView	`<PRE>`	This `View` maps a single line of a block of text delimited by `<PRE>`, `</PRE>` tags. It has the ability to expand tabs by looking for a `TabSet` property in the mapped element's `AttributeSet` (see Chapter 3 for a discussion of tabbing). If there is no such property, tabs are deemed to be set every eight characters.
ListView	`<DIR>`, `<MENU>`, `<OL>`, `<UL>`	This is a subclass of `BlockView` that is used to map various list-related elements that need special painting. The actual painting is delegated to a `List-Painter` that is obtained from the document's `StyleSheet` object, the intention being that you can change the way in which these lists are drawn by implementing your own `List-Painter` and installing a `StyleSheet` subclass with an overridden `getListPainter` method that returns an instance of your `List-Painter`. The default `ListPainter` in the `StyleSheet` class processes an LI tag associated with the block that the `ListView` is mapping and draws the appropriate decorator for the tag, which may be a circle, a square, a letter (in lower or uppercase), a number, or a Roman numeral.
NoFramesView	`<NOFRAMES>`	The `<NOFRAMES>` tag is used to provide alternative HTML for a browser that does not understand frames. Because the HTML package supports frames, any HTML inside the NOF-RAMES tag should be ignored. The `NoFramesView` accordingly renders nothing.

Table 4-9   Views in the HTML Package (continued)

ObjectView	`<OBJECT>`	This `View` is a restricted implementation of the `OBJECT` tag, which is used to include ActiveX controls, Applets, and other active content into a Web page. Browsers provide varying levels of support for this tag. The Swing HTML package supports very limited use of this tag to load a Java class file whose name is given as the `CLASSID` attribute. The class must be derived from `Component` and must have a default constructor. After loading the class, a new instance is created and any associated `PARAM` tags are used to set its properties. If the `OBJECT` tag has a `PARAM` tag with name `FONT`, for example, the class must supply a `setFont` method that takes a single argument of type `String`. This method will be invoked with the `VALUE` part of the `PARAM` tag as its argument.
Paragraph-View	`<DT>`, `<H1>`, `<H2>`, `<H3>`, `<H4>`, `<H5>`, `<H6>`, `<P>`	`ParagraphView` is derived from the `java.swing.text.Paragraph-View` class that was described in Chapter 3. It adds support for CSS attributes mapped from the HTML attributes on the corresponding `Element`.
TableView	`<TABLE>`	A `View` that maps the HTML `TABLE` tag.
Table-View.Cell-View	`<TD>`, `<TH>`	A `View` that renders a single cell of an HTML table. Most of the functionality is provided by the `BoxView` class in the text package.

Creating a Custom View

As you saw in Chapter 3, you can use custom Views to modify the way in which a document is displayed. Views are created by the editor kit's View-Factory, based on the Element that the View is mapping. The relationship between Views and the tag represented by the model Elements for HTML-Document is shown in Table 4-9. To use a custom View in place of the standard one, you need to replace the HTMLEditorKit ViewFactory. In Chapter 3, you saw how to use a replacement ViewFactory in conjunction with JTextPane by subclassing StyledEditorKit and overriding the getView-Factory method to return an instance of it (see Listing 3-3). The basic idea is the same for JEditorPane—we create a custom ViewFactory and a corresponding subclass of HTMLEditorKit with its getViewFactory method overridden. We'll see later how to make use of this editor kit. Let's first look at an example implementation of a custom HTML View.

JEditorPane has two operating modes. If you want to use JEditorPane as a cut-down browser, you set its editable property to false. In this mode, the user cannot type anything into the JEditorPane and only the usual tags that would be displayed by a browser are visible. On the other hand, you can also create an editable JEditorPane in which the user (presumably a developer) can change the content of the page. As we saw earlier in this chapter, you can arrange to write out the modified content of an HTMLDocument to an external file. Thus, you can use JEditorPane as a basic HTML editor and we'll see more about this in "The HTML Editor Kit" on page 521. You can see an example of an editable JEditorPane by typing the command

```
java AdvancedSwing.Chapter4.EditorPaneExample16
```

This program allows you to load an HTML page and, using the checkbox at the bottom of the window, you can choose whether the JEditorPane should be editable. You can toggle this checkbox before loading the page or after it has loaded. An example of a page loaded in editable mode is shown in Figure 4-18.

As you can see, when the page is editable, tags in the header block that would not normally be visible are shown as text fields with lined borders. You'll find that comments that appear anywhere in the document are also visible. The content of these text fields is actually editable and, if you provide code to write the content of the HTMLDocument to a file on demand, you can use this facility to make changes to the HTML comments or to modify the other tags that you normally cannot see. This facility may be useful for a Web page developer, but it is of less use if you want to provide a facility for the user to be able to change the text content of the page, but not its structure.

To make this possible, you need to be able to stop the structural tags being displayed even when the JEditorPane is editable. For that, you need a custom View.

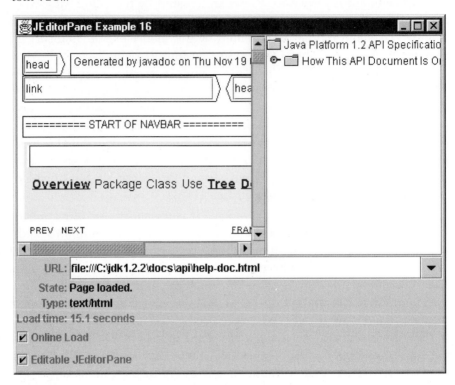

Figure 4-18   An HTML page in an editable JEditorPane.

The header and comment tags are actually rendered by the HiddenTag-View (see Table 4-9), which is derived from EditableView. EditableView is implemented to request zero space in the View layout if the JEditorPane that it resides in is not editable and the appropriate space to display whatever it contains if it resides in an editable JEditorPane. HiddenTagView extends this to supply the JTextField that will show the tag itself. CommentView is a subclass of HiddenTagView that displays the comment text instead of the tag itself, thus making it possible to change the comment. To arrange for all these tags to remain invisible even when the JEditorPane is editable, we need to change the ViewFactory to return a different View whenever it would create a HiddenTagView or a CommentView. The code to do this is very simple and is shown in Listing 4-19.

Listing 4-19 An `EditorKit` with a Modified `ViewFactory`

```
package AdvancedSwing.Chapter4;

import javax.swing.text.*;
import javax.swing.text.html.*;

public class HiddenViewHTMLEditorKit
                    extends HTMLEditorKit {
   public Object clone() {
      return new HiddenViewHTMLEditorKit();
   }

   public ViewFactory getViewFactory() {
      return new HiddenViewFactory();
   }

   public static class HiddenViewFactory extends
         HTMLEditorKit.HTMLFactory {
      public View create(Element elem) {
         Object tag = elem.getAttributes().getAttribute(
               StyleConstants.NameAttribute);
         if (tag instanceof HTML.Tag) {
            for (int i = 0; i < hiddenTags.length; i++) {
               if (hiddenTags[i] == tag) {
                  return new RealHiddenTagView(elem);
               }
            }
         }

         if (tag instanceof HTML.UnknownTag) {
            return new RealHiddenTagView(elem);
         }

         return super.create(elem);
      }

      static HTML.Tag[] hiddenTags = {
         HTML.Tag.COMMENT, HTML.Tag.HEAD,
         HTML.Tag.TITLE, HTML.Tag.META, HTML.Tag.LINK,
         HTML.Tag.STYLE, HTML.Tag.SCRIPT, HTML.Tag.AREA,
         HTML.Tag.MAP, HTML.Tag.PARAM, HTML.Tag.APPLET
      };
   }
}
```

This class extends `HTMLEditorKit` to override the `getViewFactory` method and return an extended `ViewFactory` that takes special action for the tags in Table 4-9 that would result in the creation of a `HiddenTagView` or a `CommentView`. The new `ViewFactory` is derived from `HTMLEditorKit.HTMLFactory`, which is the factory used by `HTMLEditorKit` itself. This allows us to make use of the factory's `create` method to return the appropriate `View` for all of the other tags and avoid having to repeat the tag to View mapping in the custom factory. As you can see, the affected tags are held in an array called `hiddenTags`. If the tag associated with the `Element` passed to the factory is one of the tags in `hiddenTags`, an instance of the class `RealHiddenTagView` is returned instead of the usual `HiddenTagView` or `CommentView`. The same `View` is returned if the tag is an instance of the class `HTML.UnknownTag`, which is a base class provided to allow the use of nonstandard tags in an HTML page, provided that custom `Views` are implemented to handle them. In our case, we're not going to provide such support, but we do want to hide these tags from the user.

`RealHiddenTagView` is a custom `View` that will not display anything for the `Element` that it maps. The ideal way to implement this would be to derive it from `EditableView`, which acts as an invisible view when its container is not editable. We would simply change this behavior so that the derived class would always act as if the `JEditorPane` were not editable. Unfortunately, this is not possible, because `EditableView` has package scope and so cannot be subclassed outside the `javax.swing.text.html` package (incidentally, the same is true of `HiddenTagView`). Instead, we derive `RealHiddenTagView` from `View` itself. `View` is an abstract class that requires the implementation of only a small number of methods in addition to the ones that are important for the functionality of this class. The code for `RealHiddenTagView` is shown in Listing 4-20.

Listing 4-20 A View That Is Always Invisible

```
package AdvancedSwing.Chapter4;

import java.awt.*;
import javax.swing.text.*;
import javax.swing.text.html.*;

public class RealHiddenTagView extends View {
    public RealHiddenTagView(Element elem) {
        super(elem);
    }

    public float getMinimumSpan(int axis) {
        return 0;
    }
```

Listing 4-20 A View That Is Always Invisible (continued)

```
public float getPreferredSpan(int axis) {
    return 0;
}

public float getMaximumSpan(int axis) {
    return 0;
}

public void paint(Graphics g, Shape a) {
}

public Shape modelToView(int pos, Shape a,
        Position.Bias b) throws BadLocationException {
    return a;
}

public int viewToModel(float x, float y, Shape a,
        Position.Bias[] biasReturn) {
    return getStartOffset();
}
}
```

The basic idea behind this `View` is simply that it requests no space in the `View` layout and that its `paint` method does nothing. It is easy to arrange for this—we just have to return zero from the `getMinimumSpan`, `get-PreferredSpan`, and `getMaximumSpan` methods (refer to Chapter 3 for a discussion of these methods), and we implement the `paint` method to do nothing at all. If we were able to extend `EditableView`, these would be the only methods that we would implement for ourselves. Because we have to derive this class from `View` itself, however, we are obliged to provide implementations for the `modelToView` and `viewToModel` methods. Fortunately, however, providing support for these methods for a `View` that occupies no space is trivial, as you can see.

The remaining problem is how to arrange for the `JEditorPane` to use `HiddenViewHTMLEditorKit` instead of `HTMLEditorKit` so that the correct `ViewFactory` is used. In Chapter 3, we did something similar when we created a custom editor kit for `JTextPane`; making use of it in that case was a simple matter of installing the new editor kit in the `JTextPane` when it was created. With `JEditorPane`, however, things are not quite so simple, because the appropriate editor kit is installed as each document is loaded, based on the content type of the document itself. Earlier in this chapter, we covered the mechanism by which the content type is mapped to the correct editor kit (see "The `setContentType` Method" on page 351). As you may recall, the content type is mapped to an editor kit using a registry, which is initialized using the static `registerEditorKitForContentType` method of `JEditor-Pane`. To arrange for our modified editor kit to be used instead of `HTML-EditorKit` for documents with content type `text/html`, you need the following code to have been executed before any HTML is loaded:

```
// Register a custom EditorKit for HTML
JEditorPane.registerEditorKitForContentType("text/html",
    "AdvancedSwing.Chapter4.HiddenViewHTMLEditorKit",
    getClass().getClassLoader());
```

We noted earlier in this chapter that there are two forms of `register-EditorKitForContentType`, one of which explicitly supplies a class loader to be used to load the named `EditorKit` class and another that does not specify the `ClassLoader` to be used. If the simpler form is used, when the editor kit needs to be loaded, `JEditorPane` uses the `ClassLoader` used to load the `JEditorPane` itself. In JDK 1.1, this will not cause a problem, but there are extra security checks in Java 2 that prevent this approach from working. In Java 2, `JEditorPane` will have been loaded from the so-called "boot class path" using a class loader that will only load classes from the Java core packages.

Core Note

You can find out about the boot class path and how classes are loaded in Java 2 from the online documentation supplied by Sun. If you installed the Java 2 documentation set in the directory `C:\jdk1.2.2\docs`*, point your Web browser at the file* `C:\jdk1.2.2\docs\tooldocs\findingclasses.html`*.*

If an attempt is made to use this `ClassLoader` to load a user-defined class, an exception will occur. To make it possible to load the `EditorKit`, we need to supply a different `ClassLoader` that has access to the class that contains the `EditorKit` implementation. One way to do this would be to use the expression

```
AdvancedSwing.Chapter4.HiddenViewHTMLEditorKit.class.get-
    ClassLoader()
```

which returns the `ClassLoader` that would naturally be used to load the editor kit itself. The drawback with this is that it actually causes the class to be loaded, which is not desirable in general because the editor kit may not actually be required. Instead, in this example we take advantage of the fact that the editor kit and the example code will be loaded using the same `Class-Loader` and supply the `ClassLoader` that was used to load the class that registers the `HiddenViewHTMLEditorKit`.

You can see how the modified editor kit works by typing the command

```
java AdvancedSwing.Chapter4.EditorPaneExample17
```

and loading an HTML page that has header and/or comment tags. Most of the HTML pages in the JDK API documentation have suitable tags. If you have installed the documentation in the directory `c:\jdk1.2.2\docs`, you could try using the URL

```
file:///c:\jdk1.2.2\docs\api\help-doc.html
```

This is the file that was loaded in Figure 4-18 and rendered using the standard `HTMLEditorKit` `Views`. If you load this page now, however, you'll see that the header and comment tags are no longer displayed and, if you use the Editable checkbox to toggle the `JEditorPane` between editable and read-only modes, you'll see that its appearance does not change. If you try the same with `EditorPaneExample16`, however, you'll find that toggling the editable property makes the header tags appear or disappear.

The HTML Editor Kit

To use `JEditorPane` as an HTML editor capable of anything other than simply inserting and deleting text, you need to make full use of `HTMLEditorKit`. In Chapter 1, you saw that all the text components come with a set of built-in editing features, most of which are provided by their editor kits. `HTMLEditorKit` is derived from `StyledEditorKit`, which provides a range of editing and formatting actions, as shown in Table 1-6 and these actions are, theoretically, applicable to any document (other than plain text) that can be loaded into either a `JTextPane` or a `JEditorPane`. Most of them operate by manipulating the `AttributeSets` of the `Elements` of the underlying `Document`, so the extent to which they are effective for a particular type of `Document` depends on how its associated `Views` interpret those attributes. As we've seen, the HTML `Views` use CSS attributes for rendering rather than the `StyleConstants` attributes that are manipulated by the style-related actions of `StyledEditorKit`, but many of these attributes are translated directly to their CSS equivalents as they are being stored within an `HTMLDocument` (see Table 4-8 for a list of the conversions provided at the time of writing). As a result, all of the actions supplied by `StyledEditorKit` work equally well with `HTMLEditorKit`.

Using the HTML Editor Kit Text and HTML Actions

As you saw in Chapter 1, you can get the set of editing features that a text component supports by invoking its `getActions` method:

```
public Action[] getActions();
```

The list of `Actions` that will be returned is made of the set supported by the component itself and those of its editor kit. In the case of `JEditorPane`, the exact content of this list will depend on the type of editor kit installed, which is determined by the content type of the document that has been loaded. A simple and convenient way to make the `Actions` supported by an editor kit available to the user is to add them to the application's menu bar. If you were writing an HTML page editor, for example, you would want to extract the various `Actions` supplied by `HTMLEditorKit` and build suitable menus from them, structured according to action type so that, for example, all the font related items would be held together and separated from the actions that let you create and manipulate HTML tags. Unfortunately, it's not particularly simple to build menus of related actions unless you know in advance what the complete set of `Actions` is because, although each `Action` has a name, it is difficult to see how they relate to each other without analyzing the name. Furthermore, the names themselves are not very user-friendly, as you can see from the set of `Actions` supported by `StyledEditorKit` in Table 1-6. Nevertheless, the number of different functional areas that the complete `Action` set for the editor kits in the Swing text package cover is small and the set of `Actions` does not change very often, so that it is possible to build a set of menus by assigning meaningful names to each `Action`, and then using these names to create menu items. In this section, we'll show the beginnings of a program that could be used as the basis for an HTML (or RTF, or plain text) editor.

Constructing Menus from Editor Kit Actions

To build our editor, we need to address several problems:

1. How to specify the relationship between the names to be used for the menu items and the `Actions` supported by the Swing editor kits.

2. How to arrange for the menu items to be organized into a useful menu hierarchy.

3. Because different editor kits support different sets of `Actions`, how to make sure that only the appropriate set of `Actions` is available on the menu bar for the type of document loaded into the editor.

The simplest way to address all these problems is to create a simple class that maps a meaningful name that can be added to a menu to the name of an `Action`, the idea being that a menu can be specified as an array of objects of this type. Scanning through the array would enable us to build a menu with one menu item for each entry in the array, and would also show which `Actions` to attach to them. If we call this class `MenuSpec`, we might define a menu that has entries to change the style of the font associated with text like this:

```
private static MenuSpec[] styleSpec = new MenuSpec[] {
   new MenuSpec("Bold", "font-bold"),
   new MenuSpec("Italics", "font-italic"),
   new MenuSpec("Underline", "font-underline")
};
```

In this example, the strings `Bold`, `Italics`, and `Underline` will appear on an as-yet-unnamed menu and will map to `Actions` called `font-bold`, `font-italic`, and `font-underline` respectively. If you refer to Table 1-6, you'll see that these are three of the `Actions` supplied by `StyledEditorKit`.

This simple structure allows us to build a single menu, but it is usually desirable to provide several small menus with closely related features than one large one. To do this, we need to be able to create menus that have submenus. We could achieve this by just creating several `MenuSpec` arrays like that shown earlier, using them to generate a set of `JMenu` objects and then assembling them into larger menus by hand. That, however, would be very inflexible. Instead, what we'll do is to extend `MenuSpec` so that it can also map a menu name to an array of other `MenuSpec` objects. This enables us to create a cascading menu, in which the `MenuSpec` array specifies the content of the child menu. Here, for example, is how we would specify a menu with three child menus:

```
// Menu definitions for fonts
private static MenuSpec[] fontSpec = new MenuSpec[] {
   new MenuSpec("Size", sizeSpec),
   new MenuSpec("Family", familySpec),
   new MenuSpec("Style", styleSpec)
};
```

When this array of `MenuSpec` objects is used, we'll get a menu with items labeled `Size`, `Family`, and `Style`, each of which has an associated child menu. The content of the `Style` menu, for example, will be determined by the `MenuSpec` array pointed to by the variable `styleSpec`, the definition of which you saw earlier. Figure 4-19 shows how this looks in the completed application.

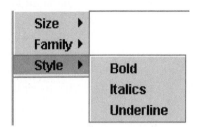

Figure 4-19 A menu created dynamically from `EditorKit` actions.

Listing 4-21 shows the simple implementation of the `MenuSpec` class. As you can see, this class has no real behavior of its own—it exists only to store information about a menu and, once the `MenuSpec` has been created, its content cannot be changed.

Listing 4-21 A Specification for Menu

```
package AdvancedSwing.Chapter4;

import javax.swing.Action;

public class MenuSpec {
    public MenuSpec(String name, MenuSpec[] subMenus) {
        this.name = name;
        this.subMenus = subMenus;
    }

    public MenuSpec(String name, String actionName) {
        this.name = name;
        this.actionName = actionName;
    }

    public MenuSpec(String name, Action action) {
        this.name = name;
        this.action = action;
    }
```

Listing 4-21 A Specification for Menu (continued)

```
    public boolean isSubMenu() {
        return subMenus != null;
    }

    public boolean isAction() {
        return action != null;
    }

    public String getName() {
        return name;
    }

    public MenuSpec[] getSubMenus() {
        return subMenus;
    }

    public String getActionName() {
        return actionName;
    }

    public Action getAction() {
        return action;
    }

    private String name;
    private String actionName;
    private Action action;
    private MenuSpec[] subMenus;
}
```

The constructors simply store their arguments for later retrieval. The first constructor allows you to create a MenuSpec that specifies a child menu that will be attached to another menu with the given name. The second constructor is for a menu item mapping a named Action from the set of Actions provided by a text component. We'll use both of these constructors in the next example in this section. The third constructor, which we won't use here, maps a menu item name to an Action. The intent here is to allow you to mix text component Actions with extra Actions that are specific to an application and which the application can create for itself. For example, if an application implements an Action in a class called DeleteAllAction, you might use the following to create a MenuSpec that can be used to add it to a menu:

```
MenuSpec deleteAllSpec = new MenuSpec("Delete All",
                         new DeleteAllAction());
```

The methods `getActionName`, `getSubMenus`, and `getAction` can be used to extract the specification for the menu or menu item that should be constructed for this `MenuSpec`. For any given `MenuSpec`, only one of these three methods will return a non-`null` result. To determine the type, the methods `isSubMenu` and `isAction` can be used.

A menu is built from an array of `MenuSpec` items. The details of this process are encapsulated in a class called `MenuBuilder`, which has a single static method called `buildMenu` that constructs a complete menu, with any necessary submenus, based on its arguments. The implementation is shown in Listing 4-22.

Listing 4-22 Building a Complete Menu

```
package AdvancedSwing.Chapter4;

import javax.swing.*;
import java.util.*;
import java.awt.event.*;

public class MenuBuilder {
   public static JMenu buildMenu(String name, MenuSpec[]
                                 menuSpecs,
                                 Hashtable actions) {
      int count = menuSpecs.length;

      JMenu menu = new JMenu(name);
      for (int i = 0; i < count; i++) {
         MenuSpec spec = menuSpecs[i];
         if (spec.isSubMenu()) {
            // Recurse to handle a sub menu
            JMenu subMenu = buildMenu(spec.getName(),
                            spec.getSubMenus(), actions);
            if (subMenu != null) {
               menu.add(subMenu);
            }
         } else if (spec.isAction()) {
            // It's an Action - add it directly to the menu
            menu.add(spec.getAction());
         } else {
```

Listing 4-22 Building a Complete Menu (continued)

```
                // It's an action name - add it if possible
                String actionName = spec.getActionName();
                Action targetAction =
                            (Action)actions.get(actionName);

                // Create the menu item
                JMenuItem menuItem = menu.add(spec.getName());
                if (targetAction != null) {
                    // The editor kit knows the action
                    menuItem.addActionListener(targetAction);
                } else {
                    // Action not known - disable the menu item
                    menuItem.setEnabled(false);
                }
            }
        }

        // Return null if nothing was added to the menu.
        if (menu.getMenuComponentCount() == 0) {
            menu = null;
        }

        return menu;
    }
}
```

The implementation is fairly straightforward. The name of the menu to be constructed is passed as the first argument, the MenuSpecs that describe the menu items on the menu as the second argument, and a set of Actions as the third. An empty JMenu is created and then a loop is entered that processes each MenuSpec in turn, creating a single menu item for each entry in the MenuSpec array. There are three possible ways for the menu item to be created, depending on the type of the MenuSpec:

- If the MenuSpec contains an Action (that is, isAction returns true), the reference to the Action stored in the MenuSpec is obtained from getAction and added directly to the menu using the JMenu add method, which creates and returns a JMenuItem.

- If isSubMenu returns true, the getSubMenus method is used to get the array of MenuSpec objects that specifies the content of the child menu and the buildMenu method is invoked again to build a new JMenu, which is then added to the original menu. In Figure 4-19, this is how the Size, Family, and Style submenus were created.

- Finally, if neither of those methods return true, the MenuSpec specifies the name of an Action, which may be in the Hashtable passed as the third argument to buildMenu. The Action name (obtained using the getActionName method) is used as the key to obtain the desired Action from the Hashtable and, if it is present, it is added to the menu under the name specified in the MenuSpec. However, not all editor kits support all the Actions you might want to add to an application menu; those that are not supported by the editor kit being used will not be passed in the Hashtable (you'll see how the Hashtable is constructed shortly). If this is the case, the menu item is still added, but it is disabled. This allows the user to see the full range of possibilities supported by the application, even if they are not available at any given time. As you'll see in our example application, as you load different document types, the set of enabled menu items will change accordingly. This addresses the third of the set of issues shown in the list above.

Because an array of MenuSpec objects can contain any mixture of these three types, the buildMenu method can be used to create a menu with any combination of menu items and submenus and the same applies to any sub-menu.

Using Editor Kit Actions

Now that we've got the means to build a set of menus from a specification, it's a relatively simple matter to add a suitable menu bar to our ongoing example. Before we look at the small amount of extra code that's needed to make the Actions supported by the various Swing editor kits available to the end user, let's try out the modified example. You can do this using the command

```
java AdvancedSwing.Chapter4.EditorPaneExample18
```

The main window of this application looks very much like that of the previous versions of this program, except that it now has a menu bar at the top and a Save button at the bottom, as shown in Figure 4-20.

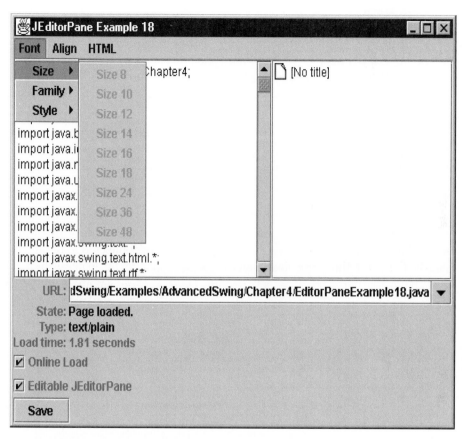

Figure 4-20 The Editor Pane example with a Font Size menu.

When the application has started, pull down all the menus in turn. You'll find that the Font menu has the three submenus for Size, Family, and Style that you saw in the code extract shown earlier. If you activate each of these menus in turn, you'll see that they are fully populated but every menu item is disabled. Figure 4-20 shows the Font Size menu, each entry on which has been created from a single MenuSpec. When a JEditorPane is created, it has a PlainDocument and a DefaultEditorKit installed, which does not support any of the Actions referenced by the set of MenuSpecs created in this example. As a result, although the menus are created, none of the Actions that they correspond to will be present in the Hashtable passed to the buildMenu method and so the menu items are all disabled. The same situation results if you actually load a plain document, as is the case in Figure 4-20.

Core Note

We're not going to show the complete set of `MenuSpec` *objects used in this example. If you want to see them, you'll find them in the source code on the CD-ROM that accompanies this book.*

Now load an HTML document into the `JEditorPane` by typing an appropriate URL and pressing RETURN. If you have installed the example code in the recommended location, you'll find a suitable HTML page at the URL

`file:///c:\AdvancedSwing\Examples\AdvancedSwing\Chapter4\SimplePage.html`

Now if you walk through the menus, you'll find that all the menu items have been activated, because they are all supported by the `HTMLEditorKit` that is now installed in the `JEditorPane`. The non-HTML `Actions` connected to the menus, namely those on the `Font` and `Layout` menus, operate by manipulating the `AttributeSets` in the `Document`'s `Elements`. These `Actions` are implemented by `StyledEditorKit`, which is the superclass of `HTMLEditorKit` and of `RTFEditorKit`, which means that the menu items created from them will be available when you load either an HTML or an RTF document. To see how they work, first select some text and then select a menu item. The `Action` associated with the menu item will then be applied to the selected text. For example, if you have loaded `SimplePage.html`, you can change font of the large red words by selecting them, and then opening the `Font` menu followed by the `Size` submenu and then clicking on the menu item for the font size that you want to apply. The `actionPerformed` method of the `Action` connected to the menu item applies the font to the `AttributeSet` of the `Elements` covered by the selected area as character attributes.

You can also use the menus to set styles for new text as it is typed into the `JEditorPane`. To do this, click anywhere inside the `JEditorPane` with the mouse, so that nothing is selected. If you start typing, the characters that appear will match the style of those already at the cursor location. You can change the style by selecting the attributes you want from the menus. For example, select a 24-point font from the `Font Size` submenu and `Bold` and `Underline` from the `Font Style` menu. As you make the menu selections, nothing appears to happen but, in fact, the *input attribute* set is being changed to reflect the attributes chosen from the menu. As you may recall from Chapter 2, the input attribute set contains character attributes that will be applied to newly inserted text. When you place the cursor, the input attribute set is initialized from the attributes at the cursor location, which is why new text inherits the appearance of the text that surrounds it. Now if you start typing, you'll find that the text is larger, is rendered in bold, and is underlined (see Figure 4-21).

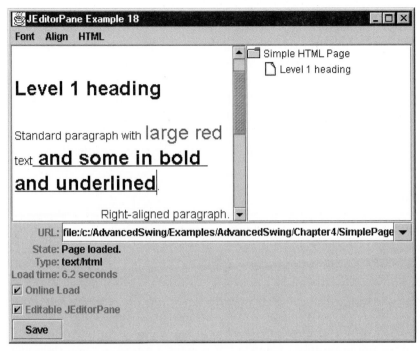

Figure 4-21   Using Editor Kit Actions to change the style of input text.

At the bottom of the window, you'll find a button labeled `save`. If you press this button, the editor kit will save the current content of the document in its usual form on standard output, which will be the window from which you started the program. If you do this now, you'll see the HTML that corresponds to what is being displayed by the `JEditorPane` and you'll notice that the text that you just typed is there, with the appropriate tags to have it displayed with the attributes set from the menu, shown here in bold:

```
<p>
        Standard paragraph with <font color="red" size="+2">
large red</font> text <u><b><font size="24">
and some in bold and underlined</font></b></u>.
</p>
```

As noted earlier in this section, this works because the `StyledEditorKit` actions apply `StyleConstants` attributes held in the `AttributeSet` to the text as it is entered. When an `HTMLEditorKit` is installed in the `JEditorPane`, these attributes will be converted directly to their CSS equivalents and stored with the content `Elements` associated with the text in the underlying `HTMLDoc-ument`. When the `HTMLEditorKit write` method is called to save the model in HTML form, these attributes cause the tags you see above to be generated.

As you can see, using only the `MenuSpec` and `MenuBuilder` classes shown in the section and the `Actions` supplied by `StyledEditorKit`, you can turn a `JEditorPane` into a simple editor that you can use to enter text in a variety of styles and fonts and, using the `Actions` on the Align menu, you can also arrange for individual paragraphs to be left-, center-, or right-aligned. Moreover, these features apply equally to HTML pages or to RTF documents, as you can see by loading the RTF document `LM.rtf` from the same directory as `SimplePage.html`. Before we look at the HTML-specific `Actions`, let's go back to our example program and complete the discussion of the implementation of the menu bar.

Core Note

If you load an RTF document, the menu items on the `Font` *and* `Layout` *menus remain enabled, but the ones on the HTML menu are no longer available, because they are provided by* `HTMLEditorKit` *but not by* `RTFEditorKit`.

Creating the Application Menu Bar

When our example program is loaded, it creates a `JMenuBar` and then calls the `createMenuBar` method to populate it. This method is shown in Listing 4-23. As you can see, it first removes whatever is currently on the menu bar, and then uses the `getActions` method of `JEditorPane` to get the current set of supported text `Actions`, which combines those provided by `JEditor-Pane` itself with the ones available from the underlying editor kit. The set of `Actions` is returned as an array, which is then converted to a `Hashtable` in which each `Action` is stored with its name as the key. The content of this `Hashtable` will, of course, be different for each editor kit. Next, the three menus that appear on the menu bar are constructed by invoking the `build-Menu` method of `MenuBuilder` with the menu name, the array of `MenuSpec` objects for that menu, and the `Hashtable` of the currently available `Actions`. The `JMenus` returned are added directly to the menu bar.

Core Note

Technically, `buildMenu` *can return* `null` *instead of a* `JMenu`. *This only happens if the* `MenuSpec` *it is given doesn't result in the creation of any menu items. In our case, this will not happen. If it did, the corresponding menu would not appear in the menu bar.*

Listing 4-23 Creating the Application Menu Bar Content

```
public void createMenuBar() {
    // Remove the existing menu items
    int count = menuBar.getMenuCount();
    for (int i = 0; i < count; i++) {
        menuBar.remove(menuBar.getMenu(0));
    }

    // Build the new menu.
    Action[] actions = pane.getActions();
    Hashtable actionHash = new Hashtable();
    count = actions.length;
    for (int i = 0; i < count; i++) {
        actionHash.put(actions[i].getValue(Action.NAME),
            actions[i]);
    }

    // Add the font menu
    JMenu menu = MenuBuilder.buildMenu("Font", fontSpec,
                                    actionHash);
    if (menu != null) {
        menuBar.add(menu);
    }

    // Add the alignment menu
    menu = MenuBuilder.buildMenu("Align", alignSpec,
                                    actionHash);
    if (menu != null) {
        menuBar.add(menu);
    }

    // Add the HTML menu
    menu = MenuBuilder.buildMenu("HTML", htmlSpec,
                                    actionHash);
    if (menu != null) {
        menuBar.add(menu);
    }
}
```

Why do we need to clear the menu bar at the start of this method? Although this operation is initially redundant the first time this method is called, we will call it again every time the installed editor kit is changed (in fact, we call it after each document has been loaded). We need to do this because changing the editor kit implies a possible change in the set of available `Actions`. When the set of `Actions` changes, we need to change the enabled state of the menu items to reflect what is now available. Because in this example we are dealing with a fixed set of `MenuSpecs`, the actual set of menu items on all the menus on the menu bar will not change, so we could do this by creating the menu hierarchy once and simply walking through them on subsequent occasions, changing the enabled state as appropriate. The implementation shown here is, however, much clearer and easier to understand. It does, however, have the consequence that we repeatedly add the same menus to the menu bar, so to avoid duplicates we need to remove all the menus each time this method is invoked.

Using HTML `Actions`

When you load an HTML document into the `JEditorPane`, you'll find that the menu items on the HTML menu are enabled. These menu items, which represent all the `Actions` provided by `HTMLEditorKit` at the time of writing (in Swing 1.1.1 and Java 2 version 1.2.2), are as follows:

Menu Label	Action Name
Table	InsertTable
Table Row	InsertTableRow
Table Cell	InsertTableDataCell
Unordered List	InsertUnorderedList
Unordered List Item	InsertUnorderedListItem
Ordered List	InsertOrderedList
Ordered List Item	InsertOrderedListItem
Preformatted Paragraph	InsertPre
Horizontal Rule	InsertHR

All these `Actions` insert HTML into the document. To use them, place the cursor where you want the insertion to take place and then click on the menu item. To insert a table, for example, place the cursor and click the `Table` menu item to get a table with one empty cell. Once you've got a cell, you can add content to it directly just by typing it in and you can apply the styles and layout constraints on the other menus as necessary. The `Table Cell` menu item adds a new cell to the right of the cursor location, moving any cells already to the right of the cursor over by one position to make room for it. Similarly, `Table Row` inserts a complete new row. The newly created row is not fully populated with cells—only a single cell is added, leaving any other positions in the row blank, as shown in Figure 4-22. You can fill out these unoccupied locations using `Table Cell`. To remove a cell, place the cursor inside it and press the DELETE key until its content has been removed, and then press it once more to delete the cell itself. Cells to the right of the deleted cell are moved left to occupy the newly created space, leaving blank space at the right side of the row; deleting the last cell in a row removes the entire row. You can also select multiple cells and delete them together.

The other menu items all work in the same way, allowing you to insert lists with bullets or numbers, a horizontal separator, or create a paragraph for pre-formatted text which uses a monospaced font and is suitable for entering content that must appear exactly as it is typed, such as a code listing. The current set of `Actions` allows you only limited access to the underlying HTML support, but may be expanded as the Swing HTML package is developed. To take advantage of any new `Actions` that might be added, you will only need to modify the `MenuSpecs` for the HTML menu by adding the new `Action` names, along with the labels that should appear on the associated menu items.

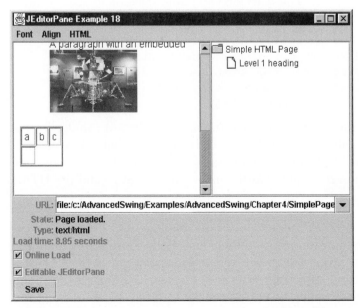

Figure 4-22 Using `HTMLEditorKit` actions to add a table.

Adding Custom HTML Actions

All the HTMLEditorKit Actions that appear on the HTML menu in our example application are derived from an inner class of HTMLEditorKit called InsertHTMLTextAction. One instance of this class is returned from the HTMLEditorKit getActions method for each of the available HTML Actions. You can use this class to create new Actions of your own and in this section we'll demonstrate how to do this by adding to our example application a Headings menu that contains menu items to insert level 1 and level 2 headings into an HTMLDocument.

To provide new HTML Actions, we need to do two things:

- Implement the Actions to perform the required operation on the HTMLDocument.
- Arrange for the new Actions to appear in the set returned by the HTMLEditorKit getActions method.

Once we've done both of the above, it is a simple matter to extend our example application to expose the new Actions in the menu hierarchy.

Creating New HTML Actions

For relatively simple operations like inserting pre-defined HTML sequences, the easiest way to expand the capabilities of HTMLEditorKit is to use InsertHTMLTextAction. This class has two public constructors:

```
public InsertHTMLTextAction(String name, String html,
        HTML.Tag parentTag, HTML.Tag addTag);
public InsertHTMLTextAction(String name, String html,
        HTML.Tag parentTag, HTML.Tag addTag,
        HTML.Tag alternateParentTag,
        HTML.Tag alternateAddTag)
```

In both cases, the name argument is the name of the Action itself, while the second argument is the actual string of HTML tags that will be inserted into the document. In terms of some examples that you have already seen, the Action that inserts a table has the name InsertTable and the HTML that it inserts is

```
<table border=1><tr><td></td></tr></table>
```

which creates a table with a single empty cell. Both constructors then have two arguments of type HTML.Tag called parentTag and addTag. The parentTag argument effectively specifies the level within the document Element structure at which the HTML will be inserted, while addTag is the

HTML.Tag value for the first inserted tag. For the InsertTable Action, these arguments have the values HTML.Tag.BODY and HTML.Tag.TABLE, which specifies that a TABLE tag should be inserted in the body of the document. It may seem confusing that you have to explicitly state the first tag to be inserted when that tag appears in the HTML string given as the second argument and that you need to specify that the HTML should be inserted in the document body. To understand why these two arguments are necessary and why there is a second constructor that has an alternate pair of tag and parent tags, let's look at an example that shows how these arguments are used.

Suppose the following simple HTML page has been loaded into the JEditorPane:

```
<HTML>
<BODY>
<H1>Heading</H1>
<P>
First paragraph text.
</BODY>
</HTML>
```

This page contains a level 1 heading and a single line of text. Now suppose you want to insert a table above the text but below the heading. You start by placing the cursor to the left of the text as shown in Figure 4-23, and then open the HTML menu and select the Table Action. This invokes the InsertTable Action to insert the HTML string shown earlier at the cursor location. This sounds straightforward, but there is a complication.

Heading

First paragraph text.

Figure 4-23 Inserting a table into an HTML page.

To see what the complication is, we need to look at the HTMLDocument that is created for this page. The part of the document content relevant to this example is shown here.

```
===== Element Class: HTMLDocument$BlockElement
  Offsets [3, 34]
  ATTRIBUTES:
   (name, body) [StyleConstants/HTML$Tag]
    ===== Element Class: HTMLDocument$BlockElement
    Offsets [3, 11]
    ATTRIBUTES:
     (name, h1) [StyleConstants/HTML$Tag]
      ===== Element Class: HTMLDocument$RunElement
      Offsets [3, 10]
      ATTRIBUTES:
       (name, content) [StyleConstants/HTML$Tag]
      [Heading]
      ===== Element Class: HTMLDocument$RunElement
      Offsets [10, 11]
      ATTRIBUTES:
       (name, content) [StyleConstants/HTML$Tag]
       [
]
    ===== Element Class: HTMLDocument$BlockElement
    Offsets [11, 33]
    ATTRIBUTES:
     (name, p) [StyleConstants/HTML$Tag]
      ===== Element Class: HTMLDocument$RunElement
      Offsets [11, 32]
      ATTRIBUTES:
       (name, content) [StyleConstants/HTML$Tag]
      [First paragraph text.]
```

When you place the cursor just before the content of the first paragraph, it is located at offset 11 within the document. When the InsertTable Action is activated from the menu, it uses this offset as the position at which the table is to be inserted. If you look at the Element structure shown previously, you'll see that there are actually three Elements that occupy document offset 11:

- The body element, which covers offsets 3 to 34.
- The block element for the paragraph containing the single line of text in this document, which begins at offset 11 and ends at offset 33.
- The run element containing the text itself, which runs from offset 11 to 32.

Clearly, it's not enough to specify that the HTML should be inserted at the current location of the cursor (or, actually, at the start of the current selection if there is one) because this is ambiguous. In practice, it only makes sense to insert the table at the body level of the document and that's what the parentTag argument is for—it resolves the ambiguity by determining which of the possible insertion locations is correct. Every Action created using InsertHTMLTextAction specifies a parent tag; the InsertTable Action, like all Actions that insert a major structural element, specifies insertion at the body level. Here's exactly how this Action is defined:

```
new InsertHTMLTextAction("InsertTable", INSERT_TABLE_HTML,
                         HTML.Tag.BODY, HTML.Tag.TABLE),
```

As yet we haven't explained why there is a need to include the HTML.Tag.TABLE argument, or why there is an alternative constructor that allows you to specify a pair of alternate tags. To see why these are needed, consider what happens if you want to insert a new row into your newly created table. The Action that inserts a table row is defined as follows:

```
new InsertHTMLTextAction("InsertTableRow", INSERT_TABLE_HTML,
                         HTML.Tag.TABLE, HTML.Tag.TR,
                         HTML.Tag.BODY, HTML.Tag.TABLE)
```

You might expect that when a table row is to be inserted the HTML string argument would be

```
<TR><TD></TD></TR>
```

which produces a new row with an empty cell in it. In fact, the HTML in the Action shown earlier is exactly the same as that used to insert a complete table, namely

```
<TABLE BORDER=1><TR><TD></TD></TR></TABLE>
```

However, if you actually use the HTML menu to insert a new row, you'll see that it does just insert a table row, not an entire new table—in other words, not all the HTML string in the InsertHTMLTextAction is being used. This poses two questions:

1. Why bother specifying the HTML to create an empty table when only a new row is needed?

2. How did the code that updated the document know which part of the HTML string should actually be used and which parts should be ignored?

The answer to the first question lies in what happens if you try to create a new table row before creating a table at all. This seems like a strange thing to do, but nothing stops you from selecting the Table Row" item from the menu before selecting Table. If you run the last version of our `JEditorPane` example, load up the `SimplePage.html` page, position the cursor at the bottom of the page, and select Table Row from the HTML menu, you'll find that a new table is created with one empty cell. In fact, the complete HTML string associated with the `InsertTableRow Action` has been inserted. However, as you know, if there had already been a table present, only the part of the HTML needed to create a new row would have been used.

Here, you've seen the same `Action` used in two different contexts; on both occasions, the correct results were obtained. That's the reason why there are two sets of tags in the `InsertHTMLTextAction`. The first parent tag/insert tag pair is intended to be used when the `Action` is applied in its expected context, while the second is used in an alternate context. In the case of the `InsertTableRow Action`, the primary tag pair is:

```
HTML.Tag.TABLE, HTML.Tag.TR,
```

which states that the expected context for this `Action` is at the level of the `TABLE` element and that the inserted HTML should start with a `<TR>` tag. The alternate pair looks like this:

```
HTML.Tag.BODY, HTML.Tag.TABLE
```

which says that if the `Action` is used at the `BODY` level, the inserted HTML should begin with a `<TABLE>` tag. In fact, wherever you insert HTML in the part of an HTML page displayed in a `JEditorPane`, there will always be a surrounding `BODY` element, so a tag pair of this type will always permit insertion to take place because there is a surrounding body tag at every location. In fact, a tag pair of this type specifies the default operation if the primary tag context does not apply.

The remaining issue is what the second tag of the pair is used for. Looking at the primary tag pair, it specifies that the inserted HTML should start with a `<TR>` tag. The HTML string provided with this `Action` does, of course, contain a `<TR>` tag:

```
<TABLE BORDER=1><TR><TD></TD></TR></TABLE>
```

The effect of the `HTML.Tag.TR` is to specify that everything preceding it in the HTML string should be excluded from the tags inserted in the document. Likewise, the matching `</TR>` tag and the `</TABLE>` tag will be excluded. This is why the same HTML string can be used whether the HTML will be inserted in its expected context or at the `BODY` level. Of course, if the alternate tag pair is used, the start tag is `<TABLE>`, so the entire HTML string will be used, resulting in the creation of a new table to enclose the table row. The `Action` that adds a new table cell is similar:

```
new InsertHTMLTextAction("InsertTableDataCell", INSERT_TABLE_HTML,
                    HTML.Tag.TR, HTML.Tag.TD,
                    HTML.Tag.BODY, HTML.Tag.TABLE),
```

The same HTML string is specified here as for the previous two actions. The primary context for this operation is with an `HTML.Tag.TR Element`, which is a table row as you might expect, and the HTML inserted begins with the `<TD>` tag. As a result, only the `<TD></TD>` pair will be used. The fallback is to create a complete new table, which would be the correct behavior.

Now that you've seen how the `InsertHTMLTextAction` class works, using it to add new `Actions` is simple. Suppose you wanted to add an `Action` to allow a level 1 header to be inserted. The tags you need to have added to the document are

```
<H1></H1>
```

If you specify this as the HTML string in the constructor of an `Insert-HTMLTextAction` object, it will work, but it won't be visible to the person trying to insert the heading. To make it more obvious that the heading tags have been inserted, you can supply some default heading text that makes the header visible. To do this, just change the HTML to

```
<H1>[H1]</H1>
```

Headings should be included at the body level, so the parent tag should be `<BODY>` and the whole HTML string should be used, so the start tag should be `HTML.Tag.H1`. Here's how the `InsertHTMLTextAction` object for this `Action` should be created:

```
new InsertHTMLTextAction("Heading 1", "<h1>[H1]</h1>",
                    HTML.Tag.BODY, HTML.Tag.H1)
```

The same technique works for other heading levels; for good measure, we'll also create an `Action` to insert a level 2 heading that looks like this:

```
new InsertHTMLTextAction("Heading 2", "<h2>[H2]</h2>",
                    HTML.Tag.BODY, HTML.Tag.H2)
```

Returning New Actions from the `getActions` Method

You've seen how to create the `Actions` to insert HTML. The next problem is how to use them from an application. There are two ways to do this. The simplest way is just to create an instance of the action and add it to a menu. If you create the two `Actions` as shown earlier, you can add them to menu simply by doing this:

```
JMenu headings = new JMenu("Headings");
headings.add(new InsertHTMLTextAction("Heading 1",
           "<h1>[H1]</h1>",
           HTML.Tag.BODY, HTML.Tag.H1);
headings.add(new InsertHTMLTextAction("Heading 2",
           "<h2>[H2]</h2>",
           HTML.Tag.BODY, HTML.Tag.H2);
```

This is not a very general solution, however. Instead, it is better to arrange for these `Actions` to be returned from the `JEditorPane`'s `getActions` method when an HTML document is loaded. To do this, you need to have the `HTMLEditorKit getActions` method return them along with its usual set of `Actions`, which means creating a subclass of `HTMLEditorKit` and overriding the `getActions` method, and then installing the subclass as the editor kit that `JEditorPane` will use when loading HTML documents.

You've already seen how to arrange for a different editor kit to be used when we looked at how to create a different `ViewFactory` so that we could arrange for hidden tags to be invisible when an HTML document is being edited. For convenience, we'll use the editor kit from Listing 4-19 as the base class from which to create one with our new `Actions` installed, so that hidden tags will remain invisible. The implementation is shown in Listing 4-24.

Listing 4-24 Adding New HTML Actions to an Editor Kit

```
package AdvancedSwing.Chapter4;

import javax.swing.*;
import javax.swing.text.*;
import javax.swing.text.html.*;

public class EnhancedHTMLEditorKit extends
      HiddenViewHTMLEditorKit {
   public Object clone() {
      return new EnhancedHTMLEditorKit();
   }

   public Action[] getActions() {
      return TextAction.augmentList(super.getActions(),
         extraActions);
   }

   private static final InsertHTMLTextAction[]
      extraActions =
```

**Listing 4-24 Adding New HTML Actions to an
                  Editor Kit (continued)**

```
      new InsertHTMLTextAction[] {
        new InsertHTMLTextAction("Heading 1",
                      "<h1>[H1]</h1>",
              HTML.Tag.BODY, HTML.Tag.H1),
        new InsertHTMLTextAction("Heading 2",
                      "<h2>[H2]</h2>",
              HTML.Tag.BODY, HTML.Tag.H2),
    };


  }
```

The new `Actions` are created and installed in a static array; like all editor kit actions, the same set is shared by every instance of the editor kit. We need to have these `Actions` included in the set returned by `getActions`, so we override the `getActions` method and use the static `augmentList` method of the `TextAction` class (which was described in Chapter 1) to merge the our `Actions` with those provided by our superclass, which inherits its `getActions` method directly from `HTMLEditorKit`. Now any `JEditorPane` that uses `EnhancedHTMLEditorKit` will have `Actions` to insert level 1 and level 2 headings available to it. To see how this works, use the following command:

```
java AdvanceedSwing.Chapter4.EditorPaneExample19
```

and load an HTML page (such as `SimplePage.html`). If you open the HTML menu, you'll find that it has a submenu labeled Headings, on which there are menu items labeled Heading 1 and Heading 2, as shown in Figure 4-24.

If you place the cursor at the end of the document and activate the Headings 1 menu item, you'll find that a level 1 heading with the text `[H1]` will appear and that you can overwrite the text with your own, which will appear in the appropriate font for a level 1 heading. The same also works for level 2 headings and, if you press the `Save` button, you'll see that the HTML has the correct tags added to it.

This example is almost unchanged from `EditorPaneExample18`. To register the editor kit to be used for all HTML documents, the line

```
JEditorPane.registerEditorKitForContentType("text/html",
        "AdvancedSwing.Chapter4.EnhancedHTMLEditorKit",
        getClass().getClassLoader());
```

was added. The menus were included by adding a new `MenuSpec` array:

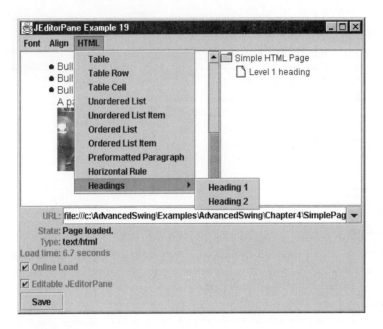

Figure 4-24   A JEditorPane with actions to add headings.

```
private static MenuSpec[] headingSpec = new MenuSpec[] {
   new MenuSpec("Heading 1", "Heading 1"),
   new MenuSpec("Heading 2", "Heading 2")
};
```

which causes menu items that refer to the new Actions to be created. Finally, this menu is added to the HTML menu by adding the highlighted line to the MenuSpec array for that menu:

```
private static MenuSpec[] htmlSpec = new MenuSpec[] {
    new MenuSpec("Table", "InsertTable"),
    new MenuSpec("Table Row", "InsertTableRow"),
    new MenuSpec("Table Cell", "InsertTableDataCell"),
    new MenuSpec("Unordered List", "InsertUnorderedList"),
    new MenuSpec("Unordered List Item",
                 "InsertUnorderedListItem"),
    new MenuSpec("Ordered List", "InsertOrderedList"),
    new MenuSpec("Ordered List Item",
                 "InsertOrderedListItem"),
    new MenuSpec("Preformatted Paragraph", "InsertPre"),
    new MenuSpec("Horizontal Rule", "InsertHR"),
    new MenuSpec("Headings", headingSpec)
};
```

Summary

This long chapter examined in great detail the most powerful of the Swing text controls. You saw that, without too much work, you can treat JEditor-Pane as an out-of-the-box editor for various types of document including HTML and RTF. The power and flexibility of JEditorPane comes from the way in which it exploits the Swing text component architecture, which cleanly separates the tasks of holding the document content, the attributes used to control the way in which it is displayed, the editor kit that controls how the user can interact with the document, and the View objects that determine how the document is actually rendered on the screen. We've looked at each of these pieces in their own right in earlier chapters of this book and in this chapter you saw exactly how JEditorPane uses the text architecture to store and display HTML and how you can leverage this support to parse and manipulate HTML documents without directly involving JEditorPane and without having to display the document to the user. Finally, you saw how to programmatically change the HTML once it has been loaded into the JEditorPane's Document model and how to extend the HTML editor kit to include more actions that can be used to extend its editing capabilities. Using these techniques, you can write code to create and modify HTML documents on-the-fly or turn the basic JEditorPane into a more complete HTML editor.

BI-DIRECTIONAL TEXT

Topics in this Chapter

- Bi-Directional Text

- Physical Fonts

- Bi-Directional Text and the Caret

Chapter 5

With the introduction of the Java 2D application programming interface (API), Java 2 provides enhanced text handling facilities that you can take advantage of using the Swing text components. A complete discussion of Java 2D would be well beyond the scope of this book, so in this chapter, we'll focus on one specific piece of the Java 2D functionality that is exposed by the Swing text components and that you can easily make use of: bi-directional text. As you'll see, the support provided by the text package for text that might not all be read in a single direction is sufficiently comprehensive that, as a developer, most of the time you can take it for granted that the consequences of using it are taken care of for you. The material in this chapter explains how the text components handle bi-directional text and the differences that the user will see when it is in use.

Bi-Directional Text

So far in this book, we've assumed that text is always read from left to right. In many languages, this is true, but both Java 2D and the Swing text components support the rendering of text in either left-to-right or right-to-left order. In fact, it is permissible to mix text ordering within a single paragraph, or even within the same line, so this feature is commonly referred to as *bi-directional text*. The most obvious example of a writing system that requires the use of bi-directional text is Arabic. Here, the text is read from right to left, apart from numerals, which use the more familiar left-to-right ordering. To display Arabic text properly, you need Java 2 and a font that can render Arabic script. Fortunately, however, you usually don't have to do anything special in your code to handle bi-directional text because the Swing text components do all the hard work for you.

Core Note

Even if you ignore the problems of ordering, properly rendering Arabic script is a complex operation because the appearance of many of the characters in the alphabet (glyphs in Java 2D terminology) depends in part on their context: Some characters have several different glyph representations. This is rather like drawing the letter "a" differently depending on which characters it is adjacent to. These details are taken care of by the Java 2D implementation of the `Graphics drawString` *method, so we don't really need to be concerned with them here.*

Some of the operating systems supported by Java 2 do not provide Arabic fonts unless you buy a version of the platform intended for a market in which Arabic script is used. Nevertheless, Java 2 provides a set of platform-independent fonts that do include Arabic characters, so you can make use of these fonts to render Arabic text. However, because Arabic characters are probably not familiar to you, we'll substitute the more usual Roman alphabet in the figures in this chapter where you would expect to see Arabic script, but we'll make it clear from the accompanying descriptions which characters should be considered to be Arabic.

Core Note

The extra fonts that Java 2 supplies are referred to as physical fonts to distinguish them from the virtual fonts that were supported by the Abstract Window Toolkit (AWT). Whereas virtual fonts have idealized names such as "Serif" or "Monospace" and are mapped to real fonts on the host platform through a mapping held in a resource file installed as part of the Java Developer's Kit (JDK) or Java Runtime Environment (JRE), physical fonts are referred to by their real names. The physical fonts that come with Java 2 are all TrueType fonts stored in the lib/fonts directory. They have the following names:

- *Lucida Sans Regular*
- *Lucida Sans Bold*
- *Lucida Sans Oblique*
- *Lucida Sans Bold Oblique*
- *Lucida Bright Regular*
- *Lucida Bright Bold*
- *Lucida Bright Italic*
- *Lucida Bright Bold Italic*
- *Lucida Sans Typewriter Regular*
- *Lucida Sans Typewriter Bold*
- *Lucida Sans Typewriter Oblique*
- *Lucida Sans Typewriter Bold Oblique*

These fonts cover several different pages of the Unicode code set, including the Arabic characters that we'll be using in the examples in this chapter.

Model Order and Visual Order

In all the examples that you have seen so far, we have been assuming that the characters that a text component contains are displayed in the same order in which they are stored. That is to say, the character at offset 0 is displayed to the left of that at offset 1, which appears to the left of the character at offset 2, and so on. As you saw in the last chapter, by creating a custom `View`, you can arrange to vary this a little by rendering characters that aren't actually in the model at all and, using similar means, you could also display fewer characters than are actually present. Nevertheless, so far we have not seen a case in which a `View` renders text in any order other than that suggested by the storage order within the model, which we will refer to as the logical order. The order in which a text component actually displays its content is referred to as its visual order. Figure 5-1 shows an example of what has, so far, been the rule—the logical order matching the visual order.

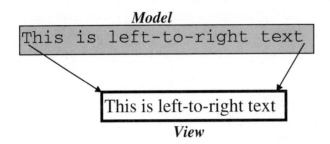

Figure 5-1   A text component displaying left-to-right text.

The upper part of this diagram represents the model, containing the text in logical order. If you think of the model as being represented in concrete terms as an array of characters, the representation shown here will seem quite natural and matches what you have seen in earlier chapters. The visual order, shown at the bottom of the diagram, is how the text component will actually display these characters. Here, the text has a natural left-to-right ordering and is displayed that way. Compare this with Figure 5-2. Here, the model contains three distinct regions of text. The leftmost and rightmost regions have left-to-right ordering and are rendered in that way by the View. However, the word "bi-directional" has right-to-left ordering and, as you can see, the View reverses the order of the model characters when displaying them. This is an example of bi-directional text.

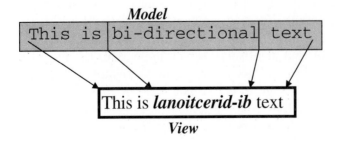

Figure 5-2   A text component displaying bi-directional text.

In the real world, the part of the text that has been shown in right-to-left order might be Arabic characters rendered using glyphs from an Arabic font, such as one of the physical fonts listed in the previous Core Note. As noted earlier, so that you can see that there is a change of order involved and because we're using exclusively Roman script in this figure (and in the others in this section), the part of the text that should be shown in a different font is instead shown in italics.

What is it that determines whether characters have left-to-right or right-to-left ordering? So far, we've made the rather imprecise (and incomplete) statement that some (but not all) Arabic characters require a right-to-left visual ordering. This, of course, is not of much use to the person implementing the rendering algorithm—how are Arabic characters going to be recognized and what about other writing systems that also don't use left-to-right ordering?

The key to this problem is the fact that Java represents all characters internally in Unicode. Unicode assigns a unique 16-bit value to every character that it can represent and this value is actually stored in a Java `char` variable inside the text component's model. Every Unicode character is classified according to whether it belongs to a set of characters that needs left-to-right rendering or the reverse. This classification, along with the rules for handling bi-directional Unicode text, actually appears in the Unicode 2.0 specification published by the Unicode Consortium (see http://www.unicode.org for further information) and equivalent information is encoded into static data compiled into the Swing text classes. Although this data is stored in the compiled class files in a compressed form (using a simple compression technique called run-length encoding), it is expanded at runtime into a form that makes it simple to determine quickly, given any Unicode character, whether its natural rendering order is left-to-right or right-to-left. As you'll see later, this information is used to mark runs of text within the model according to their rendering requirements.

Caret Position and the Selection

One consequence of the fact that the logical order and the visual order of characters in a bi-directional string do not always match is that the mapping between model offset and view position is not as simple as it is when the text is rendered left to right throughout. To see the consequences of the presence of right-to-left text, type the following command:

```
java AdvancedSwing.Chapter5.BidiTextExample
```

This example creates a frame with a `JTextPane` containing a (nonsensical) sequence of mixed Roman and Arabic characters. When the program starts, you'll see a pretty meaningless representation of the pane's content, which will look something like the screen shot shown on the left of Figure 5-3.

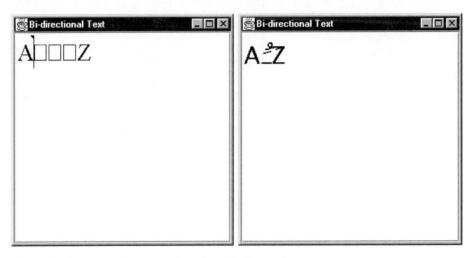

Figure 5-3   A `JTextPane` with bi-directional text.

Depending on the exact fonts in use on your system, what you actually see may well be different from Figure 5-3. The first and last characters are actually the letters A and Z; these are also the first and last characters in the model. Because these are ASCII characters, their natural display order is left to right. The three characters in the middle are the representation of the Arabic characters with Unicode values `0xFE76`, `0xFE77`, and `0xFE78` given by the font that is selected for the virtual font name Serif on my machine. These characters all have the right-to-left display attribute. Unfortunately, on my system they all have the same glyph in the font, so it is impossible to tell which of the three squares corresponds to which Arabic character. For now, just take it as read that the leftmost character on the screen is the one with Unicode value `0xFE78`, the middle one is `0xFE77`, and the right one `0xFE76`. This represents a right-to-left rendering of the middle part of the string, which is actually created as follows:

```
String s = new String(new char[] { (char)'A',
                    (char)0xFE76,
                    (char)0xFE77,
                    (char)0xFE78,
                    (char)'Z' });
```

As you can see, the display order and the model order for the middle three characters are different.

Core Note

As well as the frame, you'll also see some diagnostic information displayed in the window in which you started this program; we'll examine this information when we look under the hood of the Swing text components' bi-directional text support later in this chapter.

There is another way to use this example that shows the Arabic characters as they should be represented. To do this, type the command

```
java AdvancedSwing.Chapter5.BidiTextExample Arabic
```

When you do this, the example selects a 32-point Lucida Sans Regular font instead of the Serif font used by default. Because this font contains glyphs for Arabic characters, you'll see something like the right side of Figure 5-3. The code that selects the font looks like this:

```
if (args.length > 0 && args[0].equalsIgnoreCase("Arabic")) {
    GraphicsEnvironment.getLocalGraphicsEnvironment().getAllFonts();
    System.out.println("Using physical font");
    Font font = new Font("Lucida Sans Regular", Font.PLAIN, 32);
    tp.setFont(font);
} else {
    Font font = new Font("Serif", Font.PLAIN, 32);
    tp.setFont(font);
}
```

The first part of this "if" statement selects the physical font. The only strange part of this is the first line, which uses the getAllFonts methods of the Java 2D GraphicsEnvironment class to load the physical fonts from the file system. This line is actually a workaround for a bug in the first few customer releases of the Java 2 platform, which would not recognize physical fonts unless you force them to be loaded in this way, and may no longer be necessary by the time you read this chapter.

You'll probably notice that, whereas the left screen shot in Figure 5-3 clearly shows five characters, there appear to be only three characters when the text is rendered properly. We'll see later why this happens. In the rest of this chapter, we'll describe character and caret positions with reference to the left screen shot in Figure 5-3, because this makes it easier to visualize the connection between the five characters on the screen and the five in the underlying text component. For that reason, you are recommended to run the example program with the command line

```
java AdvancedSwing.Chapter5.BidiTextExample
```

so that what you see matches the descriptions in the text.

Now let's see how bi-directional text affects the mapping between the model and the view. As well as displaying bi-directional text, this program also registers a `CaretListener` so that it can detect changes in the position of the `Caret`. Each time the `Caret` moves, it prints its new location as reported in the resulting `CaretEvent`, which is the offset of the `Caret` in the model. With the example program running, click to the left of the letter A— that is, at the extreme left of the text component. When you do this, you should see the `Caret`'s model offset reported as 0, which is consistent with its being at the beginning of the model.

Core Note

When a text component contains bi-directional text, it would be misleading to try to describe a location using the words before or after, because the interpretation of these words depends on the reading order of the text. To avoid any confusion, we'll specify position using the terms left and right, where these refer to the visual ordering that you see on the screen. Therefore, the start of the text component in Figure 5-3 is to the left of the letter A and the letter Z is four characters to its right.

Next, click to the right of the letter z; as you might expect, this positions the `Caret` at the end of the model and returns a model offset of 5. No surprises so far, but now click to the immediate right of the letter A, immediately to the left of the leftmost Arabic character. You might have expected that this would be model position 1 but, in fact, depending on exactly where you click, it reports itself either as position 1 (if you click nearer the A) or as position 4 if the mouse is nearer to the first Arabic character. By varying the position of the mouse slightly and then clicking, you should be able to get both offsets reported in the window from which the program was started. Next, click one position to the right— between the first and second Arabic characters counting from the left and, perhaps not surprisingly, the model offset now becomes 3. Finally, click to the left of the letter z; this time, the `Caret` is apparently at offset 4 or 1 again, depending on the exact location of the mouse, despite the fact that the position immediately to the right of the letter A was earlier reported as being model offset 4 or 1. Clearly, something strange is going on here. To see what is happening, look at Figure 5-4.

Model offset

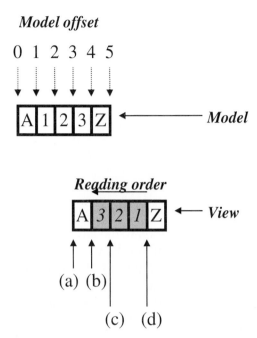

Figure 5-4 A model-to-view mapping with bi-directional text.

The boxed characters in the upper part of this figure show the logical ordering within the model. For clarity, the three Arabic characters are represented by the numerals 1, 2, and 3. The correct model offset for each character position is shown above the model. Recall that a position offset actually refers to the offset not of a character within the model, but of the gap before that character so that, for example, the model offset corresponding to the letter A in this example is 0 and for the letter Z is 4. As far as the Arabic characters are concerned, the character denoted as 1 has model offset 1 (that is, the gap before it has this offset) and so on. The model offset is, of course, completely independent of the way the text is rendered on the screen.

The lower half of the figure shows how this model is rendered in Java 2. The middle three characters have right-to-left ordering so their visual order is the reverse of the logical order shown at the top of the figure and an Arabic reader would read them right to left, as shown by the arrow labeled reading order. When you click somewhere between within the text component, the coordinates of the mouse are converted to a model location using the View's viewToModel method as you saw in Chapter 3. Clearly, clicking to the left of the A will always result in model offset 0 being returned. But what happens if you click to the right of the A and to the left of the 3 in Figure 5-4? Suppose you draw a vertical line where the Caret now resides, as shown in Figure 5-5; there are actually two ways to describe this location.

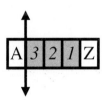

Figure 5-5   An ambiguous model location.

If you read the figure from left to right, the position to the left of the letter A (location (a)) obviously has model offset 0, so if you move your eye one character position to the right (location (b)), you would expect to encounter model position 1. However, this location is immediately to the left of the Arabic character denoted as 3 and earlier we saw that this location reported itself as having offset 4. At this point, an Arabic reader would skip to the character denoted by 1, in the position labeled (d) and begin reading from right to left. We know that the character 1 actually has model offset 1, so if we now move from the location of the character 1 toward the left (following the reading order arrow), we would expect the gap between the characters 1 and 2 to have offset 2 (which we know to be correct) and that between 2 and 3 (location (c)) to have offset 3. What happens if we now read one more character position to the left—that is, we move to location (b)? Having moved one position further through the model from offset 3, it can only be that this position has offset 4. This is, of course, exactly what was reported when the mouse was clicked in this location. It also seems to contradict the earlier description of this as being model location 1.

Actually, when a text component contains bi-directional text, the boundaries at which the text flow reverses always have two possible model offsets, depending on whether you regard that point as being part of the flow to the left of that point or of the flow to its right. That is why the visual position denoted as (b) in Figure 5-4 could be thought of as corresponding to model offset 1 if you consider it to be part of the left-to-right flow that terminates with the letter A or to model offset 4 if it is regarded as belonging to the right-to-left flow that follows it. Internally, the View objects describe a location using two attributes—the model offset and a *bias* that has the value *forward* or *backward*. The combination of a model offset and a bias always produces a unique visual position. You'll see some of the implementation details of this later in this section, but you can see the concept in action by looking again at the example program.

With the example running, click again at the left edge of the JTextPane, so that the Caret moves to model offset 0. Now press the right arrow key once to move the Caret one position right. Here, the Caret is on the boundary at which the text flow changes from left to right to right to left. Clicking to bring the Caret to this location caused the model offset to be reported as 4 but, in this case, you'll find that the model offset displayed in the window from which you started the example is 1. Notice also that the Caret is not shown as a simple vertical line—there is a small black box at the top, on the right of the Caret line, as shown in Figure 5-6.

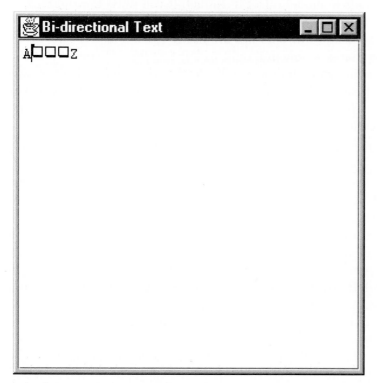

Figure 5-6   The caret showing a text direction indicator.

This box shows the direction of flow of the text that the Caret is associated with. Because it's on the right side of the Caret line, you can tell that this is left-to-right text. However, because the Caret is actually at the location at which the text flow changes, it could legitimately adopt either orientation. In fact, because it was last in a left-to-right flow, it continues to indicate that the text flow is left to right, because it still associates itself with the flow that it was last in. This, of course, is why the model offset is currently being reported as 1, not 4. In this position, the Caret is at visual offset 1 with its bias set to backward.

Now press the right arrow key one more time. Because the Caret is currently at the crossover point between flows, what should be the effect of pressing the right arrow key? Should it move right one character in terms of the model, or in terms of the View? The difference is important. If it moves one model location to the right, its model offset would be 2 which, as you saw earlier, would make it jump to the location between the 1 and the 2 in Figure 5-4. On the other hand, if it moved one character to the right visually, it would occupy the position in Figure 5-4 labeled (c), which corresponds to model offset 3. In fact, if you press the right arrow key, you'll find that it does neither of these things—instead, it stays where it is and the black indicator box flips around to the left side of the Caret line, indicating that it is now in a right-to-left text flow. If you look at the output in the command window, you'll see that the model offset is now reported as 4! Instead of moving anywhere, then, the Caret hopped over the imaginary gap between the two directions of flow, but stayed in the same visual location.

Press the right arrow key again and you'll see that the Caret continues to move to the right, increasing its visual offset but decreasing the model offset. Theoretically, the implementers of the text components could have chosen to make the right arrow key increase the model offset instead of the visual offset, but that would make the Caret move to the left in response to the right arrow key when it is in a right-to-left flow, which would be very confusing for the user. If you keep pressing the right arrow key, the Caret continues to move in that direction until it reaches the end of the right-to-left flow to the left of the letter z, at which point it reports its model offset as 1. At this point, the right arrow key causes the Caret to switch over into the left-to-right flow; as happened on the previous direction change, the Caret does not physically move. Instead, the directional indicator moves back to the right side and the model offset changes to 4 again. Finally, pressing the right arrow key once more moves the Caret to the end of the text, with model offset 5.

Before we look at the implementation details of bi-directional text, there is one more wrinkle you need to know about. Recall that when you create a selection using the JTextComponent select method or the set-SelectionStart and setSelectionEnd methods, you specify the model offsets of the two ends of the selection. When the component contains only left-to-right text, it is easy to visualize how this works. Things are not so simple with bi-directional text, however. Refer again to Figure 5-4.

Suppose we create a selection that starts at model offset 1 and ends at model offset 3. Which part of the text component will actually be highlighted? There is no ambiguity about model offset 3—it is the gap between the digits 2 and 3 in the diagram. Offset 1, however, is ambiguous: Is it to the right of the letter A or to the right of the digit 1? These two interpretations produce different results. With the first, the selection highlight will cover the digit 3 only, while the latter would highlight the digits 1 and 2. The correct interpretation is obvious when you think in terms of the model, of course: the selection extends from offset 1 to offset 3, so it must correspond to the two characters at offsets 1 and 2, which are the digits 1 and 2. Indeed, if you click between the digits 2 and 3, which is offset 3, and then drag the mouse to the right until the Caret is to the left of the letter z, which is offset 1, you'll see that the selection appears in the correct place, as shown in Figure 5-7.

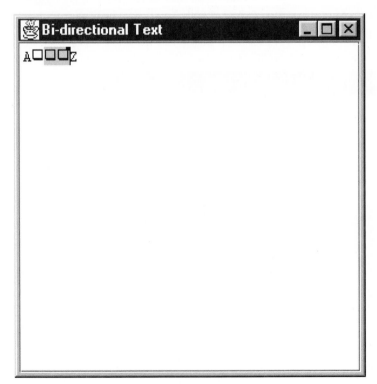

Figure 5-7   A selection in a right-to-left text flow.

That, however, was a simple case. What happens if, instead, you create a selection that starts at offset 0, with the same ending location as before (offset

3)? Whereas in the previous example the whole selection was in the right-to-left flow, this one starts in the left-to-right flow and then crosses the boundary into the right-to-left flow. The characters covered by these offsets are A, 1, and 2, as you can see from the diagram of the model in Figure 5-4. However, if you look at the visual representation at the bottom of that figure, you'll see that these characters are not displayed as a contiguous block! This is a problem, because the selection highlight is usually a continuous colored rectangle. If that were the case here, it would cover not only the characters that it should highlight, but also the character shown in Figure 5-4 as 3, which is not part of the selection at all! In fact, this does not happen. To see this, click to the left of the character A and then drag it two character positions to the right, so that the Caret occupies the location shown as (c) in Figure 5-4, which has model offset 3. When you do this, you'll see that you have two selection rectangles, which cover only the characters that are actually selected in the model, as shown in Figure 5-8. This is, of course, the correct result. You'll see, in implementation terms, why this actually happens in the next section.

Figure 5-8   A selection in bi-directional text.

How Bi-Directional Text Is Handled in the Swing Text Components

Now that you've seen the practical implications of using bi-directional text, this section looks at how the Swing text components represent bi-directional text internally and how the API is affected by the need to handle it.

Representation of Bi-Directional Text within `AbstractDocument`

The first thing to know about bi-directional text is that it does not have any special representation when stored in the `Document` model. The text components store Unicode and, because the Arabic character set (and other character sets that need to be rendered right to left) is just a subset of Unicode, the characters are stored directly in the model in the same way as the more familiar left-to-right text. The key to understanding how bi-directional text works is the `Element` framework that was introduced in Chapter 3. If you refer to the section entitled "The Element Structure of the Simple Text Components" in Chapter 3, you'll recall that a text component's data is logically grouped into sections using `Element`s that form a tree structure. In Chapter 3, we looked exclusively at the `Element`s that describe the line and paragraph structure of the data together with any attributes that might be attached to it. There is, however, a parallel `Element` structure that maps the same data content and has a separate root within the `Document`.

To see how this second tree is constructed, type the following command:

```
java AdvancedSwing.Chapter5.BidiTextExample
```

and look at the output that appears in the window in which you run the example.

Core Note

If you are running this example in a DOS window, you may need to redirect the output to a file because it will probably run off the top of the window. If you do this, let the program run for 10 seconds before looking at the output file, because it waits 10 seconds before writing the document structure to the file.

The output from this command shows both the Document structure and the Views that are created for display purposes. Here, we are only interested in the Document structure, which is reproduced here.

```
<section>
  <paragraph
    resolver=NamedStyle:default {name=default,nrefs=1}
  >
    <content>
      [0,5][A???Z]
    <content>
      [5,6][
]
<bidi root>
  <bidi level
    bidiLevel=0
  >
    [0,1][A]
  <bidi level
    bidiLevel=1
  >
    [1,4][???]
  <bidi level
    bidiLevel=0
  >
    [4,6][Z
]
```

The first part of this output shows the usual Document structure that you saw in Chapter 3. As you might expect for a JTextPane with one line of text and no attributes, all you get is a Section Element containing a single Paragraph Element that has two associated content Elements—one for the data and another for the newline that marks the end of the data. Following this is a second Element structure, beginning with the tag bidi root. Up to now, we have completely ignored the Elements in this tree because we have only been interested in how to build lines and paragraphs and attach attributes that determine the font and colors used to display the text. In fact, these Elements contain the information that describes the orientation of the text independently of its logical structure.

In this example, the text consists of the letter A, three Arabic characters, the letter Z, and the terminating newline. If you look at the Element structure descending from the bi-directional root, you can see that each Element corresponds to a range of characters that all run in the same direction. The first Element maps the letter A that has left-to-right orientation, the second maps the three right-to-left Arabic characters, and the last one contains the left-to-right sequence consisting of the letter z and the newline.

You saw in Chapter 3 that you can use the `getRootElements` method to get an array that holds the root `Element`s of any `Element` trees within a `Document`. `AbstractDocument` supports two parallel `Element` structures and therefore its implementation of `getRootElements` returns an array containing two entries, the first of which is the root of the usual `Element` tree that describes the content structure and the second is the root of the bi-directional text tree:

```
JTextPane tp = new JTextPane();

// Add text and attributes (not shown here)

Document doc = tp.getDocument();
Element[] rootElements = doc.getRootElements();
Element bidiRootElement = rootElements[1];    // Root of bidi
Element tree
```

Another way to get the root of the bi-directional `Element` tree is to use the `getBidiRootElement` method:

```
JTextPane tp = new JTextPane();

// Add text and attributes (not shown here)

AbstractDocument doc = (AbstractDocument)tp.getDocument();
Element bidiRootElement = doc.getBidiRootElement()
                         // Root of bidi Element tree
```

Notice that the second code extract casts the returned `Document` reference to an `AbstractDocument`, whereas the first does not. The `Document` interface contains a `getRootElements` method because the generic `Document` model allows the concept of multiple `Element` trees but does not specify how they are used. It does not, however, have the concept of bi-directional text, so it doesn't supply a `getBidiRootElement` method. To get the notion of bi-directional text, you have to use a concrete implementation of `Document` derived from `AbstractDocument`, so the second code extract casts the returned `Document` reference accordingly. Both of these code extracts are, of course, assuming that the `JTextPane` has been built with a model that is a subclass of `AbstractDocument`—the first extract assumes this, even though it doesn't use a cast, because it knows that the array returned by the `getRootElements` method has at least two entries and that the second entry is for the bi-directional text `Element` tree.

The bi-directional `Element` tree is made of objects of type `Abstract-Document.BidiElement`, which are derived from `AbstractDocument.LeafElement`. `BidiElements` are leaf elements, not branch elements, because they do not need to be nested. As a result, the bi-directional `Element` tree is only a single level deep and each entry in the tree maps all of a single range of the `Document`. In the example shown earlier, there are three `BidiElements`, two of which cover the left-to-right text at the beginning and end of the `Document` and a third covering the right-to-left section in the middle.

A `BidiElement`, like all `Elements`, has an associated `AttributeSet`, which contains only one attribute called the "bidi level" (see Table 2-1 in Chapter 2 for the definition of this attribute). The value of this attribute is the nesting level of bi-directional text; text with an even nesting level is to be rendered left to right, while an odd level implies right-to-left rendering. In the case of the example that we have been using in this section, the first and last characters have a nesting level of 0, while the Arabic characters are at level 1. However, because `BidiElements` are not directly concerned with the rendering of the text, it is not possible (or useful) to add other attributes to their `AttributeSets`.

Core Note

This simple example shows only two bi-directional levels. However, the Swing text components can support up to 16 levels of nested direction directional changes.

Bi-directional text has a certain amount of overhead in terms of memory and the time taken to determine which parts of a `Document` should be drawn in which direction. If you don't need to support bi-directional text, you can minimize these overheads by setting the document property i18n to `false`:

```
JTextPane tp = new JTextPane();
tp.getDocument().putProperty("i18n", new Boolean(false));
```

Core Note

In the Swing 1.1.1 and the first Java 2 releases, this property is `false` by default, thus disabling bi-directional text. If you are using either of these releases, you need to set the `i18n` property to `true` to enable it. The example we have been using in this section displays the initial value of this property when it starts and then switches on bi-directional text support.

Rendering Bi-Directional Text

You saw in Chapter 3 that a single `Element` maps a run of characters with a constant set of character attributes and that the `View` structure usually contains one `View` for each leaf `Element` in the `Document` model. For simplicity, some `Views`, such as `LabelView`, create fragments to restrict themselves to drawing text on only one screen line, an example of which was shown in Figure 3-9. The presence of bi-directional text is another reason for a `View` to create a fragment and the example that we have been using in this section demonstrates this. If you look at the output in the window from which you run it, you'll see that it displays the `View` structure of the `JTextPane`, which looks like this:

```
javax.swing.plaf.basic.BasicTextUI$RootView; offsets [0, 6]
   javax.swing.text.BoxView; offsets [0, 6]
      javax.swing.text.ParagraphView; offsets [0, 6]
         javax.swing.text.ParagraphView$Row; offsets [0, 6]
            javax.swing.text.LabelView$LabelFragment; offsets [0, 1]
               [A]
            javax.swing.text.LabelView$LabelFragment; offsets [1, 4]
               [???]
            javax.swing.text.LabelView$LabelFragment; offsets [4, 5]
               [Z]
            javax.swing.text.LabelView; offsets [5, 6]
               [
]
```

Here you can see the usual structure for a `JTextPane`, with a single `Row` fragment nested inside a single `ParagraphView`. Even though there is enough horizontal space to display the five characters in this `Document` on one screen line, the `LabelView` has created three fragments (of type `LabelView.Label-Fragment`) that correspond to the same line of text. Each of these `Views` maps a region in which the text flows in only one direction. In fact, if you look at the `BidiElements` for this `Document` (shown previously), you'll see that each fragment maps directly to a `BidiElement`. This happens because `LabelView` is coded to look at the `BidiElement` structure as part of the process of determining whether to create a `View` fragment. Notice that the newline at the end of the `Document` has its own `LabelView`, even though it is considered to be left-to-right text like the character z that appears before it in the model. This happens because these two characters are actually mapped by different `Elements` and so cannot share a `View`.

The reason for this `View` structure is, of course, that it makes the implementation of `LabelView` easier. As you saw in Chapter 3, each `View` independently renders only the part of the text component that it covers. If a single

`View` mapped a run of characters that contained changes of direction, its `paint` method would need to take into account the direction change boundaries as well as take note of whether some or all of the text is selected and so should use a different foreground color. With this implementation, the `paint` method only has to deal with left-to-right text or with right-to-left text, not with a mixture.

In Chapter 3, you also saw that the `paint` method of the `FieldView` used by `JTextField` uses convenience methods in the `javax.swing.text.Utilities` class to render text. Currently, `JTextField` supports only left-to-right text, so it does not have the complications of having to handle text flowing in the reverse direction. `LabelView` does not have this luxury, however. It has to use a more different text rendering algorithm. In fact, although the details are somewhat complex, the technique used by `LabelView` in Java 2 is very simple. In Chapter 3, you saw that `FieldView` obtained a reference to the text from the model that it needs to draw by calling the `Document getText` method and then calling the `Utilities.drawTabbedText` method to render it. What `LabelView` does is slightly different.

Core Note

In Java 2, `LabelView` uses some of the facilities of the Java2D API. A proper discussion of these features is beyond the scope of this book. Instead of doubling the size of this chapter with an overview of Java2D text handling, we'll content ourselves here with a simple description of how the Java2D features are used. For a more in-depth description, refer to Core Java 2, Volume 2: Advanced Features *by Cay Horstmann and Gary Cornell (Prentice Hall).*

In Java 2, when a `LabelView` is created, it extracts the portion of text that it maps from the `Document` and builds a separate object that contains the `Glyphs` that will be drawn for that text on the screen. A `Glyph` is simply a character from a font. In simple terms, what this process does is to use the Unicode characters from the `Document` to access the font used over the part of the text component mapped by the `LabelView` and extract the corresponding `Glyphs`. These are then organized into an object called a `GlyphVector`, which can be drawn directly by the Java2D feature of Java 2. There are several complications that can cause the arrangement of `Glyphs` in the `GlyphVector` to differ from the Unicode characters held in the `Document`, of which the following are examples:

- Adjacent characters may be merged together into a single `Glyph`. For example, it is common practice to merge the letters "fi" into a single `Glyph` in which the horizontal bar of the letter "f" joins to the top of the letter "i."
- In some writing systems, of which Arabic is an example, the `Glyph` used to represent a character may depend on the characters that it is adjacent to. You can think of this as being somewhat similar to longhand writing, where the exact shape of a character depends on those adjacent to it, because of the need to join the characters up. The merging of the three Arabic characters in our example program into one glyph in the right screen shot of Figure 5-3 is an example of this.
- The order of `Glyphs` may be reversed.

The last of these examples is actually the way in which `LabelView` handles right-to-left text—when it extracts the characters from the `Document`, it assembles them in the `GlyphVector` in reverse order! Having done this, it can simply use the following `Graphics2D` method to draw the text in the correct order (actually rendering it left to right):

```
public void drawGlyphVector(GlyphVector g, int x, int y);
```

Core Note

In Swing 1.1.1, there is no support in `LabelView` *for bi-directional text. All text is rendered left to right, using the same* `drawTabbedText` *method used by* `FieldView`.

`Views` and Position Bias

Earlier in this section, you saw that mapping between model and `View` positions when there is bi-directional text present is not a simple matter. At the boundaries where the direction change takes place, it is apparently possible to assign two model offsets for the corresponding `View` location (and vice versa), while in a right-to-left run of characters, the model offsets decrease as the `View` offset increases. Having two possible model offsets for a single `View` offset is not very convenient because the `View modelToView` method can only return a single offset and the same is true of `viewToModel`. To solve this problem, the text components have the notion of *bias*.

To understand how bias is used to select a single offset at a bi-directional text boundary, look at the situation shown in Figure 5-9.

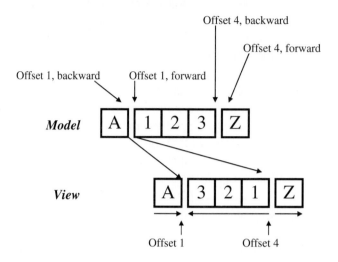

Figure 5-9 Using bias to select an unambiguous location in a text component.

This diagram is another representation of a JTextPane with three right-to-left characters surrounded by the more usual left-to-right text flow. The top of the diagram shows the model representation in logical order, while the bottom shows how these characters would be rendered in Java 2. For clarity, small gaps have been left at the direction change boundaries and arrows have been used to show the direction of the text flow. The diagram clearly shows how the model locations map to View offsets.

Consider the location just after the letter A in the model. Conventionally, this location would be called model offset 1 but, as you can see, because of the bi-directional text, it may map to View offset 1 or to View offset 4. In fact, the way to obtain an unambiguous View offset is to qualify the model offset by specifying whether you are referring to the end of the previous character in the model or the beginning of the next. This is done by using a bias value, which may take the value *forward* or *backward*. In Figure 5-9, the location just after the A is labeled offset 1, backward. This model offset maps to View position 1. By contrast, the position just before the right-to-left character shown here as 1 is labeled offset 1, forward and has View offset 4. As you can see, the combination of a model offset and a bias leads to a unique View position.

In implementation terms, the concept of bias is provided by the inner class Bias of the javax.swing.text.Position class, which, as you saw in Chapter 1, is used to anchor a logical location within a document so that its model offset can be retrieved at a later time. The `Position.Bias` class simply declares two constants that are used to refer to forward and backward bias:

```
public static final Bias Forward;
public static final Bias Backward;
```

Forward bias (or `Bias.Forward`) is used when you want to refer to the right side of a model location at which there is a change in the direction of text flow, as you can see from Figure 5-9. In this context, because we are referring to the model and dealing with logical ordering, the term right side is not ambiguous. To see how bias is used in practice, consider the implementation of a `View`'s `modelToView` method. If you refer to Table 3-2, you'll see that this method has two variants, defined as follows:

```
public abstract Shape modelToView(int pos, Shape a, Position.Bias b)
                              throws BadLocationException
public Shape modelToView(int p0, Position.Bias b0, int p1,
                              Position.Bias b1, Shape a)
                              throws BadLocationException
```

Let's look at the first of these two methods, which maps a single model position to a `Shape` whose bounding rectangle occupies the corresponding location on the screen. As you saw in Chapter 3, the standard implementations of this method return a `Rectangle` of width 1, whose height matches that of the space allocated to the `View` and whose horizontal position corresponds to the screen location of the character at the given model offset. Suppose that, in the case of the text component represented by Figure 5-9, this method were called with offset 1, which is the first boundary at which a change of text direction occurs. As you know, for this component the mapping from model offset 1 to a `View` position is ambiguous unless a bias value is also supplied. If the bias argument passed to `modelToView` in this case is `Bias.Backward`, the `Shape` returned by this method will be a `Rectangle` whose left edge lies at the boundary between the characters A and 3 in the representation of the `View` shown at the bottom of the figure. On the other hand, if the bias argument is given as `Bias.Forward`, the returned `Shape` will correspond to the location between the characters 1 and z.

The situation is similar for the reverse mapping, which is performed by the `viewToModel` method:

```
public abstract int viewToModel(float x, float y, Shape a,
                              Position.Bias[] biasReturn);
```

Here, the x and y values give the location of a point within the text component and the returned value is the corresponding model offset.

Looking again at Figure 5-9, as you know there would be an ambiguity if the `View` position passed to this method corresponded to either of the locations at which the text changes direction. If, for example, the user clicked in the gap between the A and the 3, should the returned offset be 1 or 4? We actually tried this earlier in this chapter and discovered that the result was 4. As well as the offset, this method also returns, in the `biasReturn` array passed as the last argument, the corresponding bias value that, taken together with the returned model offset, would produce the same `View` location if they were both supplied to the `modelToView` method. In this case, the returned offset would be 4 and the returned bias `Bias.Backward`.

Core Note

A return offset of 4 with `Bias.Forward` *would correspond to the forward (that is, the right-hand) side of the gap at the change of text direction— that is, the location between the* `1` *and the* `z` *in Figure 5-9.*

You should be able to see straight away that the returned model offset and bias are consistent with the initial `View` location. However, the same `View` position could also have been described as having model offset 1 with bias value `Bias.Backward`—that is, the location immediately after the character A. Why was the offset 4 chosen? The reason for this is simple. When the user clicks over a text component, the x and y coordinates from the `MouseEvent` are used to find the single leaf `View` at that location. In this case, there are two possible `View`s that could correspond to this location—the one mapping the character A and the adjacent one mapping the reverse text characters 1 through 3. If the exact location of the click matches the first of these `View`s, it will see the event as having occurred at its right boundary. This would give a model offset of 1 with `Bias.Backward`. On the other hand, if the event occurs within the boundary of the other `View`, it will be seen as having happened at its left end and will produce a model offset of 4 with bias `Bias.Backward`. Notice that in both of these cases, the bias returned is `Bias.Backward`. The `viewToModel` method returns `Bias.Backward` whenever the point it is given is at the right end of the portion of the model that it represents, speaking in terms of logical ordering, and `Bias.Forward` in *all* other cases. In the case of right-to-left text, the right end of the logical ordering (shown at the top of Figure 5-9) is, of course, the left side as seen in visual order (the lower part of the figure).

It is worth noting that in this section we have been discussing the `modelToView` and `viewToModel` methods of the `View` class. `View`s are, of course, objects that are internal to a Swing text component and usually an application would not be aware of their existence, much less try to invoke their methods. Should an application want to map between `model` and `view` locations, it would use the `modelToView` and `viewToModel` methods of `JTextComponent`, which are defined as follows:

```
public Rectangle modelToView(int pos)
        throws BadLocationException;
public int viewToModel(Point pt);
```

The interesting point about these methods is that neither of them concerns itself with the issue of bias. We know that this cannot yield an unambiguous result unless some convention is used to choose between the two possible mappings that can occur in the boundary cases. In fact, if you use the `modelToView` method, the bias is taken to be `Bias.Forward`. In the case of `viewToModel`, the underlying `view` will return the appropriate bias, but there is no way to communicate it to the application. Therefore, `viewToModel` may not give expected results if used on a boundary between different text flow directions.

The Caret

You saw in "Caret Position and the Selection" on page 551 that both the movement and the appearance of the `Caret` are affected by the presence of bi-directional text. Now that you've seen some basic implementation of bi-directional text, we'll look a bit more closely at the details of the `Caret` handling in the presence of mixed left-to-right and right-to-left text.

In Chapter 3, we said that moving the `Caret` left and right (or up and down in a two-dimensional text component) is not simply a matter of changing its x (or y) coordinate by a fixed amount each time an arrow key is pressed, or even as simple as adjusting a coordinate by the width of the character that is passing over. As an example of this, the custom `View` that was implemented in Chapter 3 included characters that were not in the model; moving the `Caret` left and right through a `View` that contains virtual characters like these involves skipping over the virtual text that is not actually in the model. In fact, what exactly needs to happen to do something as simple as move the `Caret` one position in any direction depends entirely on the `View` that is responsible for drawing the text that the `Caret` is moving through. This is why `Views` implement a `getNextVisualPositionFrom` method, which is defined like this:

```
int getNextVisualPositionFrom(int pos, Position.Bias b,
            Shape a, int direction, Position.Bias[] biasRet,
            boolean rightToLeft, int startOffset,
```

```
            int endOffset)
        throws BadLocationException
```

The meaning of the arguments should be obvious. The `pos` argument is the current model position of the `Caret`; as you might expect by now, it is qualified by a bias. The `Shape` argument represents the area of screen allocated to the text component. The `direction` indicates which way the `Caret` needs to move (NORTH, SOUTH, EAST, or WEST) and depends on which arrow key was pressed. The `rightToLeft` argument is `true` when the text associated with the `View` is to be rendered from right to left and the two offsets are the bounding offsets of the region of the model mapped by this `View`. The return value is the offset in the model that represents the next position that the `Caret` should occupy given the direction in which it was asked to move; this value is qualified by the bias value returned in the `biasRet` argument, in the same way as positions returned by the `viewToModel` method discussed in the last section require both a model offset and a returned bias to completely describe them.

Let's consider first a simple case. Suppose, in Figure 5-9, the `Caret` is currently placed between the characters 3 and 2. Relating the visual representation at the bottom of the diagram to the logical representation at the top, you can see that this means that the `Caret` is currently at model offset 3 and has bias `Bias.Forward`.

Core Note

When the `Caret` is not at a boundary at which a direction change occurs, its bias is arbitrarily considered to be forward. Because a `View` never crosses a direction change boundary, the bias of the `Caret` is always forward except when the `Caret` is at the end offset of the `View`, at which point it may have a backward bias. However, if the end of the `View` does not correspond to a change in direction flow (perhaps because some attribute such as the font changed or the end of the screen line was reached), the `Caret` will still have forward bias there.

Now suppose the user presses the right arrow key. The expectation is that the `Caret` will move to the right. In response to this action, the `getNextVisualPosition` method of the `LabelView` mapping the Arabic text will be called, with the model offset initialized to 3, the bias set to `Bias.Forward`, the direction set to EAST, and the `rightToLeft` set to `true`. Under normal circumstances, you would expect pressing the right arrow to increase the model offset by one. When there is a `rightToLeft` text flow, however, this does not happen—instead, the model offset is *decreased* by one, in this case giving it the value 2. If you refer again to the top half of Figure 5-9, you'll see that this places it between the 2 and the 1. Relating this to the visual representation at the bottom of the figure, it is clear that this corresponds to a movement to the right. Furthermore, because the Caret has not yet reached the end of the area mapped by this View (which spans model offsets 1 to 4), its bias remains forward. Thus, in this case, getNextVisualPosition returns the value 2 and the biasRet value is set to Bias.Forward. Similarly, when there is right-to-left text, pressing the left arrow key causes the model offset to be *increased* by one instead of being decreased, as would be the case in a left-to-right flow.

The Selection

When the user clicks and drags left or right to create a selection, the Caret is responsible for setting the values of its dot and mark attributes to record the endpoints of the selected region. These values are model offsets, so you won't be surprised to discover that both the dot and mark actually store both a model offset and the corresponding bias. When the user begins a selection, the dot and mark, which are attributes of the Caret (in this case implemented by the DefaultCaret class), are both set to the model offset and bias returned by the viewToModel method of the View underneath the mouse location. To illustrate the discussion with some typical values, let's look again at the JTextPane example that we've been using throughout this section. Start the program using the command

```
java AdvancedSwing.Chapter5.BidiTextExample
```

and click to the left of the character A, thus starting a new (empty) selection. As you've already seen, with the mouse in this location, the viewToModel method will return a model offset of 0 with a bias of Bias.Forward. Now drag the mouse to the right until the Caret is between the second and third characters (reading from left to right); at this point, the text component should look like Figure 5-8. As the mouse was dragged, the viewToModel method was called in response to each MouseMotionEvent to get the location and bias for the changing dot attribute. At the end of the operation, the dot will be at model offset 3 with bias Bias.Forward while the mark, which denotes the other end of the selection, has model offset 0 and bias Bias.Forward. As we saw earlier in this section, the interesting thing about this example is that the selection is displayed as two separate highlighted regions, reflecting the actual characters from the model that are selected. The Highlighter that is supplied with the

Swing text package, however, can highlight only a single rectangular region. So how does this work?

The key to understanding how this works is to realize that there are actually two `View`s involved in rendering the characters that are part of the selection in this example—the `LabelView.LabelFragment` mapping the left-to-right character `A` and another one covering the right-to-left Arabic characters. Because the default `Highlighter` is a layered `Highlighter`, each `View` is responsible for rendering its own part of the selection highlight. Therefore, the first `View` highlights the character `A`, which is its part of the selection, while the second one needs to highlight the Arabic characters at model offsets 1 and 2. As you saw in Chapter 3, layered highlights are drawn using the `paintLayer` method of the `LayeredPainter` responsible for the highlight. In this case, the default layered highlight painter supplied with Swing is being used. The `paintLayer` method of this object works by taking two model offsets that bound the highlight and the `Shape` allocated to the `View` it is rendering on and calls the `View`'s `modelToView` method, from which it gets a `Rectangle` that represents the screen area appropriate for the highlight. Because the `View` in this case is `LabelView.LabelFragment`, which is aware of bi-directional text, the returned `Rectangle` will occupy the right end of the `View`'s screen area, so the second part of the selection will be drawn there.

As well as user-generated selections, it is possible to create a selection programmatically using the `JTextComponent select` method, or as a two-step process using `setCaretPosition` followed by `moveCaretPosition`. All these methods require a model offset, but none of them accept a `Position.Bias` argument. In fact, when you use these methods, the start offset is implicitly given the bias `Bias.Forward` and the end offset uses `Bias.Backward`. The same is true of the `Caret setDot` and `moveDot` methods, which can also be used to specify a selection. Similarly, when you retrieve the model locations of the boundaries of the selection, the start and end offsets have the same implicit bias values.

Core Note

Code within the Swing text package is not restricted in this way, however, because the `DefaultCaret` class has variants of the `setDot` and `moveDot` method that accept a model offset and a bias as argument and methods called `getDotBias` and `getMarkBias` that return the bias values of the two extremes of the selection. These are of no use to an application programmer, however, because they are package private and, hence, not accessible outside the text package.

Summary

This chapter examined in detail the support provided by the text components for bi-directional text, a feature that is based on new facilities provided by Java 2D. We started by looking at the difference between logical fonts and physical fonts and demonstrated that Unicode characters have an inherent rendering direction that varies from language to language. We saw examples of Arabic text mixed with Roman characters and looked at how the difference between the character ordering in the model and the visual ordering on the screen affects the way on which the text is rendered and how the caret reacts when the user moves it over direction-change boundaries.

CREATING CUSTOM TABLE RENDERERS

Chapter 6

J Table is one of the most important components in the Swing toolkit. With very little effort, you can use it to display rows of column-centric data to the user. However, sophisticated users expect more than the relatively simple presentation that you get from the default behavior of JTable. In this chapter and the next, you'll see how to use the rendering and editing techniques provided by JTable to change its behavior in several ways. Although these mechanisms are inherently very simple, they are also extremely flexible and, with a little work, you can produce some very impressive effects. Best of all, in most cases, you can implement renderers and editors that are generic enough that they can be considered as separate building blocks that can be used to apply a particular effect to an existing table. With good design, you can even create renderers that can be used in combination with others to add several enhancements at one time.

Table Rendering

Swing controls delegate the job of painting themselves to look-and-feel specific UI classes. The JTable UI classes in turn use helper classes called renderers to draw the contents of the table cells and the column headers, if there are any. Because most of the drawing functionality is implemented by render-

577

ers and not directly by the table's UI classes, it is much easier for a developer to customize the way in which the table's content is presented.

Rendering Basics

Drawing a table is a multi-step process carried out by the table's UI class when some or all of the table needs to be repainted. Here's how it works:

1. The table is filled with its background color.
2. The grid lines, if any, are drawn in the appropriate color (as set using the `JTable setGridColor` method). A table may have no grid lines, horizontal lines, vertical lines, or both. By default, these lines are solid and one pixel wide.
3. The table cells are drawn, one by one. If the whole table is being redrawn, this operation works from top to bottom in rows and from left to right across each row. Often, only a portion of the table is visible or only a part of the table needs to be redrawn, in which case only the cells in the affected area will be re-rendered. Because of this, you should not make any assumptions about the order in which cells will be drawn when implementing a custom renderer.

The Swing package includes renderers that can be used to draw cells that contain various types of data. Without any extension, the table can display data of the following types:

- Numbers. That is, objects derived from `java.lang.Number`, which includes all the Java numeric types like `Integer`, `Float`, and `Double`. Numbers are displayed right-justified in their table cells.
- Booleans. A `Boolean` is represented by a check box, which is selected if the cell contains the value `true` and deselected if it contains `false`.
- Dates. A date is rendered using a `DateFormat` object (from the `java.text` package) in a format suitable for the system's default locale.
- Icons. If a cell contains an object that is derived from `ImageIcon`, the icon will be displayed, centered, in the cell.

Although this allows you an easy way to incorporate a bare image in a table, you will often want to add some text to the icon. To do this, you'll need to implement your own renderer, an example of which will be shown later in this section.

Any object that doesn't fall into any of the categories above is displayed, left-aligned, in the form of a text string obtained by calling the object's `toString` method. While this might produce acceptable results in some cases, many objects need a custom renderer to display them properly. The most obvious (and common) case in which this is not true is a cell containing a string, for which the default behavior is perfectly acceptable.

As well as the type of the object being displayed, there are two other criteria that partly determine how a particular cell should look, namely whether the cell is selected and whether it has the focus. These criteria are taken into consideration by all the default renderers and cause the background and foreground colors of the cell to be changed. In addition, the single cell that has the current focus (that is, the one that the user last clicked) is usually shown with a border.

Core Note

Starting with Swing 1.1.1 and Java 2 version 1.2.2, it is possible to supply an HTML string as the text for a `JLabel`. The default renderers for `JTable` are based on `JLabel` and, as a result, it is possible to store HTML in the `TableModel` and have it displayed in the table. Alternatively, you can write a custom renderer that takes the content of a cell from the `TableModel`, wraps it in HTML, and then uses it to set the text of the `JLabel` that does the actual rendering. There is, however, extra overhead involved in using the HTML support. Whether this overhead is acceptable depends on the performance requirements of your application. In general, implementing a custom renderer is probably more efficient than using HTML to achieve the same effect, but requires more development effort.

There are two ways to control the choice of renderer for a given cell in a `JTable`:

- Override the table's `getCellRenderer` method to choose a specific renderer for an individual cell. This requires you to subclass `JTable`, which is not always desirable.

- Use the default mechanism, which chooses the renderer based on the cell's column or the class of the object in that column. As mentioned earlier, there are default renderers installed in the table that will render many types of objects properly without the need to explicitly configure custom renderers or to specify special action for individual columns. As you'll see later in this chapter, it is possible using this mechanism to select a specific renderer for each cell in the table without overriding `getCellRenderer` and hence without needing to subclass `JTable`.

In this chapter, we'll use the column-based mechanism because it does not require subclassing `JTable`.

Core Note

You may be wondering why I consider subclassing `JTable` to select a cell-specific renderer a big issue. In many cases, there is no problem with doing this and, if you need to have different renderers for each cell, you should certainly consider subclassing `JTable` and overriding `getCellRenderer` to do so. Sometimes, though, it is better not to subclass `JTable`. This can be the case if you are using an integrated development environment (IDE) with a graphical user interface (GUI) builder that allows you to drag components and drop them onto a form and generates the Java code to create the corresponding layout for you. In this case, the IDE will generate code to instantiate `JTable` objects. Unless you want to edit the IDE's code, which will make it harder for you to change the layout in the GUI builder at a later date, you can't arrange for this code to use a `JTable` subclass with an overloaded `getCellRenderer` method. Instead, you have to get a reference to the table and use that to set up the correct renderers using the techniques you'll see here. In general, for the application developer, it is usually better, wherever possible, to tailor components by setting properties rather than by subclassing them.

Selecting the Renderer for a Column

If you don't override the `getCellRenderer` method, the table selects a cell's renderer based on the column that the cell resides in. When choosing a renderer for a column, the table first looks at the `TableColumn` object that represents that column in the table's `TableColumnModel`. This object contains a renderer attribute that selects a particular renderer for that column, which can be set and retrieved using the following `TableColumn` methods:

```
public void setCellRenderer(TableCellRenderer renderer);

public TableCellRenderer getCellRenderer();
```

   TableCellRenderer is an interface that must be implemented by every renderer; you'll see how this interface is defined in "Implementing a Custom Renderer" on page 589. Although you can use this mechanism to select a specific renderer for a particular column, most simple tables are created with a default `TableColumnModel` that is built automatically from the table's data model. The columns in this `TableColumnModel` do not have specific renderers configured. When a column does not have a particular renderer selected, the table user interface (UI) class chooses a renderer based on the class of the objects that the column holds. To make this possible, the `TableModel` interface includes a method called `getColumnClass` that returns a `Class` object that is supposed to indicate the type of data that resides in that column. It is used to select a renderer from the default set configured when the table is created. Because these renderers are chosen using the column data's class, they are referred to as class-based renderers to distinguish them from the column-based renderers configured in a `TableColumn` object. In this chapter, you'll see examples of both class-based and column-based renderers.

Core Note

When it comes to the implementation, there is no inherent difference at all between class-based and column-based renderers—indeed, a particular renderer could be used as both a class-based or a column-based renderer. In any particular table, the term used to describe a specific renderer depends only on how that renderer was chosen. Usually, however, a column-based renderer is a more refined version of a class-based one. For example, you might want to use the default number renderer for all numbers apart from those in the rightmost column of a table, which may, for some reason, need to show numbers in a larger font or in a different color. You can't make this distinction based on the class of the object in the column, because all the numeric columns will be of some type derived from Number, *such as* Integer, *and so will all default to the same renderer. Instead, you need to override the default choice for the column that needs special treatment by assigning a column-based renderer that can do the special formatting for you.*

The default class-based renderers were listed earlier in this chapter. If you need to, you can add a new class-based renderer to a table using the `JTable` `setDefaultRenderer` method:

```
public void setDefaultRenderer(Class columnClass,
                            TableCellRenderer renderer);
```

The `columnClass` argument determines the class of the objects that this renderer can draw. Similarly, you can find out which renderer will be used to display an object of a given class by using the `getDefaultRenderer` method:

```
public TableCellRenderer getDefaultRenderer(
                        Class columnClass);
```

Because the default renderers installed by `JTable` include a generic renderer for `java.lang.Object`, this method will always return a renderer no matter what argument it is given. Note that the names of these methods refer not to class-based renderers but to default renderers. The terms class-based renderer and default renderer are, in fact, used interchangeably and mean the same thing.

The process of determining which class-based renderer to use is a recursive one. First, the set of default renderers is searched for one whose assigned class matches exactly the one given as the argument to the `getDefaultRenderer` method. If there isn't a renderer for this class, `getDefaultRenderer` invokes itself, passing the superclass of the class it was given as its argument. Ultimately, if no renderer is registered for any of the superclasses of the class it was originally passed, it will find and return the renderer for `java.lang.Object`. As an example, suppose a table contains two columns, one of which has objects of type `java.math.BigDecimal` and the other of type `java.lang.String`. Suppose also that no custom class-based or column-based renderers have been installed in this table, so that only the default class-based renderers will be used. When the first column is being drawn, a renderer for `java.math.BigDecimal` is needed. Because there isn't one, the next step is to look for a renderer associated with the superclass of `BigDecimal`, which is `java.lang.Number`. This search succeeds, finding the default renderer for `Number` objects installed by the table. Similarly, drawing the cells for a column containing strings first entails a search for a renderer for `java.lang.String`; again, this fails, but the search for the superclass, `java.lang.Object`, will find the last-ditch `Object` renderer.

A Simple Rendering Example— the Currency Table

Let's see how the default renderers operate by looking at a simple example. The table in Figure 6-1 shows (fictional) exchange rates (against the US dollar) for a selection of currencies on two successive days. The columns in this table show the currency name, the exchange rate on the first and second days, and the amount by which the exchange rate changed between the two days. You can run this example using the command

```
java AdvancedSwing.Chapter6.CurrencyTable
```

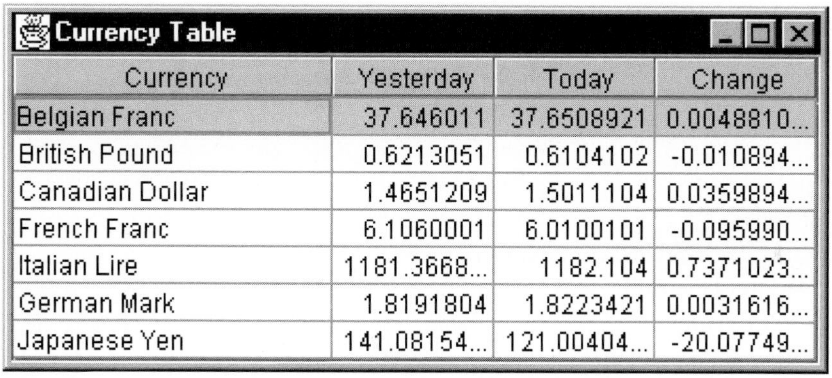

Currency	Yesterday	Today	Change
Belgian Franc	37.646011	37.6508921	0.0048810...
British Pound	0.6213051	0.6104102	-0.010894...
Canadian Dollar	1.4651209	1.5011104	0.0359894...
French Franc	6.1060001	6.0100101	-0.095990...
Italian Lire	1181.3668...	1182.104	0.7371023...
German Mark	1.8191804	1.8223421	0.0031616...
Japanese Yen	141.08154...	121.00404...	-20.07749...

Figure 6-1 The basic currency table with no custom renderers.

The table model that was used to create this example is shown in Listing 6-1. This model will be used throughout this section and will remain unchanged as the table's appearance is enhanced by using custom renderers.

Listing 6-1 The Currency Table Model

```
package AdvancedSwing.Chapter6;

import javax.swing.*;
import javax.swing.table.AbstractTableModel;

// Data for table examples
public class CurrencyTableModel extends AbstractTableModel {
```

Listing 6-1   The Currency Table Model (continued)

```
protected String[] columnNames =
           {"Currency", "Yesterday", "Today", "Change" };

// Constructor: calculate currency change to
// create the last column
public CurrencyTableModel() {
   for (int i = 0; i < data.length; i++) {
      data[i][DIFF_COLUMN] =
         new Double(
                 ((Double)data[i][OLD_RATE_COLUMN]).
                  doubleValue() -
                 ((Double)data[i][NEW_RATE_COLUMN]).
                  doubleValue());
   }
}

// Implementation of TableModel interface
public int getRowCount() {
   return data.length;
}

public int getColumnCount() {
   return COLUMN_COUNT;
}

public Object getValueAt(int row, int column) {
   return data[row][column];
}

public Class getColumnClass(int column) {
   return (data[0][column]).getClass();
}

public String getColumnName(int column) {
   return columnNames[column];
}
protected static final int OLD_RATE_COLUMN = 1;
protected static final int NEW_RATE_COLUMN = 2;
protected static final int DIFF_COLUMN = 3;
protected static final int COLUMN_COUNT = 4;
protected static final Class thisClass =
                              CurrencyTableModel.class;
```

Listing 6-1 The Currency Table Model (continued)

```
protected Object[][] data = new Object[][] {
    { new DataWithIcon("Belgian Franc",
        new ImageIcon(thisClass.getResource(
          "images/belgium.gif"))), new Double(37.6460110),
          new Double(37.6508921) , null },
    { new DataWithIcon("British Pound",
        new ImageIcon(thisClass.getResource(
          "images/gb.gif"))), new Double(0.6213051),
          new Double(0.6104102), null },
    { new DataWithIcon("Canadian Dollar",
        new ImageIcon(thisClass.getResource(
          "images/canada.gif"))), new Double(1.4651209),
          new Double(1.5011104), null },
    { new DataWithIcon("French Franc", new ImageIcon(
        thisClass.getResource("images/france.gif"))),
        new Double(6.1060001), new Double(6.0100101) ,
        null },
    { new DataWithIcon("Italian Lire",
        new ImageIcon(thisClass.getResource(
          "images/italy.gif"))), new Double(1181.3668977),
          new Double(1182.104), null },
    { new DataWithIcon("German Mark",
        new ImageIcon(thisClass.getResource(
          "images/germany.gif"))), new Double(1.8191804),
          new Double(1.8223421), null },
    { new DataWithIcon("Japanese Yen",
        new ImageIcon(thisClass.getResource(
          "images/japan.gif"))), new Double(141.0815412),
          new Double(121.0040432), null }
    };
}
```

This is a straightforward implementation of the `TableModel` interface, in which the data is held in a two-dimensional array of `Objects` and the column names are held in a separate string array. As usual, the `getColumnName` method provides the name associated with each column and the `getValueAt` method the data for each individual cell. The interesting pieces of this particular example are the `getColumnClass` method and the data array. The `getColumnClass` method is supposed to return the Java `Class` object representing the type of data held in a given column; this information is used to select a default renderer if the corresponding column does not have a specific renderer assigned to it. Here, the getColumnClass method extracts the data entry for the top row of the column and calls getClass on it to determine its data type. This is a useful technique that you can use to avoid hard-coding specific classes for each column in your table models.

Core Alert

While this is a useful shorthand when you know that all the entries in a column will be of exactly the same type, there are cases where you need to be careful. Suppose, for example, that a column contains a mixture of objects all derived from java.lang.Number. *If the first row contains an object of type* java.math.BigDecimal, *using this technique would result in* getColumnClass *returning* java.math.BigDecimal *as the column class for this column. Now suppose the second row contains an object of type* java.lang.Integer. *Although this type is derived from* Number, *it is not derived from* BigDecimal. *If you have installed custom class-based renderers for* BigDecimal *and* Integer, *they will override the default* Number *renderer and you will find that the* BigDecimal *renderer is called for all the rows in this column, while the* Integer *renderer is never invoked. This is probably not what you intended. In fact, there is no simple way to get the correct renderer invoked for each cell (because the selection is based only on the column and so only one renderer can be chosen for each column) and the best you could do would be to create a merged renderer that could deal with either of these types and return* java.lang.Number *as the column class. You would also need to assign your merged renderer as the default for objects of type* Number. *Later in this chapter, you'll see how to create renderers that behave differently for individual cells within a column.*

The table data is held in the data array, in row order. Each row has data for a single currency and contains four entries:

- DataWithIcon object
- Double representing the exchange rate for the currency on the first day
- Double holding the exchange rate on the second day
- Double representing the change in exchange rate over the two days

The DataWithIcon class holds a text string and an Icon. In this example, only the text string, which represents the currency name, will be used; the icon will be used later to demonstrate a custom renderer. The exchange rates are coded directly into the table data (in a real-world program, of course, all this data would be retrieved from some external source, such as a database) and the data model's constructor runs through the data to fill in the fourth column, which contains the difference between the two rates, when the table model is created. This task could have been deferred to the `getValueAt` method, which would have been implemented to return the difference between columns 2 and 1 when asked for the value of column 3. Because the data in this particular table model is constant, it is slightly more efficient to calculate the difference once, but this would not be possible if the table data were dynamically updated from an external source.

When the table is drawn, the table UI class checks each column for a column-based renderer. In this example, the source code for which is shown in Listing 6-2, the table's column model is created automatically so there are no column-based renderers installed. Instead, default renderers will be used for all of the data in the table.

Listing 6-2 The Currency Table Example

```
package AdvancedSwing.Chapter6;

import javax.swing.*;
import javax.swing.table.*;
import java.awt.*;
import java.awt.event.*;

public class CurrencyTable {
    public static void main(String[] args) {
        JFrame f = new JFrame("Currency Table");
        JTable tbl = new JTable(new CurrencyTableModel());

        TableColumnModel tcm = tbl.getColumnModel();
        tcm.getColumn(0).setPreferredWidth(150);
        tcm.getColumn(0).setMinWidth(150);

        tbl.setAutoResizeMode(JTable.AUTO_RESIZE_OFF);
        tbl.setPreferredScrollableViewportSize(
                            tbl.getPreferredSize());

        JScrollPane sp = new JScrollPane(tbl)
```

> **Listing 6-2 The Currency Table Example (continued)**

```
    f.getContentPane().add(sp, "Center");
    f.pack();
    f.addWindowListener(new WindowAdapter() {
        public void windowClosing(WindowEvent evt) {
            System.exit(0);
        }
    });
    f.setVisible(true);
  }
}
```

Let's look first at what happens to the last three columns. All these contain `Doubles`, so `getColumnClass` returns `java.lang.Double` in all three cases. There is no renderer installed for `Double`, but there is a default renderer for its superclass, `Number`, which will be used for these three columns. As noted earlier and as can be seen in Figure 6-1, this renderer displays numbers right-justified within the space allocated to each cell.

The first class is slightly more interesting. The type returned by `get-ColumnClass` for this column is `DataWithIcon`. Because this is a custom type (the implementation of which is shown in Listing 6-4), there is certainly no default renderer installed for it. However, `DataWithIcon` is derived from `java.lang.Object`, so the `Object` renderer will be used to draw the cells in the first column.

As you already know, the `Object` renderer displays the text returned by the `toString` method of the data that it is rendering. For this to display the currency name, `DataWithIcon` implements `toString` in such a way as to directly return the name of the currency, which was one of the two objects used to initialize each instance of it in the `data` array.

You'll notice from the code in Listing 6-2 that the first column is explicitly sized to ensure that there is enough room to show all of the currency name. There is no simple way to know exactly how wide a table column should be to safely accommodate all the data that it will display and, in most cases, it is best to set the size based on trial and error. Of course, this only works if you can be sure that you know in advance the maximum length of the data in the column and the font that will be used to display it. In the next section, you'll see how to calculate an appropriate size for a column based on the actual data that it holds.

Implementing a Custom Renderer

As the example you have just seen demonstrates, the default renderers give you an easy way to build tables that you can get by with, but you can create much more usable tables if you implement your own renderers. In this section, you'll see how to extend the default renderers to improve the appearance of the currency table a little; after that, we'll show you how to create some more interesting effects by implementing your own renderers from scratch.

How the Default Renderers Work

All table renderers (custom or otherwise) implement the `TableCellRenderer` interface. This interface has only one method, which is defined as follows:

```
public Component getTableCellRendererComponent(JTable table,
                    Object value, boolean isSelected,
                    boolean hasFocus, int row, int column);
```

The arguments passed to this method are almost self-explanatory:

`table`	The `JTable` being rendered
`value`	The data value from the cell being drawn
`isSelected`	true if this cell is currently selected
`hasFocus`	true if this cell has the input focus
`row`	The row number of the cell being drawn
`column`	The column number of the cell being drawn

The `getTableCellRendererComponent` method returns a `Component` that is used to draw the content of the cell whose row and column numbers and data value were passed as arguments. Although a `Component` of any kind can be returned, the return value is usually a `JComponent` and, most often, is a class derived from `JLabel` (although you will see examples later that return other components). When the table UI class is drawing the table, it calls the `getTableCellRendererComponent` method of the renderer appropriate for the column in which a particular cell resides; this method can take whatever steps it needs to return a suitably-configured component, which is then used to draw the cell. Typically, the component might be customized by having suitable foreground and background colors set, along with an appropriate font and, if the component is a JLabel, the text to be displayed in the cell will be associated with it using the JLabel setText method. The table UI class is not actually concerned with the exact customization performed; when the component is returned, it adjusts its size to suit that of the cell in which its content is to be displayed and then renders it by simply calling its paint method.

Note that the column argument to getTableCellRendererComponent is expressed in terms of the table's *column* model, not in terms of the column numbers of the TableModel. Therefore, if the user reorders the table columns, this number will change.

All the default renderers installed by JTable when it is created (apart from the renderer for Booleans) are derived from a prototypical Table-CellRenderer implementation called DefaultTableCellRenderer, which is derived from JLabel. Here are the public methods of the DefaultTable-CellRenderer class:

```
public class DefaultTableCellRenderer extends JLabel
         implements TableCellRenderer, Serializable {
   public DefaultTableCellRenderer();
   public void setForeground(Color c);
   public void setBackground(Color c);
   public Component getTableCellRendererComponent(JTable table,
            Object value, boolean isSelected,
            boolean hasFocus, int row, int column);
}
```

Because this class is derived from JLabel, it has the ability to paint its own background, draw text in any given color, and with a user-defined font, display an icon and align the text and/or the icon as required. However, because the default renderers are actually installed by the table, you don't get the chance to directly configure them. In the example shown in Listing 6-2, the renderer used for the first column was a DefaultTableCellRenderer configured to show left-aligned text, while the renderer in the other three displays its text right-aligned.

The default renderers do not have specific foreground and background colors or fonts assigned to them. The DefaultTableCellRenderer obtains its background and foreground colors and its font from the table that it is drawing on, using the table argument to the getTableCellRendererCom-ponent method to access them. However, you can override these attributes by using the setForeground, setBackground, and setFont methods (the latter of which is inherited from JLabel). Although you would normally do this when creating your own renderer, you can, if you want, apply color or font changes to the default renderers by using the `getDefaultRenderer` method to obtain references to them. Here's an example:

```
TableCellRenderer renderer =
            table.getDefaultRenderer(java.lang.Object.class);
if (renderer instanceof DefaultTableCellRenderer) {
   ((DefaultTableCellRenderer)renderer).setFont(
                           new Font("Dialog", Font.BOLD, 14));
}
```

When this code has been executed, any cells rendered in this specific table by the default renderer for `Objects` will use a 14-point, bold font. Notice that it is necessary to check first that the renderer is a `DefaultTableCellRenderer`, because the `setFont` method is not part of the `TableCellRenderer` interface.

`DefaultTableCellRenderer` takes special action when the cell that it is drawing is selected or has the input focus. When the cell is selected, the default colors (or any specifically installed ones) are ignored and the cell is rendered with foreground and background colors configured in the table using the `JTable` `setSelectionForeground` and `setSelectionBackground` methods.

When the cell has the input focus, a border is installed to make it stand out. You can see this border surrounding the cell in the first column of the first row in Figure 6-1. The specific border used is obtained from the Swing look-and-feel `UIManager` class like this:

```
Border border = UIManager.getBorder(
                 "Table.focusCellHighlightBorder");
```

If the cell has the focus and the underlying data in the model is editable, the usual colors are replaced by a pair of look-and-feel specific colors that can also be obtained from the `UIManager` class as follows:

```
Color foreground = UIManager.getColor("Table.focusCellForeground");
Color background = UIManager.getColor("Table.focusCellBackground");
```

Creating a Renderer That Displays Decimal Numbers

Now that you have seen how the `DefaultTableCellRenderer` works, it is a relatively simple matter to enhance it to create a custom renderer. If you look back to Figure 6-1, you'll notice that the figures shown in the rightmost three columns of the table are a little haphazard—you probably wouldn't describe this as a neatly arranged or readable layout. These columns are drawn by the default renderer for objects derived from `Number`, which converts the number's value to text using the `toString` method of the class that it is actually displaying (in this case `java.lang.Double`) and then arranges for the text to be drawn by using the `setText` method, which `DefaultTableCellRenderer` inherits from `JLabel`.

The problem with this approach, as far as this example is concerned, is that the `toString` method of `Double` shows as many decimal places as are necessary to represent the number that the `Double` contains (at least until the total number of digits in the number is no more than 16). This means that the decimal points in the rows of the table don't line up very well, resulting in an untidy appearance. In practice, you would probably prefer to show exchange rates with a fixed number of decimal places visible; if you could create a renderer that did this, your table would look much neater, because the decimal points would be much closer together and you would not be displaying digits that the user doesn't need to see.

Core Note

Even if you use a renderer that shows a fixed number of decimal places, the decimal points still won't necessarily line up unless you use a constant-width font. Even with a proportional font, however, the table looks much better with this approach.

To create a custom renderer that displays a fixed number of decimal places, there are actually two problems to solve:

1. How to create a string that represents the value of a `Number` with a specified number of decimal places.
2. How to arrange for the renderer to draw that string when presented with a `Number` from the table model.

The first problem can be solved using the `java.text.NumberFormat` class, which allows you to format numbers in various different ways. Among the constraints that you can apply when formatting numbers using this class are the maximum and minimum number of decimal places to be shown and the maximum and minimum number of digits used to represent the complete number. Using this class, you can arrange for exactly three decimal digits to be shown as follows:

```
Number number = new Double((double)123.45678);
NumberFormat formatter = NumberFormat.getInstance();
```

```
formatter.setMaximumFractionDigits(3);
formatter.setMinimumFractionDigits(3);
String formattedNumber = formatter.format(number.doubleValue());
```

With this code, the formatted result in the variable `formattedNumber`
would be `123.456`. If the variable `number` had been initialized to the value
`123.4`, then the result would have been padded to the right with zeroes, giving `123.400`.

Core Note

*If you are not familiar with the `java.text` package in general or the
`NumberFormat` class in particular, you'll find a good description of them
in* Core Java 2, Volume 2: Advanced Features *(Prentice Hall).*

Once you've got a string that represents the number as you want it to, the
next problem is to arrange for the renderer to display it. Because we are creating a custom renderer, we have a choice between creating a completely new
class that implements the `TableCellRenderer` interface or simply subclassing `DefaultTableCellRenderer`. Usually, it is simpler to take the latter
course. By doing so, you get the benefits of the special action that `Default-
TableCellRenderer` takes for selected and focused cells and the ability to
configure different background and foreground colors. This renderer is sufficiently simple that it can be implemented as a subclass of `DefaultTable-
CellRenderer` and that is the approach that we'll adopt. Later, you'll see
examples in which it isn't convenient to subclass `DefaultTableCellRen-
derer`. The code for this particular renderer is shown in Listing 6-3.

Listing 6-3 A Renderer for Decimal Numbers

```
package AdvancedSwing.Chapter6;

import java.text.*;
import javax.swing.*;
import javax.swing.table.*;

// A holder for data and an associated icon
public class FractionCellRenderer extends
        DefaultTableCellRenderer {
    public FractionCellRenderer(int integer, int fraction,
                                            int align) {
```

Listing 6-3 A Renderer for Decimal Numbers (continued)

```
        this.integer = integer;      // maximum integer digits
        this.fraction = fraction;    // exact number of fraction
                                     // digits
        this.align = align;          // alignment (LEFT,
                                     // CENTER, RIGHT)
    }

    protected void setValue(Object value) {
        if (value != null && value instanceof Number) {
            formatter.setMaximumIntegerDigits(integer);
            formatter.setMaximumFractionDigits(fraction);
            formatter.setMinimumFractionDigits(fraction);
            setText(formatter.format(
                    ((Number)value).doubleValue()));
        } else {
            super.setValue(value);
        }
        setHorizontalAlignment(align);
    }

    protected int integer;
    protected int fraction;
    protected int align;
    protected static NumberFormat formatter =
                            NumberFormat.getInstance();
}
```

You can see this renderer in action using the command

```
java AdvancedSwing.Chapter6.FractionCurrencyTable
```

The result you get will look like Figure 6-2.

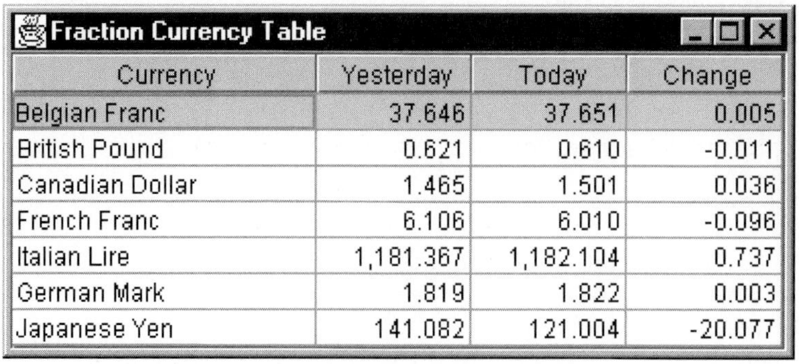

Fraction Currency Table			□ ×
Currency	Yesterday	Today	Change
Belgian Franc	37.646	37.651	0.005
British Pound	0.621	0.610	-0.011
Canadian Dollar	1.465	1.501	0.036
French Franc	6.106	6.010	-0.096
Italian Lire	1,181.367	1,182.104	0.737
German Mark	1.819	1.822	0.003
Japanese Yen	141.082	121.004	-20.077

Figure 6-2 A custom renderer for decimal numbers.

The code for the `FractionCurrencyTable` class is almost identical to that shown in Listing 6-2, except that the `FractionCellRenderer` was added as a class-based renderer for objects derived from `java.lang.Number`:

```
JTable tbl = new JTable(new CurrencyTableModel());
tbl.setDefaultRenderer(java.lang.Number.class,
      new FractionCellRenderer(10, 3, SwingConstants.RIGHT));
```

Because there is only one class-based renderer for each class, our new renderer will displace the default one for numbers installed by the table and will be used to render all cells containing objects derived from `java.lang.Number`, which, in this example, means all of the rightmost three columns.

Now let's look at Listing 6-3 and see exactly how this renderer works. If you've been following the discussion up to this point, you will probably be surprised at what you see. Given that the core of a renderer is its `getTableCellRendererComponent` method, you might be wondering why our renderer doesn't override this method to set the text of the label to the string created by formatting the number obtained from the table. Other than the constructor, which just stores a few parameters, this renderer only has a `setValue` method, which doesn't seem to get invoked anywhere and wasn't listed among the public methods of `DefaultTableCellRenderer` earlier in this chapter. So what's happening here?

To understand how this renderer works, you need to look a little more closely at the `getTableCellRendererComponent` method of `DefaultTableCellRenderer`. Because our renderer extends `DefaultTableCellRenderer`, this is the method that will be invoked to configure a component for each cell. When this method is called, it does the following:

1. If the cell is selected, it sets the foreground and background colors using those configured in the table.

2. If the cell is not selected, it sets the foreground and background colors from those configured using `setForeground` and `setBackground`. If either (or both) of these methods has not been called, the table foreground and/or background color is used instead.

3. If the cell has the focus, a border to highlight the focus is installed. Otherwise, an empty border is used.

4. The label font is set to the font used by the table.

5. The label is configured by invoking the `setValue` method, passing the value obtained from the table.

It is the last of these steps that is the important one for renderers derived from `DefaultTableCellRenderer`. As you can see from Listing 6-3, `set-Value` is a protected method that takes the `Object` value from the table cell as its only argument. The default implementation just applies the `toString` method to this object and uses the result as the text of the label, like this:

```
setText((value == null) ? "" : value.toString());
```

The advantage of the `setValue` method is that you don't need to replace all of the `getTableCellRendererComponent` method and rewrite the code that implements the first four steps in the previous list when you want to create a custom renderer—instead, you override `setValue` and just replace as much of the tailoring of the attributes of the label as you need to. Our renderer behaves differently from the default one by applying special formatting for objects derived from `Number`. As you can see from Listing 6-3, the overridden `set-Value` method verifies that the object it is passed is a subclass of `Number` and, if it is, uses the technique you saw earlier to create a string representation with the appropriate number of decimal places, uses `setText` to arrange for the `JLabel` from which the renderer is derived to draw it. The number of decimal places, and the maximum number of digits to the left of the decimal point, are supplied as arguments to the constructor and are supplied directly to the `Num-berFormat` class. The required text alignment (`SwingConstants.LEFT`, CEN-TER, or `RIGHT`) is also a parameter to the constructor and is applied directly to the component using the `setHorizontalAlignment` method.

You can see from the example code shown earlier that the table shown in Figure 6-2 was drawn by a default renderer constrained to show three decimal places, with the text right –aligned, and Figure 6-2 confirms that each of the currency values has exactly three decimal places, with zero-padding on the right where necessary.

There is one final point to be made about Listing 6-3. Notice that if the object to be rendered is not a `Number`, the superclass `setValue` method is invoked. This is absolutely necessary, of course, because our new code will only work if it is passed a `Number`. However, it is possible that this renderer will be configured in a column or on a table that returns other types (perhaps only in some rows of the table) and in that case we want to at least display something. Invoking the superclass `setValue` method causes a string representation of the object to be drawn.

A Renderer for Text and Icons

A common requirement in tables is the ability to draw icons to supplement or replace text. The table directly supports the rendering of icons in table cells when the cell contains an `ImageIcon` object—that is, if you arrange for get-

`ColumnClass` to return `ImageIcon.class` for a particular column, the `ImageIcons` held in that column of the table will be drawn, centered, into their cells. However, this functionality does not provide for mixing text and icons in the same cell.

The first column of the currency table holds the name of each currency. It would make the table look much nicer if the national flag of the appropriate country could be displayed alongside the currency name. One way to achieve this is just to add an extra column to the model and store an `ImageIcon` of the country's flag in it. Because the table has a default renderer for icons, this is all you would need to change—the table column for the flag would be generated automatically and the flag would be drawn by the `ImageIcon` renderer. While this would be simple, it would give an inferior result, because the flag and the currency name would be in separate columns. To arrange for them to appear in the same column requires another new renderer.

Before looking at how this renderer is implemented, let's think a little about the basic requirement. What we want to do is display some text and an icon together in a cell. This is a very basic task that a `JLabel` is able to perform without needing any extra code. Given that `DefaultTableCellRenderer` is derived from `JLabel`, it is clearly a good choice to derive the new renderer from `DefaultTableCellRenderer` and use the `setValue` method to configure the label with both the text and the icon. Recall that `setValue` gets only the object value stored in the table model for the cell being rendered so, to make our approach possible, this object must contain both the text and the icon together. This, of course, is why the `CurrencyTableModel` shown in Listing 6-1 used the class `DataWithIcon` to populate the first column of the table instead of a simple `String` holding the currency name. Listing 6-4 shows the definition of the `DataWithIcon` class.

Listing 6-4 The `DataWithIcon` Class

```
package AdvancedSwing.Chapter6;

import javax.swing.*;

// A holder for data and an associated icon
public class DataWithIcon {
    public DataWithIcon(Object data, Icon icon) {
        this.data = data;
        this.icon = icon;
    }
```

Listing 6-4 The `DataWithIcon` Class (continued)

```
   public Icon getIcon() {
      return icon;
   }

   public Object getData() {
      return data;
   }

   public String toString() {
      return data.toString();
   }

   protected Icon icon;
   protected Object data;
}
```

As you can see, this is a pure container class that just stores the opaque data and the `Icon` that are passed to its constructor and allows them to be retrieved later. Also, and very importantly, it implements a `toString` method that delegates directly to the `toString` method of whatever the data object happens to be. This `toString` method has been used by the default renderer for the `Object` class to arrange for the currency name to appear in the tables that you have seen in the earlier examples in this chapter.

With the appropriate data in place and the decision to subclass `Default-TableCellRenderer` made, the actual implementation, shown in Listing 6-5, is very straightforward.

Apart from the fact that this renderer deals with an icon as well as text, it is pretty much identical to the last renderer you saw. The `setValue` method receives an object to render. If the object reference is not `null` and refers to a `DataWithIcon` instance, the text and icon are extracted from it and configured into the `JLabel` superclass of the renderer using the usual `setText` and `setIcon` methods. The label then takes care of displaying them both when the table UI class actually paints the cell.

Of course, the implementation shown here is a pretty basic one. For one thing, it hard-codes the relative alignment of the text and the icon, both horizontally and vertically. A more complete implementation would allow these to be supplied as arguments to the constructor, much as the text alignment was made a parameter of the constructor of the `Fraction-CellRenderer` shown in Listing 6-3.

Listing 6-5 A Renderer for Text and Icons

```
package AdvancedSwing.Chapter6;

import javax.swing.*;
import javax.swing.table.*;

public class TextWithIconCellRenderer
        extends DefaultTableCellRenderer {
    protected void setValue(Object value) {
        if (value instanceof DataWithIcon) {
            if (value != null) {
                DataWithIcon d = (DataWithIcon)value;
                Object dataValue = d.getData();

                setText(dataValue == null ? "" :
                                    dataValue.toString());
                setIcon(d.getIcon());
                setHorizontalTextPosition(SwingConstants.RIGHT);
                setVerticalTextPosition(SwingConstants.CENTER);
                setHorizontalAlignment(SwingConstants.LEFT);
                setVerticalAlignment(SwingConstants.CENTER);
            } else {
                setText("");
                setIcon(null);
            }
        } else {
            super.setValue(value);
        }
    }
}
```

To demonstrate this renderer, it needs to be connected to the first column of the currency table. You could choose to install this renderer as a class-based renderer for class `DataWithIcon`; in this case, to show the use of a column-based renderer, an instance of `TextWithIconCellRenderer` is installed as the renderer for column 0 of the table, thus overriding the default renderer that has been used for that column in the previous examples in this chapter:

```
TableColumnModel tcm = tbl.getColumnModel();
tcm.getColumn(0).setPreferredWidth(150);
tcm.getColumn(0).setMinWidth(150);
TextWithIconCellRenderer renderer = new TextWithIconCellRenderer();
tcm.getColumn(0).setCellRenderer(renderer);
```

You can see the effect that this renderer has on the table using the following command:

```
java AdvancedSwing.Chapter6.IconCurrencyTable
```

This produces the result shown in Figure 6-3.

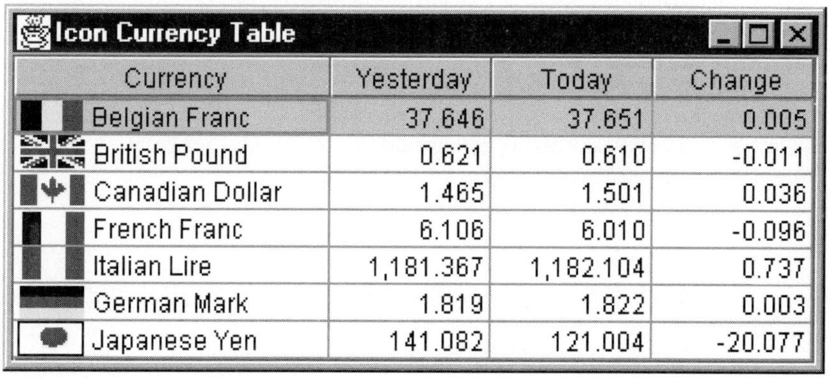

Currency	Yesterday	Today	Change
Belgian Franc	37.646	37.651	0.005
British Pound	0.621	0.610	-0.011
Canadian Dollar	1.465	1.501	0.036
French Franc	6.106	6.010	-0.096
Italian Lire	1,181.367	1,182.104	0.737
German Mark	1.819	1.822	0.003
Japanese Yen	141.082	121.004	-20.077

Figure 6-3 Rendering text and an icon in the same table column.

Calculating the Width of a Table Column

As you can see from Figure 6-3, the first column of the table now contains both the currency name and a national flag. It so happens that this column was manually sized to ensure that there is room for both the text and the icon to be visible at the same time. In fact, it is always necessary to explicitly set a column's width if you want to be sure that the content of each cell in that column is completely visible. However, it is possible to calculate the appropriate width for a table column, as the code in Listing 6-6 shows.

Listing 6-6 Calculating Table Column Widths

```
package AdvancedSwing.Chapter6;

import javax.swing.*;
import javax.swing.table.*;
import java.awt.*;

public class TableUtilities {
   // Calculate the required width of a table column
   public static int calculateColumnWidth(JTable table,
                                          int columnIndex) {
      int width = 0;          // The return value
```

Listing 6-6 Calculating Table Column Widths (continued)

```java
      int rowCount = table.getRowCount();

      for (int i = 0; i < rowCount ; i++) {
         TableCellRenderer renderer =
                     table.getCellRenderer(i, columnIndex);
         Component comp =
                     renderer.getTableCellRendererComponent(
                        table, table.getValueAt(i, columnIndex),
                        false, false, i, columnIndex);
         int thisWidth = comp.getPreferredSize().width;
         if (thisWidth > width) {
            width = thisWidth;
         }
      }

      return width;
   }

   // Set the widths of every column in a table
   public static void setColumnWidths(JTable table,
         Insets insets, boolean setMinimum,
         boolean setMaximum) {
      int columnCount = table.getColumnCount();
      TableColumnModel tcm = table.getColumnModel();
      int spare = (insets == null ? 0 : insets.left +
                                             insets.right);

      for (int i = 0; i < columnCount; i++) {
         int width = calculateColumnWidth(table, i);
         width += spare;

         TableColumn column = tcm.getColumn(i);
         column.setPreferredWidth(width);
         if (setMinimum == true) {
            column.setMinWidth(width);
         }
         if (setMaximum == true) {
            column.setMaxWidth(width);
         }
      }
   }

}
```

The `TableUtilities` class provides two static methods that allow you to determine the appropriate widths for table columns. The `calculateColumnWidth` method works out how wide a single column needs to be to fit the data that it will contain, while `setColumnWidths` is a convenience method that calculates the appropriate width for all the columns in a given table and configures their `TableColumn` objects appropriately. Let's look first at how `calculateColumnWidth` works.

The width of a column depends both on the data that it will contain and on the renderer used to draw it. To find out how much space a column needs, you need to process every cell in the column and work out how wide its representation will be when drawn on the screen with the renderer that will be used for that column. That's exactly what `calculateColumnWidth` does.

Because each cell in a table can theoretically have its own renderer, for each row in the column concerned the `JTable getCellRenderer` method is invoked to get the appropriate renderer for that row. Of course, unless the table has been subclassed and this method has been overridden, the same renderer will actually be returned for each row in the column, but this code cannot make that assumption. After locating the renderer, the rest of the loop walks down the column from the first row to the last, extracting the data value from each cell and invoking the renderer's `getTableCellRendererComponent` method to obtain a `Component` configured to draw the cell's data. Because this is an ordinary AWT component, you can find out how big it needs to be by calling its `getPreferredSize` method and, from the result, extract the width. To comfortably display all its data, the column would need to be no narrower than the largest width required by any of the components returned by the renderer. This width is the value returned by `calculateColumnWidth`.

The second method uses `calculateColumnWidth` to configure the column widths for a complete table, by processing each column in turn. There are three attributes in the `TableColumn` object that influence the size of a column—the preferred width, the minimum width, and the maximum width. The preferred width of the column is always set to the calculated width plus some optional extra space specified by an `Insets` object. Only the `left` and `right` members of this object are actually used to determine the additional space to be added on top of the room needed for the data. You can also supply a pair of booleans that determine whether the maximum and/or minimum widths should also be set to the same value. Setting the minimum width stops the user from making the cell any smaller, while setting the maximum stops the column from being made wider than the initial size.

You can see how these methods work by running a modified version of the `IconCurrencyTable` in which the columns are automatically sized using `setColumnWidths`. The code that configures this table looks like this:

```
TableColumnModel tcm = tbl.getColumnModel();
TextWithIconCellRenderer renderer = new TextWithIconCellRenderer();
tcm.getColumn(0).setCellRenderer(renderer);

// Automatically configure the column widths
TableUtilities.setColumnWidths(tbl, new Insets(0, 4, 0, 4),
                    true, false);

// Diagnostics: display the chosen column widths
for (int i = 0; i < tcm.getColumnCount() ; i++) {
  System.out.println("Column " + i + ": width is "
            + tcm.getColumn(i).getPreferredWidth());
}
```

The first column is no longer explicitly sized as it has been in all the earlier examples. Instead, the initial and minimum widths of all the columns are set so that there is enough room for all the data, plus a spare 8 pixels so that the table doesn't look too cluttered. You can run this example using the following command:

```
java AdvancedSwing.Chapter6.CalculatedColumnTable
```

So that you can see the process in operation, the preferred width of each column, as set by the `setColumnWidths` method, is shown in the window from which you run this program. Here is a typical set of results:

```
Column 0: width is 138
Column 1: width is 67
Column 2: width is 67
Column 3: width is 54
```

You'll probably notice that the table is smaller than the one in the last example. The first column is 12 pixels narrower than the 150 pixels that were hard-coded into the earlier examples and the last three columns are also smaller than the default column size of 75 pixels that has applied up to now.

While this approach works and can help to create an optimally sized table, it does have a drawback. To work out the exact sizes needed for a column, every cell in the column must be processed by its renderer. Even though this is cheaper than actually drawing all the cells, it can still represent a considerable overhead that is incurred when the table is created. Whether this overhead is acceptable depends on how much data the table contains—obviously, the more rows the table has, the more delay there will be before the table appears. Also, the column width that `calculateColumnWidth` returns is good only for the table data that it is presented with. If the data in the table can change after the table has been created, you'll have to recalculate the size again. Whether any of this is worthwhile, therefore, depends on how your application works. In many cases, the best approach is to set the column widths manually by trial and error, or perhaps by using `setColumnWidths` during development to determine the appropriate widths and then hard-coding them.

Customizing Cells and Rows

`JTable` directly supports column and class-based rendering, examples of which you have just seen. Sometimes, however, you'll want to create tables in which rendering decisions are based not on which column a cell is in or on the type of data that it contains, but on other criteria. In this section, you'll see how to create renderers that operate differently for different rows within a table, or produce effects that depend on which individual cell is being drawn.

A Row-Based Renderer: The Striped Table

The next renderer you're going to see is one that will draw alternate rows of a table in different colors, producing a striping effect that can make it easier for the eye to follow related information in the table, particularly if the table is wide or if it needs to be scrolled to bring everything into view. You can see how this renderer looks when applied to the currency table in Figure 6-4.

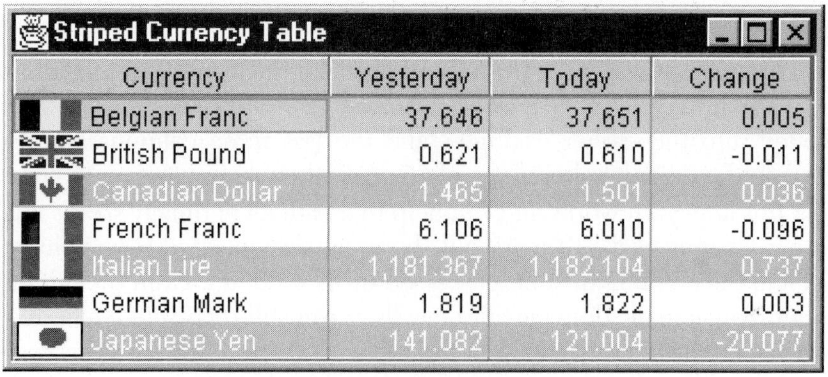

Striped Currency Table			
Currency	Yesterday	Today	Change
Belgian Franc	37.646	37.651	0.005
British Pound	0.621	0.610	-0.011
Canadian Dollar	1.465	1.501	0.036
French Franc	6.106	6.010	-0.096
Italian Lire	1,181.367	1,182.104	0.737
German Mark	1.819	1.822	0.003
Japanese Yen	141.082	121.004	-20.077

Figure 6-4   Using a renderer to create a striped table.

This particular renderer is configured with two pairs of foreground and background colors that are used to create the striping effect. In Figure 6-4, the rows are alternately white on light gray and black on white. How would you go about creating such a renderer? You know that the table draws each table cell separately by obtaining a suitably configured table from a renderer's `getTableCellRendererComponent` method and drawing it into the screen space allocated to the cell. To create a striped effect, you need to set the foreground and background differently for different rows in the table, keeping the same colors for all the cells within any given row. Because the `getTableCellRendererComponent` method gets the row number as one of its arguments, it is simple enough to use one set of colors whenever the renderer is called for a cell in an even-numbered row and the other set to draw cells in odd-numbered rows and, in principle, that's all that this renderer does.

However, that's not the only problem you need to solve. Here's the real issue: Renderers are selected on a per-column basis, but, in this case, you need to take the same action in *every* column. What this means is that you must install your renderer in every column of the table. Having done this, you can be sure that your renderer will be used to draw each cell in the table. However, this leads to a different problem. The first column contains text and an icon, so it must be drawn by a renderer that knows how to format a cell with an icon next to some text and also pick the appropriate foreground and background colors to give the striped effect. The other three columns were originally drawn by a renderer that deals with `Numbers` and displays a specific number of decimal places. Because the striping renderer has to draw the cells in these columns as well, it would seem that it must also have the same functionality as the `FractionCellRenderer`. This problem quickly gets out of hand—each time you wanted to use a different renderer in a table that has striped rows, you would need to add the functionality of that renderer to the one that does the striping. Of course, this isn't really practical and it is, to say the least, an expensive price to pay just to get a striped table. The alternative—instead of adding the drawing functionality of every other renderer into the striping renderer, adding the row-based coloring effect into all the other renderers is, of course, a problem of the same order of magnitude.

There is, however, a simple solution to this problem—by *cascading* one renderer in front of another, you can arrange to properly format each cell and also get the striped effect. In principle, what will happen is that the striped renderer will be installed on every column of the table. When it is called to get a component to draw a particular cell, it will invoke the `getTableCellRendererComponent` of the renderer that would been used for that cell and then change the foreground and background color of the component that the original renderer returns. The adjusted component will then be returned from the striping renderer. The result is that the effects produced by both renderers are applied to the cell.

Our earlier renderers have been implemented by extending the `Default-TableCellRenderer` class. When you do that, the renderer returns a new component from its `getTableCellRendererComponent` method.

Core Note

In fact, what `DefaultTableCellRenderer's` `getTableCellRendererComponent` *method returns is* `this`. *This works because* `DefaultTableCellRenderer` *is derived from* `JLabel`, *which is, of course, a* `Component`.

When you are cascading renderers, you want the first renderer to create a new component, while all the subsequent ones just modify its attributes. It follows then that, because our striping renderer won't be returning a new component from its `getTableCellRendererComponent` method, it shouldn't be derived from `DefaultTableCellRenderer`. Instead, it will provide its own implementation of the `TableCellRenderer` interface.

The problem with creating a renderer that uses another renderer is how to know which other renderer it should use. In the currency table, the striped renderer in the first column would need to invoke the `TextWithIconCell-Renderer`, while in the last three columns it should use the `FractionCell-Renderer`. How can it work out which renderer to call? The table UI class does this by first looking at the `TableColumn` object for the column that it is drawing. If this has a column renderer configured, it uses that; otherwise it uses the class-based renderer for the type of object in that column. To make the striping renderer work, it has to be installed as a column renderer for every column in the table that needs the stripe effect. If this column already needed a column-based renderer, it won't be possible for the striped renderer to consult the `TableColumn` object to find out which one that was, because all it will find there is an instance of itself! To solve this problem, this renderer supplies two convenience methods that allow you to install it on a specific column or on every column in a table. As it installs itself in a column, it will look to see whether that column already has a renderer configured for it and, if it does, it will store a reference to that renderer and use it when it's time to render a cell from that column. The details are in Listing 6-7.

Listing 6-7 A Striped Table Renderer

```
package AdvancedSwing.Chapter6;

import javax.swing.*;
import javax.swing.table.*;
import java.awt.*;

public class StripedTableCellRenderer
                    implements TableCellRenderer {
   public StripedTableCellRenderer(
                TableCellRenderer targetRenderer,
                Color evenBack, Color evenFore,
                Color oddBack, Color oddFore) {
      this.targetRenderer = targetRenderer;
      this.evenBack = evenBack;
      this.evenFore = evenFore;
      this.oddBack  = oddBack;
      this.oddFore  = oddFore;
   }

   // Implementation of TableCellRenderer interface
   public Component getTableCellRendererComponent(
                JTable table, Object value,
                boolean isSelected, boolean hasFocus,
                int row, int column) {
      TableCellRenderer renderer = targetRenderer;
      if (renderer == null) {
         // Get default renderer from the table
         renderer = table.getDefaultRenderer(
                            table.getColumnClass(column));
      }

      // Let the real renderer create the component
      Component comp = renderer.getTableCellRendererComponent(
                                    table, value,
                                    isSelected,
                                    hasFocus, row, column);

      // Now apply the stripe effect
      if (isSelected == false && hasFocus == false) {
         if ((row & 1) == 0) {
            comp.setBackground(evenBack != null ? evenBack :
                      table.getBackground());
            comp.setForeground(evenFore != null ? evenFore :
                      table.getForeground());
         } else {
```

Listing 6-7 A Striped Table Renderer (continued)

```
               comp.setBackground(oddBack != null ? oddBack :
                       table.getBackground());
               comp.setForeground(oddFore != null ? oddFore :
                       table.getForeground());
        }
     }

     return comp;
  }

  // Convenience method to apply this renderer to single column
  public static void installInColumn(JTable table,
                        int columnIndex,
                        Color evenBack, Color evenFore,
                        Color oddBack, Color oddFore) {
     TableColumn tc =
           table.getColumnModel().getColumn(columnIndex);

     // Get the cell renderer for this column, if any
     TableCellRenderer targetRenderer = tc.getCellRenderer();

     // Create a new StripedTableCellRenderer and install it
     tc.setCellRenderer(new StripedTableCellRenderer(
                       targetRenderer,
                       evenBack, evenFore,
                       oddBack, oddFore));
  }
  // Convenience method to apply this renderer to an
  // entire table
  public static void installInTable(JTable table,
                     Color evenBack, Color evenFore,
                     Color oddBack, Color oddFore) {
     StripedTableCellRenderer sharedInstance = null;
     int columns = table.getColumnCount();
     for (int i = 0 ; i < columns; i++) {
        TableColumn tc = table.getColumnModel().getColumn(i);
        TableCellRenderer targetRenderer =
                          tc.getCellRenderer();
        if (targetRenderer != null) {
           // This column has a specific renderer
           tc.setCellRenderer(new StripedTableCellRenderer(
                       targetRenderer,
                       evenBack, evenFore,
                       oddBack, oddFore));
        } else {
```

Listing 6-7 A Striped Table Renderer (continued)

```
                // This column uses a class renderer - use a
                // shared renderer
                if (sharedInstance == null) {
                    sharedInstance = new StripedTableCellRenderer(
                                    null, evenBack,
                                    evenFore, oddBack, oddFore);
                }
                tc.setCellRenderer(sharedInstance);
            }
        }
    }

    protected TableCellRenderer targetRenderer;
    protected Color evenBack;
    protected Color evenFore;
    protected Color oddBack;
    protected Color oddFore;
}
```

The constructor is simple enough; it takes the two foreground and background color pairs that will be used alternately on even- and odd-numbered rows and a *target* renderer, which it stores for later use. The target renderer is the one that should be used to obtain the component that can draw the cell and to which this renderer will apply its own foreground and background colors; it should be the original column-based renderer for the column into which the striped renderer is being installed, or `null` if there was no column renderer for that column. You can see how the target renderer is used in the getTableCellRendererComponent method. Because the striped renderer is going to be installed in a TableColumn object, this method will be invoked directly by the table UI class to draw every cell in the corresponding column. Its first job is to get the cell drawing component from the original renderer for the cell. If there was a column-based renderer, the targetRenderer member variable will be non-null and its getTableCellRendererComponent method is called. On the other hand, if this column didn't have its own renderer, the appropriate default renderer, obtained from the JTable getDefaultRenderer method, is used instead. Either way, a component correctly configured to draw the table cell (without the stripes) is obtained. Now, all that needs to be done is to set the foreground and background colors to get the striped effect. In principle, this just involves using the setForeground and setBackground methods on the rendering component to set either the even or odd color pairs. Having customized the rendering component that it gets from the target renderer, the striped renderer's getTableCellRendererComponent method returns that component to its caller, so that it will be used, in its modified form, to render the cell currently being drawn.

There are, however, some niceties to be observed here. First, if the cell is selected or has the focus, we don't want to change the colors at all, because to do so would lose the highlighting effect that the user would be familiar with. Because the isSelected and hasFocus arguments of the getTableCellRendererComponent method indicate these states, it is a simple matter to skip the color setting for either of these cases. The second thing to be careful of is a feature offered by this renderer that allows you to default the colors for a given row to the foreground and/or background colors of the table. This allows you to, for example, arrange for even rows to have black text on a light gray background, while leaving the odd-numbered rows unchanged. This behavior is configured by passing the appropriate arguments to the constructor as null. For example, the following line:

```
StripedTableCellRenderer renderer =
              new StripedTableCellRenderer(
                  null, Color.lightGray, Color.black,
                  null, null);
```

creates a renderer that applies a light gray background and a black background to the even-numbered rows and uses the table's own colors in the odd-numbered rows.

If you look at the getTableCellRendererComponent method, you'll notice that it always sets both the foreground and background colors, even if one or both of them has been supplied as null. You might think that you wouldn't have to set an explicit color if you just wanted the table's own foreground or background to be used, but you would be wrong. To see why this is, suppose you have a table with two columns, both of which contain strings and both of which are rendered using the default renderer for Objects. Now, if you install the striping renderer on this table, when rendering any given cell it will first invoke the Object renderer to get the component for that cell, and then set the appropriate attributes. Suppose also that the striped renderer has been configured to produce a light gray background on even-numbered rows and to leave odd-numbered rows in the table's background color. When the striping renderer is drawing the second column of the top row, it will call the setBackground method of the component returned by the

`Object` renderer and set the background to light gray. The next cell to be drawn will be the first column of the second row, which should be drawn in the background color of the table. Here again, the striped renderer's `get-TableCellRendererComponent` method will call the `getTableCellRendererComponent` method of the `Object` renderer. This is, of course, the *same* `Object` renderer that was used in the last column of the first row, so it will return the *same* component again. This component will, of course, have a light gray background. If the striped renderer did not explicitly set the background color to that of the table, this cell would also be drawn with a light gray background and, in fact, all the cells in the table would also be drawn in light gray! The moral of this story is to always set all the attributes that your renderer controls, even if the renderer supports some kind of default color setting as the striped renderer does. When you are cascading renderers like this, you can't really make any assumptions about how many different components will be returned from the renderers that you are calling, so you can't know what state the component that you are given will be in.

The rest of the `StripedTableCellRenderer` consists of two convenience methods that allow you to install it in a single column of a table, or on an entire table. Both of these methods are given the even and odd foreground colors for both the odd and even rows and a reference to the `JTable` itself. The `installInColumn` method is also given the index of the column in which to install itself. This method is very simple. Using the column index, it gets the `TableColumn` object for that column and extracts that column's renderer, if it has one, and then creates a new `StripedTableCellRenderer` and installs it in the column. If the column originally had a column renderer, it will be passed as the first argument to the `StripedTableCellRenderer` constructor and stored for later use. If there was no column renderer configured, the `getCellRenderer` call on the `TableColumn` object will return `null` and this value will be passed to the `StripedTableCellRenderer` constructor as the target renderer. In this case, when a cell is being rendered, the striped renderer's `getTableCellRendererComponent` method will see that the target renderer is `null` and will invoke the default renderer for the objects in that column to get the component to which the stripe will be applied, which is the desired effect.

You can use the `installInColumn` method to get striped effects for one or more individual columns. If you want to stripe an entire table (which is more likely), you can instead use the `installInTable` method, which has the same arguments, except that it doesn't need a column index. This method is basically just a loop that does the same job as `installInColumn` over each column in the table. There is, however, a minor optimization that is possible for columns that do not have a column renderer installed. If you use `installInColumn`, it creates a new `StripedTableCellRenderer` for each column. However, if there is no column renderer for a column, the first argument to the `StripedTableCellRenderer` constructor will be `null`. If you have several columns like this, they will all create different instances of the same renderer. To avoid this, the `installInTable` method creates only one such renderer on the first occasion that a column with no column renderer is encountered and then installs that single renderer in all such columns. In the case of the currency table, there is a column renderer in the first column, while the last three columns use default renderers. The first column, therefore, will have its own dedicated `StripedTableCell-Renderer`. However, thanks to the optimization performed by `install-InTable`, the last three columns will share the same `StripedTableCellRenderer` object. This would be true even if they used different default renderers to draw their contents, because the correct default renderer is determined dynamically as each cell is drawn.

When using a cascading renderer like `StripedTableCellRenderer`, you must first set up the table as you want it, with the usual renderers configured for every column that needs one, then install the striping renderer. This order is essential so that the `StripedTableCellRenderer` `installInColumn` or `installInTable` methods can work out which renderers they need to have called when the table is being drawn. It is, however, very simple to add striping to a table that doesn't already have it, as you can see from Listing 6-8, which shows how striping is added to the currency table—only the line highlighted in bold has been added to stripe the table. You can try this example using the command

```
java AdvancedSwing.Chapter6.StripedCurrencyTable
```

and the result you get will look like that shown in Figure 6-4.

Listing 6-8 Adding Striping to an Existing Table

```
package AdvancedSwing.Chapter6;

import javax.swing.*;
import javax.swing.table.*;
import java.awt.*;
import java.awt.event.*;

public class StripedCurrencyTable {
    public static void main(String[] args) {
```

Listing 6-8 Adding Striping to an Existing Table (continued)

```
    JFrame f = new JFrame("Striped Currency Table");
    JTable tbl = new JTable(new CurrencyTableModel());
    tbl.setDefaultRenderer(java.lang.Number.class,
        new FractionCellRenderer(10, 3, SwingConstants.RIGHT));

    TableColumnModel tcm = tbl.getColumnModel();
    tcm.getColumn(0).setPreferredWidth(150);
    tcm.getColumn(0).setMinWidth(150);
    TextWithIconCellRenderer renderer = new
                            TextWithIconCellRenderer();
    tcm.getColumn(0).setCellRenderer(renderer);
    tbl.setShowHorizontalLines(false);

    // Add the stripe renderer.
    StripedTableCellRenderer.installInTable(tbl,
                        Color.lightGray, Color.white,
                        null, null);

    tbl.setAutoResizeMode(JTable.AUTO_RESIZE_OFF);
    tbl.setPreferredScrollableViewportSize(
                    tbl.getPreferredSize());

    JScrollPane sp = new JScrollPane(tbl);
    f.getContentPane().add(sp, "Center");
    f.pack();
    f.addWindowListener(new WindowAdapter() {
        public void windowClosing(WindowEvent evt) {
            System.exit(0);
        }
    });
    f.setVisible(true);
    }
}
```

Cell-Based Rendering

Now that you've seen how to simulate row-based rendering, it is simple to take one more step and produce a renderer that does different things for each individual cell. The same principle is used here as with row-based rendering: You create a renderer that can be installed in a column (or in all columns of the table if you want a table-wide effect) and that cascades to other renderers to handle the mundane details of routine formatting, and then adds the appropriate variation for individual cells.

Let's create a simple example of a cell-based renderer that can be used in the currency table. The last column of this table shows the change in exchange rates between two successive days. For many users of the table, this will be the most important column for them to see, so we might want to make it stand out by changing its background color. Better still, how about making the cells that contain negative currency change values easier to see by changing both their foreground and background colors? To do this, the renderer has to examine the content of each cell and choose between two sets of foreground and background colors. This is very much like the striped renderer, except that the choice of attributes to be used depends not so much on where the cell is in that table, but instead on the data in the cell.

As with the `StripedTableCellRenderer`, this one will directly implement the `TableCellRenderer` interface and will delegate to other renderers to do most of the work. To do its job, it must be configured with the original column-based renderer for any column it will be installed in (or `null` if the column uses a class-based renderer), the foreground and background colors to use for ordinary cells, and those that need to be highlighted. All this information will be stored for use when the renderer's `getTableCellRendererComponent` method is called. However, this particular renderer needs one more piece of information to do its job.

We said that this renderer would highlight cells that contain negative values (representing currencies that are gaining value against the US dollar) by changing their foreground and background colors. One way to do this is to directly check the value of the number in a cell when that cell is being rendered. If we did this, however, we would end up with a renderer that worked, but would not be very reusable. Instead, it is better to factor out the decision-making process so that the same renderer could be used to highlight table content based on other criteria. Having done this, it would then be simple, for example, to create a renderer that highlights only values that had moved by more than 10 percent of the original value without having to rewrite all the rendering code. To make this possible, we invent a new interface called `Comparator`, defined as follows:

```
public interface Comparator {
    public abstract boolean shouldHighlight(JTable tbl,
                             Object value, int row, int column);
}
```

The `shouldHighlight` method has access to the table, the value of the cell currently being rendered, and the row and column indices of that cell. Its job is simply to return `true` if the cell should be drawn with highlighted colors and `false` if it should not. Listing 6-9 shows how the renderer is implemented.

**Listing 6-9 A Cell Renderer That Does
Value-Based Highlighting**

```java
package AdvancedSwing.Chapter6;

import java.awt.*;
import javax.swing.*;
import javax.swing.table.*;

// A holder for data and an associated icon
public class HighlightRenderer implements TableCellRenderer {
    public HighlightRenderer(Comparator cmp,
                    TableCellRenderer targetRenderer,
                    Color backColor, Color foreColor,
                    Color highlightBack, Color highlightFore) {
        this.cmp = cmp;
        this.targetRenderer = targetRenderer;
        this.backColor = backColor;
        this.foreColor = foreColor;
        this.highlightBack = highlightBack;
        this.highlightFore = highlightFore;
    }

    public Component getTableCellRendererComponent(JTable tbl,
                    Object value, boolean isSelected,
                    boolean hasFocus, int row, int column) {
        TableCellRenderer renderer = targetRenderer;
        if (renderer == null) {
            renderer = tbl.getDefaultRenderer(
                    tbl.getColumnClass(column));
        }
        Component comp =
                renderer.getTableCellRendererComponent(tbl,
                    value, isSelected, hasFocus, row, column);
        if (isSelected == false && hasFocus == false && value
                                                    != null) {
            if (cmp.shouldHighlight(tbl, value, row, column)) {
                comp.setForeground(highlightFore);
                comp.setBackground(highlightBack);
            } else {
                comp.setForeground(foreColor);
                comp.setBackground(backColor);
            }
        }
        return comp;
    }

    protected Comparator cmp;
```

Listing 6-9 A Cell Renderer That Does
Value-Based Highlighting (continued)

```
    protected TableCellRenderer targetRenderer;
    protected Color backColor;
    protected Color foreColor;
    protected Color highlightBack;
    protected Color highlightFore;
}
```

The constructor is simple—it just stores its parameters for later use. As with the striped renderer, the `targetRenderer` parameter should be the column renderer for the column into which this renderer is being installed if there is one, or `null` if there is not. The `cmp` argument is the `Comparator` that will be used to decide whether the content of a particular cell should be highlighted. The `getTableCellRendererComponent` method first obtains the component that will render the cell from the target renderer or the appropriate default renderer, and then invokes the `Comparator`'s `shouldHighlight` method, the return value from which determines which set of foreground and background colors will be used. Notice that, as always, the colors are not changed if the cell is selected or has the focus.

Installing this renderer in a table is very simple. Here's how to add it to the currency table example:

```
// Add the highlight renderer to the last column.
// The following comparator makes it highlight
// cells with negative numeric values.
Comparator cmp = new Comparator() {
    public boolean shouldHighlight(JTable tbl, Object value,
                            int row, int column) {
        if (value instanceof Number) {
            double columnValue = ((Number)value).doubleValue();
            return columnValue < (double)0.0;
        }
        return false;
    }
};
tcm.getColumn(3).setCellRenderer(new HighlightRenderer(cmp,
                        null,
                        Color.pink, Color.black,
                        Color.pink.darker(), Color.white));
```

The last line of this example creates an instance of the renderer that will display cells with black foreground on a pink background if they should not be highlighted and white on dark pink if they should be. The decision as to whether to highlight any given cell is made by the anonymous inner class shown at the beginning of the extract. This inner class implements the Comparator interface. Its shouldHighlight method checks to see that the value passed to it is a Number and, if it is, returns true if it has a negative value. If the value is zero or positive, or if the cell does not contain a Number, it will not be highlighted.

You can try this example using the command

```
java AdvancedSwing.Chapter6.HighlightCurrencyTable
```

and the result will look like Figure 6-5.

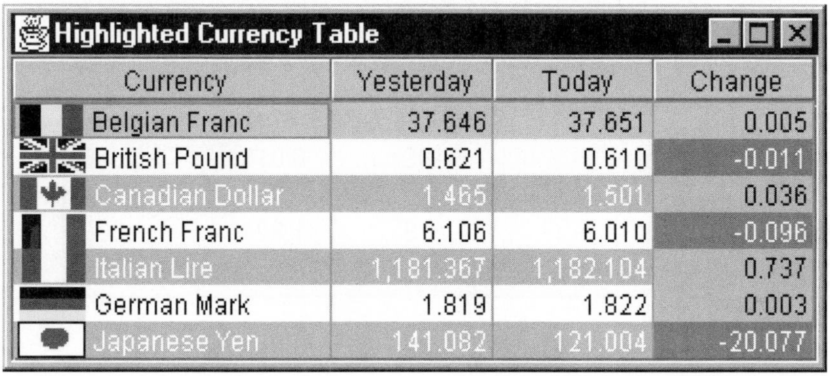

Figure 6-5   Highlighting individual cells based on their content.

While this example looks only at the value of the cell it is rendering, it is just as easy to create an example that takes other criteria into account. For example, you could, as hinted earlier, implement a renderer that showed currencies that change by more than 10 percent of their original value by using a different Comparator:

```
// Add the highlight renderer to the last column.
Comparator cmp = new Comparator() {
   public boolean shouldHighlight(JTable tbl, Object value,
                       int row, int column) {
      if (value instanceof Number) {
         Object oldValueObj = tbl.getModel().getValueAt(row, 1);
         if (oldValueObj instanceof Number) {
            double oldValue = ((Number)oldValueObj).doubleValue();
            double columnValue = ((Number)value).doubleValue();
            return Math.abs(columnValue) >
                           Math.abs(oldValue/(double)10.0);
```

```
            }
        }
        return false;
    }
};
```

If you try this modified `Comparator` using the command

`java AdvancedSwing.Chapter6.HighlightCurrencyTable2`

you'll see a table that looks like Figure 6-6.

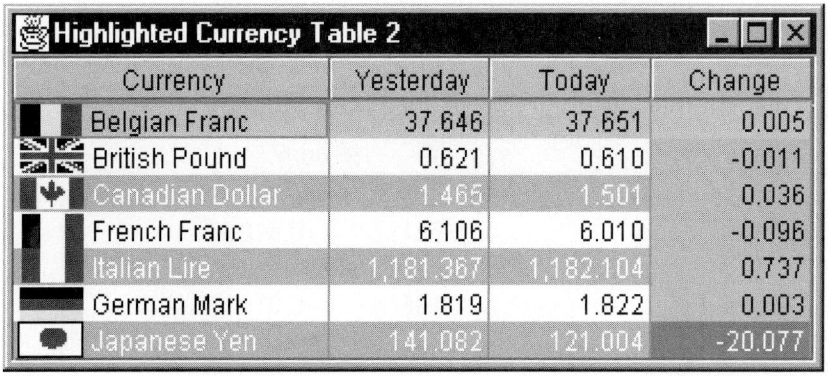

Figure 6-6   Highlighting a cell containing a significant value change.

Header Rendering

Although a table and its header are actually distinct components, they share the same `TableColumnModel` so that the column headers appear over the correct columns and to ensure that a column and its header have the same width. While the width of a table header cell is determined by the width of the corresponding column in the table, table header cells have their own renderers that are independent of those used to render the cells in the body of the table. Consequently, as you'll see in this section, you can directly control the way the header of a table looks in just the same way as you can manage the rendering of table cells.

A Multi-Line Column Header Renderer

Header renderers are simpler to deal with than the ones used in the body of the table, because every header cell has one and only one renderer, configured in the column's `TableColumn` object. When a `TableColumn` object is constructed, a default renderer is installed. This renderer is an instance of `DefaultTableCellRenderer` that draws the column name in the center of the column with a raised border around the outside. It defines its own `get-TableCellRendererComponent` method that sets the cell's background and foreground colors and its font using the colors and font configured for the table header. Usually, when you create a `JTable` and connect it to its data model, the appropriate `TableColumnModel` is constructed automatically, so unless you take specific action, your tables will be drawn with the default table header renderer. However, you can, if you wish, use the `TableColumn setHeaderRenderer` method to install a custom renderer of your own for any or all the columns in your table.

All the tables that you have seen so far in this book have had one line of text over each column. For many tables, this is just not enough. Taking the currency table as an example, the three rightmost columns are labeled Yesterday, Today, and Change. What you would probably prefer to do, if you were able, would be to write Yesterday's Rate, Today's Rate, and Rate Change and, of course, you could easily do this by changing the data model so that the `getColumnName` method returned these strings for the last three columns of data. The problem, of course, is that these long headings would make the columns too wide for the actual data that they contain, which would detract from the overall effect of the table. It would be nice to be able to supply more verbose column names without making the columns too wide by expanding the column header vertically—in other words, by creating a column header renderer that is able to accommodate multiple lines of text instead of just one. In this section, you'll see how to create such a renderer.

As you know, a renderer simply returns a component that knows how to draw whatever should appear in its cell. In the case of the header, the renderer is usually a `DefaultTableCellRenderer` that draws one line of centered text by using the features built into the `JLabel` component from which `DefaultTableCellRenderer` is derived. The most direct way to create a renderer that displays more than one line of text would be to use the HTML-based multi-line display capability of `JLabel`, which requires you to wrap the text in the appropriate HTML tags. While this is not difficult to do, it has a couple of disadvantages:

- Using HTML means using the HTML support supplied by the Swing text components. While this will work, it is a relatively heavyweight solution.
- Strictly speaking, HTML doesn't give you full control over how the text is rendered. Furthermore, if you want to mix text with

other elements such as graphics or if you want to nest Swing components inside the column header, the HTML method does not make it simple to do so.

Instead, we'll show you an alternative implementation that uses several `JLabels`, each of which will draw one line of text. To get the multi-line effect, we'll stack these `JLabels` one above the other in a container that will be the component returned from our renderer's `getTableCellRendererCompo-nent` method. The usual Swing painting mechanics will then take care of drawing all the labels (and hence the text) for us to produce the desired effect. You can easily generalize this to get more complex column headers by replacing some or all the `JLabels` with another component if necessary.

Before looking at the implementation, let's consider how the text for the column headers will be specified. The existing column renderer gets the text from the column's `TableColumn` object by invoking the `getHeaderValue` method, which returns an `Object`. If you use the default table columns created automatically for you by the table, the value that this method returns for a given column actually comes from the return value of the `getColumnName` method of `TableModel`. Thus, for example, in the case of the currency table, `getColumnName` for column 1 would return the `String` Yesterday. When the table's column model is created, this string will be stored as the header value for the table column mapping this column in the data model which, because the default column model maps the table model one for one, will be column 1 in the table column model. When the header for column 1 is rendered, it will therefore use the string Yesterday. When it comes to multi-line headers, what is the best way to supply the header text?

One approach (and probably the one that springs immediately to mind) is to change nothing—just store a longer column header in the table data model and let the renderer decide how to split the text over multiple lines given the space available to it. This is certainly simpler for the application programmer, but it gives the writer of the renderer more of a headache. The programmer of the renderer would prefer the application programmer split the text into multiple strings, one for each line. These strings could then be applied directly to `JLabels` without any messy tokenizing and font handling to work out how best to distribute the text over multiple lines. Splitting the text at compilation time is a small task to impose on the application programmer, which saves much complex renderer programming. It also has two other benefits.

First, along with the saving in programming complexity comes a performance improvement. Working out how to split the text is a costly business that requires splitting the text string into individual words and calculating how much space each would take in whichever font is being used to render the header cell, and then adding the lengths of the words to be placed on each line until the line is full. This process must be repeated for each column header cell. Requiring the application programmer to do this manually during application development avoids this performance penalty entirely.

Second, by handing responsibility to the application programmer, we can actually make another functionality improvement. The `getHeaderValue` method returns an `Object`. In Java, an array is a perfectly good `Object`, so one way to achieve the desired effect is to store an array of `String`s in the table column header, for example:

```
String[] multiLineText = { "Yesterday's", "Rate" };
TableColumn col = tbl.getColumnModel().getColumn(1);
col.setHeaderValue(multiLineText);
```

This certainly works, but we can do better. Because `getHeaderValue` and `setHeaderValue` can handle arrays, there is no reason to be restricted to `String`s—you can, theoretically, supply an array of `Object`s of any type, or of any combination of types. The only constraint is that the renderer must be able to do something useful with the array of `Object`s when it is time to draw the column header to which the data is attached. One obvious way to make use of this is to create multi-line headers that mix text and icons on separate lines. For example:

```
ImageIcon icon = new ImageIcon(…);          // URL not shown
Object[] multiLineHeader = {icon, "Yesterday's", "Rate" };
TableColumn col = tbl.getColumnModel().getColumn(1);
col.setHeaderValue(multiLineHeader);
```

You'll notice that both of these examples directly store the values to be used for the heading in the `TableColumn` object. This is unavoidable, because the `TableModel getColumnName` method can only return a `String`, so the column titles can't be stored in the data model when the multi-line renderer is in use. This is not really a problem—the column name returned by `getColumnName` is really intended to be used as a symbolic reference to the column for use within an application program; that it doubles as the content of the header cell is only due to the fact that this is the default behavior of the table.

The implementation of the renderer is shown in Listing 6-10.

Listing 6-10 A Multi-Line Header Renderer

```
package AdvancedSwing.Chapter6;

import javax.swing.*;
import javax.swing.border.*;
import javax.swing.table.*;
import java.awt.*;

public class MultiLineHeaderRenderer extends JPanel
                        implements TableCellRenderer {
   public MultiLineHeaderRenderer(int horizontalAlignment,
                                  int verticalAlignment) {
      this.horizontalAlignment = horizontalAlignment;
      this.verticalAlignment = verticalAlignment;
      switch (horizontalAlignment) {
      case SwingConstants.LEFT:
         alignmentX = (float)0.0;
         break;

      case SwingConstants.CENTER:
         alignmentX = (float)0.5;
         break;

      case SwingConstants.RIGHT:
         alignmentX = (float)1.0;
         break;

      default:
         throw new IllegalArgumentException(
                 "Illegal horizontal alignment value");
      }
      setBorder(headerBorder);
      setLayout(new BoxLayout(this, BoxLayout.Y_AXIS));
      setOpaque(true);

      background = null;
   }
   public void setForeground(Color foreground) {
      this.foreground = foreground;
      super.setForeground(foreground);
   }

   public void setBackground(Color background) {
      this.background = background;
      super.setBackground(background);
   }
```

Listing 6-10 A Multi-Line Header Renderer (continued)

```java
public void setFont(Font font) {
    this.font = font;
}

// Implementation of TableCellRenderer interface
public Component getTableCellRendererComponent(
                    JTable table, Object value,
                    boolean isSelected, boolean hasFocus,
                    int row, int column) {
    removeAll();
    invalidate();

    if (value == null) {
        // Do nothing if no value
        return this;
    }

    // Set the foreground and background colors
    // from the table header if they are not set
    if (table != null) {
        JTableHeader header = table.getTableHeader();
        if (header != null) {
            if (foreground == null) {
                super.setForeground(header.getForeground());
            }

            if (background == null) {
                super.setBackground(header.getBackground());
            }
        }
    }

    if (verticalAlignment != SwingConstants.TOP) {
        add(Box.createVerticalGlue());
    }

    Object[] values;
    int length;
    if (value instanceof Object[]) {
        // Input is an array - use it
        values = (Object[])value;
    } else {
        // Not an array - turn it into one
        values = new Object[1];
```

Listing 6-10 A Multi-Line Header Renderer (continued)

```
            values[0] = value;
        }
        length = values.length;

        // Configure each row of the header using
        // a separate JLabel. If a given row is
        // a JComponent, add it directly..
        for (int i = 0 ; i < length ; i++) {
            Object thisRow = values[i];

            if (thisRow instanceof JComponent) {
                add((JComponent)thisRow);
            } else {
                JLabel l = new JLabel();
                setValue(l, thisRow, i);
                add(l);
            }
        }

        if (verticalAlignment != SwingConstants.BOTTOM) {
            add(Box.createVerticalGlue());
        }
        return this;
    }

    // Configures a label for one line of the header.
    // This can be overridden by derived classes
    protected void setValue(JLabel l, Object value,
                            int lineNumber) {
        if (value != null && value instanceof Icon) {
            l.setIcon((Icon)value);
        } else {
            l.setText(value == null ? "" : value.toString());
        }
        l.setHorizontalAlignment(horizontalAlignment);
        l.setAlignmentX(alignmentX);
        l.setOpaque(false);
        l.setForeground(foreground);
        l.setFont(font);
    }
    protected int verticalAlignment;
    protected int horizontalAlignment;
    protected float alignmentX;
```

Listing 6-10 A Multi-Line Header Renderer (continued)

```
    // These attributes may be explicitly set
    // They are defaulted to the colors and attributes
    // of the table header
    protected Color foreground;
    protected Color background;

    // These attributes have fixed defaults
    protected Border headerBorder = UIManager.getBorder(
            "TableHeader.cellBorder");
    protected Font font = UIManager.getFont(
            "TableHeader.font");
}
```

The constructor allows you to specify both the horizontal and vertical alignment of the text within the header, given as values from the set provided by the SwingConstants class. The horizontal alignment determines whether the text in each line is centered (SwingConstants.CENTER) or left- or right-aligned (SwingConstants.LEFT or SwingConstants.RIGHT); the same constraint is applied to each line. The vertical alignment is more interesting. If all the column headers have the same number of lines, there would be no need to describe how to align them. Suppose, however, that one or more of the headers has fewer lines. Should these lines be placed at the top of the header cell leaving blank space beneath, or at the bottom? The vertical alignment allows you to control this, using the values SwingConstants.TOP to place the first line at the top of the cell or SwingConstants.BOTTOM to place the last line at the bottom of the cell. There is a third possibility, SwingConstants.CENTER, which distributes the spare space evenly between the top and bottom of the cell. This might not always be desirable, however, because the text in these cells will probably not align well with that in the other cells.

The renderer is derived from JPanel, which is a simple container that can paint its own background. The labels that hold each line of the column header will be stacked vertically within the panel. The simplest way to create this arrangement is to replace the JPanel's default FlowLayout manager with a BoxLayout, specifying a vertical arrangement. BoxLayout determines the horizontal alignment of components within its container by looking at their x-alignment attributes, which are controlled using the JComponent setAlignmentX method. This attribute specifies where a given component's alignment point resides. If the component has an x-alignment of 0.0, the alignment point is on its left edge; a component with an alignment of 1.0 has its alignment point at its right edge. Values in between place the alignment point somewhere between the two edges so that, for example, an alignment value of 0.5 specifies that the alignment point is in the middle. With a vertical arrangement, BoxLayout arranges its components so that their alignment points are directly above each other. To create the horizontal alignment requested in the constructor, the alignment values must be translated to the values 0.0 for left alignment, 0.5 for center alignment, and 1.0 for right alignment. The appropriate value is stored for use when the components of the header are added to the JPanel.

Finally, a default border is configured. This border is the same as that which has been used for the column headers that you have already seen so far. In fact, the actual border depends on the selected look-and-feel. You can, of course, use a different border or completely remove the border by using the setBorder method, which MultiLineHeaderRenderer inherits from JComponent. Here is how you might create a column header with the text left- and top-aligned and with no border:

```
MultiLineHeaderRenderer renderer = new MultiLineHeaderRenderer(
                    SwingConstants.LEFT, SwingConstants.TOP);
renderer.setBorder(BorderFactory.createEmptyBorder());
```

The BorderFactory createEmptyBorder method returns a border that occupies no space. You can also customize other attributes of the JPanel. For example, you can use setBackground to change the background color and setFont to control the font used to render each line of the header.

The real work of this renderer is done in the getTableCellRendererComponent method. This method is going to return the JPanel from which the renderer is derived as the component that will draw the cell, but before doing that, it must add the necessary JLabels and configure them properly. Because the same renderer will be called several times each time the table headers are rendered (once for each visible column), the first job is to remove the components that were added last time using the removeAll method. Then, the new components are added one by one, using the value parameter provided as the second argument. In the case of a table header renderer, this parameter is the value returned from getHeaderValue for the column being drawn. As we said earlier, to make proper use of the renderer, this value should be initialized to contain an array of Objects, each of which will form one line of the header; it is also possible to supply a single Object, in which case a single-line header will be created, with the horizontal and vertical alignments as specified to the constructor.

Usually, the array items will either be Strings or Icons. In both cases, a JLabel is created and customized using the setValue method, the default implementation of which simply installs the text or icon in the label and initializes the label's foreground and background colors, its font, and its x-alignment. The configured `JLabel` is then added to the renderer `JPanel`. As with earlier renderers, you can change some or all this behavior by implementing a subclass and overriding the `setValue` method.

If any of the values in the array is not a `String` or an `Icon`, its `toString` method is used to create a `String`, which is then used as the label text. There is one exception to this rule that makes this renderer potentially very powerful. By placing a `JComponent` in the value array, you can arrange for an arbitrary component to appear in the column header. This allows you, for example, to include a header line that contains both text and an icon. When the renderer finds a `JComponent`, it adds it directly to the `JPanel` instead of creating a `JLabel`. However, it does not customize any of the component's attributes, because you can do this directly if necessary. If you want the component to have the same background color as the column header, you should use its `setOpaque` method to make it transparent, or explicitly set its background color. You should also set its x-alignment value to match that used for the other components added by the renderer.

Figure 6-7 shows the currency table with multi-line headers. You can try this example for yourself using the command:

```
java AdvancedSwing.Chapter6.MultiLineHeaderTable
```

Currency	Yesterday's Rate	Today's Rate	Rate Change
Belgian Franc	37.646	37.651	0.005
British Pound	0.621	0.610	-0.011
Canadian Dollar	1.465	1.501	0.036
French Franc	6.106	6.010	-0.096
Italian Lire	1,181.367	1,182.104	0.737
German Mark	1.819	1.822	0.003
Japanese Yen	141.082	121.004	-20.077

Figure 6-7 Table columns with multiple heading lines.

Here is the code that was added to install the column headers:

```
// Add the custom header renderer
MultiLineHeaderRenderer headerRenderer =
          new MultiLineHeaderRenderer(SwingConstants.CENTER,
          SwingConstants.BOTTOM);
headerRenderer.setBackground(Color.blue);
```

```
headerRenderer.setForeground(Color.white);
headerRenderer.setFont(new Font("Dialog", Font.BOLD, 12));
int columns = tableHeaders.length;
for (int i = 0 ; i < columns ; i++) {
   tcm.getColumn(i).setHeaderRenderer(headerRenderer);
   tcm.getColumn(i).setHeaderValue(tableHeaders[i]);
}
```

As you can see, the column headers have white text on a blue background and the font is changed to a 12-point, bold dialog font. The header values are held in a static array, defined as follows:

```
public static Object[][] tableHeaders = new Object[] [] {
   new String[] { "Currency" },
   new String[] { "Yesterday's", "Rate" },
   new String[] { "Today's", "Rate" },
   new String[] { "Rate", "Change" }
};
```

Each entry in this array is itself an array that specifies the header for one column of the table, while each item in the array for a given column provides the data for one line of the column header. In this case, the values are all Strings. Notice that the first column has only one associated line of text, whereas the others have two. Because this table uses header renderers configured with the vertical alignment set to SwingConstants.BOTTOM, the text for this column will appear on the lowest line of the header, as you can see in Figure 6-7. How is this achieved?

If we took the simple approach of simply adding each line of text as a JLabel, the first column would have one JLabel and the last two columns would have two. BoxLayout would then place the single JLabel for the first column at the top of the header cell, not at the bottom. To persuade BoxLayout to push the labels to the bottom, as is necessary when the vertical alignment requested is SwingConstants.BOTTOM, vertical glue is added before the first label, like this:

```
if (verticalAlignment != SwingConstants.TOP) {
   add(Box.createVerticalGlue());
}
```

Glue is a JComponent that expands to fill the space available to it. When the vertical alignment is SwingConstants.BOTTOM, glue is added at the top only, so that all the spare vertical space appears at the top. When the vertical alignment is SwingConstants.TOP, the spare space should be allocated at the bottom, so that is where the glue is placed and, finally, in the case of

`SwingConstants.CENTER`, the glue is placed at both the top and the bottom to allocate spare room evenly between these two regions.

You may be wondering how the size of the areas allocated to the column headers is actually determined. The width of each header is determined by the width of the corresponding column in the table; this should, of course, be obvious—otherwise, the column header would not line up properly with the columns. The header height is determined by the table UI class, which invokes the header renderer of each column to get the component that will draw the cell and then asks for its preferred size. The height of the header is then set to the maximum requested height of all the column header components.

A Multi-Line Cell Renderer

Now that you've seen how to create a multi-line renderer for the table header, it's a relatively simple matter to turn the same renderer into one that works in the body of the table instead, although there are a few tricky points to be careful of. The main difference between creating a renderer for the table body and one for the header is that the header renderer does not have to take account of color handling for selected cells or the cell that has the focus. In addition, you'll also see that you need to be careful about color handling if you want your renderer to work with other ones such as the striping renderer shown earlier in this chapter. The implementation of this renderer is shown in Listing 6-11.

Listing 6-11 A Multi-Line Table Cell Renderer

```
package AdvancedSwing.Chapter6;

import javax.swing.*;
import javax.swing.table.*;
import javax.swing.border.*;
import java.awt.*;

public class MultiLineCellRenderer extends JPanel
                          implements TableCellRenderer {
   public MultiLineCellRenderer(int horizontalAlignment,
                                int verticalAlignment) {
      this.horizontalAlignment = horizontalAlignment;
      this.verticalAlignment = verticalAlignment;
      switch (horizontalAlignment) {
      case SwingConstants.LEFT:
         alignmentX = (float)0.0;
         break;

      case SwingConstants.CENTER:
```

Listing 6-11 A Multi-Line Table Cell Renderer (continued)

```
         alignmentX = (float)0.5;
         break;

   case SwingConstants.RIGHT:
      alignmentX = (float)1.0;
      break;

   default:
      throw new IllegalArgumentException("Illegal
                             horizontal alignment value");
   }

   setLayout(new BoxLayout(this, BoxLayout.Y_AXIS));
   setOpaque(true);
   setBorder(border);

   background = null;
   foreground = null;
}

public void setForeground(Color foreground) {
   super.setForeground(foreground);
   Component[] comps = this.getComponents();
   int ncomp = comps.length;
   for (int i = 0 ; i < ncomp; i++) {
      Component comp = comps[i];
      if (comp instanceof JLabel) {
         comp.setForeground(foreground);
      }
   }
}

public void setBackground(Color background) {
   this.background = background;
   super.setBackground(background);
}

public void setFont(Font font) {
   this.font = font;
}

// Implementation of TableCellRenderer interface
public Component
        getTableCellRendererComponent(JTable table,
            Object value, boolean isSelected,
            boolean hasFocus, int row, int column) {
   removeAll();
   invalidate();
```

Listing 6-11 A Multi-Line Table Cell Renderer (continued)

```
if (value == null || table == null) {
   // Do nothing if no value
   return this;
}

Color cellForeground;
Color cellBackground;

// Set the foreground and background colors
// from the table if they are not set
cellForeground = (foreground == null ?
                  table.getForeground() : foreground);
cellBackground = (background == null ?
                  table.getBackground() : background);

// Handle selection and focus colors
if (isSelected == true) {
   cellForeground = table.getSelectionForeground();
   cellBackground = table.getSelectionBackground();
}

if (hasFocus == true) {
   setBorder(UIManager.getBorder(
           "Table.focusCellHighlightBorder"));
   if (table.isCellEditable(row, column)) {
           cellForeground = UIManager.getColor(
                   "Table.focusCellForeground");
           cellBackground = UIManager.getColor(
                   "Table.focusCellBackground");
   }
} else {
   setBorder(border);
}

super.setForeground(cellForeground);
super.setBackground(cellBackground);

// Default the font from the table
if (font == null) {
   font = table.getFont();
}

if (verticalAlignment != SwingConstants.TOP) {
   add(Box.createVerticalGlue());
}

Object[] values;
int length;
```

Listing 6-11   A Multi-Line Table Cell Renderer (continued)

```
        if (value instanceof Object[]) {
           // Input is an array - use it
           values = (Object[])value;
        } else {
           // Not an array - turn it into one
           values = new Object[1];
           values[0] = value;
        }
        length = values.length;

        // Configure each row of the cell using
        // a separate JLabel. If a given row is
        // a JComponent, add it directly..
        for (int i = 0 ; i < length ; i++) {
           Object thisRow = values[i];

           if (thisRow instanceof JComponent) {
              add((JComponent)thisRow);
           } else {
              JLabel l = new JLabel();
              setValue(l, thisRow, i, cellForeground);
              add(l);
           }
        }

        if (verticalAlignment != SwingConstants.BOTTOM) {
           add(Box.createVerticalGlue());
        }
        return this;
     }

     // Configures a label for one line of the cell.
     // This can be overridden by derived classes
     protected void setValue(JLabel l, Object value,
                    int lineNumber, Color cellForeground) {
        if (value != null && value instanceof Icon) {
           l.setIcon((Icon)value);
        } else {
           l.setText(value == null ? "" : value.toString());
        }
        l.setHorizontalAlignment(horizontalAlignment);
        l.setAlignmentX(alignmentX);
        l.setOpaque(false);
        l.setForeground(cellForeground);
        l.setFont(font);
     }
```

Listing 6-11 A Multi-Line Table Cell Renderer (continued)

```
    protected int verticalAlignment;
    protected int horizontalAlignment;
    protected float alignmentX;

    // These attributes may be explicitly set
    // They are defaulted to the colors and attributes
    // of the table
    protected Color foreground;
    protected Color background;
    protected Font font;

    protected static Border border = new EmptyBorder(
                                          1, 2, 1, 2);
}
```

As you can see, the constructor is virtually identical to that of the header renderer. The only significant difference is that the cell renderer installs a small empty border instead of the look-and-feel specific border that the table header uses. This border will be used in all the cells drawn by this renderer, except when a cell has the focus, when a line border will be substituted.

The setForeground method also has a more complex implementation here. The mechanics of this method are simple to understand—because the component that this renderer uses to draw each cell is a JPanel that will hold one or more child components, changing the cell's foreground color and making it effective for every line of the cell's content means setting the foreground color for each of the components that the JPanel contains. This is why the setForeground method is implemented as a loop that processes all the JPanel's components. As you'll see shortly, this complication is only necessary for a cell renderer and was avoided for the simpler header renderer.

Most of the changes appear in the getTableCellRendererComponent method. In principle, the same mechanism is being used here—several JLabels (or explicitly supplied components) are placed onto a single JPanel to create the multi-line effect and you'll notice that the last part of this method is the same for both renderer implementations. There are two major changes in the cell renderer:

- The color handling is more complex.
- The setValue method has an extra argument that specifies the foreground color for the child component being configured.

The reason for all of this complication is that table cells have three possible states, whereas header cells only have one state. Each separate state has different colors associated with it. Here are the three states that a table cell can be in:

1. It can be neither selected nor have the input focus.
2. It can be selected.
3. It can have the input focus.

The first case is the most usual and the easiest to deal with. Here, the background and foreground colors may be either explicitly set using the setForeground and setBackground methods, or inherited from the table. You'll see that the getTableCellRendererComponent method uses two local variables (cellForeground and cellBackground) to hold the appropriate colors for the cell and that these are initialized to those that would be expected in this state. If, however, the cell is selected, these variables are changed to the selected foreground and background colors configured in the table.

The most complex case is the last one, in which the cell has the input focus. In this case, nothing special is done unless the cell is editable, because the focus doesn't mean anything for a non-editable cell. If the cell is editable, two different colors, obtained from the selected look-and-feel, are substituted. In addition (whether or not the cell is editable), a different border is used, as noted earlier.

When the correct cell colors have been determined, the foreground and background attributes of the JPanel are set using the selected colors.

Core Note

You may wonder why the foreground color of the JPanel is set, because JPanel doesn't use this attribute. Usually, this is a redundant step. However, it is possible, as you know, to supply a custom component instead of text or an icon as part of the content to be rendered in the cell and such a component could be written to take its own foreground color from that of its container, which would be our JPanel. Setting the JPanel's foreground ensures that such a component would acquire the correct foreground attribute. The same argument also works for the background color.

When it comes to adding the components that make up the multi-line cell, each of them needs to use the same foreground color. This is why the setValue method for this renderer requires a foreground argument—because of the possibility of the cell being selected or having the focus, the appropriate foreground color is not necessarily the color configured using setForeground or inherited from the table; the only way for this method to know the correct color is to pass it as an argument from getTableCellRendererComponent. The header renderer did not have this complication because it has only one possible foreground color. Note that there is no need to take special action for the background, because the JLabels that are added to the JPanel are made transparent, so automatically acquire the correct background color.

Before explaining the reason for the more complicated setForeground method, let's see what a table with multi-line cells looks like. You can see a table that includes this renderer using the following command:

```
java AdvancedSwing.Chapter6.MultiLineTable
```

The result will look like Figure 6-8.

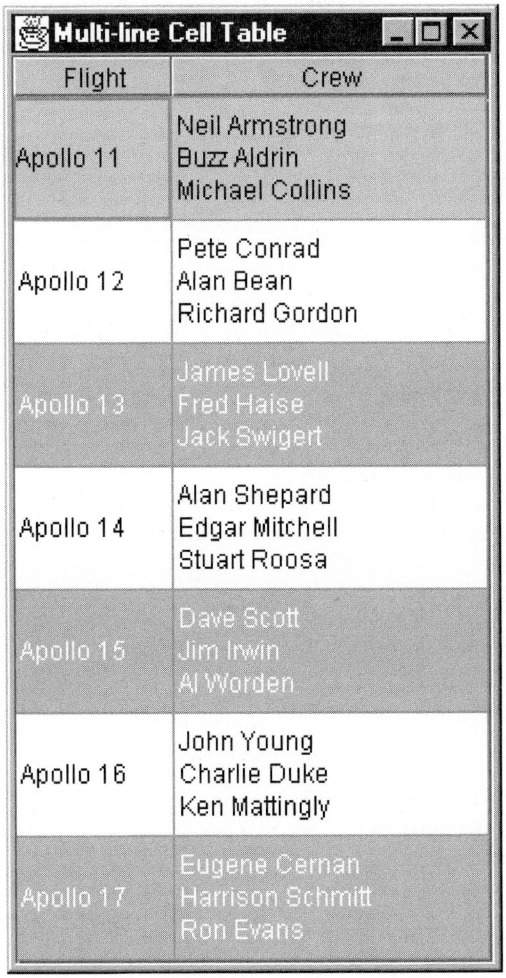

Figure 6-8   A table with multi-line cells.

This table shows the seven Apollo lunar landing flights (including the ill-fated Apollo 13, which did not land), along with the names of the crew members. You'll see that each crew's names are listed vertically, one per line, in single cell. This effect is, of course, obtained using the multi-line cell renderer. It is less obvious that the same renderer is also used in the first column, which contains only the flight name. The renderer for both these columns is configured with the vertical alignment set to `SwingConstants.CENTER`. In the case of the second column, this has no real effect because the three lines of text fill the cell. However, because there is only one line in the first column, the glue components that are added above and below the single `JLabel` force the flight name to appear in the middle of the cell. In fact, the same renderer instance is shared between both columns of this table. For reference, the code that creates this table (apart from the data model) is shown in Listing 6-12.

Listing 6-12 Installing the Multi-Line Cell Renderer

```
package AdvancedSwing.Chapter6;

import javax.swing.*;
import javax.swing.table.*;
import java.awt.*;
import java.awt.event.*;

public class MultiLineTable {
    public static void main(String[] args) {
        JFrame f = new JFrame("Multi-line Cell Table");
        JTable tbl = new JTable(new MultiLineTableModel());

        // Create the custom cell renderer
        MultiLineCellRenderer multiLineRenderer =
                new MultiLineCellRenderer(
                    SwingConstants.LEFT,
                    SwingConstants.CENTER);

        TableColumnModel tcm = tbl.getColumnModel();
        tcm.getColumn(0).setPreferredWidth(75);
        tcm.getColumn(0).setMinWidth(75);
        tcm.getColumn(1).setPreferredWidth(150);
        tcm.getColumn(1).setMinWidth(150);

        // Install the multi-line renderer
        tcm.getColumn(0).setCellRenderer(multiLineRenderer);
        tcm.getColumn(1).setCellRenderer(multiLineRenderer);
```

Listing 6-12 Installing the Multi-Line Cell Renderer (continued)

```
        // Set the table row height
        tbl.setRowHeight(56);

        // Add the stripe renderer.
        StripedTableCellRenderer.installInTable(tbl,

                    Color.lightGray, Color.white,
                    null, null);

        tbl.setAutoResizeMode(JTable.AUTO_RESIZE_OFF);
        tbl.setPreferredScrollableViewportSize(
                        tbl.getPreferredSize());

        JScrollPane sp = new JScrollPane(tbl);
        f.getContentPane().add(sp, "Center");
        f.pack();
        f.addWindowListener(new WindowAdapter() {
            public void windowClosing(WindowEvent evt) {
                System.exit(0);
            }
        });
        f.setVisible(true);
    }
}
```

Notice that a single `MultiLineCellRenderer` is created and shared between the two columns. This is appropriate in this case, and saves resources. If, however, you wanted the flight names in the left column to appear against the top of each cell instead of in the center, you would create separate renderers for the two columns with different alignment attributes.

The most important point to note about this code is the following line:

```
tbl.setRowHeight(56);
```

This shows a very important difference between table cells and header cells. Whereas the size of the component returned by the header renderer determined the height of the cells in the table header, this is not true for the table. The height of every row in this table is the same and is explicitly set using the `setRowHeight` method. By default, table rows are 16 pixels high. In this case, a 56-pixel row happens to allow enough space for three lines of text in the default font used by this table. In a production application, you would probably compute the required height by extracting the table's selected font using the `get-`

Font method (inherited by JTable from Component) and then using the font's metrics to deduce the space required to draw however many lines of text will appear in the table. If your multi-line cells contain icons or custom components, the calculation method will, of course, be different. The important thing to realize is that, if you don't set the appropriate height, the content of the cell will be confined to the fixed space allocated to each table row, with the result that the lower part of each cell will be clipped if it is too large to fit in the row.

Core Note

The restriction that all rows in a table have the same height will be removed in Java 2, version 1.3.

What about the complications in the setForeground method? You'll see from this example that the multi-line renderer is used in conjunction with the striped renderer that was developed earlier in this chapter. As you know, the striped renderer operates by first calling the getTableCellRendererComponent of each cell's actual renderer, and then changing the returned component's foreground and background colors to get the striping effect. In this case, the getTableCellRendererComponent method of MultiLineCellRenderer will first be called and will return a JPanel with its foreground and background colors set according to whether the cell being drawn has the focus or is selected, or neither. Assuming that the cell is neither selected nor focused, the striped renderer will change the foreground and background colors to white on gray or black on white (in the case of this table) by calling the MultiLineCellRenderer setForeground and setBackground methods. To effect the required foreground color change, the foreground colors of all the JLabels mounted in the JPanel must be changed, as noted earlier. This is not required, of course, for the multi-line header renderer because it will never be used in conjunction with another renderer that will change the foreground color after the getTableCellRendererComponent method has set it.

Finally, you may be wondering how the data for this table is represented in the table model. The data model is implemented in a class called MultiLineTableModel, derived from AbstractTableModel. The methods of this class are almost identical to those of the currency data model shown in Listing 6-1. The only interesting part of this model is the getValueAt method and the way in which the data is stored. Here is the implementation of the getValueAt method:

```
public Object getValueAt(int row, int column) {
    return data[row][column];
}
```

This method simply returns whatever is in the `data` array, indexed by row and column. Because a multi-line renderer is being used, you know that the values in the model must be an array of `Objects`, each of which will occupy one line of the rendered cell. Bearing this in mind, the initialization of the `data` array should come as no surprise; here's part of the statement that creates the data:

```
protected Object[][] data = new Object[][] {
    {       "Apollo 11",
            new String[] {
                "Neil Armstrong", "Buzz Aldrin", "Michael Collins"
            }
    },
    {       "Apollo 12",
            new String[] {
                    "Pete Conrad", "Alan Bean", "Richard Gordon"
            }
    },
    // More data not shown
};
```

Each row in this two-dimensional array contains the data for a single row of the table. The data for the first column of the first row is, therefore, the single `String` Apollo 11. Although the `MultiLineCellRenderer` usually expects to receive an array of objects, as you saw earlier when the implementation of the `MultiLineHeaderRenderer` was discussed, it is prepared to accept a single `Object` and treat it as an array with one entry. This simplifies the initialization of the data model. The second column of the first row is, however, an array, consisting of three `Strings`. When drawing this cell, the renderer's `getTable-CellRendererComponent` method will be passed this array as the table model value for the cell and will place each string on its own line. The part of the data model that is not shown previously follows the same pattern. You can find the source for the entire data model in the file `MultiLineTable.java` included with this book's sample code.

Renderers and Tooltips

By default, a `JTable` displays only a single tooltip that you can set using its `setToolTipText` method, which it inherits from `JComponent`. However, by using a custom renderer, you can arrange for different cells to have their own tooltips. This can often be a useful feature. To see how to implement it, let's consider again our hard-working currency table example. The first time you saw this table in Figure 6-1, it showed all the currency figures with as many decimal places as it could. However, this produced an untidy table, so we added a renderer that showed a smaller, fixed number of decimal places, sacrificing precision for presentation. Now, suppose you want the user to be able to see, on demand, the exact value of a particular currency's exchange rate, as originally displayed in Figure 6-1. One way to do this is to provide a button outside the table that would change to a renderer that showed more or less digits. But there is a more convenient way—why not show the exact value in a tooltip? If you do this, a more accurate version of an exchange rate will appear automatically when the user allows the mouse to hover for a short time over a cell containing an exchange rate. You can see an example of this in Figure 6-9 and you can try out the program that was used to generate this screen shot using the command

```
java AdvancedSwing.Chapter6.ToolTipTable
```

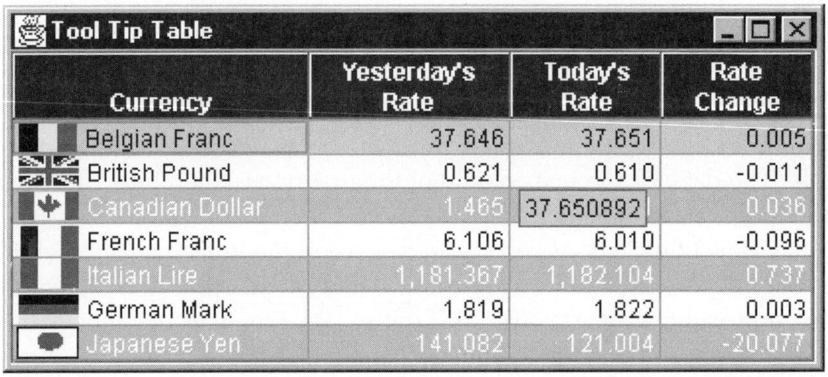

Figure 6-9 Using a cell-specific tooltip.

In Figure 6-9, the mouse was placed over the top row of the Today's Rate column; after a short delay, a tooltip containing a more precise exchange rate of the Belgian Franc appeared. If you compare this with Figure 6-1, you'll see that the tooltip does indeed contain the correct exchange rate to six decimal places, which is the arbitrary higher limit placed on the number of decimal places shown in tooltips for this table. You can, of course, set the number of digits you want to display when you create the renderer.

To create this effect, the `FractionCellRenderer` that was installed as the class-based renderer for `java.lang.Number` in the earlier examples in this chapter has been replaced by a new renderer called `ToolTipFractionCell-Renderer`, the implementation of which is shown in Listing 6-13.

Listing 6-13 A Renderer That Creates a Tooltip

```java
package AdvancedSwing.Chapter6;

import java.text.*;
import java.awt.*;
import javax.swing.*;
import javax.swing.table.*;


// A holder for data and an associated icon
public class ToolTipFractionCellRenderer extends
                                    FractionCellRenderer {
    public ToolTipFractionCellRenderer(
                int integer, int fraction,
                int maxFraction, int align) {
        super(integer, fraction, align);
        this.maxFraction = maxFraction;   // Number of tooltip
                                          // fraction digits
    }

    public Component
            getTableCellRendererComponent(
            JTable table, Object value, boolean isSelected,
                    boolean hasFocus, int row, int column) {
        Component comp =
                super.getTableCellRendererComponent(
                            table, value, isSelected,
                            hasFocus, row, column);
        if (value != null && value instanceof Number) {
            formatter.setMaximumIntegerDigits(integer);
            formatter.setMaximumFractionDigits(maxFraction);
            formatter.setMinimumFractionDigits(maxFraction);
            ((JComponent)comp).setToolTipText(
                    formatter.format(
                            ((Number)value).doubleValue()));
        }

        return comp;
    }

    protected int maxFraction;
}
```

As you can see, this renderer is created by extending `FractionCellRenderer`. This is logical because, apart from its ability to generate a tooltip, it has the same functionality as `FractionCellRenderer`. By subclassing an existing renderer in this way, you get to reuse all its code and minimize the new work to be done. The constructor of the new renderer accepts the same parameters as that of the old one and simply passes them through to the superclass constructor. In addition, it requires an extra parameter, `maxFraction`, which specifies the maximum number of decimal places that should be shown in the tooltip. In this example, of course, this will be larger than the number actually shown in the table cells. This value is stored for later use.

As with all renderers, the interesting part is the `getTableCellRendererComponent` method. This method simply invokes the existing method of its superclass, which means that it returns a `JLabel` with the same text as `FractionCellRenderer` and so the cell will be drawn in the same way by both renderers. As well as that, however, `ToolTipFractionCellRenderer` also sets the tooltip of the `JComponent` returned from the original renderer. This is the crucial step that enables the correct tooltip to be displayed for this cell, because the table invokes the renderer when it needs to draw the content of a cell and when it needs a tooltip for a cell. When the table is asked for a tooltip, it first attempts to get one from the renderer of the cell under the mouse, if any, by calling its `getTableCellRendererComponent` method and, when this method completes, it invokes the `getToolTipText` method on the `JComponent` that is returned and uses the value that it gets, if it is not `null`, as the tooltip for the cell.

Core Note

This mechanism only works, of course, if the `getTableCellRendererComponent` method returns a `JComponent`, as it does in all the examples in this chapter. You could, if you wished, write a renderer that returned an object derived from `Component`, not `JComponent`, in which case it would not be able to supply a tooltip for its individual cells and the global tooltip set for the table using the `JTable` `setToolTipText` method, if any, would be used instead. This also happens if the cell's renderer returns a `JComponent` but does not set a tooltip by calling `setToolTipText`, as was the case with the earlier examples in this chapter.

In this example, the tooltip is the value from the table cell, which is passed into the `getTableCellRendererComponent` method in the usual way. Formatting the value for the tooltip, which must be a `String`, is simply a matter of using the `NumberFormat` object created by the `FractionCellRenderer` superclass, adjusting the precision to supply the required number of decimal digits. The string returned from the `NumberFormat format` method is stored as the rendering `JComponent`'s tooltip using the `setToolTipText` method, allowing the table UI class to extract it later. This is a relatively simple example that shows how to supply cell-specific tooltips for a table; the same mechanism, of course, also works for trees.

Core Note

In early releases of Swing, when the table needed a tooltip, it invoked the renderer's `getTableCellRendererComponent` *with the value argument set to* `null`. *This had the advantage that it was not necessary to incur the overhead of generating a tooltip when the renderer was being used to draw the cell. It did, however, have the disadvantage that if, as in this case, you needed to access the cell's associated value from the* `TableModel`, *you had to get it for yourself using code like this:*

```
value = table.getValueAt(row, column);
```

The new API is simpler for the renderer, but results in extra overhead when the table is being drawn.

Summary

We started this chapter by examining how table cell renderers work and how the table selects the renderer to be used as it draws each cell and we illustrated this by showing a table containing, among other things, currency exchange rates. To demonstrate how simple it is to create a basic renderer, we showed how to improve the presentation of the exchange rates in the table by implementing a renderer that displays a numeric value with a (configurable) fixed number of decimal places. Having seen the basic mechanism, which is column-based, we moved on to describe the technique of renderer cascading which allows you to apply extra effects to a table that the original cell renderers do not supply, without having to modify or subclass them. One simple, but effective, use of renderer cascading is adding row-based effects such as colored stripes by changing the background color of alternate rows of the table. A natural progression from here is to use the layered rendering technique to control rendering at the cell level instead of on a row or column basis. The table also provides a more direct way to get specific effects in individual cells, although you need to subclass `JTable` and override its `getCellRenderer` method to use this mechanism.

Custom renderers can also be used to provide sophisticated table column headers, one example of which is a heading containing more than one line of text. The same technique can, as we showed, also be used to provide the same feature in the table cells themselves. Finally, we showed how to arrange for the table's tooltips to depend on the content of the cell that the user places the mouse on.

TABLE EDITING

Topics in this Chapter

Chapter 7

All the tables that you have seen so far in this book have displayed static data. However, `JTable` allows the user to edit the table data if the underlying table model permits it. In this chapter, you'll see how to turn a read-only table into an editable one by using the editors that are installed by default in every table. You'll also see how to enhance your tables beyond the capabilities of the default editors by creating editors of your own and how to add useful mechanisms like the ability to use the TAB key to move between cells while editing.

Overview of the Table Editing Mechanism

So far, you've seen several changes to the currency table that we've been using in this book that have enhanced its appearance and usability. The table as it stands now is useful for showing exchange rate changes for reference only, but suppose you wanted to allow the user to enter more recent values than the table currently contains. With this capability, you could use the same table to allow privileged users to update whatever information source lies behind the table's data model (perhaps a database). You can add this facility by making use of the editors that are built into the `JTable` control.

An Editable Currency Table

Making a table editable involves two steps:

1. Deciding which columns contain data that could be modified and enhancing the table model to allow those columns to be edited.
2. Choosing and installing the editors that will control the editing of information in the table.

In our first implementation of an editable table, we'll look mainly at what is involved in the first of these two steps. You'll learn about table editors later in this section—for now, we'll rely entirely on the default editors that every table has available to allow the user to make changes to the data.

Implementing an Editable Table Model

Ultimately, the table model controls which cells, if any, of a table are editable. There are two `TableModel` methods that work together to control cell editability:

```
public boolean isCellEditable(int row, int column);
public void setValueAt(Object value, int row, int column);
```

When the user tries to change the value in a table cell (by means that you'll see later), the `JTable` user interface (UI) class calls the `JTable isCellEditable` method, passing it the cell's row and column number. If this method returns `true`, an appropriate editor is assigned to the cell and the user is allowed to change the value displayed in the cell. When the user has updated the cell, the new value is stored in the model by passing it to the `setValueAt` method, which is also given the cell's row and column number, together with the new value in the form of an `Object`. If `isCellEditable` returns false, the data cannot be edited and the user won't be able to type anything into the cell.

All of the examples you have seen so far have used the `CurrencyTableModel` shown in Listing 7-1, which didn't directly implement either `isCellEditable` or `setValueAt`. Instead, it inherited these methods from `AbstractTableModel`, which implements them as follows:

```
public boolean isCellEditable(int row, int column) {
   return false;
}
```

```
public void setValueAt(Object value, int row, int column) {

}
```

As implemented here, the isCellEditable method ensures that none of the table's cells can have their values changed, which is why all the tables in the previous chapter were not editable. When isCellEditable returns false for a cell, the table will not attempt to change the cell's value, so the default implementation of setValueAt just does nothing because, of course, it will never be called.

To make the CurrencyTableModel editable, suitable implementations of isCellEditable and setValueAt need to be added. Because Currency-TableModel is useful as a read-only currency model, instead of changing it, the new methods will be implemented in a derived class called Editable-CurrencyTableModel, the implementation of which is shown in Listing 7-1.

Listing 7-1 An Editable Table Model

```
package AdvancedSwing.Chapter7;

import javax.swing.*;
import AdvancedSwing.Chapter6.*;

// An editable version of the currency table model
public class EditableCurrencyTableModel
                          extends CurrencyTableModel {
   public boolean isCellEditable(int row, int column) {
      return column == OLD_RATE_COLUMN ||
                      column == NEW_RATE_COLUMN;
   }

   public void setValueAt(Object value, int row, int column) {
      try {
          if (column == OLD_RATE_COLUMN ||
                      column == NEW_RATE_COLUMN) {
             Double newObjectValue; // New value as an Object
             double newValue; // double, for validity checking
             if (value instanceof Number) {
                // Convert Number to Double
                newValue = ((Number)value).doubleValue();
                newObjectValue = new Double(newValue);
             } else if (value instanceof String) {
```

Listing 7-1 An Editable Table Model (continued)

```
                    // Convert a String to a Double
                    newObjectValue = new Double((String)value);
                    newValue = newObjectValue.doubleValue();
                } else {
                    // Unrecognized - ignore
                    return;
                }

                if (newValue > (double)0.0) {
                    // Store new value, but reject zero or
                    // negative values
                    data[row][column] = newObjectValue;
                    data[row][DIFF_COLUMN] =
new Double(((Double)data[row][NEW_RATE_COLUMN]).doubleValue()
        - ((Double)data[row][OLD_RATE_COLUMN]).doubleValue());

                    fireTableRowsUpdated(row, row);
                }
            }
        } catch (NumberFormatException e) {
            // Ignore a badly formatted number
        }
    }
}
```

As you can see, this class inherits most of its behavior from the existing `Cur-rencyTableModel`, as well as the initial currency values. The `isCellEditable` method is very simple: The editable version of the currency table will allow only today's or yesterday's exchange rates to be edited. Obviously, it makes no sense to allow the user to edit the difference between the two rates, while changing the currency name really implies the need to change all the values in the affected row, which is really a delete operation followed by the insertion of a new row, rather than an edit. These constraints are applied by arranging for `isCellEditable` to return `true` if, and only if, the cell being edited is in column 1 or 2, which were symbolically defined (by `CurrencyTableModel`) as `OLD_RATE_COLUMN` and `NEW_RATE_COLUMN` respectively. In this case, the decision as to whether a cell's contents can be modified is based entirely on which column it is in, but you can, if you need to, control editability on a cell-by-cell basis by using the row number as well as the column index.

The `setValueAt` method is slightly more complex. This method is given the new value (as an `Object`) and the row and column index of the cell to be updated. In terms of the actual implementation of the `CurrencyTable-`

`Model`, the new value needs to be assigned to the element `data[row][col-umn]` of the two-dimensional array that holds the data. There are, however, a few other things that need to be taken into account.

First, `setValueAt` checks again that the cell to be changed is in columns 1 or 2. Of course, this repeats the same test made by `isCellEditable` and it may appear to be redundant. In terms of direct table editing, this check is, indeed, superfluous because the table will never attempt to update a cell for which `isCellEditable` returns `false`. However, other software can get direct access to the `TableModel` by calling the `JTable` `getModel` method and attempt to modify parts of the data that should be read-only. This check prevents such unauthorized access.

Next, the actual value needs to be stored in the table model. The `value` argument to `setValueAt` is defined as an `Object`, so exactly what is its actual data type? As you'll see in the next section, the type of the value passed to `set-ValueAt` depends on the editor being used to modify the table. Ideally, because the table model holds `Doubles`, the editor would supply the new value as a `Double` (or at least as a `Number`). However, none of the editors installed in the table by default do this—in fact, the editor that would be used for both of the editable columns in this table supplies the modified value as a `String`.

The implementation of `setValueAt` used here accepts either a `String` or a `Number` as the new value. If the value is supplied as a `Number`, it is converted directly to a `Double` by extracting the `double` value from the `Number` and then passing it to the constructor of `Double`. When a `String` is supplied, it is passed directly to the `Double` constructor that accepts a `String` argument and the result is stored in the data array.

Once the new value has been stored, there is one final item of business to be attended to. The last column of the table always contains the difference between the old and new currency rates, so when either of these values is changed, it is necessary to calculate a new value for this column. The same code is used to perform this calculation as that used in the constructor of `CurrencyTableModel` shown in Listing 7-1 in the previous chapter. Once the new difference has been stored, the table is self-consistent again.

Once the editor has completed its job and `setValueAt` has been called, the table will update the cell with the new value automatically, as you'll see shortly. However, using an editor is not the only way to change the table model. If the `setValueAt` method is called from elsewhere, any changes to the model that it makes will not automatically be reflected in the table's on-screen appearance. To make sure that the table updates itself, the `fireTableRowsUpdated` method of `AbstractTableModel` is called. This sends a `TableModelEvent` to any listeners registered to receive events from the model, one of which is the JTable. On receipt of this event, the table repaints itself as necessary.

That's all there is to the implementation of the editable table model. There is, however, one small point that was glossed over in this description. Suppose the user types an illegal value into one of the editable cells. For example, suppose the user tries to store the value ABCDEF as an exchange rate. Obviously, this can't be allowed. The default cell editor won't perform any validity checking on the value that the user types—it will just pass it directly to the setValueAt method. The validity checking is, in fact, performed by the constructor of the Double class when the String is given to it for conversion. If the String does not represent a valid Double, this constructor throws a NumberFormatException. As you can see, this exception is caught and the setValueAt method will return without storing a new value. The table editor framework doesn't provide any way to propagate back to the editor that an attempt was made to store an illegal value, so there is no other reasonable course to take. You might wish to display an error message to the user (using the JOptionPane class, for example), but for simplicity we have chosen to ignore illegal values, with the result that the user will simply see the cell revert to its old content on completion of the edit. The same action is taken if the new exchange rate converts to a value Double, but is negative or zero.

Having implemented an editable version of the CurrencyTableModel, it is very simple to change the example programs that we have been using so that they provide an editable table. You can experiment with such a table using the command

```
java AdvancedSwing.Chapter7.EditableHighlightCurrencyTable
```

This table is the same as the one that was shown in Figure 7-6 and, at first, will appear indistinguishable from it. The only line of code that was changed to make this table editable is this one:

```
JTable tbl = new JTable(new EditableCurrencyTableModel());
```

which replaces the original

```
JTable tbl = new JTable(new CurrencyTableModel());
```

The code that modifies the data model is, of course, in the modified data model, while the editors and the editing capability were always available in the table but were deactivated by the isCellEditable method of CurrencyTableModel.

To change the value of a cell, double-click with the mouse in one of the editable columns (the middle two columns). A text editor will appear in the cell and you'll find that you can change the cell's content. Figure 7-1 shows how the table appears when the third column of the top row is being edited. To make the change permanent, click in another cell or press the RETURN key. Notice when you do so that the cell that has been edited is updated and the currency change is also recalculated. Furthermore, you should also see that, if the currency difference becomes negative, the corresponding cell in the third column is highlighted by the renderer installed in that column, demonstrating that the table view is being properly updated (you will, in fact, need to move the row selection away from the row containing the modified cell to see that the difference value has changed color).

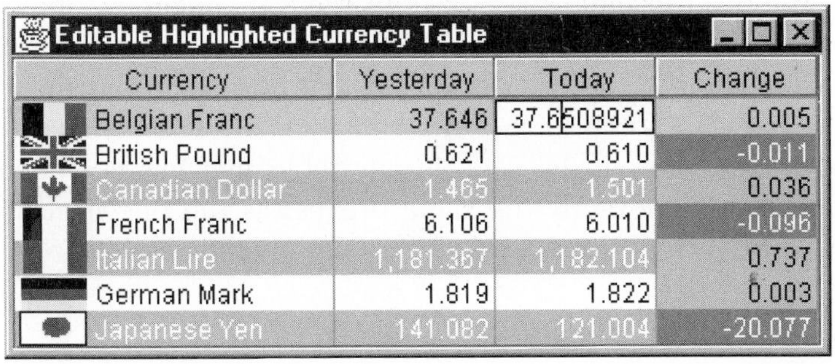

Figure 7-1   Editing a table cell.

The Table Editing Process—How It Works

In the last section, you saw that double-clicking in an editable cell activates an editor that allows you to change the cell's contents and that to take advantage of this you only need to implement a suitable table data model. In many cases, the default editors that the table installs are sufficient for your needs, but having an understanding of the table editing process will help you to create custom editors that let you go beyond the basic capabilities that you've seen so far. In this section, you'll see how the editing process works; later in this chapter, you'll use this information to create a custom editor and to control the editing mechanism in such a way as to make it easier for the user to quickly make a large number of changes to a table.

Selecting an Editor

As with renderers, the table chooses the appropriate editor for each editable cell. The mechanism used to choose an editor is, in fact, the same as that used for renderers. At the top level, the following `JTable` method is invoked to select the editor for a given cell:

```
public TableCellEditor getCellEditor(int row, int column);
```

As was the case with renderers, you can subclass `JTable` and override this method to select a cell-specific editor if you need to. If you use the default implementation, the table first looks in the `TableColumn` object for the column containing the cell to be edited. If there is no specific renderer configured here, a default class-based editor is used instead. Because `TableColumns` do not have editors associated with them by default, a class-based editor will be used in any table that has not been specifically tailored. This is exactly the same process as the one used to select a cell's renderer.

Core Note

Should you choose to override the `getCellEditor` method, be sure to take into account that the column number refers to the `TableColumnModel` column index and not to the number of the column in the `TableModel`. If you need to refer to the `TableModel` data, you can map the column index passed to the `getCellEditor` method to the one needed to access the data using the `JTable` `convertColumnIndexToModel` method.

When it is instantiated, the table creates default editors for the following object types:

- `Booleans`
- `Numbers`
- `Objects`

The editor for a column containing `Boolean` values is a `JCheckBox`, initialized as selected or not depending on whether the cell being edited contains `true` or `false`. When you click in an editable cell containing a `Boolean` value, the state of the checkbox is toggled and the new value is written back.

Numbers and `Objects` have a `JTextField` as their default editor. Both of these editors have a thin black border to clearly show the outline of the cell being edited, as you can see in Figure 7-1. The only difference between these two is that the `Number` editor shows its contents right-justified, while the `Object` editor is left-justified. By default, the `Object` editor is used for any cell in columns for which the table model's `getColumnClass` method returns something other than `Boolean.class` or `Number.class`.

If you want to create a custom editor for specific classes, you can use the `JTable setDefaultEditor` method to associate the editor with the class of object it can handle; similarly, the `getDefaultEditor` method retrieves the editor for a given class:

```
public void setDefaultEditor(Class objectClass,
                             TableCellEditor editor);
public TableCellEditor getDefaultEditor(Class objectClass);
```

As with renderers, if the `getDefaultEditor` method does not find an exact match for a given class, it looks for an editor for the superclass and so on, until it finds a match. Because every class is ultimately derived from `Object`, as a last resort the editor for `Object` will be used to edit a cell whose content type does not have a specific editor configured for it.

Core Note

You can, in fact, remove a default editor by passing a `null` editor reference to `setDefaultEditor`. If you remove the default editor for `Object`, cells containing data types that would otherwise select the `Object` editor will no longer be editable. This course of action is not recommended because there are clearer ways to arrange for a cell to be read-only, as you have already seen.

Similarly, you can set or get an editor for a specific column using the following `TableColumn` methods:

```
public void setCellEditor(TableCellEditor editor);
public TableCellEditor getCellEditor();
```

In the example shown in Listing 7-1, no column editors were configured so clicking in either of the editable columns caused a default editor to be invoked. The table model's `getColumnClass` method shown in Listing 7-1 returns `java.lang.Double` for both of these columns (because the data held in the first row of the table is always of type `Double`). Because there is no default editor for `Double`, the editor for its superclass, `java.lang.Number`, is used instead. This means that the editing of currency values is performed using a right-justified `JTextField`, as you can verify by running the last example again.

The *TableCellEditor* and *CellEditor* Interfaces

All the methods that configure editors or obtain references to them deal with the type `TableCellEditor`, which is an interface that must be implemented by any class used as a table editor. `TableCellEditor` is derived from a more primitive interface called `CellEditor` that contains methods that are common to table editors and to the cell editors for trees (which implement the `TreeCellEditor` interface). This is how the `CellEditor` and `Table-CellEditor` interfaces are defined:

```
public interface CellEditor {
   public Object getCellEditorValue();
   public boolean isCellEditable(EventObject evt);
   public boolean shouldSelectCell(EventObject evt);
   public boolean stopCellEditing();
   public void cancelCellEditing();
   public void addCellEditorListener(CellEditorListener l);
   public void removeCellEditorListener(CellEditorListener l);
}


public interface TableCellEditor extends CellEditor {
   Component getTableCellEditorComponent(JTable table,
                       Object value,
                       boolean isSelected,
                       int row, int column);
}
```

The `TableCellEditor` interface on its own is very similar to the `Table-CellRenderer` interface used by renderers. Fundamentally, an editor manages an editing component that is used in much the same way as the component returned to the table by a renderer. The editing component is obtained by calling the `getTableCellEditorComponent` method, which may choose to configure the editing component using the parameters that are supplied to it.

Core Note

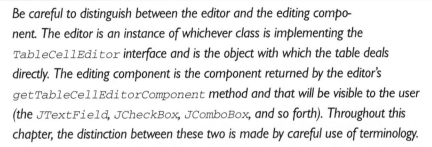

Be careful to distinguish between the editor and the editing compo-
nent. The editor is an instance of whichever class is implementing the
`TableCellEditor` interface and is the object with which the table deals
directly. The editing component is the component returned by the editor's
`getTableCellEditorComponent` method and that will be visible to the user
(the `JTextField`, `JCheckBox`, `JComboBox`, and so forth). Throughout this
chapter, the distinction between these two is made by careful use of terminology.

You'll see exactly how the table uses the editor and editing component in the discussion of the mechanics of the editing process next, in which the methods of the `CellEditor` interface, which are used to control the editing process rather than to manipulate the editing component, will also be described.

The *DefaultCellEditor* Class

You've already seen that the table configures default editors that are implemented as check boxes and text fields and that all table editors must implement the `TableCellEditor` interface. You also know, however, that no Swing component implements `TableCellEditor`, which means that you can't directly install a `JComponent` as a table editor. Instead, the table's default editors are instances of the `DefaultCellEditor` class, which implements the `TableCellEditor` interface (and the similar `TreeCellEditor` interface). The job of the `DefaultCellEditor` class is to delegate control of the actual editing to a Swing component, while providing the common code that interacts with the table to start and end the editing process. `Default-CellEditor` provides all the methods of the `TableCellEditor` interface and a few more that can be used to configure its exact behavior.

`DefaultCellEditor` has three constructors, each of which takes a different Swing component:

```
public DefaultCellEditor(JTextField editor);
public DefaultCellEditor(JComboBox editor);
public DefaultCellEditor(JCheckBox editor);
```

Each of these takes the component that you give it and arranges for that component to be returned when the `getTableCellEditorComponent` method is invoked by the table. If you are creating a custom editor by subclassing `DefaultCellEditor`, you can, if you wish, perform specific customization of these components before passing them to the DefaultCellEditor constructor. Indeed, the standard table editors are instances of Default-CellEditor, with either a JCheckBox or a JTextField configured with left- or right-aligned text depending on which class of data is to be edited.

The rest of the methods provided by DefaultCellEditor, excluding those required to implement the TableCellEditor interface, are shown here:

```
public Component getComponent();
public void setClickCountToStart();
public int getClickCountToStart();
protected void fireEditingStopped();
protected void fireEditingCanceled();
```

Because these methods are not in the TableCellEditor interface, none of them are used by the table. Instead, the first three methods are intended for use either when setting up the editor or, during the editing process, by software that is aware that it is dealing with a DefaultCellEditor. The most important of these methods is setClickCountToStart, which determines how many clicks are required before the editing component starts editing. In the case of a text field editor, for example, the user needs to double-click in a cell to activate the editing process—a single click simply selects the cell (if cell selection is enabled). By contrast, the other two default editors are activated by a single mouse click. It is important to note that it is DefaultCellEditor that determines when the edit will start, using the mouse click count and the value set by setClickCount-ToStart, rather than the table, or the editing component.

The last two methods are used internally by DefaultCellEditor to generate the events that are required when the editing process is completed or is canceled. More will be said about all of these methods in the next section.

If you want to create a custom editor that uses a JTextField, Jcom-boBox, or JCheckBox as the basic editing component, the simplest way to do it is to subclass DefaultCellEditor. You'll see a simple example of this later in this chapter. However, if your editor needs to use a different Swing component, you'll soon notice some shortcomings in the implementation of DefaultCellEditor that make subclassing it in this case slightly artificial. There is an example that demonstrates the problems and looks at the options available for working around them in "Using Table Editors" on page 669. One of these options is to avoid using Default-CellEditor and instead create a new class that directly implements the TableCellEditor interface for itself. Keep in mind, therefore, when reading the rest of this chapter that while many of the editors that the table uses will be based on DefaultCellEditor (and all the default ones are), this will not always be the case. When the editor directly implements the `TableCellEditor` interface, you cannot assume that it also supplies the `DefaultCellEditor` methods listed above.

The Mechanics of the Editing Process

The editing process has three distinct phases:

1. Detecting that the user wants to edit a cell and installing the correct editor.
2. Editing the data in the cell.
3. Completing the edit, updating the table's data model, and removing the editor.

In this section, you'll see exactly what happens in each of these phases and which pieces of the table are involved at each point.

Starting the Edit

You've seen that the first phase can be initiated by the appropriate number of mouse clicks (two for a text editor, one for a combo box or a check box) in an editable cell, but there are two additional ways to begin editing. The most obvious way, which you can try by running the `EditableHighlightCurrencyTable` example that was shown earlier, is to move the focus to the cell to be edited using the cursor keys or with a *single* click and then just start typing a new value into the cell. The table UI class registers listeners that detect mouse presses and key presses and react to either by checking whether an edit should be initiated as a result. The other way to start an edit is for an application program to call one of the `JTable editCellAt` methods:

```
public boolean editCellAt(int row, int column);
public boolean editCellAt(int row, int column, EventObject evt);
```

The `EventObject` argument is used to allow the `editCellAt` method to decide whether an edit should be started based on some aspect of the event that caused it to be invoked. Application programs that want to programmatically start an edit will usually want to do so unconditionally and will therefore call the first variant of this method.

Beginning an Edit on Mouse Action

Let's first consider what happens when the user clicks somewhere in the table. When this happens, the mouse listener registered by the table UI class receives a MOUSE_PRESSED event. If the left mouse button is pressed, the listener uses the mouse coordinates to work out which cell has been clicked; right and middle button clicks are ignored and are usually used by application code to post pop-up menus. If the click occurred inside a cell (as opposed to in the inter-cell gaps), the mouse handler calls the JTable editCellAt method, passing it the row and column indices of the cell and the MouseEvent. This method decides whether the click should start an edit and, if so, returns true. If false is returned, the click does not cause editing to begin but it may instead cause the cell or its containing row and/or column to be selected, depending on the selection criteria in use.

So, how does the JTable editCellAt method determine whether a click should actually cause editing to start? First, it calls the JTable isCellEditable method using the row and column indices that it has been passed to find out whether the user has clicked in a cell that can be modified. This call simply maps the column index, which is in terms of the column order displayed on the screen, to the TableModel column index and then calls the TableModel isCellEditable method to find out whether the model considers the cell to be editable.

Assuming that the cell is inherently editable, the next step is to get the appropriate editor for the cell, following the procedure described earlier in "Selecting an Editor" on page 654. If there is a suitable editor (which there always will be unless the default editor for java.lang.Object has been deliberately removed), the table then calls the editor's isCellEditable method. Don't confuse the CellEditor isCellEditable method with the isCellEditable method of TableModel, which determines editability based *only* on the nature of the data model and may use the cell's row and column index as part of the decision-making process. The CellEditor isCellEditable method is defined as follows:

```
public void isCellEditable(EventObject evt);
```

In other words, this method can base its decision *only* on the event that caused the table to consider editing the cell and on criteria specific to the editor; it does not have direct access to the table data, unless a reference was stored with the editor when it was created. The default editors (and all these created using DefaultCellEditor) allow the edit to start if the event they are passed is not a mouse event *or* if the number of mouse clicks is at least the number required for the type of component that the editor will use. The actual number of clicks required is configured when the editor is created using the setClickCountToStart method of DefaultCellEditor; as you know, by default this number defaults to two clicks for a text editor and one click for others. Editors that are not derived from `DefaultCellEditor` use their own criteria to determine whether to allow editing to begin, as you'll see later when we look at the implementation of a custom editor.

Core Note

For now, it is being assumed that editing is triggered by a mouse event. Later, you'll see how this process changes if editing is being started for other reasons.

When it is determined that both the `TableModel` and the editor agree that editing is going to performed, the editor's `getTableCellEditorComponent` method is called to get a suitably configured editing component, and then the editing component is sized to match the size of the cell being edited and moved to that cell's location. The editor component is then added to the `JTable`, so becomes a child component of the table. This, of course, is different from renderers, which are used to draw table cells but are never added to the table.

When the edit is initiated from a mouse click (and *only* in this case), the last step in attaching the editor to the table is to call the `CellEditor shouldSelectCell` method, which also receives the initiating event as its argument. If this method returns `true`, the cell being edited is selected—that is, it becomes the selected cell if the CTRL and SHIFT keys are not pressed, or is added to the selection in the usual way if either of these keys is pressed.

Core Warning

The editing sequence described here is slightly different from that used in Swing 1.0, where the `shouldSelectCell` method was always called when the editor was added to the table and it was convenient to use it as a common point at which to initialize the editor. This is no longer possible because this method is not invoked when the edit is started either from the keyboard or programmatically and, when it is invoked now, it happens much later in the sequence. The only point at which the editor can be initialized in the new editing sequence is in its `isCellEditable` method, which, unfortunately, does not receive any information about the row and column to which the cell is being assigned. If you need this information, you will have to defer its use to the invocation of the `getTableCellEditorComponent` method.

During the process of installing the editor, the table stores useful information that can be retrieved using the methods shown in Table 7-1.

Table 7-1 Editor-Related Information Available from `JTable`	
Information	*Method*
Row being edited	`public int getEditingRow();`
Column being edited	`public int getEditingColumn()`
Current editor	`public TableCellEditor getCellEditor()`
Editor Component	`public Component getEditorComponent()`
Is table edit active?	`Public boolean isEditing()`

Note that most of this information is only valid once editing has started and becomes invalid when editing completes. After the editor has done its job, the editor and editor component will be returned as `null` and the row and column values will both be -1. However, the `isEditing` method always returns the correct result—`true` if there is an edit in progress, `false` if not.

Finally, the table registers itself with the editor as a `CellEditorListener` to receive notification when editing is completed. You'll see how this works (and the definition of the `CellEditorListener` interface) in "Ending the Edit" on page 665.

Beginning an Edit Using the Keyboard

When editing is initiated by typing into an editable cell that has the focus, the same steps as just described are performed with some slight differences. In this case, the initial event will be `KeyEvent`, caught by a `KeyListener` registered on the `JTable` by its UI class. When starting an edit from a mouse click, the table UI class passes the mouse event to `editCellAt`. However, in response to a key click, the table UI class invokes the variant of `editCellAt` that takes only two arguments (the cell's row and column index). This causes a `null` event to be given to the three-argument variant of `editCellAt`. As a result, the `TableCellEditor` method `isCellEditable` receives a `null` event parameter, so it has no information at all on which to base a decision about whether to start editing, except the knowledge that editing was not initiated by a mouse click. The `DefaultCellEditor` implementations of this method returns `true` in this case, meaning that editing will be allowed to begin.

Core Note

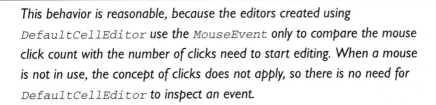

This behavior is reasonable, because the editors created using `DefaultCellEditor` *use the* `MouseEvent` *only to compare the mouse click count with the number of clicks need to start editing. When a mouse is not in use, the concept of clicks does not apply, so there is no need for* `DefaultCellEditor` *to inspect an event.*

As noted earlier, when editing is initiated using a keystroke, the `should-SelectCell` method is not called. However, the editing information listed above is still set up and the table registers itself with the editor as a `CellEditorListener`.

Explicitly Starting an Edit from Application Code

The final case to consider is starting an edit from an application program. Usually, an application will invoke the two-argument form of `editCellAt`, which is the same as starting the edit from a keystroke. However, an application may also choose to supply an arbitrary event and call the three-argument `editCellAt`, in which case the action taken will depend on the event passed and the cell editor in use. Unless the application programmer is in complete control of the table editors in use, it is recommended that the two-argument `editCellAt` method is used to programmatically initiate an edit. This case is otherwise the same as starting an edit using the keyboard—in other words, the `shouldSelectCell` method is not called. You'll see an example that programmatically starts an edit in "Tabbing Between Editable Cells" on page 696.

Editing the Cell Data

Once the editor has been installed, the user interacts directly with it to edit the cell's data content. When the data has been modified, the new content will be written to the table model and the editing process terminates; the latter part of the editing mechanism will be discussed later.

The only interesting part of the editing phase is how the events that the editing component needs actually get to it. The events that are of most interest to editing components are keyboard and mouse events. Let's look first at keyboard events. As you know, keyboard events always go to whichever (single) component has the input focus. Usually, a table consists of only one component—the JTable. Therefore, at any give time, the input focus will be on the JTable or elsewhere in the application. If you are driving the JTable using the keyboard, you would give the table the focus by clicking somewhere inside its boundary with the mouse (which the table reacts to by grabbing the focus using the JComponent requestFocus method), so all keyboard events go to the JTable.

When the table is being edited, however, there are two components to be considered—the JTable and the editing component. If the editor is a text component, it needs to receive the user's keystrokes, so it would appear that the table should pass the focus to the editing component when it is installed. In fact, though, the JTable does *not* pass the focus to the editing component. As a result of this, keystrokes intended for the editing component will actually go to the JTable, not to the editing component, so you would not expect the user to be able to type anything into the text component, which is clearly not what happens.

However, this is not the end of the story. The table UI class registers itself as a KeyListener of the JTable and so receives notification of all keys pressed while the table has the focus. When editing is in progress, this listener takes all KEY_PRESSED events and performs special handling that works only if the editing component is a JTextField (or a class derived from JTextField). The result of this processing is that the key event will be redirected to the editor kit behind the text field, thus achieving the same effect as if the key press had been passed directly to the editor.

Keystrokes, therefore, get to the editing component only if it is a JTextField. Other editors, including the standard JComboBox and JCheckBox editors, do not receive keystrokes at all—for these editors, only the initial keystroke that activates editing is processed and even then it is not passed to the editing component. This means that it is not always possible to drive an editing component to its full potential using the keyboard.

Core Note

At least this is the case at the time of writing. The situation may improve in the future.

Mouse events are, however, potentially a different matter. Mouse events are not controlled by where the input focus is directed—instead, they usually go directly to whichever component the mouse is over, the exception being when the mouse is being dragged, in which case the MOUSE_DRAGGED and MOUSE_RELEASED events go to the component that received the MOUSE_PRESSED event at the start of the drag operation. Therefore, once the editor is installed, clicking it with the mouse will cause the event generated to go directly to the editing component, not to the JTable. There is, however, a subtlety involved here.

The mouse click that starts the edit generates a MOUSE_PRESSED event that is passed to the JTable. This event, and subsequent mouse events, need to be delivered to whichever editing component is finally installed in the table. To make this possible, the table UI class remembers the component that is under the mouse when editing starts and redirects all mouse events it receives to that component, until editing is completed. This is necessary because all events after the MOUSE_PRESSED and up to the matching MOUSE_RELEASED (including MOUSE_CLICKED and MOUSE_DRAGGED, if any) will go to the JTable, not the newly installed editing component. As a result of this special handling, if you highlight the content of the editor by dragging the mouse over it, the events that this generates are passed to the editing component. This means that editor components behave normally with respect to mouse events and you can do anything with these components when they are installed inside a table that you can do when they are used on their own.

Ending the Edit

Once editing has started, there are only two ways to terminate it:

1. Performing some gesture that the editing component can interpret as marking the end of the editing operation.
2. Clicking with the mouse somewhere inside the table but outside the editing component.

Let's first look at what happens when the conditions for ending the edit have been satisfied; later, we'll describe how these two conditions are detected.

No matter why the edit is being completed, the cleanup operation is begun by invoking the stopCellEditing method of the current cell editor; this method is part of the CellEditor interface, so it is implemented by every editor. This method is defined as follows:

```
public boolean stopCellEditing();
```

The fact that this method returns a `boolean` means that it can, in theory, refuse to stop editing at any given time by returning `false`. If this happens, the table ignores whatever caused it to attempt to terminate the edit. The standard editors (all created using `DefaultCellEditor`) always return `true` from this method, which means that the editing operation will be terminated. The `stopCellEditing` method can do whatever it needs to do to clean up the editing component, but it must not lose the new value that the user selected for the cell. If this method is going to return `true`, it must also notify all `CellEditorListeners` that editing is complete. For editors derived from `DefaultCellEditor`, this obligation can be discharged by calling its `fireEditingStopped` method. Here is the definition of the `CellEditorListener` interface:

```
public interface CellEditorListener
                        extends java.util.EventListener {
    public void editingStopped(ChangeEvent e);
    public void editingCanceled(ChangeEvent e);
}
```

Any class can register as a `CellEditorListener` by implementing this interface and calling the `addCellEditorListener` method of `CellEditor`. Because all editors implement the `CellEditor` interface, they all support registration of `CellEditorListeners`. Editors derived from `DefaultCellEditor` inherit its `addCellEditorListener` and `removeCellEditorListener` methods and do not need to provide their own implementation.

Notice there appear to be two ways to report to a listener that editing has terminated; either the edit has stopped, or been canceled. The distinction between these two is what should happen to the table data model. When the `editingStopped` method is called, the edit has been ended cleanly and it is expected that the new value will be stored in the table data model. By contrast, if `editingCanceled` is called, any changes that the user made should be discarded. In fact, the default table editors never call the `editingCanceled` method, so there is no way to abandon a table edit. This interface is also used by `JTree`, which does call the `editingCanceled` method under some circumstances.

Core Note

If you implement a custom table editor, you can define a key sequence for that editor that would cancel the edit. The appropriate way to implement this is just to call the `editingCanceled` method of all registered `CellEditorListeners`, which can be done using the `cancelCellEditing` method of `DefaultCellEditor` if your editor is derived from it.

JTable implements the `CellEditorListener` interface and, as you saw in "Starting the Edit" on page 659, registers itself to receive these events with the editor when it starts the edit. Therefore, its `editingStopped` method will be invoked. You'll note from the definition of the `editingStopped` method that its only argument is a `ChangeEvent`, which carries no information at all other than a reference to its source. The meaning of the source for these events is not formally defined in the Swing API. Although the editors derived from `DefaultCellEditor` all supply the editor as the source, `JTable` cannot rely on this when a custom editor is installed, so it uses its own `getCellEditor` method to retrieve the current editor. It then invokes the `CellEditor getEditorValue` method on the editor to get the new value of the table cell. The editor itself, of course, does not know what the new cell value is; to get this value, it extracts it from the actual editing component. In the case of a `JTextField`, for example, this involves calling the `getText` method. `DefaultCellEditor` has the appropriate code to get the new value for the three component types that it supports.

With the new value available, `JTable` uses the `TableModel setValueAt` method to update the table model. At this point, no validation of the data has been performed (unless a custom editor has performed some kind of validity checking—the default editors do not do this). It is up to the `TableModel` to reject values that are not legal, according to its own criteria. As you saw earlier in the discussion of the code in Listing 7-1, there is no way for the `TableModel` to provide feedback when it receives an illegal value—it just discards the data and leaves the cell unchanged.

The last step is to disconnect the editor from the table. This job is performed by the `JTable removeEditor` method, which does the following:

1. Deregisters the table as a `CellEditorListener` of the editor.
2. Removes the editing component from its parent container, the `JTable`.
3. Returns the input focus to the `JTable` if the editing component had grabbed it.
4. Schedules a `repaint` of the cell that has just been edited.

The repaint is limited to the area of the table occupied by the edited cell. Because all table painting is handled by renderers, this operation will actually be performed by the cell's usual renderer. While the table is editing, the editor component is responsible for drawing the content of the cell. It is possible that the renderer and the editor will display the same data in different ways, so there will be an obvious difference between the cell's appearance when it is editing. This is certainly the case for data that is edited by the standard text editors, which show a lined border when an edit is active. The default renderers for the same data types do not have a border.

Finally, having seen what happens when editing is complete, let's return to the two ways in which the table detects that the current edit should be stopped. The most obvious way is for the user to directly signal the fact as part of the editing process. If the cell editor is a JTextField, for example, the user can press RETURN to complete the edit. This will generate an ActionEvent, which must be caught and the cell editor's stopCellEditing method called in response. The DefaultCellEditor implementation includes the code to register an ActionListener on the JTextField and calls stopCellEditing in its actionPerformed method. The same arrangement works if the editor is a JCheckBox: or a JComboBox: because these components also generate an ActionEvent when their state is changed.

The other way in which the user can signal the end of an edit is to click somewhere else in the table. This generates a mouse event that is caught by the table UI class. This event is actually treated in the same way as mouse events that start an edit—in fact, the same code is used. This means that the table's editCellAt method will be called, this time to determine whether to start an edit in a different cell. The description of this method that you saw earlier omitted one important fact: before deciding whether a new edit should be started, it checks whether a cell is currently being edited (using the JTable isEditing method). If so, it is immediately stopped by calling the editor's stopCellEditing method directly. When this method returns, the current edit will have been stopped and the editor removed. Any value typed into the cell will have been saved in the table's data model (assuming it was valid).

Core Note

Actually, as you know, stopCellEditing *could return* false, *in which case the active edit continues.*

There are actually several other ways to cause the current edit to be stopped, all of which do not save the current value in the table (but nevertheless do not invoke the editingCanceled method of CellEditorListeners). These are:

- Adding a column to the table model.
- Removing a column from the table model.

- Changing the margin of a table column.

- Moving a column.

Of these, only the last can be performed directly by the user. This is the only way for the user to abandon a table edit without changing the data in the table model and without having to retype the previous content.

Using Table Editors

Now that you've seen how the table manages the editing process, it's time to look at a couple of examples. The first example you'll see is a very straightforward demonstration of a JComboBox as a table cell editor. Because the table component includes support for combo box editors, this example is little more than a demonstration of how to make straightforward use of existing features. The second example, however, is more complex. Here, you'll see how to give the appearance of adding a button to a table. As you know, the table cells are not actually individual components, so you can't just add a button to a table and have it behave like a fully functioning button. Using the knowledge gained in the last section, however, you'll see how to create the illusion that your table has an embedded JButton. This technique can also be applied to "add" more sophisticated controls to your table.

A Table with a Combo Box Editor

Using a JComboBox as a table editing component is very simple—all you need to do is create and populate the combo box and wrap it with an instance of DefaultCellEditor, and then assign the editor to the appropriate table column or install it as the default editor for a specific data type. The table and DefaultCellEditor jointly provide the code to arrange for the combo box to appear when necessary and for the selected item to be written back to the table model. You can see an example of a combo box being used to edit a table cell in Figure 7-2. To try this example for yourself, use the command:

```
java AdvancedSwing.Chapter7.ComboBoxTable
```

Listing 7-2 A Table with a Combo Box Editor Installed

```
package AdvancedSwing.Chapter7;

import javax.swing.*;
import javax.swing.table.*;
import java.awt.event.*;

public class ComboBoxTable {
    public static void main(String[] args) {
        JFrame f = new JFrame("Combo Box Table");
        JTable tbl = new JTable(new ComboBoxTableModel());

        // Create the combo box editor
        JComboBox comboBox = new JComboBox(
                        ComboBoxTableModel.getValidStates());
        comboBox.setEditable(true);
        DefaultCellEditor editor =
                        new DefaultCellEditor(comboBox);

        // Assign the editor to the second column
        TableColumnModel tcm = tbl.getColumnModel();
        tcm.getColumn(1).setCellEditor(editor);

        // Set column widths
        tcm.getColumn(0).setPreferredWidth(200);
        tcm.getColumn(1).setPreferredWidth(100);

        // Set row height
        tbl.setRowHeight(20);

        tbl.setAutoResizeMode(JTable.AUTO_RESIZE_OFF);
        tbl.setPreferredScrollableViewportSize(
                        tbl.getPreferredSize());
        f.getContentPane().add(new JScrollPane(tbl), "Center");
        f.pack();
        f.addWindowListener(new WindowAdapter() {
          public void windowClosing(WindowEvent evt) {
            System.exit(0);
          }
        });
        f.setVisible(true);
    }
}

class ComboBoxTableModel extends AbstractTableModel {
    // Implementation of TableModel interface
```

Listing 7-2 A Table with a Combo Box Editor Installed (continued)

```java
public int getRowCount() {
   return data.length;
}

public int getColumnCount() {
   return COLUMN_COUNT;
}

public Object getValueAt(int row, int column) {
   return data[row][column];
}

public Class getColumnClass(int column) {
   return (data[0][column]).getClass();
}

public String getColumnName(int column) {
   return columnNames[column];
}

public boolean isCellEditable(int row, int column) {
   return column == 1;
}

public void setValueAt(Object value, int row, int column) {
   if (isValidValue(value)) {
      data[row][column] = value;
      fireTableRowsUpdated(row, row);
   }
}

// Extra public methods
public static String[] getValidStates() {
   return validStates;
}

// Protected methods
protected boolean isValidValue(Object value) {
   if (value instanceof String) {
      String sValue = (String)value;

      for (int i = 0; i < validStates.length; i++) {
         if (sValue.equals(validStates[i])) {
            return true;
         }
```

Listing 7-2 A Table with a Combo Box Editor Installed (continued)

```
          }
      }

      return false;
   }

   protected static final int COLUMN_COUNT = 2;

   protected static final String[] validStates = {
      "On order", "In stock", "Out of print"
   };

   protected Object[][] data = new Object[][] {
      { "Core Java Volume 1", validStates[0] },
      { "Core Java Volume 2", validStates[0] },
      { "Core Web Programming", validStates[0] },
      { "Core Visual Basic 5", validStates[0] },
      { "Core Java Foundation Classes", validStates[0] }
   };

   protected static final String[] columnNames = {
      "Book Name", "Status"
   };
}
```

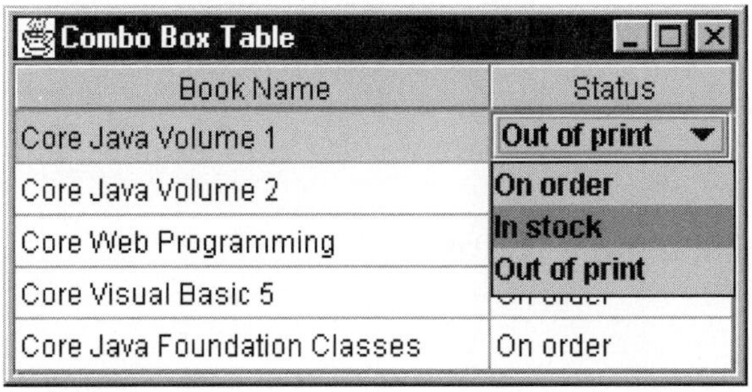

Figure 7-2 Using JComboBox as a cell editor.

The implementation of this example is shown in Listing 7-2, which combines the table and its data model. Let's look first at the data model, which is provided by the ComboBoxTableModel class. Like the other data models that have been used in this chapter, this one is derived from AbstractTableModel and stores its data in a two-dimensional array, each entry of which is a

`String`. This table lists some of the more popular Java books and their current stock state in an imaginary bookstore. The second column of the table can have one of three values:

- On order
- In stock
- Out of print

The table model must be able to supply a book's current state and allow the user to change the state of any book to one of the three legal values (but no other). Most of the table model implementation should be familiar from previous examples. The `isCellEditable` method allows only the second column to be edited. Editable tables also require a suitable `setValueAt` method; here, `setValueAt` makes use of the protected method `isValidValue` to make sure that the book's state can only be assigned a legal value—an attempt to supply a value that is not a `String` or not from the list shown previously is ignored. The only other method of any interest is `getValidStates`, which returns an array of `Strings` that represent the valid book states. These are the only values that will be acceptable to `setValueAt`.

Now let's look at the `ComboBoxTable` class, which sets up the table. Most of this code deals with creating the table, fixing its column sizes, and mounting it in a `JScrollPane` within the main `JFrame` of the application. Here is the most important part of this setup:

```
// Create the combo box editor
JComboBox comboBox = new JComboBox(
                    ComboBoxTableModel.getValidStates());
comboBox.setEditable(true);
DefaultCellEditor editor = new DefaultCellEditor(comboBox);

// Assign the editor to the second column
TableColumnModel tcm = tbl.getColumnModel();
tcm.getColumn(1).setCellEditor(editor);
```

The `JComboBox` will be used in the second column and initialized with its set of legal state values. To avoid hard-wiring these states outside the table model itself, the table model's `getValidStates` method is used to get the set of possible stock states. The next step is to create a `DefaultCellEditor` and associate the combo box with it. As you saw in the last section, this causes the `DefaultCellEditor` to register an `ItemListener` to receive notification when the combo box's selection is changed. Lastly, the editor is installed in the table's second column.

Core Note

This is, of course, a highly simplified example. In a real-world application, the table model would probably be populated from a database, using an SQL SELECT statement that would generate one row of two columns for each book in the imaginary bookstore. The values returned by the getValidStates method would most likely be obtained on demand using another SQL SELECT statement the first time they were required and cached for subsequent calls of getValidStates. Keeping the data in a table model and providing an interfacing method like getValidStates allows details like this to be kept out of the graphical user interface (GUI) implementation.

The last thing to note about the ComboBoxTable class is the following line of code:

```
tbl.setRowHeight(20);
```

The rows in a JTable are all the same height. In this case, each row will be 20 pixels high. Using a JTable is not the same as using a container with a layout manager—you cannot rely on the table to choose the correct height for its rows based on the data that its model contains and the renderers that will be used to displays its contents. If you don't set an explicit row height, you get a default value, which may or may not be suitable for your application. In this case, because a JComboBox is being used, it is necessary to add some vertical space to account for the selection window of the combo box.

If you run this example and click the mouse over a cell in the second column, you'll find that the cell content is replaced by the combo box and its drop-down menu appears, as shown in Figure 7-2. You can use the mouse to select one of the three legal book states and install it by clicking. When you do this, the new value is written to the table and the editing process ends, because the JComboBox generates an event that is caught by the Default-CellEditor and causes the editing process to terminate, as described in "The Mechanics of the Editing Process" on page 659.

Another way to end the edit is to click in another cell of the table. This also causes the drop-down menu to disappear and the cell's usual renderer will redraw the cell with the original value installed.

Core Note

For the sake of illustration, the combo box in this example has been made editable, which means that you can edit the selected value in the combo box selection window. If you do this, you could attempt to install a value that is not one of the legal stock states for books in this bookstore. However, you'll find that the table won't allow you to select an illegal state, because the `setValueAt` *method accepts only the values in the combo box drop-down list.*

Including Buttons in a Table

Having seen how to use a standard editor, let's now look at a more complex problem that requires a proper understanding of how table editing works to produce a working solution. A common misconception among developers using JTable for the first time is that the table's cells are components that are added to a container. Because of this, there is an expectation that you can use a JButton as a cell renderer and have the button behave like a real button. Unfortunately, this is not the case. If you use a renderer that draws a button, all you get is a static image of the button—the button is not actually present and can't be clicked. However, with a little ingenuity, you can give the illusion of a working button.

To see how this is done, let's return to our currency table example. The last version of this example changed the original read-only table model to an editable one. Changing the data is not of any use, of course, unless you can save the changes somewhere. Assuming that this data was loaded into the table model from a database server, it would be a good idea to write back any updated values. One way to do this might be to have a single button outside the table that would trigger the update process. Implementing that solution would not, of course, show us any new JTable features, so we'll adopt a slightly different solution here: each row of the table will be given its own button. The intent of this is that the person performing updates would press the button to commit the change on a particular line to the original data source. You can see what this arrangement looks like in Figure 7-3. To keep this example as simple as possible, the code that would, in real application, load the table model from the database and commit the updates when the buttons are pressed will not be shown. Instead, we'll just print a message when an update is requested.

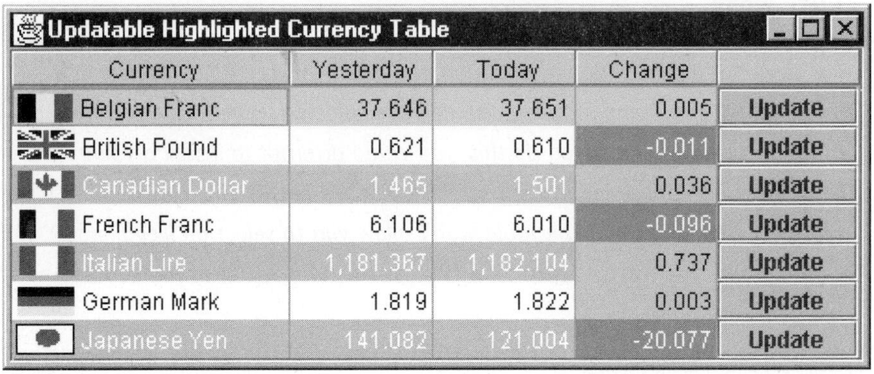

Figure 7-3   A JTable with active buttons.

To create this table, three enhancements need to be made to the editable version of the currency table:

1. A column needs to be added for the "Update" button.
2. A renderer must be written to draw the button.
3. The code that handles the user's button "press" must be written.

Lets look at these changes one by one.

Adding the Update Button Column

The simplest way to add a column for the Update button is just to add a column to the table's TableColumnModel. However, every column in the TableColumnModel must correspond to a column in the TableModel, so that the data for the column can be obtained. At first, this seems like an unnatural and clumsy arrangement—after all, the button is not really part of the table data. In fact, though, as you'll see when we look at how to implement the button in "Activating the Button" on page 683, having a TableModel column for it simplifies the implementation and also allows the action taken when it is pressed to be dependent on the model, which is exactly as it should be. Aside from this as yet unexplained advantage, the most direct benefit of having a column for the button is that the button's label can be held in the data model.

Core Note

> You might not consider this last point to be such a worthwhile gain, and you would probably be right. It does, however, avoid the need to hard-code the button label in the source code and allows you, if you wish, to use a different button label for each row. While this flexibility doesn't really fit very well for the currency table, it might be useful in other contexts. In any case, there really is no choice about adding an extra column to the `TableModel`, so it might as well be put to some use.

Fortunately, adding a column to the `TableModel` is a very simple matter. The existing functionality can be preserved by deriving the new model from `EditableCurrencyTableModel`, as shown in Listing 7-3.

Listing 7-3 An Updatable Currency Table Model

```
package AdvancedSwing.Chapter7;

import javax.swing.*;

// An updatable version of the currency table model
public abstract class UpdatableCurrencyTableModel
                extends EditableCurrencyTableModel {
   public int getColumnCount() {
      return super.getColumnCount() + 1;
   }

   public Object getValueAt(int row, int column) {
      if (column == BUTTON_COLUMN) {
         return "Update";
      }
      return super.getValueAt(row, column);
   }

   public Class getColumnClass(int column) {
      if (column == BUTTON_COLUMN) {
         return String.class;
      }
      return super.getColumnClass(column);
   }
```

Listing 7-3 An Updatable Currency Table Model (continued)

```
public String getColumnName(int column) {
   if (column == BUTTON_COLUMN) {
      return "";
   }
   return super.getColumnName(column);
}

public boolean isCellEditable(int row, int column) {
   return column == BUTTON_COLUMN ||
                 super.isCellEditable(row, column);
}

public void setValueAt(Object value, int row, int column) {
   if (column == BUTTON_COLUMN) {
      // Button press - do whatever is needed to update
      // the table source
      updateTable(value, row, column);
      return;
   }

   // Other columns - use superclass
   super.setValueAt(value, row, column);
}

// Used to implement the table update
protected abstract void updateTable(
                        Object value, int row, int column);

protected static final int BUTTON_COLUMN = 4;
}
```

Most of this code should be self-explanatory. This table model creates the extra column while preserving the existing data by delegating anything that concerns the first four columns of the table to `EditableCurrencyTableModel` and handling the last column itself. The `getColumnCount` method returns the correct number of columns by invoking the same method in its superclass and then adding 1 to account for the button column. The `getValueAt` method is enhanced to return the string Update for any row in the button column. The value returned from this method will actually be used to set the button's label; as noted above you can, if you wish, make the label dependent on the row number. For example, you might do this:

```
public Object getValueAt(int row, int column) {
   if (column == BUTTON_COLUMN) {
```

```
      return "Update row " + row;
   }
   return super.getValueAt(row, column);
}
```

As you can see, data for the other columns in the table is obtained directly from the `EditableCurrencyTableModel`.

There is a similar pattern in the `getColumnClass`, `getColumnName`, and `isCellEditable` methods, which directly handle requests for the last column and delegate others to the superclass. The `getColumnClass` method returns `String.class` for the button's column, because the data used to supply the button's label is a `String`. In this example, a column-based renderer will be used to draw the button, so the exact class returned by this method is not critically important. The `getColumnName` method returns an empty string for the last column, so the column heading will be empty as you can see in Figure 7-3. Finally, the `isCellEditable` method returns `true` for the column occupied by the button's data and whatever the superclass returns for the other columns. It might seem strange to return `true` for the button's column, but there is a good reason for this, as you'll see shortly.

The most important methods in this class are the last two. The `setValueAt` method is called when the table content is being updated. Updates for most columns go directly to the `EditableCurrencyTableModel` `setValueAt` method. What does it mean to update the button column's data and why does `isCellEditable` return `true` for this column? The reason for making this column editable is tied to the implementation of the button, which you'll see in "Activating the Button" on page 683. For now, notice that calling the `setValueAt` method to change the button column's content does not affect the button label—this much is obvious anyway, because `getValueAt` returns a constant value for that column. Instead, attempting to update this column results in a call to the abstract `updateTable` method. This method can be implemented in a concrete subclass of `UpdatableCurrencyTableModel` to provide the code needed to save the affected row's contents back to its original source.

The Button Renderer

The second thing you need for this table is a cell renderer that can draw a button. This is the simplest part, because everything you need to know to create this renderer was covered in the previous chapter. Because the renderer will draw a button, the simplest implementation is just to implement it as a subclass of JButton and return this from `getTableCellRendererComponent`. The code is shown in Listing 7-4.

Listing 7-4 A Button Renderer

```java
package AdvancedSwing.Chapter7;

import javax.swing.*;
import javax.swing.border.*;
import javax.swing.table.*;
import java.awt.*;
import AdvancedSwing.Chapter6.DataWithIcon;

// A holder for data and an associated icon
public class ButtonRenderer extends JButton
                implements TableCellRenderer {
   public ButtonRenderer() {
      this.border = getBorder();
      this.setOpaque(true);
   }

   public void setForeground(Color foreground) {
      this.foreground = foreground;
      super.setForeground(foreground);
   }

   public void setBackground(Color background) {
      this.background = background;
      super.setBackground(background);
   }

   public void setFont(Font font) {
      this.font = font;
      super.setFont(font);
   }

   public Component getTableCellRendererComponent(
                JTable table, Object value,
                boolean isSelected,
                boolean hasFocus,
                int row, int column) {
      Color cellForeground = foreground !=
                null ? foreground : table.getForeground();
      Color cellBackground = background !=
                null ? background : table.getBackground();
      setFont(font != null ? font : table.getFont());
```

Listing 7-4 A Button Renderer (continued)

```
      if (hasFocus) {
         setBorder(UIManager.getBorder(
                        "Table.focusCellHighlightBorder"));
         if (table.isCellEditable(row, column)) {
         cellForeground = UIManager.getColor(
                        "Table.focusCellForeground");
         cellBackground = UIManager.getColor(
                        "Table.focusCellBackground");
         }
      } else {
         setBorder(border);
      }

      super.setForeground(cellForeground);
      super.setBackground(cellBackground);

      // Customize the component's appearance
      setValue(value);

      return this;
   }

   protected void setValue(Object value) {
      if (value == null) {
         setText("");
         setIcon(null);
      } else if (value instanceof Icon) {
         setText("");
         setIcon((Icon)value);
      } else if (value instanceof DataWithIcon) {
         DataWithIcon d = (DataWithIcon)value;
         setText(d.toString());
         setIcon(d.getIcon());
      } else {
         setText(value.toString());
         setIcon(null);
      }
   }

   protected Color foreground;
   protected Color background;
   protected Font font;
   protected Border border;
}
```

Because you should by now be thoroughly familiar with writing renderers, not much needs to be said about this code. The only points worth noting are the border and label handling. Every button is created with a border that depends on the current look-and-feel. The table, however, uses its own border (also look-and-feel specific) to indicate the cell that currently has the focus. To preserve this mechanism for the button renderer, a reference to the button's original border is saved by the constructor. In the `getTableCell-RendererComponent` method, this original border is installed unless the button cell has the focus, when the same border as that used by the other table cells is used instead. The label is controlled by the `setValue` method, which is called from `getTableCellRendererComponent`.

Core Note

Here, as with the other renderers that you have seen in this book, a `setValue` method is implemented for the benefit of potential subclasses of `ButtonRenderer`, avoiding the need for them to re-implement the entire `getTableCellRendererComponent` method to make a small change to the way the button looks.

The value argument passed to `getTableCellRendererComponent` method (and hence to `setValue`) comes from the button's column in the table model. Using the `UpdatableCurrencyTableModel`, this value will always be a `String`. As you can see, `String` values are simply used to set the button's label. The `setValueAt` implementation is, however, more powerful. If you wish, you can subclass `UpdatableCurrencyTableModel` and have its `getValueAt` method return an `ImageIcon` or a `DataWithIcon` object to get a button with an icon or a button with an icon and accompanying text. Using Java's compact inner class notation, you can even embed this kind of extension directly into the code that creates the table. For example:

```
JTable tbl = new JTable(new UpdatableCurrencyTableModel() {
   public void updateTable(Object value, int row, int column)  {
      // Code not shown
   };

   public Object getValueAt(int row, int column) {
      if (column == BUTTON_COLUMN) {
         return new DataWithIcon("Save",
                  new ImageIcon(getClass().
                  getResource("images/save.gif")));
```

```
    }
    return super.getValueAt(row, column);
  }
});
```

This modified table would display buttons with the label Save and whatever the icon in the file `images/save.gif` represents.

Activating the Button

Now we come to the tricky part. If you created a new version of the `EditableHighlightCurrencyTable` example with the changes made so far, you would see a table with five columns, the rightmost of which contained a button with the label Update in every row. However, if you click any of these buttons with the mouse or tab over to one of them using the keyboard and press SPACE or RETURN, you wouldn't get a very useful response.

Core Note

Actually, the table would respond if you double-click the button or if you start typing into it, because a text editor would be used for the button column. This happens because the UpdatableCurrencyTableModel *returns the type* String *and* isCellEditable *returns* true *for this column, so the default editor for* Object, *a text editor, will be used. If you committed the edit by pressing* RETURN, *the table model* setValueAt *method would be called and the table update would actually occur. This would, of course, be very confusing for the user, who would expect the button to click, not offer its label to be edited!*

The question is, how to get the button to click? When you click the button's drawn image with the mouse, the table will consider starting an editor. If you implement an editor that looks like a button, with the same label as the one shown by the renderer and that activates itself on the first mouse click, you could give the illusion that the table contains a real button and, for the short period of time during which the button is active, there really would be a button in the table cell. To make this work, you need to implement an editor that returns a `JButton` as its editing component.

It would be nice to be able to implement this editor by extending `DefaultCellEditor`. This would make it possible to reuse existing code that registers CellEditorListeners and fires events when editing is stopped or abandoned. However, DefaultCellEditor has three constructors that require as arguments a JTextField, a JComboBox, or a JCheckBox. There is no default constructor and no way to supply a JButton, not even as a Component. This leaves three choices:

1. Extend DefaultCellEditor and supply a dummy JText-Field, JcomboBox, or JCheckBox just to satisfy its constructors.

2. Implement a class that provides the CellEditor interface with a constructor that accepts a JButton and add the logic required for a button editor to that class.

3. Implement a new base class that provides the CellEditor interface but which accepts an arbitrary component passed to its constructor.

The first of these would be the cheapest and fastest in implementation terms. Its drawbacks are that it requires more resource (in the shape of an addition component that is never used) and that it is not a neat and tidy solution. The difference between the second and third options is largely one of code reuse. The second option is undoubtedly faster to implement, but it would be very difficult to reuse, for the same reasons as DefaultCellEditor is hard to use in this case. The approach adopted here is to take the third alternative and implement a new base class called BasicCellEditor that is more flexible than DefaultCellEditor.

Creating a Custom Editor Base Class

The code for the new custom editor base class, which will be the basis for our button editor, is shown in Listing 7-5.

There is little to say about most of this code, because much of it will be overridden by derived classes. There are two constructors, one of which accepts any Component as its argument and a default constructor that doesn't require you to supply a Component. If a Component is supplied, its reference is simply stored as a convenience for derived classes. In most cases, a derived class will create a suitable Component and pass it to the constructor. However, if this is not possible because, for example, the Component's attributes need to be explicitly set, the default constructor can be used and the setComponent method used to register the editing component later.

Listing 7-5 A Cell Editor Base Class

```
package AdvancedSwing.Chapter7;

import javax.swing.*;
import javax.swing.table.*;
import javax.swing.event.*;
import java.awt.*;
import java.beans.*;
import java.util.*;

public class BasicCellEditor implements CellEditor,
            PropertyChangeListener {
    public BasicCellEditor() {
        this.editor = null;
    }

    public BasicCellEditor(Component editor) {
        this.editor = editor;
        editor.addPropertyChangeListener(this);
    }

    public Object getCellEditorValue() {
        return null;
    }

    public boolean isCellEditable(EventObject evt) {
        editingEvent = evt;
        return true;
    }

    public boolean shouldSelectCell(EventObject evt) {
        return true;
    }

    public boolean stopCellEditing() {
        fireEditingStopped();
        return true;
    }

    public void cancelCellEditing() {
        fireEditingCanceled();
    }

    public void addCellEditorListener(CellEditorListener l) {
        listeners.add(CellEditorListener.class, l);
    }
```

Listing 7-5 A Cell Editor Base Class (continued)

```
public void removeCellEditorListener(CellEditorListener l) {
   listeners.remove(CellEditorListener.class, l);
}

// Returns the editing component
public Component getComponent() {
   return editor;
}

// Sets the editing component
public void setComponent(Component comp) {
   editor = comp;
}

// Returns the event that triggered the edit
public EventObject getEditingEvent() {
   return editingEvent;
}

// Method invoked when the editor is installed in the table.
// Overridden in derived classes to take any convenient
// action.
public void editingStarted(EventObject event) {
}

protected void fireEditingStopped() {
   Object[] l = listeners.getListenerList();
   for (int i = l.length - 2; i >= 0; i -= 2) {
      if (l[i] == CellEditorListener.class) {
         if (changeEvent == null) {
            changeEvent = new ChangeEvent(this);
         }
         ((CellEditorListener)l[i+1]).
                 editingStopped(changeEvent);
      }
   }
}

protected void fireEditingCanceled() {
   Object[] l = listeners.getListenerList();
   for (int i = l.length - 2; i >= 0; i -= 2) {
      if (l[i] == CellEditorListener.class) {
         if (changeEvent == null) {
            changeEvent = new ChangeEvent(this);
```

Listing 7-5 A Cell Editor Base Class (continued)

```
            }
            ((CellEditorListener)l[i+1]).
                    editingCanceled(changeEvent);
        }
    }
}

// Implementation of the PropertyChangeListener interface
public void propertyChange(PropertyChangeEvent evt) {
    if (evt.getPropertyName().equals("ancestor") &&
        evt.getNewValue() != null) {
    // Added to table - notify the editor
    editingStarted(editingEvent);
    }
}

protected static JCheckBox checkBox = new JCheckBox();
protected static ChangeEvent changeEvent;
protected Component editor;
protected EventListenerList listeners =
                                new EventListenerList();
protected EventObject editingEvent;
}
```

The other CellEditor methods of interest are addCellEditorListener, removeCellEditorListener, fireEditingStopped, and fireEditingCanceled, all of which provide the event handling for the editor; the code used in these methods is taken almost directly from DefaultCellEditor. All CellEditorListeners for an instance of an editor are registered with an instance of the EventListenerList class, which is part of the javax.swing.event package. When registering a listener, you supply the listener's reference (that is, the CellEditorListener reference in this case) and the class that represents the listener, which, in this case, will always be CellEditorListener.class. The same arguments are used to remove a listener. This calling interface makes the implementation of the addCellEditorListener and removeCellEditorListener methods trivial.

Internally, the EventListenerList maintains its state as an array of Objects that are manipulated in pairs. The first item in each pair is the type of listener (for example, CellEditorListener.class) and the second is the listener's reference (that is, the reference passed to addCellEditorListener). Storing the type and reference together allows objects that support multiple event types to use a single `EventListenerList` to hold all listener details in one place.

Although `EventListenerList` provides the means for storing listeners, it doesn't have any code that can be used to deliver the events. This code is provided here in the editor's `fireEditingStopped` and `fireEditingCanceled` methods, which process the array returned by the `EventListenerList` `getListenerList` method. Because this list could (theoretically) contain multiple listener types, the first item of each pair is checked to see whether it represents a `CellEditorListener` and, if so, the second item is used as the listener reference (after appropriate casting). Notice that only a single `ChangeEvent` is created, no matter how many listeners there are and how many events actually occur. This is possible because a `ChangeEvent` only holds the event source, which is constant for a given `CellEditor`.

The implementations of `fireEditingStopped` and `fireEditingCanceled` process the listener list from the end to the front, because `DefaultCellEditor` does it that way. This is done for compatibility. It does, however, cause a problem for our button editor, as you'll see shortly. Changing the listener invocation order would make it difficult to migrate to an improved version of `DefaultCellEditor` if one is ever produced, so we choose to live with some slightly odd behavior to avoid potential problems in the future.

In addition to implementing the methods required by the `CellEditor` interface, this class also supplies a little extra functionality that we'll use to implement our button editor. Although the table calls the editor's `isCellEditable` method to determine whether an edit should start and its `getTableCellEditorComponent` method to obtain the editing component, the editor is not actually notified that the editing process has started. In Swing 1.0, the editor could rely on the table to call its `shouldSelectCell` method after the editor had been assigned to the table, which constituted notification that an edit was in progress. However, later versions changed this, so that now `shouldSelectCell` is only called if the editing process is started in response to a mouse click; if the user begins editing using the keyboard or if the application calls `editCellAt`, then `shouldSelectCell` will *not* be called. It is often useful to be able to arrange for some work to be done once it is known that editing is in progress, so to make this possible the `BasicCellEditor` class includes the following method:

```
public void editingStarted(EventObject evt);
```

This method is invoked after the editing component has been added to the table. It is called no matter how the editing process was started. If you need to know what caused the edit to be initiated, you need to override the `editingStarted` method in your custom edit and use the `evt` argument, which is a copy of the originating event, or `null` if the edit was caused by the application invoking the two-argument form of `editCellAt`. We'll see shortly how to make use of this method. As an alternative, `BasicCellEditor` also provides the method

```
public EventObject getEditingEvent()
```

which returns the same event. This method can be used at any time during the editing process.

The implementation of this feature is simple. To invoke the `editing-Started` method, the editor needs to know that the editing component has been added to the table. To do this, it listens to `PropertyChangeEvents` generated by the editing component. When a `JComponent` is added to a container, it sends a `PropertyChangeEvent` for a property called `ancestor` in which the new value is a reference to its new parent. `BasicCellEditor` registers itself as a `PropertyChangeListener` of the editing component and monitors these events, calling `editingStarted` when the `ancestor` property changes to a non-null value. Because the `editingStarted` method needs the event that started the edit, a reference to it is saved by `BasicCellEditor`'s `isCell-Editable` method for use in the `PropertyChangeListener propertyChange` method. As a result, if you subclass `BasicCellEditor` and override its `isCellEditable` method, you must remember to invoke `super.isCell-Editable` so that the edit event will be saved.

Extending the Base Class to Create a Button Editor

Having implemented a base class, the next task is to subclass it to create the button editor. The real problem to solve here is how to actually make the button work. To see what needs to be done, let's recap on what the table will do for us.

First, when the user clicks the button image, the `JTable editCellAt` method will be called. Because the button column in the `UpdatableCurrencyTableModel` is editable, it will allow editing to commence and the `getTableCellEditorComponent` method of the button editor will be called. This method will return a suitably configured `JButton`, which will subsequently be added to the table. If nothing else were done, the button would appear in the table and, if the user started the "edit" using a mouse, the mouse event would be passed to the button, causing it to click—its appearance will change as the user expects and an `ActionEvent` will be generated. Unfortunately, this would not happen if the user attempts to activate the button using the keyboard by pressing the space key, for example, which is the usual shortcut for activating a focused button.

Having arranged for the button to click, at least when using the mouse, we now need to stop the editing phase immediately because there is nothing more for the user to do with the button—it should be removed and the usual renderer restored. Also, the action implied by the button press, which is actually implemented by the table model, needs to be performed. To stop the edit, the editor's `stopCellEditing` method needs to be called. This can be done by arranging for the button editor to be an `ActionListener` of the button and invoking `stopCellEditing` from its `actionPerformed` method, which will be called when the button is clicked.

The `stopCellEditing` method of `BasicCellEditor` calls `fireEditing-Stopped`, which in turn invokes the `editingStopped` method of all registered `CellEditorListeners`. In this case, only the `JTable` is registered. As you saw in "Stopping the Edit" earlier in this chapter, when the edit terminates it removes the editing component from the table and stores the value from the component in the table's data model. What does this mean for the button editor? There really is no "value" to store, but the editor's `getEditorValue` method will still be called to get whatever the value might be. Fortunately, when the editor component is obtained using `getTableCellEditorCompo-nent`, it is given an initial value from the table model. As you know, this will usually be the button's label. Whatever it might be, the button editor just returns it when `getEditorValue` is called. The `JTable` then calls the `setValueAt` method of the table model with this value, which results in no change.

The table model that we'll use in our example will be derived from `UpdatableCurrencyTableModel`. You know that the `setValueAt` method of this class calls the abstract `updateTable` method, which will be implemented in the model subclass. This is how the row content would be written back to the database, or whatever persistent storage it was loaded from.

You can see the implementation of the button editor in Listing 7-6.

Listing 7-6 A Button Cell Editor

```
package AdvancedSwing.Chapter7;

import javax.swing.*;
import javax.swing.table.*;
import java.awt.*;
import java.awt.event.*;
import java.util.*;
import AdvancedSwing.Chapter6.DataWithIcon;
```

Listing 7-6 A Button Cell Editor (continued)

```java
public class ButtonEditor extends BasicCellEditor
                implements ActionListener,
                TableCellEditor {
   public ButtonEditor(JButton button) {
      super(button);
      button.addActionListener(this);
   }

   public void setForeground(Color foreground) {
      this.foreground = foreground;
      editor.setForeground(foreground);
   }

   public void setBackground(Color background) {
      this.background = background;
      editor.setBackground(background);
   }

   public void setFont(Font font) {
      this.font = font;
      editor.setFont(font);
   }

   public Object getCellEditorValue() {
      return value;
   }

   public void editingStarted(EventObject event) {
      // Edit starting - click the button if necessary
      if (!(event instanceof MouseEvent)) {
         // Keyboard event - click the button
         SwingUtilities.invokeLater(new Runnable() {
            public void run() {
               ((JButton)editor).doClick();
            }
         });
      }
   }

   public Component getTableCellEditorComponent(
         JTable tbl,
         Object value, boolean isSelected,
         int row, int column) {
      editor.setForeground(foreground != null ? foreground :
                                    tbl.getForeground());
      editor.setBackground(background != null ? background :
                                    tbl.getBackground());
```

Listing 7-6 A Button Cell Editor (continued)

```
      editor.setFont(font != null ? font : tbl.getFont());

      this.value = value;
      setValue(value);
      return editor;
   }

   protected void setValue(Object value) {
      JButton button = (JButton)editor;
      if (value == null) {
         button.setText("");
         button.setIcon(null);
      } else if (value instanceof Icon) {
         button.setText("");
         button.setIcon((Icon)value);
      } else if (value instanceof DataWithIcon) {
         DataWithIcon d = (DataWithIcon)value;
         button.setText(d.toString());
         button.setIcon(d.getIcon());
      } else {
         button.setText(value.toString());
         button.setIcon(null);
      }
   }

   public void actionPerformed(ActionEvent evt) {
      // Button pressed - stop the edit
      stopCellEditing();
   }

   protected Object value;
   protected Color foreground;
   protected Color background;
   protected Font font;
}
```

Creating a table that uses this editor is a simple matter of installing the editor in the column occupied by the buttons and creating a subclass of `Updat-ableCurrencyTableModel` with a suitable implementation of the `updateTable` method. The code for the application is shown in Listing 7-7 and for the table model in Listing 7-8.

Listing 7-7 An Updatable Currency Table

```
package AdvancedSwing.Chapter7;

import javax.swing.*;
import javax.swing.table.*;
import javax.swing.event.*;
import java.awt.*;
import java.awt.event.*;
import AdvancedSwing.Chapter6.*;

public class UpdatableHighlightCurrencyTable {
    public static void main(String[] args) {
        JFrame f = new JFrame("Updatable Highlighted Currency
                                                    Table");

        JTable tbl = new JTable(
                        new TestUpdatableCurrencyTableModel());
        tbl.setDefaultRenderer(java.lang.Number.class,
            new FractionCellRenderer(10, 3,
            SwingConstants.RIGHT));

        TableColumnModel tcm = tbl.getColumnModel();
        tcm.getColumn(0).setPreferredWidth(150);
        tcm.getColumn(0).setMinWidth(150);
        TextWithIconCellRenderer renderer =
                                new TextWithIconCellRenderer();
        tcm.getColumn(0).setCellRenderer(renderer);
        tbl.setShowHorizontalLines(false);
        tbl.setIntercellSpacing(new Dimension(1, 0));

        // Add the stripe renderer in the leftmost four columns.
        StripedTableCellRenderer.installInColumn(tbl, 0,
                Color.lightGray, Color.white,
                null, null);
        StripedTableCellRenderer.installInColumn(tbl, 1,
                Color.lightGray, Color.white,
                null, null);
        StripedTableCellRenderer.installInColumn(tbl, 2,
                Color.lightGray, Color.white,
                null, null);
        StripedTableCellRenderer.installInColumn(tbl, 3,
                Color.lightGray, Color.white,
                null, null);

        // Add the highlight renderer to the difference column.
        // The following comparator makes it highlight
        // cells with negative numeric values.
```

Listing 7-7 An Updatable Currency Table (continued)

```
        Comparator cmp = new Comparator() {
           public boolean shouldHighlight(JTable tbl, Object
                                    value, int row, int column) {
              if (value instanceof Number) {
                 double columnValue =
                              ((Number)value).doubleValue();
                 return columnValue < (double)0.0;
              }
              return false;
           }
        };
        tcm.getColumn(3).setCellRenderer(
                              new HighlightRenderer(cmp,
                              null, Color.pink,
                              Color.black, Color.pink.darker(),
                              Color.white));

        // Install a button renderer in the last column
        ButtonRenderer buttonRenderer = new ButtonRenderer();
        buttonRenderer.setForeground(Color.blue);
        buttonRenderer.setBackground(Color.lightGray);
        tcm.getColumn(4).setCellRenderer(buttonRenderer);

        // Install a button editor in the last column
        TableCellEditor editor = new ButtonEditor(new JButton());
        tcm.getColumn(4).setCellEditor(editor);

        // Make the rows wide enough to take the buttons
        tbl.setRowHeight(20);

        tbl.setAutoResizeMode(JTable.AUTO_RESIZE_OFF);
        tbl.setPreferredScrollableViewportSize(
              tbl.getPreferredSize());

        JScrollPane sp = new JScrollPane(tbl);
        f.getContentPane().add(sp, "Center");
        f.pack();
        f.addWindowListener(new WindowAdapter() {
           public void windowClosing(WindowEvent evt) {
              System.exit(0);
           }
        });
        f.setVisible(true);
     }
}
```

Listing 7-8 An Updatable Currency Table Model

```
package AdvancedSwing.Chapter7;

import AdvancedSwing.Chapter7.UpdatableCurrencyTableModel;

public class TestUpdatableCurrencyTableModel
             extends UpdatableCurrencyTableModel {
  public void updateTable(Object value, int row, int column) {
    System.out.println("Update for row " + row + "
                                              required.");
    System.out.println("Values are " +
            getValueAt(row, 1) +
            ", " + getValueAt(row, 2) +
            "; diff is " + getValueAt(row, 3));
  }
}
```

For this simple application, the `updateTable` method simply records that it has been called and shows the value, row, and column numbers passed from the table. Typically, in a real application, the row number might be used to extract all the data for that row and write it back to a database using Java Database Connectivity (JDBC).

That almost completes the implementation of the button editor and its sample application, but there is one small catch. As we said earlier, when the button editor is activated, the button will be automatically clicked by the mouse event that caused the table to start the edit. However, what happens if the user navigates to the button using the keyboard and presses a key? Here, the editor will be installed correctly, but the key press will not be passed to it, as you saw in "Editing the Cell Data" on page 663. As a result, the button won't click if you try to activate it with a key press and the edit will not end until you move the focus to another cell and activate that instead. Fortunately, there is a simple way to solve this problem. It is possible to programmatically click a button by calling its `doClick` method, which causes the button's appearance to change as the user would expect and generates the `ActionEvent`. When can the `doClick` method be called? It must be called some time after the button has been added to the table. Fortunately, the button editor is subclassed from our `BasicCellEditor` class, which calls its `editingStarted` method when the editing component has been added to the `JTable`. As you can see from Listing 7-6, the button cell editor overrides this method to get control at this point and calls the button's `doClick` method to simulate pressing the button. Note, however, the following two points:

1. The call is not unconditional—it happens only if the event passed to it is not a `MouseEvent`.
2. The call is not made inline—it is deferred using the `Swing-Utilities invokeLater` method.

The reason for the event check is simple—there is no need to programmatically click the button if the edit was started by a mouse click because the `MouseEvent` will be passed directly to the button by the `JTable` and cause the button to clock of its own accord. This check ensures that button will be clicked if the edit is started from the keyboard or (for some reason) as a result of an application calling `editCellAt` directly on a cell in the button column.

The reason for deferring `doClick` is slightly more subtle. If `doClick` were called inline, it would immediately call the `actionPerformed` method of the editor, which, in turn, would call the `editingStopped` method of `BasicCellEditor`. This would result in the table trying to remove the button from the table and clean up the entire edit, while it was still setting that edit up in `editCellAt`! Not surprisingly, this just doesn't work. Deferring the button click allows the edit setup to complete before starting the cleanup process. This is a technique that is generally useful and you'll see another example of it in the next section.

Tabbing Between Editable Cells

Now that the currency table has the ability to be edited and updated, there is one more usability feature you might want to add to it. Suppose you wanted the user to be able to quickly update several of the exchange rates in the body of the table. As the table currently stands, the user would have to click with the mouse in each cell to be changed, type the new value, and then click in the next cell and so on. Alternatively, the user could use the arrow keys to move between the cells whose values need to be changed. While this would work, it would be more convenient if it were possible to use the TAB key to jump around between the editable cells, skipping over those which are not editable. This would be faster than using the mouse and much better than using the cursor keys because it avoids the need to manually move the focus over cells that cannot be edited. The table does not directly support the use of the TAB key in this way, but with a little work this feature can be implemented.

Designing the Edit Traversal Mechanism

Let's first look at how you might want this to work. In terms of the currency table, the old and new exchange rate values are both directly editable. Typically, you might want the user to update the old rate and then the new rate for one currency, followed by the old rate for the next and so on. The user would start by editing the previous exchange rate. Pressing the TAB key should then cause that edit to be complete, and the new value written to the table model, and then the cell holding the new currency value should automatically get the focus and install its editor. The next TAB key press should take the focus to the old exchange rate for the next currency, and so on.

This description highlights the fact that there are two separate (but related) parts to this problem:

1. Determining which cells should be involved in the TAB order for automatic editing.

2. Arranging for the TAB key to be detected and cause the termination of the current edit, followed by starting the next one.

Let's tackle these issues separately. Assume first that the mechanism to change the editing cell has been implemented and the TAB key is detected. Where should the edit focus be moved? In the currency table data model used in the last example, there are three editable columns in each data row:

- The old exchange rate column.
- The new exchange rate column.
- The column containing the update button.

The simplest approach would be to define the tabbing order to be left to right across each row, moving between cells for which the data model isCellEditable method returns true. This would be simple to implement—given the row and column number of the cell being edited, the next one would be found by repeatedly incrementing the column number and calling the JTable isCellEditable with the same row and the new column number until an editable cell was found.

Core Note

As ever, when dealing with table column indices, you need to be careful because the user can reorder the table columns, or because there may be columns in the `TableModel` *that are not displayed. In general, the column indices used by view-related operations are not the same as those in the model. In this case, to determine whether the cell to be edited is editable, we need to use the column number, which is view-based and call the* `TableModel isCellEditable` *method, which uses model-based column indices. Fortunately,* `JTable` *has its own* `isCellEditable` *method that maps between the two sets of column indices. Alternatively, you can use the* `JTable convertColumnIndexToModel` *and* `convertColumnIndexToView` *methods to perform these mappings. You'll see how these methods are used when we look at the implementation of this example.*

If the end of the row is reached, the algorithm would continue by incrementing the row number and resetting the column number to 0. This simple approach would suffice for many tables, but it is not always good enough.

In many cases, you would want to be able to limit the editable cells reachable using the TAB key as an accelerator. In the case of the table in the last example, the tab order generated by this simple algorithm would be from the old exchange rate to the new one and then to the update button. The problem with this is that you want the TAB key to move the focus to each cell *and* start its editor. As you know, starting the editor in the table's update button column actually causes the content of that row to be updated in the database (if there is one) without further intervention from the user. This might not always be appropriate. To give yourself the chance to avoid this side effect, you need some way to specify which of the editable columns should be included in the automatic tabbing mechanism.

Now let's move on to the second issue—how to detect the TAB key during an edit and arrange for it to move to the next editable cell. For the table to be in edit mode, the user must first start an edit by double-clicking or directly typing a new value in an editable cell. Once the table is in this state, you need to be able to catch the TAB key and react to it in the proper way. This implies that you need to get key events from the editing component. However, as you already know, by default the input focus during editing is directed to the table not to the editing component, so the TAB key would actually be handled by the `JTable`, not by the editor. To be notified of a `TAB` key event, then, it is necessary to register a `KeyListener` on the `JTable`. Even this is not sufficient, however, because it is possible for custom editors to grab the focus for themselves, so it is necessary to register a `KeyListener` on the editor component as well. The intent of this design is that the `KeyListener` would grab `TAB` keys and do whatever is necessary to stop the current edit and start editing in the next editable column. There is, however, one more step that needs to be taken.

`TAB` key presses are special because they are used to move the keyboard focus between components. In fact, Swing components filter out `TAB` key presses at a very low level and pass them to the Swing focus manager, where they are consumed. Because of this, our `KeyListener` would never actually be notified of `TAB` keys. Also, pressing `TAB` would actually move focus away from the table, which is not the desired effect. To avoid both problems, it is necessary to disable the Swing focus manager when editing a cell in a table that supports movement between cells using the `TAB` key. You'll see exactly how this is done shortly.

Implementing a Table with `TAB` *Edit Traversal*

Now it's time to look at the actual implementation. As noted earlier, you need to be able to configure which columns of the table will be editable and react to the `TAB` key. Because this information needs to be stored in the table object, the simplest way to do this is to subclass `JTable` and provide a method that allows the programmer to specify the list of tabbable columns. The implementation shown in Listing 7-9 creates a subclass of `JTable` called `TabEditTable` that contains all the logic for handling `TAB` traversal between editable cells.

Listing 7-9 A Table with TAB Edit Traversal

```
package AdvancedSwing.Chapter7;

import javax.swing.*;
import javax.swing.FocusManager;
import javax.swing.table.*;
import javax.swing.event.*;
import java.awt.*;
import java.awt.event.*;
import java.util.*;
import AdvancedSwing.Chapter6.TableUtilities;
```

Listing 7-9 A Table with TAB Edit Traversal (continued)

```java
public class TabEditTable extends JTable {
   public TabEditTable() {
      super();
   }

   public TabEditTable(TableModel dm) {
      super(dm);
   }

   public TabEditTable(TableModel dm,
                       TableColumnModel cm) {
      super(dm, cm);
   }

   public TabEditTable(TableModel dm,
                       TableColumnModel cm,
                       ListSelectionModel sm) {
      super(dm, cm, sm);
   }

   public TabEditTable(int numRows, int numColumns) {
      super(numRows, numColumns);
   }

   public TabEditTable(final Vector rowData, final Vector
                                              columnNames) {
      super(rowData, columnNames);
   }

    public TabEditTable(final Object[][] rowData, final
                                       Object[] columnNames) {
      super(rowData, columnNames);
   }

   // Set the columns that contain tabbable editors
   public void setEditingColumns(int[] columns) {
      editingColumns = columns;
      convertEditableColumnsToView();
   }

   public int[] getEditingColumns() {
      return editingColumns;
   }
```

┌───┐
│ Listing 7-9 A Table with TAB Edit Traversal (continued)   │
└───┘

```
// Overrides of JTable methods
public boolean editCellAt(int row, int column,
                                   EventObject evt) {
    if (super.editCellAt(row, column, evt) == false) {
        return false;
    }

    if (viewEditingColumns != null) {
        // Note: column is specified in terms
        // of the column model
        int length = viewEditingColumns.length;
        for (int i = 0; i < length; i++) {
            if (column == viewEditingColumns[i]) {
                Component comp = getEditorComponent();
                comp.addKeyListener(tabKeyListener);
                this.addKeyListener(tabKeyListener);
                focusManager = FocusManager.getCurrentManager();
                FocusManager.disableSwingFocusManager();
                inTabbingEditor = true;
                comp.requestFocus();
                break;
            }
        }
    }

    return true;
}

public void editingStopped(ChangeEvent evt) {
    if (inTabbingEditor == true) {
        Component comp = getEditorComponent();
        comp.removeKeyListener(tabKeyListener);
        this.removeKeyListener(tabKeyListener);
        FocusManager.setCurrentManager(focusManager);

        inTabbingEditor = false;
    }

    super.editingStopped(evt);
}

protected void convertEditableColumnsToView() {
    // Convert the editable columns to view column numbers
    if (editingColumns == null) {
```

Listing 7-9 A Table with TAB Edit Traversal (continued)

```
            viewEditingColumns = null;
            return;
        }

        // Create a set of editable columns in terms of view
        // column numbers in ascending order. Note that not all
        // editable columns in the data model need be visible.
        int length = editingColumns.length;
        viewEditingColumns = new int[length];
        int nextSlot = 0;

        for (int i = 0; i < length; i++) {
            int viewIndex =
                    convertColumnIndexToView(editingColumns[i]);
            if (viewIndex != -1) {
                viewEditingColumns[nextSlot++] = viewIndex;
            }
        }

        // Now create an array of the right length
        // to hold the view indices
        if (nextSlot < length) {
            int[] tempArray = new int[nextSlot];
            System.arraycopy(viewEditingColumns, 0,
                             tempArray, 0, nextSlot);
            viewEditingColumns = tempArray;
        }

        // Finally, sort the view columns into order
        TableUtilities.sort(viewEditingColumns);
    }

    protected void moveToNextEditor(int row, int column,
                                       boolean forward) {
        // Column is specified in terms of the column model
        if (viewEditingColumns != null) {
            int length = viewEditingColumns.length;

            // Move left-to-right or right-to-left
            // across the table
            for (int i = 0; i < length; i++) {
                if (viewEditingColumns[i] == column) {
                    // Select the next column to edit
                    if (forward == true) {
                        if (++i == length) {
                            // Reached end of row - wrap
```

Listing 7-9 A Table with TAB Edit Traversal (continued)

```
                    i = 0;
                    row++;
                    if (row == getRowCount()) {
                        // End of table - wrap
                        row = 0;
                    }
                }
            } else {
                if (--i < 0) {
                    i = length - 1;
                    row--;
                    if (row < 0) {
                        row = getRowCount() - 1;
                    }
                }
            }
            final int newRow = row;
            final int newColumn = viewEditingColumns[i];

            // Start editing at new location
            SwingUtilities.invokeLater(new Runnable() {
                public void run() {
                    editCellAt(newRow, newColumn);
                    ListSelectionModel rowSel =
                        getSelectionModel();
                    ListSelectionModel columnSel =
                        getColumnModel().getSelectionModel();
                    rowSel.setSelectionInterval(
                        newRow, newRow);
                    columnSel.setSelectionInterval(
                        newColumn, newColumn);
                }
            });
            break;
        }
    }
}

// Catch changes to the table column model
public void columnAdded(TableColumnModelEvent e) {
    super.columnAdded(e);
    convertEditableColumnsToView();
}
```

```
public void columnRemoved(TableColumnModelEvent e) {
   super.columnRemoved(e);
   convertEditableColumnsToView();
}

public void columnMoved(TableColumnModelEvent e) {
   super.columnMoved(e);
   convertEditableColumnsToView();
}

public class TabKeyListener extends KeyAdapter {
   public void keyPressed(KeyEvent evt) {
      if (evt.getKeyCode() == KeyEvent.VK_TAB) {
         if (inTabbingEditor == true) {
            TableCellEditor editor = getCellEditor();
            int editRow = getEditingRow();
            int editColumn = getEditingColumn();
            if (editor != null) {
               boolean stopped = editor.stopCellEditing();
               if (stopped == true) {
                  boolean forward = (evt.isShiftDown() ==
                                                  false);
                  moveToNextEditor(editRow, editColumn,
                                                  forward);
               }
            }
         }
      }
   }
}

protected boolean inTabbingEditor;
protected FocusManager focusManager;
protected int[] editingColumns;        // Model columns
protected int[] viewEditingColumns;    // View columns
protected TabKeyListener tabKeyListener =
                                  new TabKeyListener();
}
```

Although there seems to be quite a lot of code, it is easy to see how this table works by breaking the implementation into pieces that mirror the design aspects that were covered earlier. Notice that this class has a set of constructors that mirros those of JTable, so that the programmer can create a TabEditTable in exactly the same way as creating an ordinary table. Having created the table, the only extra step needed is to specify which table columns participate in the tab traversal mechanism by calling the `setEditingColumns` method. The other public methods of this class are actually part of the logic that controls the tab traversal; they don't need to be directly called by the programmer. In most cases, then, the programmer can convert a table without tab support by simply replacing the construction of `JTable` by construction of a `TabEditTable` and then invoking `setEditingColumns`.

Specifying the Table Columns

The `setEditingColumns` method is supplied with an array of integers that specifies the column numbers of the columns that participate in tab traversal editing. Relating this to the currency table in which the two exchange rate columns should support tab traversal, you might invoke this method as follows:

```
int[] tabColumns = { 1, 2 };
tbl.setEditingColumns(tabColumns);
```

However, this code hides a subtlety that we've mentioned already in this chapter in different contexts. Are the column numbers specified in terms of the column order in the data model or as indices in the table's `TableColumn-Model`? Initially, columns 1 and 2 in the data model might actually be displayed in columns 1 and 2 of the table, but this needn't always be the case and, even if it is, the user could reorder the table columns at any time. From the programmer's point of view, the most sensible option is to specify the column indices in terms of the columns in the data model, because these indices are invariant—the exchange rates are always in columns 1 and 2 of the data model. This is, in fact, how the `setEditingColumns` model method in Listing 7-9 is implemented. As you can see, it stores the column list in an instance variable called `editingColumns`, which can be retrieved at any time using the `getEditingColumns` method.

The problem with saving data column model indices is that the table methods that deal with editing and use a column number (such as `editCellAt`) all work in terms of the `TableColumnModel` indices. As you'll see, this means that when the TAB key is being used to move the edit focus around the table you'll have the `TableColumnModel` index to work from, not the data model index. For this reason, it is necessary to map from data model indices to `TableColumnModel` indices, which can be done using the `JTable` `convert-ColumnIndexToView` method.

The most natural way for the tabbing operation to work is for the TAB key to move the editing focus across each row from left to right and to wrap back to the leftmost participating column at the end of the row. If TAB is used with SHIFT, this order would be reversed. When the decision is being made as to which cell to edit next, it would be useful to have an array of column indices in TableColumnModel order. Then, to move the edit focus to the right, you would just move to the next element in the array from the one currently in use and to move to the left you move back by one entry. Thus, when set-EditingColumns is called, the array of column numbers is converted to an array of TableColumnModel indices and stored in the instance variable viewEditingColumns for use when the TAB key is being processed. The conversion is performed by using the convertEditableColumnsToView method.

The convertEditableColumnsToView method is fairly simple. It first creates a new array of the same size as the one passed to setEditingColumns and walks down the array of data model indices converting each to the corresponding TableColumnModel index and storing it in the next slot in the new array. Because not all the data model columns need be included in the table column model for a particular table, it is possible that one or more of the columns designated as participating in tabbing might not have a corresponding TableColumnModel index. In this case, convertColumnIndexToView returns -1 and that column is ignored. As a result, the final array may be shorter than the one initially passed to setEditingColumns and, if it is, it is truncated by copying it to a new array of the appropriate size. Finally, the new array is sorted into ascending order, so that the leftmost participating column comes first, followed by the next one to its right and so on. This makes it possible to see the tabbing order in terms of the indices of the table columns as they are displayed by reading the array from the start to the end.

Core Note

The sort method used by convertEditableColumnsToView *is a simple-minded sort whose implementation is not interesting and which is not shown here. If you are using Java 2, you could instead use the* sort *method of the* java.lang.Arrays *class, which would almost certainly be more efficient.*

When setEditingColumns returns, then, the viewEditingColumns variable contains the tabbing columns in sorted order. However, this is not quite the end of the story. Suppose the user reorders the table columns. If this happens, the mapping created by setEditingColumns might become incorrect.

For example, in the initial configuration of the currency table, the data model column indices map directly to the `TableColumnModel` indices, so the `viewEditingColumns` array would initially contain the values {1, 2}. Now, if the leftmost exchange rate column were dragged to the left of the table, its `TableColumnModel` index would become 0 instead of 1 and it would be necessary to change `viewEditingColumns` to {0, 2} instead. Furthermore, if the rightmost exchange rate column were now dragged to the left to occupy position 0, the correct value of `viewEditingColumns` would now be {0, 1} and the tab order between the two exchange rate columns would be reversed in terms of their column headings, but would still be left to right across the table. To recompute the array values it is necessary to gain control whenever the order of columns in the `TableColumnModel` changes.

To be notified of changes to the `TableColumnModel`, it is necessary to implement a `TableColumnModelListener`. Fortunately, `JTable` already implements this interface and registers itself as a `TableColumnModelListener` of its own `TableColumnModel`. To receive notification of column order changes, `TabEditTable` simply overrides the following `TableColumnModelListener` methods of `JTable`:

- `columnAdded`
- `columnRemoved`
- `columnMoved`

Each of these methods simply calls the `JTable` implementation and then invokes `convertEditableColumnsToView` to convert the data column model indices (stored in `editingColumns`) to the `TableColumnModel` indices that are correct for the new column order.

Changing the Editing Cell

It remains to actually implement the code that will capture the TAB key and move the edit focus elsewhere. As noted above, it is necessary to gain control when editing is started and add a listener to receive the TAB key. Because editing is always begun by calling the `JTable editCellAt` method, the natural thing to do is to override this method in `TabEditTable`. If you look at the implementation of `editCellAt` in Listing 7-9, you'll see that it first checks whether the edit is actually going to start. If so, it then verifies that the cell about to be edited is in the list of columns for which tabbing should be active. Note that, because `editCellAt` receives a column number expressed in terms of the `TableColumnModel` ordering, this check is made by looking at the `viewEditingColumns` array, not the original array of data model indices supplied to `setEditingColumns`. If the cell is in this list, the following steps are taken:

1. The editor component installed by the superclass `editCellAt` method is obtained using `getEditorComponent`.
2. A `KeyListener` is added to this component and to the table.
3. The Swing focus manager is disabled so that TAB keys are not lost.
4. A flag is set indicating that the current editor should have special actions when the TAB key is detected.
5. The input focus is passed to the editing component.

The last step attempts to ensure that keys are passed directly to the editing component, but it is not sufficient because the table sometimes grabs the focus back. Hence, it is still necessary to install a `KeyListener` on the table as well.

As each key is passed to the editor component, the `KeyListener` implemented by the inner class `TabKeyListener` is notified. The `keyPressed` method of this class checks whether the key is a TAB key and if it is, the current edit is stopped by invoking the editor's `stopCellEditing` method. If this works, the editor has been removed and the edit focus is moved to the next eligible cell by calling the `TabEditTable moveToNextEditor` method.

The `moveToNextEditor` method is given the row and column number of the cell last edited and a flag indicating whether it should move forward or backward in the tabbing order; this flag is set to indicate backward movement if the SHIFT key was pressed together with TAB. This method can be overridden to provide any kind of tabbing behavior that you want. The default implementation provides the natural left-to-right or right-to-left tabbing order described earlier in this section. It does this by using the editing column number, which is a `TableColumnModel` index, to locate its current place in the `viewEditingColumns` array. If it is moving forward, it selects the column in the next entry of the array; otherwise, it selects the previous entry. If this would involve moving off the end of the array in either direction, the row number is incremented or decremented as necessary and the next column is taken as the one in the first or last entry of the `viewEditingColumns` array. Either way, the last step is to call `editCellAt` to start an edit in the new cell. However, this is not done directly—instead, the operation is deferred using the `SwingUtilities invokeLater` method, which allows key processing to complete before the new edit starts. Notice also that the new cell being edited is made the currently selected cell by manipulating the table's row and column selection models.

You can see how this works in practice using the following command:

```
java AdvancedSwing.Chapter7.TabbableCurrencyTable
```

First, start an edit by double-clicking somewhere in the column headed Yesterday, make a change, and then press TAB. When you do this, you'll find that the new value is written to the table and the cell in the Today column to its right starts editing. As you continue to press TAB, you'll find that you can access all the exchange rate values in turn, but not any of the other cells. Also, you'll find that you can use SHIFT and TAB to traverse the table in the other direction and that the operation wraps when you reach the top or bottom of the table.

To verify that this mechanism is resilient to column order changes, try dragging the currency rate columns to various locations within the table and then start an edit and press the TAB key. You'll find that tabbing still works, that it still allows you to access only the exchange rate columns, and that TAB continues to move you from left to right and top to bottom, even if you swap the order of the two editable columns.

Summary

In this chapter we examined closely the JTable cell editing mechanism. As with rendering, there is default editing support built into JTable that is adequate for the most common types of data that you might include in a table. However, as we showed, if you know how the table controls the editing process, you can extend its capabilities.

After looking at the basic editing support and using it to create an editable version of the currency table that we first saw in the last chapter, we went on to examine how the editing process starts, what editing involves, and how a cell editing session is ended. Armed with this knowledge, we saw how to give the illusion that a table contains an active component such as a combo box or a button, even though the component is not actually there until an editing session starts. Finally, you saw how to take control during and at the end of an editing session to allow the user to edit a cell and then move to the next editable cell by pressing the TAB key, and have the table automatically complete the editing process for the first cell before initiating an edit on the target cell. This example is typical what you can achieve once you understand the internals of the table's editing support.

DRAG-AND-DROP

Topics in this Chapter

8
Chapter

This chapter looks at the drag-and-drop feature that was introduced in the Java 2 platform. Although it isn't strictly part of Swing, drag-and-drop comes within the somewhat larger scope of the Java Foundation Classes and there is no doubt that making proper use of this feature can greatly enhance the user interface of all but the simplest of applications. Drag-and-drop builds on the data transfer feature originally introduced to support cut-and-paste in Java Developer's Kit (JDK) 1.1. Because of this dependency, there is extensive coverage of the data transfer mechanism in this chapter and much of what you'll read here will also be of use if you plan to implement a cut-and-paste mechanism beyond that provided by the Swing text components. Note that drag-and-drop is not supported by JDK 1.1, so you won't be able to compile or run the examples in this chapter if you are still working with JDK 1.1.

Drag-and-Drop Overview

In JDK 1.1, JavaSoft introduced a new Abstract Window Toolkit (AWT) sub-package called `java.awt.datatransfer` that provided the platform-dependent software and the Java classes necessary to allow Java applications to participate in the exchange of data via an intermediate location referred to as a *clipboard*. This package also allowed access to the system clipboard provided by the platform's host windowing system, allowing a Java application to exchange data with another Java application running in a separate virtual machine (VM) on the same machine or, perhaps more interestingly, with a native application. This feature made it possible to copy and paste data from something like Microsoft Word directly into a text field of a graphical user interface (GUI) form in a Java program, or vice versa. Support for copy and paste, using the `java.awt.datatransfer` package, is built into the Swing text components, so that there is no need for the programmer to explicitly enable this mechanism when using Swing.

While this feature was a major step forward when it appeared, it is by no means a complete solution to the problem of making it easy for a user to move data between applications. Because of the implementation, it was only possible to place on the system clipboard data that can be represented in the form of a string. If you only need to move text, of course, this will not cause you a problem. However, if you have to copy graphics onto the system clipboard or you want to allow the user to select and replicate components from your user interface and import them into an application in a different Java VM, you have a problem. The only solution is to somehow encode what you want to transfer as a string when placing it on the clipboard and then reverse the encoding when importing the data from the clipboard to the target. This is a cumbersome process that requires you to write and debug the encoding and decoding software and, what is worse, it means that only applications that are aware of your encoding mechanism can successfully import your data.

Core Note

For an example that uses this technique to transfer images between Java applications via the system clipboard, see Core Java 2, Volume 2: Advanced Features *by Cay Horstmann and Gary Cornell (Prentice Hall).*

Another shortcoming of copy and paste is that it is a two-step process for the user: Anything that is to be transferred must first be selected, usually by dragging the mouse over it, and then exported to the clipboard in some platform—or application-dependent way. The export operation is typically performed using a command from the application's menu bar such as Copy or Cut, or using an associated keyboard shortcut (typically Ctrl-X for Cut or Ctrl-C for Copy on the Windows platform). Once the data has been placed on the clipboard, the user would move to the target application, select the location at which the data should be placed (most likely by clicking with the mouse), and then use a Paste command from the target application's menu or its keyboard equivalent (Ctrl-V on the Windows platform). Once the data has been exported to the clipboard, it will stay there until replaced by something else, so the same data can be pasted more than once to multiple locations.

This sequence of operations can be both time-consuming and inconvenient. Most GUI platforms now support a more direct mechanism for moving data called *drag-and-drop*, which allows the user to initiate and control the operation entirely using the mouse without going through an intermediate location—the data is selected and then "dragged" across the screen, to be "dropped" at its target location. The user is required only to indicate what needs to be done using platform-dependent gestures that indicate the start and end of the operation—the applications cooperate with each other and with the windowing software to transfer the data itself. As was the case with copy-and-paste, a fully general implementation of drag-and-drop in Java is not possible, because it is necessary to interface with whatever mechanism is provided by the host platform, which requires the use of native code libraries. Java 2 provides support for this in the java.awt.dnd package. In this chapter, you'll see how to use the facilities provided by this package to add drag-and-drop support to your Swing applications.

Drag-and-drop involves three logically separate pieces—the drag source, the drop target, and the data transfer itself. Depending on your application, to provide drag-and-drop functionality you will need to write code that implements at least two of them, one of which will always be the code to handle the data transfer. An application that can be both the source and the target of a drag-and-drop operation will implement both the drag source and drop target functionality, while simpler applications might require only one of these two functions. A brief description of each of these three pieces follows.

The Drag Source

As its name suggests, a drag source is a part of the application's user interface that can provide data to be transferred using the drag-and-drop mechanism. The drag source, which is always a Component, advertises the fact that it can supply data and also specifies the operations that it can perform on that data. The Java implementation of drag-and-drop recognizes three separate operations:

- Copy
- Move

- Link

Copy and move are similar in that they both cause a copy of the data to be transferred from the source to the target. At the end of a move operation, if it is successful, the original data is removed from the drag source, whereas copy leaves the source data intact. A typical use for these operations would be to copy or move files within or between file systems using a graphical file system viewer such as Windows Explorer. When operating as a drag source, this program would offer the ability to copy, move, or link files (or groups of files). The precise operation to be performed may be chosen by the user or may be imposed by the nature of the application receiving the data.

The precise meaning of each operation depends entirely on the source and target applications. While the interpretation of copy and move within a given application context will usually be fairly intuitive for the user, the meaning of the link operation may not be and, in fact, many applications will not support this operation at all. The intent of the link operation is to allow a reference to data in one context to be placed in a different context so that it can be accessed from the receiving context without having been moved or copied there. The precise details of this are very dependent on the applications involved and the nature of the data itself. Perhaps the simplest case that illustrates this operation is, again, a graphical file viewer, where dragging a file from one location to another and specifying link as the operation would make a hard or soft link from the new location to the old one, thus creating another way to get to the same file system object without relocating or copying the original. Not all platforms will necessarily have the concept of a file system link and, on these systems, the drag source corresponding to the file viewer would not offer it as a valid choice.

The Drop Target

A drop target is a region of the application's GUI that can receive data from a drag source. An application may support any number of drop targets. In the Java 2 implementation of drag-and-drop, a drop target always corresponds to a GUI `Component`. Like drag sources, drop targets can offer to support any of the three available drag-and-drop operations. It is permissible for distinct drop targets within an application to support different operations. When a drag operation is in progress and the user drags the mouse over a drop target, the set of available operations is limited to the intersection of the set offered by the drag source and that supported by the drop target. It is quite common for this intersection to be empty, in which case a drop on the target from the active drag source will not be possible. At any given time, a drop target may or may not be active. For example, you might want to create an editor that can receive text dragged from an external source by registering the editor component as a drop target. However, if the editor supports a read-only mode, it should not be possible for the user to drag text into it when this mode is selected and the drop target should behave as if it were inactive in this case.

Data Transfer

The drag-and-drop mechanism is outwardly concerned mainly with the graphical representation of the user's request to move data from one location to another, but the actual transfer of the data is ultimately the most important aspect. In fact, once the drag source and the drop target are known, the problem of moving the data itself from one to the other is very similar to that solved by the JDK 1.1 data transfer mechanism used to implement copy-and-paste, except that an intermediate clipboard is not used with drag-and-drop. As far as the drag source and drop target are concerned, the movement of the data requires two things:

- Agreement on the format in which the information will be transmitted.
- The existence of a channel between the two through which the information can be passed.

To agree on the transmission format of the data, both parties must have a common way of specifying individual data formats. The drag-and-drop mechanism uses the `java.awt.datatransfer.DataFlavor` class to describe the way in which the information is represented, in exactly the same way as the JDK 1.1 cut-and-paste feature does. There is a predefined set of `DataFlavors` that are understood to represent specific ways of encoding information, such as `DataFlavor.stringFlavor`, representing a Unicode string and `DataFlavor.plainTextFlavor` for plain text encoded in a specific character set. The drag source can offer the data in one or more of the standard flavors or can invent flavors of its own that, if used, might convey more information to the receiver, but may only be understood by a cooperating drop target. Usually, a drag source will offer its content in several flavors and allow the drop target to pick the best form that it understands. We'll say more about `DataFlavors` later in this chapter.

The communication channel through which the data is actually moved is managed by the drag-and-drop mechanism itself. Neither the drag source nor the drop target need be aware of the precise details of what is going on, which is helpful because the implementation details are very platform-dependent. At the level of the drag source, the data to be transferred must be packaged in the form of an object that implements the `java.awt.datatransfer.Transferable` interface. Again, this is the same mechanism used for copy and paste. A `Transferable` needs to be able to return a list of the `DataFlavor`s that it supports and must return the actual data in a form suitable for the `DataFlavor` selected by the drop target. When the data is dropped, the drop target can get a reference to the `Transferable` and use it to determine the actual `DataFlavor` that it wants to use and to get the data itself. You'll see several examples of this in this chapter.

Architecture of the Java Drag-and-Drop Subsystem

To illustrate the architecture of the Java drag-and-drop subsystem and to get a clearer idea of how the pieces fit together, let's walk through a specific drag-and-drop example. Whereas up to now the discussion has been fairly abstract, here we'll get right to specifics and describe exactly what happens from the point of view of the Java developer implementing both the drag source and the drop target. Because we're going to describe this from the programmer's viewpoint, we're no longer going to talk in generic terms—the description here assumes that the developer is using the Java 2 drag-and-drop feature. It's worth bearing in mind, however, that it is by no means always the case that both the drag source and drop target will be implemented in Java—either of them could be provided as part of a native application and, as we go through the scenario we're about to describe, we'll point out what differences might exist if one party in the transfer operation is a native application. Indeed, in the next section, when we start implementing a drop target in Java, we'll assume that you have available a native drag source to test it with.

The scenario that we're going to explore involves a graphical file system viewer, such as Windows Explorer, which will act as a drag source, and a file editor that can open a file dropped onto it for display or for editing. Let's assume for now that the file system viewer is implemented in Java rather than being a platform-native application. Building an application that displays a file system using a `JTree` component is not too difficult a task and, later in this chapter, you'll see how to add drag source functionality to such a component. The editor in this example will be an instance of the Swing `JEditor-`

`Pane` component, which, as we've already seen, can handle text files encoded in various different ways. Opening a file in a `JEditorPane` can be done by supplying a `URL`, reading the file into a `String`, and passing that to the `JEditorPane` or passing the content via an `InputStream` or a `Reader`. `JEditorPane` does not, however, directly support opening a file by dropping it from a drag source. Our aim here is to sketch out what is involved in providing this feature and to introduce the most important classes in the `java.awt.dnd` package. In the next section, we'll go a step further and show the actual implementation.

Drag Source Architecture

As we said earlier, the drag source is the object that is responsible for providing the data that will be dragged by the user to a drop target. You can think of the drag source either in terms of a region of the GUI that will react to the platform-specific gesture to initiate a drag, or as the set of classes within the application (both application-specific and those provided by the Java platform) that implement the drag source functionality. For clarity, in this chapter we'll use the term *drag source component* when we mean the former and *drag source* for the latter. A drag source is implemented using a set of objects, most of which are instances of classes in the `java.awt.dnd` package. In most cases, to create a drag source that you can use in your application you only need to supply two classes of your own—implementations of the `DragGestureListener` and `DragSourceListener` interfaces that we'll see later in this section. In practice, the `DragGestureListener` is very dependent on the nature of the drag source component and you will probably create a single `DragGestureListener` implementation for a component that you can reuse whenever you need a drag source component of that type. Later in this chapter, you'll see how to create a `DragGestureListener` that responds to user requests to drag information from a `JTree` component. The specific example that we'll show will use a `JTree` populated with nodes that represent a view of a file system, but the `DragGestureListener` will be general enough to be reused with any kind of `JTree`. By contrast, the `DragSourceListener` is more likely to be tied to the specifics of the drag source component, in that it might behave differently for a `JTree` containing file system objects than for one containing library records. However, as we'll see, it is often possible to implement a `DragSourceListener` that does nothing, because all the methods of the `DragSourceListener` convey information that need not be acted upon. The architecture of the drag source, in terms of the most important classes and the runtime relationships between them, is shown in Figure 8-1.

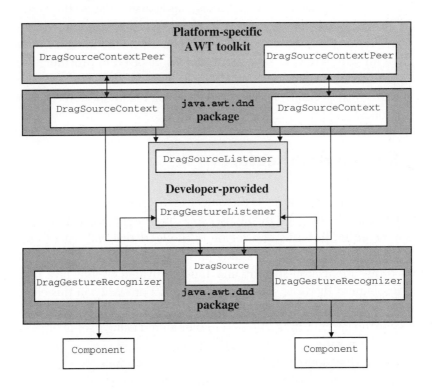

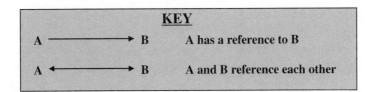

Figure 8-1 Architecture of the drag source.

This diagram shows an application with two drag source components concurrently active. For the sake of this example, these components will be assumed to be JTrees showing a view of a file system, like the one shown in Figure 8-2. JTree does not have any built-in support for drag-and-drop. To add it, you need to register the JTree with an instance of the class java.awt.dnd.DragSource, as shown in Figure 8-1.

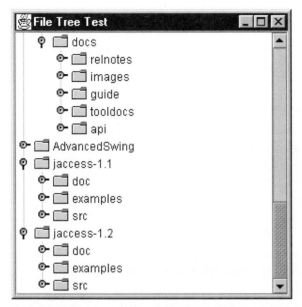

Figure 8-2   A `JTree` showing a view of a file system.

The `DragSource` class provides the following functionality:

- The ability to create a `DragGestureRecognizer`.
- Methods to allow the developer to specify whether a drag that the user has requested should actually be initiated.
- A repository for mappings between the types of data that the host platform can use in a drag-and-drop operation to the `DataFlavors` that the Java drag-and-drop subsystem uses to represent them.

Of these, you'll usually only be directly concerned with the first two; the flavor mapping is used internally by the drag-and-drop subsystem and is of little interest to most applications. As we go through the description of this example, you'll see how these features of the `DragSource` are used.

There are two ways to get a `DragSource`. The most obvious way is just to create one for your dedicated use:

```
DragSource ds = new DragSource();
```

This is perfectly acceptable, but it is strictly unnecessary. A single `Drag-Source` can support interaction with any number of drag source components—in fact, it has no direct relationship with a drag source component, as you can see from Figure 8-1. Because of this, you only need a single `Drag-Source` no matter how many components you have with drag capability. The easiest way to ensure that you only ever use one `DragSource` is to use the static `DragSource getDefaultDragSource` method:

```
DragSource ds = DragSource.getDefaultDragSource();
```

You can invoke this method as many times as you like and you'll get the same `DragSource` reference each time. In most cases, you'll only need the `DragSource` reference for long enough to register a drag source component. As the drag operation proceeds, events will be delivered to report on its progress. Should you need a reference to the `DragSource` while handling these events, you can use the `getDefaultDragSource` method to recover it. If, for some reason you elect to create your own `DragSource` objects, you can get a reference to the one involved in the operation that caused the event from information provided by the event itself. Because of this it will not usually be necessary to keep a long-term reference to the `DragSource` in an application object.

Obtaining a `DragSource` object is not enough to enable a `Component` to serve as a source for drag operations because there is, as yet, no connection between the two. To enable the `Component`, you have to create a `DragGestureRecognizer`. The `DragGestureRecognizer` is associated with both the `DragSource` and the `Component` and so forms the bridge between the two and is tied to a particular `Component`. In other words, as Figure 8-1 shows, if you have two drag source components, you need to create a separate `DragGestureRecognizer` for each of them.

`DragGestureRecognizer` is an abstract class in the `java.awt.dnd` package, whose job is to monitor the drag source `Component` for events that constitute a request by the user to initiate a drag. What exactly will be recognized as a request to start a drag depends on the concrete implementation of `DragGestureRecognizer`. You probably think of drag-and-drop as an operation that is initiated and controlled entirely using the mouse and, not surprisingly, the drag-and-drop subsystem supplies a `DragGestureRecognizer` subclass that monitors mouse events on its associated `Component` to detect a drag request. It is, however, perfectly possible to implement a `DragGestureRecognizer` that triggers a drag based on some other events, such as a combination of key strokes, or on command from the application. Such an implementation would not be very useful, however, because the user would still need to drag with the mouse to continue the operation.

If you're happy to use the built-in `DragGestureRecognizer`, you can get one using the `DragSource createDefaultDragGestureRecognizer` method:

```
public DragGestureRecognizer createDefaultDragGestureRecognizer(
                Component c, int actions, DragGestureListener 1);
```

The Component argument is, of course, the drag source component that is to be monitored. The second argument (actions) is a mask that indicates which of the three possible drag actions the drag source component can support. It consists of an OR of any of the following values:

- DnDConstants.ACTION_NONE
- DnDConstants.ACTION_COPY
- DnDConstants.ACTION_MOVE
- DnDConstants.ACTION_LINK
- DnDConstants.ACTION_REFERENCE
- DnDConstants.ACTION_COPY_OR_MOVE

ACTION_NONE has value 0 and indicates that no action is being offered. This, of course, is useless when creating a drag source. The values ACTION_LINK and ACTION_REFERENCE are synonyms referring to the link operation, while ACTION_COPY_OR_MOVE is shorthand for (ACTION_COPY | ACTION_MOVE). The last object passed when creating a DragGestureRecognizer is a DragGestureListener. DragGestureListener is an interface with one method:

```
public interface DragGestureListener extends EventListener {
    void dragGestureRecognized(DragGestureEvent dge);
}
```

You are responsible for writing a class that implements this interface; its dragGestureRecognized method will be called when the events that trigger the start of the drag have been detected by the DragGestureRecognizer. You'll see a typical implementation of a DragGestureListener in "Implementing a Drag Source" on page 792.

Assuming that you use the standard mouse gesture recognizer, the events that are recognized as a request to start a drag are platform-dependent. The first thing that must happen is for the user to press a mouse button over the drag source component. The exact state of the mouse when the MOUSE_PRESSED event is generated must be as follows:

- On Solaris, any single mouse button must be pressed.
- On Win32, the left mouse button must be pressed. (Strictly speaking, the button recognized as button 1 is required, which may not be the left button if you have reconfigured your mouse because, perhaps, you are left-handed).

This event on its own is not enough for a drag request to be recognized. In addition, the user must do one of the following:

- Drag the mouse outside the boundary of the drag source component.
- Move the mouse more than a certain number of pixels away from the point at which the initial event occurred. The exact distance is obtained as the value of a desktop property called `DnD.gestureMotionThreshold`. If this property is not defined, it defaults to five pixels.

If the mouse is released or the ESCAPE key is pressed before these conditions are met, the drag will not be initiated at all.

When the conditions for the drag to start have been met, your `DragGestureListener`'s `dragGestureRecognized` method will be called. The job of this method is to decide whether a drag operation will actually be initiated. If this method does nothing, the drag will not proceed; to actually begin a drag operation, the `DragSource startDrag` method must be called. If you look at the definition of the `dragGestureRecognized` method, however, you'll see that it doesn't get the `DragSource` as a parameter—instead, it gets a `DragGestureEvent`. Because you don't have a direct reference to the `DragSource`, how can you invoke any of its methods? One way is to call the static `getDefaultDragSource` method, but that only works if you used this method to create your `DragSource` in the first place. Fortunately, the drag-and-drop application programming interface (API) is designed with programmer convenience in mind and here we see the first example of a very useful design pattern that is repeated for all the events that you'll need to handle when implementing drag-and-drop. Instead of requiring you to jump through hoops to get a reference to the `DragSource`, the `DragGestureEvent` has its own `dragStart` method that you can call instead. In fact, it has a whole host of cover methods that save you having to obtain any external state at all when deciding whether to start the drag. If you look at the API reference for `DragGestureEvent`, you'll find the following amongst the set of useful methods that it defines:

- `public Component getComponent();`
- `public int getDragAction();`
- `public DragSource getDragSource();`
- `public void startDrag(Cursor dragCursor, Transferable transferable, DragSourceListener dsl) throws InvalidDnDOperationException;`

- ```
  public void startDrag(Cursor dragCursor, Image
      dragImage, Transferable transferable,
      DragSourceListener dsl) throws
      InvalidDnDOperationException;
  ```

Why are you required to invoke the `startDrag` method to approve the drag? Surely if the user makes the correct platform-dependent gesture over a part of the GUI that's occupied by a drag source component, that should be reason enough to start the drag? That's not the view taken by the drag-and-drop subsystem, and with good reason. To see why you might not want to automatically start a drag operation, look back to Figure 8-2. Suppose the user clicks in the window using the mouse and starts a drag operation. The `JTree` itself occupies almost all of the window shown in Figure 8-2, but if the user clicked in the empty area to the right of the set of directories shown in the visible part of the `JTree`, you wouldn't want to permit a drag, because the file or directory to drag would not have been selected. In fact, you only want to allow a drag operation to begin if the user attempts to drag from an area of the component occupied by one of the nodes of the tree. Even then, you may want to make further checks. You may, for example, not want to allow the user to drag certain types of files or disallow attempts to move or link directories. Because these decisions are dependent not on the drag-and-drop mechanism nor on the `JTree` itself, they can only be made by code that is aware of what the drag source component represents and this is why the decision must be made in the `dragGestureRecognized` method. Refusing a drag operation is, by the way, very easy—just return from the `dragGestureRecognized` method without invoking `startDrag`.

Suppose that the user has selected a file and made the gesture to start the drag and that you want to check whether the user wants to perform a copy, a move, or a link to enforce the restrictions mentioned in the previous paragraph. You can get find out which operation is being performed from the `DragGestureEvent getDragAction` method, which returns `ACTION_COPY`, `ACTION_MOVE`, or `ACTION_LINK`. But how does the user indicate which operation is required? The selected action is actually determined by the `DragGestureRecognizer` and so is, theoretically, platform-dependent (as well as being dependent on the gesture type if you use a custom recognizer). In fact, though, the action is selected in the same way on both Solaris and Windows and is determined by the state of the `SHIFT` and `CTRL` keys, as follows:
  ```

Neither pressed	ACTION_MOVE
CTRL pressed, SHIFT not	ACTION_COPY
CTRL and SHIFT both pressed	ACTION_LINK

If you press SHIFT without CTRL, the default recognizer will not signal the start of a drag operation and your dragGestureRecognized method will not be called.

Core Warning

The drag gesture and the conventions used to select an operation as described here apply only when the drag source is implemented using the Java drag-and-drop mechanism. If you want to drag from a native application to a Java drop target, you may find that different conventions apply. You'll see an example of this later in this chapter.

As you can see from the API extract shown earlier, the startDrag method has several arguments that you can supply. Two of them, cursor and image, allow you control over the way the cursor appears as the user drags it toward a drop target. We won't say any more about those two arguments until we look in detail later in this chapter at how to customize the feedback that is provided to the user. The other two arguments are, however, worth mentioning at this point. The Transferable argument is a reference to an object that can provide the data that is actually being dragged to the drop target. The fact that you have to provide this argument when the drag is initiated might seem surprising, but there is a good reason for it. Usually, the user will select what is to be dragged using the mouse and then initiate the drag. Because the drag operation may continue for some time before a drop occurs and is asynchronous to the source application, there is the possibility, depending on the way in which the application is implemented, that the source data within the application might change before the drop takes place. Supplying the Transferable at the start of the operation makes it possible to take a frozen copy of the data that represents exactly what the user selected to be transferred. It also makes the actual drop operation somewhat simpler, because the drag-and-drop subsystem doesn't have to go back to the source application to request the data when the drop itself occurs.

Core Note

Transferable is just an interface that requires its implementing class to indicate the forms in which the data can be delivered and has a method that can be used to obtain the data on demand. Theoretically, if you implement your own Transferable, you have the choice as to whether to copy the data into an internal buffer when the Transferable is created and supply the value from the buffer when asked, or whether to simply save a reference to the data within the application and fetch it on demand. Choosing the latter might be confusing for the user if the original data can change during the drag. It may be more efficient, however, if you know that the source data will remain unchanged until it is dropped.

The last argument to startDrag is an object of type DragSourceListener. DragSourceListener is another interface that you are required to supply an implementation of to start a drag operation. The methods of this interface, which we'll see later in this chapter, are entered to report the operation's progress once the user has dragged the cursor over a valid drop target. As with the DragGestureListener, the events that are passed to the methods of this interface contain all the state information to process them, so your DragSourceListener does not need to be permanently associated with a particular drag source component or DragSource; it is sufficient to create only one DragSourceListener for all drag source components of a particular type.

Core Note

In fact, it can actually be better than that. In the simplest cases, you won't actually need to do anything at all to handle the events that the DragSourceListener receives because the default handling provided by the drag-and-drop subsystem is perfectly satisfactory. As a result, a trivial implementation in which all the methods have empty bodies will be good enough and such an implementation can be shared among an arbitrary number of different drag source components.

Once the startDrag method has been called, the drag operation has been initiated and nothing more happens from the point of view of the drag source until the drag is ended by the user or encounters a drop target.

Figure 8-1 shows two other classes that we haven't yet mentioned—DragSourceContext and DragSourceContextPeer. In most cases, you won't need to interact with these two classes at all—they are used by the drag-and-drop subsystem itself. `DragSourceContext` does have some useful methods, but the ones that you commonly need to use are accessible indirectly via cover methods in the events that are delivered to your `DragSourceListener`, so there is little reason to access the `DragSourceContext` directly. The only operation that absolutely requires you to bypass the cover methods and use the `DragSourceContext` itself is changing the drag cursor to provide custom feedback to the user, a topic we'll cover later. Every `DragSourceContext` has a `DragSourceContextPeer` associated with it. This object is part of the platform-specific drag-and-drop implementation and cannot be accessed directly from within application code.

Core Note

Only one drag-and-drop operation can be active at any given time, so there will never be more than one set of `DragSourceContext`/ `DragSourceContextPeer` *objects concurrently active, even though Figure 8-1 would seem to suggest that there can be. The diagram is intended to emphasize the point that each drag operation has its own dedicated* `DragSourceContext`/`DragSourceContextPeer` *pair which is created when the drag starts and discarded when it ends. The next drag operation does not reuse the previous objects.*

Drop Target Architecture

As the user drags the mouse over the desktop, eventually a drop target will be encountered. Like the drag source, in Java a drop target is always a `Component`. To avoid confusion, we'll use the term *drop target component* when referring to the region of the screen occupied by the drop target and reserve the term *drop target* to mean the collection of objects that work together to provide the drop target functionality. The architecture of the drop target is shown in Figure 8-3.

You can see that this is a little different from the arrangement of objects that make up the drag source. Whereas you could use one `DragSource` object to manage as many different drag sources as you have, you need a dedicated `DropTarget` object for each drop target component. There is no convenience method to create a `DropTarget`—instead, you use one of its five constructors:

- `public DropTarget();`
- `public DropTarget(Component c, DropTargetListener dtl);`

- ```
  public DropTarget(Component c, int ops,
      DropTargetListener dtl);
  ```
- ```
  public DropTarget(Component c, int ops,
      DropTargetListener dtl, boolean act);
  ```
- ```
  public DropTarget(Component c, int ops,
      DropTargetListener dtl, boolean act, FlavorMap fm);
  ```

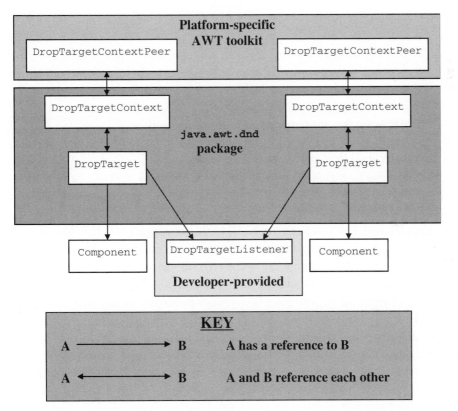

Figure 8-3 Architecture of the drop target.

The last of these constructors is the most general. If you use one of the others, the arguments that you don't specify are defaulted and can be changed later if required using a mutator method. For example, if you use the default constructor, you get a `DropTarget` that is not associated with any `Component` and is therefore not of any immediate use. You can connect it a `Component` and set the other attributes using the following methods:
  ```

- `public void addDropTargetListener(`
  `DropTargetListener dtl) throws`
  `TooManyListenersException;`
- `public void setActive(boolean isActive);`
- `public void setComponent(Component c);`
- `public void setDefaultActions(int ops);`
- `public void setFlavorMap(FlavorMap fm);`

The `ops` argument specifies the actions that this drop target will accept. Like the similar parameter to the `DragSource startDrag` method, it is an OR of the values `ACTION_COPY`, `ACTION_LINK`, and `ACTION_MOVE`. For example, if you want to allow the user to copy or move data to your drop target but you can't support the link operation, you should set the `ops` argument to `ACTION_COPY_OR_MOVE` or use the `setDefaultActions` method to set the same value. If you use one of the constructors that does not have an `ops` argument, this is, in fact, the default value that will be used.

As noted earlier, the drag-and-drop system uses a `FlavorMap` to map between `DataFlavors` that have meaning only inside the Java VM and the native data transfer formats used on the host platform. Usually, you don't need to concern yourself with the details of the `FlavorMap` because a default one is installed automatically for you. If you wish to create your own `FlavorMap` for a specific `DropTarget`, you can use the `setFlavorMap` method to arrange for it to be used.

A drop target may be either active or inactive. By default, the drop target is active, but you can use the `setActive` method to temporarily or permanently disable it or re-enable it at any time. When the drop target is inactive, the drop target component is not considered a valid target for a drop and the user will not get the usual feedback from the cursor when it encounters the inactive drop target component. Depending on the nature of your application, you might want to tie the active or inactive state of the drop target to the enabled state of the component itself. If, for example, your drop target component is a text component, you might not want to allow the user to drag text into it if it is inactive or if it is not editable. By setting the initial state of the drop target from that of the component and monitoring `Property-ChangeEvents` for the editable and enabled properties, you can keep the states of the component and the drop target synchronized.

Core Note

This is only possible for Swing components, because AWT components do not have bound properties for the editable and enabled states.

The last attribute of the `DropTarget`, and the most important one, is the `DropTargetListener`. `DropTargetListener` is an interface that has methods that allow you to receive notification of events that relate to a drag in progress over the drop target component. To construct a `DropTarget`, you need to create a class that implements `DropTargetListener` and register an instance of it with the `DropTarget` either via the constructor or with the `addDropTargetListener` method. As is often the case with the drag-and-drop API, the state and cover methods that are available from the events delivered to the `DropTargetListener` are sufficiently comprehensive that you don't need to retain any state information with your `DropTargetListener`, which means that you can share a single instance of it with more than one `DropTarget`. However, each `DropTarget` can have only one `DropTargetListener` at any given time; if you try to add a new listener to a `DropTarget` that already has one, you'll get a `TooManyListenersException`. This restriction is applied because the primary function of the listener is to cooperate with the drag-and-drop subsystem to control the progress of the drag operation. The listener will have to decide whether a drop from the current drag source and with the current conditions is acceptable. Obviously, it makes no sense to allow more than one listener to try to control the same operation.

Having seen how to create a `DropTarget`, let's look at how the drop part of the drag-and-drop operation works in practice. Suppose that the user has selected a file from a Windows Explorer-like program and is dragging it toward a Java application containing a `JEditorPane` that has been enabled as a drop target component by connecting a custom `DropTarget` object to it (you'll see the actual implementation of this later in this chapter). When the user drags the cursor over the boundary of the `JEditorPane`, the drag-and-drop subsystem creates a `DropTargetContext`, which it will use to manage the drop while it is over the `JEditorPane`, and a corresponding `DropTargetContextPeer` which is used by the native code part of the subsystem. These objects are associated one-to-one with a `DropTarget` but, as was the case with the `DragSourceContext` and the `DragSourceContextPeer`, you don't really need to deal with either of them.

Core Note

*A `DropTarget` only ever has one `DropTargetContext` that is created
the first time a drag moves over its associated `Component`. The
`DropTargetContextPeer` is connected to the `DropTargetContext`
at the same time, but is disconnected when the drop completes or when
the user drags the cursor outside the component. The next drag to enter
the component will use the same `DropTargetContext`, but a new
`DropTargetContextPeer` will be created.*

To signal the fact that the drag operation has entered the drop target component, the drag-and-drop subsystem calls the `DropTargetListener`'s
`dragEnter` method, passing it a `DropTargetDragEvent`. There are three
types of event that can be delivered to the `DropTargetListener`:

- A `DropTargetDragEvent`, which is used when the drag first
  moves over the drop target component, as the cursor moves
  within the boundary of the component, and when the user
  changes the state of the SHIFT and CTRL keys, thus affecting the
  drag action.
- A `DropTargetEvent`, which is delivered just before a drop
  occurs or when the cursor is dragged outside the bounds of the
  drop target component without a drop having taken place.
- A `DropTargetDropEvent`, used when the user requests a drop
  over the drop target.

These three events are related by the class hierarchy shown in Figure 8-4.

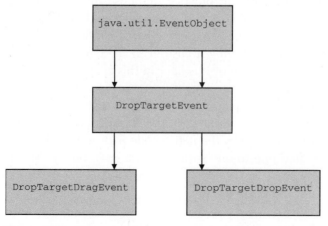

Figure 8-4 Hierarchy of drop target event classes.

The principal job of the `DropTargetListener dragEnter` method is to determine whether a drop operation from the drag source that initiated it would be allowed. To make this decision, the listener can use several pieces of information, including the state of the drop target component itself and the following attributes that can be obtained from the `DropTargetDrag-Event`:

- The current location within the drop target component of the cursor.
- The set of actions offered by the drag source.
- The action currently selected by the user.
- The list of `DataFlavors` in which the data being transferred can be obtained.

In deciding whether a drag operation should be considered valid, the `DropTarget` is most likely to take into account the format in which the data is available and the action that the user wants to perform. The cursor location may not seem very important at the point at which the drag enters the component because there is no suggestion that a drop will definitely occur at this position. However, while the cursor is over the drop target component, movement of the mouse will cause the `DropTargetListener`'s `dragOver` method to be called. This method is also given a `DropTargetDragEvent` and may also decide to accept or reject the drag operation on the same basis as the `dragEnter` method. In fact, there is no real difference between the `dragEnter` and `dragOver` methods in this regard, except that the `dragEnter` method is called only once while the cursor is over the drop target and therefore is the logical place to examine the data types available, which do not change over the entire course of the drag operation.

Let's consider the case of our `JEditorPane`. When the drag operation moves over the `JEditorPane`, the `DropTarget` implementation will extract the list of `DataFlavors` and decide whether the `JEditorPane` can handle data of that type. If it can't, the drag should be immediately rejected by calling the `DropTargetDragEvent`'s `rejectDrag` method. Calling this method does *not* terminate the drag operation from the point of view of the drag source, because the user might choose to drag the cursor to a different program that might be able to accept data of that type. Neither does it stop the `DropTarget`'s `dragOver` method being called while the cursor remains over the drop target component. It does, however, cause the drag-and-drop subsystem to ensure that the cursor shows that the drop target has rejected the drag.

Core Note

You'll see an example that shows how to check the list of `DataFlavor`s for acceptable types in "Implementing a Drop Target" on page 738.

Assuming that the data format is acceptable, the `DropTargetListener` will also check that the proposed operation, obtained using the `getDropAction` method, is valid. For a `JEditorPane`, it is likely that both `ACTION_COPY` and `ACTION_MOVE` would be acceptable but that `ACTION_LINK` would not, because there is no sensible meaning for the link operation in connection with an editor. If the current operation is not acceptable, the `DropTargetListener` has two choices:

- Reject the drag outright by calling `rejectDrag`.
- Accept the drag but suggest that a different operation would be more acceptable.

If the user suggests a link operation, the `DropTargetListener` for our `JEditorPane` could determine whether an alternative, more acceptable operation is available by calling the `getSourceActions` method of the `DropTargetDragEvent`, which returns the complete set of operations that the `DragSource` is prepared to perform with the available data. If this set contains either `ACTION_COPY` or `ACTION_MOVE`, the `DropTargetListener` can invoke the `acceptDrag` method passing its preference from these two operations. If not, it will call `rejectDrag`. Both of these actually belong to the `DropTargetContext`, but there are cover methods provided by `DropTargetDragEvent` that allow more convenient access to them. Here is how they are defined:

- `public void acceptDrag(int dragOperation);`
- `public void rejectDrag();`

The parameter supplied to `acceptDrag` is the drop target's preferred action, which may or may not coincide with the operation that the user is currently trying to perform. As we said earlier, if the `rejectDrag` method is called, the cursor is changed to indicate that the drop operation is not valid under the current conditions. At the time of writing, calling `acceptDrag` with an operation that is different to the one implied by the user's drag gesture does *not* affect the cursor if the drag source is a native application (at least not on the Windows platform), so the user has no clue that the drop, if were performed now, would actually fail. For this reason, it might be preferable to reject the drag under these circumstances. If you choose this option, you can still accept the drag later if users change their gestures to request an acceptable operation because the DropTargetListener's dragOver method will still be called. Note that the cursor *is* changed to signal rejection if you offer an alternative operation when the drag source is a Java application.

What about considering the state of the underlying drop target component when deciding whether to accept or reject a drag? This looks like it might be a problem, because the list of attributes available from the DropTargetDrag-Event does not include the original Component, which seems inconvenient it you use one DropTargetListener to manage several drop target components. Fortunately, there are two ways to get a reference to the Component under the cursor:

1. As shown in Figure 8-4, the DropTargetDragEvent is sub-
    classed (via DropTargetEvent) from java.util.Event-
    Object, which provides a getSource method to obtain the
    source of the event; for these events, the event source is the
    DropTarget object associated with the drop target component.
    You can use the DropTarget's getComponent method to obtain
    a reference to the component itself.

2. DropTargetEvent (and hence DropTargetDragEvent) also
    has a getDropTargetContext method that returns a reference
    to the DropTargetContext object associated with the drop
    operation. This class also has a getComponent method that you
    can use to get a reference to the component. This is a more
    type-safe method than using the source of the event because
    you don't need to cast the return value of getSource to
    DropTarget to use it.

In the case of our JEditorPane example, you might want to examine the JEditorPane to determine whether it is editable before accepting a drag that would copy or move text from another editor into the JEditorPane's current content. However, you might not want to apply this restriction if the user were trying to drag an entire file, because you would probably want to allow the user to open a new file in read-only mode by dragging it over the JEditorPane.

After the dragEnter method has completed, as long as the cursor remains over the drop target component, the DropTargetListener's dragOver method will be entered as the mouse is moved around, perhaps because the user is moving it to a suitable location before activating the drop. As we said earlier, this method also receives a `DropTargetDragEvent` and you should examine the attributes available from this event to determine whether the drag should be accepted and call either `acceptDrag` or `rejectDrag` as before. It is not worth wasting time checking the available data flavors in the `dragOver` method, however, because they will remain the same as the ones offered by `dragEnter`. It follows that if you reject the drag for this reason in the `dragEnter` method, you should continue to do so from `dragOver`. On the other hand, if your decision to accept or reject the drag depends on the location of the cursor or on the action being offered, you can use the `dragOver` method to re-examine whether a drop would be acceptable given the position returned from the `DropTargetDragEvent` `getLocation` method or the action returned from `getDropAction`.

If the user drags the cursor outside the bounds of the drop target component, the `DropTargetListener`'s `dragExit` method is invoked. Unlike `dragEnter` and `dragOver`, this method is passed a `DropTargetEvent`, which only has methods that allow access to the `DropTargetContext` or to the event source. However, there is usually very little to do in the `dragExit` method. If you allocated any resources for the potential drop in the `dragEnter` method, you should free them here. Note carefully, though, that the `dragExit` method is also called immediately before the user performs a drop and you can't tell whether it has been called because the user has elected to drop or because the cursor has left the area controlled by the `DropTarget`. Another possible task for the `dragExit` method is to remove any "drag-under feedback" effects that might have been applied to the drop target component to make it obvious to the user that the cursor is over a valid drop target (in addition to cursor feedback, which is the job of the drag-and-drop subsystem and the `DragSource`). You'll see an example of this in "Providing Drag-Under Feedback" on page 773.

There is one more method provided by the `DropTargetListener` that we haven't yet mentioned. The `dropActionChanged` method is called when users change the operation that they want to be performed. On both Solaris and Windows, this method is called when the state of the CTRL or SHIFT keys is changed so that a new operation would be selected. If, for example, the drag begins with neither key pressed, an `ACTION_MOVE` action will be offered. If, while the cursor is over the drop target component, the user pressed the CTRL key, the `DropTargetListener`'s `dropActionChanged` method would be called. This method, like `dragEnter` and `dragOver`, is given a `Drop-TargetDragEvent` and, typically, it will call `getDropAction` to examine the action now being offered which, in this example, will now be `ACTION_COPY`. The `dropActionChanged` method may, like the other two methods, call either `rejectDrag` to reject the drag or `acceptDrag` to accept it or to offer a different operation. In fact, it probably won't surprise you to know that a typical `DropTargetListener` implementation will share the same code for the `dragOver` and `dropActionChanged` methods and will probably reuse it in `dragEnter`, while adding an extra check for the `DataFlavors` available from the `DragSource`.

Note carefully, however, that the action returned from the `getDrop-Action` method will be `ACTION_NONE` if the user selects an action that is not one of those in the source actions offered by the drag source. Thus, if the drag source is prepared to perform `ACTION_COPY` or `ACTION_MOVE` and the user presses both `CTRL` and `SHIFT` to select a link action, `getDropAction` will return `ACTION_NONE` instead of `ACTION_LINK`.

Transferring Data

If the user drags the cursor over a drop target and releases the mouse buttons, a drop will occur and the drag-and-drop subsystem will call the `DropTargetListener`'s `dragExit` method followed by its `drop` method. We've already described the `dragExit` method and how you should handle it; the `drop` method is where you actually perform the data transfer itself. This method is defined as follows:

```
public void drop(DropTargetDropEvent dtde);
```

As you can see from the class hierarchy shown in Figure 8-4, `DropTarget-DropEvent` is, like `DropTargetDragEvent`, derived from `DropTargetEvent`. Many of the methods of `DropTargetDropEvent` are cover methods for those of `DropTargetContext` and almost all of them are the same as those of `DropTargetDragEvent`. This is partly because the `drop` method, like `dragEnter` and `dragOver`, has first to decide whether the drop should be accepted before it can transfer the data and so it needs access to the same information as the other two methods.

Core Note

If the user elects to drop over a drop target, the `DropTargetListener`*'s* `drop` *method will be called, even if the drop target has previously accepted the "drop only on condition that an alternative drag operation be selected." This means that you should check that the correct conditions for the drop apply before attempting the data transfer itself and call* `rejectDrop` *if the drop is not acceptable. The* `drop` *method is not called, however, if the last* `dragOver` *or* `dragEnter` *invocation called* `rejectDrag`*.*

The most important `DropTargetDropEvent` methods that might be used in the `drop` method are:

- `public void dropComplete(boolean success);`
- `public DataFlavor[] getCurrentDataFlavors();`
- `public List getCurrentDataFlavorsAsList();`
- `public int getDropAction();`
- `public Point getLocation();`
- `public int getSourceActions();`
- `public Transferable getTransferable(DataFlavor df)`
- `public boolean isLocalTransfer();`
- `public void rejectDrop();`

The first thing that the `drop` method will usually do is to check whether to accept the drop. At this stage, the user is committed to the drop and the operation will end whether the data is transferred, but the `drop` method is still able to refuse to perform the transfer operation. In most cases, the initial checks in the `drop` method will be the same as those in the `dragOver` method—that is, the drop operation will be checked, along with perhaps the location of the cursor if the drop target uses this to decide where to put the data from the drag source. If the conditions that relate to these checks are not met, the `drop` method can simply call `rejectDrop` and return.

The next criterion of interest will be the `DataFlavor` to be used to transfer the data. The complete set of `DataFlavors` was made available to the `DropTargetListener` in the `dragEnter` and `dragOver` methods and the listener will already have rejected the drop in these methods if there is no suitable transfer format. However, rejecting the drop in this way does not cancel it—the user can still go ahead and attempt the drop, so it is still necessary to verify, using the `DropTargetDropEvent getCurrentDataFlavors` or `getCurrentDataFlavorsAsList` methods, that there is a data transfer format that is compatible with the needs of the drop target component. In the `drop` method, however, this check will also result in the selection of the transfer format to be used. If there is no mutually agreeable `DataFlavor`, the `rejectDrop` method should be called.

Having decided on the transfer flavor, the `drop` method will use the `DropTargetDropEvent getTransferable` method to obtain a reference to the `Transferable` that can provide the drag source's data and then invoke its `getTransferData` method to obtain the data content:

```
public Object getTransferData(DataFlavor flavor);
```

Once the data transfer is complete, the `DropTargetDropEvent dropComplete` method should be called with argument `true` if the drag source is to consider the operation to have been a success, or `false` if it should not. Completing the operation and deciding whether to notify a success or a failure is not always a straightforward matter, however. You'll see some examples that demonstrate exactly how this is done in the rest of this chapter. For now, bear the following points in mind:

- The data returned from the `getTransferData` method is in the form of an `Object`. In fact, what this `Object` actually is depends on the `DataFlavor`. In some cases, such as when transferring a Unicode string using `DataFlavor.stringFlavor`, the `Object` returned is the actual data which simply needs to be cast to the appropriate type (`String`) and used directly. In other cases, though, the `Object` returned is an `InputStream` which the `DropTargetListener` must arrange to read from to get the actual data. Any time you read from an `InputStream`, there is the possibility of an `IOException` that would cause the drop to fail and, in this case, you should call `dropComplete(false)` to indicate this to the drag source. We'll say more about the various data formats later in this chapter.
- If you're transferring a file or a set of files from a program like Windows Explorer, the transfer takes place using a flavor called `DataFlavor.javaFileListFlavor`. The `Object` returned from `getTransferData` is of type `java.util.List` and contains a list of objects of type `File`, one for each file involved in the transfer. Having obtained the file list, the `DropTargetListener` might apply additional checks to some or all of the files, such as verifying that it is dealing with files that it can read or is not dealing with directories if this is not appropriate in the context of the operation. Only if these checks succeed will the actual operation proceed and the `DropTargetListener` call `dropComplete(true)`.

When the drop operation is completed and the `dropComplete` or `rejectDrop` method has been called, the drag source is notified of the result in the `dragDropEnd` method of its `DragSourceListener`. We haven't said much about the events delivered to the `DragSourceListener` so far in this chapter because they are usually of more importance to the drag-and-drop subsystem than to application code. If the application needs to find out whether the operation succeeded, however, it can do so in the `dragDropEnd` method by

calling the getDropSuccess method of the DragSourceDropEvent delivered to it, which returns the same value passed by the DropTargetListener
to the dropComplete method. The drag source can also use the getDrop-
Action method to find out which of its offered actions was actually accepted.
This information is important if the drag source is a text editor and the user
has dragged text elsewhere. If the ACTION_MOVE operation was selected and
the operation succeeded (and under no other conditions), the Drag-
SourceListener will have to arrange for the source text component to
delete the selected text.

Implementing a Drop Target

Now that you've had an overview of the drag-and-drop subsystem and seen
the major classes and how they work together, it's time to start looking at
some real code. In this section, you'll see how to implement a working drop
target that can be used with a JEditorPane. The first version of this example
will be very rudimentary, but will show the basic features of a working drop
target. In the sections that follow, we'll enhance this example by adding more
facilities until the fourth version has everything you need to be able to drop
files and text onto a JEditorPane including appropriate feedback to the user
and the ability to scroll the JEditorPane until the required location for the
drop comes into view.

   Because at this point we don't have a drag source written in Java, we'll
assume that you have suitable platform-native applications that can act in this
role. On the Windows platform, for example, you can use the Windows
Explorer as a source for files and either WordPad or Microsoft Word for
dragging text.

A Simple Drop Target

The aim of our first example is to create a class that can be used as a drop target for a JEditorPane. Before we start looking at the code that implements
the drop target support, there is an important choice that we need to make—
namely whether we should create a whole new component derived from
JEditorPane with drop target support included, or whether this support
should be part of a separate class that can be connected as required to existing JEditorPanes. How you make this choice is probably determined mainly
by the environment that you are working in. If you build a new component
derived from JEditorPane that automatically behaves as a drop target, you

won't need to worry about this feature as you build your application—just slot in your component and let it do its job. The flip side of this picture is what you should do if you already have an application to which you have been asked to add drag-and-drop support. If you're in that position, you might find it simpler to have the drop target functionality as a separate item and connect the drop target to each `JEditorPane` as required. The benefits of this are clearer if your application uses subclassed `JEditorPane`s: Because Java does not have multiple inheritance, if you have created your drop target as a subclass of `JEditorPane`, you have to do some extra, perhaps nontrivial, work if you want to add the same feature to a class that is already subclassed from `JEditorPane`. In this book, we take the view that it is generally more useful to implement the drop target support in a separate object that you can use in conjunction with a `JEditorPane` or any subclass of `JEditorPane`. If you prefer the other approach, you can always build your own `JEditorPane` subclass that incorporates the code that you see here by instantiating a drop target object in its constructor and connecting it to the `JEditorPane`.

The drop target that we're going to implement in this section will demonstrate how to interact with the drag-and-drop subsystem to allow a single file to be dragged from elsewhere on the desktop and dropped onto a `JEditorPane`, where it will be opened and displayed. You've already seen in this book how to arrange for a `JEditorPane` to open a file and you'll know that, if you can obtain a URL to describe the location of the file, the `JEditorPane` will work out for itself the file's content type and will install the correct `EditorKit` to display its content properly. In essence, then, all the drop target needs to do when the file is dropped on the `JEditorPane` is to get the location of the file as a URL and call the `JEditorPane setPage` method and that's exactly what the code shown in Listing 8-1 does. There is, of course, slightly more to it than that but, although it may appear that there is quite a lot of code to implement something that sounds so straightforward, most of it is pretty simple.

Listing 8-1 A Drop Target for a `JEditorPane`

```
package AdvancedSwing.Chapter8;

import javax.swing.*;
import java.awt.*;
import java.awt.event.*;
import java.awt.datatransfer.*;
import java.awt.dnd.*;
import java.io.*;
import java.net.*;
import java.util.List;
```

Listing 8-1 A Drop Target for a `JEditorPane` (continued)

```java
public class EditorDropTarget implements DropTargetListener
{
   public EditorDropTarget(JEditorPane pane) {
      this.pane = pane;

      // Create the DropTarget and register
      // it with the JEditorPane.
      dropTarget = new DropTarget(pane,
                DnDConstants.ACTION_COPY_OR_MOVE,
                this, true, null);
   }

   // Implementation of the DropTargetListener interface
   public void dragEnter(DropTargetDragEvent dtde) {
      DnDUtils.debugPrintln("dragEnter, drop action = "
               + DnDUtils.showActions(dtde.getDropAction()));

      // Get the type of object being transferred and
      // determine whether it is appropriate.
      checkTransferType(dtde);

      // Accept or reject the drag.
      acceptOrRejectDrag(dtde);
   }

   public void dragExit(DropTargetEvent dte) {
      DnDUtils.debugPrintln("DropTarget dragExit");
   }

   public void dragOver(DropTargetDragEvent dtde) {
      DnDUtils.debugPrintln("DropTarget dragOver,
                drop action = " + DnDUtils.showActions(
                dtde.getDropAction()));

      // Accept or reject the drag
      acceptOrRejectDrag(dtde);
   }

   public void dropActionChanged(DropTargetDragEvent dtde) {
      DnDUtils.debugPrintln("DropTarget dropActionChanged,
                drop action = " + DnDUtils.showActions(
                dtde.getDropAction()));

      // Accept or reject the drag
      acceptOrRejectDrag(dtde);
   }
```

Listing 8-1 A Drop Target for a `JEditorPane` **(continued)**

```
public void drop(DropTargetDropEvent dtde) {
    DnDUtils.debugPrintln("DropTarget drop, drop action = "
            + DnDUtils.showActions(dtde.getDropAction()));

    // Check the the drop action
    if ((dtde.getDropAction() &
            DnDConstants.ACTION_COPY_OR_MOVE) != 0) {
        // Accept the drop and get the transfer data
        dtde.acceptDrop(dtde.getDropAction());
        Transferable transferable = dtde.getTransferable();

        try {
            boolean result = dropFile(transferable);

            dtde.dropComplete(result);
            DnDUtils.debugPrintln("Drop completed,
                            success: " + result);
        } catch (Exception e) {
            DnDUtils.debugPrintln("Exception while handling
                            drop " + e);

            dtde.dropComplete(false);
        }
    } else {
        DnDUtils.debugPrintln("Drop target rejected drop");
        dtde.rejectDrop();
    }
}

// Internal methods start here

protected boolean acceptOrRejectDrag(
                        DropTargetDragEvent dtde) {
    int dropAction = dtde.getDropAction();
    int sourceActions = dtde.getSourceActions();
    boolean acceptedDrag = false;

    DnDUtils.debugPrintln("\tSource actions are " +
                    DnDUtils.showActions(sourceActions) + ",
                    drop action is " +
                    DnDUtils.showActions(dropAction));

    // Reject if the object being transferred
    // or the operations available are not acceptable.
```

Listing 8-1 A Drop Target for a `JEditorPane` (continued)

```
     if (!acceptableType ||
        (sourceActions &
              DnDConstants.ACTION_COPY_OR_MOVE) == 0) {
        DnDUtils.debugPrintln("Drop target rejecting drag");
        dtde.rejectDrag();
     } else if ((dropAction & DnDConstants.ACTION_COPY_OR_MOVE)
                                                     == 0) {
        // Not offering copy or move - suggest a copy
        DnDUtils.debugPrintln("Drop target offering COPY");
        dtde.acceptDrag(DnDConstants.ACTION_COPY);
        acceptedDrag = true;
     } else {
        // Offering an acceptable operation: accept
        DnDUtils.debugPrintln("Drop target accepting drag");
        dtde.acceptDrag(dropAction);
        acceptedDrag = true;
     }

     return acceptedDrag;
  }

  protected void checkTransferType(DropTargetDragEvent dtde) {
     // Only accept a list of files
     acceptableType =
     dtde.isDataFlavorSupported(DataFlavor.javaFileListFlavor);

     DnDUtils.debugPrintln("File type acceptable - " +
                           acceptableType);
  }

  // This method handles a drop for a list of files
  protected boolean dropFile(Transferable transferable)
              throws IOException, UnsupportedFlavorException,
              MalformedURLException {
     List fileList = (List)transferable.getTransferData(
                        DataFlavor.javaFileListFlavor);
     File transferFile = (File)fileList.get(0);
     final URL transferURL = transferFile.toURL();
     DnDUtils.debugPrintln("File URL is " + transferURL);

     pane.setPage(transferURL);

     return true;
  }
```

Listing 8-1 A Drop Target for a `JEditorPane` **(continued)**

```
    public static void main(String[] args) {
        final JFrame f = new JFrame("JEditor Pane Drop Target
                                    Example 1");

        JEditorPane pane = new JEditorPane();

        // Add a drop target to the JEditorPane
        EditorDropTarget target = new EditorDropTarget(pane);

        f.addWindowListener(new WindowAdapter() {
            public void windowClosing(WindowEvent evt) {
                System.exit(0);
            }
        });

        f.getContentPane().add(new JScrollPane(pane),
                               BorderLayout.CENTER);
        f.setSize(500, 400);
        f.setVisible(true);
    }

    protected JEditorPane pane;
    protected DropTarget dropTarget;
    protected boolean acceptableType;   // Indicates whether
                                        // data is acceptable
}
```

You can try out this example using the command

```
java AdvancedSwing.Chapter8.EditorDropTarget
```

which creates a frame with an empty `JEditorPane`. You'll also need to start Windows Explorer (or, on Solaris, an equivalent graphical file display program such as `dtfile`) and select a file containing some plain text (such as a Java source file) or an HTML file. With the file selected, use whatever your platform recognizes as the gesture necessary to initiate a drag to drag the file over the `JEditorPane` and then drop it. In the case of Windows Explorer, you can use either the left of right mouse button to drag the file over the desktop; when you're ready to drop it on the `JEditorPane`, just release the mouse button. As you drag the file, you should get feedback from the cursor to indicate that a drag is in progress. What exactly you see depends not only on the operating system you are using, but also on whether the application thinks you are requesting a copy, move, or a link operation. The standard cursors that you'll see when using Windows are shown in Figure 8-5.

Figure 8-5   Drag cursors on the Windows platform.

In order from left to right, the leftmost three cursors are used when the user has selected a copy, move, or a link operation and the cursor is currently over a location (that is, over a drop target) that could perform that operation on the data selected from the drag source. The rightmost cursor, which looks like no-entry sign, is used when the cursor is not over a drop target or is over a drop target that has rejected the drop for some reason. The drag source is responsible for selecting the correct cursor at all times, based on feedback from the drag-and-drop subsystem. When the drag source is a native application, you can't control the cursor that is displayed but, if you write a drag source for a Java component, you have the choice of using the default cursors shown previously or using your own. You'll see how to use custom drag cursors later in this chapter.

Creating and Using the `DropTarget`

The `EditorDropTarget` class shown in this example provides all the code needed to implement a basic drop target for a `JEditorPane`. As you can see from the main method, all you need to do to add this functionality to an existing editor is to create an instance of it, passing the `JEditorPane` as a constructor argument:

```
JEditorPane pane = new JEditorPane();
EditorDropTarget target = new EditorDropTarget(pane);
```

The constructor creates a `DropTarget` object that is associated with the component that is passed to it, thus activating that component as a drop site within the drag-and-drop subsystem. In this simple example, the drop site is always active and will accept copy or move operations; in a more sophisticated implementation, you would probably make the acceptable actions a constructor parameter and you would want to arrange for the drop site to be active only when the editor is enabled. In later versions of this example, we'll add more sophisticated features.

Core Note

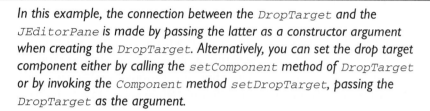

In this example, the connection between the `DropTarget` and the `JEditorPane` is made by passing the latter as a constructor argument when creating the `DropTarget`. Alternatively, you can set the drop target component either by calling the `setComponent` method of `DropTarget` or by invoking the `Component` method `setDropTarget`, passing the `DropTarget` as the argument.

Apart from instantiating a `DropTarget` object and connecting it to the `JEditorPane`, the only other thing you need to supply is an implementation of the `DropTargetListener` interface, a reference to which you pass when creating the `DropTarget` (refer to Figure 8-3 to see how these classes fit together). The `DropTargetListener` could be implemented as a separate class but, for simplicity, we implement the code as part of the `Editor-DropTarget` class. This has the advantage of keeping all our code in one class, which makes life easier for the developer using `EditorDropTarget`. An alternative and equally acceptable approach would be to implement the `DropTargetListener` as an inner class of `EditorDropTarget`, but there seems to be little reason to do that. Implementing `DropTargetListener` requires us to supply code for the `dragEnter`, `dragOver`, `dragExit`, `drop-ActionChanged`, and `drop` methods that we described under "The Drop Target" on page 714. These methods are all relatively simple and, in fact, because three of them are almost exclusively concerned with deciding whether the operation that the user is performing should be allowed, these three methods share a lot of common code.

The `dragEnter` Method

When the user drags the cursor over the `JEditorPane`, the first `DropTar-getListener` method that gets called is `dragEnter`. The implementation of this method in this example looks like this:

```
public void dragEnter(DropTargetDragEvent dtde) {
   DnDUtils.debugPrintln("dragEnter, drop action = "
             + DnDUtils.showActions(dtde.getDropAction()));

   // Get the type of object being transferred and determine
   // whether it is appropriate.
   checkTransferType(dtde);
```

```
    // Accept or reject the drag.
    acceptOrRejectDrag(dtde);
}
```

The first method that `dragEnter` calls is a utility routine that prints debug output to the window from which the application was started. You can use this debugging information to see when the various `DropTargetListener` methods are invoked and what the result of calling each of them is. To enable the debugging, you need to define a property called `DnDExamples.debug`, which you can do by invoking the example like this:

```
java -DDnDExamples.debug AdvancedSwing.Chapter8.EditorDropTarget
```

You might find it useful to start the example program with debugging enabled and try dragging a file over the `JEditorPane` to become familiar with the sequence of events that are delivered to the `DropTargetListener`. You'll also see what happens when you do different things such as dragging the mouse away from the drop target without performing a drop, or pressing the ESC key, which cancels the drag, while the cursor is over the `JEditor-Pane`. Here's some sample output obtained in this way:

```
dragEnter, drop action = Move
File type acceptable - true
Source actions are Copy Move Link, drop action is Move
Drop target accepting drag
DropTarget dragOver, drop action = Move
Source actions are Copy Move Link, drop action is Move
Drop target accepting drag
DropTarget dragOver, drop action = Move
Source actions are Copy Move Link, drop action is Move
Drop target accepting drag
DropTarget dragExit
```

The start of this trace shows the `dragEnter` method being called, with the user's drop action being `ACTION_MOVE`; the drop action is obtained from the `getDropAction` method of the `DropTargetDragEvent` that is created by the drag-and-drop subsystem and passed to the drop target. A little further down the trace, you can see that the `dragOver` method was invoked twice as the cursor was moved over the `JEditorPane`, followed finally by `dragExit`, which ends the interaction between the `JEditorPane` drop target and the drag-and-drop subsystem for this drag. In fact, this call resulted from the ESC key being pressed which terminated the drag, but it is impossible to distinguish this from the case where the user simply drags the cursor out of the `JEditorPane`'s screen space (and, of course, the drop target doesn't need to be able to tell these two cases apart).

Ultimately, the `dragEnter` method must decide whether to accept or reject the drag operation by invoking either the `acceptDrag` or `rejectDrag` method of `DropTargetDropEvent`, both of which are covered for the same methods in the `DropTargetContext` object associated with the drop. The `dragEnter` method decides which method to call based on:

1. whether any of the `DataFlavors` offered by the drag source is acceptable, and
2. whether the drag operation is acceptable to the drop target.

Because the first check is only really required in the `dragEnter` method while the second will also be made from `dragOver`, `dropActionChanged` and `drop`, the code that implements these two cases is separated into two separate methods, both of which the `dragEnter` method invokes (see Listing 8-1).

The `DataFlavor` check is performed in the `checkTransferType` method, which, in the case of this example, is very simple:

```
protected void checkTransferType(DropTargetDragEvent dtde) {
    // Only accept a list of files
    acceptableType =
        dtde.isDataFlavorSupported(DataFlavor.javaFileListFlavor);

    DnDUtils.debugPrintln("File type acceptable - " +
                            acceptableType);
}
```

The drop target in this implementation is only going to allow us to drop a file onto the `JEditorPane`—it won't permit you to drag text from another editor, although you will see how to allow this in the next section. To check whether a particular `DataFlavor` is available from the drag source, you call the `DropTargetDragEvent` method `isDataFlavorSupported`, passing it a reference to the `DataFlavor` type that you would like to use, in this case the well-known value `DataFlavor.javaFileListFlavor`. If this type is available, the drag source and the drop target have a compatible transfer format for the date. To record this fact, the instance variable `acceptableType` is set to `true`. On the other hand, if this flavor is not being offered by the drag source, `acceptableType` is set to `false`. Before returning, `checkTransfer-Type` writes the result of the check to your output window if you started the program with debugging enabled, as you can see from the trace extract shown earlier.

Next, `dragEnter` invokes the `acceptOrRejectDrag` method, which actually determines whether the drag operation will be accepted or rejected. Here is how the `acceptOrRejectDrag` method is implemented:

```
protected boolean acceptOrRejectDrag(DropTargetDragEvent dtde) {
    int dropAction = dtde.getDropAction();
    int sourceActions = dtde.getSourceActions();
    boolean acceptedDrag = false;

    DnDUtils.debugPrintln("\tSource actions are " +
                    DnDUtils.showActions(sourceActions) +
                    ", drop action is " +
                    DnDUtils.showActions(dropAction));

    // Reject if the object being transferred
    // or the operations available are not acceptable.
    if (!acceptableType ||
        (sourceActions & DnDConstants.ACTION_COPY_OR_MOVE) == 0) {
        DnDUtils.debugPrintln("Drop target rejecting drag");
        dtde.rejectDrag();
    } else if ((dropAction & DnDConstants.ACTION_COPY_OR_MOVE) ==
                                                              0) {
        // Not offering copy or move - suggest a copy
        DnDUtils.debugPrintln("Drop target offering COPY");
        dtde.acceptDrag(DnDConstants.ACTION_COPY);
        acceptedDrag = true;
    } else {
        // Offering an acceptable operation: accept
        DnDUtils.debugPrintln("Drop target accepting drag");
        dtde.acceptDrag(dropAction);
        acceptedDrag = true;
    }

    return acceptedDrag;
}
```

The first step is to check whether the `checkTransferType` method found an acceptable transfer type; if it did not, `rejectDrag` is called immediately. This test is performed here rather than in `checkTransferType` itself because `checkTransferType` is called only once each time a drag operation moves over the drop target component, whereas `acceptOrRejectDrag` is invoked continuously while the drag is in progress. Because the data flavors offered cannot change once the drag has started, the result of the tests performed by `checkTransferType` will remain valid throughout the drag. Furthermore, this check must be made each time `acceptOrRejectDrag` is called because calling `rejectDrag` does not terminate the drag, or even prevent the other `DropTargetListener` methods being called; invoking `rejectDrag` once in `dragEnter` is therefore not sufficient.

Assuming that there is a compatible data transfer flavor, the next test is whether the drag source is prepared to carry out either a copy or a move operation. Note that this check involves the value returned by the `get-SourceActions` method, which is also constant for the duration of a drag. Because this drop target will only perform a copy or move, if neither of these is available from the drag source, there is no possibility that the drop would succeed, so `rejectDrag` should be called. This test would result in the drag being the rejected if the drag source offers only a link operation.

At this point, we know that the drop could succeed because the drag source is prepared to transfer a file list and perform either a copy or move operation. The only remaining thing to check is the action implied by the user's current gesture, which is obtained from the `DropTargetDropEvent` `getDropAction` method. The drop would succeed, and should be accepted, if the user has requested either a copy or a move operation but if both the CTRL and SHIFT keys are pressed to indicate a link, the drop would not be accepted. Because we know that the drag source is prepared to perform either a copy or a move, both of which would be acceptable, if a link operation is requested, instead of calling `acceptDrag` with the currently selected operation, we instead call `acceptDrag` with argument `ACTION_COPY`, which expresses our preference to perform a copy instead.

Core Note

As noted earlier, calling `acceptDrag` *with an operation that does not reflect the one in progress causes the cursor change to the "no entry" sign shown in Figure 8-5 (or its equivalent on your platform) if the drag source is a Java implementation, but may or may not have any effect in the case of a native drag source.*

The last thing that `acceptOrRejectDrag` does is return `true` if it accepted the drag (whether or not it suggested an alternative operation) and `false` if it did not. If you look at the `dragEnter` method, however, you'll see that having done its job, it just returns when it receives control back from `acceptOrRejectDrag`, without inspecting the return value. In fact, nothing in this example uses this return value—it's there only so that we can use it when we enhance this code to provide feedback from the drop target to the user later in this chapter.

Returning from the `dragEnter` method returns control to the drag-and-drop subsystem. There is no need to return any kind of status from the `dragEnter` method (and, indeed, there is no way to do so)—the only requirement is that `dragEnter` invoke either `acceptDrag` or `rejectDrag` as appropriate.

The `dragOver`, `dragExit`, and `dropActionChanged` Methods

While the user continues to drag the cursor over the drop target component, the `DropTargetListener` `dragOver` method will be called in response to movement of the mouse. As with `dragEnter`, the main job of this method is simply to call either `acceptDrag` or `rejectDrag` depending on the parameters of the drag. The only difference between `dragEnter` and `dragOver` is that there is no need for the latter to examine the list of `DataFlavors` available from the drag source because this will not change, so the initial setting of the `acceptableType` instance variable will apply throughout the drag operation. To implement `dragOver` in this simple case, then, it is sufficient to simply call `acceptOrRejectDrag` again. In more complex cases, however, the implementation of `dragOver` might not be quite so simple. As an example, whereas the exact location of the cursor is not important when dragging a new file over a `JEditorPane`, this would not be the case if you were instead trying to copy or move a file by dragging it over a graphical file viewer such as the one shown in Figure 8-2. Furthermore, in addition to the checks made by `acceptOrRejectDrag`, if the drag cursor were placed over a node in the `JTree` that represents a directory to which the user does not have write access, you would probably want to call `rejectDrag`.

The same rationale applies to the `dropActionChanged` method—here, there is the possibility that the new drop action will be more acceptable than the previous one or will not be acceptable at all. Either way, just calling `acceptOrRejectDrag` is still the correct thing to do. The `dragExit` method implementation in this example is extremely simple. As we'll see later in this chapter, you can use the `dragExit` method to remove any drag-under feedback effects that were applied during `dragEnter` or any of the other `DropTargetListener` methods. In this simple case, however, there is nothing more to do.

Transferring the Data—the `drop` Method

In general, when the `drop` method is entered, you know two things:

1. There is at least one `DataFlavor` supported by both the drag source and the drop target that could be used to transfer the data being dragged by the user.
2. At least one of the source actions available from the drag source is acceptable to the drop target.

The first task of the `drop` method is to decide whether the drop will be accepted or rejected and to select the format in which the data will be transferred. Because there is a common data format between the drag source and the drop target, there is no need to recheck this, but it is necessary to ensure that the selected drop operation is acceptable. The `drop` method is passed as its only argument a `DropTargetDropEvent`, the methods of which you saw earlier in this chapter. This event, like `DropTargetDragEvent`, has a `get-DropAction` method that returns the operation that the user last selected before the drop. If this operation is not compatible with the drop target, the drop should be rejected by calling the `DropTargetDropEvent rejectDrop` method. In this example, the drop target is prepared to perform a copy or a move operation so it checks that the value returned by `getDropAction` is one of these. For ease of reference, the implementation of the `drop` method is repeated here.

```
public void drop(DropTargetDropEvent dtde) {
    DnDUtils.debugPrintln("DropTarget drop, drop action = "
                + DnDUtils.showActions(dtde.getDropAction()));

    // Check the drop action
    if ((dtde.getDropAction() &
                        DnDConstants.ACTION_COPY_OR_MOVE) != 0) {
        // Accept the drop and get the transfer data
        dtde.acceptDrop(dtde.getDropAction());
        Transferable transferable = dtde.getTransferable();

        try {
            boolean result = dropFile(transferable);

            dtde.dropComplete(result);
            DnDUtils.debugPrintln("Drop completed, success: " +
                            result);
        } catch (Exception e) {
```

```
              DnDUtils.debugPrintln("Exception while handling drop
                             " + e);
              dtde.dropComplete(false);
         }
    } else {
         DnDUtils.debugPrintln("Drop target rejected drop");
         dtde.rejectDrop();
    }
}
```

Before the data can be transferred, a reference to the `Transferable` that gives access to it must be obtained from the drag-and-drop subsystem via the `getTransferable` method of the `DropTargetDropEvent`. However, before you can call this method, you must accept the drop operation by calling `acceptDrop`. Notice that `acceptDrop`, unlike `acceptDrag`, has no arguments, because there is no scope at this late stage for offering an alternative operation if the one suggested by the user is not acceptable. Once you call `acceptDrop`, you are not committed to actually accepting the drop data or performing the requested operation on it, but you are obliged to call `drop-Complete` before the `drop` method ends to inform the drag source that the drop has ended, successfully or otherwise.

In this example, we already know that the data that will be returned from the `Transferable` will be a list of `File` objects representing the files that were dragged by the user from the drag source, so the `drop` method immediately calls another method called `dropFile`, the code for which we'll examine shortly, to perform the drop. This method returns a boolean indicating whether the drop succeeded, which is used as the argument to the `drop-Complete` method. If an exception occurs, `dropComplete` is invoked with argument `false`. In more complex cases, there will be more than one possible `DataFlavor` for the transfer and the `drop` method will need to select one and act appropriately. You'll see an example of this in the next section.

The `dropFile` method (which is part of the implementation of this example and not a drag-and-drop method) is very straightforward. To obtain the list of files from the `Transferable`, the `getTransferData` method is called with argument `DataFlavor.javaFileListFlavor`. Because we know that this flavor is available, it is safe to do this without further checks and to cast the returned `Object` to type `java.util.List`, which is the type used by `DataFlavor.javaFileList`:

```
List fileList = (List)transferable.getTransferData(
                DataFlavor.javaFileListFlavor);
File transferFile = (File)fileList.get(0);
final URL transferURL = transferFile.toURL();
```

Because the user may have selected more than one file, the `List` may have more than one entry, but this code simply extracts the first item in the list. Once we have the file, we need to invoke the `JEditorPane`'s `setPage` method to have it load and display the file content, for which we need a URL. Fortunately, the items of the `List` returned by `getTransferData` are of type `java.io.File`, and, as of Java 2, this class has a `toURL` method from which you can obtain a URL that refers to the same file as the `File` object itself. The last step is to pass this URL to the `setPage` method. Of course, you can only safely call Swing component methods from the AWT event thread. This, however, is not a problem, because the drag-and-drop subsystem always arranges to invoke the methods of all its listeners from the event thread. This means that you don't have to take any special steps to ensure thread safety when using drag-and-drop with Swing components.

Having called `setPage`, the `dropFile` method returns `true` to the `drop` method so that it can signal a successful drop to the drag source. Strictly speaking, of course, there is still a possibility that the `JEditorPane` will fail to open or display the file, but it is not practical to attempt to determine whether this will happen.

A Multi-Functional Drop Target

The example that you have just seen allows you to drag a single file from Windows Explorer onto a `JEditorPane`. Because there is only one possible transfer operation here, the code is fairly simple and demonstrates without too much complication how to implement a basic drop target. In the real world, however, drop targets are rarely as simple as this, and here and in the next two sections we'll complicate the code more and more by introducing extra features, while keeping the same overall code layout so that you can see more easily how the implementation changes as we enhance the functionality. The first change we're going to make is to enhance the drop target so that, as well as dragging an entire file onto the editor, you can also select text from another application and drag it directly into the `JEditorPane`'s text flow. Adding this capability requires us to make several changes to the code, of which the most obvious are the following:

- As well as accepting a complete file transfer using the Java file list `DataFlavor`, we have to be able to handle the transfer of blocks of text from an external source. Text, of course, uses a different `DataFlavor` from files, so we'll need to be able to enhance the `checkTransferType` method to accept a drop that offers one of the possible flavors for text as well as `DataFlavor.javaFileListFlavor`.

- When the user completes a drop with text, we need to select the appropriate DataFlavor from the offered set, extract the text itself, and then paste it into the JEditorPane. As you'll see, this is a little more involved than arranging for a complete new file to be opened.

In the last example, although we implemented all the DropTargetListener methods, most of the code was actually contained in helper methods that dealt with checking the available data transfer flavors (checkTransferType), choosing whether to accept or reject a drag based on the user's selected action (acceptOrRejectDrag), and completing the drop by opening a new file in the JEditorPane (dropFile). Adding the ability to support a new DataFlavor affects only the first of these three methods and requires us to write an additional method that is similar to dropFile. It must handle text instead, while leaving the rest of the code almost unchanged. Because the changes are confined to well-defined areas of the original example, in this section we'll show only those methods that are affected by the enhancements that we're making; if you want to see all of the source code, you can find it on the CD-ROM that accompanies this book.

Text and Data Flavors

Before we look at the code for this example, we need to examine the way in which the drag-and-drop subsystem handles transferring text. Drag-and-drop relies entirely on the java.awt.datatransfer package for the means to describe the data that a drag source wishes to export and for transferring that data to the drop target. The mechanism that this package supplies is the DataFlavor class. Up to now, you have only seen one instance of this class in use, DataFlavor.javaFileListFlavor, which represents a list of File objects. The code in Listing 8-1 simply used DataFlavor.javaFileListFlavor as a constant, which is exactly what it is. Using this constant, you can easily find out whether the drag source can supply a list of files simply by passing it as an argument to the DropTargetDragEvent isDataFlavorSupported method:

```
if (dtde.isDataFlavorSupported(DataFlavor.javaFileListFlavor)) {
    // Drag source can supply a file list
}
```

or by obtaining a list of available flavors from the DropTargetDragEvent getCurrentDataFlavors method and walking down the list looking for the correct type:

```
DataFlavor[] flavors = dtde.getCurrentDataFlavors();
for (int i = 0; i < flavors.length; i++) {
   if (flavors[i].equals(DataFlavor.javaFileListFlavor)) {
      // File list flavor is available
   }
}
```

If you want to find out whether the drag source supports the transfer of text, you would probably look for a similar constant in the `DataFlavor` class that looks like it might represent text and then write code like that shown earlier to see if the drag source supports the transfer of data in that flavor. In fact, there is such a constant (`DataFlavor.plainTextFlavor`), but there is actually a little more to managing the transfer of text than there is to presenting a list of files. The complication arises from the fact is that there isn't just one type of text, so a single `DataFlavor` constant just won't do.

Suppose you open a basic file editor such as the UNIX `vi` editor or the Windows Notepad program. These programs deal only in plain, unformatted text—they don't concern themselves with presentation issues such as font, text color, subscripting, and so on. When you save a file created by one of these editors, you just get a simple sequence of bytes in which each byte maps to a single character in the file. There are, however, several more sophisticated forms of text in common use. Two that we've seen quite a lot of in this book are Hypertext Markup Language (HTML) and Rich Text Format (RTF). Both of these formats store not only the text itself, but also attributes that indicate how the text should be displayed and, possibly, graphics and hyperlink information as well. Now suppose that you start a Web browser and a plain text editor on your machine and load a Web page into the browser, select some text from the Web page, and copy it onto the system clipboard with a view to importing it into the text editor. When you copy the text onto the clipboard, the browser exports an object (the platform-specific equivalent of a `Transferable`) that carries with it information describing the formats in which the selected data can be made available. These formats actually depend on the Web browser that you are using. Internet Explorer 5, for example, can export text from a Web page as plain text, HTML, or enriched text. Assuming that your browser supported export in all these formats, what would happen when you attempt to paste the data from the clipboard into your text editor? Because the editor understands only simple plain text, it would naturally choose to receive the data in plain text format. The result of this, of course, would be that any formatting applied by the HTML from which the text was originally created will be lost and there is little point in the browser supplying any of this text when it is asked for the data in plain text form, because the HTML tags would just be interpreted as part of the text.

Suppose, on the other hand, that you wanted to paste the same selection into an HTML editor, which, of course, understands HTML as well as plain text. In this case, you would expect the receiving editor to ask for the selection in HTML format. This time, the browser would export the text and the HTML tags so that the editor could display it in the same form as the browser, or in the form of raw HTML for the user to edit directly.

Expressing this in terms of the `java.awt.datatransfer` package, there need to be different `DataFlavor` objects corresponding to the different types of text that are available. In fact, there are two constants in the `DataFlavor` class that represent text without formatting:

`DataFlavor.plainTextFlavor`   Plain text encoded in Unicode and presented as an `InputStream`.

`DataFlavor.stringFlavor`   Plain text encoded in Unicode and returned as a `String` object.

Although these are the only predefined text `DataFlavors`, it is possible to create others. The key to creating new ones is to realize that each `DataFlavor` is distinguished by three characteristics:

1. The type of data that is represents.
2. The class used to return the data when the `getTransferData` method of a `Transferable` is called, referred to as its *representation class*.
3. A human-presentable name, which can be used for display purposes.

The data format is expressed as a multipurpose Internet mail extension (MIME) type and may include optional parameters such as the character set in which the data is encoded. The `plainTextFlavor`, for example, is described by the following MIME type:

`text/plain; charset=unicode`

and its representation class is `java.io.InputStream`. By contrast, the MIME type of `stringFlavor` is

`application/x-java-serialized-object`

and its representation class is `java.lang.String`—in other words, the `getTransferData` method of a `Transferable` that handles data of type `stringFlavor` would return the `String` directly to the caller.

Creating a new `DataFlavor` is simply a matter of invoking one of the `DataFlavor` constructors and passing the required values for these three attributes. As a developer working with drag-and-drop at the application level, you will need to create a new `DataFlavor` when you implement a drag source if you need to supply the data in a form for which there is no existing `DataFlavor`. Note that `DataFlavor` only describes the format and representation of data—it does not actually contain the data itself. As a result, inventing a new `DataFlavor` does not require you to write the code that actually transfers data in that form—that job belongs to the `Transferable`, which needs to be able to encapsulate the data in the form described by the `DataFlavor`'s representation class and return an instance of that class when its `getTransferData` method is called.

When implementing a `DropTarget`, you don't need to be concerned about creating a `DataFlavor`—your problem will be interpreting it to discover the format of the data that it contains. `DataFlavor` has several methods that you can use to do this:

- `public String getMimeType();`
- `public String getPrimaryType();`
- `public String getSubType();`
- `public Class getRepresentationClass();`
- `public String getParameter(String paramName);`
- `public boolean isMimeTypeEqual(String mimeType);`
- `public boolean equals(Object o);`
- `public boolean equals(String s);`

The `getMimeType` method returns the complete MIME definition of the data type starting with the type and subtype, followed by any accompanying parameters; if you just want the primary type or the subtype, use `getPrimaryType` and `getSubType` instead. The `getRepresentationClass` method gives you a `Class` object for the type of object that will be returned by the `getTransferData` method of any `Transferable` when this `DataFlavor` is passed as the argument. This method is most often used when you need to carry out the data transfer implied by the drop operation, as you'll see later in this section. The values returned by these four methods for the built-in `DataFlavor plainTextFlavor` are as follows:

getMimeType	Text/plain; class=java.io.InputStream; charset=unicode
getPrimaryType	Text
getSubType	Plain
getRepresentationClass	Java.io.InputStream

whereas the values returned when these methods are invoked against the `DataFlavor.stringFlavor` object are:

getMimeType	Application/x-java-serialized-object; class=java.lang.String
getPrimaryType	application
getSubType	x-java-serialized-object
GetRepresentationClass	java.lang.String

The `getParameter` method returns the value of a specific parameter from the MIME description of the `DataFlavor`. This method is commonly used when the representation class of the data is `java.io.InputStream` to get the character set used to encode the data, so that it can be properly converted to Unicode as it is read. Typical usage for this method would something like this:

```
DataFlavor flavor = DataFlavor.plainTextFlavor;
String charSet = flavor.getParameter("charset");
```

In this case, the value returned would be `unicode`. You'll see this method in use later in this section when we show the code that implements the transfer of text to the `JEditorPane`.

The last three methods in the earlier list are useful for comparing a `DataFlavor` to a MIME type or another `DataFlavor`. For example, if you want to know whether a specific `DataFlavor` is the same as the built-in `DataFlavor.plainTextFlavor`, you could use the following expression:

```
flavor.equals(DataFlavor.plainTextFlavor)
```

This expression evaluates to `true` if flavor has the same representation class as `plainTextFlavor` (that is, `java.io.InputStream`) and the MIME types match according to the `isMimeTypeEqual` method. The `isMimeType-Equal` method is a weaker test that does not require the representation class of the two `DataFlavors` to match. It returns `true` if the primary of the two `DataFlavors` are the same and either the subtypes match or one of them is a wildcard (represented by a "`*`"), so that for example, the MIME types `text/plain` and `text/*` match according to this method. Note that, because only the MIME type and subtype are taken into account, any optional parameters are ignored, so that `DataFlavors` with the following MIME descriptions:

```
text/plain; charset="unicode"
text/plain; charset="cp1251"
```

would be considered equal, even though they do not use the same character encoding. We'll make use of this fact later in this section.

The two built-in `DataFlavors` that represent plain text aren't the only `DataFlavors` that you are likely to come across when attempting to drag text from a native platform application to a Java drop target. To see some of the other types of text available, type the following command:

```
java -DDnDExamples.debug AdvancedSwing.Chapter8.EditorDropTarget2
```

This command runs the example program whose code we'll be looking at shortly. In addition to allowing you to drop files onto the `JEditorPane`, this program also allows you to drag and drop text from a platform-native application. When debugging is enabled, as it is by the command line shown previously, the `checkTransferType` method prints the MIME types of all the `DataFlavors` that are offered by the drag source when the drop target's `dragEnter` method is called. To try this out, start an editor, type and select some text, and drag it over the `JEditorPane`. Using WordPad on the Windows platform, you should get a result something like this:

```
Drop MIME type text/enriched; class=java.io.InputStream; charset=ascii
                                                        is available
Drop MIME type text/plain; class=java.io.InputStream; charset=ascii
                                                        is available
```

Internet Explorer 5 offers an even larger set of transfer flavors if you select some text from a Web page that it's displaying. Here is some typical output:

```
Drop MIME type text/enriched; class=java.io.InputStream; charset=ascii
                                                        is available
Drop MIME type text/html; class=java.io.InputStream; charset=unicode
                                                        is available
Drop MIME type text/plain; class=java.io.InputStream; charset=ascii
                                                        is available
Drop MIME type text/plain; class=java.io.InputStream; charset=unicode
                                                        is available
```

As you might expect of a Web browser, IE5 is prepared to supply HTML, rich text, and plain text, depending on the capabilities of the receiving program. Notice that two different forms of plain text are offered, one encoded in Unicode, the other in `ascii`, whatever that means. There is actually no Java-supported character encoding called `ascii`—in fact, if you tried to convert the data from an `InputStream` with data of this type by creating an `InputStreamReader` with this character encoding, you'll get an `Unsupport-edEncodingException`. In fact, describing the encoding as `ascii` is somewhat misleading—what it actually means is that the input stream from a `Transferable` using a `DataFlavor` with this MIME definition will use the platform's default encoding.

FlavorMap and the `SystemFlavorMap`

Of the `DataFlavors` in the set returned by IE5, only the last one looks like one of the built-in flavors that describe plain text although, in fact, even that is not actually `DataFlavor.plainTextFlavor`. Given that IE5 is a platform-native application, it can't create new `DataFlavor` objects, so where did these come from?

Core Note

The discussion that follows covers an advanced topic that you don't need a complete understanding of to make use of the drag-and-drop subsystem and the rest of this chapter does not depend on it. If you are not interested in how the set of `DataFlavors` that is available for a specific drag operation is obtained, you should skip forward to the next section.

The drag-and-drop subsystem is responsible for converting the data formats offered by native applications into `DataFlavor` objects that Java programs can understand. The native drag-and-drop mechanism has a platform-dependent way of describing data formats that is much like the `DataFlavor` scheme. When the Java VM is started, it creates a `FlavorMap` that maps the platform-native representation of the supported data transfer types from the local platform into the corresponding `DataFlavor`. This `FlavorMap` is used to map the types offered by the drag source when a drag operation begins into a list of `DataFlavor` objects. By default, all `DragSources` and `DropTargets` use this system-created `FlavorMap`, but you can supply your own if you want to change the mapping from platform type to `DataFlavor`. The constructor of the `DragSource` class provides a parameter that sets a new `FlavorMap` for that drag source, while `DropTarget` has both a constructor argument and a `setFlavorMap` method. The `FlavorMap` in use for a given drag operation can be obtained from the `getFlavorMap` method of the `DragSource` or the `DropTarget` objects that are managing it.

`FlavorMap` is actually an interface that defines two methods:

```
public Map getFlavorsForNatives(String[] natives);
public Map getNativesForFlavors(DataFlavor[] flavors);
```

The drag-and-drop subsystem uses the first of these methods to convert the available platform data types into `DataFlavor` objects; application code can use the second to get the list of native data types from one or more `DataFlavors` (although this information is probably only of use to highly specialized applications with native code that interacts directly with the platform's drag-and-drop provider). Supplying `null` as the argument for either of these methods returns a `Map` of all the known values of that type, so that the call

```
Map flavorMap = getFlavorsForNatives(null);
```

gives a `Map` with the `DataFlavors` corresponding to all the native drag-and-drop data formats on the platform that the Java drag-and-drop subsystem supports.

The `FlavorMap` interface does not specify how the mapping that it describes is stored or how it is initially created. The system default `Flavor-Map` is an instance of the class `SystemFlavorMap`, which initializes itself from a text file called `flavormap.properties` that is stored in the `jre/lib` directory of the Java installation on your machine. This file simply maps platform-specific data type names to the MIME definitions that will be used to build the corresponding `DataFlavor` objects. Its content is, of course, platform-specific; here's what the Windows version of this file looks like:

```
TEXT=text/plain; charset=ascii
UNICODE\ TEXT=text/plain;charset=unicode
HTML\ Format=text/html;charset=unicode
Rich\ Text\ Format=text/enriched;charset=ascii
HDROP=application/x-java-file-list;class=java.util.List
```

You should recognize from this file the `DataFlavors` that were shown as being returned from IE5 when dragging text over a Java drop site and the standard `DataFlavor` that represents a list of files that we used in the first example in this chapter. You can extend the default `SystemFlavorMap` by creating another file in the same format as the one shown previously and setting the property `AWT.DnD.flavorMapFileURL` to a string URL which points to it. Entries from this file that have the same key as those from the system default file will overwrite the default entry, which allows you to redefine the MIME type returned for any of the standard types or to add new definitions.

Establishing a Transfer Format when Several `DataFlavors` Are Available

Now let's look at the code for our second drag-and-drop example. The main difference between this program and the one shown in Listing 8-1 is that we want to be able to allow the user to drag text from a native application (or any Java application that can act as a drag source and supply text) onto a `JEditorPane`, where it will be inserted in place of anything currently selected in the editor. As you've already seen in this section, dragging text onto a drop target can result in a choice of `DataFlavors`. In the most general implementation, you might want to make the choice of transfer flavor dependent on the type of data that the JEditorPane is currently displaying. As an example of this, suppose the text is being dragged from IE5, so that you have a choice of two different encodings of plain text, enriched text, and HTML. JEditorPane can, of course, display all these formats. If it currently has an HTML page loaded, you might prefer to transfer the text from the drag source in HTML format if it is available and accept plain text if it isn't. Similarly, when the JEditorPane has an RTF document installed, you would probably want to select enriched text in preference to plain text and, finally, if the document is itself plain text then you would naturally elect to accept plain text from the drag source.

Because you can easily obtain the content type of the document in the JEditorPane from its getContentType method, it is a relatively easy matter to work out the most appropriate transfer format given access to the list of flavors available from the drag source. However, for the purposes of this example, we are not going to attempt to select the best possible transfer format. The reason for this choice is to avoid the complexity that would be involved when actually transferring the data during the execution of the DropTargetListener drop method, which would overly complicate the implementation to the point that it would be difficult to see the most important details. In fact, to keep things simple, we're going to accept only three flavors—DataFlavor.javaFileListFlavor (to preserve the ability to drop files), DataFlavor.stringFlavor, and DataFlavor.plainTextFlavor. In other words, we're always going to import either an entire file or a string selection in the form of plain text.

Core Note

The complexity involved in importing more general forms of text arises partly from the fact that neither JEditorPane nor the underlying EditorKit implementations offer a single method of importing data to an arbitrary location in the document that works equally well for plain text, RTF, and HTML. Because of this, the drop method would have to be implemented with special case code for all three text types. Showing this code would not, of course, help you to understand drag-and-drop.

In the previous example, we checked whether there was an acceptable DataFlavor in the checkTransferType method, which was invoked from the DropTargetListener dragEnter method. We keep the same structure for this example, but this time we need slightly more complicated code, as shown in Listing 8-2.

Listing 8-2 Working with Multiple Transfer Flavors

```
protected void checkTransferType(DropTargetDragEvent dtde) {
    // Accept a list of files, or data content that
    // amounts to plain text or a Unicode text string
    acceptableType = false;
    draggingFile = false;

    if (DnDUtils.isDebugEnabled()) {
        DataFlavor[] flavors = dtde.getCurrentDataFlavors();
        for (int i = 0; i < flavors.length; i++) {
            DataFlavor flavor = flavors[i];
            DnDUtils.debugPrintln("Drop MIME type "
                    + flavor.getMimeType() + " is available");
        }
    }

    if (dtde.isDataFlavorSupported(
                DataFlavor.javaFileListFlavor)) {
        acceptableType = true;
        draggingFile = true;
    } else if (dtde.isDataFlavorSupported(
                DataFlavor.plainTextFlavor)
        || dtde.isDataFlavorSupported(DataFlavor.stringFlavor)) {
        acceptableType = true;
    }
    DnDUtils.debugPrintln("File type acceptable - " +
                        acceptableType);
}
```

Forgetting about the debugging code, this method is changed from the previous version shown in Listing 8-1 in two respects:

1. As well as checking whether the user is dragging a file, it also allows for the possibility of plain text or a Unicode string. If any of these three flavors is available, it will set the instance variable `acceptableType` to `true`.

2. In addition to determining whether there is a common transfer flavor, this method also initializes another instance variable called `draggingFile`, which it sets to `true` if `DataFlavor.javaFileListFlavor` is available and `false` if we are dragging text.

As with the previous example, the value of `acceptableType` is used in the decision to accept or reject the drag. The `draggingFile` variable is used to allow the `DropTargetListener` to use different criteria for accepting a drag or a drop depending on whether the user is dragging text or a file. You'll see why this is necessary shortly.

As before, the checkTransferType method is only called when the cursor moves into the space occupied by the drop target component and makes a once-and-for-all decision as to whether it is feasible to transfer the data offered by the current drag operation. The acceptOrRejectDrag method is again the one that determines whether the drag will be accepted or rejected. Like checkTransferType, there is a little extra complication in this method because of the need to support both importing of text and reading entire files. The modified version of this method is shown in Listing 8-3.

Listing 8-3 Determining Whether to Accept or Reject a Drag Operation

```
protected boolean
acceptOrRejectDrag(DropTargetDragEvent dtde) {
    int dropAction = dtde.getDropAction();
    int sourceActions = dtde.getSourceActions();
    boolean acceptedDrag = false;

    DnDUtils.debugPrintln("\tSource actions are " +
            DnDUtils.showActions(sourceActions) +
            ", drop action is " +
            DnDUtils.showActions(dropAction));

    // Reject if the object being transferred
    // or the operations available are not acceptable
    if (!acceptableType ||
       (sourceActions & DnDConstants.ACTION_COPY_OR_MOVE) == 0) {
        DnDUtils.debugPrintln("Drop target rejecting drag");
        dtde.rejectDrag();
    } else if (!draggingFile && !pane.isEditable()) {
        // Can't drag text to a read-only JEditorPane
        DnDUtils.debugPrintln("Drop target rejecting drag");
        dtde.rejectDrag();
    } else if ((dropAction & DnDConstants.ACTION_COPY_OR_MOVE) ==
                                                              0) {
        // Not offering copy or move - suggest a copy
        DnDUtils.debugPrintln("Drop target offering COPY");
        dtde.acceptDrag(DnDConstants.ACTION_COPY);
        acceptedDrag = true;
    } else {
        // Offering an acceptable operation: accept
        DnDUtils.debugPrintln("Drop target accepting drag");
```

> Listing 8-3 Determining Whether to Accept or
>   Reject a Drag Operation (continued)

```
        dtde.acceptDrag(dropAction);
        acceptedDrag = true;
    }

    return acceptedDrag;
}
```

   The code that has been added to this method is highlighted in bold. The rationale behind this modification is simple. A `JEditorPane` can be in either an editable or noneditable state; when it is editable, the document that it is displaying can be modified by the user but, when it `setEditable(false)` is called, the document should be considered read-only. We didn't worry about this issue in our first example, because it is perfectly acceptable to open different documents in a read-only editor—the read-only state only stops us changing the content of the document once it has been opened. Therefore, when dropping a file onto a `JEditorPane`, you don't need to check whether it is read-only. On the other hand, dragging text into an editor amounts to changing the content of the document and should be prohibited if the editor is read-only. The extra code that has been added to the `acceptOrReject-Drag` method will reject the drag if the editor is not editable and the user is not dragging a file onto it. The need to make this test conditional on whether the user is dragging a file is, of course, the reason the `checkTransferType` method sets the new instance variable `draggingFile`.

Core Note

Another issue that we have sidestepped here is whether the `JEditorPane` *is enabled. Strictly speaking, if the editor is disabled, the drop should be rejected unconditionally. We'll attend to this detail in the next version of this example drop target.*

Transferring Text from the Drag Source to the Drop Target

When the user finally commits to the drop, the `DropTargetListener`'s `drop` method is called. In Listing 8-1, the `drop` method simply verified that the user's drop action was either a move or a copy, called `acceptDrop`, obtained a reference to the `Transferable` and then passed it to the helper method `dropFile` to actually open the file in the editor. Most of that code still applies in version of the example. The only difference is that now there is the possibility that the user is dragging text instead of a file. To cater for this, the `drop` method checks the `draggingFile` variable and calls the original `dropFile` method if it is `true` or the new `dropContent` method if it is not. Here's the affected part of the code, with the changes highlighted:

```
try {

    boolean result = false;

    if (draggingFile) {
        result = dropFile(transferable);
    } else {
        result = dropContent(transferable, dtde);
    }

    dtde.dropComplete(result);
    DnDUtils.debugPrintln("Drop completed, success: " + result);
} catch (Exception e) {
    DnDUtils.debugPrintln("Exception while handling drop " + e);
    dtde.dropComplete(false);
}
```

The actual transfer of text from the drag source to the drop target takes place in `dropContent`. The most important things that this method has to do are:

1. Determine which flavor to use for the data transfer (either `stringFlavor` or `plainTextFlavor`).
2. Obtain the data from the `Transferable`, converting it to Unicode if necessary.
3. Insert the text into the `JEditorPane`.

The implementation of this method is shown in Listing 8-4.

The first thing that this method does is check that the `JEditorPane` is editable—if it is not, it returns immediately without attempting to transfer any data. You may be wondering whether it is necessary to make this check here because the drag will have been rejected in the `dragEnter` and `dragOver` methods if the editor is not editable and, as we said earlier, if the last call to `dragOver` before the user initiated the drop calls `rejectDrop`, then the `drop` method will not be called at all.

Listing 8-4 Dropping Text onto a JEditorPane

```
protected boolean dropContent(Transferable transferable,
                              DropTargetDropEvent dtde) {
   if (!pane.isEditable()) {
      // Can't drop content on a read-only text control
      return false;
   }

   try {
      // Check for a match with the current content type
      DataFlavor[] flavors = dtde.getCurrentDataFlavors();

      DataFlavor selectedFlavor = null;

      // Look for either plain text or a String.
      for (int i = 0; i < flavors.length; i++) {
         DataFlavor flavor = flavors[i];

         if (flavor.equals(DataFlavor.plainTextFlavor)
            || flavor.equals(DataFlavor.stringFlavor)) {
            selectedFlavor = flavor;
            break;
         }
      }

         if (selectedFlavor == null) {
            // No compatible flavor - should never happen
            return false;

         }

         DnDUtils.debugPrintln("Selected flavor is " +
                 selectedFlavor.getHumanPresentableName());

         // Get the transferable and then obtain the data
         Object data =
              transferable.getTransferData(selectedFlavor);

         DnDUtils.debugPrintln("Transfer data type is " +
                 data.getClass().getName());

         String insertData = null;
         if (data instanceof InputStream) {
```

Listing 8-4 Dropping Text onto a `JEditorPane` (continued)

```
        // Plain text flavor
        String charSet =
                selectedFlavor.getParameter("charset");
        InputStream is = (InputStream)data;
        byte[] bytes = new byte[is.available()];
        is.read(bytes);
        try {
           insertData = new String(bytes, charSet);
        } catch (UnsupportedEncodingException e) {
           // Use the platform default encoding
           insertData = new String(bytes);
        }
     } else if (data instanceof String) {
        // String flavor
        insertData = (String)data;
     }

     if (insertData != null) {
        int selectionStart = pane.getCaretPosition();
        pane.replaceSelection(insertData);
        pane.select(selectionStart,
           selectionStart + insertData.length());
        return true;
     }
     return false;
  } catch (Exception e) {
     return false;
  }
}
```

This logic is almost flawless, except for the fact that the drag operation is performed asynchronously from the execution of the application itself. While the user drags the mouse over the drop target component, the application continues to execute and could, theoretically, change the state of the `JEditorPane` from editable to read-only after the last `dragOver` call but before `drop` is entered. If this happens, the last call to `dragOver` will invoke `acceptDrop`, so that `drop` *will* eventually be called, by which time the `JEditorPane` will have been switched to read-only mode. Of course, this is very unlikely to happen, but the window of opportunity does exist.

Having verified that the `JEditorPane` is in an appropriate state to import the data, the next step is to determine the transfer flavor. Because we are only going to accept `stringFlavor` or `plainTextFlavor`, this method gets the list of available `DataFlavors` from the `DropTargetDropEvent` and iterates through each flavor, looking for one that matches either `stringFlavor` or `plainTextFlavor` and uses whichever of these appears first in the list.

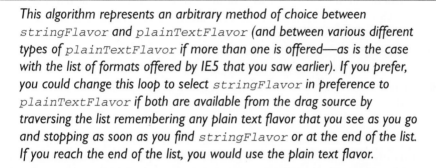

Core Note

This algorithm represents an arbitrary method of choice between `stringFlavor` *and* `plainTextFlavor` *(and between various different types of* `plainTextFlavor` *if more than one is offered—as is the case with the list of formats offered by IE5 that you saw earlier). If you prefer, you could change this loop to select* `stringFlavor` *in preference to* `plainTextFlavor` *if both are available from the drag source by traversing the list remembering any plain text flavor that you see as you go and stopping as soon as you find* `stringFlavor` *or at the end of the list. If you reach the end of the list, you would use the plain text flavor.*

What may not be immediately obvious from the code is that there is a subtlety about the way in which we check for the availability of a plain text flavor. Here is the code that does this:

```
if (flavor.equals(DataFlavor.plainTextFlavor)
        || flavor.equals(DataFlavor.stringFlavor)) {
    selectedFlavor = flavor;
    break;
}
```

Notice that we use the `equals` operator to test whether a flavor from the available flavors list matches `DataFlavor.plainTextFlavor`. It would clearly be presumptuous to replace this by a test of this form:

```
if (flavor == DataFlavor.plainTextFlavor)
```

because there is no guarantee that the `DataFlavor` object that the drag-and-drop subsystem supplies in the list of flavors available from the drag source is exactly the same object as the constant `DataFlavor.plainTextFlavor`. That, however, is not the subtlety in this test. The fact of the matter is that the constant object `DataFlavor.plainTextFlavor` is a flavor that has the following properties:

- It has primary MIME type text with subtype plain.
- Its representation class is `java.io.InputStream`.

- Its MIME type has a `charset` parameter set to `unicode`, indicating that the data stream is encoded in Unicode.

These attributes match exactly those of the `DataFlavor` that will be created by default by the drag-and-drop subsystem for text from a native application that claims to supply Unicode text. However, many applications do not offer Unicode text—they provide the data in the platform's default encoding. In this case, the drag-and-drop subsystem creates a `DataFlavor` which matches the first two attributes of `plainTextFlavor`, but with the charset parameter set to `ascii` instead of Unicode. Nevertheless, this still represents plain text and our drop target can handle it just as easily as if it were encoded in Unicode. Obviously we don't want to have to complicate the `dropContent` method by extracting the MIME type and subtype from the `DataFlavors` offered and explicitly checking to see if they are `text` and `plain` respectively, thereby ignoring the character encoding to match on any kind of plain text. Fortunately, we don't need to do this because, as we noted under "Text and Data Flavors" on page 754, the `DataFlavor` `equals` operator performs exactly this check, ignoring the `charset` parameter, if it is present. Therefore, the test

```
flavor.equals(DataFlavor.plainTextFlavor)
```

evaluates to true if `flavor` is plain text in any encoding, which is exactly what we want here.

Having selected the appropriate transfer format, the next step is to obtain the data by invoking the `getTransferData` method of the `Transferable` returned by the drag-and-drop subsystem, passing it the `DataFlavor` that we have chosen to use. This method returns an `Object`, the type of which matches the representation class of the `DataFlavor`. To insert the data into the `JEditorPane`, we need to have it in the form of a `String`. If the data is being transferred as `DataFlavor.stringFlavor`, `getTransferData` returns it in the form of a `String`, so there is nothing more to do in this case. However, if we are using `DataFlavor.plainTextFlavor`, the `getTransferData` method will return a `java.io.InputStream`. To get the data in the form of a `String`, we need to read it from the `InputStream` and convert it to Unicode. As you know, an `InputStream` delivers a sequence of bytes with a particular encoding and the byte stream must be converted to Unicode using the appropriate character set converter. One way to do this is to create an `InputStreamReader` with the correct encoding and wrap it around the `InputStream`. We've already seen several example of this in earlier chapters. Here, we use an alternative method provided by the `String` class, through the following constructor:

```
public String(byte[] bytes, String encoding);
```

which constructs a `String` from an array of bytes and an encoding name. As Listing 8-4 shows, the first step is to create a byte array of the appropriate size (using the `InputStream available` method to find out how many bytes of data there are) and then read the data from the `InputStream` into the array. The remaining problem is to get the correct encoding. The encoding can be obtained by asking for the `charset` parameter of the `DataFlavor`'s MIME type using the `getParameter` method, so the code should look something like this, assuming that the data has been read into an array called `bytes`:

```
String charSet = selectedFlavor.getParameter("charset");
String insertData = new String(bytes, charSet);
```

However, there is a small problem with this. As we noted earlier, the default `DataFlavor` for plain text specifies the character set `ascii`, which is not a valid Java character encoding. Passing `ascii` to the `String` constructor will cause an `UnsupportedEncodingException`. However, this `charset` value actually means that the data is in the platform's default encoding, which could be handled automatically by creating a `String` using the byte array and without specifying an encoding:

```
insertData = new String(bytes);   // OK if "bytes" in
                                   // platform default encoding
```

Rather than explicitly checking for the value `ascii`, we simply allow the exception to be thrown and then revert to using this simpler constructor:

```
String insertData;
try {
   String charSet = selectedFlavor.getParameter("charset");
   String insertData = new String(bytes, charSet);
} catch (UnsupportedEncodingException e) {
   insertData = new String(bytes);
}
```

Incidentally, this method also works for those applications (such as IE5) that offer data in Unicode. In this case, the data is still read from an `Input-Stream`, in which each byte pair represents a Unicode character. Creating a `String` with `unicode` as the character set will correctly convert such an `InputStream` to Unicode characters, simply by assigning each pair of bytes to a Java `char`.

Finally, having obtained the transfer data as a `String`, we insert it into the `JEditorPane` using its `replaceSelection` method, which replaces whatever is selected with the new data, or inserts it at the location of the cursor if there is no selection. So that you can see exactly what has been dragged, the new text is highlighted by using the JTextComponent select method. In a production environment, you would almost certainly not want to do this.

You can try this example using the command

```
java AdvancedSwing.Chapter8.EditorDropTarget2
```

Once the program has started, drag a file from Windows Explorer onto it to show that the functionality of the first example is still available. Next, start a text editor or a Web browser, select some text from it and drag that over the JEditorPane. You'll find that the drag cursor indicates that a drop could be performed, provided you are not holding down both the CTRL and SHIFT keys to indicate a link operation. When you release the mouse buttons, the text will be transferred to the JEditorPane, as shown in Figure 8-6. Note that if you drag the text from a text editor and indicate a move operation, the text in the editor will be deleted after being dropped on the JEditorPane. Deleting the text is the job of the drag source; it should only be done if the drop target accepted the move operation and the subsequent transfer of data worked. This is why the DropTargetListener drop method must invoke dropComplete with the appropriate success or failure indication.

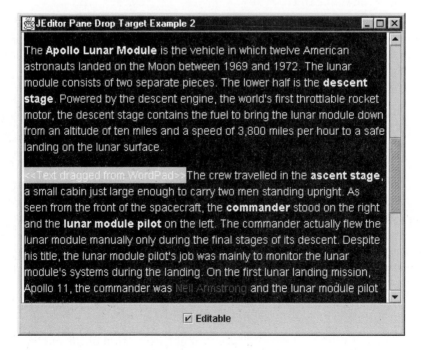

Figure 8-6 Text dragged into JEditorPane.

Incidentally, this example incorporates a checkbox that you can use to switch the JEditorPane between editable and read-only modes. If you make the JEditorPane read-only by clearing this checkbox, you'll find that you can still drag a new file from Windows Explorer but, if you try to drag text, the drag cursor will indicate that the operation is not acceptable and an attempt to drop the text will be ignored.

Providing Drag-Under Feedback

As far as managing the transfer of files or text from an external application to a JEditorPane is concerned, our example drop target is now basically complete. However, we are not finished with it yet. In this section and the next, we're going to add a couple of features that make the drop target more useful from the user's point of view, starting with adding some feedback to indicate that the cursor is over a valid location for the drop. As you know, the drag cursor is automatically changed to indicate whether the currently selected operation is valid, but this isn't always sufficient. Although the drag-and-drop subsystem operates at the component level and therefore the drop target also has the same physical scope, it isn't always the case that the whole area occupied by a component should be considered valid as a drop site.

Consider the case of a JTree displaying a view of a file system, as shown in Figure 8-2. If the user wants to move a file from one location in the file system to another, it is usual to highlight the node of the tree that the file would be dropped into as the user moves the cursor over the view of the file system. When the cursor is not over (or at least near) a node representing a directory, there should be no visible highlighting, so that the user can see that a drop would not succeed. In a proper implementation, of course, in this case, rejectDrag would be called and the cursor would be changed, so that it will be clear to the user that the drop location is unacceptable.

Later in this chapter, you'll see the implementation of a drop target for a JTree and the code that provides the appropriate drop target or drag-under feedback, as it is usually called. In this section, we'll demonstrate how to implement drag-under feedback in the context of the JEditorPane. When it comes to implementing the drop target for the JTree, we'll place the code that triggers the feedback in the same place but the details will, of course, be different.

The JEditorPane drop target can now cope with two different types of data transfer. These two modes of operation are sufficiently different that they merit completely different kinds of drag-under feedback. What we'll implement is the following:

- If the user is dragging a file, the entire JEditorPane is the drop target. In a case like this, it makes sense either to provide no drag-under feedback and to rely solely on the change of cursor shape to indicate to the user that the drop would succeed, or to make a change to the drop target's state that clearly indicates that the whole component would be affected by the drop. In this example, we'll provide the feedback by changing the background color of the editor when the cursor is over it and the drag operation is acceptable; and we'll revert to the original color when the operation is not acceptable, when the drop occurs, or when the user drags the file out of the bounds of the JEditorPane.

- When text is being dragged, the feedback should reflect exactly what will happen when the text is dropped. In the previous version of this example, it was necessary to select the text in the JEditorPane that was to be replaced, or click with the mouse at the point at which the text was to be dropped. Because you can't do this while a drag is in progress, it was necessary to select the insertion point before the drag operation starts. This is not the most convenient interface for the user. In this example, we're going to improve on this by having the insertion point track the cursor as the user drags the text over the JEditorPane. The feedback to the user will be the movement of the caret through the text as the user performs the drag.

The feedback that we give to the user depends on the type of transfer being performed and whether the user's selected operation is acceptable. Because we want to move the editor's insertion caret to track the mouse if the user is dragging text, the drag-under feedback for this case also depends on the location of the mouse. In general, then, we need to be able to switch the feedback on and off when the drag enters the component, each time the mouse moves, when the user's selected operation changes, and when the drag operation leaves the component. To make it easier to replace the details of the feedback should you decide to subclass EditorDropTarget or, more likely, if you decide to use it as the basis for your own drop target, we'll implement the code that provides the feedback in a separate method and call it from dragEnter, dragOver, dropActionChanged, and dragExit. Listing 8-5 shows the code that provides the drag-under feedback for this example.

Listing 8-5 Drag-Under Feedback for a `JEditorPane`

```
protected void dragUnderFeedback(DropTargetDragEvent dtde,
                                 boolean acceptedDrag) {
    if (draggingFile) {
        // When dragging a file, change the background color
        Color newColor = (dtde != null && acceptedDrag ?
                          feedbackColor : backgroundColor);
        if (newColor.equals(pane.getBackground()) == false) {
            changingBackground = true;
            pane.setBackground(newColor);
            changingBackground = false;
            pane.repaint();
        }
    } else {
        if (dtde != null && acceptedDrag) {
            // Dragging text - move the insertion cursor
            Point location = dtde.getLocation();
            pane.getCaret().setVisible(true);
            pane.setCaretPosition(pane.viewToModel(location));
        } else {
            pane.getCaret().setVisible(false);
        }
    }
}
```

The arguments supplied to the `dragUnderFeedback` method represent the information that we would need to pass to it in the most general case. Most of the information about the drag operation is made available to the `DropTargetListener` methods that will invoke `dragUnderFeedback` in the `DropTargetDragEvent` that they receive, including the location of the drag cursor relative to the drop target component and the user's current action. For this reason, we pass the `DropTargetDragEvent` directly to dragUnderFeedback. There is a small problem with this, however—the `dragExit` event is passed a `DropTargetEvent`, not a `DropTargetDragEvent`. DropTargetEvent is the superclass of `DropTargetDragEvent` and carries much less state. Fortunately, in `dragExit` all we need to do is remove whatever dragunder feedback effects have been applied, which does not require contextdependent information available from a `DropTargetDragEvent`. Therefore, when `dragUnderFeedback` is invoked from `dragExit`, we'll pass `null` for the first argument. There is no issue with the `drop` method, which receives a `DropTargetDropEvent`, because you don't concern yourself with drag-under feedback in this method; in fact, by the time `drop` is called, `dragExit` will already have removed the drag-under effects. The second argument to this method indicates whether the drag operation in progress is acceptable to the drop target and is used to decide whether to show or remove the drag-under effects.

Core Note

Purists might prefer to pass a `DropTargetEvent` as the first argument to this method to avoid the use of a `null` reference for the special case of `dragExit`. The drawback with this approach is that it requires you to cast the `DropTargetEvent` to a `DropTargetDragEvent` if you want to get the cursor location or any other context-dependent information from it, which is likely to offend other purists.

The `dragUnderFeedback` method behaves differently depending on whether the object being dragged is a file or some text, which it can determine from the `draggingFile` instance variable. Providing feedback for file dragging is the simpler case—here, all that is necessary is to set the `JEditor-Pane`'s background color. If the drag has not been accepted or we are being called from `dragExit`, which is the case when the first argument is `null`, we need to revert to the component's original background color, which is obtained and stored in the drop target class' constructor. Otherwise, we set a (fixed) background color that indicates that the drop is valid. In the case of this example, the background is changed to gray. Note that before and after the `setBackground` call we toggle the state of an instance variable called `changingBackground`. You'll see later why this is necessary.

When the user is dragging text, a little more work is involved. Here, we want to move the insertion caret to the nearest valid location in the editor to the position of the mouse. To do that, we get the mouse location relative to the `JEditorPane` using the `getLocation` method of `DropTargetDrag-Event`, and then use the `JEditorPane viewToModel` method to convert the mouse position to an offset within the editor pane's document. Finally, the caret is moved to this location using `setCaretPosition`. There is one other point to take note of. Swing text components hide the insertion caret when they don't have the focus, which means that the caret will not be visible during the drag operation. For this reason, before setting the caret location we make the caret visible; conversely, if we are removing the drag-under effect, we switch the caret off again.

With the implementation of the `dragUnderFeedback` method complete, the only other change is to call it at the appropriate times. As we said earlier, we need to call this method whenever the selected drop operation or the position of the cursor might have changed and when the drag operation is terminated. This means that we need to call it from `dragEnter`, `dragOver`, `dropActionChanged`, and `dragExit`. In all cases, this requires the addition of one line of code. Because nothing else in those methods needs to change for this example, we're not going to bother to reproduce the entire source listing here. Instead, for the purposes of illustration we'll show only the change to the `dragExit` method:

```
public void dragExit(DropTargetEvent dte) {
    DnDUtils.debugPrintln("DropTarget dragExit");


    // Do drag-under feedback
    dragUnderFeedback(null, false);
}
```

The `dragExit` method is, as noted earlier, a special case because it doesn't receive a `DropTargetDragEvent`, so the first argument passed to `dragUnderFeedback` here is `null`. The second argument is also fixed—it's `false` to indicate that the drag has not been accepted. Both of these settings indicate to `dragUnderFeedback` that it should remove any drag-under effects previously applied.

You can try this example by typing the command:

```
java AdvancedSwing.Chapter8.EditorDropTarget3
```

and then dragging a file over the editor component. As you do so, the component's blank background will change from white to gray, as shown in Figure 8-7; if you drag the cursor out of the component without dropping the file, you'll see that it will revert to its original color. The same thing happens if you cancel the drag while the file is over the editor by pressing the ESCAPE key. If you now drop a file onto the editor, and then drag some text over it, you'll see that the insertion caret tracks the mouse as you move it over the component and, when you drop the text, it will be inserted where the caret last appeared. Because our drag-under feedback code moves the insertion caret as you move the mouse, there is no need to modify the `dropContent` method to have the text inserted at this location.

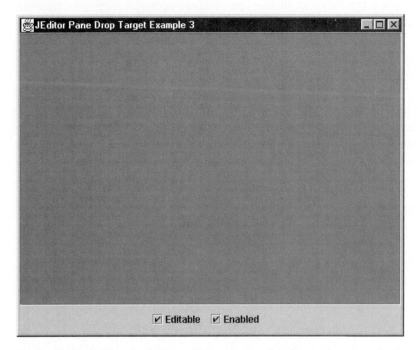

Figure 8-7   Drag-under feedback while dragging a file over `JEditorPane`.

Like the last example, this one has a checkbox that enables you to make the editor editable or read-only and it also has a second one that you can use to enable or disable the `JEditorPane`. The effect of making the editor read-only depends on the drag operation being performed—that is, we do not allow text to be dragged onto a read-only editor, but it is acceptable to drag a file and open it in read-only mode. When the editor is disabled, however, it should not be possible to do either of these things. If you look back to the previous example, you'll see that we explicitly took into account whether the drop target component was editable when deciding to accept or reject both the drag and the drop operations. We could handle a disabled component by adding similar checks to the same methods, but there is a better way. The `DropTarget` object itself has an `active` attribute that you can set when it is created and subsequently change as required. If you make the `DropTarget` inactive, it behaves as if it is not a drop target at all. In other words, the `DropTargetListener`'s `dragEnter`, `dragOver`, `dragExit`, `dropAction-Changed`, and `drop` methods will never be called for an inactive `DropTarget`. We take advantage of this by setting the `DropTarget`'s active attribute in its constructor, as shown in Listing 8-6.

Listing 8-6 Setting the Active Attribute for a `DropTarget`

```
public EditorDropTarget3(JEditorPane pane) {
   this.pane = pane;

   // Listen for changes in the enabled property
   pane.addPropertyChangeListener(this);

   // Save the JEditorPane's background color
   backgroundColor = pane.getBackground();

   // Create the DropTarget and register
   // it with the JEditorPane.
   dropTarget = new DropTarget(pane,
      DnDConstants.ACTION_COPY_OR_MOVE,
      this,
      pane.isEnabled(), null);
}
```

Here, the `DropTarget` will be active if the editor is enabled and inactive if it is not. This, however, is not sufficient because the enabled state of the editor could change later and we need the active attribute of the `DropTarget` to track the change. Fortunately, the enabled state of a `JComponent` is exposed as a bound property, which allows us to receive notification of changes to it by registering a `PropertyChangeListener`, as you can see from Listing 8-6. The `propertyChange` method then simply reflects the state of the enabled attribute of the component in the active state of the `DropTarget`, as shown in Listing 8-7.

Listing 8-7 Tracking the Enabled and Background Attributes of a Component

```
public void propertyChange(PropertyChangeEvent evt) {
   String propertyName = evt.getPropertyName();
   if (propertyName.equals("enabled")) {
      // Enable the drop target if the JEditorPane is enabled
      // and vice versa.
      dropTarget.setActive(pane.isEnabled());
   } else if (!changingBackground &&
             propertyName.equals("background")) {
      backgroundColor = pane.getBackground();
   }
}
```

This method also serves another purpose. As noted earlier, to toggle the background color of the drop target component between its original color and the color needed for drag-under feedback, we store the initial background color as an instance variable of our drop target class. This, of course, is not sufficient because the program could change the background color after the original value has been saved. The solution for this problem is the same as for the `DropTarget` active state because the background color is also a bound property of the editor, so we can update the saved background color from the `propertyChange` method as the change is made. There is a catch, however, because the drag-under feedback causes the background color to change, which will result in `propertyChange` being invoked. If we did nothing about this, we would store the feedback color as the original background color. This is why the `dragUnderFeedback` method used the `changingBackground` instance variable to indicate that this background color change is to be ignored; when the background property changes, it is ignored if `changingBackground` is `true`. You can try this by clearing the enabled checkbox and then attempting to drag both text and a file onto the `JEditorPane`. In both cases, you'll find that the drag cursor will show that the operation is invalid, there will be no drag-under feedback, and dropping the file or text will be ignored.

Scrolling the Drop Target

The final enhancement that we're going to make to our drop target example will make it possible for the user to drag text to a location in the editor that is not actually visible when the drag operation begins. With the current implementation, as you drag text over the `JEditorPane`, the insertion caret tracks the mouse so that you can indicate exactly where you would like to drop the text. However, a `JEditorPane` is usually enclosed in a `JScrollPane` and, if there is enough text in the editor, at any given time a certain amount of it will not be visible. When this is the case, the user will try to drag the text in the direction of the part of the document where the insertion should take place by moving the mouse to the top, bottom, left, or right of the `JScrollPane`, in the expectation that this will cause the editor's content to be scrolled to bring the drop position into view. Unfortunately, although the drag-and-drop subsystem has autoscrolling built in, it does not work automatically—you have to implement an interface called `java.awt.dnd.Autoscroll` through which you can be notified when the user's drag gesture might require to scroll the drop target component. It is your responsibility to decide the direction and distance of the scroll and to carry it out.

In the first three drop target examples in this chapter, to maximize reusability, the code was part of a separate class that could be used to provide the drop target functionality for any JEditorPane. Unfortunately, autoscrolling is different and cannot easily be made part of a separate class in this way. Autoscrolling is supported by the DropTarget and is enabled only if the Component that you register via its constructor or its setComponent method directly implements the Autoscroll interface. In other words, an unmodifed JEditorPane cannot have autoscrolling switched on simply by using another class, which provides the autoscrolling capability, as an adapter as we have been doing in this chapter to add its drop target functionality. Therefore for this example, instead of modifying the EditorDropTarget class, we'll be developing a subclass of JEditorPane, called AutoScrollingEditorPane, which implements the Autoscroll interface, and using that instead of an ordinary JEditorPane. By doing this, we'll be able to keep the example simple enough so that we can concentrate on showing how the drag-and-drop mechanism interacts with the component to tell it when to scroll.

The Autoscroll interface has only two methods:

```
public interface Autoscroll {
    public Insets getAutoscrollInsets();
    public void autoscroll(Point cursorLocn);
}
```

The idea is that when the drag cursor is close to the edge of the component, the autoscroll method is called to allow the component to be scrolled. The getAutoscrollInsets method is used to determine how close the cursor must be to the edge of the component before the DropTarget will call the autoscroll method; in fact, there are also other constraints that must be satisfied but, to avoid complicating things, we'll postpone looking at those until later. Let's first see how this works in practice by looking at an example. Type the following command:

```
java AdvancedSwing.Chapter8.EditorDropTarget4
```

and then drag a fairly large file onto the editor, such as its own source code from the file EditorDropTarget4.java, as shown in Figure 8-8.

With the source file displayed in the editor, select some text from another application and drag it over the editor. The drag cursor should indicate that the drop operation is valid. Now drag the text down toward the bottom of the visible area. As you reach the last line of the text, providing you don't drag the mouse too quickly, the content of the editor will begin to scroll upward, bring text from further down the file into view. This will continue to happen as long as you keep the drag cursor relatively motionless near the position that it occupied when scrolling commenced. If you drag the cursor up to the top of the editor, you'll find that the source file will scroll in the opposite direction. Similarly, dragging the text to the right will scroll the content a very small distance horizontally, an effect that can be reversed by dragging the text back over to the left. This is the autoscroll feature in action—if you try to do this with the previous example (EditorDropTarget3), which does not have autoscroll suport, you'll find that the editor does not scroll when you drag text to its edges.

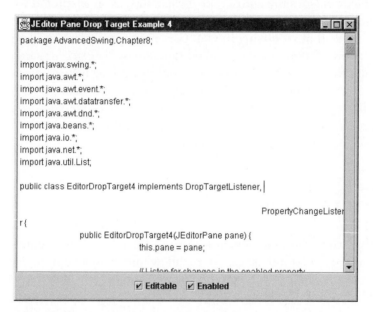

Figure 8-8   Supporting drop target autoscroll.

To trigger the scrolling action, you have to drag the text close to the edge of the editor's visible area. Let's look at the components involved in this example to see exactly how this works.

Figure 8-9 shows a JEditorPane wrapped in a JScrollPane. This is a rather unusual view of this arrangement; when you see this on the screen, only the part of the JEditorPane that falls within the viewing area of the JScrollPane is actually visible, whereas Figure 8-9 shows the whole JEditorPane, including the parts of it that are not in view. For most purposes, the JEditorPane neither knows nor cares that it is enclosed in a JScrollPane. When mouse events are reported to the JEditorPane, for example, the coordinates are given relative to the top left of the JEditorPane, rather than relative to the JScrollPane. When it comes to autoscrolling, this is a very important point. The user expects autoscrolling to be triggered when the mouse approaches the edge of the visible area of the scrolled area, which is the region shown darkly shaded in Figure 8-9, and the `Autoscroll` interface provides the `getAutoscrollInsets` method, which returns the insets that represent the critical area within which the autoscrolling operation should be performed.

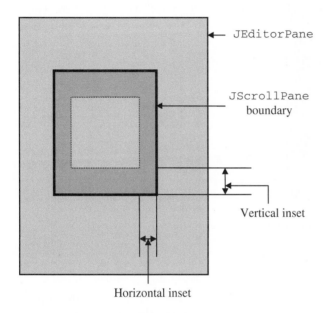

Figure 8-9   The apparent insets that trigger drop target autoscrolling.

You might at first think that this would be the highlighted area shown in Figure 8-9, but that is not the case. The drag-and-drop mechanism works with respect to the drop target component, not the `JScrollPane`—it is, in fact, unaware of the `JScrollPane`. Suppose your intended effect is for autoscrolling to happen when the mouse is within eight pixels of the boundary of the `JScrollPane`. The obvious thing to do would be to implement the `getAutoscrollInsets` method like this:

```
public Insets getAutoscrollInsets() {
   return new Insets(8, 8, 8, 8);
}
```

If you do this, however, the autoscrolling region you set up will be as shown in Figure 8-10.

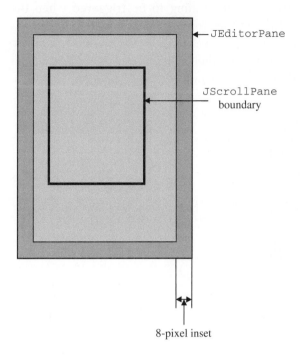

JEditorPane

JScrollPane
boundary

8-pixel inset

Figure 8-10 Incorrect autoscrolling insets.

The eight-pixel insets returned from `getAutoscrollInsets` are applied to the `JEditorPane` itself, *not* to the visible area of the `JScrollPane`. This means that, in general, most or all of the autoscrolling region will be inaccessible to the user. In fact, the correct insets to return from `getAutoscrollInsets` are illustrated in Figure 8-11.

As you can see, to calculate the correct insets, you need to take into account both the position of the origin of the `JEditorPane` relative to the viewable area of the `JScrollPane` and the size of the viewable area, as well as the apparent eight-pixel insets that you want the user to perceive. Because of this, the required insets change as the user scrolls the viewable area of the `JEditorPane`, because the scrolling action moves the location of the `JScrollPane` relative to the `JEditorPane`. Fortunately, the `getAutoscrollInsets` method is invoked each time the drag-and-drop subsystem tries to determine whether the mouse is within the autoscroll area and you can return different insets on each call if necessary.

Now let's look at the code for the `AutoScrollingEditorPane` class to see how the `getAutoscrollInsets` method is actually implemented; the code is shown in Listing 8-8.

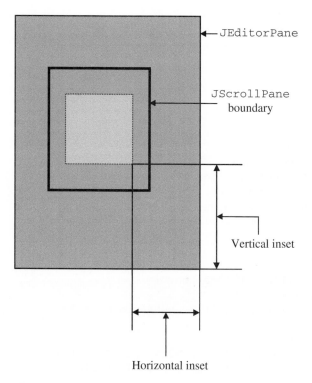

```
                                    ←─ JEditorPane



                                    JScrollPane
                                      boundary






                                    Vertical inset




                    Horizontal inset
```

Figure 8-11 Correct autoscrolling insets.

Listing 8-8 A `JEditorPane` with Autoscrolling Support

```java
package AdvancedSwing.Chapter8;

import javax.swing.*;
import java.awt.*;
import java.awt.dnd.*;

public class AutoScrollingEditorPane extends JEditorPane
                                    implements Autoscroll {
    public static final Insets defaultScrollInsets =
                                    new Insets(8, 8, 8, 8);
    protected Insets scrollInsets = defaultScrollInsets;

    public AutoScrollingEditorPane() {
    }

    public void setScrollInsets(Insets insets) {
        this.scrollInsets = insets;
    }
```

> **Listing 8-8 A `JEditorPane` with Autoscrolling Support (continued)**

```
public Insets getScrollInsets() {
  return scrollInsets;
}

// Implementation of Autoscroll interface
public Insets getAutoscrollInsets() {
  Rectangle r = getVisibleRect();
  Dimension size = getSize();
  Insets i = new Insets(r.y + scrollInsets.top,
        r.x + scrollInsets.left,
        size.height - r.y - r.height + scrollInsets.bottom,
        size.width - r.x - r.width + scrollInsets.right);
  return i;
}

public void autoscroll(Point location) {
  JScrollPane scroller =
        (JScrollPane)SwingUtilities.getAncestorOfClass(
        JScrollPane.class, this);
  if (scroller != null) {
    JScrollBar hBar = scroller.getHorizontalScrollBar();
    JScrollBar vBar = scroller.getVerticalScrollBar();
    Rectangle r = getVisibleRect();
    if (location.x <= r.x + scrollInsets.left) {
      // Need to scroll left
      hBar.setValue(hBar.getValue() -
                            hBar.getUnitIncrement(-1));
    }
    if (location.y <= r.y + scrollInsets.top) {
      // Need to scroll up
      vBar.setValue(vBar.getValue() -
                            vBar.getUnitIncrement(-1));
    }
    if (location.x >= r.x + r.width - scrollInsets.right) {
      // Need to scroll right
      hBar.setValue(hBar.getValue() +
                            hBar.getUnitIncrement(1));
    }
    if (location.y >= r.y + r.height - scrollInsets.bottom) {
      // Need to scroll down
      vBar.setValue(vBar.getValue() +
                            vBar.getUnitIncrement(1));
    }
  }
}
}
```

AutoScrollingEditorPane is a subclass of JEditorPane that has a default autoscroll insets of eight pixels on each side of the JScrollPane that it is wrapped in. The setScrollInsets method can be used to set a different value for this property on a per-component basis. The only other difference between this component and JEditorPane is the fact that it implements the Autoscroll interface. When you construct a DropTarget and pass it a component that implements Autoscroll, or use the Drop-Target setComponent method to associate it with such a component, autoscrolling is automatically enabled and the getAutoscrollInsets and autoscroll methods of the Autoscroll interface will be called at the appropriate times.

Let's look first at the getAutoscrollInsets method, which must return an Insets object that corresponds to the darker shaded area of Figure 8-11. To calculate the correct insets, you need to know the coordinates of the visible area of the JEditorPane relative to its origin, which corresponds to the dark-outlined rectangle in Figure 8-11. You can obtain this from the JEditorPane getVisibleRect method, which returns a Rectangle describing the shape of the visible area. In terms of the variables used in the implementation of getAutoscrollInsets shown in Listing 8-8, the attributes of this Rectangle are illustrated in Figure 8-12.

In the implementation of getAutoscrollInsets, the variables used are as follows:

r A Rectangle describing the visible area of the JEditorPane. The x and y coordinates are measured relative to the origin of the JEditorPane and are shown as the values r.x and r.y in Figure 8-12. Similarly, the values r.width and r.height correspond to the width and height of the visible area and measure the size of the dark-outlined area in the diagram.

size A Dimension object that holds the actual size of the JEditorPane as returned by the getSize method. The size.width value, for example, gives the width of the JEditorPane, as indicated in Figure 8-12.

scrollInsets An Insets object that describes the *apparent* insets of the autoscroll area as seen by the user. Figure 8-12 shows the measurements represented by two instance variables of this object, scrollInsets.bottom and scrollInsets.right. As you can see, these inset values describe the autoscroll area by reference to the dark-outlined area, which represents the JScrollPane.

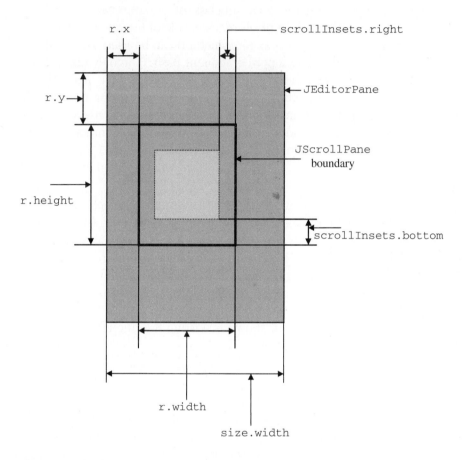

Figure 8-12 Calculating autoscrolling insets.

From the previous definitions and Figure 8-12, it is easy to see how to calculate the insets of the autoscroll area relative to the JEditorPane, which is what getAutoscrollInsets needs to return. The left inset, for example, is the sum of the horizontal distance from the left of the JEditorPane to the left side of the JScrollPane's viewing area (represented by the dark outline) and the left inset of the region represented by scrollInsets or, in other words

```
r.x + scrollInsets.left
```

Similarly, the top inset is the sum of the distance from the top of the JEditorPane to the top of the JScrollPane and the top inset of scrollInsets, that is

```
r.y + scrollInsets.top
```

These are exactly the values used in the implementation of the getAuto-scrollInsets method in Listing 8-8. The right and bottom insets values are slightly more difficult to compute. The right inset is the distance from the right edge of the JEditorPane to the right edge of the area shown in the JScrollPane, plus the right inset of scrollInsets. From Figure 8-12, you can see that the distance to the right edge of the JEditorPane is given by size.width, while the distance to the right edge of the JScrollPane is (r.x + r.width), from which it follows that the right inset is

```
(size.width - (r.x + r.width)) + scrollInsets.right
```

which simplifies (on removal of the parentheses) to the value used in Listing 8-8. Similarly, the bottom inset is given by

```
(size.height - (r.y.+ r.height)) + scrollInsets.bottom
```

which again matches with the expression used in Listing 8-8.

The other method that you need to implement is the autoscroll method, which is responsible for actually moving the visible area of the JEditorPane within the window of the JScrollPane so that it scrolls in the direction in which the user is trying to drag the text to be dropped. The autoscroll method is passed only a single Point object that describes the location of the drag cursor, relative to the JEditorPane. Given only this single piece of information, the autoscroll method needs to determine:

1. In which direction (or directions) the JEditorPane should be scrolled.
2. By how much the JEditorPane should scroll, if at all.

The answer to the first of these questions can be expressed as follows:

- If the drag cursor is near the top of the visible area, scroll the content downward.
- If the drag cursor is near the bottom of the visible area, scroll the content upward.
- If the drag cursor is near the left of the visible area, scroll the content to the right.
- If the drag cursor is near the right of the visible area, scroll the content to the left.

These descriptions are all expressed in terms of the visible area of the JEditorPane, but the location that the autoscroll method is given is relative to the origin of the JEditorPane, not relative to its visible region. However, we know that it is within the autoscroll insets area, which is also expressed relative to the origin of the JEditorPane, so it is possible to compare the cursor position with the insets returned by getAutoscrollInsets. As an example, the drag cursor is near the top of the visible area if its y coordinate places it within the top inset of the dark shaded area in Figure 8-12, which, from the calculation used for the left inset returned by getAutoscrollInsets, is given by the value r.y + scrollInsets.top. In other words, we should scroll downward if the condition

```
location.y <= r.y + scrollInsets.top
```

is true. Similarly, the drag cursor is near the left of the visible area if its x coordinate is less than r.x + scrollInsets.right. The expressions used for determining whether the drag cursor is near the bottom or right of the visible area can similarly be deduced from the expressions used to compute the right and bottom insets in getAutoscrollInsets. Note that, if the drag cursor is in a corner of the visible area, it will be close enough to two sides to cause more than one of these conditions to be satisfied which will cause the JEditorPane to scroll both horizontally and vertically.

Having determined in which direction or directions the JEditorPane must be scrolled, the only remaining question is how far to scroll it. The obvious answer to this question is to scroll up and down by the height of one line of text, or left and right by the width of a character. However, while this could be made to work for JEditorPane, it is not a very generic solution—it would be better if the autoscroll method could be made independent of such concepts as lines or characters of text, so that the same code could be reused for other components. So far, all the code that you have seen in connection with implementing autoscrolling depends only on the drop target component being a JComponent (because getVisibleRect is actually a JComponent method and so is not specific to JEditorPane). Fortunately this is quite easy to do. The JScrollBar component has two attributes that determine how far the component that it contains is moved when the user clicks on the scrollbar—the *unit increment* and the *page increment*. The former corresponds most closely to the concepts of line and character for a text component. In fact, the Swing text components implement an interface called Scrollable that allows scrollbars to interrogate them to find out how far they should be scrolled each time a scrolling movement is necessary. This makes it possible for them to scroll by different amounts depending on the font in use, or even to continue to scroll a line at a time if different lines use different fonts and so require different scroll distances. By using the scrollbar getUnitIncrement method to obtain the scrolling distance, we allow the component itself to determine how far it will be scrolled, and we have a solution that will work for any drop target component, whether or not it implements the `Scrollable` interface.

Core Note

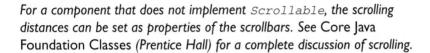

For a component that does not implement Scrollable, *the scrolling distances can be set as properties of the scrollbars. See* Core Java Foundation Classes *(Prentice Hall) for a complete discussion of scrolling.*

For convenience, the code for the `autoscroll` method is reproduced next. This method is, of course, an instance method of the `JEditorPane` and has no direct knowledge of the `JScrollPane` that the editor might be wrapped in. The first task, therefore, is to obtain a reference to that `JScrollPane`, which is done using the `SwingUtilities getAncestorOf-Class` method. This method searches the component hierarchy of the component passed as its second argument to find an ancestor component of the class given as the first argument. The code shown here will find the first `JScrollPane` enclosing the `AutoScrollingEditorPane`. From here, the scrollbars themselves can be found using the `getHorizontalScrollBar` and `getVerticalScrollBar` methods.

```
public void autoscroll(Point location) {
   JScrollPane scroller =
               (JScrollPane)SwingUtilities.getAncestorOfClass(
               JScrollPane.class, this);
   if (scroller != null) {
      JScrollBar hBar = scroller.getHorizontalScrollBar();
      JScrollBar vBar = scroller.getVerticalScrollBar();
      Rectangle r = getVisibleRect();
      if (location.x <= r.x + scrollInsets.left) {
         // Need to scroll left
         hBar.setValue(hBar.getValue() -
                  hBar.getUnitIncrement(-1));
      }
      if (location.y <= r.y + scrollInsets.top) {
         // Need to scroll up
         vBar.setValue(vBar.getValue() -
                  vBar.getUnitIncrement(-1));
      }
      if (location.x >= r.x + r.width - scrollInsets.right) {
         // Need to scroll right
         hBar.setValue(hBar.getValue() +
         hBar.getUnitIncrement(1));
```

```
      }
      if (location.y >= r.y + r.height - scrollInsets.bottom) {
         // Need to scroll down.setValue(vBar.getValue() +
                                    vBar.getUnitIncrement(1));
      }
   }
}
```

Once the scrollbars have been located, the code uses the getUnitIncrement method with argument +1 if it needs to scroll the JEditorPane right or down or –1 to scroll left or up. This method returns the amount by which the scrollbar's value should be changed to move a distance of one unit in the requested direction. The returned value is, however, always positive and is either added to (to move right or down) or subtracted from (to move left or up) the current value of the scrollbar to properly adjust the view of the JEditorPane.

Note that the value +1 or –1 passed to the getUnitIncrement method does *not* determine the sign of the returned value, which is always zero or positive. Instead, it is used to allow the scrollbar to return a different value for movement in different directions. This might be required, for example, if the JScrollPane contained a Scrollable that manages a text component in which each line is a different height, so that moving up one line would require a movement by a different distance than would moving one line downward.

Implementing a Drag Source

Now that you've seen how to implement a drop target, the next step is to create a drag source. We've already covered most of the information that you need to build a drag source (refer back to "Architecture of the Java Drag-and-Drop Subsystem" on page 716 if you need to remind yourself of drag source basics) and, in the next section, we'll see how to build a drag source for a tree that's showing a graphical view of a file system. Here, we'll implement a simple (but not very useful) drag source to show you the basics and to demonstrate how to create a customized Transferable object to allow data to be moved to the drop target.

Before looking at the code, let's first see the drag source in action. Type the following command:

```
java AdvancedSwing.Chapter8.JLabelDragSource
```

This creates a small frame with a single JLabel mounted on it, as shown in Figure 8-13.

Figure 8-13   A drag source for a JLabel.

The JLabel in this example is functioning as a drag source, making its text available to drop targets that can accept either a Unicode string or plain text. To demonstrate this, start a text editor, and then click with the mouse on the JLabel and drag it over the text editor. If the editor supports drag-and-drop, the cursor should change to indicate that there is data to be dropped and releasing the mouse will copy the label's text into the editor. The result of performing this operation on the Windows platform with WordPad as the drop target is shown in Figure 8-14.

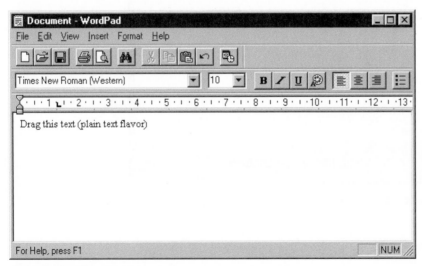

Figure 8-14   Text dragged from a JLabel to WordPad.

In this case, the data that has actually been transferred is the label's text plus a description of the flavor used to perform the data transfer. As you'll see, the Transferable that this example uses offers two flavors, the choice between these two being made by the drop target. So that you can see which one was chosen, the `Transferable` adds this debugging information to the data that it is asked to move. WordPad accepts the data in plain text format, but if you start our last `JEditorPane` drop target example using the command

```
java AdvancedSwing.Chapter8.EditorDropTarget4
```

and drop the text over the `JEditorPane`, you'll see that it chooses to accept the data as a Unicode string, as shown in Figure 8-15. The fact that this choice is made is determined entirely by the order in which the available flavors are presented to our drop target implementation, which, as you saw in Listing 8-4, chooses the first flavor that it understands from the list presented to it.

Figure 8-15   Text dragged from a `JLabel` to `JEditorPane`.

Implementing the *JLabel* Drag Source

The code for the drag source is shown in Listing 8-9. As was the case with the drop target, we choose to implement the drag source as a separate class instead of subclassing `JLabel` to produce a label with built-in drag source support. As noted earlier, this makes it easier to plug drag-and-drop functionality into existing GUI interfaces without having to replace any of the components.

Listing 8-9 A Drag Source for a `JLabel`

```
package AdvancedSwing.Chapter8;

import java.awt.*;
import java.awt.datatransfer.*;
import java.awt.dnd.*;
import java.util.*;
import javax.swing.*;

public class JLabelDragSource implements DragGestureListener,
                          DragSourceListener {
   public JLabelDragSource(JLabel label) {
      this.label = label;

      // Use the default DragSource
      DragSource dragSource = DragSource.getDefaultDragSource();

      // Create a DragGestureRecognizer and
      // register as the listener
      dragSource.createDefaultDragGestureRecognizer(
               label, DnDConstants.ACTION_COPY_OR_MOVE, this);
   }

   // Implementation of DragGestureListener interface.
   public void dragGestureRecognized(DragGestureEvent dge) {
      if (DnDUtils.isDebugEnabled()) {
         DnDUtils.debugPrintln("Initiating event is " +
                             dge.getTriggerEvent());
         DnDUtils.debugPrintln("Complete event set is:");
         Iterator iter = dge.iterator();
         while (iter.hasNext()) {
            DnDUtils.debugPrintln("\t" + iter.next());
         }
      }
      Transferable transferable = new JLabelTransferable(label);
      dge.startDrag(null, transferable, this);
   }

   // Implementation of DragSourceListener interface
   public void dragEnter(DragSourceDragEvent dsde) {
       DnDUtils.debugPrintln("Drag Source: dragEnter,
                   drop action = " + DnDUtils.showActions(
                   dsde.getDropAction()));
   }
```

Listing 8-9 A Drag Source for a `JLabel` (continued)

```
public void dragOver(DragSourceDragEvent dsde) {
    DnDUtils.debugPrintln("Drag Source: dragOver,
                drop action = " + DnDUtils.showActions(
                dsde.getDropAction()));
}

public void dragExit(DragSourceEvent dse) {
    DnDUtils.debugPrintln("Drag Source: dragExit");
}

public void dropActionChanged(DragSourceDragEvent dsde) {
    DnDUtils.debugPrintln("Drag Source: dropActionChanged,
                drop action = " + DnDUtils.showActions(
                dsde.getDropAction()));
}

public void dragDropEnd(DragSourceDropEvent dsde) {
    DnDUtils.debugPrintln("Drag Source: drop completed,
                drop action = " + DnDUtils.showActions(
                dsde.getDropAction()) + ", success: " +
                dsde.getDropSuccess());
}

public static void main(String[] args) {
    JFrame f = new JFrame("Draggable JLabel");
    JLabel label = new JLabel("Drag this text", JLabel.CENTER);
    label.setFont(new Font("Serif", Font.BOLD, 32));
    f.getContentPane().add(label);
    f.pack();
    f.setVisible(true);

    // Attach the drag source
    JLabelDragSource dragSource = new JLabelDragSource(label);
}

protected JLabel label;    // The associated JLabel
}
```

The basic support from the drag-and-drop subsystem for a drag source is provided by the `DragSource` class, which was described in outline earlier in this chapter. To implement a drag source for a component, you need to create a `DragSource` and then register a `DragGestureRecognizer` that ties together the `DragSource` and the component itself.

As we said in our earlier discussion of the `DragSource` class, you can opt to use a single `DragSource` for each component that you want to add drag source capability to. To do this, you simply use the default constructor:

```
DragSource dragSource = new DragSource();
```

However, the `DragSource` does not need to have a one-to-one relationship with the drag source component and, in fact, there is no direct connection to the drag source component at all. Because of this, it is possible to use a single `DragSource` to manage all the drag source components in an application, and the `DragSource` class provides a static method that returns a reference to a default instance that is created automatically for you:

```
DragSource dragSource = DragSource.getDefaultDragSource();
```

The connection between a `DragSource` and a specific drag source component is made by a `DragGestureRecognizer`. The job of the `DragGesture-Recognizer` is to monitor the drag source component for events that indicate that the user wants to start a drag operation. You need a different instance of `DragGestureRecognizer` for each drag source component; when you create it, it registers itself to receive the events from the component that will enable it to recognize the user's drag gesture. The drag-and-drop subsystem provides a subclass of `DragGestureRecognizer` that listens to mouse events delivered to the drag source component and triggers notification according to the platform-specific criteria described in "The Drag Source" on page 713. Using this predefined class is simple—you just use the `DragSource create-DefaultDragGestureRecognizer` method:

```
dragSource.createDefaultDragGestureRecognizer(
        label, DnDConstants.ACTION_COPY_OR_MOVE, this);
```

The first argument specifies the drag source component on which the default `DragGestureRecognizer` will register to receive mouse events. The second argument supplies the list of operations that the drag source will support. In this example, we allow the user to drag text from the label using either a copy or a move gesture although, in fact, the semantics of the operation will be the same whichever operation the user chooses, because we won't delete the label's text in the case of a move operation. We make this choice because it is more convenient for the user to select a move than a copy, which requires the CTRL key to be held down in addition to the mouse gesture.

The third argument to this method is the most important one because it supplies a reference to the `DragGestureListener` that will be notified when the `DragGestureRecognizer` detects a request by the user to start a drag operation. The `DragGestureListener` interface is a very simple one, consisting of a single method. As shown in Figure 8-1, it is possible to associate a single `DragGestureListener` instance with more than one `DragGesture-Recognizer` (and therefore with more than one drag source component), but in this case the `DragGestureListener` functionality is implemented directly within the `JLabelDragSource` object itself, so that the third argument to `createDefaultDragGestureRecognizer` is this.

Core Note

The `DragSource` *class has another method that you can use to create a* `DragGestureRecognizer`:

```
public DragGestureRecognizer createDragGestureRecognizer(
            Class recognizerAbstractClass, Component c,
            int actions, DragGestureListener dgl);
```

The interesting thing about this method is that its first argument is described as an abstract subclass of `DragGestureRecognizer` *and the returned object is described as an instance of a class derived from this abstract subclass. What does this mean? In practice, in the current implementation of drag-and-drop, this method only works if the first argument has value* `java.awt.dnd.MouseDragGestureRecognizer.class` *and, when you call it with this value, it returns an instance of the platform-specific class that recognizes mouse gestures. This is, of course, the same as if you had simply called* `createDefaultDragGestureRecognizer`. *Any other value passed as the first argument will cause* `createDragGestureRecognizer` *to return* `null`. *This method will only be potentially useful to application developers when the drag-and-drop subsystem supplies more than one drag gesture recognizer.*

Implementing the `DragGestureListener` interface requires you to provide only the `dragGestureRecognized` method, which is called when the user has made the appropriate gesture to initiate a drag operation. This method must decide whether to allow the drag operation to start and to invoke the `startDrag` method if it should. Returning from `dragGesture-Recognized` without calling `startDrag` will cause the user's drag gesture to be ignored. Here is how this method is implemented in `JLabelDragSource`:

```
// Implementation of DragGestureListener interface.
public void dragGestureRecognized(DragGestureEvent dge) {
    if (DnDUtils.isDebugEnabled()) {
```

```
    DnDUtils.debugPrintln("Initiating event is " +
                          dge.getTriggerEvent());
    DnDUtils.debugPrintln("Complete event set is:");
    Iterator iter = dge.iterator();
    while (iter.hasNext()) {
        DnDUtils.debugPrintln("\t" + iter.next());
        Transferable transferable =
                          new JLabelTransferable(label);
    }
    dge.startDrag(null, transferable, this);
}
```

As you can see, this implementation always accepts the drag operation because there are no extra conditions to be met before we allow the user to drag the label's text. In a more complex drag source, the `dragGestureRecognized` method might want to perform some extra checks before allowing the drag to proceed. We said earlier that it is possible to share a single `DragGestureListener` among multiple drag sources, but you will almost certainly need some context to carry out validity checks. The `DragGestureEvent` passed to `dragGestureRecognized` has methods that provide the following state information:

- The component acting as the drag source.
- The `DragSource` object associated with the `DragGestureListener`.
- The user's selected drag action (copy, move, or link).
- The position of the mouse within the drag source component at the point that the drag was initiated.
- The `DragGestureRecognizer` handling the event.
- The first event that triggered the gesture that started the drag.
- An iterator that can be used to retrieve all the events that were part of the gesture recognition process.

In the next section, you'll see a drag source that makes use of some of this state information to decide whether to allow a user to drag entries from a `JTree`. The most obvious check to make in this case is whether the mouse is over a tree node and whether that node represents something that could be dragged. Making this check requires access to a reference to the drag source component and the coordinates of the mouse within that component, both of which can be obtained from the `DragGestureEvent`.

In some circumstances, it can be useful to have the set of events that caused the drag gesture to be recognized. As far as the mouse gesture recognizer is concerned, the `DragGestureEvent` `getTriggerEvent` method returns a `MouseEvent` for the mouse press that started the gesture, which includes the initial location of the cursor. You can also get this information more easily from the `getDragOrigin` method. If you need all the events, you can get them using the `iterator` method, which allows you to step through the events in the order in which they were delivered. The `dragGestureRec-ognized` method of `JLabelDragSource` prints the complete list of events if you run it with the `DnDExamples.debug` property defined:

```
java -DDnDExamples.debug AdvancedSwing.Chapter8.JLabelDragSource
```

If you start a drag and release the mouse as soon as the drag has been recognized, you'll see a stream of events printed in the window in which you typed the above command. The event list always begins with a `MOUSE_PRESSED` event (the same event returned by `getTriggerEvent`) and contains all the `MOUSE_DRAGGED` events up to the point at which the gesture was recognized which, as described earlier, occurs when the cursor has moved five pixels horizontally or vertically from its initial location, or when the mouse is dragged outside the component.

The most important `DragGestureEvent` method is `startDrag`, which has two variants:

- `public void startDrag(Cursor dragCursor,`
    `    Image dragImage, Point imageOffset,`
    `    Transferable transferable, DragSourceListener dsl)`
    `    throws InvalidDnDOperationException`
- `public void startDrag(Cursor dragCursor,`
    `    Transferable transferable, DragSourceListener dsl)`
    `    throws InvalidDnDOperationException`

These two methods achieve the same thing, with the exception that the second version does not specify an image or an image offset. In our simple drag source, we use this second variant. The arguments are used as follows:

`dragCursor`   Specifies the cursor shape to be used when the drag is not accepted by the drop target or when the cursor is not over a drop target. You can specify any cursor here, including an animated cursor. If you don't want to use a special cursor, you can use the platform default one (which is usually a no-entry sign) by supplying this argument as `null`.

dragImage   Some platforms enable you to supply an image that is displayed in addition to the drag cursor when a drag is in progress. If you need to provide extra feedback to the user in this way, you can use this argument to supply the Image object. If you don't need to use this feature, supply null for this argument (or use the simpler variant of startDrag).

imageOffset   If an image is supplied, this argument gives the initial location at which the image is to be drawn. The position is given relative to the origin of the coordinate system of the drag source component and will usually be calculated as a fixed offset from the location of the cursor at the point at which the drag gesture is recognized. If the platform supports the rendering of the image, the intent is that its position relative to the cursor will remain fixed as the cursor moves, with the separation determined by this initial offset. If you don't want to supply an image, this argument should be null.

transferable   This argument supplies the Transferable that can be used to get the data to be supplied to the drop target. Depending on the type of data you need to transfer, you may be able to use one of the standard Transferables supplied by the java.awt.datatransfer package, or you may need to create your own. Shortly, you'll see an example of a custom Transferable.

dsl   The DragSourceListener that will monitor the drag operation on behalf of the drag source.

Not all platforms support the rendering of an image in addition to normal cursor feedback. You can find out whether the platform your application is running on supports this by calling the DragSource isDragImageSupported method.

In our example, the startDrag method is called with the Cursor argument set to null so that the default cursor is used and the DragSourceListener argument is supplied as this, because JLabelDragSource implements this interface itself. The Transferable is an instance of the class JLabelTransferable, the implementation of which we'll show later in this section.

The rest of the JLabelDragSource class is the implementation of the DragSourceListener interface. The methods of this interface are very similar to this of DropTargetListener and, as you might expect, there is a direct parallel between the activities of the drop target and those of the drag source while a drag operation is in progress. Here are the methods that make up the `DragSourceListener` interface:

- `public void dragEnter(DragSourceDragEvent dsde);`
- `public void dragOver(DragSourceDragEvent dsde);`
- `public void dragExit(DragSourceEvent dse);`
- `public void dropActionChanged(`
        `DragSourceDragEvent dsde);`
- `public void dragDropEnd(DragSourceDropEvent dsde);`

Once the drag has been initiated by calling the `DragGestureEvent` `startDrag` method, nothing happens until the cursor moves over a valid drop target and the `DropTargetListener` for that drop target calls `accept-Drag`. If both of these events happen, the `DragSourceListener` `dragEnter` method is called, to inform the drag source that the cursor is now over a drop target. The `dragOver` method is called as the cursor moves while it remains within the drop target and `dragExit` is invoked when the cursor leaves the drop target, if the ESCAPE key is pressed to cancel the operation, or just before the drop occurs. The `dropActionChanged` method will be invoked if the user's gesture changes the operation being offered to the drop target and, finally, the `dragDropEnd` method informs the `DragSourceListener` that the drop occurred, but does not imply that it was successful.

The events that are passed to the `DragSourceListener` methods have the same hierarchy as those used by the drop target, as shown in Figure 8-16.

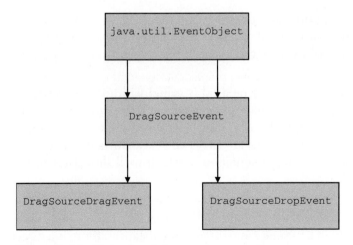

Figure 8-16   Hierarchy of drag source event classes.

All the events delivered are instances of `DragSourceEvent` or one of its two subclasses. `DragSourceEvent` itself has only one method:

```
public DragSourceContext getDragSourceContext();
```

The relationship between the `DragSourceContext` and the other classes that make up the drag source was shown in Figure 8-1. Most applications will not need to directly access the `DragSourceContext` because the `Drag-SourceDragEvent` and `DragSourceDropEvent` classes have cover methods that allow you to access the functionality of the `DragSourceContext` without needing to explicitly get a reference to it.

The `DragSourceDragEvent` that is passed to `dragEnter`, `dragOver`, and `dropActionChanged` has four methods that allow you to get the current state of the drag operation:

- `public int getGestureModifiers();`
- `public int getTargetActions();`
- `public int getUserAction();`
- `public int getDropAction();`

The first of these methods just returns the state of the modifiers in the mouse event corresponding to the event being delivered to the `Drag-SourceListener`. You can use this information to determine which mouse buttons are pressed should you need to. In practice, there should be little reason to do this because the relationship between mouse button state and the implied user gesture should be considered to be platform-dependent, so assumptions about the meanings of particular buttons should not be hard-coded into your application.

The `getTargetActions` method returns the drop action last suggested by the drop target, while `getUserAction` gives you the action implied by the user's current gesture. Finally, `getDropAction` is the action implied by the combination of the drag source actions, the user action, and the target action. This will, of course, be `ACTION_NONE` if there is no common action among these three. For example, if the drop target suggests `ACTION_COPY` and the user action is currently `ACTION_MOVE`, `getDropAction` will return `ACTION_NONE`. On the other hand, if the drop target suggested `ACTION_MOVE` instead and the drag source actions include `ACTION_MOVE`, `getDropAction` will return `ACTION_MOVE`.

After the drag has started, the `DragSourceListener` has two main duties:

1. To change the cursor shape to provide drag-over feedback to the user.

2. When the drop completes, to perform any actions on the drag source that are implied by the operation that was actually carried out.

Although you can explicitly change the cursor as the drag operation proceeds, the drag-and-drop subsystem will do this for you automatically based on whether the cursor is currently over a drop target, whether the drop target considers the operation acceptable, and what the selected operation actually is. If you want to change the cursor, you can do this from the `dragEnter`, `dragOver`, `dropActionChanged`, and `dragExit` methods by obtaining a reference to the `DragSourceContext` using the `getDragSourceContext` method of `DragSourceEvent` and then calling its `setCursor` method. Note that this is probably the only case that requires you to obtain a direct reference to the `DragSourceContext`, because the drag source events do not have cover methods for the cursor control functionality. By default, the cursor state is set based on the intersection of the current drop action and the drop target's suggested action, as returned by the `DragSourceDragEvent` `getDropAction` and `getTargetActions` methods.

When the drag operation completes, the `dragDropEnd` method is called with a `DragSourceDropEvent`. This class has two methods that allow the drag source to determine the outcome of the drop:

- `public boolean getDropSuccess();`
- `public int getDropAction();`

The first of these returns `true` if the drop target performed the data transfer without error. In this case, the `getDropAction` method can be used to determine the actual operation (copy, move, or link) that the drop target performed. Although the example code in Listing 8-9 does nothing in the `dragDropEnd` method other than print debugging information (if the `DnDExamples.debug` property is defined), in many cases you will need to take some action here. For example, if you implement a drag source for a text component, you'll need to delete the text that has been dragged if, and only if, the `getDropSuccess` method returns `true` and `getDropAction` returns `ACTION_MOVE`.

The implementation of the `DragSourceListener` in our example is very simple—it only displays diagnostic information if debugging is enabled. You'll see a more complete example when we look at creating a drag source for a `JTree` component.

Creating a Transferable for a `JLabel`

The last step in implementing our drag source is providing the `Transferable`. Actually, because all we strictly need to transfer in this example is the text from the label, you might think that we could simply have used the `StringSelection` class from the `java.awt.datatransfer` package, which implements `Transferable`, and passed the object created as the result of the following statement to the `startDrag` method:

```
new StringSelection(label.getText())
```

This, however, does not work in all cases. If you modify the source of `JLabelDragSource` to use a `StringSelection`, you'll find that you can successfully drag the label's text onto our `JEditorPane` drop target, but not onto platform-native applications. This happens because, although `StringSelection` claims to be able to supply its data in both `String` and plain text formats, the representation classes that it uses for both of these flavors is not compatible with export to the platform drag-and-drop subsystem:

- In the case of the `String` flavor, the representation is a Java class, which is only suitable for transfer to another Java application (such as `JEditorPane`).

- The plain text flavor supplies its data as a `java.io.StringReader` so that it returns Unicode characters when read. This is inconsistent with the Java drag-and-drop implementation, which requires data exported to the platform to be in the form of a `java.io.InputStream`.

To transfer the label text to platform native applications, we are forced to implement our own `Transferable`. Because we're taking the trouble to do this, we might as well take the next logical step and provide the code necessary to all the `JLabel` itself to be transferred, so that the user can drag the complete label and drop it onto a suitable drop target. If the drop target is a container, this might result in a copy of the `JLabel` being added to the container. If you've used a Java integrated development environment that allows you to build a user interface, you'll recognize this as the beginnings of an implementation of a component toolbar; although the example shown here will be a trivial one, all the code you need for creating your own toolbar with draggable components is present here.

The `Transferable` will support three flavors:

- The label text supplied as a Unicode string. The object returned from the `getTransferData` method for this flavor will be of type `java.lang.String`.

- The label text supplied as plain text characters in the platform's default encoding. This flavor is provided specifically to allow the text to be exported to native applications and, therefore, the `getTransferData` method must return an object of type `java.io.InputStream` when asked for the data in this flavor.

- A copy of the `JLabel` itself. Here, the object returned from `getTransferData` will be of type `javax.swing.JLabel`. This flavor is only usable when dragging the label between two Java VMs.

To create a `Transferable`, you need to implement the following three methods:

`getTransferDataFlavors`	to provide a list of the supported flavors
`isDataFlavorSupported`	to indicate whether the `Transferable` supports a given flavor
`getTransferData`	to return the data in the requested flavor

All three of these methods either require a `DataFlavor` object as an argument or return objects of type `DataFlavor`, so we need a `DataFlavor` object to represent each of the three flavors that the `Transferable` supports. The first of these is easy—for a Unicode string, we just use `DataFlavor.stringFlavor`, which is already defined in the `java.awt.datatransfer` package. The other two are not so obvious, however.

Getting a type for plain text sounds simple, but in fact there is no predefined `DataFlavor` that expresses the actual type of the data that our `Transferable` will return. The obvious choice would be `DataFlavor.plainTextFlavor`, but this is defined to return an object of type `java.io.InputStream`, which supplies its data in Unicode, as we saw earlier when creating the `JEditorPane` drop targets. In fact, what we want to return is an object of type `java.io.InputStream` in which the character stream is in the platform local encoding. The drag-and-drop subsystem uses the MIME type

```
text/plain; charset=ascii
```

to represent text with this encoding, so a suitable `DataFlavor` for the plain text variant of our `Transferable` can be created like this:

```
new DataFlavor("text/plain; charset=ascii", "ASCII Text");
```

Finally, the `DataFlavor` that corresponds to transferring the whole `JLabel` is created using the following statement:

```
new DataFlavor(JLabel.class, "Swing JLabel");
```

Here, the first argument supplies the flavor's representation class and the second is its human-readable name. A `DataFlavor` created in this way actually has a MIME type of `application/x-java-serialized-object` because the data will be transferred using the Java object serialization mechanism, which requires that the object itself be serializable. Like all Swing components, `JLabel` is serializable.

Now that we have definitions for the three flavors, the implementation of the `Transferable` is straightforward. The code is shown in Listing 8-10.

Listing 8-10 A Transferable for a `JLabel`

```java
package AdvancedSwing.Chapter8;

import java.awt.datatransfer.*;
import java.io.*;
import javax.swing.*;

public class JLabelTransferable implements Transferable {
    public JLabelTransferable(JLabel label) {
        this.label = label;
    }

    // Implementation of the Transferable interface
    public DataFlavor[] getTransferDataFlavors() {
        return flavors;
    }

    public boolean isDataFlavorSupported(DataFlavor fl) {
        for (int i = 0; i < flavors.length; i++) {
            if (fl.equals(flavors[i])) {
                return true;
            }
        }
```

Listing 8-10 A Transferable for a `JLabel` **(continued)**

```
      return false;
   }

   public Object getTransferData(DataFlavor fl) {
      if (!isDataFlavorSupported(fl)) {
         return null;
      }

      if (fl.equals(DataFlavor.stringFlavor)) {
         // String - return the text as a String
         return label.getText() + " (DataFlavor.stringFlavor)";
      } else if (fl.equals(jLabelFlavor)) {
         // The JLabel itself - just return the label.
         return label;
      } else {
         // Plain text - return an InputStream
         try {
            String targetText = label.getText() + "
                     (plain text flavor)";
            int length = targetText.length();
            ByteArrayOutputStream os =
                     new ByteArrayOutputStream();
            OutputStreamWriter w = new OutputStreamWriter(os);
            w.write(targetText, 0, length);
            w.flush();
            byte[] bytes = os.toByteArray();
            w.close();
            return new ByteArrayInputStream(bytes);
         } catch (IOException e) {
             return null;
         }
      }
   }

   // A flavor that transfers a copy of the JLabel
   public static final DataFlavor jLabelFlavor =
                  new DataFlavor(JLabel.class, "Swing JLabel");

   private JLabel label;        // The label being transferred
   private static final DataFlavor[] flavors =
      new DataFlavor[] {
         DataFlavor.stringFlavor,
         new DataFlavor("text/plain; charset=ascii",
                    "ASCII text"), jLabelFlavor
      };
}
```

The constructor takes as its only argument a reference to the `JLabel` being transferred. This reference is stored until the transfer data is requested in the `getTransferData` method. The `getTransferDataFlavors` method is trivial—it simply returns an array containing `DataFlavor` objects for the three flavors that are supported by the `Transferable`. Similarly, `isDataFlavorSupported` compares the `DataFlavor` supplied as its argument to the three supported flavors and returns `true` if a match is found and `false` otherwise.

The `getTransferData` method, however, is a little more complex. Because the `Transferable` recognizes three different flavors, there are three different cases to consider, based on the `DataFlavor` passed by the caller. The two easiest cases are where the flavor requested is `DataFlavor.stringFlavor` or the flavor for the `JLabel` itself because this require us to return the `String` or the `JLabel` as an object. In the case of `stringFlavor`, we extract the text from the label and add the string `"(DataFlavor.stringFlavor)"` so that you can see that this flavor was requested; if the `JLabel` is required, it is just returned directly from the reference held within the `JLabelTransferable`.

Returning the label in plain text form is a little more difficult. Here, we need to create and return an object of type `java.io.InputStream` which, when read, will return the characters of the text label. There is no `InputStream` class in the `java.io` package that takes a Unicode string as input and returns bytes in the platform local encoding (apart from `StringBufferInputStream`, which is deprecated), so we need to simulate one using two streams. This is done by taking the text label (adding the extra string `"(plain text flavor)"` for diagnostic purposes) and converting it to an array of bytes by using a `ByteArrayOutputStream`, wrapped with an `OutputStreamWriter`. The `OutputStreamWriter` takes the input string and converts each character to a byte in the platform's local encoding, and then passes them to the `ByteArrayOutputStream`, which stores them in an internal byte array. Because the `getTransferData` method has to return an `InputStream`, the final step is to create and return a `ByteArrayInputStream`, which takes the byte array from the `ByteArrayOutputStream` as its input.

This completes the implementation of the `Transferable` for the `JLabel`. You've already seen that it works when dragging text to either a platform-native application or to a `JEditorPane`, which demonstrates the transfer both of plain text and a Unicode string. To see that it also correctly transfers the complete `JLabel`, you need to start two Java VMs in two separate command windows using the following commands:

```
java AdvancedSwing.Chapter8.JLabelDragSource
java AdvancedSwing.Chapter8.PanelDropTarget
```

The first of these commands brings up the draggable JLabel, while the second creates a frame with a JPanel in it, to which a drop target has been added. This drop target is capable of accepting dragged objects derived from java.awt.Component; when such an object is dropped on it, it simply adds it to the JPanel. To see this in action, click the mouse in the JLabel and drag it over the frame, and then drop it. You should see a copy of the label appear in the frame. You can repeat this as many times as you like—each time you do so, another copy of the label appears in the frame, as shown in Figure 8-17.

Figure 8-17   Dragging a JLabel onto a drop target.

The implementation of the drop target for the JPanel in the Panel-DropTarget class is very similar to the one for JEditorPane except that, instead of looking for a list of files or text, it accepts a transferable whose representation class is java.awt.Component or a subclass thereof. We're not going to show the complete source code for this drop target here because most of it has been shown already; if you want to see the complete implementation, you'll find it on the book's CD-ROM. The main differences between PanelDropTarget and EditorDropTarget are in the checkTransferType and drop methods, the PanelDropTarget versions of which are both shown in Listing 8-11, with the changes from the EditorDropTarget implementation highlighted in bold.

Listing 8-11 A Drop Target That Can Accept Components

```
protected void checkTransferType(DropTargetDragEvent dtde) {
    // Only accept a flavor that returns a Component
    acceptableType = false;
    DataFlavor[] fl = dtde.getCurrentDataFlavors();
    for (int i = 0; i < fl.length; i++) {
        Class dataClass = fl[i].getRepresentationClass();
        if (Component.class.isAssignableFrom(dataClass)) {
```

Listing 8-11 A Drop Target That Can Accept Components (continued)

```
            // This flavor returns a Component - accept it.
            targetFlavor = fl[i];
            acceptableType = true;
            break;
        }
    }
    DnDUtils.debugPrintln("File type acceptable - " +
                        acceptableType);
}

public void drop(DropTargetDropEvent dtde) {
    DnDUtils.debugPrintln("DropTarget drop, drop action = "
            + DnDUtils.showActions(dtde.getDropAction()));
    // Check the drop action
    if ((dtde.getDropAction() &
                    DnDConstants.ACTION_COPY_OR_MOVE) != 0) {
        // Accept the drop and get the transfer data
        dtde.acceptDrop(dtde.getDropAction());
        Transferable transferable = dtde.getTransferable();

        try {
            boolean result = dropComponent(transferable);

            dtde.dropComplete(result);
            DnDUtils.debugPrintln("Drop completed,
                                success: " + result);
        } catch (Exception e) {
            DnDUtils.debugPrintln("Exception while handling
                                drop " + e);
            dtde.dropComplete(false);
        }
    } else {
        DnDUtils.debugPrintln("Drop target rejected drop");
        dtde.rejectDrop();
    }
}

protected boolean dropComponent(Transferable transferable)
        throws IOException, UnsupportedFlavorException {
    Object o = transferable.getTransferData(targetFlavor);
    if (o instanceof Component) {
        DnDUtils.debugPrintln("Dragged component class is
                                " + o.getClass().getName());
```

Listing 8-11 A Drop Target That Can Accept Components (continued)

```
        pane.add((Component)o);
        pane.validate();
        return true;
    }
    return false;
}
```

The role of the checkTransferType is to determine whether the drag source and drop target have any compatible transfer flavors. In this case, the drop target will only accept the transfer of an object derived from java.awt.Component. To determine whether it is possible to get such an object from the drag source, checkTransferType gets the list of available DataFlavors and calls the getRepresentationClass method on each of them in turn, checking whether the class that is returned is java.awt.Component or a subclass of it, using the Class method isAssignableFrom. If any of the available flavors can return a Component, this method will set acceptableType to true and the drag operation will be accepted (provided also that the operation is either copy or move). As a side effect, it also saves a reference to the DataFlavor that can supply the Component, because this will be needed when handling the drop operation.

The drop method must select an appropriate flavor from those available and then transfer the data. Because only one flavor is acceptable and it is known that it is being offered by the drag source, drop just calls the drop-Component method, which is specific to PanelDropTarget. This method, which is also shown in Listing 8-11, uses the DataFlavor stored by check-TransferType to get the dragged object by calling getTransferData on the Transferable. If this object is of type Component (which it will be unless there is an inconsistency in the implementation), it adds it to the JPanel and invokes the validate method to have the panel's layout manager size it and allocate space for it. We are assuming here that the JPanel has its default FlowLayout manager installed, so that the JLabel will be given its preferred size. In a real application, you would do whatever is required here in the context of the operation being performed.

Using Drag-and-Drop with the JTree Component

To conclude this chapter, we're going to look at how to implement in Java one of the most common uses of drag-and-drop—the ability to copy and move files using a graphical file system viewer. In creating this example, we'll use most of the techniques that you've seen in this chapter and we'll also take a closer look at some of the detail that has so far only been mentioned only in passing.

The *FileTree* Component

To implement drag-and-drop functionality for a component that displays a file system, we first need such a component. The most natural way to display the relationship between files and folders graphically is to use a tree, in which each file or folder maps to a node; a folder would be modeled as a branch node with files or other folders as its children, while files would always be leaf nodes. Building a tree from a file system is, in principle, a relatively simple matter—you just have to create one node per object and arrange them to mirror the actual parent-child relationships in the file system itself. Such a component was implemented in Chapter 10 of *Core Java Foundation Classes* and we will use that component, called `FileTree`, as the basis for this example.

The original implementation of the `FileTree` class is described in detail in *Core Java Foundation Classes*. To build drag sources and drop targets for `FileTree`, we will need to make a few minor changes to the original code, which we'll cover in this section, but we're not going to repeat here the description of the basic implementation of the tree. If you have a copy of *Core Java Foundation Classes*, it would be a good idea to re-read Chapter 10 before proceeding with this section. If you don't have this book, a copy of Chapter 10 in PDF format has been included on the CD-ROM that accompanies this book.

Modifications to the `FileTree` Component

The original `FileTree` component was created to show how to represent a hierarchical file system using a `JTree`. A typical view of the file system that the `FileTree` component produces was shown in Figure 8-2 earlier in this chapter. While the implementation in *Core Java Foundation Classes* was perfectly adequate for its purpose, for the sake of this more advanced example, a few modifications were required. If you would like to compare the source code for the original example with that for the drag-and-drop example, you'll find both among the example code for this chapter; the file names are as follows:

`FileTree.java`	The new source code, modified for this example
`CoreJFC/FileTree.java`	The original source code, as created for *Core Java Foundation Classes*

The changes that have been made to `FileTree` are summarized below.

Inclusion of files	The original `FileTree` component only showed directories in the file system. Because it would not be very useful to restrict ourselves to dragging and dropping directories, the modified component also shows files.
Ordering of files and directories	As you can see from Figure 8-2, the ordering of nodes in the tree is essentially random. In fact, it matches the order in which the `java.io.File list` method returns the contents of each directory. This is not very satisfactory, so the new version of this component orders the nodes so that all directories precede all files and both files and directories are sorted into alphabetical order. This produces a much more useful representation of the file system.
Autoscrolling	Autoscrolling support has been added. As we said earlier in this chapter, autoscrolling support needs to be built into the target component itself rather than being a feature provided by the code that will be used to support drag and/or drop for the component. The code that was added to `FileTree` is identical to that added to `JEditorPane` and shown in Listing 8-8.
`FileTreeNode` made public	Each file or directory in the view mapped by the `FileTree` is represented by an instance of the inner class `FileTree.FileTreeNode`, which is derived from `DefaultMutableTreeNode`. In the original implementation, there was no reason to expose these nodes, so they were made protected. For the purposes of this example, it was necessary to directly manipulate the nodes that represent the file system objects that will be dragged around, so this class was made public.

Support for changing the file system view	The original implementation provided a static view of the file system. Because Java does not provide a way to receive notification of changes to the underlying file system (for example the removal or renaming of files), no provision was made to incorporate changes into the `JTree` view. It is still not possible to detect changes to the file system made externally, but it is necessary to update the view when we move or copy a file or directory from one location to another by dragging it from or dropping it onto a `FileTree` and it is feasible to do this because the code that operates on the file system is aware of the `FileTree`. Consequently, code has been added that allows the `FileTree` to update itself as the result of an object being added to or removed from the part of the file system that it is mapping.
`FileTreeNode` API extended	As well as making `FileTreeNode` public, a couple of extra methods were added to it. One of these (`isDir`) returns a boolean indicating whether the node represents a directory (`true`) or a file (`false`). The other (`getFullName`) returns the full path name of the file or folder that the node represents as a `String`.

If you'd like to try out the modified `FileTree` on its own (that is, without any code for drag-and-drop being present in the example), you can do so by typing the following command:

```
java AdvancedSwing.Chapter8.FileTreeTest pathname
```

where *pathname* is the full path name of the directory to appear at the root of the tree. If you are using the Windows platform and you want the root directory of a drive to appear as the tree's root, be sure to supply the backslash as well as the drive name—that is, type `c:\` instead of simply `c:`. A typical example of what you'll see is shown in Figure 8-18. If you compare this with Figure 8-2, you'll see that the tree now shows files as well as directories and that the files and directories appear in alphabetical order.

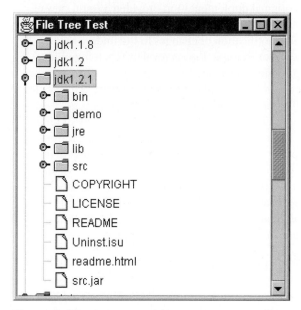

Figure 8-18   An improved file system view component.

The Drag Source Implementation

As before in this chapter, we are going to implement the drag-and-drop support for `FileTree` as separate classes that we connect to instances of the tree rather than subclassing `FileTree` and adding the code directly to it. We'll develop the drag source and the drop target separately and we'll explain them in isolation although, in reality, they do have dependencies upon each other. These dependencies, however, are not very close dependencies—all we need to ensure is that both implementations obey the usual drag-and-drop protocol in the sense that the drag source exposes the objects to be dragged in a form that is acceptable to the drop target and that the drop target properly communicates the result of the drop operation back to the drag source. In theory, because both drag source and drop targets are conforming to rules imposed by the drag-and-drop subsystem, it should be possible to use either the drag source or the drop target from this book together with the other of the pair obtained from another source.

The `FileTreeDragSource` Class

The drag source is by far the simpler of the two main pieces of code that we'll show you in this section. The drag source is implemented in a class called (not surprisingly) `FileTreeDragSource` and looks very much like the one that we created for `JLabel` in Listing 8-9. The code for `FileTreeDrag-Source` is shown in Listing 8-12.

Listing 8-12 A Drag Source for a Graphical File Viewer

```
package AdvancedSwing.Chapter8;

import java.awt.*;
import java.awt.event.*;
import java.awt.datatransfer.*;
import java.awt.dnd.*;
import java.io.*;
import java.util.*;
import javax.swing.*;
import javax.swing.tree.*;

public class FileTreeDragSource implements DragGestureListener,
                                DragSourceListener {
    public FileTreeDragSource(FileTree tree) {
        this.tree = tree;

        // Use the default DragSource
        DragSource dragSource =
                DragSource.getDefaultDragSource();

        // Create a DragGestureRecognizer and
        // register as the listener
        dragSource.createDefaultDragGestureRecognizer(
                tree, DnDConstants.ACTION_COPY_OR_MOVE, this);
    }

    // Implementation of DragGestureListener interface.
    public void dragGestureRecognized(DragGestureEvent dge) {
        // Get the mouse location and convert it to
        // a location within the tree.
        Point location = dge.getDragOrigin();
        TreePath dragPath =
                tree.getPathForLocation(location.x, location.y);
        if (dragPath != null && tree.isPathSelected(dragPath)) {
            // Get the list of selected files and create a
            // Transferable. The list of files and the is saved
            // for use when the drop completes.
            paths = tree.getSelectionPaths();
            if (paths != null && paths.length > 0) {
```

Listing 8-12 A Drag Source for a Graphical File Viewer (continued)

```
            dragFiles = new File[paths.length];
            for (int i = 0; i < paths.length; i++) {
               String pathName = tree.getPathName(paths[i]);
               dragFiles[i] = new File(pathName);
            }

            Transferable transferable =
                       new FileListTransferable(dragFiles);
            dge.startDrag(null, transferable, this);
         }
      }
   }

   // Implementation of DragSourceListener interface
   public void dragEnter(DragSourceDragEvent dsde) {
      DnDUtils.debugPrintln("Drag Source: dragEnter,
                drop action = " + DnDUtils.showActions(
                dsde.getDropAction()));
   }

   public void dragOver(DragSourceDragEvent dsde) {
      DnDUtils.debugPrintln("Drag Source: dragOver,
                drop action = " + DnDUtils.showActions(
                dsde.getDropAction()));
   }

   public void dragExit(DragSourceEvent dse) {
      DnDUtils.debugPrintln("Drag Source: dragExit");
   }

   public void dropActionChanged(DragSourceDragEvent dsde) {
      DnDUtils.debugPrintln("Drag Source:
               dropActionChanged, drop action = "
               + DnDUtils.showActions(dsde.getDropAction()));
   }

   public void dragDropEnd(DragSourceDropEvent dsde) {
      DnDUtils.debugPrintln("Drag Source: drop completed,
               drop action = " + DnDUtils.showActions(
               dsde.getDropAction()) + ",
               success: " + dsde.getDropSuccess());
      // If the drop action was ACTION_MOVE,
      // the tree might need to be updated.
      if (dsde.getDropAction() == DnDConstants.ACTION_MOVE) {
```

Listing 8-12 A Drag Source for a Graphical File Viewer (continued)

```
        final File[] draggedFiles = dragFiles;
        final TreePath[] draggedPaths = paths;

        Timer tm = new Timer(200, new ActionListener() {
            public void actionPerformed(ActionEvent evt) {
                // Check whether each of the dragged files exists.
                // If it does not, we need to remove the node
                // that represents it from the tree.
                for (int i = 0; i < draggedFiles.length; i++) {
                    if (draggedFiles[i].exists() == false) {
                        // Remove this node
                        DefaultMutableTreeNode node =
                        (DefaultMutableTreeNode)draggedPaths[i].
                            getLastPathComponent();
                        ((DefaultTreeModel)tree.getModel()).
                            removeNodeFromParent(node);
                    }
                }
            }
        });
        tm.setRepeats(false);
        tm.start();
    }
}

public static void main(String[] args) {
    JFrame f = new JFrame("Draggable File Tree");
    try {
        FileTree tree = new FileTree(args[0]);
        f.getContentPane().add(new JScrollPane(tree));

        // Attach the drag source
        FileTreeDragSource dragSource = new
                                FileTreeDragSource(tree);
    } catch (Exception e) {
    }
    f.pack();
    f.setVisible(true);
}

protected FileTree tree;          // The associated tree
protected File[] dragFiles;       // Dragged files
protected TreePath[] paths;       // Dragged paths
}
```

The tasks that `FileTreeDragSource` must perform are:

- Associate a `DragSource` with the `FileTree` and assign a `DragGestureListener` to receive notification when the user attempts to initiate a drag. This job is performed in the constructor and uses the same code as we saw in the `JLabelDragSource` class. As before, the `DragGestureListener` is directly implemented by the `FileTreeDragSource` class.
- When a drag gesture is recognized, check whether the drag should be allowed and call `startDrag` if it should.
- Create a `Transferable` for the drop target.
- When the drop completes, check whether it succeeded. If it did and the action was `ACTION_MOVE`, update the view of the file system in the `FileTree` to reflect the fact that the files and/or directories that have moved should no longer be visible in their original locations.

Each of these tasks is self-contained, so we'll describe them separately in the sections that follow.

Checking Whether the Drag Operation Is Valid

In the case of the drag source for `JLabel`, the drag operation was always considered valid because the whole surface of the component was considered to be the object being dragged. With a tree, however, this is not the case. The expected protocol when moving files using a graphical file viewer is that the user will select one or more objects from the file system and then, with the cursor over one of those objects, drag them to the drop target. In terms of this example, this means that the `dragGestureRecognized` method must check that the following conditions are satisfied before calling `startDrag`:

- The mouse is positioned over a node of the tree.
- The node over which the mouse is positioned must be selected.

If either of these criteria is not satisfied, the drag gesture will be ignored. These checks ensure, for example, that the user cannot start a drag by pressing the mouse over an area of unoccupied space in the tree.

You might be wondering how it is possible for the user to attempt to drag one or more selected items from the tree without the mouse being physically placed over one of them—the fact that we have to check that the node over which the mouse is positioned when the drag begins is selected implies that it might be possible for that node to be under the cursor and not selected. In fact, this is perfectly possible. To start a drag, you have to click the mouse over a valid node and then drag it. The act of clicking the mouse will cause the node under the mouse to be selected if it is not already selected, so both of the conditions above will be satisfied. But suppose that the node was only one of several nodes that were selected. Clicking on the node will result in that node and all the others being deselected, which means that, because there is now no selection, the drag will be rejected. But suppose the user holds down the CTRL key and then presses the mouse over one of the selected nodes, and then starts to drag the mouse. Holding down CTRL while clicking on a selected node will deselect that node, but leave the others selected. Dragging the mouse with CTRL held down is a valid drag gesture, so it will be recognized by the `DragGestureRecognizer` and the `dragGestureRecognized` method will be invoked. Now, the drag will have been started while the mouse was over a node that was not selected, but there still exists at least one other node that is selected. Although we could allow this, it seems counter-intuitive to allow the drag to start if the user is not dragging one of the selected items.

Everything that the `FileTreeDragSource` has to do to verify that the drag conditions are satisfied can be achieved using facilities provided by the `JTree` component. To work out whether the mouse is placed over a node of the tree, the position of the cursor at the time that the drag gesture started is obtained from the `DragGestureEvent` using its `getDragOrigin` method. This position is then converted to the `TreePath` for the corresponding node in the tree using the `JTree getPathForLocation` method. Because the coordinates of the drag location are specified relative the origin of the `JTree` component, it doesn't matter that the tree is actually mounted in a `JScrollPane` and that the origin of the tree may not be visible in the viewport, because `getPathForLocation` requires the position to be specified in the tree's coordinate system. If `getPathForLocation` returns a non-`null` value, the drag operation began over a node of the tree—in other words, over a directory or file in the file system.

Next, we need to work out whether the node under the mouse is selected. This is simple—the `isPathSelected` method can be used to find out if the `TreePath` that it is given as an argument is among the selected set, so we just pass it the `TreePath` returned by `getPathForLocation` and, if it returns `true`, both of the drag conditions have been met.

Creating the `Transferable`

Once the `DragGestureListener` has determined that the drag is valid, it must call the `DragGestureEvent startDrag` method, for which it will need a `Transferable` that will eventually be given to the `DropTarget`. The drag source is going to pass to the drop target a list of files and directories selected by the user. We've already seen that the `java.awt.datatransfer` package includes a `DataFlavor` called `javaFileListFlavor` that describes data in this form and we saw it in use when we developed the drop target for `JEditorPane` earlier in this chapter. In that example, however, the drag source was a native application and the `Transferable` that provided the list of files in the `javaFileListFlavor` was created internally by the drag-and-drop subsystem. In fact, there is (at the time of writing) no public implementation of such a `Transferable` in the JDK, so we need to create one of our own. Fortunately, it is very simple and the code is shown in Listing 8-13.

Listing 8-13   A Transferable for a List of File System Objects

```
package AdvancedSwing.Chapter8;

import java.awt.datatransfer.*;
import java.io.*;
import java.util.*;

public class FileListTransferable implements Transferable {
   public FileListTransferable(File[] files) {
      fileList = new ArrayList();
      for (int i = 0; i < files.length; i++) {
         fileList.add(files[i]);
      }
   }

   // Implementation of the Transferable interface
   public DataFlavor[] getTransferDataFlavors() {
      return new DataFlavor[]
                     { DataFlavor.javaFileListFlavor };
   }

    public boolean isDataFlavorSupported(DataFlavor fl) {
       return fl.equals(DataFlavor.javaFileListFlavor);
    }
```

**Listing 8-13 A Transferable for a List of
File System Objects (continued)**

```
public Object getTransferData(DataFlavor fl) {
    if (!isDataFlavorSupported(fl)) {
        return null;
    }

    return fileList;
}

List fileList;                    // The list of files
}
```

The representation class for `javaFileListFlavor` is defined to be
`java.util.List` and each entry in the list must be a `File` object corresponding to one file or directory that is part of the data being transferred.
The constructor for the `FileListTransferable` class therefore takes an
array of `File` objects and then converts it to an object of type `ArrayList`,
which implements the `java.util.List` interface. The `ArrayList` is held
within the `Transferable` until the drop target asks for it by invoking the
`getTransferData` method that, as you can see, simply verifies that the caller
is requesting the data in the appropriate flavor and then returns the store
`ArrayList`. To implement the `Transferable` interface, this class must also
provide implementations of the `getTransferDataFlavors` and `isData-
FlavorSupported` methods. Because only one flavor is supported, both of
these methods are, as you can see, very trivial.

If you return to the `dragGestureRecognized` method in Listing 8-12,
you'll see that after checking the drag conditions, it obtains a list of all the
nodes in the tree that are selected using the `JTree getSelectionPaths`
method, which returns the selected nodes as an array of `TreePath` objects,
which is stored within the `FileTreeDragSource` class for later use. Because
the `FileListTransferable` constructor needs the selected files as an array
of `File` references, it is necessary to convert each `TreePath` into the corresponding `File` object. To do this, we need the full file system path name of
the node represented by the `TreePath`. The mapping between `TreePath`
and file system name is known only within the `FileTree` class. To make it
possible to perform the conversion, `FileTree` provides a method called `get-
PathName`, which we call for each `TreePath` object, and then pass the result-
ing name to the `File` constructor to create the appropriate `File` object.

Once the `FileListTransferable` has been obtained, the `startDrag` method is called and the drag operation begins.

Note that this implementation passes the value `DnDConstants.ACTION_COPY_OR_MOVE` to `startDrag`, implying that it does not support the link operation. The reason for this is twofold. First, supporting three operations would complicate the example without making it any more useful as a demonstration of how to implement drag-and-drop for a `JTree`. The second reason is more important however—Java just doesn't provide a platform-independent way to link files! If you want to implement this operation, you'll have to write some native code to invoke the underlying operating system services.

Updating the `FileTree` on Completion of the Drag Operation

After the drop has been completed, the drag source may need to update the `FileTree` that it is associated with. The reason for doing this should be clear from the following example. Suppose the `FileTree` shows the content of the directory `c:\temp` which contains files a and b and that the user selects files a and b and drags them over a drop target using a gesture that indicates a move operation. If the drop target accepts this operation, it will move the files from their current location and put them somewhere else. The process of carrying out this operation will actually remove the files a and b in the directory `c:\temp`, but the drag source's `FileTree` will still show them as present. It is the job of the drag source to update the `FileTree` to show the correct state. This task is performed in the `dragDropEnd` method in Listing 8-12.

The `dragDropEnd` method first checks whether the drop action selected by the user was a move; if the user performed a copy, the source files in the underlying file system will not have changed, so there would be no need to change the content of the `FileTree`. However, some care is required here. Suppose that the drop operation moved file a but failed to move file b, perhaps because there was no room in the file system to which b was being moved. In this case, the drop target may or may not report success, depending on its implementation. Because we can't tell what the drop target will do when it only manages to perform part of the move, the `dragDropEnd` method does not call the `getDropSuccess` method of the `DragSourceDropEvent`, but instead checks whether the files that were the subject of the operation have actually been moved, by making use of the list of `File` objects that was created by the `dragGestureRecognized` method—it loops through this list, checking each entry to see whether it has been removed and, if it has, removes the file's node from its parent. To update the `FileTree`, the `drag-DropEnd` method needs to locate the nodes for the files that have actually been removed and remove them from their parent node (the one that represents `c:\temp`). Locating the node for each file is simple, because the `drag-GestureRecognized` method saves the `TreePath` objects for the files being dragged; from the `TreePath` object, the file node itself can be located by calling the `getLastPathComponent` method and then removed using the `DefaultTreeModel removeNodeFromParent` method, which will cause the `JTree` to redraw itself as a side effect.

Core Alert

You'll notice that the `dragDropEnd` method does not directly check whether the dragged files still exist—instead, it starts a timer for a short interval and performs the check when the timer expires. This is an unfortunate trick made necessary by the fact that when dragging files to Windows Explorer, the `dragDropEnd` method is entered before the files have actually been moved. As a result of this it looks, in the `dragDropEnd` method, as if the source files still exist as a result of which the `FileTree` view would not get updated.

You can try out the `FileTree` drag source by typing command

```
java AdvancedSwing.Chapter8.FileTreeDragSource pathname
```

where *pathname* is the absolute path name of a directory in your file system. If you select a file or a folder and start dragging it, you'll find that the cursor changes to indicate that the drop would not be accepted, which shows that the drag source is active. You can demonstrate that the drag source actually works by starting Windows Explorer (or dtfile on Solaris) and dragging some files from the `FileTree` onto it, or start one of the `JEditorPane` examples from earlier in this chapter and drag a text file or an HTML file onto the editor to see that they are opened successfully.

The Drop Target

Having seen how to implement the `FileTree` drag source, we now move on to the drop target. You won't be surprised to discover that much of the source code for this drop target is very similar to that for the `EditorDropTarget` classes that were developed earlier in this chapter. As far as interfacing with the drag-and-drop subsystem is concerned, there is very little difference between `JEditorPane` and `FileTree`. Most of the work in this class actually concerns the job of moving or copying the files from the drag source, which has little to do with drag-and-drop itself. To keep the distinction clear, we'll discuss these two aspects separately.

The `FileTreeDropTarget` Class

As we did with the `JEditorPane` drop target, we can reduce the job of implementing a drop target for the `FileTree` component into several smaller pieces:

- Ensuring that the data type of the object being dragged is acceptable. As in earlier examples, this task is performed by the `checkTransferType` method. Here, this method is trivial because only the `javaFileListFlavor` is accepted.
- Determining whether the cursor is over a valid drop location.
- Providing drag-under feedback to indicate where the drop would occur, if it is considered valid.
- When the drop occurs, obtaining the list of files involved and copying or moving them to their new locations.

We'll discuss the last three of these tasks and show the source code for them separately in the sections that follow. The overall structure of the `File-TreeDropTarget` class is the same as that of `EditorDropTarget`, so we're not going to show all the source code here. If you want to see the complete implementation, you'll find the source file on the CD-ROM that accompanies this book.

You can try out the drop target implementation by typing the command

```
java AdvancedSwing.Chapter8.FileTreeDropTarget pathname
```

where, as usual, *pathname* is the root of the directory tree to be displayed. You can try dragging from one copy of the tree to another by running both of the following commands from separate windows:

```
java AdvancedSwing.Chapter8.FileTreeDragSource c:\
java AdvancedSwing.Chapter8.FileTreeDropTarget c:\
```

Note that although you can use a move gesture when dragging files from the drag source onto the drop target, when you use `FileTreeDropTarget` as the drop target, it will just copy the files and directories that you drag—it does not delete the originals. If you want the drop target to implement the move operation properly, you need to define the property `DnDExam-ples.allowRemove`, like this:

```
java -DDnDExamples.allowRemove
                 AdvancedSwing.Chapter8.FileTreeDropTarget c:\
```

Be careful when you enable this property that you only use the move gesture when you really intend to.

The CD-ROM also contains an example that attaches both a drag source and a drop target to the same tree. You can run this example using the command

```
java AdvancedSwing.Chapter8.DragDropTreeExample pathname
```

and then drag and drop files and folders in a single window.

Checking for a Valid Drop Location

When the user drags the mouse over the drop target, the determination as to whether the cursor is over a valid drop location is made by the `acceptOrRejectDrag` method, which is called from `dragEnter`, `dragOver`, and `dropActionChanged`. For the user to be able to drop a file into the file system, the destination must be a directory to which the user has write access. To make this determination, the drop target must:

1. Convert the mouse location to a `FileTree` node.
2. Verify that the node represents a directory.
3. Check that the user has permission to write in that directory.

Because the user can attempt a drop event when the drop target has rejected it because the cursor location does not correspond to a writable directory, this functionality is also required during drop processing, so it is implemented in a separate method that can be called from either place. The code for this method, called `isAcceptableDropLocation`, is shown in Listing 8-14. As you can see, this method itself delegates responsibility to another method called `findTargetDirectory`, which returns a `File` object for the directory that will be the target for the drop if, and only if, the three conditions listed above are met. The `findTargetDirectory` method itself is used in more than one place, which is why its code is not included directly into `isAcceptableDropLocation`.

Listing 8-14 Determining the Validity of the Drop Location

```
protected boolean isAcceptableDropLocation(Point location) {
    return findTargetDirectory(location) != null;
}

protected File findTargetDirectory(Point location) {
    TreePath treePath =
            tree.getPathForLocation(location.x, location.y);
    if(treePath != null) {
        FileTree.FileTreeNode node =
        (FileTree.FileTreeNode)treePath.getLastPathComponent();
        // Only allow a drop on a writable directory
        if (node.isDir()) {
            try {
                File f = new File(node.getFullName());
                if (f.canWrite()) {
                    return f;
                }
            } catch (Exception e) {
            }
        }
    }
    return null;
}
```

Drag-Under Feedback

Drag-under feedback is very important when the user is moving or copying files using drag-and-drop, because it is essential that the user can unambiguously see the drop location. In this example, we provide drag-under feedback by selecting the node in the tree that represents the current drop target; as the user drags the cursor over the tree, the node that would act as the drop target will appear selected only if it represents a directory to which the user has write access.

By using the selection in this way, however, we are creating a conflict with the tree itself, which may already have nodes selected. This is certainly the case if we attach both a drag source and a drop target to the same tree and the user drags files from one part of the tree to another, because the file or files being dragged will, of course, be selected. To remove all ambiguity, we need to deselect the nodes that are not under the mouse cursor while the drag is in progress and reselect them when the drag operation has completed. This means:

1. When `dragEnter` is called, the current selection must be saved and all nodes in the tree must be deselected.

2. As the user moves the cursor, the dragOver method must determine whether the node under the cursor represents a valid drop site and select it if it does.
3. When dragExit is entered, the node for the drop target (if there is one) should be deselected and the nodes that were selected before dragEnter was called must be reselected.

The code that provides the drag-under feedback is shown in Listing 8-15.

Listing 8-15 Providing Drag-Under Feedback for the FileTree Drop Target

```
protected void saveTreeSelection() {
   selections = tree.getSelectionPaths();
   leadSelection = tree.getLeadSelectionPath();
   tree.clearSelection();
}

protected void restoreTreeSelection() {
   tree.setSelectionPaths(selections);
   // Restore the lead selection
   if (leadSelection != null) {
      tree.removeSelectionPath(leadSelection);
      tree.addSelectionPath(leadSelection);
   }
}

protected void dragUnderFeedback(DropTargetDragEvent dtde,
                                 boolean acceptedDrag) {
   if (dtde != null && acceptedDrag) {
      Point location = dtde.getLocation();
      if (isAcceptableDropLocation(location)) {
         tree.setSelectionRow(
            tree.getRowForLocation(location.x, location.y));
      } else {
         tree.clearSelection();
      }
   } else {
      tree.clearSelection();
   }
}
...

TreePath[] selections;      // Initially selected rows
TreePath leadSelection;     // Initial lead selection
```

The `saveTreeSelection` method is called from `dragEnter` and uses `JTree` methods to get the list of selected `TreePaths`, which it saves for later restoration. It is important to also save the lead selection, which is obtained using the `getLeadSelectionPath` method. The lead selection is usually the last path to have been selected by the user and it is rendered with a highlighting border when the tree has the focus. Having saved all necessary selection information, the `clearSelection` method is called to deselect everything.

The `restoreTreeSelection` restores the original selection state by reselecting everything originally stored by `saveTreeSelection`, and then specifically reselecting the previous lead selection path. This code works even if nothing in the tree was selected when `saveTreeSelection` was called, because it explicitly checks for the lead selection being `null` and does nothing if it is.

When the cursor first enters the space occupied by the `FileTree` component, the `dragEnter` method will be called. This method calls `saveTreeSelection`. As a result, any existing selection will be saved and then cleared, so the selection can safely be manipulated while the cursor is still over the drop target. If the drag operation is canceled by the user (by pressing the ESCAPE key) or the cursor is dragged out of the `FileTree`, the `dragExit` method will be invoked, which will result in the original selections being restored by `restoreTreeSelection`. This also happens when the user commits to the drop—in other words, when the drop target's `drop` method is entered, the selection will have been restored to the state it was in before the drag started.

The `dragEnter`, `dragOver`, `dropActionChanged`, and `dragExit` methods all call `dragUnderFeedback`. In all cases apart from `dragExit`, the first argument to this method is the `DropTargetDragEvent` that indicates where the mouse is relative to the `FileTree`. This argument is passed as `null` to `dragExit`, which results in the tree selection being cleared and no further action being taken. In the other cases, the mouse location is passed to the `isAcceptableDropLocation` method which works out whether the cursor is over a writable directory. If it is, the drop would succeed, so the path under the mouse is selected to indicate where the file (or files) being transferred would be moved or copied to by calling the `setSelectionRow` method; this has the effect of clearing any previous selection, so there will only ever be at most one node selected as the user drags the cursor over the drop target. If the cursor is not over a valid drop site, perhaps because it moved from a node representing a writable directory to one representing a file, the previous node must be deselected without the new one being selected; the `clearSelection` method is used to do this.

Performing the Drop

If the user commits to the drop operation while the cursor is over the `File-Tree`, the `drop` method will be called. This method delegates most of its work to another method called `dropFile`, which deals with the details of transferring the files or directories that the user is dragging. However, it does carry out some housekeeping functions before and after performing the drop processing itself, as you can see from Listing 8-16.

**Listing 8-16 The `FileTreeDropTarget`
          `drop` Method**

```
public void drop(DropTargetDropEvent dtde) {
    DnDUtils.debugPrintln("DropTarget drop, drop action = "
              + DnDUtils.showActions(dtde.getDropAction()));

    // Check the drop action
    if ((dtde.getDropAction() &
            DnDConstants.ACTION_COPY_OR_MOVE) != 0) {
        // Accept the drop and get the transfer data
        dtde.acceptDrop(dtde.getDropAction());
        Transferable transferable = dtde.getTransferable();
        boolean dropSucceeded = false;

        try {
            tree.setCursor(Cursor.getPredefinedCursor(
                        Cursor.WAIT_CURSOR));

            // Save the user's selections
            saveTreeSelection();

            dropSucceeded = dropFile(dtde.getDropAction(),
                        transferable, dtde.getLocation());

            DnDUtils.debugPrintln("Drop completed, success: "
                        + dropSucceeded);
        } catch (Exception e) {
            DnDUtils.debugPrintln("Exception while handling
                                        drop " + e);
        } finally {
            tree.setCursor(Cursor.getDefaultCursor());
```

Listing 8-16 The `FileTreeDropTarget`
`drop` Method (continued)

```
            // Restore the user's selections
            restoreTreeSelection();
            dtde.dropComplete(dropSucceeded);
        }
    } else {
        DnDUtils.debugPrintln("Drop target rejected drop");
        dtde.dropComplete(false);
    }
}
```

The first thing that this method does is to verify that the drop operation is acceptable and then accepts it. Having accepted the drop, the `getTransfer-able` method can be called to get the `Transferable`, which will eventually be used by `dropFile` to get the list of files to be moved. As we said earlier, when the `drop` method is called, the `dragExit` method will already have been invoked, so the drag-under feedback will have been removed and the original tree selections restored. However, because the process of moving the affecting files may take a short time, we want to continue to provide feedback to the user, so the `saveTreeSelection` method is used to save (again) the user's own selection and then the file transfer is performed by calling the `dropFile` method.

Core Note

It would be nice to be able to avoid restoring the tree selection in the `dragExit` *method only to remove it again while handling the drop, but there is no way for the drop target code to know whether* `dragExit` *is being called immediately prior to an invocation of* `drop` *or because the user has moved the drag cursor away from the* `FileTree`. *Because of this, it is not possible to perform any optimization.*

When the transfer is complete, there are two things to do:

- Restore the user's tree selection by calling `restoreTreeSelection`.
- Report on the success of the drop operation, for the benefit of the drag source, by calling `dropComplete`.

Both of these operations must be performed whether the drop proceeds normally or fails. It is also important to invoke the `dropComplete` method even if, for some reason, the `dropFile` method throws an exception. Because of this, most of this method is wrapped in a `try` block, with the operations that must be performed at the end placed in the `finally` clause to ensure that they are completed no matter what the outcome of the drop.

Performing the Movement of Files

The last piece of the puzzle as far as interaction with the drag-and-drop subsystem is concerned, is the `dropFile` method, which will actually control the movement of the files and/or directories that the user dragged onto the `FileTree`. This method has several tasks to perform:

- Obtaining the list of files to transfer.
- Getting the target directory as a `FileTreeNode` and as a `File` object. The `FileTreeNode` will be used when updating the tree's visual representation, while the `File` object will be used when actually moving the data.
- Highlighting the target directory in the tree to provide drag-under feedback to the user.
- Moving the source files to the target directory.

The code for this method is shown in Listing 8-17.

Listing 8-17 Handling the Drop Operation for the `FileTree` Component

```
// This method handles a drop for a list of files
protected boolean dropFile(int action, Transferable
            transferable, Point location)
            throws IOException, UnsupportedFlavorException,
            MalformedURLException {
  List files = (List)transferable.getTransferData(
            DataFlavor.javaFileListFlavor);
  TreePath treePath = tree.getPathForLocation(
            location.x, location.y);
  File targetDirectory = findTargetDirectory(location);
  if (treePath == null || targetDirectory == null) {
     return false;
  }
  FileTree.FileTreeNode node =
    (FileTree.FileTreeNode)treePath.getLastPathComponent();
```

```
      // Highlight the drop location while we perform the drop
      tree.setSelectionPath(treePath);

      // Get File objects for all files being
      // transferred, eliminating duplicates.
      File[] fileList = getFileList(files);

      // Don't overwrite files by default
      copyOverExistingFiles = false;
      // Copy or move each source object to the target
      for (int i = 0; i < fileList.length; i++) {
         File f = fileList[i];
         if (f.isDirectory()) {
            transferDirectory(action, f, targetDirectory,
                              node);
         } else {
            try {
               transferFile(action, fileList[i],
                            targetDirectory, node);
            } catch (IllegalStateException e) {
               // Cancelled by user
               return false;
            }
         }
      }

      return true;
   }
```

Most of this code should be self-explanatory. The mouse location passed
from the `drop` method is given to the `JTree getPathForLocation` method
to get the `TreePath` for the directory into which the user wants to drop the
files and is also passed to the `findTargetDirectory` method that we saw
earlier to get a `File` object for the same directory. In practice, given all the
checks that have been made while the drag was being carried out, neither of
these methods should return `null` because the mouse should be over a node
of the tree that represents a writable directory. However, a check is added
here to ensure that both of the returned references are valid and, in the event
of any problem, the `dropFile` method returns `false` to indicate that it
failed. The values returned by these two methods give us everything we need
to know about the directory that is the target of the drop operation.

The rest of this method is a loop that moves or copies one file or directory at a time. This, however, is not quite as simple as it sounds. To see what complications might arise, let's look at some typical cases. Consider the directory structure shown in Figure 8-18 and suppose that the user selects and drags the files `c:\jdk1.2.1\COPYRIGHT`, `c:\jdk1.2.1\LICENSE`, and `c:\jdk1.2.1\README` and drops them onto the directory `c:\temp`. When the `dropFile` method is entered, the `List` object returned from the `Transferable` `getTransferData` method will return `File` objects for each of these three files. Assuming that the user selected copy as the drag operation, the loop in the `dropFile` method needs to copy the `COPYRIGHT`, `LICENSE`, and `README` files directly into the target directory `c:\temp`. In principle, all it has to do is create the new files in the `c:\temp` directory and use the `File` objects to read the content of the source files and write it to the new files. When the copy is complete, if the operation chosen was `ACTION_MOVE`, the source file should be removed. This simple process works as long as the objects being dragged are files.

The situation is more complex when the user selects a directory, however. Copying a directory implies copying the directory itself and all the files and directories it contains. If the directory does contain subdirectories, this is a recursive operation that terminates when all the subdirectories have been processed. Furthermore, in the case of a move operation, after each directory's content has been copied, all its files and subdirectories must be deleted and the directory itself must be removed. You'll see the details of this later in this section.

The fact that handling directories is more complex than handling files is the reason why the loop in Listing 8-17 handles files and directories differently by calling a specific method for each. This, however, is not the only problem associated with copying directories. Returning to Figure 8-18, suppose the user selects and drags the following nodes from the `FileTree`:

- `c:\jdk1.2.1`
- `c:\jdk1.2.1\COPYRIGHT`

This, of course, is redundant, because dragging the node `c:\jdk1.2.1` implies copying that directory and all its content, which includes the file `c:\jdk1.2.1\COPYRIGHT`. If we did nothing about this and simply copied the directory and then the `COPYRIGHT` file, we would be doing extra work. The problem would get worse if the user selected many files from a directory that was also selected, or if subdirectories with lots of files in them were selected but, beside the extra time taken, no real harm would be done. The real problem occurs when the user makes a redundant selection and then performs a move operation. In this case, when the directory `c:\jdk1.2.1` has been copied, it will be removed, so the next pass of the loop in the `drop-File` method will not find a `c:\jdk1.2.1\COPYRIGHT` file to operate on. This looks like an error but, of course, it is not. To avoid both this problem and the redundant copying operations, before starting its loop, `dropFile` calls the `getFileList` method, passing it the `java.awt.List` returned from the `Transferable`. This method turns the `List` into an array of `File` objects, which is easier to iterate through than a `List`; it also scans the list of files and directories that the user has selected and removes redundant entries such as the `COPYRIGHT` file in the case shown earlier.

Removing Redundant File and Directory Paths

The process of removing redundant items from the set of `File` objects returned from the `Transferable` is a relatively simple one, but it requires a reasonable amount of code to implement it. The task itself is easy enough in principle—given two file system objects A and B, the path B is redundant if the absolute path names of A and B are the same or if the absolute path name of B starts with the absolute path name of A with the underlying file system's file separator character added to the end of it. Therefore, in the previous example, `c:\jdk1.2.1\COPYRIGHT` is redundant because it starts with the string `c:\jdk1.2.1\`, which is the other path name plus the file separator character. It is important to add the file separator to avoid false matches such as `c:\temp` and `c:\tempfiles`, which would otherwise meet the condition for `c:\tempfiles` to be considered redundant.

The difficulty arises because the `File` objects from the `Transferable` can theoretically be delivered in any order. In practice, they will probably appear in the order in which you see them in the tree, but you cannot rely on this. To find all the redundant paths, you have to check each one against every other one, testing the longer name against the shorter one. You can make this job easier by sorting the list of files alphabetically. This ensures that longer names appear after shorter ones, so you only have to compare each entry with the ones that follow it in the list. This is exactly what the `getFileList` method does, as you can see from Listing 8-18.

Listing 8-18 Removing Redundant Paths from the Set of Files Being Dragged

```
// Get the list of files being transferred and
// remove any duplicates. For example, if the
// list contains /a/b/c and /a/b/c/d, the
// second entry is removed.
protected File[] getFileList(List files) {
    int size = files.size();
```

Listing 8-18 Removing Redundant Paths from the Set of Files
             Being Dragged (continued)

```java
// Get the files into an array for sorting
File[] f = new File[size];
Iterator iter = files.iterator();
int count = 0;
while (iter.hasNext()) {
    f[count++] = (File)iter.next();
}

// Sort the files into alphabetical order
// based on pathnames.
Arrays.sort(f, new Comparator() {
    public boolean equals(Object o1) {
        return false;
    }

    public int compare(Object o1, Object o2) {
        return ((File)o1).getAbsolutePath().compareTo(
                    ((File)o2).getAbsolutePath());
    }
});

// Remove duplicates, retaining the results in a Vector
Vector v = new Vector();
char separator = System.getProperty(
                    "file.separator").charAt(0);
outer:
    for (int i = f.length - 1 ; i >= 0; i--) {
        String secondPath = f[i].getAbsolutePath();
        int secondLength = secondPath.length();
        for (int j = i - 1 ; j >= 0; j--) {
            String firstPath = f[j].getAbsolutePath();
            int firstLength = firstPath.length();
            if (secondPath.startsWith(firstPath)
              && firstLength != secondLength
              && secondPath.charAt(firstLength) == separator) {
              continue outer;
            }
        }
        v.add(f[i]);
    }
```

> **Listing 8-18 Removing Redundant Paths from the Set of Files Being Dragged (continued)**
>
> ```
>     // Copy the retained files into an array
>     f = new File[v.size()];
>     v.copyInto(f);
>     return f;
> }
> ```

The easiest way to sort objects in Java 2 is to put them into an array and then use the `sort` method of the `Arrays` class to do the sorting, so `get-FileList` extracts the `File` objects from the `List` that it is passed and loads them into an array of the appropriate size. There are many overloaded variants of the `Arrays` `sort` method that take arrays of different kind of objects as their first argument, along with a `Comparator`. `Comparator` is an interface with two methods defined:

- `public boolean equals(Object o);`
- `public int compare(Object o1, Object o2);`

The first of these methods allows two `Comparator`s to be compared, which is not of interest to us here. The second method compares two values and returns a negative if the first object is "less than" the second, zero if they are equal, and a positive integer if first object is "greater than" the second one. What this means, of course, depends on the type of the objects being compared and the context of the operation being performed. In terms of our example, the `compare` method is passed a pair of objects from the array that it is sorting which, in this case, will be `File` objects. We need to supply a `Comparator` that can sort `File` objects based on the alphabetical ordering of the absolute path name of the file system objects that they represent. Given a pair of these objects, we can extract the path names using the `getAbsolute-Path` method and then use the `String` `compareTo` method to do the comparison. This method returns the correct value required by the definition of the `compare` method—that is, for example, given the two paths

- `c:\jdk1.2.1`
- `c:\jdk1.2.1\COPYRIGHT`

the first is "less than" the second because it is a substring of it, so `compareTo` will return a negative value.

When the `sort` method completes, the list of `File`s will be sorted according to their absolute path names and all we need to do is go through the list from the end to the beginning (that is, *backward*) comparing the path name of each entry with those that precede it in the list, looking for entries that match some leading part of it. If we find such a path, the `File` object that we are currently working with must be redundant, so we do not need to keep it. If we reach the start of the list without finding a match, a copy of the `File` object is added to a `Vector`. Only `File` objects that do not have parent directories in the list will appear in this Vector. This operation is performed by the nested "for" loops in the code shown in Listing 8-18.

To see how this works in practice, suppose that the `getFileList` method were passed a `List` containing `File` objects for the following paths:

- `c:\jdk1.2.1\COPYRIGHT`
- `c:\jdk1.1.8\src\javax`
- `c:\jdk1.1.8\src\javax\swing`
- `c:\jdk1.1.8\src`
- `c:\temp\page1.html`
- `c:\jdk1.2.1`

The first step is to sort these entries according to path name, giving the following result:

- `c:\jdk1.1.8\src`
- `c:\jdk1.1.8\src\javax`
- `c:\jdk1.1.8\src\javax\swing`
- `c:\jdk1.2.1\src`
- `c:\jdk1.2.1\src\COPYRIGHT`
- `c:\temp\page1.html`

Now this list is processed from the bottom looking for redundancy. This process starts with `c:\temp\page1.html`. Clearly, none of the other match the beginning of this string, so this entry will be copied to the result `Vector` and will be one of the files involved in the drag operation. Next, we look at `c:\jdk1.2.1\src\COPYRIGHT` and compare it with the entries above it in the list. Here, redundancy is detected immediately, because the string before it, when the file separator character is added, becomes `c:\jdk1.2.1\src\`, which matches the beginning of the path name we are looking it. This causes `c:\jdk1.2.1\src\COPYRIGHT` to be discarded, with no further checks required. On the other hand, `c:\jdk1.2.1\src` will be copied to the result `Vector`. Of the remaining three strings, the first two are redundant because `c:\jdk1.1.8\src\javax\` matches the beginning of `c:\jdk1.1.8\src\javax\swing`, causing the latter to be discarded and similarly with `c:\jdk1.1.8\src\javax` itself, which is eliminated because of `c:\jdk1.1.8\src`. Thus, only the `File` objects with the following paths are copied to the results `Vector`:

- `c:\jdk1.1.8\src`
- `c:\jdk1.2.1\src`
- `c:\temp\page1.html`

Finally, the `Vector` of `File` objects that remain is converted to an array and is returned to the caller.

Copying a Directory

Once the `dropFile` method has the correct list of file system objects involved in the drop, it loops through them copying or moving them. A move operation is different from a copy only in that the move requires the original object to be removed when the copy is complete, so in this section we'll deal mainly with the details of the copy operation. Each item in the array returned by `getFileList` is either a directory or an array. The copying in process for these two object types is very different, so we'll examine them separately, starting in this section with how directories are handled.

Suppose we need to copy the directory `c:\a\b\c` to the directory `c:\temp`. Obviously, the first thing to do is to create the target directory `c:\temp\c`, if it does not already exist. What next? Copying a directory implies copying all its content as well, so we need to get a list of the objects in the directory `c:\a\b\c` and copy those to `c:\temp\c`. Suppose that the directory `c:\a\b\c` contains the following objects:

- A file called `c:\a\b\c\README`
- A directory called `c:\a\b\c\src`

To copy the directory, we create a loop, handling one object from the directory at a time. The first pass of the loop will copy `c:\a\b\c\README` to `c:\temp\c\README`. This is a file copy operation, which will be covered in "Copying a File" on page 844 and will call the same method that `dropFile` itself calls to copy files from its list of objects to be dragged. The second pass of the loop encounters a directory. Copying this directory involves creating the target node `c:\temp\c\src` and then copying the contents of `c:\a\b\c\src` into it. This is, of course, the same task as we are already describing, so it is performed by recursion. If this directory itself has subdirectories, there will be further levels of recursion until the deepest level of nesting is reached. The implementation of this whole process is shown in Listing 8-19.

Listing 8-19 Copying a Directory

```
protected void transferDirectory(int action, File srcDir,
            File targetDirectory,
            FileTree.FileTreeNode targetNode) {
  DnDUtils.debugPrintln(
            (action == DnDConstants.ACTION_COPY ? "Copy" :
            "Move") + " directory " +
            srcDir.getAbsolutePath() +
            " to " + targetDirectory.getAbsolutePath());

  // Do not copy a directory into itself or
  // a subdirectory of itself.
  File parentDir = targetDirectory;
  while (parentDir != null) {
    if (parentDir.equals(srcDir)) {
        DnDUtils.debugPrintln("-- SUPPRESSED");
        return;
    }
    parentDir = parentDir.getParentFile();
  }

  // Copy the directory itself, then its contents

  // Create a File entry for the target
  String name = srcDir.getName();
  File newDir = new File(targetDirectory, name);
  if (newDir.exists()) {
    // Already exists - is it the same directory?
    if (newDir.equals(srcDir)) {
        // Exactly the same file - ignore
        return;
    }
  } else {
    // Directory does not exist - create it
    if (newDir.mkdir() == false) {
        // Failed to create - abandon this directory
        JOptionPane.showMessageDialog(tree,
            "Failed to create target directory\n  " +
            newDir.getAbsolutePath(),
            "Directory creation Failed",
            JOptionPane.ERROR_MESSAGE);
```

Listing 8-19 Copying a Directory (continued)

```
            return;
        }
    }

    // Add a node for the new directory
    if (targetNode != null) {
    targetNode = tree.addNode(targetNode, name);
    }

    // Now copy the directory content.
    File[] files = srcDir.listFiles();
    for (int i = 0; i < files.length; i++) {
        File f = files[i];
        if (f.isFile()) {
            transferFile(action, f, newDir, targetNode);
        } else if (f.isDirectory()) {
            transferDirectory(action, f, newDir, targetNode);
        }
    }

    // Remove the source directory after moving
    if (action == DnDConstants.ACTION_MOVE &&
        System.getProperty(
                    "DnDExamples.allowRemove") != null) {
        srcDir.delete();
    }
}
```

As you can see, this method does broadly what was outlined earlier. There are, however, a couple of interesting points to note.

First, there is a check for the relationship between the source and target directories to make sure that the user is not trying to drag a directory "inside" itself. As an example of this would be trying to drag the directory c:\jdk1.2.1 into the subdirectory c:\jdk1.2.1\src, which is illegal because it is an operation that would recurse until the file system filled up. This is easy to check—we just take the target directory and compare it with the source. If they don't match, we move to the parent of the target and compare that with the source, repeating this operation until a match occurs, in which case the operation will be abandoned, or we reach the root of the file system. In the case of this example, we would first compare c:\jdk1.2.1\src with c:\jdk1.2.1, which does not match, and then move to the parent of `c:\jdk1.2.1\src`, which is `c:\jdk1.2.1`, at which point we match with the target and abandon the operation.

Next, the target directory is created if it does not exist and a node for the new directory is added to the `FileTree`, which will make it visible to the user when the `FileTree` repaints itself. The `FileTree` itself provides the `add-Node` method that is provided here. We're not going to describe how this method works in detail, except to say that it creates a new `FileTreeNode` for the new directory and adds it to the tree, causing an event that will make the tree repaint itself. You'll find a discussion of the topic of adding nodes to a `TreeModel` and arranging for the tree to update its screen display in Chapter 10 of *Core Java Foundation Classes* on the CD-ROM that accompanies this book.

The directory contents are copied using the loop that we described earlier, recursing if necessary to copy subdirectories. Finally, if the operation is `ACTION_MOVE`, the source directory is deleted. Deleting the original directory is actually conditional on the property `DnDExamples.allowRemove` being defined. As noted earlier, for the purposes of this example, you have to explicitly define this property when you run it to authorize removal of files or directories. This is a safeguard against accidents when running the test program.

There is also a subtlety surrounding the single line of code that deletes the source directory. In general, you can only delete a directory that is empty and this code makes no such check. In fact, the underlying platform does this for you. How do we know that the source directory is empty at this point? Consider an example in which we move the directory `c:\jdk1.2.1` to another location. This directory contains several files and subdirectories, such as:

- `c:\jdk1.2.1\bin (directory)`
- `c:\jdk1.2.1\include (directory)`
- `c:\jdk1.2.1\jre (directory)`
- `c:\jdk1.2.1\lib (directory)`
- `c:\jdk1.2.1\COPYRIGHT (file)`
- `c:\jdk1.2.1\License (file)`

and so on. As this directory is processed by the `transferDirectory` method, it will invoke itself recursively to move the four subdirectories and will invoke the `transferFile` method (described in the next section) to move the two files. The last thing that these methods do when performing a move operation is, of course, to remove the original object. Therefore, when the `c:\jdk1.2.1\bin` directory move operation completes, it will have been removed. The same happens with the other three directories and the two files. After the loop shown in Listing 8-19 completes, therefore, the directory should be empty. If any errors occur, perhaps because the user is trying to move a directory that he does not have permission to remove, that directory will remain and the parent directory will not be empty, which will cause the attempt to remove it to fail. This is, of course, exactly what you would expect.

Copying a File

Copying a file from the drag source is, in principle, simply a case of creating a new, empty file at the target location, reading the content of the original file and writing it to the new one, and then closing both files. Finally, if the file is being moved, the original should be removed. That is, indeed, exactly what the `FileTreeDropTarget` `transferFile` method does but, as with copying directories, there are a few interesting points to look out for. The implementation is shown in Listing 8-20.

Listing 8-20　Copying a File

```
// Copy or move a file
protected void transferFile(int action, File srcFile, File
        targetDirectory, FileTree.FileTreeNode targetNode) {
    DnDUtils.debugPrintln(
        (action == DnDConstants.ACTION_COPY ? "Copy" :
            "Move") + " file " +
            srcFile.getAbsolutePath() +
            " to " + targetDirectory.getAbsolutePath());

    // Create a File entry for the target
    String name = srcFile.getName();
    File newFile = new File(targetDirectory, name);
    if (newFile.exists()) {
        // Already exists - is it the same file?
        if (newFile.equals(srcFile)) {
            // Exactly the same file - ignore
            return;
        }
        // File of this name exists in this directory
        if (copyOverExistingFiles == false) {
            int res = JOptionPane.showOptionDialog(tree,
                "A file called\n " + name +
                "\nalready exists in the directory\n  " +
                targetDirectory.getAbsolutePath() +
                "\nOverwrite it?", "File Exists",
                JOptionPane.DEFAULT_OPTION,
                JOptionPane.QUESTION_MESSAGE,
                null, new String[] {"Yes", "Yes to All", "No",
                "Cancel"},   No");
```

Listing 8-20 Copying a File (continued)

```
          switch (res) {
          case 1:// Yes to all
             copyOverExistingFiles = true;
          case 0:// Yes
             break;
          case 2:// No
             return;
          default: // Cancel
             throw new IllegalStateException("Cancelled");
          }
       }
    } else {
       // New file - create it
       try {
          newFile.createNewFile();
       } catch (IOException e) {
          JOptionPane.showMessageDialog(tree,
                "Failed to create new file\n  " +
                newFile.getAbsolutePath(),
                "File Creation Failed",
                JOptionPane.ERROR_MESSAGE);
          return;
       }
    }

    // Copy the data and close file.
    BufferedInputStream is = null;
    BufferedOutputStream os = null;

    try {
       is = new BufferedInputStream(
                        new FileInputStream(srcFile));
       os = new BufferedOutputStream(
                        new FileOutputStream(newFile));
       int size = 4096;
       byte[] buffer = new byte[size];
       int len;
       while ((len = is.read(buffer, 0, size)) > 0) {
          os.write(buffer, 0, len);
       }
    } catch (IOException e) {
```

Listing 8-20 Copying a File (continued)

```
        JOptionPane.showMessageDialog(tree,
            "Failed to copy file\n  " + name + "\nto
            directory\n  " +
            targetDirectory.getAbsolutePath(),
            "File Copy Failed",
            JOptionPane.ERROR_MESSAGE);
        return;
    } finally {
        try {
            if (is != null) {
                is.close();
            }
            if (os != null) {
                os.close();
            }
        } catch (IOException e) {
        }
    }

    // Remove the source if this is a move operation.
    if (action == DnDConstants.ACTION_MOVE &&
        System.getProperty("DnDExamples.allowRemove")
                                                    != null) {
        srcFile.delete();
    }
    // Update the tree display
    if (targetNode != null) {
        tree.addNode(targetNode, name);
    }
}
```

The first part of this method checks whether the target file already exists. If it doesn't, the `File` method `createNewFile` is used to create it and any problems encountered in doing so cause an error message to be displayed in a modal dialog and the operation to be aborted. If the file already exists, there is the possibility that the user is dragging the file onto itself by, for example, dragging the file `c:\jdk1.2.1\COPYRIGHT` into the directory `c:\jdk1.2.1`. If this is the case, there is nothing to do and trying to treat this as anything other than a special case by reading and writing the file to itself would be disastrous—the first write to the file would lose any unread data!

If the file already exists, we prompt the user for confirmation that it is to be overwritten by posting a modal dialog. If the user is copying one directory tree over another and the target tree contains older versions of the files being copied from the source directory, it may be that there will be many file copy operations for which the target file will already exists. Because of this, we give the user the ability to agree that all such copies will go ahead, even if the files already exist. A typical example of the dialog that appears is shown in Figure 8-19.

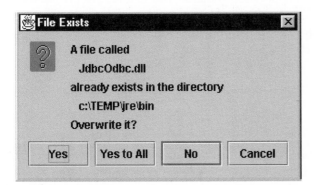

Figure 8-19 Prompting for permission to overwrite existing files.

This dialog allows the user four possible options:

Yes	The current file is copied. If another attempt is made to copy over an existing file, another dialog will appear.
Yes to All	All attempts to copy over existing files are assumed to be approved without further prompting.
No	This file should not be copied. Prompt again if another file to be copied already exists.
Cancel	Do not copy this file or any other files. In other words, abort the entire drag operation from this point.

If the user replies Yes or Yes to All, the copy is performed, overwriting the original content of the file. The difference between Yes and Yes to All is that we do not want to prompt the user again if the latter is selected. To arrange for this, the instance variable copyOverExistingFiles is set to true in this case; if this variable is true when an existing file is being copied, the copy will take place without a dialog being displayed. This variable is initialized to false in the dropFile method, so permission to overwrite existing files extends only for the duration of a single drop operation.

Selecting No aborts the current file copy or move operation. This is simple to arrange—the transferFile method just returns. Cancel is more difficult to implement. Here, the intention is to abort the current operation and to copy or move any other files involved in the operation that have not yet been processed. The problem with this is that the loop that handles the remaining files is outside the transferFile method, so it cannot be aborted directly by transferFile. To make this operation possible, the transferFile method throws an IllegalStateException when Cancel is selected, to notify dropFile that it should terminate its copying loop without processing any more files or directory, as shown in Listing 8-17.

Summary

In this chapter, we looked in detail at the drag-and-drop mechanism offered by the Java 2 platform and showed how to use it in conjunction with Swing components. We started out by explaining the architecture and showed how the responsibility for a drag-and-drop operation is divided between the drag source, the drop target, and the underlying operating system. We then looked in detail at how to implement fully functioning drop targets and drag sources that allow you to transfer files and text between Java applications or between a Java application and a program running on the native platform. One of the most important issues that the developer has to confront when adding this facility to a custom component or to an application is how to represent the data being transferred. We addressed this topic by providing a detailed discussion of the Java data transfer package, which was originally created to provide a cut-and-paste mechanism for JDK 1.1. Finally, we brought all the pieces together by building a complete implementation of a tree component that displays a representation of a file system and allows the user to move files and directories around by dragging and dropping the icons that represent them in the tree.

THE SWING
UNDO PACKAGE

Topics in this Chapter

- Using the Undo Package
- Creating Your Own `UndoableEdits`
- Extending `UndoManager`

Chapter 9

A graphical user interface (GUI) should be designed to allow the user to do what he or she needs to do with minimal effort. There is, however, another side to this coin. As well as making it possible for the user to do something, it is also important to give the user the ability, where it makes sense, to reverse an action that turned out to be inappropriate. For example, as we saw in the first few chapters of this book, the Swing text components allow the user to change the style of large stretches of text or to delete anything from a single character to entire paragraphs with only a few mouse clicks or key presses. It is not so obvious, however, what the users should do when they realize that the wrong piece of text was deleted or the heading that had just been underlined should have been left as it was.

Fortunately, Swing contains a package designed to make it possible for you to implement your application in such a way as to make it possible for the user to reverse actions that the developer considers reversible. The undo feature (which resides in the `javax.swing.undo` package) consists of a small set of interfaces, classes, and events that you can use to build your application in such a way that it is possible for one change or a group of several changes to be stored so that they can be undone, either individually or together, on request from the user. This support is not free, however. To make use of it, you have to structure the actions that you take in response to button presses or the activation of menu items so that the effects of these actions can be stored and later reversed. The undo package provides the mechanism for expressing an undoable action, but it does not do all the work for you.

This chapter looks in detail at the Swing "undo" package. Although this package is a free-standing piece of software that can be used in many different contexts, some of its most obvious applications are within the realms of text processing and, indeed, the Swing text components make use of it to provide the basis for incorporating undo functionality within your applications. As well as looking at how the text components use the undo mechanism, you'll also see how to make direct use of it by enhancing it to improve your user interface.

An Undo Example

The easiest way to understand the facilities that the undo package provides is to look at an example that shows them in use. The undo package is completely independent of anything else in Swing, but the text components have support for an undo mechanism integrated at all levels, from the underlying Content model through to the various Document classes that support different content types. When you think of undo and redo, you'll probably associate it almost immediately with the ability to correct typing mistakes in your favorite editor or word processor, be it the simple "u" key in the UNIX vi editor or the more sophisticated undo mechanism provided by Microsoft Word. The Swing text components have the ability to provide the user with a similar level of functionality to that available from Word, but this support is not immediately accessible—you have to add a small amount of code to your application to enable it. We'll see what that code is in this section.

Text Component Events Revisited

The simple example that we'll look at in this section is based on the cut-down hypertext markup language (HTML) editor that we used in Chapter 4. To make things even simpler, we'll use a JTextPane instead of a JEditorPane and we'll stick to manipulating plain text. The basic program simply creates an empty JTextPane in a frame and provides menu items that allow you to change the font and the text alignment using actions provided by the JText-Pane's editor kit. The code to create the frame and its menu is almost the same as that described in "The HTML Editor Kit" in Chapter 4, so we won't show it here.

As well as the basic editor, two other frames also appear. Both of these frames are placed alongside the editing frame and contain non-editable text areas that will display events that are generated from the JTextPane. You can try this example using the command

```
java AdvancedSwing.Chapter9.UndoExample1
```

When the three frames have appeared, try typing into the main window. As you type, you'll see that events generated by the JTextPane are reported in the other two frames. You may find that the time taken to update these windows causes the response of the JTextPane to feel a little sluggish. After you've typed a few characters into the JTextPane, you should see something like Figure 9-1.

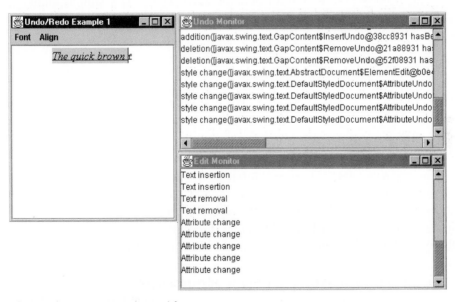

Figure 9-1 Events generated from a JTextPane.

The frame at lower right monitors the DocumentEvents that the JText-Pane's Document generates each time something is added to or removed from it, or when attributes are changed; you'll see one line of output added here each time you make a change to the input window. (DocumentEvents were discussed in Chapter 1.) The frame at the top right also changes when-ever you do anything to the input window. This frame displays another type of event that is produced by the JTextPane's Document model—the Undo-ableEditEvent. This event is the key to the Swing undo package. Each time a state change takes place in the Document, it records the details and generates an UndoableEditEvent, which is then broadcast to any registered UndoableEditListeners.

The way in which the details of the change are recorded are not specified by the undo package, because they depend on the nature of the object being modified—the information that would need to be saved to describe a text edit is obviously different to that required to flip the state of a checkbox. Nevertheless, these two very different operations are identical from the viewpoint of the undo package. The important thing is that the UndoableEditEvent contains not only a record of the state change, but also the code necessary to reverse the edit. You'll see the details of the Undoable-EditEvent and the other classes that it relies on in "Inside the Undo Package" on page 861. Catching an UndoableEditEvent is a simple matter of adding code like this:

```
pane.getDocument().addUndoableEditListener(
                    new UndoableEditListener() {
   public void undoableEditHappened(UndoableEditEvent evt) {
      UndoableEdit edit = evt.getEdit();
      textArea.append(edit.getPresentationName() + "(" +
                    edit.toString() + ")\n");
   }
});
```

The UndoableEditListener interface consists of the single undoable-EditHappened method, of which the code extract shown previously is a very simple example that just displays the edit in a separate window. A more useful listener would record the edit so that the user could reverse its effect later, if required. You'll see how simple it is to create such a listener in the next section.

As you add or delete text in the main window or change its attributes, you'll find that a single UndoableEditEvent is received for each action you perform. There is, in fact, one UndoableEditEvent corresponding to each DocumentEvent. If you look closely at the output in the top right window of Figure 9-1, you'll see that there are various different types of Undoable-EditEvent, of which the following is a selection:

```
addition([javax.swing.text.GapContent$InsertUndo@58ad501c
             hasBeenDone: true alive: true])
addition([javax.swing.text.GapContent$InsertUndo@79d9501c
             hasBeenDone: true alive: true])
```

```
deletion([javax.swing.text.GapContent$RemoveUndo@530d501c
            hasBeenDone: true alive: true])
style change([javax.swing.text.DefaultStyledDocument$
            AttributeUndoableEdit@a071501d
            hasBeenDone: true alive: true])
```

These events were generated by inserting two characters, deleting the last one and then changing the font of the remaining character. The text that appears at the start of each line is a short, human-readable description of the change that was made that is referred to as the "presentation name" of the edit. As its name suggests, this text is intended to be used in the user interface, perhaps as a tooltip associated with the button or menu item that the user would use to undo the last operation—after adding some text, the tooltip would say something like "Undo addition," while following a font change it might read "Undo style change."

The rest of each line is a summary of the edit that was performed. As you can see, each edit stores a couple of attributes (`hasBeenDone` and `alive`) that record its current state; we'll say more about these later in this chapter. The interesting thing to note about these lines is that the edits are instances of several different classes and they actually belong to different parts of the text package. Events that change the content of the `Document` model, that is insertions and deletions, are instances of inner classes of the `GapContent` class, which, as you'll recall from Chapter 1, is the class that organizes that characters that make up the `Document` model. By contrast, when you change the font or underline some characters in the text control, you aren't changing the characters themselves—you modify the attributes attached to the `Element`s that map those characters. In this case, the `UndoableEditEvent` is generated not by the `Content` class but by the `Document` itself and, again, it is an instance of an inner class of the object that is responsible for handling the change, which, in this case, is `DefaultStyledDocument`. These inner classes hold the information needed to describe the change made, but they also know how to reverse the change to restore the attributes or the content of the model to the state they were in before the user made the change that caused the event. The fact that reversing an attribute change requires a different action to undoing the insertion or removal of text explains why these different events are encapsulated as instances of different classes.

A Simple Way to Handle Undoable Edits

The ability to record edits and reverse them is the most important feature of the undo package. You could write an `UndoableEditListener` that gathered the events that it received and remembered them, so that the edits that they contain could be undone on demand, but you don't need to go quite this far because the basic mechanism to allow you to do this is provided in the built-in `UndoManager` class. `UndoManager` is an `UndoableEditListener`, so it can be attached directly to a text component to store its edit events. It also provides two methods, `undo` and `redo`, that respectively undo the last edit performed and reapply the last undone edit. The edits that the text component generates are stored internally by the `UndoManager`, so you don't need to be concerned about how many of them there are or the order in which they were generated—all you need to do is invoke the `undo` method. If the `UndoManager` has received several `UndoableEditEvents`, calling `undo` several times reverses the effect of each edit in order from the most recent to the oldest, while calling `redo` at any time restores the effect of the last edit undone. The `UndoManager` does the hard work of keeping track of which edit would be undone or redone next.

To illustrate how simple it is to use `UndoManager`, let's modify the last example so that the user can undo changes made in the `JTextPane`. If you're used to using Microsoft Word, you'll almost certainly be familiar with the key sequence CTRL+Z that allows you to undo your most recent changes, and the equally useful CTRL+Y that lets you reapply them after you've used CTRL+Z. Even though the Swing text components provide full support for undo and redo by generating the appropriate `UndoableEditEvents`, they do not provide bindings for these key sequences, because these actions have to be handled outside the text component by an `UndoManager` (or its equivalent), which the developer is responsible for providing. It is, however, trivial to add this functionality. All you have to do is:

1. Create an `UndoManager` and register it as an `Undoable-EditListener` with the component (or components) that you want it to manage.

2. Create an `Action` that will cause the `UndoManager`'s undo method to be called, and another that will invoke the `redo` method.

3. Attach these `Actions` to menus or toolbar buttons or `JButtons` that you add to the user interface.

4. Bind the actions to keystrokes on the text component so that the user can invoke them directly while typing into the component.

Listing 9-1 shows how to add undo and redo support to a `JTextPane` and bind the undo and redo actions to the usual keystrokes. This listing does not show all of this example—only the code that relates to adding the undo support. If you want to see the complete implementation, you'll find it on the CD-ROM that accompanies this book.

Listing 9-1 Adding Undo Support to `JTextPane`

```
package AdvancedSwing.Chapter9;

import java.awt.*;
import java.awt.event.*;
import java.util.*;
import javax.swing.*;
import javax.swing.event.*;
import javax.swing.undo.*;
import AdvancedSwing.Chapter4.MenuSpec;
import AdvancedSwing.Chapter4.MenuBuilder;

public class UndoExample2 extends JFrame {
    public UndoExample2() {
        super("Undo/Redo Example 2");

        pane = new JTextPane();
        pane.setEditable(true);      // Editable
        getContentPane().add(new JScrollPane(pane),
                        BorderLayout.CENTER);

        // Add a menu bar
        menuBar = new JMenuBar();
        setJMenuBar(menuBar);

        // Populate the menu bar
        createMenuBar();

        // Create the undo manager and actions
        UndoManager manager = new UndoManager();
        pane.getDocument().addUndoableEditListener(manager);

        Action undoAction = new UndoAction(manager);
        Action redoAction = new RedoAction(manager);

        // Add the actions to buttons
        JPanel panel = new JPanel();
        JButton undoButton = new JButton("Undo");
        JButton redoButton = new JButton("Redo");
        undoButton.addActionListener(undoAction);
```

Listing 9-1 Adding Undo Support to `JTextPane` (continued)

```
      redoButton.addActionListener(redoAction);
      panel.add(undoButton);
      panel.add(redoButton);
      getContentPane().add(panel, BorderLayout.SOUTH);

      // Assign the actions to keys
      pane.registerKeyboardAction(undoAction,
               KeyStroke.getKeyStroke(KeyEvent.VK_Z,
               InputEvent.CTRL_MASK),
               JComponent.WHEN_FOCUSED);
      pane.registerKeyboardAction(redoAction,
               KeyStroke.getKeyStroke(KeyEvent.VK_Y,
               InputEvent.CTRL_MASK),
               JComponent.WHEN_FOCUSED);
   }

   // The Undo action
   public class UndoAction extends AbstractAction {
      public UndoAction(UndoManager manager) {
         this.manager = manager;
      }

      public void actionPerformed(ActionEvent evt) {
         try {
            manager.undo();
         } catch (CannotUndoException e) {
            Toolkit.getDefaultToolkit().beep();
         }
      }

      private UndoManager manager;
   }

   // The Redo action
   public class RedoAction extends AbstractAction {
      public RedoAction(UndoManager manager) {
         this.manager = manager;
      }

      public void actionPerformed(ActionEvent evt) {
         try {
            manager.redo();
         } catch (CannotRedoException e) {
```

Listing 9-1 Adding Undo Support to `JTextPane` (continued)

```
            Toolkit.getDefaultToolkit().beep();
        }
    }

    private UndoManager manager;
}

// CODE OMITTED.
}
```

The constructor creates the `UndoManager` and registers it as an `Undo-ableEditListener` with the `JTextPane`'s document model. This step is sufficient to ensure that any changes made to the content of the `JTextPane`, be they insertions, deletions, or attribute changes, will be stored by the `UndoManager`. The next step is to create the undo and redo `Actions`—we'll look at the details of these `Actions` shortly. Next, two buttons labeled `Undo` and `Redo` are created and placed on a panel below the `JTextPane`. These buttons are set up so that they invoke the `actionPerformed` method of the undo and redo `Actions` when they are clicked, so that the user can use them to access the `UndoManager`. Lastly, the same `Actions` are bound to keystrokes on the `JTextPane` using the `JComponent` `registerKeyboardAction` method. The undo `Action` will be triggered whenever the user presses CTRL+Z when the `JTextPane` has the keyboard focus, while redo will be activated by the key sequence CTRL+Y.

The `Actions` themselves are very simple. When the `Action` is triggered, the `actionPerformed` method will be invoked. This method needs to call either the undo or redo method of the `UndoManager` that it is attached to. To make this possible, both `Actions` have a constructor that takes the `UndoManager` reference as its only argument and stores it; when the `actionPerformed` method is called, it uses this reference as the target of the undo or redo call.

If you type the command

```
java AdvancedSwing.Chapter9.UndoExample2
```

you'll see the same user interface as the previous example (shown in Figure 9-1), but this version includes the code shown previously. To see how this code works in practice, type a few characters into the `JTextPane` and then press the Undo button. When you do this, you'll notice that the character that you last typed is removed, while pressing Redo restores it. You can achieve the same effects using CTRL+Z and CTRL+Y, respectively. The undo feature also works if you highlight some of the text and change its font, size, style, or alignment and then press CTRL+Z or the Undo button, when the previous style is restored. You can also make several changes in succession, such as changing the font family, increasing the font size, and underlining the text and then use the Undo button to remove these changes separately in reverse order, because the UndoManager stores all the edits that occur in the correct order and allows you to undo them individually.

We got all this functionality by adding a relatively small amount of very simple code to our first example. It is very useful functionality, but it is not perfect. Here's a list of the shortcomings of this example as it stands:

- The Undo and Redo buttons should only be enabled when there is an edit to undo or redo. To maintain the proper state of these buttons, it would be necessary to be aware of the state of the UndoManager. Unfortunately, the UndoManager does not generate events when its internal state changes and it is impossible to keep these buttons in the proper state without enhancing it to add this functionality.

- The buttons should have an associated tooltip that shows the presentation name of next edit that would be undone or the edit that would be redone by pressing them. Although this information is available, it is difficult to use it properly without subclassing JButton and overriding the getToolTipText method to get the tooltip text from the UndoManager on demand. This is another case in which it would be useful to be able to receive an event when the state of the UndoManager changes, so that the tooltip text could be updated directly using setToolTipText.

- If you copy some text onto the system clipboard and then paste it into the JTextPane, you'll find that the Undo button removes all the characters that you pasted in as a single unit. On the other hand, if you type several characters directly into the JTextPane and then use the Undo button, they are deleted one at a time and, similarly, the Redo button replaces them individually. This is different from the behavior of commercial programs such as Microsoft Word, which merges together changes like this into a larger edit that can be undone or redone as a single unit. The support for this is provided by the undo package but is not exploited by the text package.

It is possible to add all this missing functionality to our example program and later in this chapter we will do so. Before we can do that, however, we need to take a closer look at the undo package itself.

Inside the Undo Package

The examples that we have used so far to illustrate the undo mechanism have both used the text package, because undo support is integrated directly into the text components. However, the undo mechanism is completely generic and can be used to allow the user to reverse actions on anything from a single GUI component to the whole user interface. It can also be used to store internal application state even when the state changes did not originate directly from the user interface, thereby facilitating a simple transactional system in which a series of changes can be made separately and then committed or rolled back as a unit. In this section, we'll look at the small number of classes and interfaces that form the basis of the undo package.

UndoableEdit and AbstractUndoableEdit

At the root of the undo mechanism is the `UndoableEdit` interface, which specifies the methods that any class, which describes a state change that can be reversed, must provide. `UndoableEdit` has 11 methods:

```
public void undo() throws CannotUndoException;
public boolean canUndo();
public void redo() throws CannotRedoException;
public boolean canRedo();
public String getPresentationName();
public String getUndoPresentationName();
public String getRedoPresentationName();
public boolean isSignificant();
public boolean addEdit(UndoableEdit anEdit);
public boolean replaceEdit(UndoableEdit anEdit);
public void die();
```

The motivation behind the first seven of these methods should be fairly obvious. The `undo` and `redo` methods cause the `UndoableEdit` to reverse or reapply whatever state changes were made that resulted in it being created. An `UndoableEdit` has two possible states—either it has been done, or it has been undone. The `undo` method can only be invoked when the edit has been done and results in the edit moving to the undone state. Similarly, the `redo` method can only be used when the edit has been undone. When an `Undo-ableEdit` is created, it will usually be in the done state, because it is typically generated at the same time as the action that it describes is performed. If you try to undo an edit that has already been undone, the `undo` method throws a `CannotUndoException` and, similarly, a `CannotRedoException` results from an attempt to redo a redone edit. The `canUndo` and `canRedo` methods can be used to deduce the current state of the edit if necessary. Note that this description applies only to simple edits that encapsulate only one logical state change—we'll see later, in the discussion of `UndoManager`, that it is possible to create edits that describe changes that have more than one state change which can be reversed or redone separately. We saw this with `UndoExample2` in which we were able to type several characters or change text attributes and then undo each action separately, in the reverse order to that in which they were performed.

The `getPresentationName` method is one of three that is intended to be used when displaying information about an `UndoableEdit` to the user, the other two being `getUndoPresentationName` and `getRedoPresentation-Name`, which supply text that should be used to describe respectively the action of undoing or redoing this particular edit. The expectation is that the string returned by `getPresentationName` will be used to create the more specific text returned from the other two methods and, in the implementation of these methods in the `AbstractUndoableEdit` class, the undo presentation name is formed by prefixing the string returned by `getPresentationName` with the word `Undo`, and the redo presentation name is similarly derived. You've already seen examples of what `getPresentationName` returns when applied to edits created by the Swing text package because both `UndoExample1` and `UndoExample2` display the string that it provides in their lower right-hand frames. Typical examples are addition, deletion, and style change.

The `isSignificant` method returns a boolean that indicates, not surprisingly, whether the edit is "significant." The best way to explain this is to consider an example. Suppose you create a user interface that consists of several text fields and you use a single `UndoManager` to catch all the changes in all the text fields, so that the user can progressively undo changes that were made field by field. Labeling these text fields A, B, and C, the user might type a name into field A, house number and street name into field B, and city name into field C. Suppose the user wanted to reverse the last two edits and type a completely different address, leaving the name unchanged. The events generated by the text fields and held in the `UndoManager` make this possible, but there are other things that happen in addition to text being typed—in particular, the user moved the focus between the text fields to type each part of the address. These events are not recorded as `UndoableEdits` by the text fields, but you could arrange to catch focus-loss events and generate an `UndoableEdit` to record them. If you did this, the `UndoManager` would store something like this:

1. Several text insertion edits in text field A
2. A focus-lost edit from text field A
3. Several text insertion edits in text field B
4. A focus-lost event from text field B
5. Text insertion edits in text field C

If the user now used CTRL+Z to reverse these edits, the text typed into field C would be removed, one character for each time the user pressed CTRL+Z. The user would press CTRL+Z again to move the focus back to text field B and several more times to clear field B. Although this represents a true reversal of exactly what happened, the user will probably find it tedious to have to press CTRL+Z to move the focus from field C to field B—this seems like something that should be reversed automatically without the user needing to specifically request it. This is why the concept of a significant edit exists—think of a significant edit as something that the user would want to have to explicitly reverse, while an insignificant edit is one that should be undone as a by-product of other actions. Here, all the text insertion edits would be significant and the focus changes would be insignificant. `UndoManager` recognizes insignificant edits and undoes them as it encounters them when told to undo something. In this example, each CTRL+Z would undo a character insertion in text field C, until the field is empty. The next CTRL+Z will cause the `UndoManager` to encounter the focus-lost edit; because this is not significant, it will undo that edit and then continue looking for a significant edit to undo, resulting in the last character of text field B being removed as well. Note that none of the edits created by the Swing text components describe themselves as insignificant.

The last two methods, `addEdit` and `replaceEdit`, are intended to be used to allow edits to be merged together. This might be appropriate when the user is typing into a text field—if the user enters a sequence of characters, these methods can be used to create a single edit that contains everything that the user typed instead of storing the edits individually as they are generated. This scheme has the advantage that a single undo operation would then remove everything that the user typed in one go. Unfortunately, the

Swing text components do not generate `UndoableEdit`s that support merging, so this does not happen in practice.

The `die` method is used to remove from `UndoManager` edits that should no longer be active. We'll describe this method, as well as `addEdit` and `replaceEdit`, in more detail when looking at compound edits later in this chapter.

There is a basic implementation of the `UndoableEdit` interface in the `AbstractUndoableEdit` class, which is also part of the `javax.swing.undo` package. `AbstractUndoableEdit` is the base class from which all the undoable edits generated by the text package are derived; specific edits override methods of `AbstractUndoableEdit` as necessary. Table 9-1 summarizes what each of the methods of `AbstractUndoableEdit` does.

Table 9-1 Implementing `AbstractUndoableEdit`

Method	*Description*
`undo()`	Checks to see whether the edit can be undone by calling `canUndo` and throws a `CannotUndoException` if it has. If it has not been undone yet, the undo methods mark it as not done by setting the instance variable `hasBeenDone` to `false`. This variable is initialized to `true` when the `AbstractUndoableEdit` is created.
`canUndo()`	If the edit is `alive` (that is, `die` has not been called) and `hasBeenDone` is true, this method returns `true`. Otherwise, it returns `false`.
`redo()`	This method is similar to undo—it calls `canRedo`, throwing a `CannotRedoException` if it returns `false`. Otherwise, it sets `hasBeenDone` to `true`.
`canRedo()`	The `canRedo` method returns `true` if the edit is `alive` and `hasBeenDone` is false. Otherwise, it returns `false` (that is, the edit cannot be redone).
`getPresentationName`	Returns an empty string.

Table 9-1 Implementing `AbstractUndoableEdit` (continued)	
`getUndoPresentationName`	Returns the string returned by `getPre-sentationName` prefixed with the word `Undo`. Typically, a subclass will override `getPresentationName` to return something meaningful and use the `Abstract-UndoableEdit` implementation of this method to get an appropriate string to use when describing this edit in a tooltip.
`getRedoPresentationName`	Returns the string returned by `getPre-sentationName` prefixed with the word `Redo`.
`isSignificant`	Returns `false`.
`addEdit`	Returns `false`, indicating that it does not support merging of edits.
`replaceEdit`	Returns `false`.
`die`	Marks the edit as being not `alive`, which prevents it being either undone or redone.

Because `AbstractUndoableEdit` does not encapsulate any real editing behavior, its `undo` and `redo` methods do not have anything to reverse—this is the responsibility of derived classes. Instead, these methods provide the logic that maintains the internal state of the edit, freeing subclass implementers from having to worry about how to keep track of whether a specific edit has been done or undone. Here's how the `undo` method of a typical real undoable edit is implemented:

```
public void undo() throws CannotUndoException {
    super.undo();
    // Now undo the edit, whatever that means
}
```

By first invoking the `undo` method of `AbstractUndoableEdit`, the proper state checking is performed without any duplication of code. There is, of course, no return value to check because `undo` doesn't return anything; instead, if there is an error, it throws a `CannotUndoException`, which is propagated directly to the caller. As a result, the programmer can assume that the edit is in the correct state to be undone if `super.undo()` returns successfully.

A Simple *UndoableEdit* Example

Let's look at a simple example of the use of the undo package with a Swing component. In this example, we are going to add undo support to the JTree component so that the user can use the CTRL+Z and CTRL+Y keys to undo and redo changes to the expanded state of tree nodes. Whenever the user expands or collapses a node, the tree will create and send an UndoableEdit that can be used to restore the node to its original state. Although this is not a feature you are likely to want to build into a real-world application, it is relatively simple to implement and illustrates how to create UndoableEdits and how to add support for them to a GUI component.

Before we describe the code, let's look at how the example works. If you type the command

```
java AdvancedSwing.Chapter9.UndoExample3
```

you'll be presented with a tree with three nodes in addition to the root node. Click first on the Apollo 8 node and then on the Apollo 12 node to expand both of them, as shown in Figure 9-2. Now if you press the Undo button or use the shortcut CTRL+Z, you'll find that the Apollo 12 node closes. Press Redo or use CTRL+Y and it expands again. Pressing Undo twice collapses both the Apollo 12 and the Apollo 8 nodes, restoring the tree to its original state. Pressing Undo again does nothing (other than causing a beep) because there are no more UndoableEdits to reverse.

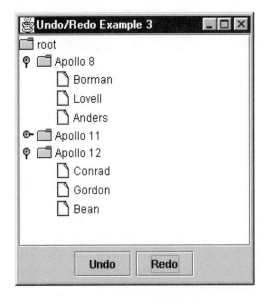

Figure 9-2   A tree with undo and redo support.

The code for this example is very simple. Listing 9-2 shows the application itself. As you can see, this code is very similar to the text-based example shown in Listing 9-1. It starts by creating an instance of a subclass of JTree called UndoableTree and uses it to build the user interface. The Undoable-Tree class, which we'll be looking at shortly, allows interested parties to register as UndoableEditListeners and receive UndoableEditEvents whenever any node in the tree is expanded or collapsed by user or programmatic action. As with the previous example, we delegate the job of catching and managing these events to UndoManager and we add Undo and Redo buttons that give access to it. We also provide the CTRL+Z and CTRL+Y shortcuts that were used in Listing 9-1, except that here we register them against the frame's content pane so that they operate whenever the focus is in the frame.

Listing 9-2 Using a JTree with Undo Support

```
package AdvancedSwing.Chapter9;

import java.awt.*;
import java.awt.event.*;
import javax.swing.*;
import javax.swing.event.*;
import javax.swing.tree.*;
import javax.swing.undo.*;

public class UndoExample3 extends JFrame {
    public UndoExample3() {
        super("Undo/Redo Example 3");

        DefaultMutableTreeNode rootNode =
                        new DefaultMutableTreeNode("root");
        DefaultMutableTreeNode node =
                        new DefaultMutableTreeNode("Apollo 8");
        rootNode.add(node);
        node.add(new DefaultMutableTreeNode("Borman"));
        node.add(new DefaultMutableTreeNode("Lovell"));
        node.add(new DefaultMutableTreeNode("Anders"));

        node = new DefaultMutableTreeNode("Apollo 11");
        rootNode.add(node);
        node.add(new DefaultMutableTreeNode("Armstrong"));
        node.add(new DefaultMutableTreeNode("Aldrin"));
        node.add(new DefaultMutableTreeNode("Collins"));
```

Listing 9-2 Using a `JTree` with Undo Support (continued)

```
node = new DefaultMutableTreeNode("Apollo 12");
rootNode.add(node);
node.add(new DefaultMutableTreeNode("Conrad"));
node.add(new DefaultMutableTreeNode("Gordon"));
node.add(new DefaultMutableTreeNode("Bean"));

UndoableTree tree = new UndoableTree(rootNode);

getContentPane().add(new JScrollPane(tree),
                    BorderLayout.CENTER);

// Create the undo manager and actions
UndoManager manager = new UndoManager();
tree.addUndoableEditListener(manager);

Action undoAction = new UndoAction(manager);
Action redoAction = new RedoAction(manager);

// Add the actions to buttons
JPanel panel = new JPanel();
JButton undoButton = new JButton("Undo");
JButton redoButton = new JButton("Redo");
undoButton.addActionListener(undoAction);
redoButton.addActionListener(redoAction);
panel.add(undoButton);
panel.add(redoButton);
getContentPane().add(panel, BorderLayout.SOUTH);

// Assign the actions to keys
((JComponent)getContentPane()).
            registerKeyboardAction(undoAction,
            KeyStroke.getKeyStroke(KeyEvent.VK_Z,
            InputEvent.CTRL_MASK),
            JComponent.WHEN_IN_FOCUSED_WINDOW);
((JComponent)getContentPane()).
            registerKeyboardAction(redoAction,
            KeyStroke.getKeyStroke(KeyEvent.VK_Y,
            InputEvent.CTRL_MASK),
            JComponent.WHEN_IN_FOCUSED_WINDOW);
}

// The Undo action
public class UndoAction extends AbstractAction {
   public UndoAction(UndoManager manager) {
      this.manager = manager;
   }
```

Listing 9-2 Using a `JTree` with Undo Support (continued)

```
        public void actionPerformed(ActionEvent evt) {
            try {
                manager.undo();
            } catch (CannotUndoException e) {
                Toolkit.getDefaultToolkit().beep();
            }
        }

        private UndoManager manager;
    }

    // The Redo action
    public class RedoAction extends AbstractAction {
        public RedoAction(UndoManager manager) {
            this.manager = manager;
        }

        public void actionPerformed(ActionEvent evt) {
            try {
                manager.redo();
            } catch (CannotRedoException e) {
                Toolkit.getDefaultToolkit().beep();
            }
        }

        private UndoManager manager;
    }

    public static void main(String[] args) {
        JFrame f = new UndoExample3();
        f.addWindowListener(new WindowAdapter() {
            public void windowClosing(WindowEvent evt) {
                System.exit(0);
            }
        });
        f.pack();
        f.setVisible(true);
    }
}
```

The `UndoableTree` class sends an event whenever a node is expanded or collapsed. To implement this, we need to do the following:

1. Allow the registration of `UndoableEditListeners` with the `UndoableTree`.

2. Get control during node expansion or collapse.
3. Create a suitable object that represents the change of node state and implements the `UndoableEdit` interface.
4. Build that object into an `UndoableEditEvent` and send it to all registered listeners.
5. When the `undo` method of the edit is called, revert the node to the state it was in before the event was generated.
6. When the `redo` method is called, put the node into the state it was in after the event.

Let's leave the registration of listeners as a task to be dealt with later and look first at the mechanics of creating the `UndoableEdit` that we'll need for this example. The first task is to get control whenever a node is expanded or contracted. There are four methods in the `JTree` API that deal with this subject:

```
public void collapsePath(TreePath path);
public void collapseRow(int row);
public void expandPath(TreePath path);
public void expandRow(int row);
```

Of these, the two that deal with row numbers actually end up calling the other two, so we only need to concern ourselves with the variants of these methods that use `TreePath` objects. These methods are used by the tree's UI classes to expand or collapse a node in response to user action (such as clicking on a branch node) and they are also the only way to change the expanded state of a node programmatically. Because these methods are effectively a single point of control for this operation, we can override them in our derived class to do whatever we want in addition to actually changing the state of the node. What we need to do, of course, is create a suitable `UndoableEdit` and then broadcast it to our listeners. Listing 9-3 shows the complete implementation of the `UndoableTree` class, including the overridden `expandPath` and `collapsePath` methods.

Listing 9-3 Adding Undo Support to a `JTree`

```
package AdvancedSwing.Chapter9;

import javax.swing.*;
import javax.swing.event.*;
import javax.swing.tree.*;
import javax.swing.undo.*;

public class UndoableTree extends JTree {
    // Only one constructor for brevity
```

Listing 9-3 Adding Undo Support to a `JTree` (continued)

```java
public UndoableTree(TreeNode root) {
   super(root);
}

public void addUndoableEditListener(UndoableEditListener l) {
   support.addUndoableEditListener(l);
}

public void removeUndoableEditListener(
                              UndoableEditListener l) {
   support.removeUndoableEditListener(l);
}

public void collapsePath(TreePath path) {
   boolean wasExpanded = isExpanded(path);

   super.collapsePath(path);

   boolean isExpanded = isExpanded(path);
   if (isExpanded != wasExpanded) {
      support.postEdit(new CollapseEdit(path));
   }
}

public void expandPath(TreePath path) {
   boolean wasExpanded = isExpanded(path);

   super.expandPath(path);

   boolean isExpanded = isExpanded(path);
   if (isExpanded != wasExpanded) {
      support.postEdit(new ExpandEdit(path));
   }
}

private void undoExpansion(TreePath path) {
   super.collapsePath(path);
}

private void undoCollapse(TreePath path) {
   super.expandPath(path);
}

private class CollapseEdit extends AbstractUndoableEdit {
   public CollapseEdit(TreePath path) {
      this.path = path;
```

Listing 9-3 Adding Undo Support to a `JTree` (continued)

```
      }

      public void undo() throws CannotUndoException {
         super.undo();
         UndoableTree.this.undoCollapse(path);
      }

      public void redo() throws CannotRedoException {
         super.redo();
         UndoableTree.this.undoExpansion(path);
      }

      public String getPresentationName() {
         return "node collapse";
      }

      private TreePath path;
   }


   private class ExpandEdit extends AbstractUndoableEdit {
      public ExpandEdit(TreePath path) {
         this.path = path;
      }

      public void undo() throws CannotUndoException {
         super.undo();
         UndoableTree.this.undoExpansion(path);
      }

      public void redo() throws CannotRedoException {
         super.redo();
         UndoableTree.this.undoCollapse(path);
      }

      public String getPresentationName() {
         return "node expansion";
      }

      private TreePath path;
   }

   private UndoableEditSupport support =
                              new UndoableEditSupport(this)
}
```

JTree has many constructors but, to avoid cluttering the listing with irrelevant details, we only implement one in our subclass. The logic for handling the expansion or collapse of a node is shown in the expandPath and collapsePath methods, which are very similar to each other, so we'll cover both cases by looking at how collapsePath works. An UndoableEdit should only be created if the node actually collapses as a result of calling this method. Although this should be guaranteed if this method is invoked as a result of user action, there is no certainty that an application will only invoke collapsePath when the node is expanded. To guard against this case, we first get the expanded state of the node using the isExpanded method, and then invoke the superclass collapsePath implementation to actually cause the node to close. When this method returns, we call isExpanded again. If these two calls return different values, the node must have been collapsed and we can generate our edit. If they return the same value, either the node was already collapsed or the TreePath was illegal; in either case, we don't want to do anything more.

The next problem is what our UndoableEdit implementation should do. We could create a class that provides a complete implementation of the UndoableEdit interface, but it is simpler to subclass AbstractUndoableEdit to get default implementations of methods like isSignificant that we don't need to add anything to. In fact, we create two subclasses of AbstractUndoableEdit called CollapseEdit and ExpandEdit that are used by collapsePath and expandPath respectively. Of course, because these events are the reverse of each other, we could have managed with only one class to which we provide a constructor parameter that tells it which way to behave but, given that the code is so simple, it is clearer to create two very simple classes than one slightly more complex one. For convenience, both of these classes are inner classes of UndoableTree. This is, in fact, a very common way to implement UndoableEdits—they naturally form a part of the object being "edited," so an inner class is a convenient and natural way to build them. In this case, it also allows easy access to the tree to which they relate and saves us having to store that information as another attribute passed to the constructor.

What should the undo and redo methods actually do? As we know, their first job is to invoke their counterparts in their superclass to verify that the edit is in the correct state. Having done this, the undo method of the CollapseEdit has to expand the TreePath that was originally collapsed when the edit was created. Similarly, the redo method must collapse that TreePath. Because we need access to the TreePath, we need to pass this object to the `CollapseEdit` constructor. It would seem, then, that we could implement the `undo` method as simply as this:

```
public void undo() throws CannotUndoException {
    super.undo();
    UndoableTree.this.expandPath(path);   // Plausible, but wrong!
}
```

Unfortunately, this is wrong. The problem is that we have overridden the `expandPath` method so that we can generate an `UndoableEditEvent` after the node is expanded. If we take this approach, when we undo a `Collapse-Edit` we'll get an `ExpandEdit` created and posted to our listeners. This is not what we want! What we actually want to do is invoke the `JTree`'s `expandPath` method, but we can't do this directly from anything other than `Undoable-Tree` itself. To solve this problem, we added to `UndoableTree` private methods called `undoExpansion` and `undoCollapse` that call the `JTree` `expandPath` and `collapsePath` methods for us (see Listing 9-2). Because `CollapseEdit` is an inner class of `UndoableTree`, it has access to these private methods. So, the final implementation of the `undo` method of `Collap-seEdit` looks like this:

```
public void undo() throws CannotUndoException {
    super.undo();
    UndoableTree.this.undoCollapse(path);
}
```

The `redo` method similarly calls `undoExpand`. The same methods are also used by `ExpandEdit`, in which the `undo` method uses `undoExpand` and `redo` calls `undoCollapse`.

Of the other `UndoableEdit` methods, the only one we can usefully override is `getPresentationName`, which, in both cases, returns a string describing the effect of the edit. We don't make any use of this string in this example, but we will see examples of its use later in this chapter.

Once we've created the correct edit, we need to be able to broadcast it to all the `UndoableTree`'s `UndoableEditListeners` in the form of an `Undo-ableEdit`. This requires three things:

- The `UndoableTree` needs to provide `addUndoableEditListener` and `removeUndoableEditListener` methods to allow the registration and removal of listeners.
- When a `CollapseEdit` or `ExpandEdit` has been created, we need to be able to turn it into an `UndoableEditEvent`.
- The `UndoableEditEvent` needs to be sent to all listeners.

Fortunately, we don't have to do much work to provide these features because the undo package contains a class called `UndoableEditSupport` that will do all this for us. Here are the public methods of this class:

```
public UndoableEditSupport();
public UndoableEditSupport(Object source);
public synchronized void addUndoableEditListener(
                        UndoableEditListener l);
public synchronized void removeUndoableEditListener(
                        UndoableEditListener l);
public synchronized void postEdit(UndoableEdit e);
public int getUpdateLevel();
public synchronized void beginUpdate();
public synchronized void endUpdate();
```

To use `UndoableEditSupport`, an event source such as `UndoableTree` creates an instance of it and delegates certain operations to it. The two constructors allow you to determine the source of the `UndoableEditEvents` that this class will generate; if you use the default constructor, the `Undoable-EditSupport` itself appears as the event source. If you want your component to be the source of the event, use the second constructor, as is shown in Listing 9-2. Similarly, the component implements the `addUndoableEditListener` and `removeUndoableEditListener` methods by delegating directly to the ones provided by `UndoableEditSupport`, which manages the registration and removal process and also handles sending events to all registered listeners.

Having created an `UndoableEdit`, there are two ways to use `Undoable-EditSupport` to create and deliver an event. The simplest way is to just invoke `postEdit`, which constructs an `UndoableEditEvent` containing the edit passed as its argument and passes it to its listeners. This is how `Undo-ableTree` delivers its `UndoableEditEvents`. There is also a slightly more advanced mechanism that makes use of the `beginUpdate`, `postEdit`, and `endUpdate` methods that we'll cover in the next section.

Compound Edits

`UndoableEdits` created from the `AbstractUndoableEdit` class represent only a single change to an object. In many cases, it is convenient to group together several actual changes in whatever it is that is being edited and represent them as a single edit that can be undone or redone as a unit. The undo package provides a subclass of `AbstractUndoableEdit` called `Compound-`

`Edit` that can be used to create edits made up of several smaller pieces, each of which is an `UndoableEdit` of some kind. The `CompoundEdit` class provides the same methods as `AbstractUndoableEdit` and adds two more of its own—`isInProgress` and `end`. As well as implementing these new methods, most of the methods inherited from `AbstractUndoableEdit` are overridden to provide behavior appropriate for an edit with multiple subedits.

To create a `CompoundEdit`, you do the following:

1. Create a `CompoundEdit` object. `CompoundEdit` acts as a container for other edits, which is initially empty and "in progress."
2. Add one or more `UndoableEdits` to it using the `addEdit` method. At this stage, the `isInProgress` method would return `true`.
3. Complete the `CompoundEdit` by calling its `end` method.

Once the `end` method has been called, the edit is no longer "in progress" and the `isInProgress` method would now return `false`. This has two consequences:

*   You can't add any more edits. If you try to do so, the `addEdit` method simply returns `false`.
*   You can now undo the edit. If you call `undo` before invoking the `end` method, you get a `CannotUndoException`. Similarly, invoking `redo` before the edit is ended results in a `CannotRedoException`.

Calling `end` is an irreversible step—you cannot subsequently "reopen" the edit and add something new.

Although a `CompoundEdit` is made up of one or more smaller units, calling `undo` results in all the edits that it contains being undone, in reverse order. In other words, a `CompoundEdit` is treated as a single atomic action. Likewise, calling `redo` reapplies all the edits in the order in which they were added. Because of this, users can't tell that they are undoing or redoing a `CompoundEdit` rather than a simple edit—the compound nature of the edit is, in fact, only for the convenience of the software as we'll see when we look at a couple of examples later in this section. Table 9-2 summarizes what the most important `CompoundEdit` methods do by comparison with those of `AbstractUndoableEdit`.

Table 9-2 Implementation of CompoundEdit

Method	Description
undo	If the end method has not been called or undo has already been called since the last redo call (in other words the edit has already been undone), a CannotUndoException is thrown. Otherwise, the last edit added is undone, followed by the one added before that and so on, until they have all been undone.
canUndo	If the end method has not been called or undo has already been called since the last redo call (in other words the edit has already been undone), this method returns false. Otherwise, it returns true.
redo	If the end method has not been called or redo has already been called since the last undo call (in other words the edit has already been redone), a CannotRedoException is thrown. Otherwise, the edits are redone in order, starting with the first one added to the CompoundEdit.
canRedo	If the end method has not been called or redo has already been called since the last undo call (in other words the edit has already been redone), this method returns false. Otherwise, it returns true.
end	Marks the edit as being no longer in progress.
die	Calls die on all the contained edits.
addEdit	If end has been called, this method returns false. Otherwise, it adds the give UndoableEdit at the end of the current set of edits and returns true. See later in this chapter for further discussion of this method.
isInProgress	Returns true if the end method has not been called. After end has been invoked, this method always returns false.
isSignificant	Returns true if the isSignificant method of any of the edits contained by this CompoundEdit returns true. Otherwise returns false.
getPresentationName	Returns the presentation name of the last edit added to the CompoundEdit.

Table 9-2 Implementation of `CompoundEdit` (continued)	
`getUndoPresentationName`	Returns the result of calling `getUndoPresentationName` on the last edit added to the `CompoundEdit`.
`getRedoPresentationName`	Returns the result of calling `getRedoPresentationName` on the last edit added to the `CompoundEdit`.

In the simplest case, the edits in a `CompoundEdit` are simply held in a list in the order in which they were added—in other words, if you create a `CompoundEdit` to which you add five `UndoableEdit`s and call `end`, you end up with a list of five `UndoableEdit`s. However, the `addEdit` method does not simply add each edit to the internal list. Instead, it does the following:

1. If the internal list is empty, the edit is placed in the list.
2. Otherwise, the `addEdit` method of the last edit in the list is called with the new edit as its argument. This gives the last edit a chance to "absorb" the new one, allowing the latest one to be discarded. If this call returns `true`, the new edit is discarded (having added its effect to the last one) and no further action is taken.
3. Otherwise, the `replaceEdit` method of the new edit is called with the last edit added as its argument, giving the new edit the chance to absorb the old edit and take its place, thus reversing the roles of the previous step. If this call returns `true`, the last edit is removed from the list (having become a part of the new edit) and the new one added in its place.
4. Finally, if none of the above applies, the new edit is added to the list.

In principle, this operation is meant to allow related edits to be merged together. As an example, suppose the user types several characters into a document being monitored by an `UndoableEditListener`, which is adding the edits from the `UndoableEditEvent`s that get generated into a `CompoundEdit` that it will subsequently close by calling its `end` method. As you already know, if you insert 10 characters, you get 10 `UndoableEditEvent`s and 10 `UndoableEdit`s will be added to the `CompoundEdit`, each able to undo or redo the insertion of a single character. However, if these `UndoableEdit`s were implemented appropriately, their `addEdit` methods could absorb another `UndoableEdit` if certain conditions were met (that is, both edits must add characters to the document in adjacent locations, or both must delete characters in adjacent locations). In this case, the 10 single-character `UndoableEdits` would be replaced by a single `UndoableEdit` containing all 10 characters. Unfortunately, the edits generated by the Swing text package do not support merging in this way because their `addEdit` and `replaceEdit` methods always return `false` and, in fact, there is no practical use of edit merging anywhere in Swing.

In any case, you might be wondering what the point of edit merging is if `CompoundEdits` can only be undone or redone as a single unit. Because of this, there is very little difference between a `CompoundEdit` containing 10 single-character edits and one with one merged 10-character edit—after all, calling `undo` on either of these results in all 10 characters being removed from the document, so the user would not be able to tell the difference between these two cases. In practice, other than the fact that merging would probably save a small amount of memory (by allowing nine `UndoableEdits` to be discarded) and the undo process would be slightly faster, there appears to be no real reason for `CompoundEdit` to have the concept of edit merging. However, this is not quite true. In fact, the edit merging code is present for the benefit of `UndoManager`, which is a subclass of `CompoundEdit` that has different rules for undoing and redoing the edits that it contains. We'll say more about this in "The `UndoManager` Class" on page 893.

A Compound Edit Example

In the last example, you saw how to create a pair of `UndoableEdits` that can handle the expansion and collapse of a tree node and a subclass of `JTree` that emits `UndoableEditEvents` containing these edits when necessary. However, there is a small problem with this example. To see what it is, run the example again and click on the expansion handle of the Apollo 8 node to expand it and reveal its three child nodes, and then select one of them as shown in Figure 9-3.

Now close the Apollo 8 node by clicking on its expansion handle again. As you know, this will cause the tree to generate an `UndoableEdit` that will be stored by the `UndoManager` so that you can undo it using the Undo button. If you now press Undo, the node reopens but, as you can see from Figure 9-4, the selection is not where it originally was in Figure 9-3. When you collapse a tree node, if any of its children were selected, they are deselected (because they are going out of view) and the collapsing node itself is selected instead. Unfortunately, although our `UndoableEdits` capture the collapse of the branch node, they do not record the fact that the selection might also change as a direct consequence of this.

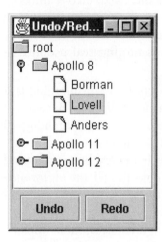

Figure 9-3   Selecting a node in a tree with undo support.

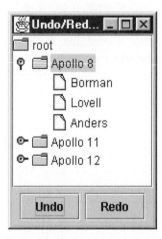

Figure 9-4   Incorrect selection behavior when undoing a node collapse operation.

One way around this is to modify the CollapseEdit and ExpandEdit classes so that they incorporate the selection information and implement the undo and redo methods so that they restore the selection as appropriate. There is, however, a more flexible solution available. Because expanding or collapsing nodes and moving the selection are two separate operations that exist independently of each other, instead of adding code to the existing classes, we implement a new UndoableEdit that deals only with the selection change. When the user expands or collapses a node, instead of creating one `UndoableEdit`, the tree would create two—one for the node state change and one for the selection change. The advantage of this over adding the functionality to the existing classes is that the new `UndoableEdit` class can be used in other contexts in which the user changes the tree selection, without expanding or collapsing a node. If we call this new class `SelectionEdit`, we could change the tree implementation to fire two `UndoableEditEvents` when a node is collapsed, like this:

1. Fire an `UndoableEditEvent` containing a `SelectionEdit`.
2. Fire an `UndoableEditEvent` containing a `CollapseEdit`.

The `UndoManager` would then store these events so that they could be undone on demand. The order in which the events are generated is essential—if they were stored the other way around, the `UndoManager` would first reverse the `SelectionEdit` and then the `CollapseEdit`. This would not achieve the desired effect, because undoing the `SelectionEdit` first would attempt to select a child node that is still invisible. The tree would ignore this, so the branch node would remain selected and would then expand, leaving the selection in the wrong place. On the other hand, storing the edits in the order shown earlier causes the operations to be reversed properly—the `CollapseEdit` is undone first, expanding the node and revealing the three child nodes, followed by the `SelectionEdit`, which will pass the selection to the original child node, which is now visible.

The disadvantage of generating an `UndoableEdit` for each state change is that the `UndoManager` only reverses one of them at a time—that is, when you click `Undo` once, the `CollapseEdit` is undone so that the branch node reopens, but it retains the selection. You need to click `Undo` again to reverse the `SelectionEdit` and have the selection move to the right place. In other words, although the tree created two edits, we want the `UndoManager` to treat them as one so that pressing `Undo` seamlessly would reverse both of them together and subsequently pressing `Redo` would reapply them both. You can achieve exactly this effect by building the two individual edits into a single `CompoundEdit` because, as we said earlier, once the `CompoundEdit` has been closed (that is, the `end` method has been invoked), calling `undo` on it results in the `undo` method of all the individual edits being called in reversed order and similarly for the `redo` method.

There are two ways to create a `CompoundEdit` from a set of `UndoableEdits`. The most direct way is to simply instantiate a `CompoundEdit` object and directly add edits to it using its `addEdit` method:

```
CompoundEdit edit = new CompoundEdit();
```

```
edit.addEdit(new SelectionEdit(/* Parameters not shown */);
edit.addEdit(new CollapseEdit(path));
edit.end();
support.postEdit(edit);          // Post the event to listeners
```

There is also a slightly more compact way to achieve the same thing using the `UndoableEditSupport` class that we used in the previous example. In that example, and in the previous code extract, we created an `UndoableEdit` object and broadcast it to our listeners by calling the `UndoableEditSupport` object's `postEdit` method. `UndoableEditSupport` also has a "batching" mode that is triggered by invoking its `beginUpdate` method, which causes it to create an empty `CompoundEdit`. Once this has been done, you can pass individual edits to it using the `postEdit` method. Instead of directly delivering these edits as `UndoableEditEvents`, `UndoableEditSupport` adds them to the `CompoundEdit`, until you call `endUpdate`, at which point it creates and broadcasts an `UndoableEditEvent` containing the entire `CompoundEdit`. Calling `endUpdate` also switches off the batching, so a subsequent call to `postEdit` would deliver the edit immediately unless preceded by another invocation of `beginUpdate`. Using this mechanism, the code extract shown earlier would be rewritten like this, where `support` is an instance of `UndoableEditSupport`:

```
support.beginUpdate();
support.postEdit(new SelectionEdit(/* Parameters not shown */);
support.postEdit(new CollapseEdit(path));
support.endUpdate();
```

What about the `UndoableEdit` that manages the change of tree selection? Implementing this is very simple—all we need to do is get the state of the tree's selection model before and after the node is expanded or collapsed and store that information in the `SelectionEdit` object which, like `ExpandEdit` and `CollapseEdit`, is derived from `AbstractUndoableEdit`. To undo the edit, we call the tree's `setSelectionPaths` method with the selection saved before the node changed state and to redo it we do the same thing but pass the state of the selection after the expansion or collapse. The details are shown in Listing 9-4, in which the changes made from our first `Undoable-Tree` implementation (in Listing 9-3) are shown in bold.

> **Listing 9-4** Creating a `CompoundEdit` with
> `UndoableEditSupport`

```
package AdvancedSwing.Chapter9;

import javax.swing.*;
import javax.swing.event.*;
import javax.swing.tree.*;
import javax.swing.undo.*;

public class UndoableTree2 extends JTree {
    public UndoableTree2(TreeNode root) {
        super(root);
    }

    public void addUndoableEditListener(UndoableEditListener l) {
        support.addUndoableEditListener(l);
    }

    public void removeUndoableEditListener(
                                  UndoableEditListener l) {
        support.removeUndoableEditListener(l);
    }

    public void collapsePath(TreePath path) {
        boolean wasExpanded = isExpanded(path);
        TreePath[] selections = getSelectionPaths();

        super.collapsePath(path);

        boolean isExpanded = isExpanded(path);
        if (isExpanded != wasExpanded) {
            TreePath[] newSelections = getSelectionPaths();
            support.beginUpdate();
            support.postEdit(new SelectionEdit(selections,
                                             newSelections));
            support.postEdit(new CollapseEdit(path));
            support.endUpdate();
        }
    }

    public void expandPath(TreePath path) {
        boolean wasExpanded = isExpanded(path);
        TreePath[] selections = getSelectionPaths();
```

```
      super.expandPath(path);

      boolean isExpanded = isExpanded(path);
      if (isExpanded != wasExpanded) {
         TreePath[] newSelections = getSelectionPaths();
         support.beginUpdate();
         support.postEdit(new SelectionEdit(selections,
                                            newSelections));
         support.postEdit(new ExpandEdit(path));
         support.endUpdate();
      }
   }

   private void undoExpansion(TreePath path) {
      super.collapsePath(path);
   }

   private void undoCollapse(TreePath path) {
      super.expandPath(path);
   }

   private class CollapseEdit extends AbstractUndoableEdit {
      public CollapseEdit(TreePath path) {
         this.path = path;
      }

      public void undo() throws CannotUndoException {
         super.undo();
         UndoableTree2.this.undoCollapse(path);
      }

      public void redo() throws CannotRedoException {
         super.redo();
         UndoableTree2.this.undoExpansion(path);
      }

      public String getPresentationName() {
         return "node collapse";
      }

      private TreePath path;
   }
```

```
private class ExpandEdit extends AbstractUndoableEdit {
   public ExpandEdit(TreePath path) {
      this.path = path;
   }

   public void undo() throws CannotUndoException {
      super.undo();
      UndoableTree2.this.undoExpansion(path);
   }

   public void redo() throws CannotRedoException {
      super.redo();
      UndoableTree2.this.undoCollapse(path);
   }

   public String getPresentationName() {
      return "node expansion";
   }

   private TreePath path;
}

private class SelectionEdit extends AbstractUndoableEdit {
   public SelectionEdit(TreePath[] oldSelections,
                        TreePath[] newSelections) {
      this.oldSelections = oldSelections;
      this.newSelections = newSelections;
   }

   public void undo() throws CannotUndoException {
      super.undo();
      UndoableTree2.this.setSelectionPaths(oldSelections);
   }

   public void redo() throws CannotRedoException {
      super.redo();
      UndoableTree2.this.setSelectionPaths(newSelections);
   }

   public String getPresentationName() {
      return "selection change";
   }
```

Listing 9-4 Creating a `CompoundEdit` **with**
`UndoableEditSupport` (continued)

```
        private TreePath[] oldSelections;
        private TreePath[] newSelections;
    }

    private UndoableEditSupport support =
                                new UndoableEditSupport(this);
}
```

You can try this code by typing the following command:

```
java AdvancedSwing.Chapter9.UndoExample4
```

When the tree appears, do the following:

1. Click the expansion handle for the Apollo 8 node.
2. Click the expansion handle for the Apollo 11 node.
3. Click the node for Armstrong.
4. Hold down the SHIFT key and click the node labeled Collins. This selects all three child nodes of the Apollo 11 node.
5. Click the expansion handle for Apollo 11 again. This causes the node to collapse and the selection will move from the three child nodes to the Apollo 11 node.

Each time you open or close a node, an `UndoableEditEvent` is delivered to the `UndoManager`, which extracts the associated `UndoableEdits` and stores them. At this point, three `UndoableEdits` have been sent to the `UndoManager`, as shown in Figure 9-5.

If you now press the Undo button, the `UndoManager` will invoke the undo method of the last `UndoableEdit` that was added to it, which is the `CompoundEdit` labeled C in Figure 9-5. Because calling undo on a `CompoundEdit` undoes all the edits it contains, this will result in the `CollapseEdit` being undone, followed by the `SelectionEdit`, thus restoring the selection to the three child nodes of the Apollo 11 node. At this point, the state of the `UndoManager` will have changed to that shown in Figure 9-6.

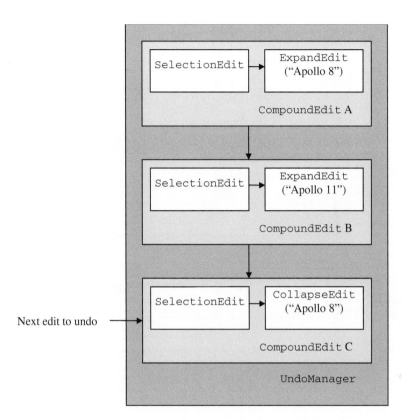

Figure 9-5 UndoableEdits generated from the tree.

Obviously, pressing Undo again will undo CompoundEdit B and collapse the Apollo 11 node again. Pressing Redo at this point will redo edit B to expand that node and restore the selection, while pressing Redo again will collapse the node again. The important points to note about this are the following:

- The individual edits of a CompoundEdit cannot be separately undone or redone—to all intents and purposes, a CompoundEdit appears to be a single edit.
- The edits stored by UndoManager can be manipulated separately, even though UndoManager is derived from CompoundEdit. This allows the user to reverse individual operations.

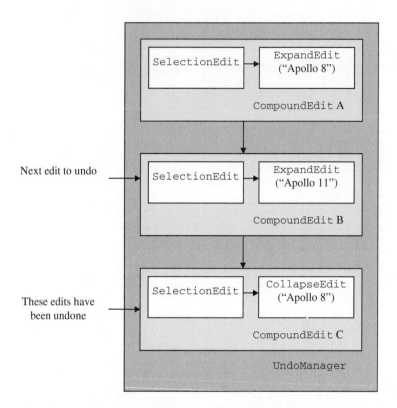

Figure 9-6 Undoing a single edit with `UndoManager`.

Compound Edits and the Text Components

The edits created by the Swing text component are very similar to the ones that you've seen in the two tree examples shown earlier in that they are `CompoundEdits` made of simpler action-specific edits derived from the base class `AbstractUndoableEdit`. The basic edits are generated by low-level code within the text package and are merged into a `CompoundEdit` at the point that the `UndoableEditEvent` is delivered to the `UndoableEditListeners` of a text component's `Document`. There is, in fact, a direct relationship between the edits, the `UndoableEditEvent` delivered to the `Undoable-EditListeners`, and the corresponding `DocumentEvent` created for `Docu-mentListeners`. The relationship between these classes for a typical change to a text component is shown in Figure 9-7.

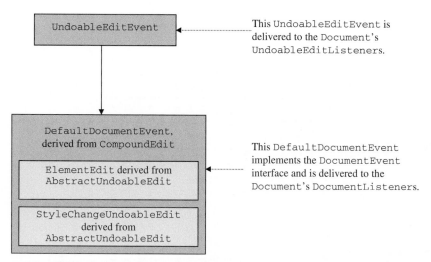

Figure 9-7   Text component events and `UndoableEdits`.

As you can see, the `DocumentEvent` that is delivered to `DocumentListeners` is actually an instance of the class `DefaultDocumentEvent`, an inner class of `javax.swing.text.AbstractDocument`. Recall from Chapter 1 that, unlike the other Swing events (and AWT events), `DocumentEvent` is actually an interface, not a class. `DefaultDocumentEvent` implements the `DocumentEvent` interface but is also derived from `CompoundEdit`, so it can contain edits described by the simpler `AbstractUndoableEdit` subclasses generated by code in the `Document` implementations. Because of this arrangement, `DocumentListeners` can get access to the `UndoableEdit` information for any change to the `Document` simply by casting the `DocumentEvent` to a `DefaultDocumentEvent`, but this is not recommended because it makes an assumption about the implementation of the text package. The same `DefaultDocumentEvent` is also delivered to `UndoableEditListeners` as the edit associated with the `UndoableEdit` passed to the listener's methods. Using an `UndoableEditListener` is the recommended way to get direct access to the `UndoableEdit`, by calling the `UndoableEditEvent`'s `getEdit` method, which returns a reference to the `DefaultDocumentEvent` object.

The text package defines four `UndoableEdit` classes, all derived from `AbstractUndoableEdit`. Table 9-3 describes what these `UndoableEdits` mean and the information that they store.

Table 9-3 UndoableEdits Defined in the Text Package

Class Name	Defining Class	Description
AttributeUndoableEdit	DefaultStyledDocument	This edit is used when changing or replacing the attributes of an Element of a document. It stores a reference to the Element, the existing elements, the new attributes being applied, and a flag indicating whether these attributes replace or merge into the existing ones. To undo the operation, the old attributes are simply used to directly replace the current attribute set of the Element. To apply or redo the operation, the new attributes are merged with the existing set, or overwrite them if total replacement is required.
StyleChangeUndoableEdit	DefaultStyledDocument	Records a change in the logical style associated with a paragraph. The new Style, the original logical style, and a reference to the paragraph's Element are stored. To perform or redo the operation, the attribute resolving parent of the Element is set to the new Style supplied. To undo the operation, the original resolving parent attribute set is restored.
ElementEdit	AbstractDocument	ElementEdit records a change to the underlying Element structure of a Document. It stores a reference to a parent Element, an index into that parent where the change starts, an array of Elements added, and an array of Elements removed. To apply the operation, the child Elements in the *removed* set, which start at the given index within the parent, are removed and then the Elements in the *added* set are inserted instead of them. The redo action reverses this process.
InsertUndo	GapContent and StringContent	This edit records the insertion of text into the Content underlying the model. The text being inserted and the offset at which it is inserted are supplied to the constructor. The operations needed to apply or redo and to undo this change are simple and are performed directly by the Content class on the data that it stores.
RemoveUndo	GapContent and StringContent	This class is the same as InsertUndo except that it represents the removal of text. Because of this, they are almost exact copies of each other with the undo and redo methods swapped over.

In many cases, the `DefaultDocumentEvent` will only contain one of these edits. Direct insertion of text, for example, will create a `DefaultDocument-Event` with a single `InsertUndo` edit. However, there are cases to which this does not apply. To see an example of this, type the following command

```
java AdvancedSwing.Chapter9.UndoExample2
```

which runs an example that we saw earlier in this chapter. Now type text into the text pane, select some (but not all) of it and use the `Font` and `Style` menus to change the selected text to bold. When you do this, you'll see the following event appear in the Undo Monitor window:

```
style change([javax.swing.text.AbstractDocument$
        ElementEdit@696fcbac hasBeenDone: true alive: true,
javax.swing.text.DefaultStyledDocument$
        AttributeUndoableEdit@698fcbac
hasBeenDone: true alive: true])
```

Here, the `DefaultDocumentEvent` contains an `ElementEdit` followed by an `AttributeUndoableEdit`, the latter of which applies the attribute change that makes the text appear bold. Why is there also an `ElementEdit` here? As we saw earlier in this book, a range of characters within the document that has the same attributes is managed by a single `Element`. When you type the original text into the text pane, it is all mapped by one leaf `Element`. However, when you change the font of some of the text to bold, not all the text will have the same attribute set, so it can no longer be covered by a single `Element`. Hence, the existing element is replaced by two or three new ones, depending on how you selected the text. Suppose you type the text `Some text` into the text pane. The initial `Element` structure will include a single leaf `Element` mapping all these characters, as shown in Figure 9-8.

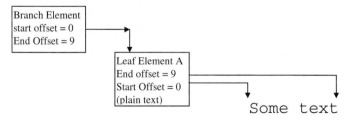

Figure 9-8 Element structure for a simple document.

If you now select the text `me te` and change its font to bold, the text will be divided into three regions, each with a different attribute set:

1. The characters `So` with the original plain font

2. The characters me te with a bold font
3. The characters xt also with the original font

Because there are three different attribute sets involved, there needs to be three Elements to cover the same text mapped by the original leaf Element, as shown in Figure 9-9.

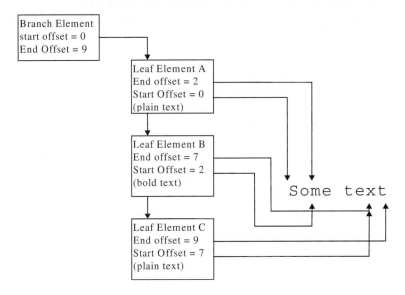

Figure 9-9   Element structure after an attribute change.

To change the font of the middle five characters to bold, the following steps are performed:

1. The original leaf Element at offset 0 of the branch Element for the paragraph is removed and three new Elements with the same attribute set are inserted instead.

2. The attribute set of the middle Element is changed to include the bold setting.

The first of these two actions generates the ElementEdit and the second results in the AttributeUndoableEdit. Both of these are encapsulated inside a single CompoundEdit, so they will always be undone or redone as a single unit. If this edit is undone, the attribute change is reversed first and then the Element change is undone by restoring the original leaf Element.

Core Note

Because ElementEdit *operates by storing references to* Elements *that are no longer in use, it is possible to use up memory very quickly if you keep a long history of document changes in your* UndoManager. *As we'll see in the next section, it is possible to configure how many updates* UndoManager *will store and to discard unwanted edits at any time.*

The UndoManager Class

Throughout this chapter we've made use of the UndoManager class to store UndoableEdits generated by the GUI components in our examples and to provide the ability for the user to undo and redo those edits. As we said earlier, UndoManager is a direct subclass of CompoundEdit, but there are a few differences between these two classes that we'll look at in this section. We'll also show you how to extend the functionality of UndoManager to make it more useful in real applications; the change that we'll make is trivial, but you'll see that the user interface will be greatly improved as a result.

Differences Between UndoManager and CompoundEdit

The principal aim of the CompoundEdit class is to allow the source of UndoableEdit events to group them together is such a way that, while being logically separate from the point of view of the originating software, they are presented as a single unit to the user. By contrast, UndoManager has an almost entirely opposite aim: It is intended to act as a last-in, first-out stack of edits that the user can undo and redo separately, so it is important that the individual edits within an UndoManager can be acted upon individually. While CompoundEdit is a convenience for the developer, UndoManager was created for the benefit of the user.

The undo and redo Methods

In the case of CompoundEdit, you cannot invoke undo or redo until all the edits have been added and the end method has been called. Once this has happened, the undo method undoes all the edits in reverse order and the redo method redoes them in their original order. With UndoManager, the situation is quite different. In most cases, end will never be invoked for UndoManager—in fact, if you call its end method, the UndoManager reverts to being a simple CompoundEdit and will only undo or redo all its edits as a unit. In the more usual case in which end has not been called, UndoManager keeps track of the location of the last edit that it undid which, by default, is the last one added to it. If you call undo, it undoes that edit and moves its internal pointer to the edit before (as we'll see below that, because of the concept of insignificant edits, this is not quite true, but we'll avoid that complication for now). Thus, for example, in Figure 9-5 edit C was originally the next edit to be reversed. When undo was called, that edit was undone and the next one to undo became edit B, as shown in Figure 9-6. Calling redo moves the pointer the other way, of course.

The die and addEdit Methods

The implementations of the die and addEdit methods of UndoManager differ from those of CompoundEdit. If you invoke die on a CompoundEdit, the die methods of all the edits that it contains are invoked, thus rendering the entire CompoundEdit useless. With UndoManager, however, calling die affects only those edits that have been undone and not redone. Furthermore, the UndoManager addEdit method, unlike that of CompoundEdit, does not necessarily add a new edit after all the existing ones. To see what actually happens and why the die method behaves as it does, let's look at an example. Suppose the user types the text Some yext into a text field monitored by an UndoManager, causing an UndoableEdit to be generated and stored for each character typed. Assuming the user really intended to type Some text, the user might now decide to back up and change the incorrect y to a t by pressing CTRL+Z four times to undo the incorrect insertions and then typing t. After last the four edits have been undone and before the t has been inserted, the state of the UndoManager will be as shown in Figure 9-10.

The four edits on the right side of Figure 9-10, edits 6 to 9, have been undone, while the five to the left have not. At this point, the user will type the letter t and the text component will send out another UndoableEditEvent containing an InsertUndo edit for the string t. Let's call this new edit number 10. What should UndoManager do with this edit? Obviously, it can't add it to the end of the list after edit 9, because that doesn't reflect the user's actions. In fact, UndoManager inserts the new edit immediately after the next edit to be undone (edit 5) and then discards all the edits that are in the undone state (edits 6 to 9), calling their die methods in the course of doing so. This leaves the UndoManager in the state shown in Figure 9-11.

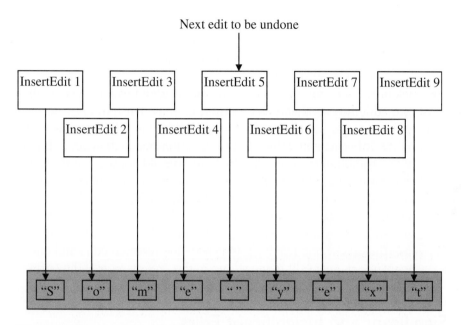

Figure 9-10 Undoing edits with `UndoManager`.

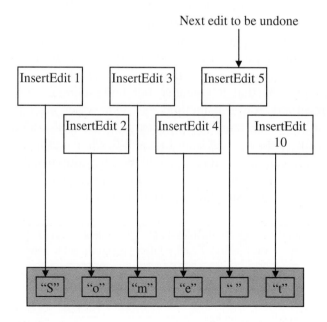

Figure 9-11 `UndoManager` state after undoing edits and inserting a new edit.

There are two important points to note about this:

- Calling `die` on an `UndoManager` results in the `die` methods of any edit that has been undone being invoked. Edits that have not been undone are not affected.
- Adding a new edit to an `UndoManager` by calling its `addEdit` method discards any edits that are in the undone state which means, of course, that these edits can no longer be redone. This is correct behavior because undoing a set of insertions using CTRL+Z and then typing something new implies that the user did not want to retain the characters whose insertions were undone. Note that this is *not* the same as removing the text by using the DELETE key instead of CTRL+Z, because character delete operations are themselves `UndoableEdits` that are held by the `UndoManager`. Deleting four characters and inserting a new one results in four new `RemoveUndo` edits and one new `InsertUndo` edit being stored in the `UndoManager`; the entire sequence can be reversed by calling undo five times.

Significant and Insignificant Edits

When we looked at the methods of `UndoableEdit`, we saw that it is possible to implement the `isSignificant` method in such a way that edits that should not require explicit action by the user to be undone can be automatically reversed as part of an undo operation. An edit of this type, typically something like a shift of the input focus, should return `false` from its `isSignificant` method. `CompoundEdit` ignores the `isSignificant` method when undoing the edits that it contains, but `UndoManager` does not—it uses the value returned from this method to decide which edits to undo. Previously, we said that `UndoManager` undoes only the edit added before the one most recently undone—that is, in Figure 9-5, when edit C has been undone, the next undo candidate would be edit B. This simple statement is true as long as all the edits have an `isSignificant` method that returns `true`. Consider, however, the situation shown in Figure 9-12.

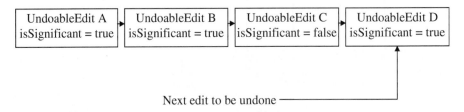

Next edit to be undone

Figure 9-12 `UndoManager` and insignificant edits.

Here, there are four `UndoableEdits`, of which three are significant and one is not. The first time `undo` is called in the `UndoManager`, edit D is undone, leaving C as the next one to undo, as shown in Figure 9-13.

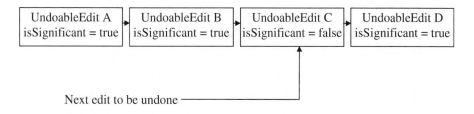

Figure 9-13 `UndoManager` after undoing a significant edit.

If `undo` is called again, edit C will, of course, be undone, but the process would not stop there. Because edit C is not significant, `UndoManager` will also undo edit B, changing its state to that shown in Figure 9-14.

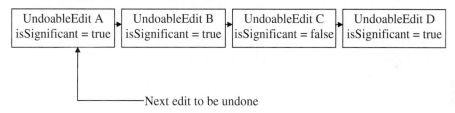

Figure 9-14 The effect of undoing an insignificant edit.

In fact, when `undo` is called, `UndoManager` undoes as many insignificant edits as it finds until it locates an edit whose `isSignificant` method returns `true`. The significant edit will also be undone and the process will stop. In other words, the logic of the undo method is something like this:

```
while there is still an edit to undo and its
        isSignificant method returns false {
    undo the edit
}
if there is still an edit to undo {
    undo it;       // Must be a significant edit
}
```

This process allows, for example, focus changes stored as insignificant edits to be reversed automatically without the user having to know about them and press CTRL+Z or an `Undo` button an extra time. The same process applies to redo—after redoing an edit, `UndoManager` looks for any insignificant edits that follow it and will undo those as well, until another significant edit is encountered (which will *not* be undone) or all the edits have been redone.

Note the subtle difference between this example, which proposes the use of insignificant edits to transparently store and reverse focus changes, and our tree example which used a `CompoundEdit` to bundle a selection change with a tree expansion or collapse edit to arrange for a selection change to happen together with the change in state of the tree node without the user having to request it. Because the selection change and the focus change are both effectively managed outside the control of the user, why are two different mechanisms used? The reason is a practical one that is connected to who generates the edits. In the case of the tree, the node collapse and the selection change are necessarily related to each other because the latter, if it happens at all, will happen only as a direct result of the former. These edits are, therefore, tightly coupled and can conveniently be placed in a single `CompoundEdit`. On the other hand, the example shown in Figure 9-12 may result from the following sequence of user actions:

1. User types A into text field 1, generating significant edit A.

2. User types B into text field 1, generating significant edit B.

3. User clicks in text field 2, moving the focus and generating insignificant edit C.

4. User types C into text field 2, generating significant edit D.

There is no necessary relationship between any of these edits—the first two are from the same text field, but they are separate `CompoundEdits`. The focus-changed edit would probably be generated by some kind of form-level logic that listens for focus changes and has no knowledge of the edits generated by the text fields. It should be obvious that there is no real way for the focus-change edit to be bundled into any of the other `CompoundEdits` and the same argument holds for the last character insertion. In cases like this, where the edits come from unrelated software components, an edit that needs to be recorded but should be invisible to the user should be implemented as an insignificant edit. When the edit is an immediate and necessary side effect of a state change that also creates an `UndoableEdit`, it is better to bundle them in the same `CompoundEdit` and both edits should return true from their `isSignificant` methods.

Other UndoManager Features

There are a couple of other UndoManager features that we'll mention in passing but otherwise say very little about:

- UndoManager supplies a set of convenience methods for the simple management of a trivial UndoManager instance that contains only one UndoableEdit. In this simple case, only one of the undo or redo methods can be successfully invoked at any given time; when undo has been called, only redo is then legal and vice versa. To save the application the trouble of having to remember which state the single edit is in, UndoManager provides the undoOrRedo method, which simply calls either undo or redo as appropriate. There is also a canUndoOrRedo method that returns true unless the UndoManager contains no edits, in which case it returns false. Calling undoOrRedo when the UndoManager has no edits results in an exception being thrown.

- It is possible to set an upper limit on the number of edits that an UndoManager will store. By default, UndoManager will hold up to 100 edits at the same time, but you can set a different limit using the setLimit method which takes the maximum number of contained edits as an integer argument. If invoking setLimit reduces the capacity of the UndoManager to the extent that it contains more edits than it is allowed to, it will discard its oldest edits (and call their die methods) and retains half of its full quota. Thus, for example, if the UndoManager contains 60 edits (numbered 0 through 59) and setLimit is called with argument 50, edits 0 through 24 will be discarded, leaving the UndoManager with 25 edits and capacity for another 25 to be added. The same happens if adding an edit exceeds the allowed capacity—half the edits are discarded. It is also possible to remove all the edits by calling the discardAllEdits method.

Extending UndoManager

To close this chapter, we're going to address what seems to be an oversight in the design of the UndoManager class. If you run any of the undo examples that we've seen so far in this chapter, you'll see that the Undo and Redo buttons are always enabled. This isn't really correct—each button should be enabled only if it can actually perform the function that it is advertising. This means, for example, that the Undo button should start in the disabled state and become enabled only when an UndoableEdit is added to the UndoManager. Furthermore, when the Undo button is pressed, an edit will be undone and, if there are no remaining edits to undo, the Undo button should be disabled again. Of course, you can tell whether there is an edit that can be undone by calling the UndoManager's canUndo method—the trouble is that there is no convenient way to know when it might be a good idea to call this method.

To address this problem, we need to arrange for UndoManager to generate an event when its state changes in such a way as to affect objects, like the Undo button, that need to know whether an UndoableEdit is available. To do this, we have to create a subclass of UndoManager and do the following:

1. Decide on the type of event to broadcast in the event of a suitable state change.
2. Provide a means for listeners to register to receive these events and to deregister themselves when necessary.
3. Work out when the event should be generated and add the code to deliver it at the appropriate points.

Event Type

Swing and AWT between them define many event types, as do other packages in the JDK. Some of these events carry state information, while others just convey the fact that a state change has happened. We could choose to reuse an existing event type for our extended UndoManager or create one of our own, but the option of inventing our own event should only be taken if there is no existing event that can properly be used to convey the meaning that we need to pass to our event's listeners. As it turns out, there are at least two existing events that fit this description, so there is no need for us to add a new event for this example. The events that are worth consideration are java.beans.PropertyChangeEvent and javax.swing.event.ChangeEvent. The distinguishing points of these events are as follows:

PropertyChangeEvent   This event notifies a change in the value of a bound property of some object. The event contains the source of the event, the name of the property (a string), together with its values before and after the change took place.

ChangeEvent   A ChangeEvent signifies a change of some kind in the internal state of its source. Other than carrying a reference to the source, this event has no qualifying information—the listener is expected to discover the nature of the change by directly querying the event source or, in simple cases where the meaning of the event is unambiguous, by inference.

We could reasonably use either of these events to satisfy the requirements of this example—there is, in fact, very little to choose between them. The implementation you'll see below actually uses ChangeEvent. The reasons for this choice were:

- A PropertyChangeEvent should carry the value of the property that changed before and after the change took place. In terms of UndoManager, this means extracting and sending the set of UndoableEdits that have not been undone before and after whatever change occurred. While this could be done, it is unlikely that these values would be of any real use to a listener—as you'll see later, all the listener really needs to know is whether the UndoManager can perform an undo or redo operation in its new state, which can be deduced by simply calling its canUndo or canRedo method—in other words, by directly querying the source, which follows the prototypical usage of a ChangeEvent.

- Using a PropertyChangeEvent implies the existence of an underlying property whose value can be obtained using a "getter" method (and perhaps changed with a "setter" method, although that clearly would be inappropriate here). In the case of UndoManager, the property would be the set of UndoableEdits that have not yet been undone. Adding a method to retrieve this set would be possible but, as noted earlier, would be of little use.

By contrast with these points, a ChangeEvent just tells listeners that they need to check back with the event source to get updated state information— there is no implication that some tangible "property" exists. Because in the UndoManager case the state that the listener is interested in is just a boolean, there is little overhead involved in requiring the listener to obtain the state from the UndoManager rather than delivering it with the event, especially as the methods to be used to retrieve it (canUndo and canRedo) already exist. Using a ChangeEvent results in a simpler implementation both for the event source and for its listeners.

Listener Registration

Having chosen to use `ChangeEvents`, it follows that listeners of our `UndoManager` subclass will need to implement the `ChangeListener` interface and to register and remove them we need to include the following methods:

```
public void addChangeListener(ChangeListener listener);

public void removeChangeListener(ChangeListener listener);
```

As you might expect, the management of listeners is a very common task within the implementation of the Swing component set and there is a core facility that provides the necessary code for this. Listing 9-5 shows the code for our subclass of `UndoManager`, called `MonitorableUndoManager`, which contains the listener management methods.

Listing 9-5 An Extended `UndoManager` Class

```
package AdvancedSwing.Chapter9;

import javax.swing.event.*;
import javax.swing.undo.*;

public class MonitorableUndoManager extends UndoManager {

    // List of listeners for events from this object
    protected EventListenerList listenerList =
                            new EventListenerList();

    // A ChangeEvent dedicated to a single MonitorableUndoManager
    protected ChangeEvent changeEvent;

    // Super class overrides
    public synchronized void setLimit(int l) {
        super.setLimit(l);
        fireChangeEvent();
    }

    public synchronized void discardAllEdits() {
        super.discardAllEdits();
        fireChangeEvent();
    }
```

Listing 9-5 An Extended UndoManager **Class (continued)**

```java
public synchronized void undo() throws CannotUndoException {
    super.undo();
    fireChangeEvent();
}

public synchronized void redo() throws CannotRedoException {
    super.redo();
    fireChangeEvent();
}

public synchronized boolean addEdit(UndoableEdit anEdit) {
    boolean retval = super.addEdit(anEdit);
    fireChangeEvent();
    return retval;
}

// Support for ChangeListeners
public void addChangeListener(ChangeListener l) {
    listenerList.add(ChangeListener.class, l);
}

public void removeChangeListener(ChangeListener l) {
    listenerList.remove(ChangeListener.class, l);
}

protected void fireChangeEvent() {
    Object[] listeners = listenerList.getListenerList();
    for (int i = listeners.length - 2; i >= 0; i -= 2) {
        if (listeners[i] == ChangeListener.class) {
            if (changeEvent == null) {
                changeEvent = new ChangeEvent(this);
            }
            ((ChangeListener)listeners[i+1]).stateChanged(
                                        changeEvent);
        }
    }
}
```

The listener management in this class is typified by the implementation of the addChangeListener method, which looks like this:

```java
public void addChangeListener(ChangeListener l) {
    listenerList.add(ChangeListener.class, l);
}
```

As you can see, it simply delegates to another object, declared like this:

```
protected EventListenerList listenerList =
                            new EventListenerList();
```

The `EventListenerList` is a class that stores information about listeners. To register a new listener, you call its `add` method, passing the `Class` object for the listener's interface and a reference to a new listener instance to be stored. A single `EventListenerList` can store all the listeners for a given object, even if that object can generate events of different types. You can, for example, have a single `EventListenerList` for an object that generates both `ActionEvents` and `ChangeEvents`. To register the listeners, you distinguish them by the listener interface class, for example:

```
public void addChangeListener(
                   ChangeListener changeListenerInstance) {
   listenerList.add(ChangeListener.class,
                   changeListenerInstance);
}
public void addChangeListener(
                   ActionListener actionListenerInstance) {
   listenerList.add(ActionListener.class,
                   actionListenerInstance);
}
```

The `removeChangeListener` method is implemented in a similar way.

Event Generation and Delivery

Once we detect a state change, we need to deliver a `ChangeEvent`. Because these events will be generated in several locations, we create a convenience method called `fireChangeEvent` that delivers the event to all our listeners:

```
protected void fireChangeEvent() {
   Object[] listeners = listenerList.getListenerList();
   for (int i = listeners.length - 2; i >= 0; i -= 2) {
      if (listeners[i] == ChangeListener.class) {
         if (changeEvent == null) {
            changeEvent = new ChangeEvent(this);
         }
         ((ChangeListener)listeners[i+1]).stateChanged(
                                    changeEvent);
      }
   }
}
```

To deliver the event, we need to get hold of the list of our registered listeners, which is maintained by the `EventListenerList` class and can be obtained, in the form of an `Object` array, from its `getListenerList` method. To understand this code, you need to know that the array that this method returns always has an even number of entries. Each entry pair consists of the event listener class in the even-numbered slot and the listener instance reference in the odd-numbered slot, as shown in Figure 9-15.

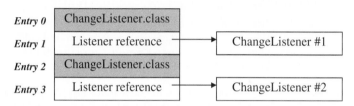

Figure 9-15 How `EventListenerList` stores listener references.

To deliver the event, this code traverses the array, checking the even-numbered entry of each pair to see if it contains the value `ChangeListener.class` that signifies a `ChangeListener` and, if it does, using the odd-numbered entry as a reference to the listener with which to call its `stateChanged` method. Note that the array is processed from the end rather than from the start, which means that the most recently added listeners will receive the event first. In practice, listeners should not depend on this ordering—it just happens to be implemented this way for all `JComponents`, so we continue the theme here.

Another point to notice is that the event actually delivered is a static member of the class that is created the first time it is needed—in other words, we only create one `ChangeEvent` that is passed on every call to every `ChangeListener`. This optimization is typical of event delivery in the Swing packages—it saves time and reduces the amount of garbage collection that needs to be done. It does, of course, assume that listeners will not modify the content of the event while processing it; because it has no useful information other than the event source, this is a reasonable assumption.

The remaining problem is where to put the calls to the `fireChangeEvent` method. As you can see from Listing 9-5, there are several such calls. The rationale behind these calls is summarized here, by method.

Methods that do not appear in this list do not need to be overridden and so are inherited directly from `UndoManager`.

setLimit	Usually, changing the number of edits that UndoManager can hold will not affect whether this an undoable or redoable edit available, but there are some cases in which it might. Suppose, for example, that the UndoManager has capacity for 100 edits and actually contains 60, of which numbers 30 through 59 have been undone and numbers 0 to 29 have not. In this case, the user could either undo edit 29 or redo edit 30, so both the Undo and Redo buttons should be enabled. If setLimit is now called to reduce the capacity to 20, only the most recent 10 edits will be retained—those numbered 50 through 59. Because all these have been undone, a redo is still possible, but there is nothing to undo, so the Undo button should be disabled. Because of this, a ChangeEvent needs to be generated.
discardAllEdits	The reasoning here is the same as for setLimit, because all the edits will be discarded and both the Undo and Redo buttons should be disabled.
undo and redo	The rationale behind generating events in these methods should be obvious—one of them increases the number of redoable edits and reduces the number of undoable edits, while the other does the reverse. Thus, an event needs to be generated.
addEdit	Calling the addEdit method adds another edit that can be undone, which means that the Undo button should be enabled. This requires the generation of an event, to give the application an opportunity to enable the button.

Using the MonitorableUndoManager Class

You can see our MonitorableUndoManager class in action by typing the following command:

```
java AdvancedSwing.Chapter9.UndoExample5
```

This program is based on one of our earlier JTextPane examples (UndoExample2) with a few minor modifications. Listing 9-6 is an extract from the code for this example, showing all the modifications made from UndoExample2 highlighted in bold. The complete source file is, of course, available on the CD-ROM that accompanies this book.

There are two fairly obvious differences between this example and its predecessor that need little comment—we create a MonitorableUndoManager instead of an UndoManager and we arrange for both the Undo and Redo buttons to be initially disabled. This is both correct (because there are initially no edits to undo or redo) and safe (because our MonitorableUndoManager will

Listing 9-6 Using the Extended UndoManager Class

```java
package AdvancedSwing.Chapter9;

import java.awt.*;
import java.awt.event.*;
import java.util.*;
import javax.swing.*;
import javax.swing.event.*;
import javax.swing.undo.*;
import AdvancedSwing.Chapter4.MenuSpec;
import AdvancedSwing.Chapter4.MenuBuilder;

public class UndoExample5 extends JFrame {
    public UndoExample5() {
        super("Undo/Redo Example 5");

        pane = new JTextPane();
        pane.setEditable(true);// Editable
        getContentPane().add(new JScrollPane(pane),
                             BorderLayout.CENTER);

        // Add a menu bar
        menuBar = new JMenuBar();
        setJMenuBar(menuBar);

        // Populate the menu bar
        createMenuBar();

        // Create the undo manager and actions
        MonitorableUndoManager manager =
                        new MonitorableUndoManager();
        pane.getDocument().addUndoableEditListener(manager);

        Action undoAction = new UndoAction(manager);
        Action redoAction = new RedoAction(manager);

        // Add the actions to buttons
        JPanel panel = new JPanel();
        final JButton undoButton = new JButton("Undo");
        final JButton redoButton = new JButton("Redo");
        undoButton.addActionListener(undoAction);
        redoButton.addActionListener(redoAction);

        undoButton.setEnabled(false);
        redoButton.setEnabled(false);
        panel.add(undoButton);
```

Listing 9-6 Using the Extended `UndoManager` **Class (continued)**

```
      panel.add(redoButton);
      getContentPane().add(panel, BorderLayout.SOUTH);

      // Assign the actions to keys
      pane.registerKeyboardAction(undoAction,
                  KeyStroke.getKeyStroke(KeyEvent.VK_Z,
                      InputEvent.CTRL_MASK),
                      JComponent.WHEN_FOCUSED);
      pane.registerKeyboardAction(redoAction,
                  KeyStroke.getKeyStroke(KeyEvent.VK_Y,
                      InputEvent.CTRL_MASK),
                      JComponent.WHEN_FOCUSED);

      // Handle events from the MonitorableUndoManager
      manager.addChangeListener(new ChangeListener() {
         public void stateChanged(ChangeEvent evt) {
            MonitorableUndoManager m =
                        (MonitorableUndoManager)evt.getSource();
            boolean canUndo = m.canUndo();
            boolean canRedo = m.canRedo();

            undoButton.setEnabled(canUndo);
            redoButton.setEnabled(canRedo);

            undoButton.setToolTipText(canUndo ?
                        m.getUndoPresentationName() : null);
            redoButton.setToolTipText(canRedo ?
                        m.getRedoPresentationName() : null);
         }
      });
   }

   // MORE CODE NOT SHOWN
}
```

inform us when the situation changes). The only other difference is that we create a `ChangeListener` and register it to receive `ChangeEvents` from the `MonitorableUndoManager`.

When such an event is received, we obtain a reference to the `MonitorableUndoManager` from the `getSource` method of `ChangeEvent`, and then invoke its `canUndo` and `canRedo` methods to work out which of the Undo and Redo buttons should now be enabled; the values returned by these methods are passed directly to the `setEnabled` methods of the two buttons. This is the minimal functionality we wanted to achieve by adding event handling to

`UndoManager`. You can see it in action by typing a single character into the `JTextPane` of the example program—as soon as you do this, an `Undoable-Edit` is created and the `Undo` button is enabled. As you type more characters, this button stays enabled and the `Redo` button is still disabled. Now press the `Undo` button or type `CTRL+Z`. When you do this, the last character you typed disappears and, more importantly, the `Redo` button is enabled. Now if you press `Redo`, the character reappears and the `Redo` button is disabled again. Finally, if you press `Undo` until all the text has gone, you'll see that the `Redo` button is enabled but, as the last character is removed, the `Undo` button will be disabled because there are no more edits to undo.

We've also added another enhancement to this example. As you can see from Listing 9-6, when a `ChangeEvent` occurs, we set the tooltip of the `Undo` button to the string returned by the `UndoManager` `getUndoPresentation-Name` and that of the `Redo` button to whatever is returned by `getRedoPre-sentationName`. In the case of `UndoManager`, these methods look at the next edit that would be undone or redone and return its undo or redo presentation name. To see how useful this is, move the mouse pointer over the `Redo` button while it is enabled and you'll see a tooltip that says `Redo addition`. This text actually comes from the `InsertUndo` edit that is generated by the `Document`'s `GapContent` object and stored in the `MonitorableUndoManager`. If you press `Redo` so that the `Undo` button is enabled and then move the mouse pointer over the `Undo` button, you'll see that it also has an appropriate tooltip, as shown in Figure 9-16.

Figure 9-16 Using `MonitorableUndoManager` to create tooltips and disabled buttons.

Summary

In this chapter, we looked at the undo package and saw how, with very little effort, you can make it possible for the user to undo and redo edits within text fields. We then moved on to describe the fundamental classes and interfaces within the undo package and saw how to apply the undo mechanism in a non-text context by developing an `UndoableEdit` for use in conjunction with a `JTree`. Finally, we saw how to improve the undo package's `UndoManager` class to make it easier to create the kind of undo support that users get in popular desktop applications.

Index

ABOUT THE CD-ROM

The CD-ROM included with *Core Swing: Advanced Programming* contains:

- The source code for all of the examples in this book.
- A copy of Chapter 10 of *Core Java Foundation Classes* in PDF format.
- Versions of the NetBeans integrated development environment for both Windows and UNIX platforms.
- Evaluation copies of SwingSoft SwingBuilder, part of SwingSoft's suite of integrated development components. SwingBuilder is a visual GUI building tool that has strong support for Swing components. Both Windows and Red Hat Linux versions of SwingBuilder are included.

The CD-ROM can be used on Microsoft Windows® 95/98/NT®, the Sun Solaris operating system and Red Hat Linux. Instructions for using this software can be found in the Introduction.

License Agreement

Use of the software accompanying *Core Swing: Advanced Programming* is subject to the terms of the License Agreement and Limited Warranty, found on the previous two pages.

Technical Support

Prentice Hall does not offer technical support for any of the programs on the CD-ROM. However, if the CD-ROM is damaged, you may obtain a replacement copy by sending an email that describes the problem to: disc_exchange@prenhall.com.